T0190341

Lecture Notes in Computer Science　　13293

More information about this series at https://link.springer.com/bookseries/558

Khalid Saeed · Jiří Dvorský (Eds.)

Computer Information Systems and Industrial Management

21st International Conference, CISIM 2022
Barranquilla, Colombia, July 15–17, 2022
Proceedings

 Springer

Editors
Khalid Saeed (iD)
Bialystok University of Technology
Bialystok, Poland

Jiří Dvorský (iD)
VSB - Technical University of Ostrava
Ostrava, Czech Republic

ISSN 0302-9743   ISSN 1611-3349 (electronic)
Lecture Notes in Computer Science
ISBN 978-3-031-10538-8   ISBN 978-3-031-10539-5 (eBook)
https://doi.org/10.1007/978-3-031-10539-5

This Springer imprint is published by the registered company Springer Nature Switzerland AG
The registered company address is: Gewerbestrasse 11, 6330 Cham, Switzerland

Preface

CISIM 2022 was the 21st event in a series of conferences dedicated to computer information systems and industrial management applications. The conference was held during July 15–17, 2022, in Barranquilla, Colombia, at the Universidad de la Costa.

Total number of papers were submitted to CISIM by researchers and scientists from a number of reputed universities around the world. These scientific and academic institutions belong to Brazil, Bulgaria, Chile, Colombia, India, Mexico, Pakistan, Peru, Poland, Spain, and Venezuela. Most of the papers were of high quality, but only Number of reviewed papers of them were sent for open peer review. Each paper was assigned to at Number of minimal reviews initially, and the acceptance decision was taken after receiving at least two positive reviews. In cases of conflicting decisions, another expert's review was sought for the respective papers. In total, about 180 reviews and comments were collected from the referees for the submitted papers. In order to maintain the guidelines of Springer's Lecture Notes in Computer Science series, the number of accepted papers was limited. Furthermore, a number of electronic discussions were held among the Program Committee (PC) chairs to reach a consensus on papers with conflicting reviews. After the discussions, the PC chairs decided to accept the 28 best papers for publication in the proceedings book the best Number of accepted papers. Briefly, a total of 55 papers were reviewed and 28 of them were accepted. The open peer review process was used, where 3+ reviews per paper were considered. The main topics covered by the chapters in this book are biometrics, security systems, multimedia, classification and clustering, and industrial management. Besides these, the reader will find interesting papers on computer information systems as applied to wireless networks, computer graphics, and intelligent systems. We are grateful to the three esteemed speakers for their keynote addresses. The authors of the keynote talks were Witold Pedrycz, University of Alberta, Canada; Diana G. Ramirez-Rios, University at Buffalo, USA; and Anita Pal, Durgapur National Institute of Technology, India.

We would like to thank all the members of the PC and the external reviewers for their dedicated efforts in the paper selection process. Special thanks are extended to the members of the Organizing Committees (both International and Local) for their great efforts to make the conference another success. We are also grateful to Andrei Voronkov, whose EasyChair system eased the submission and selection process. Finally, we would like to thank the Springer team for their help with this publication.

We hope that the reader's expectations will be met and that both the on-line and on-site participants benefited from the conference.

September 2022   Khalid Saeed
                                                                                        Jiří Dvorský

Organization

Conference Patrons

Eduardo Crissien	Universidad de la Costa, Colombia
Marta Kosior-Kazberuk	Białystok University of Technology, Poland

General Chair

Khalid Saeed	Białystok University of Technology, Poland

Conference Co-chairs

Marek Krętowski	Białystok University of Technology, Poland
Rituparna Chaki	University of Calcutta, India
Katherinne Salas	Universidad de la Costa, Colombia

Advisory Committee

Nabendu Chaki	University of Calcutta, India
Agostino Cortesi	Ca' Foscari University of Venice, Italy
Nobuyuki Nishiuchi	Tokyo Metropolitan University, Japan
Young Im-Cho	Gachon University, South Korea
Sławomir Wierzchoń	Polish Academy of Sciences, Poland
Emiro De-La-Hoz-Franco	Universidad de la Costa, Colombia

International Organizing Committee

Zenon Sosnowski (Chair)	Białystok University of Technology, Poland
Henry Maury Ardila	Universidad de la Costa, Colombia
Jiří Dvorský	VŠB-Technical University of Ostrava, Czech Republic
Pavel Moravec	VŠB-Technical University of Ostrava, Czech Republic

Local Organizing Committee

Dionicio Neira (Chair)	Universidad de la Costa, Colombia
Paola Ariza	Universidad de la Costa, Colombia
Zhoe Comas	Universidad de la Costa, Colombia

Andres Sanchez	Universidad de la Costa, Colombia
Maciej Szymkowski (Chair)	Białystok University of Technology, Poland
Miguel Jimenes	Universidad de la Costa, Colombia
Kitti Koonsanit	Tokyo Metropolitan University, Japan
Aleksander Sawicki	Białystok University of Technology, Poland

Program Committee Chairs

| Khalid Saeed | Białystok University of Technology, Poland |
| Jiří Dvorský | VŠB-Technical University of Ostrava, Czech Republic |

Program Committee

Waleed Abdulla	University of Auckland, New Zealand
Raid Al-Tahir	University of the West Indies at St. Augustine, Trinidad and Tobago
Valentina Emilia Balas	University of Arad, Romania
Mauricio Barrios	Universidad de la Costa, Colombia
Anna Bartkowiak	Wrocław University, Poland
Alessandra De Benedictis	University of Naples Federico II, Italy
Daniela Borissova	Bulgarian Academy of Sciences, Bulgaria
Rahma Boucetta	University of Sfax, Tunisia
Shariq Aziz Butt	University of Lahore, Pakistan
Nabendu Chaki	University of Calcutta, India
Rituparna Chaki	University of Calcutta, India
Young-Im Cho	Gachon University, South Korea
Melissa Acosta-Coll	Universidad de la Costa, Colombia
Agostino Cortesi	Ca' Foscari University of Venice, Italy
Fernando Crespo	Universidad Alberto Hurtado, Chile
Pierpaolo Degano	University of Pisa, Italy
Jan Devos	Ghent University, Belgium
Andrzej Dobrucki	Wrocław University of Technology, Poland
Guilherme Luiz Dotto	Santa Maria Federal University, Brazil
David Dagan Feng	University of Sydney, Australia
Pietro Ferrara	Ca' Foscari University of Venice, Italy
Riccardo Focardi	Ca' Foscari University of Venice, Italy
Margarita Gamarra	Universidad de la Costa, Colombia
Marina Gavrilova	University of Calgary, Canada
Raju Halder	Ca' Foscari University of Venice, Italy
Christopher G. Harris	University of Northern Colorado, USA
Kauru Hirota	Tokyo Institute of Technology, Japan
Valentina Janev	The Mihajlo Pupin Institute, Serbia

Additional Reviewers

Peter Ahn
Marcin Adamski
Vincenzo Arceri
Tomasz Grześ
Radek Halfar
Maciej Kopczynski
Marek Lampart
Luca Olivieri

Miroslaw Omieljanowicz
Dionicio Neira Rodado
Mariusz Rybnik
Aleksander Sawicki
Maciej Szymkowski
Marek Tabędzki
Jiří Tomčala
Sebastiaan J. van Zelst

Keynotes

A Study of Fuzzy and Neutrosophic Economic Order Quantity Model Allowing Delay in Payment

Anita Pal

Durgapur National Institute of Technology, India
anita.pal@maths.nitdgp.ac.in

Abstract. The inventory control problem is one of the most fundamental and well-known optimization problems in operation research. In this study, we develop two inventory control models under the assumption of trade credit policy. Firstly, we consider an interval type-2 fuzzy inventory control model that involves a delay in payment on the premise of a tacit agreement between retailer and supplier to obtain an entire trade credit order. In this model, we include time dependent deterioration rate. We have also introduced a fuzzy method to find maximum profit in the retailer's inventory policy for deteriorating items in a supply chain. Finally, a sensitivity analysis is carried out to get the sensitiveness of the tolerance of different input parameters. Later, we establish a neutrosophic economic order quantity (EOQ) inventory model, assuming that the market demand is sensitive to the retail price and promotional effort. The supplier and retailer both adopt a partial trade credit policy. We include preservation technology to restrict the normal deterioration. We analyse the crisp model first, and then neutrosophic logic is implemented in the proposed model, considering demand, retail cost, ordering cost, carrying cost, promotional cost, and cost for preservation technology as a triangular neutrosophic number. De-neutrosophication of total neutrosophic profit has been done based on the removal area method. The present investigation shows that the de-neutrosophic and defuzzification values of the total profit function are convex, which assures the existence of unique solution. Mathematical theorems are developed to determine the optimal inventory policy for the retailer efficiently. Finally, numerical illustrations are also provided to justify the models, and the results in this study generalize some already published results in the crisp sense.

Federated Learning and Knowledge Distillation with Granular Computing

Witold Pedrycz

Department of Electrical and Computer Engineering, University of Alberta, Edmonton, Canada
wpedrycz@ualberta.ca

Abstract. With the rapid progress encountered in data analytics, we have been witnessing important challenges. The visible and pressing requirements are inherently associated with the data and a way they are addressed in system modeling. In the landscape of data analytics, we identify three ongoing quests with far-reaching methodological implications, namely (i) modeling in the presence of existing constraints of privacy and security, (ii) efficient model building with limited data of varying quality, and (iii) deployment of advanced and computationally demanding models on computing platforms of limited computing resources. To address these challenges, federated learning and knowledge distillation have emerged as conceptual and algorithmic sound directions.

In the talk, we demonstrate how various ways of conceptualization of information granules as fuzzy sets, sets, rough sets, and others may lead to innovative augmentations of the above stated paradigms leading to interesting and efficient solutions. It is also advocated that Granular Computing enriches and augments the principles of federated learning and knowledge distillation.

To establish a sound conceptual modeling setting, we include a brief discussion of information granules-oriented design of rule-based architectures. A way of forming the rules through unsupervised federated learning is discussed along with algorithmic developments. A granular characterization of the model formed by the server vis-a-vis data located at individual clients is presented. It is demonstrated that the quality of the rules at the client's end is described in terms of granular parameters and subsequently the global model becomes represented as a granular model. The roles of granular augmentations of models in the realm of logic-oriented knowledge distillation are discussed.

Socially Optimal Solutions in Freight and Disaster Response Logistics

Diana G. Ramirez-Rios

University at Buffalo, USA
dgramire@buffalo.edu

Abstract. Today's society faces numerous challenges exacerbated by climate change, globalization, and socio-economic inequities, to name a few. These issues include heavy congestion, pollution, noise, and parking conflicts from the freight transportation perspective. In disaster logistics, the distribution of relief supplies encounters additional challenges because resources are mostly or entirely destroyed in the affected area after a disaster, and local relief supplies may not be available. In both scenarios, society is affected by the negative externalities of the movement of goods. Thus, logistical solutions must account for these negative impacts by aiming at the socially optimal.

This seminar focuses on the research developed in the disaster response logistics field, where the optimal minimizes the social costs of human suffering. This research considers the Facility Location problem, where disaster relief organizations aim for optimal points of distribution (PODs) to distribute the relief supplies to the people in need after a disaster occurs. Given a fixed distribution center where relief supplies are stored, the problem considers identifying the districts' shapes and the location of the PODs inside the district, such that it minimizes the total social costs. The social costs consider the private or logistics costs (i.e., the fixed cost of setting the POD, the transportation, and inventory holding costs) and the externalities of the distribution in the form of deprivation costs. The deprivation cost is the cost experienced by the impacted individual for the time spent without the relief. The analytical and numerical results provide unique insights that can serve as guidelines for disaster responders at the planning stage to allocate resources better and alternative distribution strategies of relief in the affected regions.

Contents

Machine Learning and Artificial Neural Networks

Biometrics and Pattern Recognition Applications

Semi-supervised Adaptive Method for Human Activities Recognition (HAR)

Fabio Mendoza Palechor[1](✉), Enrico Vicario[2], Fulvio Patara[2],
Alexis De la Hoz Manotas[1](✉), and Diego Molina Estren[1](✉)

[1] Department of Computer Science and Electronics, Universidad de la Costa, Barranquilla,
Colombia
{fmendoza1,adelahoz6,dmolina}@cuc.edu.co
[2] Department of Systems Engineering, Università degli Studi di Firenze, Firenze, Italy

Abstract. Using sensors and mobile devices integrated with hardware and software tools for Human Recognition Activities (HAR), is a growing scientific field, the analysis based on this information have promising benefits to detect regular and irregular behaviors in individuals during their daily activities. In this study, the Van Kasteren dataset was used for the experimental stage, and it all data was processed using the data mining classification methods: Decision Trees (DT), Support Vector Machines (SVM) and Naïve Bayes (NB). These methods were applied during the training and validation processes with the proposed methodology, and the results obtained showed that all these three methods were successful to identify the cluster associated to the activities contained in the Van Kasteren dataset. The Support Vector Machines (SVM) method showed the best results with the evaluation metrics: True Positive Rate (TPR) 99.2%, False Positive Rate (FPR) 0.6%, precision (99.2%), coverage (99.2%) and F-Measure (98.8%).

Keywords: HAR · Data mining · Cluster · Evaluation metric · Dataset · Van Karesten

1 Introduction

Using sensors and mobile devices integrated with hardware and software tools for Human Recognition Activities (HAR), is a growing scientific field, the results have promising benefits for detecting regular and irregular behaviors in individuals during their daily activities. Many studies related to HAR can be found, studies like [1], where authors used several computational intelligence methods to identify actions like crouch, stand up, jump, run, walk and others, and there are applications in wide areas such as healthcare, security, domotics, sports and others [2–5]. Several data mining techniques (DM), machine learning (ML), and deep learning (DL) play a relevant role inside HAR, since they provide tools to perform tasks such as classification, segmentation and hybrid systems. These methods can be compared, based on their results, as you can see in [6–9]. The implementation of these methods can be found in several studies, such as K-Nearest Neighbor (KNN) [1, 8, 10, 11], Support Vector Machine (SVM) [1, 6, 10, 12, 13], Naive

K. Saeed and J. Dvorský (Eds.): CISIM 2022, LNCS 13293, pp. 3–17, 2022.
https://doi.org/10.1007/978-3-031-10539-5_1

Bayes (NB) [14, 15], Decision Trees (DT) [1, 16], and Neural Convolutional Networks (CNN) [17]. Datasets play an important role in the process of HAR, since scientists can develop new solutions for efficient identification of activities, in the literature you can see several studies where the authors use different datasets [1, 10, 12, 18, 19]. The most representative datasets related to HAR are Van Kasteren [20], CASAS Kyoto [21], CASAS Aruba [22], CASAS Multiresident [23], Opportunity [24–26], UCI HAR [27, 28] and mHealth [29, 30]. The first five datasets, contain data captured from individual interactions with sensors deployed in indoor environments and the last two datasets, contain data collected using body sensors (wearables) or smartphones. Ensuring the high quality of a HAR model is a complex task, due to the elevated number of evaluation metrics for validation, as you can see in [17, 31, 32]. The main objective of this study is to present a model based on data mining techniques for HAR, the proposed approach integrates the unsupervised cluster method K-Means with the classification techniques SVM, DT and NB. These were compared to achieve the best results in the validation metrics: precision, coverage, False Positive Rate FPR, True Positive Rate TPR and F-Measure. The dataset chosen by this study was Van Kasteren, due the high quality of its data and, the number of existing recommended studies of this kind. The study is structured as follows: in Sect. 2 you can find previous studies related to HAR, Sect. 3 presents the materials and methods used in the current study, Sect. 4 shows the methodology, Sect. 5 presents the results obtained, and finally Sect. 6, show the conclusions and future works.

2   Related Works

Several authors propose the implementation of techniques or methods for the development of tools that can correctly identify human activities, different hardware devices and software are used to collect data, for later analysis related to HAR. Next, you can find a brief description of some contributions in this field of study.

In [7], authors manifested difficulties in activity recognition based on sensor networks in SMART HOME, usually, probabilistic models such as Markov Hidden model (HMM) and Linear Discriminant Analysis (LDA), are used to classify activities. In that study, SVM based on minority sampling (SMOTE) overcome HMM, LDA and SVM, and this approach could lead to a significant increase in performance for the classification process. The Van Kasteren dataset was used during the experimentation process, and accuracy was the chosen evaluation metric. In [8], the performance of several classification algorithms was analyzed, based on a system for recognition of online activities under Android platforms. In this study, the classification algorithm KNN was improved with clustering algorithms. Grouped KNN eliminates the computational complexity, and the performance is evaluated in four test subjects for activities like walking, running, sitting and standing up. According to [1], the recognition of human activities using automated methods has surged recently as a key research topic, in this study, authors proposed an optical flow descriptor based on features derived from movement, human action is analyzed through a histogram containing local and global cinematic features, authors used the UCF101 and Weizman datasets, and they used the classification techniques KNN, DT, SVM and DL. The classification rates obtained were 98.76% using KNN for Weizman and 70% for UCF101. In [11], the study showed the percentage of the population that owns a smartphone has increased significantly recently, and this fact can be used to collect information about the context of the user. In this study, the authors proposed a HAR model, using smartphones to obtain data, several statistics from the sensor data were calculated to model each activity and, a learning supervised technique performed classification in real time. The methods KNN and a classifier based on K-means were compared, and the activities analyzed were still, walking, running and vehicle. According to [16], human movement detection is an important task to several areas such as healthcare, physical state and elder care. This study proposed a model for human movement detection using smartphone sensors and learning automated methods. The data was obtained from the accelerometer, gyroscope, step counter and cardiac frequency sensors. The algorithms used were KNN, DT, Random Forest, SVM with PCA and evaluation metrics were f-measure, accuracy and area under curve. In [17], the study shows that HAR is a field that has attracted much attention in the last few years, based on the demand in several areas. In this study, the authors proposed the implementation of a Deep Neural Convolutional Network (Convent) with the objective of making efficient and effective HAR based on smartphone sensors. The experimentation showed that Convent derive relevant and more complex features with each extra layer, even the complexity level diminishes from layer to layer. Neural networks overcome other data mining techniques in HAR, using a dataset collected from 30 volunteer subjects, achieving a general performance of 94.79% in the test dataset and 95.75% with extra information from temporal Fast Fourier Transform in the HAR dataset. According to [19], HAR represents a great contribution for health monitoring, in the study, the authors proposed an approach based on SMART HOME, data was collected through several sensors in different locations. The dataset used was Van Kasteren and CASAS. In their approach, authors first selected a class for each activity, and then the key features are used for activity recognition. The methods used were Multi-class SVM, Correct Incorrect Distance Learning and Ranking (CIDLR) and Direct Distance Minimization (DDM). The results obtained for HAR achieved 84.24% for Van Kasteren and 97.5% for CASAS. In [33], the study showed that human activity recognition must consider the semantics of the environment and the relationship between the elements on it. The authors called this "activity space", the location and the artifacts in it (identified by RFID tags), allowed to apply PMM to recognize the activity performed by the individual. Preliminary studies indicated that the proposed model was noise tolerant and had a high accuracy to detect the activity space of the individual, and the ability to handle big volume of data. The study in [34] showed a smart home with a ubiquitous intelligent monitoring system, with 4 sensors (ECG, Environment Temperature, Location Camera, Facial and Expression Sensor) and 7 contexts (ECG, pulse, body temperature, environment temperature, location, movement and facial expression). In this study, authors used LSVM (Support Vector Machine) and association rules to analyze captured patterns. The proposed model identified with a high level of accuracy (over 70%), the service needed by the human based on the analysis of the information provided by the sensors. Authors in [35], manifested that HAR provides valuable context information for wellness, healthcare and sports applications, recently many approaches have been proposed for automated learning, to identify activities from sensor data. Nevertheless, most methods are designed for off-line processing, and not on the sensor node, the proposed approach was implemented using an application for Android devices, 4 datasets were used: ActiveMiles, WISDM v1.1., Daphnet FoG and Skoda. Crossed validation was made with 10 subsets. In [36], the authors proposed the learning of composite features formed by 2D single corners in time and space, to recognize human activities. Each corner is codified with relation to their neighbors and the whole set. The extraction of composite features was made by data mining (association rules). The final classifiers can be used to perform activity localization and classification. According to [37], gesture and movement detection for hands is quite challenging, especially in real environments. This study performed the recording of a hand, and 5 different gestures, and the gestures are replaced later using the interaction with a computer mouse. The hand silhouette was extracted as a combination of different segmentation methods, to produce an invariant affine Fourier descriptor and then to be classified by SVM. The gestures are recognized was changes by a Finite State Machine FSM. According to [38], the authors proposed a hierarchical method to detect and recognize human activities in MPEG sequences. The algorithm presented 3 stages: 1. Using PCA analysis from the movement vectors in MPEG, grouping macroblocks per speed, distance and human proportions, 2. The DC DCT components of luminance and chrominance are compared with activity templates and human skin, 3. An exhaustive analysis of the regions without compression in the previous steps through segmentation and graphs. According to [39], authors presented an approach to group human activity analysis in a smart home environment based on auto adaptive neural network called Growing Self-Organizing Maps (GSOM). The dataset used was collected from several sensors in an apartment within a period of two weeks. The results indicated that GSOM showed attractive features for interpretation and analysis of useful patterns present in the data from daily activities.

3   Materials and Methods

3.1   Dataset Description

The dataset selected for the proposed method is Van Kasteren [20]. The data was collected by different sensors such as layer switches, mercury contacts, infrared passive sensors PIR and flotation sensors. The collection process was made during two weeks in an apartment occupied by two men. For the annotation process, they used Bluetooth headsets with voice recognition and an activity log handwritten. The data are binary type, and you can see the activation, on and off, from the sensors. The actions identified were grouped in the activities: brush teeth, shower, go to bathroom, take a bath, shave, breakfast, dinner, have snack, drink, load dishwasher and unload dishwasher and others. The dataset presents a structure formed by two plain text documents called KasterenSenseData and KasterenActData, these contain the information of the sensors and the set of activities studied respectively. To start with the analysis of the data, first you must perform a depuration process. First stage involves unifying the data in one single format, storing which sensors were used in each activity. Then, the data integration is determined by the number of times that each activity is found in the dataset, and this is shown in Fig. 1.

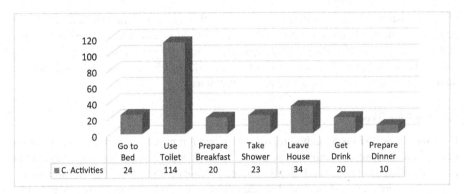

Fig. 1. Number of activities by category.

In Fig. 2, you can see the number of activities by capture date, based on the sensors installed inside the indoor environment of the study.

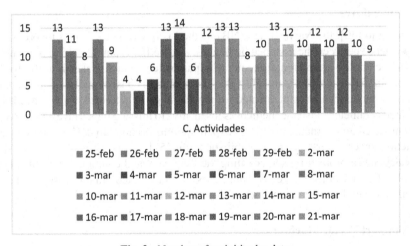

Fig. 2. Number of activities by date.

After the dataset was integrated, the process of separating and transforming the data was made, including an analysis of the distribution of the data with relation to the frequency of occurrence of each activity, considering that the dataset is unbalanced, also the authors proceeded to the segmentation of the data using the K-Means method, after obtaining the optimal selection of the number of clusters based on the elbow method. Finally, the integration of the segmentation algorithm and the classification algorithms SVM, DT and NB was introduced.

3.2 Simple K-Means

Clustering is a data mining task where analyzed data are divided in groups [40], according to [41], all data belonging to a single cluster are grouped, based on common features of the attributes. There are different methods such as partition, hierarchical, based on density. Simple K-Means is a popular clustering method, considered of hierarchical type, and it is used especially for grouping datasets of low dimension [41], highlighting its simplicity and efficiency, as mentioned by [42, 43]. In [43], authors indicated that the number of groups to create must be known previously.

3.3 Decision Trees

Decision Trees (DT) is a method used in classification processes to perform a partition of the data in subsets, usually the structure of a DT is formed by one single root node and several adjacent nodes called children, the combination of parent and children nodes allows to achieve an answer, found inside the terminal node as mentioned by [44, 45]. According to [46, 47], DT are used extensively for modelling of data in real time prediction systems inside real complex environments. In [48] you can see a DT is used to support decision making processes. In [49] DT are viewed as a supervised approach for classification processes, the most common algorithms are J48, C4.5 and Random Forest.

3.4 Naïve Bayes

According to [50], the Naïve Bayes (NB) method is based on the Bayes theorem with independence between the assumed predicates, a naïve Bayesian model is easy to build, without a complex estimation of the iterative parameters, which makes it useful for big datasets. In [51], the authors manifest that this method is based on classic mathematic theory, the model can be implemented for a wide range of activities, since it needs few estimated parameters, also the methods is insensitive to missing data. Bayesian networks are considered an alternative to classic expert systems oriented to decision making and prediction under uncertainty in probabilistic terms [52]. NB is a probabilistic classifier that calculates a probability set, counting the frequency and combination of the values given by the dataset [53]. The algorithm uses the Bayes theorem and assumes that all data are independent from the values of the class variable [54].

3.5 Support Vector Machines

Support Vector Machines (SVM) is considered a method of high level when the available data is limited, since it brings self-regulation to reduce the overfitting, it is used in many areas such as text and hypertext categorization, handwritten characters recognition, image classification and others [55–59]. Usually, SVM are used to solve classification problems efficiently, since it is an automatic learning system, based in the development of statistical learning systems [60].

4 Methodology

This study is based on the training of the methods DT, SVM and NB using the Van Kasteren dataset under the same training scenario. Previously, the dataset was integrated, as mentioned in Sect. 3.1, then all data was preprocessed and transformed to create the model under the proposed approach, where the best classification algorithm, Simple K-Means, is integrated. You can see each of the stages of the methodology below.

4.1   Data Cleaning and Preparation

In this stage, a meticulous analysis was performed on the data, after their integration, to identify atypical values, redundant and missing data. In this stage, it was noticed that the activities were unbalanced, being the most predominant the "use toilet" activity, which can create an issue of over training in that activity, and reduced accuracy capacity in the rest of the categories described in Sect. 3.1. You can see in Fig. 3, the distribution of the activities according to the dataset.

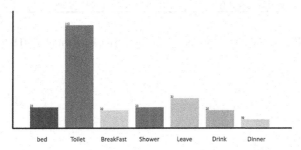

Fig. 3.   Activity distribution before data balancing

With this situation, it was necessary to perform a balancing process, on the classes, to obtain best levels in the evaluation metrics, so it was decided to implement the SMOTE algorithm [61], to allow generation of synthetic data for minority classes, based on the number of near neighbors used and the percentage needed to increase the selected class and the random seed for the random sampling. In this stage, it is perfectly clear that all data must be prepared (remove missing data, atypical data, data normalization, etc.) before using SMOTE, since the selected neighbor chosen to generate synthetic data, could contain noise or disturbances, and the data produced would have low quality. Nevertheless, the SMOTE filter has a positive impact when the data are unbalanced, since the balancing processes diminish the probability of biased learning in favor of a majority class [62]. In Fig. 4, you can see the distribution of the activities after the SMOTE filter was applied.

4.2   Cluster Adjustment and Preparation

After the preparation and transformation stage was finished, the next step was to determine the optimal number of clusters to use to create the proposed model. For this task, it was used the elbow method. According to [63], the elbow algorithm allows to determine the real number of groups in a dataset, based on [64], it is a visual method, where k is set starting in 2, the right number of generated groups. Next, in Fig. 5, you can see the results shown by the elbow method.

Based on Fig. 5, you can see the elbow shows in k = 4, which means the optimal number of clusters is 4. Then, the generation of 4 groups of the Simple K-Means was implemented. Next you can see the features of data for each group created.

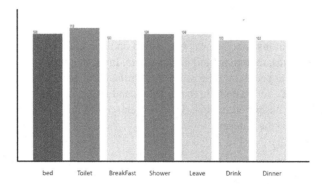

Fig. 4. Activity distribution after data balancing with SMOTE

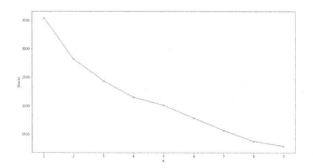

Fig. 5. Elbow method results

- Cluster No 1: Group of the activities associated with the activity "Drink", where the activation of the sensors CupsCupboard, Fridge and Freezer is present. This group has 103 records, representing 14% of the data.
- Cluster No 2: Group of the activities associated with the activity "Shower", where the activation of the sensors HallToiletDoor, HallBathroomDoor, ToiletFlush and HallBedRoomDoor is present. This group has 118 records, representing 16% of the data.
- Cluster No 3: Group of the activities associated with the activity "Bed", where the activation of the sensors HallToiletDoor, HallBathroomDoor, Fridge, FrontDoor, ToiletFlush and HallBedRoomDoor is present. This group has 319 records, representing 43% of the data.
- Cluster No 4: Group of the activities associated with the activity "Breakfast", where the activation of the sensors Microwave, CupsCupboard, Fridge, PlatesCupBoard, Freezer, GroceriesCupBoard and PansCupBoard is present. This group has 206 records, representing 28% of the data.

With these clusters, you can see the number of activities to be recognized is reduced from the data, but these groups can be related to other activities, as shown in Table 1.

Table 1. Relationship of clusters and activities

Cluster	Activity
1	Drink
2	Shower, Toilet
3	Bed, Leave
4	Breakfast, Dinner

4.3 Activity Classification

After all clusters were defined, the training and testing process was performed, using the classification methods selected: DT, SVM and NB. These are compared under the same test scenario, using crossed validation with 10 subsets to guarantee the dataset was divided randomly, one part for training and one part for test and evaluation. The evaluation metrics implemented were precision, coverage, FPR, TPR and F-Measure. Next, you can see the results obtained by the implemented methods. In Table 2, you can see the results obtained by DT for the activities classification associated with the clusters described in Sect. 4.2. The results were considered successful, with a precision rate of 98.9%, indicating a wrong classification in 8 records only.

Table 2. DT J48 results + crossed validation: 10 folds

Class	TPR	FPR	Precision	Coverage	F-measure
Cluster 0	96.1%	0.6%	96.1%	96.1%	96.1%
Cluster 1	1%	0%	1%	1%	1%
Cluster 2	99.1%	0.9%	98.8%	99.1%	98.9%
Cluster 3	99.5%	0%	1%	99.5%	99.8%
Average	98.9%	0.5%	98.9%	98.9%	98.9%

In Table 3, you can see the results obtained by SVM for the activities classification associated with the clusters described in Sect. 4.2. The results were considered successful, with a precision rate of 99.2%, indicating a wrong classification in 6 records only.

In Table 4, you can see the results obtained by NB for the activities classification associated with the clusters described in Sect. 4.2. The results were considered promising, with a precision rate of 97.6%, indicating a wrong classification in 20 records only.

With these results from the experimentation phase, the best algorithm was SVM with crossed validation 10 subsets, and it was integrated with the Simple K-means method finally. Next, you can see in Fig. 6 the comparison of the algorithms.

Table 3. SVM results + crossed validation: 10 folds

Class	TPR	FPR	Precision	Coverage	F-measure
Cluster 0	1%	0%	1%	1%	1%
Cluster 1	94.9%	0%	1%	94.9%	97.4%
Cluster 2	1%	0.14%	98.2%	1%	98.4%
Cluster 3	1%	0%	1%	1%	1%
Average	99.2%	0.6%	99.2%	99.2%	98.8%

Table 4. NB results + crossed validation: 10 folds

Class	TPR	FPR	Precision	Coverage	F-Measure
Cluster 0	99.0%	0%	1%	99.0%	99.5%
Cluster 1	99.2%	0.29%	86.7%	99.2%	92.5%
Cluster 2	94.4%	0.2%	99.7%	94.4%	96.9%
Cluster 3	1%	0.2%	99.5%	1%	99.8%
Average	97.3%	0.6%	97.6%	97.3%	97.4%

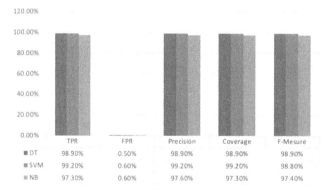

Fig. 6. Comparison results of DT, SVM and NB algorithms

5 Results and Discussion

HAR is a field of study in constant growing, and researchers are working more in the efficient identification of different activities, the technology devices have an important role in the process, since they provide the capture and compilation of the information correctly. The computational intelligence techniques framed inside the disciplines of DM, ML and DL have a substantial place inside HAR, since they all use data to discover patterns that become useful knowledge. In this study, the authors compared the classification methods DT, SVM and NB, during the processes of training and validation of the proposed approach, under the same test scenario. The results obtained showed that, all three methods are successful to recognize the cluster associated with each of the activities contained in the dataset Van Kasteren. The SVM method obtained the best result with TPR (99.2%), FPR (0.6%), Precision (99.2%), Coverage (99.2%) and F-Measure (98.8%), surpassing the results proposed by similar works as [31]. These results clearly show that it is possible to create hybrid systems where traditional classification methods can be integrated with unsupervised methods, corresponding to clustering this time, since the latter permit to segment the activities with certain degree of similarity, obtaining a reduction of the variables, which it is quite useful with datasets with a high number of attributes. Finally, the presented results showed that data mining hybrid methods represent an alternate solution inside HAR, and their findings can be used to support decision making processes.

6   Conclusions and Future Works

The recognition of human activities in daily life is research field with growing interest in recent years, different authors have decided to study monitoring several activities, using sensors connected through a network infrastructure, devices like smartphones and wearables, they also have built many datasets that permit the implementation of data mining methods with the goal of performing classification and detection processes. This study used the dataset Van Kasteren [20], in the same way as many other studies. To analyze the data, it was necessary to perform several procedures, highlighting integration and representation of the data to obtain a single format capable of being processed.

In this research, the classification methods DT, SVM and NB were compared under the same test scenario, during the training and validation processes, the results showed that all three methods are successful to identify the cluster associated to the activities contained in the dataset Van Kasteren. The SVM method obtained the best result with TPR (99.2%), FPR (0.6%), Precision (99.2%), Coverage (99.2%) and F-Measure (98.8%), surpassing the results proposed by similar works as [31].

Acknowledgment. This work was partially supported from the REMIND Project from the European Union's Horizon 2020 research and innovation program under the Marie Skłodowska-Curie grant agreement No. 734355.

References

1. Ladjailia, A., Bouchrika, I., Merouani, H.F., Harrati, N., Mahfouf, Z.: Human activity recognition via optical flow: decomposing activities into basic actions. Neural Comput. Appl. **32**(21), 16387–16400 (2019). https://doi.org/10.1007/s00521-018-3951-x
2. Banos, O., Damas, M., Pomares, H., Prieto, A., Rojas, I.: Daily living activity recognition based on statistical feature quality group selection. Expert Syst. Appl. **39**(9), 8013–8021 (2012)
3. Casale, P., Pujol, O., Radeva, P.: Human activity recognition from accelerometer data using a wearable device. In: Vitrià, J., Sanches, J.M., Hernández, M. (eds.) IbPRIA 2011. LNCS, vol. 6669, pp. 289–296. Springer, Heidelberg (2011). https://doi.org/10.1007/978-3-642-21257-4_36

4. Calabria-Sarmiento, J.C., et al.: (2018). Software applications to health sector: a systematic review of literature (2018)
5. Chen, L., Hoey, J., Nugent, C.D., Cook, D.J., Yu, Z.: Sensor-based activity recognition. IEEE Trans. Syst. Man Cybern. Part C (Appl. Rev.) **42**(6), 790–808 (2012)
6. Arifoglu, D., Bouchachia, A.: Activity recognition and abnormal behaviour detection with recurrent neural networks. Proc. Comput. Sci. **110**, 86–93 (2017)
7. Fergani, B.: Comparing HMM, LDA, SVM and Smote-SVM algorithms in classifying human activities. In: El Oualkadi, A., Choubani, F., El Moussati, A. (eds.) Proceedings of the Mediterranean Conference on Information & Communication Technologies 2015. Lecture Notes in Electrical Engineering, vol. 381, pp. 639–644. Springer, Cham (2016)
8. Paul, P., George, T.: An effective approach for human activity recognition on smartphone. In: 2015 IEEE International Conference on Engineering and Technology (Icetech), pp. 1–3. IEEE, March 2015
9. Dao, M.S., Nguyen-Gia, T.A., Mai, V.C.: Daily human activities recognition using heterogeneous sensors from smartphones. Proc. Comput. Sci. **111**, 323–328 (2017)
10. Liu, Y., Nie, L., Liu, L., Rosenblum, D.S.: From action to activity: sensor-based activity recognition. Neurocomputing **181**, 108–115 (2016)
11. Concone, F., Gaglio, S., Lo Re, G., Morana, M.: Smartphone data analysis for human activity recognition. In: Esposito, F., Basili, R., Ferilli, S., Lisi, F. (eds.) AI*IA 2017. LNCS, vol. 10640, pp. 58–71. Springer, Cham (2017). https://doi.org/10.1007/978-3-319-70169-1_5
12. Fahad, L.G., Khan, A., Rajarajan, M.: Activity recognition in smart homes with self verification of assignments. Neurocomputing **149**, 1286–1298 (2015)
13. Manzi, A., Dario, P., Cavallo, F.: A human activity recognition system based on dynamic clustering of skeleton data. Sensors **17**(5), 1100 (2017)
14. Tran, D., Sorokin, A.: Human activity recognition with metric learning. In: Forsyth, D., Torr, P., Zisserman, A. (eds.) ECCV 2008. LNCS, vol. 5302, pp. 548–561. Springer, Heidelberg (2008). https://doi.org/10.1007/978-3-540-88682-2_42
15. Robertson, N., Reid, I.: A general method for human activity recognition in video. Comput. Vis. Image Underst. **104**(2–3), 232–248 (2006). ISSN 1077-3142. https://doi.org/10.1016/j.cviu.2006.07.006
16. Balli, S., Sağbaş, E.A., Peker, M.: Human activity recognition from smart watch sensor data using a hybrid of principal component analysis and random forest algorithm. Meas. Control **52**(1–2), 37–45 (2019)
17. Ronao, C.A., Cho, S.B.: Human activity recognition with smartphone sensors using deep learning neural networks. Expert Syst. Appl. **59**, 235–244 (2016)
18. Tan, Y.E., Lo, C.C., Shieh, C.S., Miu, D., Horng, M.F.: Adaptive confidence evaluation scheme for periodic activity recognition in smart home environments. In: 2019 IEEE International Conference on Dependable, Autonomic and Secure Computing, International Conference on Pervasive Intelligence and Computing, International Conference on Cloud and Big Data Computing, Intl Conf on Cyber Science and Technology Congress (DASC/PiCom/CBDCom/CyberSciTech), pp. 1077–1081. IEEE, August 2019
19. Tahir, S.F., Fahad, L.G., Kifayat, K.: Key feature identification for recognition of activities performed by a smart-home resident. J. Ambient. Intell. Humaniz. Comput. **11**(5), 2105–2115 (2019). https://doi.org/10.1007/s12652-019-01236-y
20. van Kasteren, T.L.M., Englebienne, G., Kröse, B.J.A.: Activity recognition using semi-Markov models on real world smart home datasets. J. Ambient Intell. Smart Environ. **2**(3), 311–325 (2010). https://doi.org/10.3233/AIS-2010-0070
21. Cook, D.J., Crandall, A.S., Thomas, B.L., Krishnan, N.C.: Casas: a smart home in a box. Computer **46**(7), 62–69 (2013). https://doi.org/10.1109/MC.2012.328
22. Cook, D.J.: Learning setting-generalized activity mdoels for smart spaces. IEEE Intell. Syst. **99**(1) (2011). https://doi.org/10.1109/MIS.2010.112

23. Singla, G., Cook, D.J., Schmitter-Edgecombe, M.: Recognizing independent and joint activities among multiple residents in smart environments. J. Ambient. Intell. Humaniz. Comput. **1**(1), 57–63 (2010). https://doi.org/10.1007/s12652-009-0007-1

24. Chavarriaga, R., et al.: The Opportunity challenge: a benchmark database for on-body sensor-based activity recognition. Pattern Recogn. Lett. **34**(15), 2033–2042 (2013). https://doi.org/10.1016/j.patrec.2012.12.014

25. Roggen, D., et al.: Collecting complex activity data sets in highly rich networked sensor environments. In: Seventh International Conference on Networked Sensing Systems (2010). https://doi.org/10.1109/INSS.2010.5573462

26. Lukowicz, P., et al.: Recording a complex, multi modal activity data set for context recognition. In: 23th International Conference on Architecture of Computing Systems (2010). http://www.opportunity-project.eu/challengeDataset. Accessed 3 July 2018

27. Anguita, D., et al.: A public domain dataset for Human Activity Recognition using smartphones. In: 21th European Symposium on Artificial Neural Networks, Computational Intelligence and Machine Learning. ESANN 2013, Bruges, Belgium, pp. 437–442, April 2013

28. Ronao, C.A., Cho, S.: Human activity recognition using smartphone sensors with two-stage continuous hidden Markov models. In: 2014 10th International Conference on Natural Computation, pp. 681–686 (2014). https://doi.org/10.1109/ICNC.2014.6975918

29. Banos, O., et al.: mHealthDroid: a novel framework for agile development of mobile health applications. In: Pecchia, L., Chen, L.L., Nugent, C., Bravo, J. (eds.) IWAAL 2014. LNCS, vol. 8868, pp. 91–98. Springer, Cham (2014). https://doi.org/10.1007/978-3-319-13105-4_14

30. Banos, O., et al.: Design, implementation and validation of a novel open framework for agile development of mobile health applications. BioMed. Eng. OnLine **14**(S2:S6), 1–20 (2015)

31. Chetty, G., White, M., Akther, F.: Smart phone based data mining for human activity recognition. Proc. Comput. Sci. **46**, 1181–1187 (2015)

32. Keyvanpour, M.R., Zolfaghari, S.: Augmented feature-state sensors in human activity recognition. In: 2017 9th International Conference on Information and Knowledge Technology (IKT), pp. 71–75). IEEE, October 2017

33. Yamada, N., Sakamoto, K., Kunito, G., Yamazaki, K., Tanaka, S.: Human activity recognition based on surrounding things. In: Tomoya Enokido, L., Yan, B.X., Kim, D., Dai, Y., Yang, L.T. (eds.) EUC 2005. LNCS, vol. 3823, pp. 1–10. Springer, Heidelberg (2005). https://doi.org/10.1007/11596042_1

34. Choi, J., Shin, D., Shin, D.: Ubiquitous Intelligent Sensing System for a Smart Home. In: Yeung, D.Y., Kwok, J.T., Fred, A., Roli, F., de Ridder, D. (eds.) SSPR/SPR 2006. LNCS, vol. 4109, pp. 322–330. Springer, Heidelberg (2006). https://doi.org/10.1007/11815921_35

35. Ravi, D., Wong, C., Lo, B., Yang, G.Z.: Deep learning for human activity recognition: A resource efficient implementation on low-power devices. In: 2016 IEEE 13th International Conference on Wearable and Implantable Body Sensor Networks (BSN), pp. 71–76. IEEE, June 2016

36. Gilbert, A., Illingworth, J., Bowden, R.: Scale invariant action recognition using compound features mined from dense spatio-temporal corners. In: Forsyth, D., Torr, P., Zisserman, A. (eds.) ECCV 2008. LNCS, vol. 5302, pp. 222–233. Springer, Heidelberg (2008). https://doi.org/10.1007/978-3-540-88682-2_18

37. Okkonen, M.A., Kellokumpu, V., Pietikäinen, M., Heikkilä, J.: A visual system for hand gesture recognition in human-computer interaction. In: Ersbøll, B.K., Pedersen, K.S. (eds.) SCIA 2007. LNCS, vol. 4522, pp. 709–718. Springer, Heidelberg (2007). https://doi.org/10.1007/978-3-540-73040-8_72

38. Ozer, B., Wolf, W., Akansu, A.N.: Human activity detection in MPEG sequences. In: Proceedings Workshop on Human Motion, Austin, Texas, USA, pp. 61–66 (2000). https://doi.org/10.1109/HUMO.2000.897372

39. Zheng, H., Wang, H., Black, N.: Human activity detection in smart home environment with self-adaptive neural networks. In: 2008 IEEE International Conference on Networking, Sensing and Control, Sanya, pp1505–1510 (2008). https://doi.org/10.1109/ICNSC.2008.452 5459

40. Kaur, S.: Survey of different data clustering algorithms. Int. J. Comput. Sci. Mob. Comput. **5**(5), 584–588 (2016)

41. Virdi, G., Madan, N.: Review on various enhancements in K means clustering algorithm (2018)

42. Du, W, Lin, H., Sun, J., Yu, B., Yang, H.: A new projection-based K-means initialization algorithm. In: Proceedings of 2016 IEEE Chinese Guidance, Navigation and Control Conference, China (2016)

43. Kanungo, T., Mount, D.M., Netanyahu, N.S., Piatko, C.D., Silverman, R., Wu, A.Y.: An efficient k-means clustering algorithm: analysis and implementation. IEEE Trans. Pattern Anal. Mach. Intell. **7**, 881–892 (2002)

44. Friedl, M.A., Brodley, C.E.: Decision tree classification of land cover from remotely sensed data. Remote Sens. Environ. **61**(3), 399–409 (1997)

45. Dai, W., Ji, W.: A mapreduce implementation of C4. 5 decision tree algorithm. Int. J. Database Theory Appl. **7**(1), 49–60 (2014)

46. Lausch, A., Schmidt, A., Tischendorf, L.: Data mining and linked open data—new perspectives for data analysis in environmental research. Ecol. Model. **295**, 5–17 (2015)

47. Daszykowski, M., Korzen, M., Krakowska, B., Fabianczyk, K.: Expert system for monitoring the tributyltin content in inland water samples. Chemom. Intell. Lab. Syst. **149**, 123–131 (2015)

48. Magerman, D.M.: Statistical decision-tree models for parsing. In: Proceedings of the 33rd Annual Meeting on Association for Computational Linguistics, pp. 276–283. Association for Computational Linguistics, June 1995

49. Zhao, Y., Zhang, Y.: Comparison of decision tree methods for finding active objects. Adv. Space Res. **41**(12), 1955–1959 (2008)

50. Suresh, K., Dillibabu, R.: Designing a machine learning based software risk assessment model using Naïve Bayes algorithm. TAGA J. **14**, 3141–3147 (2018)

51. Naik, D.L., Kiran, R.: Naïve Bayes classifier, multivariate linear regression and experimental testing for classification and characterization of wheat straw based on mechanical properties. Ind. Crops Prod. **112**, 434–448 (2018)

52. Picard, R.W., et al.: Affective learning—a manifesto. BT Technol. J. **22**(4), 253–269 (2004)

53. Patil, T.R., Sherekar, S.S.: Performance analysis of Naive Bayes and J48 classification algorithm for data classification. Int. J. Comput. Sci. Appl. **6**(2), 256–261 (2013)

54. O'Reilly, K.M.A., Mclaughlin, A.M., Beckett, W.S., Sime, P.J.: Asbestos-related lung disease. Am. Family Phys. **75**(5), 683–688 (2007)

55. James, A., Abu-Mostafa, Y., Qiao, X.: Nowcasting recessions using the SVM machine learning algorithm. Available at SSRN 3316917 (2018)

56. Vapnik, V.: Statistical Learning Theory. Wiley, Hoboken (1998)

57. Papageorgiou, C., Oren, M., Poggio, T.: A general framework for object detection. In: Proceedings of the International Conference on Computer Vision (1998)

58. Joachims, T.: Text categorization with support vector machines: learning with many relevant features. In: Nédellec, C., Rouveirol, C. (eds.) ECML 1998. LNCS, vol. 1398, pp. 137–142. Springer, Heidelberg (1998). https://doi.org/10.1007/BFb0026683

59. Kim, Y., Ling, H.: Human activity classification based on micro-Doppler signatures using a support vector machine. IEEE Trans. Geosci. Remote Sens. **47**(5), 1328–1337 (2009)

60. Da Silva, F., Niedermeyer, E.: Electroencephalography: Basic Principles. Clinical Applications, and Related Fields. William & Wikins, Baltimore (1993)

61. Chawla, N.V., Bowyer, K.W., Hall, L.O., Kegelmeyer, W.P.: SMOTE: synthetic minority over-sampling technique. J. Artif. Intell. Res. **16**, 321–357 (2002)
62. Palechor, F.M., de la Hoz Manotas, A.: Dataset for estimation of obesity levels based on eating habits and physical condition in individuals from Colombia, Peru and Mexico. Data in brief **25**, 104344 (2019)
63. Ng, A.: Clustering with the k-means algorithm. Mach. Learn. (2012)
64. Kodinariya, T.M., Makwana, P.R.: Review on determining number of cluster in K-means clustering. Int. J. **1**(6), 90–95 (2013)

A New Approach for Image Thinning

Patryk Milewski[1]([⊠])[iD] and Khalid Saeed[1,2][iD]

[1] Faculty of Computer Science, Bialystok University of Technology,
Wiejska 45A, 15-351 Białystok, Poland
{patryk.milewski,k.saeed}@pb.edu.pl
[2] Department of Computer Science and Electronics – CUC, Universidad de la Costa,
Barranquilla, Colombia
https://pb.edu.pl/

Abstract. In this paper we presented a novel, general purpose thinning method with emphasis on symmetry. The proposed algorithm is of iterative character. We achieved better skeleton structure by splitting the method into 3 stages, each with a different thinning strength. We introduced an image designed for testing the thinning algorithms and the results of various skeletonization methodologies. Our tests show the proposed algorithm outperforms the current state-of-the-art methods in accuracy and symmetry. We provided implementation details and showed how the performance of the method was increased. Thinning is a basic stage in image segmentation and hence feature extraction for object recognition. Both the test image and the implementation of our method will be made publicly available.

1 Introduction

Thinning in computer vision has numerous applications. In biometrics, thinning algorithms are used for image preprocessing. For instance, biometrics based on fingerprints and iris make use of image skeleton as a step towards feature vector extraction. In optical character recognition, thinning can be used in order to reduce letters to a simpler, easier to recognize for computer systems, form.

Some thinning algorithms can be executed in parallel. Work on design of parallel iterative thinning methods began as far as 1980's [1]. Our method contains steps which are able to run in parallel.

Due to the complexity of thinning, there is no universal method which satisfies all applications. Proposed general algorithm was created with symmetry in mind. While every algorithm has its own strengths and weaknesses and produces various results for various applications it is evident that comparing them in terms of general quality is not a trivial task [2]. Moreover, in biometric systems based on fingerprint recognition algorithm susceptibility to spoofing must be taken into account. In [3] authors describe Fingerprint Liveness Detection to ensure the actual presence of live fingerprint.

In order to test overall performance of novel thinning algorithms, there are many thinning test images. A good thinning test image should have some parts already thinned, so that the applied algorithm clearly approaches the final skeleton, and troublesome pixel connections where there is no definitive answer which

K. Saeed and J. Dvorský (Eds.): CISIM 2022, LNCS 13293, pp. 18–31, 2022.
https://doi.org/10.1007/978-3-031-10539-5_2

pixel should be removed. These conditions fulfils the test image created by Zhang [4], as seen in Fig. 1.

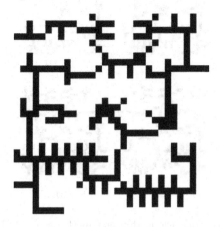

Fig. 1. One of the first thinning test images created by Zhang [4]

However, we also wanted to test symmetry in much more thick cases thus we have created our own image with broader cases.

2 Related Works

In [5] authors use Zhang–Suen thinning to improve readability of ancient papyrus library. Zhang–Suen thinning methods [1,4,6,7] are considered one of the most popular algorithms.

Thinning in MRI images [8] is used to detect Focal Cortical Dysplasia. Authors compared three different thinning algorithms, Zhang–Suen [7] thinning, Stentiford and OPTA (One Pass Thinning Algorithm). In [9], authors used segmentation aided by artificial intelligence to split the MRI image into regions of special interest.

Segmentation is a very important step which can greatly affect the outcome of skeletonization. Nowadays, AI methods [10] produce good results. Some authors join segmentation with thinning to get better results, such as [11]. Skeletonization is also used in pictures depicting real life objects. In [12], authors describe flux-based skeletonization algorithm, aided by Convolutional Neural Network. In [13] authors present a database of 3450 finger photos and compare neural networks for segmentation. By using thinning algorithms, it is possible to extract unique data, which could be used for biometrics systems of verification and identification based on fingers.

In [2,14–16] authors show various similar sequential iterative methods, while parallel thinning approaches are shown in [1,17]. In [18] is shown a completely different algorithm – thinning is done by using unsupervised learning in order to achieve skeletal representation from point clouds.

A set of thinning algorithms is shown in Fig. 2.

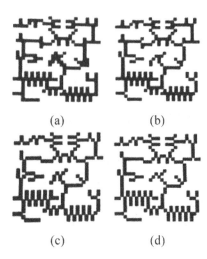

Fig. 2. Zhang test image in various thinning methods: (a) Original test image, (b) Guo-Hall, (c) Zhang, (d) KMM [19]

3   A New Thinning Algorithm - Calibrated Thinning

Authors call their proposed method CalThin, a short for Calibrated Thinning. The proposed method works on binarized images. For every non-border pixel, define neighbours as 8 adjacent pixels surrounding the tested pixel. Define $B(x)$ as the **number of non-white neighbours** for the given pixel x. Define $T(x)$ as the **number of color transitions** (that is, a transition to different color) in clockwise direction for the given pixel x. Similar definitions were used in [7].

Define a **convolution matrix** M as used in [2]:

$$\begin{bmatrix} 128 & 1 & 2 \\ 64 & 0 & 4 \\ 32 & 16 & 8 \end{bmatrix}$$

and offsets P:

$$\begin{bmatrix} 0 & 1 & 2 \\ 3 & 4 & 5 \\ 6 & 7 & 8 \end{bmatrix}$$

For each pixel, compute the sum $S(x)$ using the following formula:

$$s = \sum_{i=0}^{8} \begin{cases} M_i & \text{if } P_i \text{ is black} \\ 0 & \text{if } P_i \text{ is white} \end{cases} \tag{1}$$

Define D as the set of the following values: 5, 7, 13, 15, 20, 21, 22, 23, 28, 29, 30, 31, 52, 53, 54, 55, 60, 61, 62, 63, 65, 67, 69, 71, 77, 79, 80, 81, 83, 84, 85, 86, 87, 88, 89, 91, 92, 93, 94, 95, 97, 99, 101, 103, 109, 111, 112, 113, 115, 116,

117, 118, 119, 120, 121, 123, 124, 125, 126, 127, 133, 135, 141, 143, 149, 151, 157, 159, 181, 183, 189, 191, 193, 195, 197, 199, 205, 207, 208, 209, 211, 212, 213, 214, 215, 216, 217, 219, 220, 221, 222, 223, 225, 227, 229, 231, 237, 239, 240, 241, 243, 244, 245, 246, 247, 248, 249, 251, 252, 253, 254, 255.

Fig. 3. Example – values for the pixel at the center: $B(X) = 4$, $T(X) = 6$, $S(X) = 1 + 2 + 16 + 64 = 83$

Define **calibration** as a set of three functions, each returns true or false and takes as parameters the given pixel x and its neighbours.

Create 2 calibrations C_1, C_2 which are used for reducing given image to thinned state. Note that these calibrations are not suited for creating final skeleton due to their pixel priorities:

$$C_1 = \begin{cases} f_1(x) = T(x) < 3 \land B(x) < 5 \\ f_2(x) = T(x) < 5 \land B(x) > 4 \\ f_3(x) = T(x) < 3 \land B(x) > 2 \end{cases} \tag{2}$$

$$C_2 = \begin{cases} f_1(x) = T(x) < 3 \land B(x) < 6 \\ f_2(x) = T(x) < 4 \land B(x) > 2 \land B(x) < 6 \\ f_3(x) = T(x) = 2 \end{cases} \tag{3}$$

Create 2 calibrations C_3, C_4 which further reduces thinned image to final skeletonized output:

$$C_3 = \begin{cases} f_1(x) = T(x) < 4 \land B(x) < 6 \\ f_2(x) = T(x) < 4 \land B(x) > 2 \land B(x) < 6 \\ f_3(x) = T(x) < 3 \end{cases} \tag{4}$$

$$C_4 = \begin{cases} f_1(x) = B(x) > 1 \\ f_2(x) = T(x) < 4 \\ f_3(x) = \quad \text{true} \end{cases} \tag{5}$$

(Note that functions f_1, f_2, f_3 need only two values: $B(x)$ and $T(x)$.)

The proposed algorithm goal is to make a symmetrical skeleton. This is accomplished by calibration functions which differ in priority to remove black pixels. As authors' solution to stroke continuity detection are simple calibrations, worth considering are other approaches with parallel algorithms which preserves symmetry, although they are more complex [20].

Algorithm is implemented by the following pseudocode:

```
1  foreach calibration in C:
2      set has_changed to false
3      while has_changed is false:
4          foreach black pixel:
5              if f_1(x):
6                  mark pixel as gray
7          foreach gray pixel:
8              if f_2(x):
9                  mark pixel for deletion
10         foreach pixel for deletion:
11             if f_3(x):
12                 set pixel to white
13                 set has_changed to true
14         foreach gray pixel:
15             if (S(x) is in D)
16                 set pixel to white
```

Note that calibration C_4 could be implemented in more straightforward manner by taking advantage of $f_3(x) = $ true.

4   Experiments and Results

In order to test various troublesome cases, thinning test image was created as shown in Fig. 4.

Fig. 4. Proposed thinning test image

The proposed test image has cases for optical character recognition, silhouette and contour detection. Letters in cursive font and monospaced are present. Monospaced letters have been chosen to be one of the most similar looking after the thinning process. Thus it is easy to judge, for instance, how much similarity there is between B and 8, I and 1. Cat silhouette and contour, however, is a perfect case for recognizing how much difference there is between thinned contour, where the given algorithm cannot access image center and silhouette, where image center is available.

Figure 5 shows final output after all of the other calibrations in sequential manner. It is clear that symmetry was preserved.

Fig. 5. Proposed thinning test image after all calibrations

(a)   (b)

Fig. 6. Selected regions from the proposed test image before thinning (a) and after calibrated thinning (b). Note how skeleton preserved the structure.

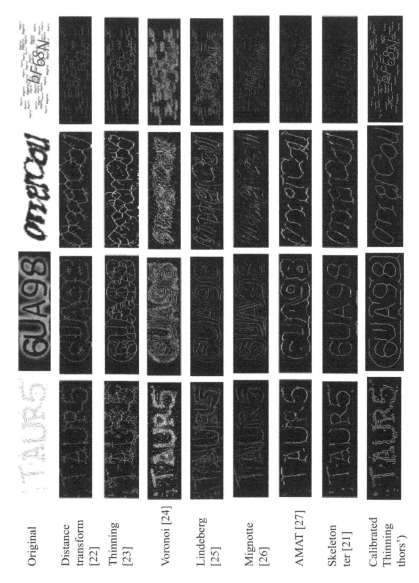

Fig. 7. Results of thinning algorithms as given in [21] with authors' appended method. Note how our proposed method has comparative results yet it's implementation is usually far simpler. Note that the authors' proposed method samples are usually binarized by maximizing contrast. Colored version is given for comparison with the other methods in color (Color figure online)

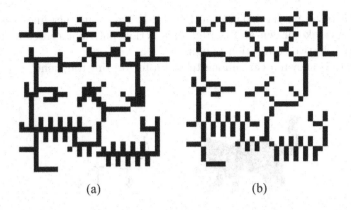

(a)   (b)

Fig. 8. Zhang test, before (a) and after calibrated thinning (b)

Figure 7 shows various thinning methods and their results from [21] with CalThin algorithm appended in it. In Fig. 8 is shown how Zhang Thinning Image is thinned using CalThin.

In Fig. 9 a–d is presented the behavior of the proposed method when additional strokes are applied to the chosen image. In Fig. 9 a a single stroke and its skeleton is presented.

In Fig. 9 b to previously drawn stroke is added another which results in crossing.

In Fig. 9 c another line is added, however, instead of passing through the center, the line is drawn from it to the upper border. This shifts the previously computed image center. As depicted in Fig. 9 d, the proposed method is able to connect many paths to a single connection point.

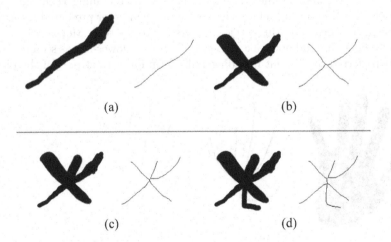

(a)   (b)

(c)   (d)

Fig. 9. Strokes before and after applying our thinning method. (a) A single stroke. (b) Two crossed strokes. (c) Three crossed strokes. (d) Four crossed strokes.

In order to retain the balance, in Fig. 9 d is drawn another line in opposing direction as stroke drawn at Fig. 9 c. This action pulls our center point down which results in two connection points.

In Fig. 10 is shown a cat silhouette and a fingerprint fragment.

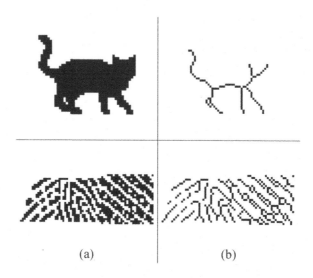

(a)   (b)

Fig. 10. Chosen regions of proposed test image before (a) and after (b) Calibrated thinning

In Fig. 11 are presented tests on a hand silhouette. It is visible that our method is the only one which branches out the fingers evenly, by firstly joining pinkie with ring and middle with index and then combining them into single stroke. It is visible that it behaves less predictable in other presented algorithms; in (b) and (c) pinkie and ring are joined directly to the root. Moreover, it is clear that our algorithm did not make additional stroke in lower-left as seen in (b) and that it preferred to thin out into diagonal line in lower right part of the picture.

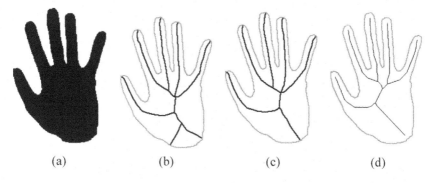

(a)   (b)   (c)   (d)

Fig. 11. Hand silhouette before (a) and after thinning algorithms: DCE-Manual [28] (b), thinning method as proposed in [29] (c), Authors' (d).

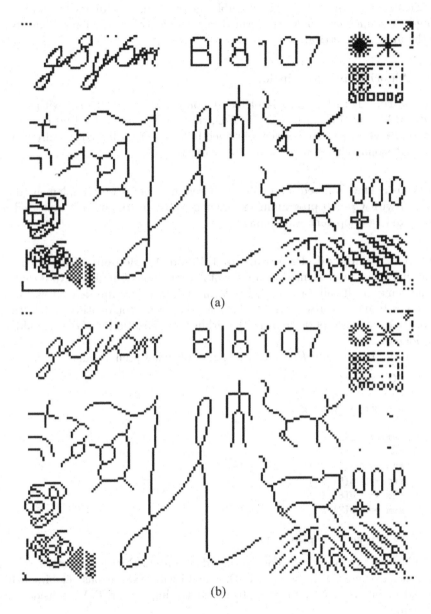

Fig. 12. Comparison of thinning methods: Zhang–Suen (a) and authors' proposed method (b).

In Fig. 12 is presented comparison of Zhang-Suen and authors' thinning algorithms. Note how in characters "BI8107" our method achieved perfectly symmetrical shapes wherever it was possible, in particular for digits "8" and "0". Note how connection points are formed in each algorithm. CalThin is shown to be the most symmetrical.

4.1 Algorithmic Description

Hardware. Algorithms were implemented on Intel Core i9-8950HK with 32 GB DDR4 RAM and 1TB SSD + 1TB HDD, running Windows 10 64-bit operating system. Fingerprint samples were obtained by using DigitalPersona U.are.U and DigitalPersona EikonTouch fingerprint scanners.

Software. The proposed method and chosen algorithms were implemented on .NET 6 with C# 9.0 programming language. Visual Studio 2022 was used as Integrated Development Environment.

Detailed Pseudocode Proposals for Efficient Implementation. Each calibration can be implemented as a class of 3 anonymous functions. Note that f_2 is the same in all calibrations. If black and white values are defined as bytes, as values 0 and 255 respectively, efficient computing could utilize bitshifting. In order to increase performance, algorithm parallelization on GPU should be considered.

In order to compute $B(X)$, consider the following pseudocode:

```
 1  int B(byte[] p):
 2
 3      int sum = ~p[0] & 1
 4
 5      sum += ~p[1] & 1
 6      sum += ~p[2] & 1
 7      sum += ~p[3] & 1
 8      sum += ~p[5] & 1
 9      sum += ~p[6] & 1
10      sum += ~p[7] & 1
11
12      return sum + (~p[8] & 1)
```

Where "p" represents 9 values in regards to offsets P with currently selected pixel at the center. & is bitwise AND, $\sim$ is bitwise NOT. Consider bitshifting instead of bitwise AND. In order to efficiently implement $T(X)$ consider the following:

```
 1  int T(byte[] p):
 2
 3      int cache1 = ~p[0] & 1
 4      int cache2
 5
```

```
 6     int sum = cache1 ^ (cache2 = ~p[1] & 1)
 7     sum += cache2 ^ (cache1 = ~p[2] & 1)
 8     sum += cache1 ^ (cache2 = ~p[5] & 1)
 9     sum += cache2 ^ (cache1 = ~p[8] & 1)
10     sum += cache1 ^ (cache2 = ~p[7] & 1)
11     sum += cache2 ^ (cache1 = ~p[6] & 1)
12     sum += cache1 ^ (cache2 = ~p[3] & 1)
13
14     return sum + cache2 ^ (~p[0] & 1)
```

Where $\hat{}$ represents XOR. Consider CPU parallelization techniques. In order to implement $S(X)$, consider the following pseudocode:

```
 1 int S(byte[] p, int[] M):
 2     int sum = M[0] & ~p[0]
 3
 4     sum += M[1] & ~p[1]
 5     sum += M[2] & ~p[2]
 6     sum += M[3] & ~p[3]
 7     sum += M[5] & ~p[5]
 8     sum += M[6] & ~p[6]
 9     sum += M[7] & ~p[7]
10
11     return sum + (M[8] & ~p[8])
```

Note that in every implementation, the value of the central pixel is omitted. Consider loop unrolling.

4.2 Applications

As seen in Fig. 10 our method makes a symmetric, simple skeleton. The proposed algorithm is versatile and is a good choice when skeleton simplicity is necessary. Our method could be used in optical character recognition as seen in Fig. 6, fingerprint thinning as seen in Fig. 10.

4.3 Conclusions

We have presented a novel approach to iterative thinning algorithms based on calibration functions.

Our method differs from the others presented in this paper by using sequential calibrations, with various conditions used for pixel manipulation. We used machine learning to obtain optimal parameters for calibrations. The algorithm was tested with many other configurations.

The proposed algorithm was tehoroughly tested in terms of execution speed on CPU whilst now we are working on GPU applications on different operating systems. Some efforts have been also put on the combination of the skeletonization with segmentation for varieties of applications. Figure 7 shows how our method compares to chosen state of the art methods.

The experiments show many opportunities for future work including creation of new techniques based on the idea of calibrations.

Acknowledgements. This work was supported by grant WZ/WI-IIT/4/2020 from Bialystok University of Technology and funded with resources for research by the Ministry of Science and Higher Education in Poland.

References

1. Zhang, Y.Y., Wang, P.S.P.: Design of parallel thinning algorithms. In: 9th International Conference on Pattern Recognition, pp. 1023–1025 (1988)
2. Saeed, K., Tabędzki, M., Rybnik, M., Adamski, M.: K3M: a universal algorithm for image skeletonization and a review of thinning techniques. Int. J. Appl. Math. Comput. Sci. (2010)
3. Zhang, Y., Gao, C., Pan, S., Li, Z., Xu, Y., Qiu, H.: A score-level fusion of fingerprint matching with fingerprint liveness detection. IEEE Access **8**, 183391–183400 (2020)
4. Zhang, Y.Y., Wang, P.S.P.: A parallel thinning algorithm with two-subiteration that generates one-pixel-wide skeletons. In: IEEE Proceedings of ICPR 1996 (1996)
5. Sudarma, M., Sutramiani, N.P.: The thinning Zhang-Suen application method in the image of Balinese scripts on the papyrus. Int. J. Comput. Appl. **91**, 9–13 (2014)
6. Ben Boudaoud, L., Solaiman, B., Tari, A.: A modified ZS thinning algorithm by a hybrid approach. Vis. Comput. **34**(5), 689–706 (2017). https://doi.org/10.1007/s00371-017-1407-4
7. Zhang, T.Y., Suen, C.Y.: A fast parallel algorithm for thinning digital patterns. Commun. ACM (1984)
8. Subashini, P., Jansi, S.: Optimal thinning algorithm for detection of FCD in MRI images. Int. J. Sci. Eng. Res. (2011)
9. Dalca, A.V., John, G., Sabuncu, M.R.: Anatomical priors in convolutional networks for unsupervised biomedical segmentation. In: IEEE/CVF Conference on Computer Vision and Pattern Recognition (CVPR) (2018)
10. Hu, R., Dollar, P., He, K., Darrell, T., Girshick, R.: Learning to segment every thing. In: IEEE Conference on Computer Vision and Pattern Recognition (CVPR) (2018)
11. Jerripothula, K.R., Cai, J., Lu, J., Yuan, J.: Object co-skeletonization with co-segmentation. In: IEEE Conference on Computer Vision and Pattern Recognition (CVPR) (2017)
12. Ke, W., Chen, J., Jiao, J., Zhao, G., Ye, Q.: SRN: side-output residual network for object symmetry detection in the wild. In: IEEE Conference on Computer Vision and Pattern Recognition (CVPR) (2017)
13. Chopra, S., Malhotra, A., Vatsa, M., Singh, R.: Unconstrained fingerphoto database. In: IEEE/CVF Conference on Computer Vision and Pattern Recognition Workshops (CVPRW) (2018)
14. Saeed, K., Rybnik, M., Tabedzki, M.: Implementation and advanced results on the non-interrupted Skeletonization algorithm. In: Skarbek, W. (ed.) CAIP 2001. LNCS, vol. 2124, pp. 601–609. Springer, Heidelberg (2001). https://doi.org/10.1007/3-540-44692-3_72
15. Tabedzki, M., Saeed, K., Szczepański, A.: A modified K3M thinning algorithm. Int. J. Appl. Math. Comput. Sci. **26**(2), 439–450 (2016)
16. Haseena, M.H.F., Roselin, C.A.: A review on an efficient iterative thinning algorithm. Int. J. Innovative Res. Sci. Eng. Technol. **6**(11) (2017). (An ISO 3297: 2007 Certified Organization)

17. Bataineh, B.: An iterative thinning algorithm for binary images based on sequential and parallel approaches. Pattern Recognit Image Anal. **28**(1), 34–43 (2018). https://doi.org/10.1134/S1054661818010030
18. Lin, C., Li, C., Liu, Y., Chen, N., Choi, Y.K., Wang, W.: Point2Skeleton: learning skeletal representations from point clouds (2020)
19. Saeed, K.: Image analysis for object recognition. Białystok University of Technology (2004)
20. Dong, J., Chen, Y., Yang, Z., Ling, B.W.-K.: A parallel thinning algorithm based on stroke continuity detection. SIViP **11**(5), 873–879 (2016). https://doi.org/10.1007/s11760-016-1034-y
21. Bai, X., Ye, L., Zhu, J., Zhu, L., Komura, T.: Skeleton filter: a self-symmetric filter for skeletonization in noisy text images. IEEE Trans. Image Process. **29**, 1815–1826 (2019)
22. Bitter, I., Kaufman, A.E., Sato, M.: Penalized-distance volumetric skeleton algorithm. IEEE Trans. Visual Comput. Graphics **7**(3), 195–206 (2001)
23. N'emeth, G., Kardos, P., Pal'agyi, K.: Thinning combined with iteration-by-iteration smoothing for 3D binary images. Graph. Models **73**(6), 335–345 (2011)
24. Ogniewicz, R., Ilg, M.: Voronoi skeletons: theory and applications in computer vision and pattern recognition. In: Proceedings CVPR 1992, 1992 IEEE Computer Society Conference on IEEE, pp. 63–69. IEEE (1992)
25. Lindeberg, T.: Edge detection and ridge detection with automatic scale selection. Int. J. Comput. Vision **30**(2), 117–156 (1998)
26. Mignotte, M.: Symmetry detection based on multiscale pairwise texture boundary segment interactions. Pattern Recogn. Lett. **74**, 53–60 (2016)
27. Tsogkas, S., Dickinson, S.: AMAT: medial axis transform for natural images. In: Computer Vision (ICCV), 2017 IEEE International Conference on IEEE, pp. 2727–2736. IEEE (2017)
28. Bai, X., et al.: Skeleton pruning by contour partitioning with discrete curve evolution. IEEE PAMI **29**(3), 449–462 (2007)
29. Yang, C., Indurkhya, B., See, J., Grzegorzek, M.: Towards automatic skeleton extraction with skeleton grafting. IEEE Trans. Visual. Comput. Graph. **27**(12), 4520–4532 (2021). https://doi.org/10.1109/TVCG.2020.3003994

Augmentation of Accelerometer and Gyroscope Signals in Biometric Gait Systems

A. Sawicki$^{(\boxtimes)}$

Faculty of Computer Science, Bialystok University of Technology, Bialystok, Poland
a.sawicki@pb.edu.pl

Abstract. This paper presents IMU augmentation method based on perturbing sensor orientation and modeling accelerometer and gyroscope readings. The algorithm aims to improve the generalization properties of CNNs and ultimately increase the performance of biometric gait systems. The novelty of the presented approach is the combination of classical mechanisms of acceleration signal augmentation combined with the analytical generation of angular velocity measurements. This paper presents a comparison of proposed and selected literature techniques for a publicly available gait corpus collected on an uneven surface. The use of the developed algorithm allowed to improve the identification metrics for samples collected for irregular surfaces such as grass and cobblestone.

Keywords: Augmentation · Gait · Accelerometer biometric

1 Introduction

This work presents the development of a novel method for the augmentation of accelerometer and gyroscope motion sensors. It aims to improve the performance of gait-based biometric person identification systems that are based on deep convolutional neural networks.

The use of Deep Learning (DL) solutions allows obtaining very good classification results in areas such as natural language processing, speech, or time series analysis. The success of such methods strongly depends on a large and diverse dataset, which will provide good generalization properties of neural networks [1]. In many cases, acquiring a large number of learning samples is time-consuming, expensive, and in some cases impossible. Data augmentation is a set of techniques and tools to artificially generate additional data based on an existing training set. It is a kind of a remedy in situations where new data cannot be acquired. It should be emphasized that in the field of image processing, data augmentation in the form of affine transform usage can be considered as a widely used standard. However, in the field of motion classification, the subject is much more challenging [2]. This demonstrates the importance of developing new algorithms.

The paper is organized as follows. Sect. 2 describes the state of the literature in the field of IMU data augmentation. Sect. 3 describes in detail the methodology of this work, including the database characteristics, proposed algorithm as well as applied classifier. Sect. 4 presents identification results for several selected augmentation methods. Sect 5 contains conclusions and a description of the planned future work.

© The Author(s), under exclusive license to Springer Nature Switzerland AG 2022
K. Saeed and J. Dvorský (Eds.): CISIM 2022, LNCS 13293, pp. 32–45, 2022.
https://doi.org/10.1007/978-3-031-10539-5_3

2 Literature Review

A review of the literature on motion sensor data augmentation shows that there is an absence of a unified standard in contrast to the field of image processing (where affine transformations are widespread). Nevertheless, two main groups of augmentation solutions can be distinguished. In the first one, the IMU signals are transformed as standard time series, while in the second one, their synthetic generation is performed on the basis of orientation and displacement time series.

The authors of the publication [3], who investigated the issue of gait analysis using a smartphone, proposed to generate new signals by rotating the accelerometer measurement data in three-dimensional space. Rotations from 0 to 45° were performed, with a step of 15° for all three rotation axes. This approach allows simulations of what measurements would be acquired if the sensor were rotated. However, this interesting approach has a drawback. The operation of rotation of signals in three-dimensional space is not able to influence the norm/magnitude of the signal. If, at time t, the norm of accelerometer readings was, for example, 1.1 g, then changing the sensor orientation will change the ratio of values on individual sensor axes. A kind of "shift of values between axes" will occur, but the magnitude will remain constant. It is not possible to generate a signal that would be amplified in any way.

On the other hand, in the paper [4] focusing on Parkinson Desis monitoring, the authors proposed a whole series of different types of transformations (Jittering, Scaling, Rotation, Permutation, MagWarp, TimerWarp and Cropping). The developed approach allows both signal rotation and gains addition. In the conducted experiments, augmentation based on rotation and rotation with premutation achieved the best classification results [4]. It should be noted that the rotation was based on randomly selecting the axis and angle of rotation in the range of 180°. The generated rotation could even model an upside-down rotation of the sensor. In the case of gait analysis, it is unlikely that the sensor will be rotated so significantly. It should also be noted that both methods [3, 4] were applied only to accelerometer signals, but with some success, can also be used for sensors such as gyroscopes.

On the other hand, in [5] a three-step augmentation mechanism to both accelerometer and gyroscope signals was proposed. In the first noise was added, in the second the signal was scaled between 0.7 and 1.1 and in the last step the sampling irregularities of the signals were modeled. In the presented approach [5], there is no connection between the gyroscope and the accelerometer signals, which may lead to the generation of samples that are not observable in real conditions. The presence of any quantity measured by the gyroscope is closely related to the rotation of the sensor and results from a change in orientation. Due to the fact that the accelerometer also measures gravitational accelerations (which depend on the orientation), a change in the orientation of the sensor should also affect its indications.

The methods described in [3–5] do not require additional information about the sensor orientation, which is their undoubted advantage. On the other hand, they do not enable simulation of orientation drift or sensor vibrations and their influence on the measured values of accelerometer and gyroscope.

The second group of solutions includes approaches related to the synthetic generation of accelerometer and gyroscope signals. A representative of this application can be the solution proposed in [6]. The authors developed an algorithm for the artificial generation of IMU measurement values from videos of YouTube platform. The gyroscope measurement values generation was done using only the sensor orientation data. In the case of accelerometer signals, the measurement values consist of the gravitational acceleration (sufficiently well modeled using orientation), and the acceleration value resulting from the motion of the object. In order to fully model the signal, information about the orientation as well as the trajectory of the motion is necessary. In [6] motion trajectory information was used directly from a video recording. In an approach [7] realizing a similar issue, the professional Vicon motion capture system was used to capture human movement.

While the work of [6, 7] generates angular velocity signals very well, the synthetic generation of accelerometer signals requires an additional source of information about body motion. However, when testing single sets of accelerometer and gyroscope, this knowledge is not available, limiting potential applications.

In this paper we develop augmentation mechanics that is a composite of previously presented techniques. First of all, in the presented approach, we focused on modifying the original orientation signals and subsequently modeling the IMU measurements. The additional rotations have small values and model the limited rotations of the IMU sensors (similar to [3] and opposite [4]). The augmentation of accelerometer signals is a twin solution to [3] and has the disadvantage of being unable to amplify the signal. The novelty of the presented solution is the fact that the output angular velocity signal is generated analytically (in accordance with [6, 7]). Therefore measurement data of the accelerometer and the gyroscope are closely connected. In contrast to [5], where modality augmentation proceeds independently, the generated data is always observable in real-world conditions.

3 Methodology

The aim of the conducted work was to investigate the effect of selected augmentation methods on the performance of gait-based biometric systems. The conducted research examined the influence of literature augmentation techniques [3, 4] and proposed solution on identification metrics. A comparison was performed for a publicly available dataset containing gait acquired on substrate such as pavement, grass, cobble stone.

3.1 Dataset

In the conducted research a publicly available gait corpus "*A database of human gait performance on irregular and uneven surfaces collected by wearable sensors*" [8] was used. The database contains IMU signals collected with 30 subjects on a few substrate types. In the presented study, samples from surfaces such as stairs and ramps were not included. Scientific research focused on four flat surfaces: pavement I, pavement II, flat even, grass and cobblestone.

Data acquisition was conducted using an inertial motion capture system MTw Awinda which contains 6 IMU sensors. The location in sequence of each of them is right and left shin, right and left thigh, wrist, and the back of the torso. In the current work as in our previous work [9], only a single sensor located on the right thigh was used. This is motivated by the fact that the collected signals with some similarity may reflect data collected with a smartphone located in the trouser pocket. This gives hope for the potential implementation of the system on mobile devices. In this research despite a single IMU exploitation, ten signals were available for further processing (3 accelerometer channels, 3 gyroscope channels, and 4 orientation quaternion time series channels).

3.2 Segmentation and Data Preprocessing

The gait cycles contained in the corpus were represented in the form of block recordings that included both gait and stillness periods. To eliminate pause periods, wavelet decomposition was used according to the methodology described in [10].

Figure 1 shows an example of a block recording in which a period of stationary was observed at the beginning and end of the data. The X-axis presents time and the Y-axis shows the magnitude of the accelerometer signals. A magnitude value close to "1" (related to the effect of gravitational acceleration) is acquired during the pause period. The occurrence of motion interruptions was marginal, however, it is worth noting that these situations occurred and the algorithm was able to process them correctly. After segmentation, the block recordings were divided into frames of fixed length of 128 samples, in order to be used for the classification.

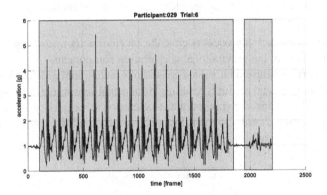

Fig. 1. Segmentation, colored background indicates periods detected as movement

Four experiments involving different types of substrate were conducted in the present study. In each of them, the classifier was trained with the use of gait collected on the pavement I substrate. Validation was carried out with samples recorded on pavement II, flat even, grass, cobblestone. This approach is closest to the real-life scenario. In an actual implementation, most likely the gait samples would be taken on a hard surface and used to create reference set. This approach seems reasonable, typically during the day city inhabitants walk more time on concrete or hard sidewalk than on grass or cobble stone. It would not be efficient to collect samples (and train system) for gait on grass, which may occur relatively infrequently.

Figure 2 shows the full characteristics of the dataset by participant and surface type. The dataset was relatively unbalanced. For example, for Participant 08, approximately

40 gait samples were recorded for the cobblestone surface, and for Participant 12, the number was approximately 85. Since the distribution of data was unbalanced, the f1-score metric was used to evaluate identification performance.

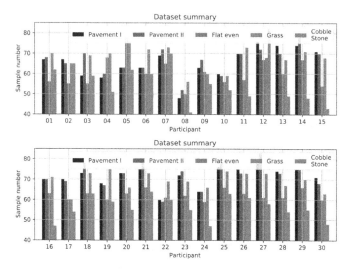

Fig. 2. Number of gait samples by participant and surface type

Before the augmentation process begins, the accelerometer measurement values are subjected to removal of the gravitational acceleration components.

Accelerometric measurement values consist of gravitational acceleration (modeled by sensor orientations) and readings resulting from actual sensor motion. Using the sensor orientation information, the gravitational acceleration value can be estimated and subtracted from the actual recorded signals. Figure 3 presents the IMU signal preprocessing diagram. The output signal is next used in the classification process.

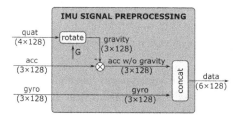

Fig. 3. Signal preprocessing block diagram

3.3 Data Augmentation

The data augmentation process was performed in two stages. In the first one, the orientation signal (*quat*) was passed through a perturbation pipeline that models constant sensor displacement, vibrations, and sensor orientation drift during the walking motion.

Modified orientation signal (*augmented quat*) was used in both the gyroscope and accelerometer signal augmentation process. First of all, together with the original orientation signal (*quat*) and accelerometer signal (*acceleration w/o gravity*), it was used for the transformation of signals between two coordinate systems. This type of transformation can be understood as obtaining information on how the accelerometer signal would look if the sensor had an artificially created orientation (*augmented quat*). On the other hand, the *augmented quat* signal was used to reconstruct the angular velocity signals. In the proposed method, 30 additional learning samples were generated for each gait sample.

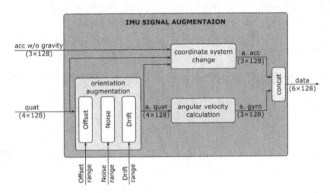

Fig. 4. Data flow diagram for the proposed augmentation technique

Figure 4 presents a block diagram of the presented data augmentation mechanism. It can be noticed that the output of the augmentation module is a data block of dimension 6×128, which is compatible with that shown in Fig. 3.

In this study, the capabilities of two settings of the augmentation module were investigated. These parameters were selected by trial and error methods. The following settings Offset: 7.5°, Noise: 0.1°, Drift: 3° and Offset: 3.5°, Noise: 0.2°, Drift: 4° were examined.

Orientation Signal Augmentation
Several typical scenarios affecting the values measured by the IMU sensors can be observed. These are the presence of rotation of the sensor with respect to the initial position (*Offset*), vibrations (*Noise*), or the slow rotation of the sensor over time (*Drift*). The proposed augmentation technique can account for all these scenarios and model them by modifying the orientation signals.

Modeling the presence of rotation of the sensor with respect to the initial position (*Offset*) was realized in the following steps: randomly select angles of rotation about three axes from the *Offset range*; create a *Q_offset* quaternion representing the orientation change; multiply the original orientation signals at each time t by the artificially created quaternion (equivalent to giving an additional constant rotation for the entire gait sample).

Modeling of sensor vibration (*Noise*) was implemented in the following steps: at each time t, randomly select angles of rotation about three axes from the *Noise range*; create a quaternion *Q_noise* representing noise; multiply the original orientation signals by the artificially created quaternion (equivalent to giving an additional random rotation at each frame of gait sample).

Modeling of slow sensor rotation during motion (*Drift*) was implemented as follows. For each of the three axes, randomly select two values from the *Drift range*. For each pair create a Bezier curve of length 128 which can model slow angle change. For each time *t*, create a quaternion Q_drift modeling rotation about the three axes. Multiply the original orientation signals by an artificially created quaternion.

Figure 5 a) shows the original orientation signal whereas Fig. 5 b) presents augmented. In the results of the manual inspection, we can see a significant change of the *w* component (quaternion), while remembering that for each data frame the quaternion is normalized. From the signal patterns we can observe that despite the addition of noise, the augmented signal Fig. 5 b) does not have significant jitter.

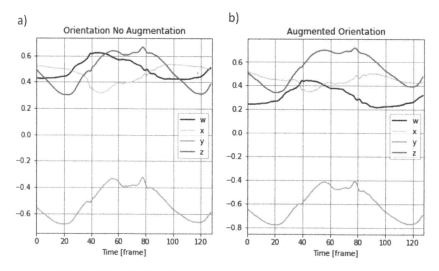

Fig. 5. Original orientation signal a) augmented orientation signal b)

IMU Signals Augmentation
Augmentation of the IMU signals was performed by changing the accelerometer measurements coordinate system and reconstructing the angular velocity signal with the use of modified orientation signals.

Augmentation of accelerometer signals involved two-step calculations. In the first one, the quaternion describing the rotation between two reference systems - original and augmented was determined (1):

$$\begin{aligned} _{aug}^{G}q &= {}_{S}^{G}q \cdot {}_{aug}^{S}q \\ _{aug}^{S}q &= {}_{S}^{G}q^{*} \cdot {}_{aug}^{G}q \end{aligned} \tag{1}$$

where:

$_{aug}{}^{G}q$–quaternion describing a rotation from global (world) coordinates to an augmented orientation;

$_{s}{}^{G}q$– quaternion describing a rotation from global (world) coordinates to sensor orientation;

$_{aug}{}^{S}q$– quaternion describing the rotation that must be performed to switch from the sensor orientation to the augmented orientation;

$_{s}{}^{G}q^{*}$ – A conjugate quaternion representing a rotation from sensor to global coordinates;

· – Hamiltonian operator/quaternion multiplication operator.

In the next step, the vector (acceleration at time t) was rotated using formula (2):

$$v' = q \cdot v \cdot q^{*} \tag{2}$$

where:

v – The original vector (in quaternion form where w = 0);

v' – vector in the new reference system (in quaternion form where w = 0);

q- quaternion representing the specified rotation.

Formula (2) could be presented in more detailed form (3):

$$\begin{bmatrix} 0 \\ a_{augx} \\ a_{augy} \\ a_{augz} \end{bmatrix} = {}_{aug}{}^{S}q \cdot \begin{bmatrix} 0 \\ a_{sx} \\ a_{sy} \\ a_{sz} \end{bmatrix} \cdot {}_{aug}{}^{S}q^{*} \tag{3}$$

where:

$_{aug}{}^{S}q$– quaternion describing the rotation that is required to switch from sensor orientation to the augmented orientation;

a_{sx}, a_{sy}, a_{sy}–accelerometer measurement values at time t;

$a_{augx}, a_{augy}, a_{augy}$– augmented accelerometer measurement values, the readings that would be measured if the sensor had an augmented quat orientation.

Augmentation of the gyroscope readings involved reconstruction of the angular velocity signals from the augmented orientation timeseries. Process is initiated by determining the quaternion differential (4):

$$\dot{q}_t = (q_{t+1} - q_t)/\Delta T, \tag{4}$$

where:

$q_{(t+1)}, q_t$ – orientation in the quaternion form at time $t + 1$ and t;

$\dot{q}_t$ – quaternion differential;

ΔT– sampling period.

In the next augmentation step, the angular velocity was reconstructed according to the equation.

$$\omega_t(q_t, \dot{q}_t) = 2 \cdot W(q_t) \cdot \dot{q}_t, \tag{5}$$

where:

ω_t – vector of angular velocities ($\omega_x, \omega_y, \omega_z$) at time t;

W – matrix mapping the quaternion q_t and its differential to angular velocities.

The value of the matrix W depends on quaternion q at time t. The coefficient of the W matrix is specified in Eq. (6):

$$W(q_t) = \begin{bmatrix} -q_x & q_w & -q_z & q_y \\ -q_y & q_z & q_w & -q_x \\ -q_z & -q_y & q_x & q_w \end{bmatrix},$$ (6)

where:

q_w, q_x, q_y, q_z – value of the quaternion w, x, y, z components at time t;

Figure 6 shows the accelerometer and gyroscope measurements and their perturbed (augmented) forms.

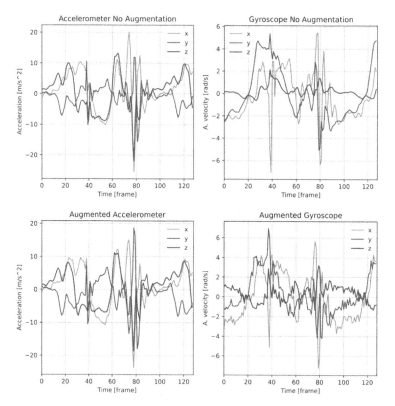

Fig. 6. Comparison of real accelerometer and gyroscope signals with their augmented forms

Several important observation can be noted from the signals presented in Fig. 6. First of all, although the augmented orientation signal (Fig. 5) has a slow-variable nature, the reconstructed angular velocity signal has a jitter noise (reconstructed signal nevertheless has the characteristics of the original signal). The *Noise* parameter has a crucial influence on perturbation process.

On the other hand, the augmented acceleration signal is remarkably similar to the original, with some distinctive differences. The maximum value of the augmented acceleration signal decreased from about 20 to about 15 m/s^2. An increase in the difference between OX and OZ can be observed over a duration of 30–60 frames. In the process of augmentation, the signal did not gain an additional offset, drift or noise, but numerous local distortions.

The effect of augmentation on the orientation signal is shown in Fig. 5. However, the analysis of the orientation signals will be omitted. The x, y, z coordinates of the quaternions represent imaginary numbers. The quaternion itself was normalized to a norm of one. In addition, the same orientation can be presented as two quaternions with negated components.

3.4 Classification

Data classification was carried out with a Deep Learning CNN classifier, in an architecture compatible with [11]. The dimensions of the last dense layer were modified to be consistent with the number of participants in the used dataset. It should be noted that the deep network structure was designed to process accelerometer and gyroscope measurement values in the form of 6 × 128 data blocks. The CNN was trained for 200 epochs using cross_entropy cost function, with the use of Adam optimization algorithms. The structure of particular network layers is presented in Table 1.

Table 1. Neural network architecture used in biometric system, ks-kernel size, p-padding, dimensions consistent to TensorFlow module documentation

#warstwy	Range	Pattern
0	Conv2D	ks = [1, 9, 1, 32], p = VALID
1	MaxPool2D	ks = [1, 2], p = VALID
2	Conv2D	ks = [1, 3, 32, 64], p = SAME
3	Conv2D	ks = [1, 3, 64, 128], p = SAME
4	MaxPool2D	ks = [1, 2], p = VALID
5	Conv2D	ks = [6, 1, 128, 128]
6	Dense	dim = [2048, 30]

This network has the general characteristics of AlexNet type architecture such as alternate convolution and max pooling layers. However, there are several significant differences. First of all, in the first layer of the network, the filter has a dimension of 1 × 9. In this case the first neural layer does not process data from several sensor axes (each filter reacts to a single sensor axis). Moreover, the consecutive conv2D layers are rather unusual.

4   Experiment Results

The experiments were conducted for 4 types of substrate: Pavement, Grass, Flat even and Cobble stone. For each, the identification performance was examined in cases:

– absence of augmentation (Baseline),
– proposed augmentation algorithm: Offset: 3.5°, Nosie: 0.2°, Drift: 4° (Proposed I),
– proposed augmentation algorithm: Offset: 7.5°, Noise: 0.1°, Drift: 3° (Proposed II),
– augmentation proposed by the Iso et al. (Iso et al. [3]),
– augmentation proposed by Um et. al. permutation and rotation (Um et al. I [4]),
– augmentation proposed by Um et al. rotation (Um et al. II [4]).

Considering the non-deterministic nature of the neural network classifiers, each experiment was repeated 50 times.

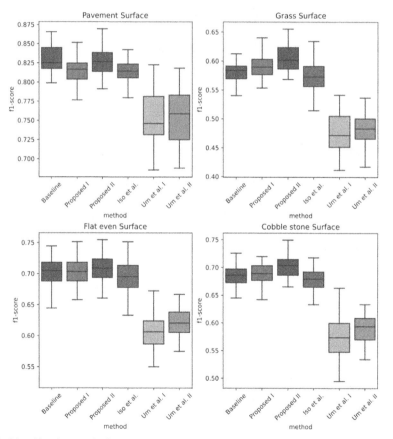

Fig. 7. Identification results for different substrate types and data augmentation algorithms based on validations repeated 50 times

Several interesting observations can be obtained from the results presented in Fig. 7. First of all, augmentation techniques in many cases have no real impact on the identification results, and in some even degrade the achieved metrics. Regardless of substrate type, the Um et al. methods provided worse identification results than baseline approach.

Application of the algorithms *"Proposed I"*, *"Proposed II"*, or *"Iso et al."* did not result in significant differences for *Pavement* and *Flat Even* surfaces identification metrics. In these cases, the use of augmentation is not recommended. A positive augmentation effect was observed for surfaces such as Grass and Pavement and generally only for the Proposed II method.

5 Conclusions and Future Work

This paper presents an analysis of the impact of motion sensor augmentation techniques on the performance of biometric identification systems. The proposed approach concern classification process with the use of triaxial accelerometer and gyroscope signals. A new augmentation technique based on modification of orientation signals, and providing simultaneous modeling of accelerometer and gyroscope signals was proposed (Fig. 4). The conducted research examined the effect of the proposed algorithm as well as literature techniques [3, 4] on biometric identification metric (Fig. 7). Validation of the augmentation algorithms was performed for a publicly available dataset containing gait recorded on a substrate such as: pavement, flat even, grass, cobblestone.

The results of the experiments (Fig. 7) indicate that the application of the augmentation mechanism is not always profitable. Methods of Um el al. [4] based on rotation (*Um et al. I*) and rotation and permutation (*Um et al. II*) significantly worsened the identification results for all examined substrates. It is speculated that due to the significant rotations ranges ($\pm 180°$ range, Sect. 2), method generated samples that were not observable under real conditions. Although these techniques have achieved very good identification rates in the field of Parkinson's disease monitoring, its use in the field of gait analysis is not recommended.

The approach of Iso et al. [3] produced significantly higher identification rates than the methods of Um et al. (Fig. 7). Due to the modeling of limited rotations, it ensures the generation of potentially observable samples. However, this approach does not allow modeling additional disturbances such as vibration or drift. It can be speculated that these factors contribute to the advantage of our proposed solution (Proposed II).

Regarding the proposed approach, which allows modeling both rotation, vibration and drift depending on the introduced parameters significant differences in results can be observed. *Proposed I* method (Offset: 7.5°, Noise: 0.1°, Drift: 3°) produced lower results than *Proposed II* (Offset: 3.5°, Noise: 0.2°, Drift: 4°) in each of the analyzed substrate. Certainly, the selected parameters are not the optimal parameters for highest identification performance. However, the purpose of the study was to show the possibility of obtaining identification scores higher than the baseline, rather than searching for a local maximum.

A major advantage of the proposed solution is that the generated accelerometer and gyroscope signals are closely associated with each other. In the presented approach, the disturbances of the gyroscope and accelerometer are not interfered independently as is the case [5]. Consequently, the generation of samples that are not observable in the real world is prevented. However, the proposed approach has two major drawbacks: computational complexity and the inability to amplify the accelerometer signal (similar to [3]). Further work is planned to create a new pre-processing block for the data augmentation module. It is expected to gain additional control by decomposing the accelerometer readings into components resulting from gravitational acceleration (orientation-dependent) and actual motion. This would allow to simulate, e.g., change in walking speed, accelerometer measurement noise. Such a solution is expected to increase the scores of gait-based biometric identification systems.

Acknowledgment. This research was funded in whole or in part by National Science Centre, Poland 2021/41/N/ST6/02505. For the purpose of Open Access, the author has applied a CC-BY public copyright licence to any Author Accepted Manuscript (AAM) version arising from this submission.

References

1. Wen, Q, Sun, L., Song, X., Gao, J., Wang, X., Xu, H.: Timeseries data augmentation for deep learning: a survey. arXiv preprint arXiv:2002.12478 (2020)
2. Eyobu, O.S., Han, D.: Feature representation and data augmentation for human activity classification based on wearable IMU sensor data using a deep LSTM neural network. Sensors **18**, 2892 (2018)
3. Iso, T., Yamazaki, K.: Gait analyzer based on a cell phone with a single three-axis accelerometer. In: Proceedings of ACM Conference on Human-Computer Interaction with Mobile Devices and Services (MobileHCI) (2006)
4. Um, T.T., Pfister, F.M.J., Pichler, D., et al.: Data augmentation of wearable sensor data for Parkinson's disease monitoring using convolutional neural networks. In Proceedings of the 19th ACM International Conference on Multimodal Interaction, Glasgow, UK (2017)
5. Delgado-Escano, R., Castro, F.M., Cozar, J.R., et al.: An end-to-end multi-task and fusion CNN for inertial-based gait recognition. IEEE Access **2019**, 7 (2019)
6. Kwon, H, Tong, C., Haresamudram, H., Gao, Y., et al.: IMUTube: automatic extraction of virtual on-body accelerometry from video for human activity recognition. arXiv:2006.05675 (2020)
7. Pellatt, L., Dewar, A., Philippides, A., Roggen D.: Mapping vicon motion tracking to 6-Axis IMU data for wearable activity recognition. In: Ahad, M.A.R., Inoue, S., Roggen, D., Fujinami, K. (eds.) Activity and Behavior Computing, Smart Innovation, Systems and Technologies, vol. 204, pp. 3–20. Springer, Singapore (2021). https://doi.org/10.1007/978-981-15-8944-7_1
8. Luo, Y., Coppola, S., Dixon, P., et al.: A database of human gait performance on irregular and uneven surfaces collected by wearable sensors. Sci. Data **7**(1), 219 (2020)
9. Sawicki, A., Saeed, K.: Application of LSTM Networks for Human Gait-Based Identification. In: Zamojski, W., Mazurkiewicz, J., Sugier, J., Walkowiak, T., Kacprzyk, J. (eds.) Theory and Engineering of Dependable Computer Systems and Networks. Advances in Intelligent Systems and Computing, vol. 1389, pp. 402–412. Springer, Cham (2021). https://doi.org/10.1007/978-3-030-76773-0_39

10. Barralon, P., Vuillerme, N., Noury. N.: Walk detection with a kinematic sensor: frequency and wavelet comparison. In: International Conference of the IEEE Engineering in Medicine and Biology Society, 1711–1714. PMID: 17945661 (2006)
11. Zou, Q., Wang, Y., Wang, Q., Zhao, Y., Li, Q.: Deep learning-based gait recognition using smartphones in the wild. arXiv:1811.00338 (2020)

Computer Information Systems
and Security

A Look into the Vulnerability of Voice Assisted IoT

Raghunath Maji[1], Atreyee Biswas[2(✉)], and Rituparna Chaki[1(✉)] (iD)

[1] AKC School of Information Technology, Calcutta University, Rajabazar, India
rituchaki@gmail.com
[2] Maulana Abul Kalam Azad University of Technology, Kalyani, West Bengal, India
atreyee11@gmail.com

Abstract. The use of 'smart' assistants in our daily life have brought a change to the user perception of the complicacy of systems involved in the Internet of Things (IoT). The smart assistants come with inherent voice-driven software aimed to improve user experience. The ease of use however, comes with the potential threat to user data security. In this paper, we studied several researches in an attempt to understand the vulnerabilities of voice-driven IoT systems. We try to find the research areas in order to secure the unsuspecting users of an IoT system.

Keywords: Voice assistants · Virtual assistant skills · Voice enabled IoT · IoT security

1 Introduction

The commonly used voice assistant software installed on Internet of Things (IoT) devices, helps the user to monitor the world by using heterogeneous sensors (e.g., cameras or microphones). They transmit sensor or user data to some cloud infrastructure for analysis and command interpretation. After analyzing these sensor data or user data/commands, the cloud server decides whether they will communicate with other online services (such as calendars, messaging systems, weather information systems, etc.) or communicate with actuators or smart devices (e.g., smart light bulbs, or other IoT household devices). The popular virtual assistants such as Siri, Cortana, Alexa, etc., have made spoken access to data and services through mobile devices a common thing. The use of voice assistants is not limited to voice search only, they are also being used to control all the smart devices within a house. Now-a-days, most home electronics devices are voice-enabled devices. For example, the fridge, Air-conditioner, lights, fans can all be controlled by voice which is increasing the demand for the use of voice assistants. All the tech giant companies like Google, Microsoft, Apple, and Samsung have created their voice assistants to target this huge potential market of the future. Online shopping is another area where the use of voice assistants has increased in the last few years [1]. The dreadful pandemic has actually forced most people to opt for online shopping. Now most online shopping sites use voice assistant

K. Saeed and J. Dvorský (Eds.): CISIM 2022, LNCS 13293, pp. 49–62, 2022.
https://doi.org/10.1007/978-3-031-10539-5_4

which makes it easy to buy things and pay for them. As these voice assistant applications support different regional languages, they are becoming more and more popular.

However, the popularity of voice assistants comes with concerning drawbacks. Currently, most Internet of Things (IoT) devices are controlled by voice assistant software and it has been observed in the past that many Internet-controlled devices are insecure and have weak standards. The Voice Assistant controls all small and large scale home appliances [2], so if the Voice Assistant is not protected, then the appliance is not protected, and may be damaged by improper use or misused by someone with unauthorized access to the Voice Assistant. Voice Assistant now controls most users' Smartphone's so the user does not have to control the IoT device manually. Thus the safety and reliability [3,4], of the voice assistant has become a point of concern from the point of user data security. In this paper, we have surveyed some of the existing works in this domain to arrive at the specific points of vulnerability of voice assistants. This survey gives a clear picture of different issues in securing IoT environment through the use of voice assistants application. We have tried to explain the variety of problems that have occurred in the use of virtual assistants in the past and what recovery process had been used in recent times to recover these problems. More specifically, our contribution is:

- Investigate and understanding of previously discovered threats against smart virtual assistants in the IoT environment.
- Analyze whether the protection mechanisms in the virtual assistants prevent the above attacks.
- identify and discuss potential defenses in situations where attackers break through old defenses and succeed in attacking.

The rest of this paper is organized as follows. Section 2 focuses on some past research works on voice assistants and their vulnerabilities in IoT environment. Section 3 focus on the aim and research questions of voice assistants. The fourth section deals with different kind of vulnerabilities in voice assistants. Finally, Section five and six includes the future work and conclusions.

2   Related Work

Voice assistants and voice enable IoT device play an important role in creating better output from IoT. In this section we shall discuss some past research works on voice assistants and their vulnerabilities in IoT environment.

In this paper [6], the author's highlights and demonstrates the three weaknesses of the voice assistant and suggests some solutions to overcome these weaknesses. According to them, even if there is no user, The voice assistants devices may be attacked by activating various audio or video sounds. They specifically point out this weakness and to prevent this they have proposed a device called "VIRTUAL SECURITY BUTTON" which will prevent the voice assistant from taking voice commands from any recorded sound source if there is no user around the voice assistant.

In [7], the author's said that the virtual assistant's microphone always listens to the end-user, which may be a violation of our privacy, although all virtual assistant companies state that they only record the user's voice when the user says "wake up". But they continue to hear conversations and background sounds to hear the "sound of awakening". Some devices have been found to save their recordings. If an attacker gains access to the device of a compromised virtual assistant, all recorded sound or voice can be sent to the attacker.

In [34], the authors focus primarily on the security and privacy challenges arising from the use of acoustic channels. Here they discuss different types of attacks and countermeasures but they mainly highlight established areas such as voice authentication and new areas such as acoustic denial-of-service which deserve more attention. In the context of this study, an obfuscated example is a signal perceived by humans as noise, while the PVA interprets a command. Here they describe the different types of loopholes where privacy can be compromised, like bypass of access control, which may lead to the loss of confidential data. Another issue is recorded speech of the user can use for misleading the voice authentication and predicting the user's emotion.

In a recent work by Wang et al. [8], anothers approach was investigated to implement speech recognition technology in IoT enabled smart home system. Smart home can be personalized by users through imposing voice command and it is therefore necessary to prohibit false voice recognition. In this paper a complete smart home system has been discussed in context of basic speech recognition and related algorithms considering minimization of error in speech recognition by IoT devices associated with smart home. The method discussed in this paper has future scope to work in a noisy environment as well as in a more improved communication technology such as 5G.

In [35], the authors state that the virtual assistant has two parts, the first is the user end where the virtual assistant collects user data and the other end is the cloud server which executes or analyzes the data and provides relevant services depending on it. In the Voice Assistant ecosystem (Fig. 1), they store this personal data temporarily or permanently in different places which makes it easier for cyber attackers to tamper with this data. This is a major privacy issue any voice assistants. To overcome this problem, they examine the type and location of data and personal information within the Voice Assistant ecosystem, and in parallel, they run IoT forensic strategies to gather valuable information about cyber-attacks. In order to examine the privacy issue more in-depth, they created their own testbed for three different voice assistants like Amazon Alexa, Google Assistant, and Microsoft Cortana. They used Xiaomi Redmi Note 6 Pro mobile phone, with Android 9 installed on it, a Lenovo Yoga 730 laptop, with Windows 10 installed on it, as well as a Raspberry Pi 4, with Raspberry Pi OS (ex. Raspbian) installed on it to simulate the functioning of voice assistant devices. They show some results where we see that the voice assistant system shares the user's confidential data.

In [33], the authors conducted a survey and followed some criteria for paper selection. They only select papers that must present an empirical study of the security or privacy aspects of the voice assistant. Another criterion is that the paper must contain information about actual privacy or security elements and be published in a journal or at a good conference. They avoid documents that may have an interest in security and privacy but do not focus on it as the main investigation. They categorized the paper based on the target audience. The audience is the end-user, developer, or both. In the end, they found that 79% of the paper focused on end-user data protection, 11% included end-users with developers, and 10% focused on developers only. The main security flaws of Voice Assistants are verified by the manufacturers through third party software.

In [14], the authors discuss some aspects of Voice Assistant that make the user's personal data more insecure. According to them, some sophisticated voice assistants are able to perform high-priority commands, such as changing the system settings of the operating system. They also say that voice assistants often belong to OS or device manufacturers, so they enjoy more privilege than regular apps. We also know that the operating system maintains the security of our system and if these voice assistants can change the operating system then those voice assistants can easily break the security of any system.

On the other hand Z. Ma et al. [9] discussed security aspects of smart IoT devices with the use of speech recognition. In this work authors proposed an outsourced privacy-preserving speech recognition framework (OPSR) for smart IoT devices in long-short term memory (LSTM) neural network and edge computing. A series of additive secret sharing based interactive protocols between two edge servers were designed for obtaining lightweight outsourced computation and in context of this protocol neural network training process of LSTM for intelligent IoT device voice control was implemented. Finally, with universal composability theory in combination with experimental results, the correctness and security of this framework, theoretically had been proved.

In future, it will be interesting to extend the idea of the proposed framework to some other types of secret sharing protocols which are not additive in nature such as secure multiplicative protocol and secure comparison protocol in preserving privacy of smart IoT devices with the use of speech recognition.

As per a report dated May 25, 2018, in The Telegraph USA [4], the user reported about their conversations being recorded and sent to a random contact by their voice assistant, which was Amazon Alexa. There are many such reports that lead to the observation that not all data/user personal information collected by Voice Assistant remain under complete control of the user only!

We observed that the attacking surface of the voice assistant is very large but the research community focuses on only a small part of it. In general, the focus is mostly on issues such as poor authentication and data protection using different data encryption algorithms. We also found that research is needed to address other issues related to Always Listening end-user conversation and the Integration of IoT Devices. In this paper we have highlighted the different areas of risk and all the vulnerabilities in each case and what preventive measures have been taken in the past and we hope that this paper will present a road-map for future research in this area.

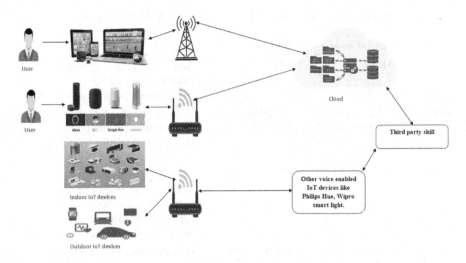

Fig. 1. Voice assistant ecosystem

3   Aim and Research Questions

To the best of our knowledge, there is a very limited number of research papers that specifically address the security and privacy challenges associated with Virtual Assistants. The lack of a comprehensive threat analysis not only prevents users from realizing the risks associated with the devices but also prevents them from creating a formal security model. In this paper, we focus on the following main research questions:

- What are the major vulnerabilities for virtual assistants that violate user privacy?
- What are the major limitations of existing countermeasures?
- What countermeasures can be taken to alleviate these weaknesses?

And our objectives of this research paper are:

- Investigate and understanding of previously discovered threats against smart virtual assistants in the IoT environment.
- Analyze whether the protection mechanisms in the virtual assistants prevent the above attacks.
- If attackers break through old defenses and succeed in attacking, identify and discuss potential defenses.

Table 1. List of some well known voice assistant application

Vendor	Virtual assistant	Enabled device	Feature
Amazon	Alexa [35]	Echo, dot, tab, fire tablet	Alexa calling and messaging, voice control, audio, Wi-Fi music, skill, smarter home
Google	Google now and Google [35]	Any phone with Android, Google home	Call and messaging, speech, recognition, Google home, Google allo, mobile integration, content control, chat assistant
Apple	Siri [36]	iPhone, iPad, Mac	Call and messaging, punctuation, voice changing, multi-language, text editing, app support, sports, entertainment, home kit
Microsoft	Assistant cortana [35]	Any PC with windows, any Mobile with window	Digital assistant, time best reminder, call and messaging, location best reminder, cloud and online service.
Samsung	Bixby [37]	Samsung android mobile, tab	Bixby voice, Bixby vision, Bixby home, Bixby reminder, QR code detection, intelligent user interface, translation function
Braina	Braina virtual assistant [38]	Any phone with Windows, android smartphone, tab	Speech to text, search information on the Internet, play the songs you want to hear, open or search files on your computer, set alarms and reminders, mathematical calculations, remember notes for you, automate various computer tasks, read ebooks

4 Vulnerabilities of Voice Assistant Systems that Increase End Users' Data Security Risks

We currently do a lot of our important work with voice assistants and for that, they collect and store our information in raw form without any encryption. Figure 1 shows the Voice Assistant ecosystem where the Voice Assistant system sends all its data to the cloud server for data analysis. If the voice assistant has various weaknesses that allow someone to access our data, then it is a very bad aspect in terms of security. so it is very important to know the vulnerability of a voice assistant

- Always Listening end user conversation
- Weak Authentication
- Easily controlled by Ultrasonic sound
- Silently install skills (apps) on a user IoT device
- Cloud server dependency
- Dependent on other edge devices

4.1 Always Listening End User Conversation

The Voice Assistant application/service for an IoT (e.g. Amazon Echo) is fast becoming part of our daily life. These digital assistants only respond when they hear a keyword ('wakeup word'). The devices are on a continuous listen mode, thus Amazon's Echo devices listen for "Alexa", iOS devices listen constantly for "Hey Siri" and Android devices listen for the words "Hey Google" unless we turn it off. Obviously, the microphones remain switched on always [10]. In [11], the authors conducted a diary study and interviewed seventeen smart speaker users and seventeen non-users to better understand these aspects that may inform future smart speaker design and privacy controls. The questions for which the authors searched for a response were: (1) factors that affect the adoption of smart speakers (2) the privacy perceptions and concerns of individuals about smart speakers (3) the effect of these privacy concerns on the user's behavior with smart speakers? Based on their answers, the authors suggested designing more usable and better-integrated privacy controls for smart speakers.

The "always on" mode of these virtual assistants drew the attention of [7], as that may be a violation of our privacy. All tech giants, such as Amazon, Apple, Google, and Microsoft, claim that their voice assist devices only record when users order the assistant to wake up [3]. In reality, they continue to hear conversations and background sounds to hear the "sound of awakening". Some devices have been found to save their recordings. If an attacker gains access to the device of a compromised virtual assistant, all recorded sound or voice can be sent to the attacker. On 13 August 2020, Dikla Barda, Roman Jaikin, and Yara Sriki posted a blog on checkpoint research "Keeping the gate locked on your IoT devices: Vulnerabilities found on Amazon's Alexa" [12]. Where they pointed that, some Amazon/Alexa subdomains are at risk for cross-origin resource sharing (CORS) incorrect configuration and cross-site scripting. These vulnerabilities allow an attacker to silently install skills (apps) on the user's Alexa account, get a list of all installed skills in the user's Alexa account, silently delete an installed skill, get the victim's personal information. In [13], The author also noticed that even when the Wake-up Word was not used, the system was still recording the voice of all the people present there. It was reported that, 61.5% of recordings were triggered by TV audio and 38.4% by human conversation. Based on this, they said that it is possible to record a private conversation and send it to the device without saying the wake-up word. As they say, if they capture all the words in the house except the user's words, it can easily find the user's daily activities and the user's geographical location.

All voice assistants are always listening, so it is not possible for us to know where they are recording our private conversations. But the easiest way to turn it off is to turn off the microphone of voice assistant device. In [13], the authors' said that they did not find evidence of recorded and transmitted any private conversations when the microphone was turned off on the device. However, if we turn off the microphone of a voice assistant device, the work it is intended to do is not complete. As we can not turn on the microphone of the voice assistant device using voice command,so we have to switch it on!

4.2   Weak Authentication

The authors [14–17], have blamed a weak authentication system for attacking the security and privacy of voice assist devices. The authentication of voice assistants is done by using wake-up words. And all voice assistants have a "wake-up" word that is the same for everyone. So everyone knows the word "wake-up" of a voice assistant. The voice assistants have no additional ways of authenticating the user. The device will accept any command succeeding the wake-up keyword. So it is very easy for hackers to activate a device using their waking sound and try to access personal information or do some illegal things using this device.

In [7], the author states that some attackers who want to attack the voice assistant device come close to the device, fooling the device and ordering it as the owner of that device. From there they are able to find out his email id, personal information, calendar details.

We know that all voice assistants are activated in the wake-up word but we often say the activation word for some other work or similar word for which the voice assistant is activated and keeps recording our conversations. This issue may affect users' privacy in situations where private or confidential conversations are accidentally leaked, or where attackers may retrieve sensitive information from these devices. Published on May 25, 2018 in The Telegraph USA, by Helena Horton "Amazon Alexa recorded owner's conversation and sent to 'random' contact, couple complains". An American couple found their Amazon Alexa voice assistant system had recorded their conversations and sent them to a contact. All of these information proves that not all data/user personal information collected by Voice Assistant is completely controlled by the user. If more than one person uses a single voice assistant, it is difficult to determine who has access to the resources and how this access should be granted. Generally in a multi-user environment, Voice Assistant gives all users the same access priority and any user can change the device setup purchase network connection word or more without the initial user's consent and this is not good for respecting privacy.

When a user tries to buy something from a shopping site which obviously involves a banking transaction, then that must be done in a very secure manner. One way to achieve security of transaction is to let the user approve/aware of the bank transaction. The case described in [18], shows how a child recently placed an unauthorized order worth about $ 300 using his mother's Amazon account. From this example, it is clear that the financial information held by a voice assistant is not completely secure.

4.3 Easily Controlled by Ultrasonic Sound

One of the major weaknesses of Voice Assistant devices is that all of these devices or applications are activated by the Silent command. Whether it's Alexa, Siri, Cortana, Google Assistant or Bixby, they can all be victims of this worryingly common hack. In [16], the authors used a technique called Dolphin Attack, (a way to translate voice commands into ultrasonic frequencies that are too high for humans to hear) to access the voice assistants device without knowing the owner of this IoT device. DolphinAttack uses inaudible voice injection to control Voice assistants Silently, the attacker used a portable transmitter that could launch a dolphin attack anywhere. The authors uses ultrasonic words that people cannot hear, but it can be heard on a microphone such as a smartphone, smart speakers, Amazon Echo, or Google Home. The basic principle of Dolphin Attack is to inject inaudible voice commands before digitizing elements. There-fore, the potential for dolphin attack depends much more on the audio hardware than on the speech recognition system. In recent times, microphones using most IoT devices have been able to receive sound signals above 20 kHz [19,20]. One way of mitigating such type of attacks is to use a microphone that will reject all kinds of ultrasonic sound. This is obviously an expensive solution, so [16], devel-oped a software solution to protect the virtual assistant from dolphin attacks. The authors claimed that a machine learning-based classifier would detect high frequencies from 500 to 1000 Hz.

4.4 Silently Install Skills (Apps) on a User IoT Device

In [12] the author shows some evidence that Voice Assistant devices install/uninstall various skills (apps) on our devices without informing us. And these skills access the voice history of voice assistants and gain personal infor-mation through skill interactions when users use installed skills . Nowadays, a lot of virtual assistant skills are hosted online, although the numbers continue to grow every day. For example, Amazon's skills market now has more than 100,000 [31], worldwide, and Google Assistant has more than 4,500 skills in the skills market [32].

4.5 Cloud Server Dependency

All voice assistants use cloud infrastructure and this infrastructure has many advantages such as it is cheaper than physical storage and using cloud storage to access your file from anywhere with internet connection, you can synchronize and update all your devices that are connected to this infrastructure. As cloud infrastructure creates all these benefits, it also opens up new opportunities for hackers [21]. The cloud infrastructure helps an user to access her or his files from anywhere that has an internet connection. Thus, it becomes extremely important to protect the unauthorized access of cloud data [22]. Since many people in Cloud Infrastructure use it simultaneously, the chances of authorization errors are much higher than any single-use device.

Cloud providers may have multiple copies of data in cloud storage for error-tolerance and data recovery in the event of a crash or system failure. The users have no idea about the number of copies of their data in cloud storage and the location of the data. Therefore, deleting data from cloud storage [23], is also a very serious problem nowadays. Once a cloud user wants to delete his data, he must make sure that the data is actually deleted from all cloud storage sources and there should be no duplicate data anywhere in the cloud storage. The user, however, is never sure whether all copies of client data have been deleted as requested [24]. In [25], the author states that Amazon mayn keep a copy of users' voice interactions with Alexa even after deleting the recordings.

In [26], the authors conducted a passive analysis of encrypted smart home traffic and found some privacy vulnerabilities when exchanging information between voice assistant devices and voice assistant cloud providers. In the case of cloud infrastructure, all user data is stored in a single point, so if the security of this point is violated, all data is leaked [27]. But if the data is stored on a single user's device and the security of that device is compromised, then that person's data is only leaked, not everyone's data is leaked.

APIs (Application user interfaces) can open lines of communications for attackers to exploit cloud resources. Some developer's build APIs without proper authentication controls and some developers do not think that attackers will see backend API calls and do not set up proper authentication controls. As a result, these APIs are completely open to the Internet and anyone can use them to access enterprise data.

4.6   Dependent on Other Edge Devices

Smart homes, smart cities, and smart cars are some of the hot topics in recent times. If we want to create smart home or smart car or smart city and control it through voice assistant then we need to connect voice assistant with all IoT devices used in smart home or smart car. If any of these devices are harmful, the vulnerability of the virtual assistant is multiplied. Some studies [29,30], show that the vulnerability of voice assistants is increased if the voice assistant is integrated with other IoT devices. Such devices are Philips Hue, Wipro smart lighting, etc.

In [26], the author has set up a smart home laboratory with a passive network to collect traffic from the actual smart home. They examined four commercially available smart homes Device: A Sense Slip Monitor, a nest cam indoor, Security camera, a Belkin WeMo switch, and An Amazon Echo. The author's noticed after installing these devices that Voice Assistant security was not being properly implemented. The another work [28], The authors tested five smart home IoT devices including Wings Smart Body Analyzer, Philips Hue Connected Bulb, Belkin Wemo Motion Sensor and Switch Kit, Nest Smoke Alarm and Withings Smart Baby Monitor. Here the authors also find that after installing all these devices, the security of smart home architecture is not going to be implemented properly and which is giving a lot of chances to man in middle attack.

Insecure interaction between apps used to control peripheral devices and third-party counterpart apps that can open a way for remote attackers.

5   Future Research Scope

In the above section, we have surveyed a variety of research works in a bid to understand the vulnerabilities associated with voice-driven smart assistants in the internet of things environment. Our study leads to the following, The above study leads to fill up following research gaps:

- Voice assistants devices like 'Amazon Echo', 'Google Now' have been widely used in every aspect of our daily lives. Although research has already begun to develop personalized and secure IoT systems using voice assistants, this requires modifying existing protocols or introducing new ones that can solve practical problems such as noisy environments, extensive command management, poor authentication and validation.
- Not much research has been done on how to prevent the voice assistant from always listening to the user's personal information without interfering with the purpose for which we use the voice assistant. Some have suggested decoupling voice input and output in order to distinguish between the use of both microphone and speaker, when only one have been granted access [14]. We need to have in-depth research considering the heterogeneity of the voice assistants across the IoT environment.
- We have seen that the voice assistant acts based on user instructions or answers the question of the user who utters the wake-up word of the voice assistant. However, the authenticity of the speaker as being the rightful owner of the system is not verified. This allows anyone to easily access another user's voice assistant and thereby gain access to privileged information. Thus authentication of the user has to be given due consideration while designing the voice-driven systems.
- The security of IoT is dealt in attack specific way. The present day voice-controlled IoT systems are vulnerable to attacks that need to be modeled effectively by using a suitable technique. The literature survey leads to the conclusion that contextual awareness is important to model the behavior profile of valid users.

6   Conclusion

Voice assistants are gaining popularity due to their ease of use. Now-a-days, they often come as a pre-installed feature in most of the IoT devices. The ease of use, however comes with a inherent problem, the problem of security breach for an unsuspecting user. In this paper, we have surveyed several research works devoted towards identifying the vulnerabilities of so-called 'smart' assistants. Voice assistants are very helpful in making our daily work easier but at the same time we need to keep in mind that it is very important to keep all our important personal data safe. There have been several incidents that have taken place around us which lead us to the observation that so far voice-controlled IoT networks are vulnerable to a variety of attacks. In this paper, we have discussed different type of previously discovered threats against smart virtual assistants in the IoT environment. We have also tried to look at what mechanisms have been used in the past to solve the problems that occurred in the past and how many problems have been solved and what problems still remain. The basic mode-of-operation of these voice assistants tend to be in an 'Always ON' mode. The always-listening problem in all the voice assistants is very dangerous for users to protect their personal information. We noticed that the voice assistant started working when someone said the wake-up word of this assistant but the assistant does not check that the user is genuine or an illegitimate person. We have highlighted all these problems in our review and we hope that this study will provide a clear direction towards finding new opportunities for improvement and innovation.

References

1. Muthukumaran, A.: Optimizing the usage of voice assistants for shopping. Indian J. Sci. Tech. **1343**, 4407–4416 (2020). https://doi.org/10.17485/IJST/v13i43.1911
2. Martin, T.: (2021). https://www.cnet.com/home/smart-home/alexa-features-you-need-to-use-in-the-kitchen/
3. Hoy, M.: Alexa, Siri, Cortana, and more: an introduction to voice assistants. Med. Ref. Serv. Q. **37**, 81–88 (2018). https://doi.org/10.1080/02763869.2018.1404391
4. Wolfson, S.: Amazon's Alexa recorded private conversation and sent it to random contact (2018). https://www.theguardian.com/technology/2018/may/24/amazon-alexa-recorded-conversation
5. Tu, Y.-H., Du, J., Lee, C.-H.: Speech enhancement based on teacher-student deep learning using improved speech presence probability for noise-robust speech recognition. IEEE/ACM Trans. Audio Speech Lang. Process. **27**(12), 2080–2091 (2019)
6. Lei, X., Tu, G.-H., Liu, A.X., Li, C.-Y., Xie, T.: The insecurity of home digital voice assistants - vulnerabilities, attacks and countermeasures. In: IEEE Conference on Communications and Network Security (CNS), pp. 1–9 (2018). https://doi.org/10.1109/CNS.2018.8433167
7. Chung, H., Iorga, M., Voas, J., Lee, S.: Alexa, can I trust you? Computer **50**(9), 100–104 (2017). https://doi.org/10.1109/MC.2017.3571053
8. Wang, P., Lu, X., Hongyu, S., Lv, W.: Application of speech recognition technology in IoT smart home. In: 2019 IEEE 3rd Advanced Information Management, Communicates, Electronic and Automation Control Conference (IMCEC) (2019). https://doi.org/10.1109/IMCEC46724.2019.8984175
9. Ma, Z., Liu, Y., Liu, X., Ma, J., Li, F.: Privacy-preserving outsourced speech recognition for smart IoT devices. IEEE Int. Things J. **6**(5), 8406–8420 (2019)
10. JAMEY (2021). https://www.whatthetech.tv/voice-assistants-are-always-listening-should-you-be-worried/
11. Lau, J., Zimmerman, B., Schaub, F.: Alexa, are you listening? privacy perceptions, concerns and privacy-seeking behaviors with smart speakers. Proc. ACM Hum.-Comput. Interact. **2**(CSCW), 31 (2018). https://doi.org/10.1145/3274371, Article 102

12. Barda, D., Zaikin, R., Shriki, Y.: Keeping the gate locked on your IoT devices: vulnerabilities found on Amazon's Alexa (2020). https://research.checkpoint.com/2020/amazons-alexa-hacked/
13. Ford, M., Palmer, W.: Alexa, are you listening to me? an analysis of Alexa voice service network traffic. Pers. Ubiquit. Comput. **23**(1), 67–79 (2018). https://doi.org/10.1007/s00779-018-1174-x
14. Alepis, E., Patsakis, C.: Monkey says, monkey does: security and privacy on voice assistants. IEEE Access **5**(2017), 17841–17851 (2017). https://doi.org/10.1109/access.2017.2747626
15. Lei, X., Tu, G.H., Liu, A.X., Ali, K., Li, C.Y., Xie, T.: The insecurity of home digital voice assistants: Amazon Alexa as a case study (2017). https://arxiv.org/pdf/1712.03327.pdf
16. Zhang, G., Yan, C., Ji, X., Zhang, T., Zhang, T., Xu, W.: DolphinAttack: inaudible voice commands. In: Proceedings of the 2017 ACM SIGSAC Conference on Computer and Communications Security (CCS 2017). Association for Computing Machinery, New York, pp. 103–117 (2017). https://doi.org/10.1145/3133956.3134052
17. Zhang, N., Mi, X., Feng, X., Wang, X., Tian, Y., Qian, F.: Dangerous skills: understanding and mitigating security risks of voice-controlled third-party functions on virtual personal assistant systems. In: 2019 IEEE Symposium on Security and Privacy (SP), pp. 1381–1396 (2019)
18. Lai, A.: Sneaky kid orders $350 worth of Toys on Her Mom's Amazon account (2018). https://mom.me/news/271144-sneaky-kid-orders-350-worth-toys-her-moms-amazon-account/
19. STMicroelectronics: MP23AB02BTR MEMS audio sensor, high-performance analog bottom-port microphone (2014). http://www.mouser.com/ds/2/389/mp23ab02b-955093.pdf
20. STMicroelectronics: . MP34DB02 MEMS audio sensor omnidirectional digital microphone (2016). http://www.mouser.com/ds/2/389/mp34db02-955149.pdf
21. Modi, C., Patel, D., Borisaniya, B., Patel, A., Rajarajan, M.: A survey on security issues and solutions at different layers of Cloud computing. J. Supercomput. **63**(2), 561–592 (2013). https://doi.org/10.1007/s11227-012-0831-5
22. Picchi, A.: Amazon workers are listening to what you tell Alexa (2019). https://www.cbsnews.com/news/amazonworkers-are-listening-to-what-you-tell-alexa/
23. Ramokapane, K.M., Rashid, A., Such, J.M.: Assured deletion in the cloud: requirements, challenges and future directions. In: Proceedings of the 2016 ACM on Cloud Computing Security Workshop, pp. 97–108 (2016)
24. Ramokapane, K.M., Rashid, A., Such, J.M.: I feel stupid I can't delete... : a study of users' cloud deletion practices and coping strategies. In: Thirteenth Symposium on Usable Privacy and Security (SOUPS 2017), pp. 241–256 (2017)
25. Kelly, M., Statt, N.: Amazon confirms it holds on to Alexa data even if you delete audio files (2019). https://www.theverge.com/2019/7/3/20681423/Amazon-Alexa-echo-chris-coons-data-transcripts-ecording-privacy
26. Apthorpe, N., Reisman, D., Feamster, N.: A smart home is no castle: privacy vulnerabilities of encrypted IoT traffic. arXiv preprint arXiv:1705.06805 (2017)
27. Tabassum, M., Kosinski, T., Lipford, H.R.: I don't own the data : end user perceptions of smart home device data practices and risks. In: Fifteenth Symposium on Usable Privacy and Security (SOUPS 2019). USENIX Association, Santa Clara, CA (2019). https://www.usenix.org/conference/soups2019/presentation/tabassum

28. Sivaraman, V., Gharakheili, H.H., Vishwanath, A., Boreli, R., Mehani, O.: Network-level security and privacy control for smart-home IoT devices., In: IEEE 11th International Conference on Wireless and Mobile Computing, Networking and Communications (WiMob), pp. 163–167 (2015). https://doi.org/10.1109/WiMOB.2015.7347956

29. Ronen, E., Shamir, A., Weingarten, A.-O., O'Flynn, C.: IoT goes nuclear: creating a Zigbee chain reaction. IEEE Secur. Priv. **16**(1), 54–62 (2018). https://doi.org/10.1109/MSP.2018.1331033

30. Suarez-Tangil, G., Tapiador, J.E., Peris-Lopez, P., Ribagorda, A.: Evolution, detection and analysis of malware for smart devices. IEEE Commun. Surv. Tutor. **16**(2), 961–987 (2014). https://doi.org/10.1109/SURV.2013.101613.00077

31. Wiggers, K.: The Alexa skills store now has more than 100,000 voice apps (2019). https://venturebeat.com/2019/09/25/the-alexa-skills-store-now-has-more-than-100000-voice-apps/

32. Kinsella, B.: Google Assistant Actions rose about 2.5 times last year compared to 2.2 times growth for Amazon Alexa skills (2019). https://voicebot.ai/2019/02/15/google-assistant-actions-total-4253-in-january-2019-up-2-5x-in-past-year-but-7-5-the-total-number-alexa-skills-in-u-s/

33. Bolton, T., Dargahi, T., Belguith, S., Al-Rakhami, M.S., Sodhro, A.H.: On the security and privacy challenges of virtual assistants. Sensors **21**, 2312 (2021). https://doi.org/10.3390/s21072312

34. Cheng, P., Roedig, U.: Personal voice assistant security and privacy—a survey. Proc. IEEE **110**(4), 476–507 (2022). https://doi.org/10.1109/JPROC.2022.3153167

35. Germanos, G., Kavallieros, D., Kolokotronis, N., Georgiou, N.: Privacy issues in voice assistant ecosystems. In: IEEE World Congress on Services (SERVICES), pp. 205–212 (2020). https://doi.org/10.1109/SERVICES48979.2020.00050

36. Brill, T.M., Munoz, L., Miller, R.J.: Siri, Alexa, and other digital assistants: a study of customer satisfaction with artificial intelligence applications. J. Mark. Manag. **35**, 1401–1436 (2019). https://doi.org/10.1080/0267257X.2019.1687571

37. Hainis, R.: Bixby, digital voice assistant in Samsung phone (2022). https://www.androidauthority.com/bixby-879091/

38. Ways, M.: AI virtual assistant for windows (2022). https://www.typinglounge.com/braina-review

A Systematic Review of Highly Transparent Steganographic Methods for the Digital Audio

Jerzy Pejaś⬤ and Łukasz Cierocki$^{(\boxtimes)}$⬤

Faculty of Computer Science and Information Technology, Department of Software Engineering and Cybersecurity, West Pomeranian University of Technology, 49 Żołnierska Street, 71-210 Szczecin, Poland
jpejas@wi.zut.edu.pl, lukasz.cierocki@zut.edu.pl

Abstract. Audio steganography is a rapidly growing aspect of broad information protection. This paper presents an overview of steganographic methods using audio as a medium. As an additional aspect during the review, an effort was made to focus on the transparency requirement of the considered methods used in the steganography process. Previous literature reviews have not focused on a single aspect of method evaluation in sufficient depth. Data for the review were collected from papers published between 2018 and 2022 and gathered from three source databases, i.e. Web of Science, IEEE, and ACM, resulting in a total of 32 entries. The obtained methods were classified according to one of the approaches previously proposed in the literature. A systematic comparative analysis of the retrieved methods has been done, comparing their capacity, robustness, and transparency, with particular emphasis on transparency. In addition, a few of the most promising methods were selected and thoroughly analyzed for transparency behavior.

Keywords: Audio steganography · Transparency · Literature review · Impreceptibility

1 Introduction

We refer to a steganographic system as three successive processes. The first involves embedding confidential information in a carrier, the second is sending this crafted message through a public channel, and the third is recovering the previously embedded message. Each method of audio steganography includes a way of inserting/extracting a secret message in/from an audio signal.

Along with cryptography, steganography is one of the most widely used ways to protect information. Cryptography hides the meaning of information, while steganography hides the very fact of its existence [6]. Such crafted media containing confidential information can be sent to the recipient through a public channel, as it does not present any value to a person not authorized to read it.

K. Saeed and J. Dvorský (Eds.): CISIM 2022, LNCS 13293, pp. 63–77, 2022.
https://doi.org/10.1007/978-3-031-10539-5_5

We can evaluate each steganographic method in terms of three basic requirements: transparency, capacity, and robustness. These requirements can be represented as a triangle like in Fig. 1, where each requirement lies on one of the
vertices. Steganographic methods are characterized by the fact that a change in
one parameter does not leave the others unaffected. Thus, an increase in capacity
is associated with a change in transparency and robustness, and an improvement
in transparency will not remain without effect on the capacity [25].

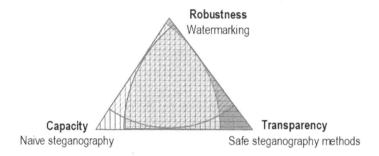

Fig. 1. Audio steganography triangle of requirements

2 Transparency

This paper focuses on the concept of transparency in the context of steganographic methods. The use of audio raises many challenges and research issues;
however, it also represents a research gap. As a digital audio signal is a carrier
used, the knowledge of limitations and subtle features of the sense of hearing
as such allows creating more and more interesting methods using this particular
container. The human auditory sense (HAS) is an extremely complex mechanism
consisting of many anatomical structures and closely related processes [12].

2.1 Human Auditory System

Hearing perception can be described as a process that begins when sound waves
travel through the air to the auricle, then through the external auditory canal to
the tympanic membrane. Under the influence of the air vibrations, the eardrum
moves the malleus adjacent to it. Vibrations from the malleus are transmitted
to the incus and stapes and travel through the auditory tube to the inner ear,
where they are converted into nerve impulses that travel through the auditory
nerve to the hearing centers in the cerebral cortex [12].

As we can read in [36] and in [12], the "typical" human hearing range is 20 Hz
to 20 kHz, with the highest sensitivity in the 1 kHz to 3 kHz range, perfectly
matching the frequency range of human speech, which is 500 Hz to 3 kHz.

Chen, et al. write in their paper [16], that International Federation of the
Phonographic Industry (IFPI) has its own set of requirements with respect to

method transparency. The method should be characterized by, inaudibility of the embedded message, offer an SNR of more than 20 dB. Furthermore, it is necessary that the capacity is at least 20 bps and that the embedded information is protected against typical stegoanalytic attacks e.g. re-sampling, re-quantization, compression attack etc.

2.2   Measures

As mentioned in the previous paragraph, transparency can be defined by a number of measures. We use two sets of measures to evaluate the transparency of the methods: objective tests, and subjective tests. The most commonly used are objective measures like MSE, PSNR, SNR and PRD, while less frequently used are PESQ, SDG and ODG.

PSNR (Peak to Signal Noise Ratio) is used to evaluate the stego audio quality compared to the cover audio and is expressed in decibels (dB). A higher PSNR value means higher audio quality. The formula gives PSNR:

$$PSNR = 10 \times log\left(\left(\frac{255^2}{MSE}\right)\right) \quad \text{where} \quad MSE = \frac{1}{M \times N} \sum_{0}^{M-1} \sum_{0}^{N-1} \|c - s\|^2 \tag{1}$$

where M, N are the width and height of the signal and c, s are the carrier and stego audio, respectively [4].

In audio specifications, SNR tells us the difference in the maximum volume we can get from the device's own noise. At low SNR and higher volumes this unwanted noise can be heard. A high SNR value is especially desirable for music with high dynamics such as classical or electronic music. SNR is given by formula:

$$SNR = 10 \times log_{10}\left(\frac{\sum_{i=1}^{N} c_i^2}{\sum_{i=1}^{N} (c_i - s_i)^2}\right) \tag{2}$$

where N are the number of signal samples and c, s are the carrier and stego audio, respectively [4].

PRD is a measure that determines the Percentage mean square Root of the Difference between two signals and takes values from 0 to 1 [39]. It is given by the formula,

$$PRD = \sqrt{\left(\frac{\sum_{i=1}^{N} (c_i - s_i)^2}{\sum_{i=1}^{N} c_i^2}\right)} \tag{3}$$

where N are the number of signal samples and c, s are the carrier and stego audio, respectively [4].

An interesting measure of transparency is the Pearson and Kendal correlation also called the normalized correlation (NC). This measure takes values from -1 to 1 with 1 indicating full cross-correlation of the signals and 0 indicating no such correlation and -1 indicating full negative correlation [41]. We calculate this correlation by the formula:

$$\rho(c, s) = \frac{\sum_{i=1}^{N}(c_i - \bar{c})(s_i - \bar{s})}{\sqrt{\sum_{i=1}^{N}(c_i - \bar{c})^2}\sqrt{\sum_{i=1}^{N}(s_i - \bar{s})^2}} \tag{4}$$

Among other objective measures, the following PEAQ (Perceptual Evaluation of Audio Quality) [1] and PESQ (Perceptual Evaluation of Speech Quality) [2] standards developed by ITU are worth noting. These are standardized algorithms for objective evaluation of sound quality. The result of the PEAQ algorithm is an objective difference grade (ODG) measured on a 5-point scale from 0 (inaudible), −1 (audible but not annoying), −2 (mildly annoying), −3 (annoying) and −4 (very annoying). The generally accepted standard is for steganographic algorithms to achieve values in the range 0 a −1 [42].

2.3   Related Works

In the field of steganography using digital audio, at least a dozen valuable review articles have been created over the years [6, 13, 17–19].

One of the most recent is an article [6] where the authors conducted a systematic review of the literature, along with a proposed categorization of the methods, recognition of the key features of each method, and a detailed description of the measures and data sets used. Particularly valuable seems to be the methodological description of the approach to the analysis performed, in which the individual steps of the review are listed along with the keywords used.

In an interesting paper [19] authors gave an overview of the methods for audio and speech. Proposals were offered to classify the methods based on the type of embedding operation performed. Particularly interesting are methods that are based on the principals of human auditory sense (HAS).

A paper [18] where the authors also performed a systematic literature review, with an emphasis on grouping methods by information embedding domain, also deserves mention. In addition, the authors revealed the advantages and disadvantages of the described steganographic methods and made a classification based on the robustness of the method. A performance evaluation has also been made.

Almost every review article tries to bring up how to categorize steganographic methods. Some focus on the medium used, others try to assign methods by the type of embedding operation performed, and others by the domain in which the embedding operations are performed.

Compared to existing review articles, the classification proposed in the [6] article allows an unambiguous distinction between the embedding methods used, thus avoiding the problem of overlapping or low-level segregation of these methods. In particular, this approach allows to clearly distinguish classification of codec-based methods for which an additional coded domain has been introduced [18].

This paper uses during the analysis the categorization method proposed in the article [6]. Based on [6] we can distinguish 8 classes of methods that are applicable to audio steganography. Each of these classes is based on the key idea of information embedding.

In the following, the article is organized as follows. Section 3 describes the motivations and basic information about the steganographic process. In turn, Sect. 4 describes the methodology for conducting this review. Section 5 presents the results of the literature review performed. The final Sect. 6 describes a summary with conclusions and an outline of future work.

3   Motivation

Typically, research in the field of steganography addresses one of three aspects, viz: the domain of embedding, the type of carrier used, and the method of embedding. The first aspect defines the signal domain in which the information is embedded. The most commonly used domains are time, frequency, and wavelets. It is worth mentioning that each domain has different properties regarding the basic requirements of the method. The second aspect involves the type of media used. In steganography involving audio signals, digital lossless audio formats WAV, AAC, FLAC or the lossy compressed MP3 format are most commonly used as a carrier. Rarely, formats beyond this set are used, but there are known examples of VOiP being used as a carrier. The third aspect and, we believe, the most important is the method of embedding information.

There are many ways to embed information in a signal. It usually comes down to manipulating the signal at the bit level (LSB), or changing the values of the coefficients of the different types of transforms. There are also embedding methods that take advantage of changes in codewords used in the process of, for example, audio compression. There have been at least a dozen review articles trying to summarize and classify methods in audio steganography, but none of them has focused on the key requirement of transparency of a given method.

This paper extends the previous reviews with an important aspect such as transparency. During the literature overview, more attention was also paid to codecs-based methods. Due to their practical suitability for real-time transmission of audio information, it was proposed to assign these methods to the coded domain.

Due to this requirement, the data embedded in the audio signal can affect the quality of the signal and can be captured by humans because of the sensitivity of their HAS system. Hence, finding the trade-off between changes resulting from data embedding and signal quality has significant practical importance and is the main focus of the analysis presented later in this paper. For the purposes of the analysis, we propose a systematic division of methods according to the domain in which a given method works and the embedding method used. This allows for a better understanding of the extremely subtle differences between the proposed approaches.

4   Methodology

The methodology of the following literature review includes three steps: information gathering, identification of basic method features, and comparative analysis. On the basis of comparative analysis methods were objectively selected that

have a set of characteristics, allowing them to be called the best and their tests
were carried out using a uniform set of data. Methods were taken from three
databases: Web of Science, IEEE Explore, ACM based on a unified query performed through the advanced search tool.

The executed query included three parts. The first defined, the main idea of
the search, the second, defined the embedding domain and the third, where the
feature of the methods is described, which was emphasized in this review. The
study was based on articles published between 2018 and 2022. Figure 2 shows
the results of data collection and filtering process.

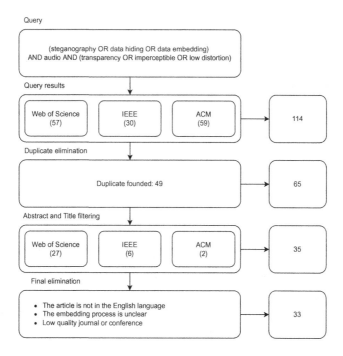

Fig. 2. Literature review methodology and filtering process

In the step where each method was analyzed, an effort was made to extract
the main idea behind each method and to determine details such as the domain
of embedding (DoE), the method of data injection (MODI) to be performed,
the type of carrier, the secret message type, supporting techniques, and evaluation metrics. Finally, each method was classified into one of the categories that
describe in general terms how the method works.

5   Review Results

The resulting literature search yielded 30 methods that were analyzed. The types of methods, the domain of embedding (DoE), and the main mode of embedding (MODI) were defined. In addition, parameters such as capacity, transparency, and robustness are taken into account. The type of media used was verified and the embedded message was characterized. Various supporting techniques and metrics used for each method were characterized.

Method types are determined by their general characteristics related to how the secret message is embedded in a cover file. The proposal of such types are described in the paper [6]. In our analysis, however, we focus primarily on those steganography methods that accord higher priority to transparency and capacity compared to robustness. Hence, among the 9 groups of methods defined in the paper [6] the first column of Table 1 presents only the 6 most prominent group of methods of embedding secret messages, whose main objective is to improve transparency followed by capacity, while keeping robustness at a desired level.

1. **Linear or sequential embedding.** The methods in this group are based on sequential, or linear access to data and then performing embedding operations. Methods that just use sequential data access are among the most commonly developed methods. Methods in this category have one significant feature - they often have high embedding rates. Speaking about the context of disadvantages, it is necessary to point out that this kind of methods is characterized by almost complete lack of resistance to typical attacks in which the signal is processed such as compression or filtering attack. Often the embedded data can succumb to simple stegoanalytic attacks.

2. **Selective embedding.** Selective methods stand, so to speak, in opposition to the linear methods described in the previous paragraph. In this type of methods, a selection of an appropriate, usually the least carrier-altering fragment is made in order to perform an embedding operation on it. The biggest advantage of this category of methods is to increase the security of the method by developing a nonlinear way to access the data during the embedding. This allows the development of methods with higher resistance to stegoanalytic attacks, but results in losses on the capacity side. Methods in this class also have high PSNR and SNR, but this may be due to the lower frequency of embedding.

3. **Frequency Masking and Amplitude Thresholding.** In this group of methods, deposition most often occurs in connection with the use of different acoustic properties of the carrier signal, moreover, different properties of the human sense of hearing are used. The biggest difference between the methods in this group and the selective methods is due to the fact that in the selective methods, the criterion for site selection is not based on a purely acoustic fact. The obvious advantage of these methods is that they have relatively high safety, resulting from the selection of sites where human hearing is less effective. However, as we can read in [6], it is necessary to test these methods against statistical tests.

4. **Error minimization embedding.** Minimization methods use techniques to minimize interference between the stegoobject and the carrier signal. This approach has the advantage of reducing the error, which directly improves the security and robustness of the stegoanalytic tests. In the context of capacity, we can talk about high variability and it depends on the method. Further research is needed on the possibility of increasing resistance to transformational type attacks like filtering or compression.

5. **Pattern - matching embedding.** The way this group of methods works is based on looking for patterns of the embedded message in the carrier signal. The patterns are in binary form. Obvious advantage of the methods used is relatively high security and transparency resulting not from the fact of embedding itself but rather appropriate "description" of carrier. This category of methods contains also a number of disadvantages, with computational and time complexity at the top.

6. **Phase coding.** The methods in this group are based on modifying the phase values of the frequency components. This is because the human sense of hearing is not immune to changes occurring in the phase domain. The biggest advantage of this type of methods is the resistance to various types of transformation attacks. This type of methods has the best balance between the three requirements to steganographic methods presented on Fig. 1.

7. **Spread spectrum.** Spectrum spreading methods, were originally developed to improve transmission quality in wireless media. The biggest advantage of this type of approach is the increased resistance to data loss during transmission, but these methods cause a lot of perceptual interference.

8. **Tone insertion.** This group of methods targets only music, as it uses specific musical elements such as drum sounds, or percussion sounds, tempo for embedding. Methods are known that take advantage of these properties and embed morse code into subtle changes in the tempo of a music track.

9. **Others.** This category includes methods that cannot be clearly assigned to any of the above categories. Very often they are single methods with a specific DoE. One such method is one that uses the encoder as its domain of operation and modification of codewords (MODI) and is shown in Table 1.

The second column of the Table 1 shows the method reference, and the publication year of the article. The third, on the other hand, describes the domain of embedding (DoE). We can distinguish between the time domain, labeled T, the frequency domain, F, and the wavelet domain, labeled W. Furthermore, some method was found whose embedding domain is changing encoding parameters, and this method is labeled as C.

The fourth column contains data about the embedding operation - MODI. For the methods emerged in this review, we can distinguish 5 modification methods:

1. LSB substitution (LSB)
2. coefficient modification (CM)
3. sample digit modification (SDM)

4. spectrum addition (SA)
5. Code word modification (CWM).

The next three columns of the table contain information about the basic parameters of each method - capacity, transparency, and robustness. Although most methods have variable capacitance we tried to evaluate the relative capacitance by averaging the values and assigning them to one of 3 groups. The group L (Low), has an average capacity between 0–250 bps, the group M (Medium) - between 250 and 750 bps, while the group H (High) has more like 750 bps.

The transparency of a given method can be expressed by a number of measures, i.e. PSNR, SNR, PESQ and others. For the purpose of this review, we defined 4 ranges of transparency values: UA (Unacceptable) when SNR is less than 20 dB, L (Low) for SNR between 20 and 40 dB, M (Medium) for 40–60 dB, and H (High) for values greater than 60 dB. The other measures, also are not without influence on the final evaluation.

The issue of method robustness is almost always problematic. Nearly 50% of methods have not been tested for robustness to typical transformational or statistical attacks. In the case of robustness, the rule of thumb is that if the method contains a robustness rating and the meaning of the message is preserved after the attack, it is assigned a rating of G (Good) and if the meaning of the message is lost, it is assigned a rating of W (Weak)

The next two columns of Table 1 contain information about the medium and the message being embedded. Within the media information, the format of the audio file used is determined. Within the context of the embedded message, it is determined whether the embedded message is audio, video or text. If the type of message being embedded is not explicitly specified, it is assumed to be bitstream.

The last two columns provide information on the various techniques supporting the method such as cryptography, compression, or scrambling, and make specifications of the methods used to evaluate the method.

According to Table 1 it is worth noting that most methods operating in the frequency domain have a high or medium level of transparency, with the time domain being dominated by methods having a low to medium level.

Figure 3 shows the ratio between the different types of methods. The largest percentage of methods are based on sequential or linear access to data, or on selective selection based on a specific access scheme. To a lesser extent, methods based on error minimization, phase coding and spectrum spreading are used. It seems interesting that sequential and selective methods appear overly frequently. Thus, we should suppose that minimization, phase coding, and spread spectrum methods seem to be interesting research directions. It has been observed that these methods have interesting properties in terms of transparency preservation with a satisfactory level of robustness.

Figure 4 presents the percentage of each embedding domain used. Significantly, the frequency domain and wavelet domain dominate among the methods found. This allows us to conclude that in methods that in their essence are supposed to provide a high transparency factor, it is these two domains that provide it.

Table 1. Review results

Method type	Ref., Year	DoE	MODI	Capacity	Transparency	Robustness	Carrier type	Message type	Supportive techniques	Evaluation features
Linear or sequential embedding	[8], 2021	T	SDM	L	H	N/A	WAV	Image	Encryption	PSNR SNR NC HC
	[16], 2021	W	CM	L	L	G	N/A	Bitstream	Scrambling	SNR BER BPS
	[3], 2020	W	CM	L	M	G	WAV	Audio	Chaotic maps scrambling	MSE SNR HC BPS NC PSNR SDG
	[44], 2020	T	SDM	L	L	N/A	N/A	Bitstream	None	ODG, SNR
	[29], 2019	W	LSB	M	H	G	N/A	Image	None	SNR SDG ODG BER, NC
	[23], 2019	W	CM	H	L	G	N/A	Audio	None	SNR, SDG, PSNR, HC
	[4], 2018	T	LSB	H	H	N/A	N/A	Audio	Chaotic maps fractal coding	SNR SDG HC PSNR
	[11], 2018	W	LSB	H	L	N/A	WAV	Bitstream	None	SNR
	[37], 2018	F	CM	M	H	N/A	WAV	Bitstream	Noise reduction	MSE, SNR, PSNR, MOS
	[30], 2018	W	CM	M	M	G	WAV	Image	None	MOS SNR NC BER
	[40], 2018	T	LSB	L	M	N/A	N/A	Bitstream	Compression encryption	PSNR MSE
	[26], 2018	C	CWM	H	H	N/A	WAV	Bitstream	N/A	PESQ
Selective embedding	[31], 2022	C	LSB	M	H	G	WAV	AMR	SIAE	PESQ, Test error rate
	[24], 2021	F	CM	M	H	G	WAV	Image	Encryption	PSNR SNR NC HC
	[34], 2021	F	CM	M	M	G	WAV	Image	Fuzzy logic, SVD	SNR BPS BER NC
	[45], 2020	F	CM	H	M	N/A	WAV	Bitstream	Scrambling	ODG BPS
	[33], 2020	T	SDM	L	M	G	MP3	Bitstream	None	ODG NC
	[35], 2019	T	SDM	M		N/A	WAV	Text	Encryption	SNR
	[32], 2019	W	CM	M	L	G	WAV	Audio, WAV	None	MSE, SNR, UACI
	[22], 2019	F	CM	N/A	M	N/A	WAV, MP3	Bitstream	None	PSNR, ODG, PEAQ
	[43], 2019	C	CWM	H	M	N/A	WAV, MP3	Bitstream	None	ODG, HC
	[27], 2018	F	CM	H	H	G	WAV	Bitstream	SVD	SNR, SDG, BPS
	[28], 2018	F	CM	H	H	G	N/A	Image	None	SNR, BER, SDG
	[9], 2018	T	LSB	M	H	N/A	WAV	Bitstream	Chaotic maps, Encryption	SNR
	[21], 2018	T	LSB	M	H	G	WAV	Image	Chaotic maps	PSNR, MSE, BER, SSIM
Error minimizing	[15], 2020	F	SA	L	L	N/A	N/A	Bitstream	None	BPS
	[38], 2019	C	CM	L	N/A	G	AMR	Bitstream	PDM-AFS pulse model	PESQ, Test Error Rate
Phase coding	[5], 2019	F	CM	M	M	NA	NA	Image	SVD	BER, SNR, ODG
	[7], 2019	F	SDM	H	L	M	WAV	Bitstream	Encryption	BER, SNR, SegSNR, Time
Spread spectrum	[14], 2019	F	CM	L	L	NA	NA	Image	SVD	BER SNR ODG
	[10], 2019	W	CM	L	L	G	MP3, WAV	Bitstream	None	SNR, ODG, BPS
Frequency masking and amplitude thresholding	[42], 2020	F	SA	L	L	W	N/A	Bitstream	None	PEAQ, ODG, SNR time
	[20], 2019	F	SA	M	M	NA	FLAC	Bitstream	None	BER

As shown in the Fig. 5, the most commonly used media type is WAV format. However, there are methods that use a hybrid approach, i.e., applicable to several media formats such as WAV, FLAC, MP3, AAC. Figure 6, on other hand, shows that over 50% of methods do not have a clearly defined type of embedded message narrowing down to simply specifying the message as a bitstream.

The metrics used to assess the quality of message embedding were also looked at carefully during the literature analysis conducted. As has been shown in Fig. 7, the most typical metric is the SNR metric, which was used in 21 articles analyzed. Next, ODG, PSNR metrics were used about 10 times. The other measures SDG, NC, MSE, MOS and PEAQ were not very popular.

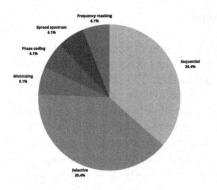

Fig. 3. Method types

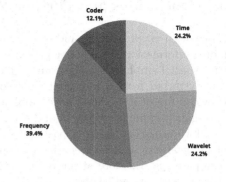

Fig. 4. Methods domains

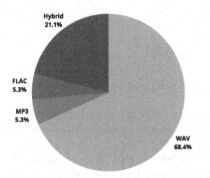

Fig. 5. Carrier types

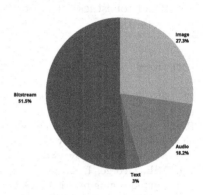

Fig. 6. Messages types

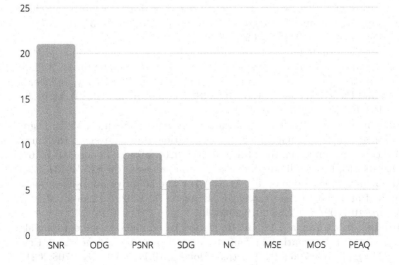

Fig. 7. Measures bar chart

6   Conclusions and Further Works

Along with cryptography, audio steganography is one of the main methods of hiding information. This paper presents an overview of steganographic methods with special emphasis on the transparency parameter. The data for this review was extracted from 3 large databases of scientific articles with unified query. Previous literature reviews have ambiguously described the various parameters of steganographic methods. In addition, this review systematically reviews metrics, for evaluating the transparency of given methods. Note the small number of publications in the categories of non-sequential and non-selective methods (compare Fig. 3). More attention to this category of methods is needed in further research. As noted, most methods operating in the frequency domain, have a higher degree of transparency than methods operating in the time domain. In the context of robustness, it is worth noting that if a method has it tested, it has good robustness.

References

1. BS.1387: Method for objective measurements of perceived audio quality. https://www.itu.int/rec/R-REC-BS.1387/en
2. P.862: Perceptual evaluation of speech quality (PESQ): an objective method for end-to-end speech quality assessment of narrow-band telephone networks and speech codecs. https://www.itu.int/rec/T-REC-P.862
3. Ali, A.H., George, L.E., Mokhtar, M.R.: An adaptive high capacity model for secure audio communication based on fractal coding and uniform coefficient modulation. Circ. Syst. Signal Process. **39**(10), 5198–5225 (2020). https://doi.org/10.1007/s00034-020-01409-7
4. Ali, A.H., George, L.E., Zaidan, A.A., Mokhtar, M.R.: High capacity, transparent and secure audio steganography model based on fractal coding and chaotic map in temporal domain. Multimed. Tools Appl. **77**(23), 31487–31516 (2018). https://doi.org/10.1007/s11042-018-6213-0
5. Allwinnaldo, Budiman, G., Novamizanti, L., Alief, R.N., Ansori, M.R.R.: QIM-based audio watermarking using polar-based singular value in DCT domain. In: 2019 4th International Conference on Information Technology, Information Systems and Electrical Engineering (ICITISEE), pp. 216–221 (2019). https://doi.org/10.1109/ICITISEE48480.2019.9003921
6. AlSabhany, A.A., Ali, A.H., Ridzuan, F., Azni, A., Mokhtar, M.R.: Digital audio steganography: systematic review, classification, and analysis of the current state of the art. Comput. Sci. Rev. **38**, 100316 (2020). https://doi.org/10.1016/j.cosrev.2020.100316, https://linkinghub.elsevier.com/retrieve/pii/S1574013720304160
7. Alsabhany, A.A., Ridzuan, F., Azni, A.H.: The adaptive multi-level phase coding method in audio steganography. IEEE Access **7**, 129291–129306 (2019). https://doi.org/10.1109/ACCESS.2019.2940640
8. Altinbaş, A.E., Yalman, Y.: Bit Reduction based audio steganography algorithm. In: 2021 6th International Conference on Computer Science and Engineering (UBMK), pp. 703–706 (2021). https://doi.org/10.1109/UBMK52708.2021.9558943

9. Alwahbani, S.M.H., Elshoush, H.T.I.: Chaos-based audio steganography and cryptography using LSB method and one-time pad. In: Bi, Y., Kapoor, S., Bhatia, R. (eds.) IntelliSys 2016. LNNS, vol. 16, pp. 755–768. Springer, Cham (2018). https://doi.org/10.1007/978-3-319-56991-8_54

10. Attari, A.A., Shirazi, A.A.B.: Robust and transparent audio watermarking based on spread spectrum in wavelet domain. In: 2019 IEEE Jordan International Joint Conference on Electrical Engineering and Information Technology (JEEIT), pp. 366–370 (2019). https://doi.org/10.1109/JEEIT.2019.8717415

11. Avci, D., Tuncer, T., Avci, E.: A new information hiding method for audio signals. In: 2018 6th International Symposium on Digital Forensic and Security (ISDFS), pp. 1–4 (2018). https://doi.org/10.1109/ISDFS.2018.8355361

12. Ballou, G.: Handbook for Sound Engineers. Taylor & Francis (2013)

13. Bilal, I., Kumar, R., Roj, M.S., Mishra, P.K.: Recent advancement in audio steganography. In: 2014 International Conference on Parallel, Distributed and Grid Computing, pp. 402–405 (2014). https://doi.org/10.1109/PDGC.2014.7030779

14. Budiman, G., Suksmono, A.B., Danudirdjo, D.: FFT-based data hiding on audio in LWT-domain using spread spectrum technique. Elektron. Elektrotech. **26**(3), 20–27 (2020). https://doi.org/10.5755/j01.eie.26.3.23950, https://eejournal.ktu.lt/index.php/elt/article/view/23950

15. Chen, K., Zhou, H., Li, W., Yang, K., Zhang, W., Yu, N.: Derivative-based steganographic distortion and its non-additive extensions for audio. IEEE Trans. Circ. Syst. Video Technol. **30**(7), 2027–2032 (2019). https://doi.org/10.1109/TCSVT.2019.2918511

16. Chen, S.T., Huang, T.W., Yang, C.T.: High-SNR steganography for digital audio signal in the wavelet domain. Multimed. Tools Appl. **80**(6), 9597–9614 (2021). https://doi.org/10.1007/s11042-020-09980-6

17. Dastoor, S.K.: Comparative analysis of Steganographic algorithms intacting the information in the speech signal for enhancing the message security in next generation mobile devices. In: 2011 World Congress on Information and Communication Technologies, pp. 279–284 (2011). https://doi.org/10.1109/WICT.2011.6141258

18. Djebbar, F., Ayad, B., Meraim, K.A., Hamam, H.: Comparative study of digital audio steganography techniques. **2012**(1), 25 (2012). https://doi.org/10.1186/1687-4722-2012-25, https://asmp-eurasipjournals.springeropen.com/articles/10.1186/1687-4722-2012-25

19. Dutta, H., Das, R.K., Nandi, S., Prasanna, S.R.M.: An overview of digital audio steganography. **37**(6), 632–650 (2020). https://doi.org/10.1080/02564602.2019.1699454, https://www.tandfonline.com/doi/full/10.1080/02564602.2019.1699454

20. Eichelberger, M., Tanner, S., Voirol, G., Wattenhofer, R.: Imperceptible audio communication. In: ICASSP 2019–2019 IEEE International Conference on Acoustics, Speech and Signal Processing (ICASSP), pp. 680–684 (2019). https://doi.org/10.1109/ICASSP.2019.8682262

21. El-Khamy, S.E., Korany, N.O., El-Sherif, M.H.: Chaos-based image hiding scheme between silent intervals of high quality audio signals using feature extraction and image bits spreading. In: 2018 35th National Radio Science Conference (NRSC), pp. 266–273 (2018). https://doi.org/10.1109/NRSC.2018.8354372

22. Garcia-Hernandez, J.J.: On a key-based secured audio data-hiding scheme robust to volumetric attack with entropy-based embedding. Entropy **21**(10), 996 (2019). https://doi.org/10.3390/e21100996, https://www.mdpi.com/1099-4300/21/10/996

23. Gupta, A., Kaur, A., Dutta, M.K., Schimmel, J.: Perceptually transparent & robust audio watermarking algorithm using multi resolution decomposition & Cordic QR decomposition. In: 2019 42nd International Conference on Telecommunications and Signal Processing (TSP), pp. 313–317 (2019). https://doi.org/10.1109/TSP.2019.8768894

24. Hameed, A.S.: A high secure speech transmission using audio steganography and duffing oscillator. Wirel. Pers. Commun. **120**(1), 499–513 (2021). https://doi.org/10.1007/s11277-021-08470-8

25. Hassaballah, M.: Digital Media Steganography: Principles, Algorithms, Advances (2020). https://doi.org/10.1016/C2018-0-04865-3

26. He, J., Chen, J., Xiao, S., Huang, X., Tang, S.: A novel AMR-WB speech steganography based on diameter-neighbor codebook partition. **2018**, e7080673 (2018). https://doi.org/10.1155/2018/7080673, https://www.hindawi.com/journals/scn/2018/7080673/

27. Kanhe, A., Aghila, G.: A DCT-SVD-based speech steganography in voiced frames. Circ. Syst. Signal Process. **37**(11), 5049–5068 (2018). https://doi.org/10.1007/s00034-018-0805-9

28. Kanhe, A., Gnanasekaran, A.: Robust image-in-audio watermarking technique based on DCT-SVD transform. EURASIP J. Audio Speech Music Process. **2018**(1), 16 (2018). https://doi.org/10.1186/s13636-018-0139-3

29. Karajeh, H., Khatib, T., Rajab, L., Maqableh, M.: A robust digital audio watermarking scheme based on DWT and Schur decomposition. Multimed. Tools Appl. **78**(13), 18395–18418 (2019). https://doi.org/10.1007/s11042-019-7214-3

30. Kaur, A., Dutta, M.K.: High embedding capacity and robust audio watermarking for secure transmission using tamper detection. Etri J. **40**(1), 133–145 (2018). https://doi.org/10.4218/etrij.2017-0092, https://onlinelibrary.wiley.com/doi/abs/10.4218/etrij.2017-0092

31. Kheddar, H., Megías, D.: High capacity speech steganography for the G723.1 coder based on quantised line spectral pairs interpolation and CNN auto-encoding (2022). https://doi.org/10.1007/s10489-021-02938-7

32. Liao, M., Dong, X., Chen, J., Zeng, D.: An audio steganography based on Twi-DWT and audio-extremum features. In: 2019 Chinese Control Conference (CCC), pp. 8882–8888 (2019). https://doi.org/10.23919/ChiCC.2019.8866035

33. Masmoudi, S., Charfeddine, M., Ben Amar, C.: A semi-fragile digital audio watermarking scheme for MP3-encoded signals using Huffman data. Circ. Syst. Signal Process. **39**(6), 3019–3034 (2020). https://doi.org/10.1007/s00034-019-01299-4

34. Mosleh, M., Setayeshi, S., Barekatain, B., Mosleh, M.: A novel audio watermarking scheme based on fuzzy inference system in DCT domain. Multimed. Tools Appl. **80**(13), 20423–20447 (2021). https://doi.org/10.1007/s11042-021-10686-6

35. Mostafa, R.M., Mohamed, M.H., Sewsey, A.A.: A hybrid system for securing data communication. In: 2019 15th International Computer Engineering Conference (ICENCO), pp. 56–61 (2019). https://doi.org/10.1109/ICENCO48310.2019.9027464

36. Noll, P.: Wideband speech and audio coding. IEEE Commun. Mag. **31**(11), 34–44 (1993). https://doi.org/10.1109/35.256878

37. Pal, D., Ghoshal, N.: Secured and imperceptible data transmission through digital audio signal with reduced internal noise. Wirel. Pers. Commun. **100**(2), 505–518 (2018). https://doi.org/10.1007/s11277-017-5095-1

38. Ren, Y., Wu, H., Wang, L.: An AMR adaptive steganography algorithm based on minimizing distortion. Multimed. Tools Appl. **77**(10), 12095–12110 (2018). https://doi.org/10.1007/s11042-017-4860-1

39. Renza, D., Ballesteros L., D.M., Lemus, C.: Authenticity verification of audio signals based on fragile watermarking for audio forensics. Expert Syst. Appl. **91**, 211–222 (2018). https://doi.org/10.1016/j.eswa.2017.09.003, https://www.sciencedirect.com/science/article/pii/S0957417417305997

40. Teotia, S., Srivastava, P.: Enhancing audio and video steganography technique using hybrid algorithm. In: 2018 International Conference on Communication and Signal Processing (ICCSP), pp. 1059–1063 (2018). https://doi.org/10.1109/ICCSP.2018.8524182

41. Torcoli, M., Kastner, T., Herre, J.: Objective measures of perceptual audio quality reviewed: an evaluation of their application domain dependence. IEEE/ACM Trans. Audio Speech Lang. Process. **29**, 1530–1541 (2021). https://doi.org/10.1109/TASLP.2021.3069302

42. Wang, S., Yuan, W., Unoki, M.: Multi-subspace echo hiding based on time-frequency similarities of audio signals. IEEE/ACM Trans. Audio Speech Lang. Process. **28**, 2349–2363 (2020). https://doi.org/10.1109/TASLP.2020.3013785

43. Yi, X., Yang, K., Zhao, X., Wang, Y., Yu, H.: AHCM: adaptive Huffman code mapping for audio steganography based on psychoacoustic model. IEEE Trans. Inf. Forensics Secur. **14**(8), 2217–2231 (2019). https://doi.org/10.1109/TIFS.2019.2895200

44. Yu, H., Wang, R., Dong, L., Yan, D., Gong, Y., Lin, Y.: A high-capacity reversible data hiding scheme using dual-channel audio. IEEE Access **8**, 162271–162278 (2020). https://doi.org/10.1109/ACCESS.2020.3015851

45. Zhang, Z., Yi, X., Zhao, X.: An AAC steganography scheme for adaptive embedding with distortion minimization model. Multimed. Tools Appl. **79**(37), 27777–27790 (2020). https://doi.org/10.1007/s11042-020-09344-0

Industrial Management and Other Applications

Software Product Maintenance: A Case Study

Shariq Aziz Butt[1]([✉]), Acosta-Coll Melisa[2], and Sanjay Misra[3]

[1] The University of Lahore, Lahore, Pakistan
Shariq2315@gmail.com
[2] Universidad de La Costa, Barranquilla, Colombia
macosta10@cuc.edu.co
[3] Østfold University College, Halden, Norway
sanjay.misra@hiof.no

Abstract. Maintenance is the most important part of software product development. It is a major component of all software development life cycle models (SDLC). Several variables are being used as intermediaries for software systems' maintainability throughout software development. The goal of this study is to see whether these variables are consistent between themselves and how well they anticipate maintenance efforts at the system stage. The maintenance of software products includes error checking, proper functionality of the system, improving performance, making the system adaptive, and follow up the change request that come from the client side. To perform all these types of actions to enhance the product quality 4 types of maintenance are normally followed Corrective, Preventive, Adaptive, and Perfective maintenance. The maintenance activity is the most time taking activity when change requests come from the client. This paper is explaining the concept of maintenance with an iterative model and its 4 types. Case studies are also discussed in the paper to explain the maintenance activities performed in software organizations and their impact on the product. The performance measures are not aligned with one another. Only the size of the system and its lack of consistency are found to be highly linked to greater maintenance effort. Maintainability measurements, aside from size, may well not accurately indicate additional maintenance effort. Parts of the project must be assessed in the situations where they will be deployed. Conventional factors are being used to indicate problematic places in the code, but improving the worst parts may mistakenly cause further problems throughout the system. Our findings show that local changes must be supported by a system-wide examination.

Keywords: First maintenance · Types of maintenance · Case study

1 Introduction

Software maintenance is quite well known to be expensive and time-consuming. As a result, software systems must be upgradeable. But how can we know which systems would be able to be maintained? What are the best maintainable designs and solutions

---

The original version of this chapter was revised: the affiliation of Sanjay Misra was presented incorrectly. This has been corrected. The correction to this chapter is available at https://doi.org/10.1007/978-3-031-10539-5_29

K. Saeed and J. Dvorský (Eds.): CISIM 2022, LNCS 13293, pp. 81–92, 2022.
https://doi.org/10.1007/978-3-031-10539-5_6

for a certain set of requirements? What can be done to make source code better manageable [1, 2]? Most software development studies have been undertaken on software maintenance indicators over the years to support answer these issues. The Maintainability Index, the CK metrics, such as coupling and cohesiveness, and numerous code smells are examples. Earlier validation work on such measures and methodologies looked at functionally distinct systems. Because of the variations throughout functioning, it's difficult to differentiate the impacts of design decisions from the systems' functioning [3, 4]. On the other hand, are in a remarkable position since we have accessibility to four industry-quality, functionally equivalent systems. Software maintenance is the process to manage the software application after the delivery of the product. The maintenance of the software product includes error correction, proper functionality of the system, improve performance, making the system adaptive, and following the change request that comes from the client-side [5]. Maintenance is major and important part of software development because it deals with the changes in the software after the delivery also known as post-delivery activities. Maintenance is of four types, corrective, preventive, adaptive, and perfective. Maintenance is the process to improve the quality of the software product. It also impacts software products and organizations with different contexts and organizations do different types of maintenance according to their defined procedure. To better understand the maintenance and its activities we conduct a case study to define and explain activities in an organization. The case study will explain how these activities are performed and their impact on the product [6, 7].

In general, the following are the research questions addressed in this study:

RQ1: At the system level, are widely accepted software maintainability variables generally stable?
RQ2: Are there any correlations between commonly used software manageability metrics and the overall maintenance efforts shown in our research?

In the paper Sect. 2 is explaining the literature on maintenance, Sect. 3 is explaining the phases of the model, Sect. 4 is explaining the result and analysis, and Sect. 7 is the conclusion.

2 Literature Work

The IEEE standard (729-1983) defined maintenance "as a modification of software product after the delivery of the product to correct the faults, make the system adaptive, improve the performance and fulfill change request". Maintenance is an old traditional phase of the software development life cycle [8, 9]. Every product needs modification after development because of the change request from the client, not meeting the requirement of the customer, improving the performance of the system, and making it adaptive to the new environment (hardware, software, etc.) [10]. This is the reason that maintenance effort/activities in the software life cycle range from 65%- to 75% of the total software development life cycle and become a crucial part of software development. Every software system needs to modify to meet the requirements of the customer, users, and new technologies. As different types of modification and improvement activities can perform to maintain the software such as corrections, error faults removal, improvements, etc. all these activities of maintenance include four types corrective maintenance, perfective maintenance, preventive maintenance, and adaptive maintenance. For maintenance, there are many models/frameworks reported by many popular researchers and practitioners to support efficient maintenance such as quick-fix, Boehm, Osborne, iterative-enhancement, full reuse, and the IEEE-1219 and ISO/IEC 14764 IEEE standards. A flow of task-oriented maintenance [11–13] is shown in Fig. 1.

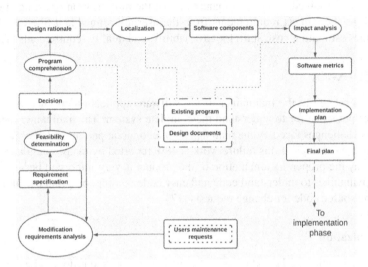

Fig. 1. Flow of task-oriented maintenance model [2].

3   Phases of Model

The above-mentioned Fig. 1 has different phases related to maintenance activities that are explained below [14].

3.1   Modification Requirement Analysis

In this modification, requests are welcomed by the operating system. The user/client uses the system and after the evaluation, the change arises. In the modifications phase, the activities include adding new functionality, improving the performance of the system, and shifting the system to another platform to make it adaptive and compatible for all types of environments. In this phase, any type of request is analyzed in detail for the current system in such a way those modification requirements can be well understood by the user and staff who are involved in the maintenance [15].

3.2 Feasibility Determination

This is an imperative component in the maintenance process. In this stage, the client prerequisites are inspected as far as technical and economical feasibility. Two vital issues are broken down first one, Is whether it was extremely essential and significant to introduce this modification/change with the current system. Furthermore second is how much effort will be required to execute the change. The solutions to these two issues will decide if the proposed modification will be presented or not. Hence the cost to benefit ratio is assumed as a determinant factor of the modification or change process. At this stage, the request requirements from the user are refined and filtered. Further, this includes estimating cost, staff, tool availability, and quality requirements [16].

3.3 Code – X-Ray

This task is related to the maintainer of the software application/product. In this, the maintainer put some for to understand the complete system. The maintainer faced any issues and challenges faced by the maintainers due to incompatible and poor document design. The percentage of this failure work is 48% reported by many candidates. In the Code-X-Ray the proper documentation of the product is very important because it will help the maintainer to understand code and easy code reading, program execution, and change the source code for change requests [17].

3.4 Localization

In this phase location of the code that has to change or modified is done. The maintainer identifies the location where the code has to change and form what part of code the current change request relates. This phase is also known as spotting. Mean that spot the exact code from the source code. It's a very important and most sensitive part of maintenance activities because the wrong identification of code and then code changes can ruin the other modules/functionalities/phase or whole project [18].

3.5 Impact Analysis

In this phase, the impact of modification is calculated. The maintainer examines how much and how will the modification request will impact the system and in what ways. To properly examine and evaluate the impact the maintainer needs a proper and accurate design of the project so that he/she can understand the flow and functionalities (Inter-Related or Non-Inter-Related). The overall system's complexity is examined in this phase [19].

3.6 Implementation Plan

The implementation plan is designed for the intended modifications. It incorporates how to modify the existing specifications and design documents, and how to re-code and design the new and changed parts of the software product. The implementation plan is the last phase of the maintenance. At the point when every one of these phases is finished the standard thing advancement process is enacted then the maintenance process triggers the necessity evaluation phase in the development process, in which the whole process is divided into smaller steps/phases that can be created by teams [20].

4 Types of Maintenance

There are different types of maintenance that are done in software industries to make product maintenance more efficient and correct [21, 22].

4.1 Corrective Maintenance

In the corrective maintenance bug fixing is done in the software product to remove all bugs and improve the software quality and functionality [23–25].

4.2 Perfective Maintenance

In the perfective maintenance new user requirements handle by the maintainer. At this phase, all the requirements or modifications are added to the system and make sure that the other system's functionality is working properly or not. The current new added changes are affecting the system or not [26–28].

4.3 Adaptive Maintenance

Adaptive maintenance is done in a software product to make it adaptive for the environment. In this phase modification or updating has been done to make it compatible with any environment. In adaptive maintenance modification of a product, an item is performed after conveyance to keep a product item usable in a changed or evolving condition [29, 30].

4.4 Preventive Maintenance

In this phase future bugs, errors or modifications have already been considered. The developer makes some changes in the system to future perspectives so that whenever the need to modify or change anything in the product can do easily [30, 31].

4.5 Performance Measures of Maintenance

This section explains the metrics which have been chosen since they are among the more widely used and identified.

4.6 Maintainability Index

For evaluating the maintainability of whole systems, the Maintainability Index (MI) has already been developed. The basic three MI combines the averages per module of three traditional code metrics (lines of code, cyclomatic difficulty, and Halstead Volume) into a single-value indication of maintainability using a quadratic. A lot of comments are included in an upgraded four-metrics version of MI [32].

The enhanced MI values have already been categorized in non-object-oriented applications as described in the following: >85 indicates good maintainability; 65–85 indicates moderate maintainability; and 65 and less suggests poor maintainability with really poor parts of code (big, uncommented, and unstructured). There are no strategies for MI categorization levels for object-oriented systems that researchers are aware of. Moreover, because classifiers in such systems are fewer than modules in the existing method, academics have proposed that object-oriented processes must have larger thresholds.

4.7 Structural Measures

Structural measures (SM), which include the CK metrics [33], seem to be the most commonly used metrics for evaluating code maintainability. An earlier study [3] evaluated the primary factors which are also the topic of this research using an updated version of a component of the CK metrics. The coupling measure OMMIC (calling to procedures in an irrelevant class), the cohesion measure TCC (tight class cohesion), the measurement of class size WMC1 (numbers of techniques per class; every technique seems to weight 1), and the length of inheritance tree are all included in this subset (DIT). Table 2 displays the statistics of the various systems.

4.8 The Detect of Code

The term "code smells" is developed to describe a symptom of a software design flaw. Code detection has proven itself as a reliable method of identifying faults with software designs that may create future development and maintenance concerns. Only five pieces of research on the influence of code detection on maintenance are identified in a systematic study. Nonetheless, we previously published research that looked at the impacts of 12 code identification on maintainability in the systems studied above. These Only 2 are proven to have a negative impact on maintenance efforts. Moreover, we didn't account for file size or the number of modifications before arriving at this conclusion. We identified no effect after adjusting for these factors. Still, we have included the estimated amount per KLOC of such identification in the systems in Table 2 to demonstrate the utility of code components.

It's worth noting that the research looked at the amount of identification and maintenance efforts at the file level to determine the influence of different code identification upon maintainability. We didn't look at the differences between the systems in particular. We also didn't look into whether reworking files to minimize identification, which could result in smaller individual files, would raise the entire system size and hence make the system less maintainable. The research presented here, on the other hand, functions at the system level [34, 35].

5 Maintenance Case Study

The four systems are subjected to a variety of maintenance measurements, which are mentioned above. Furthermore, how well do such measures reflect actual manageability (the ease with which the systems can be maintained in practice)?

The 4 products throughout this sample taken are web-based data systems mostly written in Java that have been functionally identical (having the same requirements and specifications). They cost €17,000, €22,000, €48,000, and €62,000 to build separately through 4 main companies. The lengths of the 4 system applications, designated as Systems A through D in Table 2, are displayed in the first two rows. The systems have been created as part of a research project on software development variation and reproducibility (Table 1).

Table 1. Shows the companies that are targeted for the current study.

Companies	Projects	No. employees	Type of services	Location	Sub-locations
Company 1	1	200–250	Govt. software applications	Pakistan	Australia
Company 2	2	200–220	IT solutions consultancy	Pakistan	UK
Company 3	3	250–300	Android applications	Pakistan	U.A.E
Company 4	4	150–270	IT solutions consultancy	Pakistan	Colombia

We ran a controlled maintenance assessment on the 4 methods to find out. For a total of €45,000, we engaged six programmers to do 3 maintenance jobs on two of the 4 functionally comparable but individually designed Java systems. 3 of the programmers performed for a software company in Colombia, while the other 3 worked for a development organization in Pakistan. The developers are chosen from a group of 65 people who took part in previous research on programming competence which also includes maintenance responsibilities. The outcomes of the previous study are being used as pre-test measurements in this situation. It is generally advised to use pre-test measures to increase the interoperability of the findings. Two adaptive activities are added by the programmers to enable the system to become functional again once updates to the web platform are performed. A third function, which has been required by the customers, has also been implemented by the programmers. A plug-in for an Eclipse IDE automatically logged the period the developer spends on every file. In Colombia, the research lasted 3 to 4 weeks, whereas in Pakistan, it extended 3 weeks. On 2 different systems, every developer completed the same 3 activities. There are 2 reasons that the same programmer is responsible for both systems. First, the relative influence of a system can be distinguished from the developer's effect. Second, we can examine the developers' process of learning when they repeated the identical projects. Such two cycles also correlate to two distinct methods of maintainers often encountered in maintenance work:

beginners to a system and experienced maintainers. Although the systems are allocated to every developer randomly, every developer retained the 4 systems the same amount of times (two), so all of the systems are maintained at least once in every round. The total length of effort spent by the programmers on each of the modules is shown in the next lower row of Table 2. The programmers took 39% lesser time in total to complete the assignments in the second round. Table 2's average values have been changed to account for this variation. In most human-centric software development research, the performance of the activities completed by the subjects is measured in addition to the time (effort). The amount of faults is the most often used quality metric. In our situation, though, the acceptability tests revealed that the systems had fewer problems once the maintenance chores are completed. As a result, using faults as a measure of quality is pointless. Rather, we have used the number of changes performed during the work as a quality metric. The quantity of modifications is often shown to be a strong predictor of later problems, with much more changes indicating a higher risk of failure. As a result, the number of changes (revisions) made to complete the tasks was added as the final control variable. The figures were calculated with the help of SVNKit, a Java framework for extracting data from the Subversion version management system.

The total number of modifications per system is shown in the last row of Table 2. Table 2 demonstrates that System C is the highest maintained system when the efforts and performance values are added together. System B, on the other hand, has the weakest quality and requires the most care.

Table 2. Shows the maintenance measurements and the results of a maintenance analysis for the four systems. Brown denotes the best system, while blue represents the worst.

Category	Metrics	System A	System B	System C	System D
Size	Number of Java files	58	174	28	127
	Java lines of code (LOC)	6124	32457	2872	8450
Maintainability Index ments, cyclomatic (MI) Halstead's volume	LOC, # of com- complexity,	124	104	127	111
Structural measures (SM)	Coupling (OMMIC)	8.5	6.2	7.5	4.5
	Cohesion (TCC)	0.19	0.25	0.22	0.25
	Size of classes (WMC1)	6.7	6.4	12.2	5.8
	Depth of inheritance tree (DIT)	0.32	0.58	0	0.61
Code smells	Feature Envy (# per KLOC of code)	5.22	1.35	4.20	2.42
	God Class (# per KLOC of code)	0.11	0.25	0.51	0.22
Study of actual main- tainabil- ity	Average effort (hours)	25	30	16	22
	Predictor of quality (avg. # changes)	129	115	65	117

6 Explanation and Comparing

Maintained criteria rated the system which functioned well in the maintenance experiment (System C) also as the finest, as shown in Table 2. Table 3 shows the Spearman rank correlation between the maintainability measures and the reported maintenance efforts and performance. High MI, TCC, and DIT scores are expected to imply high maintainability. It's worth noting that higher DIT levels are regarded as positive approximately to 3 [6].) In our experiment, the DIT values range from 0 to .96 overall. As a result, we inverted the MI, TCC, and DIT to evaluate the factors explicitly with maintainability, as measured by the number of hours performed on routine maintenance.

It's not noteworthy that the size of the code corresponds to the results of the maintenance assessment. According to software development history, decreasing functionality reduces maintenance issues. The systems in our analysis show that decreasing size (expressed in the number of the file or overall LOC) has a beneficial influence on functioning.

Size and the inversion of cohesiveness (1/TCC) have been the only two measures that are substantially connected with efforts. The additional alternative measures for manageability are adversely linked with the measured efforts. Three of them showed a strong inverse relation: 1/MI, OMMIC, and FE.

The disparity in the measurements is remarkable. One cause for the discrepancy is that certain metrics are highly interrelated; that is, enhancing the values of one metric can result in lower values for others in the same system. When attempting to obtain minimal coupling while also attempting to obtain strong cohesion, for example, it becomes more challenging, and vice versa. It is often easier to achieve strong cohesion and minimal coupling between parts or subclasses by increasing their length, however, the entire maintainability of the component or class will worsen as a result of the increased size.

Table 3. Shows a matrix of rank correlations.

	LOC	1/MI	OMMIC	1/TCC	WMC1	1/DIT	FE	GC	Hours	Changes
LOC	1	−0.6	−0.8	0.5	−0.3	0.5	−0.7	−0.2	1	0.6
1/MI	−0.5	1	0.6	−1	0.5	1	0.6	−0.5	−0.4	0.5
OMMIC	−0.5	0.5	1	−0.7	0.7	1	0.5	0.1	−0.7	−0.3
1/TCC	0.7	−1	−0.5	1	−0.2	−1	−0.6	0.5	0.5	−0.4
WMC1	−0.2	0.2	0.6	−0.5	1	0.6	0	0.3	−0.5	−0.6
1/DIT	−0.6	1	1	−1	0.3	1	0.7	−1	−0.6	1
FE	−0.5	0.7	0.5	−0.6	0	0.4	1	−0.1	−0.5	0.3
GC	−0.2	−0.5	0.3	0.5	0.5	−1	−0.1	1	−0.2	−1
Hours	1	−0.5	−0.7	0.4	−0.6	−0.5	−0.5	−0.5	1	0.5
# changes	0.2	0.3	−0.3	−0.5	−0.5	1	0.3	−1	0.5	1

7   Conclusion

Software product maintenance is a very hard and most important part of any software product development. To maintain the software there are 4 types for this activity. In our case study organization is using only perfective and corrective maintenance. The organization usually removes bugs from the software product but more spend time and use efforts for software enhancements, its rating is almost 80% in their products. The findings of this case study conducted show that current software management measures are incompatible, except for length and the inversion of cohesiveness, neither of which are coherent with the findings of a management study of four programs that performed the identical function. Nonetheless, these measurements are used to validate a wide range of support and maintenance solutions (procedures, methodologies, strategies, and solutions). The conclusion of the research may be determined by the metrics used instead of the overall maintainability. By using Maintainability Indexes as an example, one might claim that employing a costly company with complicated procedures (System D) enhances maintainability. From the other perspective, one may argue that hiring a low-cost organization with lightweight methods (System C) is preferable because it would result in fewer platforms that are easier to manage.

References

1. Jangra, P., Das, S., Khurana, S.K.: Remote software maintenance system for telecom network. In: 2017 International Conference on Advances in Computing, Communications, and Informatics (ICACCI), pp. 1356–1359. IEEE (2019)
2. Rashid, M.A., Lo, B.: W: A task-oriented software maintenance model. Malays. J. Comput. Sci. **9**(2), 36–42 (1996)
3. Ahmad, M.O., Kuvaja, P., Oivo, M., Markkula, J.: Transition of software maintenance teams from Scrum to Kanban. In: 2016 49th Hawaii International Conference on System Sciences (HICSS), pp. 5427–5436. IEEE (2016)
4. Sirisomboonsuk, P., Gu, V.C., Cao, R.Q., Burns, J.R.: Relationships between project governance and information technology governance and their impact on project performance. Int. J. Project Manag. **36**(2), 287–300 (2018)
5. Acar, Y., et al.: Comparing the usability of cryptographic APIs. In: IEEE Symposium on Security and Privacy (2017)
6. Acar, Y., Backes, M., Fahl, S., Kim, D., Mazurek, M.L., Stransky, C.: You get where you're looking for: the impact of information sources on code security. In: IEEE Symposium on Security and Privacy. https://doi.org/10.1109/SP.2016.25
7. Acar, Y., Backes, M., Fahl, S., Kim, D., Mazurek, M.L., Stransky, C.: How internet resources might be helping you develop faster but less securely. IEEE Secur. Priv. **15**(2), 50–60 (2017)
8. Acar, Y., Fahl, S., Mazurek, M.L.: You are not your developer, either: a research agenda for usable security and privacy research beyond end users. In IEEE Cybersecurity Development. https://doi.org/10.1109/SecDev.2016.013
9. Acar, Y., Stransky, C., Wermke, D., Weir, C., Mazurek, M.L., Fahl, S.: Developers need support, too: a survey of security advice for software developers. In: Cybersecurity Development (SecDev) (2017)
10. Assal, H., Chiasson, S.: Motivations and amotivations for software security. In SOUPS Workshop on Security Information Workers (WSIW). USENIX Association (2018)

11. Butt, S.A., Misra, S., Piñeres-Espitia, G., Ariza-Colpas, P., Sharma, M.M.: A cost estimating method for agile software development. In: Gervasi, O., et al. (eds.) ICCSA 2021. LNCS, vol. 12955, pp. 231–245. Springer, Cham (2021). https://doi.org/10.1007/978-3-030-87007-2_17

12. Assal, H., Chiasson, S.: Security in the software development lifecycle. In Symposium on Usable Privacy and Security. USENIX (2018)

13. Ayewah, N., Hovemeyer, D., Morgenthaler, J.D., Penix, J., Pugh, W.: Using static analysis to find bugs. IEEE Softw. **25**, 5 (2008). https://doi.org/10.1109/MS.2008.130

14. Butt, S.A.: Study of agile methodology with the cloud. Pac. Sci. Rev. B: Humanit. Soc. Sci. **2**(1), 22–28 (2016)

15. Baca, D., Boldt, M., Carlsson, B., Jacobsson, A.: A novel security-enhanced agile software development process applied in an industrial setting. In: International Conference on Availability, Reliability and Security (2015)

16. Baca, D., Petersen, K., Carlsson, B., Lundberg, L.: Static code analysis to detect software security vulnerabilities - does experience matter? In: International Conference on Availability, Reliability and Security (2009)

17. Przybyłek, A.: Systems evolution and software reuse in object-oriented programming and aspect-oriented programming. In: Bishop, J., Vallecillo, A. (eds.) International Conference on Modelling Techniques and Tools for Computer Performance Evaluation, TOOLS 2011. LNCS, vol. 6705, pp. 163–178. Springer, Heidelberg (2011). https://doi.org/10.1007/978-3-642-21952-8_13

18. Bartsch, S.: Practitioners' perspectives on security in agile development. In: International Conference on Availability, Reliability and Security. https://doi.org/10.1109/ARES.2011.82

19. Butt, S.A., Jamal, T.: Frequent change request from user to handle cost on project in agile model. Proc. Asia Pac. J. Multidiscip. Res. **5**(2), 26–42 (2017)

20. Berisha, G., Pula, J.S.: Defining small and medium enterprises: a critical review. Acad. J. Bus. Adm. Law Soc. Sci. **1** (2015)

21. Aziz Butt, S., Piñeres-Espitia, G., Ariza-Colpas, P., Tariq, M.I.: Project management issues while using agile methodology. In: Przybyłek, A., Jarzębowicz, A., Luković, I., Ng, Y.Y. (eds.) LASD 2022. LNBIP, vol. 438, pp. 201–214. Springer, Cham (2022). https://doi.org/10.1007/978-3-030-94238-0_12

22. Przybyłek, A.: An empirical study on the impact of AspectJ on software evolvability. Empir. Softw. Eng. **23**(4), 2018–2050 (2017). https://doi.org/10.1007/s10664-017-9580-7

23. Boone, H.N., Boone, D.A.: Analyzing likert data. J. Ext. **50**(2), 1–5 (2012)

24. Chess, B., McGraw, G.: Static analysis for security. IEEE Secur. Priv. **2**, 6 (2004). https://doi.org/10.1109/MSP.2004.111

25. Dillman, D.A.: Mail and Internet Surveys: The Tailored Design Method. Wiley, Hoboken (2000)

26. Fischer, F., et al.: Stack overflow considered harmful? the impact of copy paste on android application security. In: IEEE Symposium on Security and Privacy. https://doi.org/10.1109/SP.2017.31

27. Garfinkel, S., Lipford, H.R.: Usable Security: History, Themes, and Challenges. Synthesis Lectures on Information Security, Privacy, and Trust, vol. 5, no. 2 (2014)

28. Tariq, M.I., Diaz-Martinez, J., Butt, S.A., Adeel, M., De-la-Hoz-Franco, E., Dicu, A.M: A learners experience with the games education in software engineering. In: Balas, V., Jain, L., Balas, M., Shahbazova, S. (eds.) Soft Computing Applications, SOFA 2018. Advances in Intelligent Systems and Computing, vol. 1222, pp. 379–395. Springer, Cham (2018). https://doi.org/10.1007/978-3-030-52190-5_27

29. Gorski, P.L.: Developers deserve security warnings, too: on the effect of integrated security advice on cryptographic API misuse. In: Fourteenth Symposium on Usable Privacy and Security (SOUPS 2018), pp. 265–281. USENIX Association, Baltimore (2018). https://www.use nix.org/conference/soups2018/presentation/Gorski

30. Butt, S.A., Gochhait, S., Andleeb, S., Adeel, M.: Games features for health disciplines for patient learning as entertainment. In: Das, S., Gochhait, S. (eds.) Digital Entertainment, pp. 65–86. Palgrave Macmillan, Singapore (2021). https://doi.org/10.1007/978-981-15-972 4-4_4

31. Green, M., Smith, M.: Developers are not the enemy!: the need for usable security APIs. IEEE Secur. Priv. **14**(5), 40–46 (2016). https://doi.org/10.1109/MSP.2016.111

32. Grieco, G., Grinblat, G.L., Uzal, L., Rawat, S., Feist, J., Mounier, L.: Toward large-scale vulnerability discovery using machine learning. In: ACM Conference on Data and Application Security and Privacy 12 (2016). https://doi.org/10.1145/2857705.2857720

33. Butt, S.A., Misra, S., Luis, D.M.J., De la Emiro, H.F: Efficient approaches to agile cost estimation in software industries: a project-based case study. In: Misra, S., Muhammad-Bello, B. (eds.) Information and Communication Technology and Applications, ICTA 2020. Communications in Computer and Information Science, vol, 1350, pp. 645–659. Springer, Cham (2020). https://doi.org/10.1007/978-3-030-69143-1_49

34. Butt, S.A., Tariq, M.I., Jamal, T., Ali, A., Martinez, J.L.D., De-La-Hoz-Franco, E.: Predictive variables for agile development merging cloud computing services. IEEE Access **7**, 99273–99282 (2019)

35. Tian, F., Wang, T., Liang, P., Wang, C., Khan, A.A., Babar, M.A.: The impact of traceability on software maintenance and evolution: a mapping study. J. Softw.: Evol. Process **33**(10), e2374 (2021)

Digital Transformation and the Role of the CIO in Decision Making: A Comparison of Two Modelling Approaches

Daniela Borissova[1,2]($\boxtimes$) , Zornitsa Dimitrova[1] , Vasil Dimitrov[1] ,
Radoslav Yoshinov[3] , and Naiden Naidenov[1]

[1] Institute of Information and Communication Technologies at the Bulgarian Academy of Sciences, 1113 Sofia, Bulgaria
{daniela.borissova,zornitsa.dimitrova,vasil.dimitrov,
naiden.naidenov}@iict.bas.bg
[2] University of Library Studies and Information Technologies, 1784 Sofia, Bulgaria
[3] Laboratory of Telematics at the Bulgarian Academy of Sciences, Sofia, Bulgaria
yoshinov@cc.bas.bg

Abstract. Digital transformation imposes to transform different business processes in order to improve their efficiency and bring organizational and operational innovations. In this regard, the role of the Chief Information Officer (CIO) becomes more important and required. It should be able to cope with different challenges related to decision-making under the lack of enough time or sometimes under uncertain conditions. To overcome such challenging situations some proper models should be used to make the right decisions. For the goal, the current article deals with the problem of group decision-making. The proposed two mathematical models are compared toward their suitability to be applied for evaluation and selection of collaborative software tools for remote working. The results show that both models based on group multi-criteria decision analysis may be used to aid the CIO in the analysis of complex problems considering different experts' opinions to make the decision-making process more transparent and objective when forming a final decision. Both models could be used not only for the selection of software tools for remote collaboration but also in cases of Internet provider selection, selection of vendor under public procurements, different software types selection, selection of conference location, etc.

Keywords: CIO · Digital transformation · Group decision-making · Mathematical models · Collaborative software tools

1 Introduction

Today the role of Chief Information Officer (CIO) is rapidly changing. This is due to not only the need for digital transformation but also due to innovation to create a more customer-centric approach is clear. CIO's dominant focus has been shown to have a direct and positive impact on corporate performance [1]. Recent research has shown that

© The Author(s), under exclusive license to Springer Nature Switzerland AG 2022
K. Saeed and J. Dvorský (Eds.): CISIM 2022, LNCS 13293, pp. 93–106, 2022.
https://doi.org/10.1007/978-3-031-10539-5_7

the responsibility of the CIO includes general and domain-specific demands to perform a digital transformation. The role of top management is essential for planning and to make significant success the CIO should provide motivated alternative decisions to cope with different challenges [2]. The CIO along with top managers should discuss the challenges and requirements toward the strategic IT innovations and select suitable and reliable IT-enabled software tools [3]. The role of CIO is to governance with multifunctional teams to combine different business aspects. To be competitive, any organization have to implement good practices and innovative IT [4]. In this way, the duties of the CIO can take on a wide range of responsibilities, which determines their important role in the organization [5]. The CIO along with chief information security officer (CISO) should make enough efforts to increase the level of network and information security. To realize reliable information security, the different methods of artificial intelligence in cyberspace could be used [6]. Special attention is needed to provide the requested cybersecurity for some critical information infrastructure [7]. The CIO with digital service team has to cope with cybersecurity policy at different levels [8].

CIO should be able to estimate the applicability of new technologies in the context of specifics hardware requirements and to determine the required short-term and long-term changes [9]. CIO should be able to propose suitable models for decision-making including group decision-making in cases of Internet provider selection, selection of vendor under public procurements, different software types selection, selection of conference location, etc. Gartner recommends evaluating the technology trends to identify the impact on people, businesses, and the IT estate [10]. Taking into account all of these and the current pandemic situation, the article aims to analyse some software tools to make possible collaboration between team members at distance. Due to the lack of sufficient time, these decisions should be well justified and based on some mathematical models. The current article aims to compare the suitability of the proposed group decision-making model for fast evaluation and selection of software tools for collaborative remote working described in [11] with a new group decision-making model based on extended simple additive weighting and combinatorial optimization.

The article is structured as follows: Sect. 2 describes the basic parameters of some widely used videoconferencing tools, learning management systems, and tools for project management; Sect. 3 contains a description of the two group decision-making modelling approaches for evaluation and selection; Sect. 4 describe the obtained numerical results and discuss the conducted comparison between two modelling approaches; while Sect. 5 summarizes the advantages and possible applications of the proposed group decision-making modelling approaches.

2 Software Tools for Remote Collaboration

In the age of digitalization, the use of various technological and business solutions, allowing remote access between members, is becoming more common today. This due to the increased level of network and information security involving different tools including artificial intelligence too [12]. We identify that a minimum of three software platforms is needed to motivate persons to stay at home and to continue collaborative work. These are videoconferencing, LMS and project management. Some new trends enable the home to become a space for entrepreneurship [13]. This involves different software tools that make possible the remote real-time collaboration between teams located in different geographical regions [14]. In the context of the remote collaboration, the current article aims to determine three essential aspects of remote collaboration namely videoconferencing, e-learning, and project management tools. These collaborative software platforms are applicable for the business companies, universities and research organizations.

2.1 Software Tools for Videoconferencing

The latest achievements in ICT make it possible to change the communication patterns by using the videoconferencing tools [15]. The usage of such tools is constantly growing in the modern digital era. The videoconferencing tools are a part of business activities that allow establishing strong relationships providing accessibility, flexibility, and clear from participants' perceptions. These tools support business-to-business commitment and suppliers and customers and speed up the innovation in SMEs [16, 17]. Among the existing platforms for videoconferencing the current article investigates a restricted number of them. The main parameters of these videoconferencing tools used during the evaluation are given in Table 1.

Table 1. Videoconferencing tools' current parameters

Parameters	Zoom	Webex	Skype	Google Hangouts	UMeetin	Lifesize
Number of participants	100	100	50	25	25	25
HD video	Yes	--	Yes	--	--	--
HD audio	Yes	--	--	--	--	--
Screen sharing	Yes	Yes	Yes	Yes	--	Yes
Group chat	Yes	--	Yes	Yes	--	Yes
Video meeting recordings	Yes	Yes	Yes	Yes	--	--
Time duration limit per meeting	40 min	40 min	Unlimited	Unlimited	30 yesmin	24 h

Among the investigated freeware tolls for videoconferencing, the most critical criteria of these tools are the number of participants and the time duration of meetings. For example, some of them provide up to 100 users like Zoom and Webex, but the Google Hangouts, UMeetin, and Lifesize accommodate no more than 25 users. There exist also major differences between the time duration of meetings among the tools given – form 30 min to 24 h. Some additional parameters such as HD video, HD audio, screen sharing, group chat, and video recording could contribute to the meetings' effectiveness. Some of these parameters are not supported in the freeware versions and this makes the selection of a proper video conferencing tool complex including different quantitative and qualitative evaluation criteria.

2.2 Learning Management System Software

The learning management systems (LMS) are applicable in the field of education and business training due to their numerous advantages [18]. The improvement of the efficiency of online courses can benefit from personalized learning supporting [19]. This involves also an integration of gamification elements in the e-learning environment too [20]. The interactive multimedia e-learning system should allow customizing to reflect different aspects of problems of learning and training [21]. The use of an appropriate system for testing the acquired knowledge and skills is also required. For generating e-tests some aspects of intelligence involving gamification elements could be used [22, 23]. In the area of business, the LMSs are related to different training courses including cyber-security education and training [24–26]. The latest versions of LMS with mobile applications is another circumstance that contributes to students' motivation incensement. The main parameters of some free and popular LMS are shown in Table 2.

Table 2. Learning management systems' current parameters

Parameters	Moodle	Chamilo	ILIAS	Forma LMS
SCORM 1.2	Yes	Yes	Yes	Yes
SCORM 2004	Yes	--	Yes	Yes
xAPI	Yes	--	--	--
Mobile application	Yes	Yes	--	--
Self-hosted cloud-based	Yes	Yes	--	--
Self-hosted system	Yes	Yes	--	Yes
SaaS/cloud	--	Yes	Yes	Yes
WordPress	--	Yes	--	Yes
Google calendar	--	Yes	--	Yes

All of the examined LMSs are compatible with Linux, Mac, and Windows plat-forms and are supported by browsers like Apple Safari, Google Chrome, Internet Explorer and Mozilla Firefox. The parameters related with supported standards are SCORM 1.2/2004 and xAPI. The parameters concerning the deployment are related to a mobile application, self-hosted, cloud-based, self-hosted system, and SaaS/cloud. It should notice, that cloud natives allow a better adaptation to the new normal. The parameters WordPress and calendar are focused on the possibility to integrate additional useful applications for the learning content visualization.

2.3 Software Platform to Support Project Management

The project management (PM) software provides a flexible solution by combining different sets of tools thus helping to achieve the goals by managing project activities, time, resources, and costs. Project management practices are diverse, as the projects are, which involve a variety of partners like business and research organizations. Therefore, the best practices should be made following the particular project characteristics and partners to improve the performance [27]. The project management tool can prioritize the processes and progress tracking that contributes to proper resource distribution [28]. The collaboration between project team members allows files and knowledge sharing thus improve better project planning. In presence of multiple alternatives, a set of baseline schedules at the project planning phase could be used to simulate different disruption types [29]. The basic parameters of a predefined set for PM are given in Table 3.

Table 3. Project management tools current parameters

Parameters	Jira	Bitrix24	Infolio	GitHub
Collaborators limit	Up to 10	Up to 12	Unlimited	Unlimited
Storage limit	2 GB	5 GB	1 GB	0.5 GB
Custom workflow	Yes	Yes	Yes	--
Timeline tracking	Yes	Yes	--	--
Calendar	Yes	Yes	Yes	--
Chat	Yes	Yes	Yes	Yes
Portfolio manage	--	Yes	--	Yes
Gantt chart	--	Yes	--	--
Version control	--	--	--	Yes

All of the presented PM alternatives could be deployed and realized as software as a service (SaaS) including a mobile application interface. Except for the storage limit, collaborators, and chat, the rest of the parameters vary – to be present or no for all investigated alternatives (Table 3).

3   Group Decision-Making Models in Determination of Software Tools for Remote Collaboration

The expanding ICT today imposes to make business decisions at different levels and to consider multiple stakeholders [30]. To consider the different stakeholders' points of view toward the mentioned above alternatives, an expert group of decision-makers is to be formed. Each DM should determine coefficients for the importance of evaluation criteria to the given set of alternatives. In some cases, combined weighed criteria [31] could be used as additional coefficients given by CIO to express DMs competence.

3.1   Group Decision-Making Model for Fast Evaluation and Selection

In such way, the mathematical model for evaluation and selection of software tools for collaborative remote working could be expressed similarly to the classic SAW and modified SAW [32]. Instead of evaluations scores usage, the proposed mathematical model (M-1) consider the parameters of software tools as variables [11]:

$$maxA_i = \sum_{e=1}^{E} \lambda^e \sum_{j=1}^{N} w_j^e p_{ij}, \, i = \{1, 2, \ldots, M\} \tag{1}$$

$$\sum_{j=1}^{N} w_j^e = 1 \tag{2}$$

$$\sum_{e=1}^{E} \lambda^e = 1 \tag{3}$$

where index $i = 1, \ldots, M$ is used to represent the number of alternatives; evaluation criteria are denoted by index $j = 1, \ldots, N$; parameters performance of i-th alternative in respect to the j-th criterion is expressed by p_{ij}; the coefficients expressing the importance of j-th criterion regard the e-th expert point of view are w_j^e; and weighted coefficients λ^e are express the importance of e-th expert' opinion.

The weighted coefficients w_j^e express the relative importance between evaluation criteria should comply the relation (2) and additional coefficients that make difference between the importance of group members' opinions λ^e are restricted within the range of $[0, 1]$. The alternatives performance represents the sum of the multiplication of parameter performance taking into account the experts' opinions by the relation (1). The most appropriate suitable alternative should have maximum performance.

3.2 Group Decision-Making Model for Evaluation and Simultaneous Selection of Several Software Tools for Remote Collaboration

The second modelling approach relies also on the SAW, but utility function includes an additional two types of coefficients. First of them represents binary integer variables for selection of the best alternative/s as an aggregated group decision, while the second type of coefficients expresses the importance of the expert' opinions. Taking into account these considerations, the selection of 3 collaborative software types could be done by the following group decision-making model with combinatorial optimization formulation (M-2) as follows:

$$max \left(\sum_{i}^{M} x_i \left(\sum_{e=1}^{E} \lambda^e A_i^e \right) + \sum_{s}^{S} y_s \left(\sum_{e=1}^{E} \lambda^e A_s^e \right) + \sum_{t}^{T} z_t \left(\sum_{e=1}^{E} \lambda^e A_t^e \right) \right) \tag{4}$$

subject to

$$\forall i = 1, 2, \ldots, M : (\forall e = 1, 2, \ldots, E : A_i^e = \sum_{j}^{N} w_j^e a_{i,j}^e) \tag{5}$$

$$\forall s = 1, 2, \ldots, S : (\forall e = 1, 2, \ldots, E : A_s^e = \sum_{p}^{P} w_p^e a_{s,p}^e) \tag{6}$$

$$\forall t = 1, 2, \ldots, T : (\forall e = 1, 2, \ldots, E : A_t^e = \sum_{q}^{Q} w_q^e a_{t,q}^e) \tag{7}$$

$$\sum_{i=1}^{M} x_i = 1, x_i \in \{0, 1\} \tag{8}$$

$$\sum_{s=1}^{S} y_s = 1, y_s \in \{0, 1\} \tag{9}$$

$$\sum_{t=1}^{T} z_t = 1, z_t \in \{0, 1\} \tag{10}$$

$$\sum_{j=1}^{N} w_j^e = 1 \tag{11}$$

$$\sum_{p=1}^{P} w_p^e = 1 \tag{12}$$

$$\sum_{q=1}^{Q} w_q^e = 1 \tag{13}$$

$$\sum_{e=1}^{E} \lambda^e = 1 \tag{14}$$

where A_i^e express the aggregated assessment of the i-th alternative against all criteria considering the point of view of the e-th expert, and respectively for the next two selection types A_s^e and A_t^e, while $a_{i,j}^e$ denotes the evaluation score from e-th expert for i-th alternative toward j-th criterion and the evaluation scores for the rest next two selection types are respectively $a_{s,p}^e$ and $a_{t,q}^e$. The relations (8)–(10) guarantee the only one selection from each software type and are based on three types of binary integer variables for each software type. The weighted coefficients representing the importance of criteria for different groups of selection are expressed by the equalities (11)–(13). The last Eq. (14) shows that the sum of weighted coefficients for experts' opinions importance should be exactly equal to 1.

The advantage of this modelling approach is the fact that the optimal group decision about the selected alternative for all three types of collaborative tools is determining as a single run of the optimization task. This is due to the used binary integer variables x_i, y_s, z_t, that make the formulated model a combinatorial one.

4 Numerical Application

The inputs from Table 1, Table 2, and Table 3 are used to compare the applicability of the proposed two group decision-making models when selecting software tools for collaboration remotely. These software tools are evaluated by a formed group that involves CIO (E-1), IT (E-2), and an expert from a digital service team (E-3). Evaluation of the VCT, LMS, and PM is done by using of same evaluation criteria for both models, and by using the same weighted coefficients that express the relative importance between criteria for the alternatives evaluation.

4.1 Evaluation of Collaborative Software Tools by Group of Experts

To get a group decision, each expert should determine corresponding weighted coefficients that express the relative importance between evaluation criteria (parameters) of videoconferencing tools. These weighted coefficients are given in the first 3 rows of Table 4, while the rest rows contain the evaluation scores for each alternative toward evaluation criteria.

Table 4. Weighted coefficients for the evaluation criteria and scores for the alternatives of videoconferencing tools from a group of 3 experts

Experts & alternatives	Number of participants	HD video	HD audio	Screen sharing	Group chat	Video meeting recordings	Time duration limit per meeting
	w_1	w_2	w_3	w_4	w_5	w_6	w_7
E-1	0.2	0.08	0.07	0.13	0.05	0.15	0.32
E-2	0.1	0.13	0.18	0.15	0.07	0.15	0.22
E-3	0.13	0.1	0.2	0.19	0.1	0.08	0.2
A-1	0.78	0.91	0.93	0.98	0.79	0.69	0.19
A-2	0.65	0.12	0.15	0.92	0.21	0.70	0.08
A-3	0.50	0.89	0.12	0.95	0.81	0.66	0.97
A-4	0.25	0.11	0.19	0.90	0.73	0.62	0.94
A-5	0.25	0.09	0.07	0.02	0.31	0.11	0.06
A-6	0.25	0.05	0.10	0.89	0.84	0.13	0.81

For the first modelling approach (1)–(3) the normalizing is within the range between 0 and 1, where 1 means present of a feature and 0 in the opposite situation [11]. The supported maximum participants' number is chosen to be equal to 1 and the same is valid for the videoconferencing time duration expressed by "unlimited". The other existing values are normalized proportionally.

The weighted coefficients for the relative importance between criteria determined from group members' along with evaluation scores for the alternatives in respect to the evaluations criteria about the LMS are shown in Table 5.

Table 5. Weighted coefficients for the criteria and evaluation scores for the LMS alternatives from a group of 3 experts

Experts & alternatives	Supported specifications					Deployment			
	SCORM 1.2	SCORM 2004	xAPI	Mobile application	Self-hosted cloud-based	Self-hosted system	SaaS/cloud	Word-press	Google Calendar
	w_1	w_2	w_3	w_4	w_5	w_6	w_7	w_8	w_9
E-1	0.08	0.15	0.16	0.12	0.09	0.13	0.07	0.10	0.10
E-2	0.07	0.13	0.17	0.11	0.08	0.20	0.10	0.08	0.06
E-3	0.07	0.10	0.05	0.10	0.13	0.15	0.10	0.10	0.20
A-1	0.88	0.94	0.94	0.86	0.95	0.92	0.15	0.72	0.13
A-2	0.84	0.17	0.27	0.90	0.88	0.90	0.92	0.89	0.92
A-3	0.91	0.79	0.25	0.42	0.25	0.21	0.88	0.15	0.09
A-4	0.92	0.88	0.23	0.18	0.31	0.88	0.91	0.75	0.69

For the first modelling approach (1)–(3), the normalizing is simple and uses 0 for absence and 1 for the presence of the corresponding LMS feature.

The determined from the experts weighted coefficients for the relative importance between criteria along with evaluation scores for the alternatives concerning the criteria for the PM are shown in Table 6.

Table 6. Weighted coefficients for the evaluation criteria and scores for the alternative of PM tools from a group of 3 experts

Experts & alternatives	Collaborators limit	Storage limit	Custom workflow	Timeline tracking	Calendar	Chat	Portfolio manage	Gantt chart	Version control
	w_1	w_2	w_3	w_4	w_5	w_6	w_7	w_8	w_9
E-1	0.09	0.1	0.05	0.18	0.19	0.05	0.1	0.11	0.13
E-2	0.18	0.09	0.07	0.07	0.07	0.1	0.02	0.13	0.27
E-3	0.12	0.1	0.17	0.14	0.17	0.06	0.02	0.11	0.11
A-1	0.1	0.4	0.83	0.93	0.79	0.76	0.2	0.14	0.25
A-2	0.12	0.9	0.92	0.88	0.84	0.86	0.93	0.98	0.12
A-3	0.95	0.2	0.87	0.23	0.91	0.72	0.17	0.11	0.19
A-4	0.98	0.1	0.12	0.21	0.11	0.92	0.88	0.09	0.99

For the first modelling approach (1)–(3), the normalization is also within the range between 0 and 1 and express the presence or not of parameters except the parameters for the collaborators limit and storage limit. The unlimited of collaborators limit is considered equal to 1, while the maximum storage limit (5 GB) takes the value of 1, and the rest are proportionally calculated.

4.2 Comparison Between Group Decision-Making Approaches

The obtained results for the selected combination of VCT, LMS, and PM by using both approaches along with the coefficients for the experts' opinions importance under three scenarios are shown in Table 7.

Table 7. Group decision for the selected combination of VCT, LMS, and PM under three scenarios for the importance of experts' opinions

	E-1	E-2	E-3	Model M-1			Model M-2		
				VCT	LMS	PM	VCT	LMS	PM
Case-1	0.33	0.33	0.34	A-3	A-2	A-2	A-3	A-1	A-2
Case-2	0.20	0.35	0.45	A-1	A-2	A-2	A-1	A-2	A-2
Case-3	0.50	0.40	0.10	A-3	A-1	A-2	A-3	A-1	A-2

The Case-1 represents the scenario where experts' opinions are with equal importance; the Case-2 illustrate scenario with the most important opinion of the expert E-3, followed by E-2 and E-1, while Case-3 emphasises on the opinion of the expert E-1 closely followed by E-2 and then E-3.

The empirical comparison of the results when using model M-1 and M-2 under the same coefficients for the criteria importance w_j^e, along with the evaluation of the parameters for VCT, LMS, and PM from Table 4, Table 5, and Table 6 are graphically illustrated in Fig. 1.

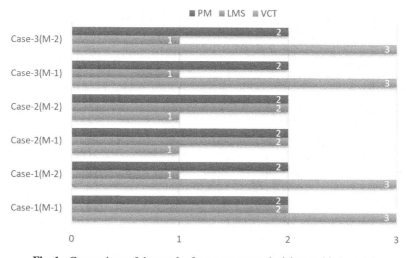

Fig. 1. Comparison of the results from two group decision-making models

When all experts take part with equal importance (Case-1) to form the final group decision, the selection of VCT is the same for both mathematical models. In Case-1 the selection of PM determines also identical results and decisions from both models recommend selecting the alternative A-2 (Bitrix24). Determination of the most suitable LMS via two models shows different solutions for Case-1 (Fig. 1). The usage of model M-1 that is suitable for fast evaluation by group decision-making determine as preferable alternative A-2 (Chamilo) for LMS. In contrast to model M-1, the M-2 model is a more precisely formulated group decision-making model for evaluation and selection via combinatorial optimization. The obtained solution using model M-2 for Case-1 determines as the most preferable selection alternative A-1 (Moodle) for LMS. This difference is due to the more informed evaluations based not only on the presence or not of the functional features but including the evaluation score for their particular alternative's performance versus given criteria.

In Case-2 and Case-3, where the experts' opinions are considered with different importance in the final group decision, both models show that identical results. Considering the experts' importance expressed by Case-2, the selected alternative for VCT is A-1 (Zoom), for LMS the decision is to select alternative A-2 (Chamilo) and for PM alternative A-2 (Bitrix24). In Case-3, which represents another combination of experts' opinion importance, the selection of collaboration software tools is as follows: for VCT to be chosen alternative A-3 (Skype), for LMS – alternative A-1 (Moodle), and for PM – alternative A-2 (Bitrix24).

The empirical comparison of the results from the described two different group decision-making modelling approaches shows their applicability for the selection of collaborative tools for remote working. The first modelling approach (1)–(3) based on the parameters of software tools used as variables and expressed by 0 or 1 if the functional features are present or not is suitable for fast group decision-making. The advantages of this model are the possibility to consider not only the coefficients for relative importance between evaluation criteria (software parameters) but also to take into account the weighted coefficients used to differentiate the experts' opinion importance. The second modelling approach (4)–(14) requires more attention to evaluate in respect to some scale to get the corresponding score that expresses the performance of the alternatives toward given criteria. The advantage of this modelling approach is the fact that the optimal selection of the interesting combination of software item is obtained as a single run of the optimization task. This is due to the used binary integer variables that make a possible selection of a single representative item from different software tools.

Despite the difference between describe approaches both of them could be successfully applied for group decision-making. This is proved by the obtained numerical results illustrated in Fig. 1 where the decision for selection of VCT, LMS and PM are identical in Case-2 and Case-3, while Case-1 differs in the selection only in MLS. Depending on the selected strategy that is the core of each of the models, it is possible to use one of them on different stages to determine reasonable group decision-making. It should be pointed out some essential elements of both models namely the number and qualification of the experts, and their opinions' importance when aggregating the final group decision. All this is possible only with the active role of the CIO in organizing the decision-making process. That is why the CIO plays an important role in the organization, especially in providing a variety of effective solutions that contribute to the satisfaction of managers and employees. On the other hand, this will provide the necessary market flexibility and lead to better economic sustainability.

After selection the needed software tools for collaborative remote working it is needed to determine their way of deployment (self-hosted, cloud-based, SaaS, etc.) and access. For this purpose, it should carefully to consider available access points and configuration of the existing wireless network to avoid additional expenses and from another hand to don't increase the radio frequency pollution from these devices that have a negative effect on the human body.

5 Conclusions

The role of CIO become more important due to the ongoing digital transformation and is extremely needed considering by the current pandemic situation and the requirements to work at the home office. To make possible such remote collaboration, the proper software tools are to be selected. In a similar situation, the CIO should be able to provide proper mathematical models to make reasonable decisions. For such purposes, the current article deals with an empirical comparison between two modelling approaches for group decision-making. First of them aims to make fast evaluation and selection based on the availability or not of parameters of the items (software tools) from which the selection should be done. The second modelling approach includes also evaluation expressed by corresponding score (from given scale) and require the formulation of more complex optimization task, and is more time consuming compared to the first modelling approach.

The conducted numerical experiments demonstrated that both of described approaches could be applied for the purposes of CIO for selection of different software tools. In both mathematical models, the opinions of the experts that form a group could take part with different importance. This feature is important when forming the final group decision, where different experts' points of view toward evaluation criteria importance could be integrated with different weights. The advantage of the second model is the possibility for simultaneous selection of several software tools.

The proposed two mathematical models could be used for other similar problems. For example, the problems of evaluation and selection of IT hardware or infrastructure equipment. The CIO should determine a proper group of experts qualified in the area of IT equipment. This will give a more transparent solution to the executive managers about the particular selection, where the final decision will be based on different experts' opinions. In such a way, it is possible to achieve better economic sustainability.

Acknowledgment. This work is supported by the Bulgarian National Science Fund by the project *"Mathematical models, methods and algorithms for solving hard optimization problems to achieve high security in communications and better economic sustainability"*, KP-06-N52/7/19-11-2021.

References

1. Chan, R.Y.K.: Do chief information officers matter for sustainable development? Impact of their regulatory focus on green information technology strategies and corporate performance. Bus. Strateg. Environ. **30**(5), 2523–2534 (2021). https://doi.org/10.1002/bse.2761

2. Jarvelainen, J.: Understanding the stakeholder roles in business continuity management practices – a study in public sector. In: 53rd Hawaii International Conference on System Sciences, pp. 1966–1975, Maui, Hawaii (2020)

3. Gogan, J.L., Conboy, K., Weiss, J.W.: Dangerous champions of IT innovation. In: 53rd Hawaii International Conference on System Sciences, pp. 6144–6153, Hawaii (2020)

4. Gerth, A.B., Peppard, J.: The dynamics of CIO derailment: how CIOs come undone and how to avoid. Bus. Horiz. **59**, 61–70 (2016)

5. Dawson, G.S., Ho, M.-W., Kauffman, R.J.: How are c-suite executives different? A comparative empirical study of the survival of American chief information officers. Decis. Support Syst. **74**, 88–101 (2015)

6. Trifonov, R., Tsochev, G., Manolov, S., Yoshinov, R., Pavlova, G.: Increasing the level of network and information security using artificial intelligence. In: Fifth International Conference on Advances in Computing, Communication and Information Technology (2017). https://doi.org/10.15224/978-1-63248-131-3-25

7. Tsochev, G., Yoshinov, R., Iliev, O.: Key problems of the critical information infrastructure through SCADA systems research. SPIIRAS Proc. **18**(6), 1333–1356 (2019)

8. Kianpour, M., Kowalski, S.J., Overby, H.: Advancing the concept of cybersecurity as a public good. Simul. Model. Pract. Theory **116**, 102493 (2022). https://doi.org/10.1016/j.simpat.2022.102493

9. Shen, S., Chen, O., Sun, J., Mok, L., Gao, A., Wan, D.D.K.: Coronavirus (COVID-19) outbreak: short- and long term actions for CIOs. Gartner report ID G00720647 (2020)

10. Cearley, D., Burke, B., Smith, D., Jones, N., Chandrasekaran, A., Lu, CK., Karamouzis, F.: Top 10 strategic technology trends for 2020: a Gartner trend insight report. ID: G00467123, pp. 1–21 (2020)

11. Borissova, D., Dimitrova, Z., Dimitrov, V.: How to support teams to be remote and productive: group decision-making for distance collaboration software tools. Inf. Secur.: Int. J. **46**(1), 36–52 (2020). https://doi.org/10.11610/isij.4603

12. Alhayani, B., Mohammed, H.J., Chaloob, I.Z., Ahmed, J.S.: Effectiveness of artificial intelligence techniques against cyber security risks apply of IT industry. Mater. Today: Proc. (2021). https://doi.org/10.1016/j.matpr.2021.02.531

13. Reuschke, D., Mason, C.: The engagement of home-based businesses in the digital economy. Futures (2020). https://doi.org/10.1016/j.futures.2020.102542

14. Oyekana, J., Prabhua, V., Tiwari, A., Baskaran, V., Burgess, M., Mcnally, R.: Remote real-time collaboration through synchronous exchange of digitised human-workpiece interactions. Futur. Gener. Comput. Syst. **67**, 83–93 (2017)

15. Julsrud, T.E., Hjorthol, R., Denstadli, J.M.: Business meetings: do new videoconferencing technologies change communication patterns? J. Transp. Geogr. **24**, 396–403 (2012)

16. Hardwick, J., Anderson, A.R.: Supplier-customer engagement for collaborative innovation using video conferencing: a study of SMEs. Ind. Mark. Manag. **80**, 43–57 (2019)

17. Ghosh, S., Hughes, M., Hodgkinson, I., Hughes, P.: Digital transformation of industrial businesses: a dynamic capability approach. Technovation, 102414 (2021). https://doi.org/10.1016/j.technovation.2021.102414

18. Chtouka, E., Guezguez, W., Amor, N.B.: Reinforcement learning for new adaptive gamified LMS. In: Jallouli, R., Bach Tobji, M.A., Bélisle, D., Mellouli, S., Abdallah, F., Osman, I. (eds.) ICDEc 2019. LNBIP, vol. 358, pp. 305–314. Springer, Cham (2019). https://doi.org/10.1007/978-3-030-30874-2_24

19. Yoshinov, R., Arapi, P., Christodoulakis, S., Kotseva, M.: Supporting personalized learning experiences on top of multimedia digital libraries. Int. J. Educ. Inf. Technol. **10**, 152–158, (2016)

20. De la Pena, D., Lizcano, D., Martinez-Alvarez, I.: Learning through play: gamification model in university-level distance learning. Entertain. Comput. **39**, 100430 (2021). https://doi.org/10.1016/j.entcom.2021.100430

21. Borissova, D., Mustakerov, I.: A framework of multimedia e-learning design for engineering training. In: Spaniol, M., Li, Q., Klamma, R., Lau, R.W.H. (eds.) ICWL 2009. LNCS, vol. 5686, pp. 88–97. Springer, Heidelberg (2009). https://doi.org/10.1007/978-3-642-03426-8_11

22. Petrova, P., Kostadinova, I.: An approach for embedding intelligence in a system for automatic test generation and a 3D result model. In: Proceedings of 10th International Conference on Intelligent Systems, pp. 358–363. IEEE, Varna (2020). https://doi.org/10.1109/IS48319.2020.9199969

23. Kostadinova, I., Rasheva-Yordanova, K., Garvanova, M.: Analysis of algorithms for generating test questions in e-testing systems. In: 11th International Conference on Education and New Learning Technologies, EDULEARN 2019, pp. 1714–1719 (2019). https://doi.org/10.21125/edulearn.2019.0498

24. Beuran, R., Tang, D., Tan, Z., Hasegawa, S., Tan, Y., Shinoda, Y.: Supporting cybersecurity education and training via LMS integration: CyLMS. Educ. Inf. Technol. **24**(6), 3619–3643 (2019). https://doi.org/10.1007/s10639-019-09942-y

25. Shalamanov, V.: Organising for IT effectiveness, efficiency and cyber resilience in the academic sector: national and regional dimensions. Inf. Secur.: Int. J. **42**, 49–66 (2019)

26. Tagarev, T.: Towards the design of a collaborative cybersecurity networked organisation: identification and prioritisation of governance needs and objectives. Future Internet **12**(4), 62 (2020). https://doi.org/10.3390/fi12040062

27. Barbosa, A.P.F.P.L., et al.: Configurations of project management practices to enhance the performance of open innovation R&D projects. Int. J. Project Manag. (2020). https://doi.org/10.1016/j.ijproman.2020.06.005

28. Kreuzer, T., Roglinger. M., Rupprecht. L.: Customer-centric prioritization of process improvement projects. Decis. Support Syst. **133**, 113286 (2020)

29. Burgelman, J., Vanhoucke, M.: Project schedule performance under general mode implementation disruptions. Eur. J. Oper. Res. **280**(1), 295–311 (2020)

30. Garvanova, M., Shishkov, B.: Capturing human authority and responsibility by considering composite public values. In: Shishkov, B. (ed.) BMSD 2019. LNBIP, vol. 356, pp. 290–298. Springer, Cham (2019). https://doi.org/10.1007/978-3-030-24854-3_22

31. Petrov, I.: Combined criteria weighting in MCDM: AHP in blocks with traditional Entropy and novel Hierarchy in TOPSIS evaluation of Cloud Services. In: Proceedings of Big Data, Knowledge and Control Systems Engineering (BdKCSE), pp. 1–9 (2021). https://doi.org/10.1109/BdKCSE53180.2021.9627221

32. Korsemov, D., Borissova, D.: Modifications of simple additive weighting and weighted product models for group decision making. Adv. Model. Optim. **20**(1), 101–112 (2018)

Low-Cost Voice Assistant Design and Testing for Older Adults

Bárbara Farías-Barraza[1], Marcelo Reyes-Rogget[1]([⊠]), Felipe A. López[2],
Ignacio N. López-Martínez[3], Carlos Contreras-Bolton[4], Rodrigo Linfati[5],
and Gustavo Gatica[1]

[1] Engineering Faculty, Universidad Andres Bello, Antonio Varas 880, Providencia, Santiago de Chile, 7500971 Santiago, Chile
{marcelo.reyes,ggatica}@unab.cl
[2] Instituto de Humanidades, Universidad Academia Humanismo Cristiano, Av. Condell 282, Providencia, Santiago de Chile, Chile
felipe.lopez@uacademia.cl
[3] Instituto de Física, Pontificia Universidad Catolica de Chile, Avda. Libertador Bernardo O'Higgins 340, Santiago de Chile, Chile
inlopez1@uc.cl
[4] Universidad de Concepción, Concepción, Chile
carlos.contreras.b@udec.cl
[5] Universidad del Bio-Bio, Concepción, Chile
rlinfati@ubiobio.cl

Abstract. By the year 2050, at least 2 billion people will be over 60 years of age, making it one of the age groups of greatest concern. One of the biggest concerns of this group is loneliness and as a consequence of it, loss of autonomy and decreased daily activity. For this reason, we propose a virtual voice assistant made with open-source software and available technologies, allowing them to have accompaniment and improve interaction with technologies are proposed. Our development test had 89% correct answers and an estimated sale price of less than 150 USD. To test the assistant, we did tests with a group of older adults, who have no previous experience with this type of technology. Within our conclusions, the high willingness to use technologies by older adults is pointed out. Moreover, we conclude that the continuous use and greater confidence in technology motivates a more frequent use of it. Older adults have complexities with other languages, so voice assistants should prefer short, concise, and intuitive commands. Finally, it is concluded that social norms must be taken into account in this technology, otherwise, the error rate will increase.

Keywords: Smart home · Assistive technology · Older adults · Ambient assisted living · Voice assistant

1 Introduction

With the development of medicine, there has been an increase in the life expectancy of the population. By 2050 the world's population over 60 years old will reach 2 billion,

K. Saeed and J. Dvorský (Eds.): CISIM 2022, LNCS 13293, pp. 107–122, 2022.
https://doi.org/10.1007/978-3-031-10539-5_8

representing 22% of the world's population [1]. In the case of Chile, the 2017 census indicated that older adults represented 16.2% of the population and it is estimated that by 2025 they will represent 20.11% [2]. These data show that the population of older adults will be increasingly numerous.

Chile has the highest life expectancy in Latin America; however, 61% of Chileans associate old age with obsolescence, exclusion and loneliness, hence unhappiness [3].

The fifth national survey on quality of life in old age [4], in which 2,132 people participated, shows that 43.5% of older people perceive some degree of loneliness. According to the same survey, the feeling of loneliness increases to 47.9% in people over 70 years old and in people with lower educational levels [4]. Another survey in which 2,033 people over 60 years old participated, showed that 23,8% of them feel that they often or always lack company [5]. Also, depicted that 14,5% feel that they often or always are ignored by others, and 23,9% feel that they never or hardly ever part of a group of friends [5].

The above figures indicate that both, the population of older adults and loneliness feeling have been on the rise, which speaks of a real problem that requires attention. In particular, it harms the well-being and quality of life of older adults, even causing premature death [3]. This scenario has been exacerbated by the Covid-19 pandemic, which has affected different dimensions of their quality of life [3, 6–12]. Also, care practices have had to be rearticulated, changing the relationship between caregiver and cared-for [13].

For this situation, a low-cost solution that allows for care and support for older adults hasn't been presented by technology. Existing solutions aren't focused on this segment of users, considering their specific needs.

Therefore, it is necessary to contribute with technologies to analyse and seek solutions to this problem. The motivation of this research is to reflect on the use of technology and how it can contribute to the processes of care, quality of life, and emotional well-being. The objective of this work is to develop a low-cost technological assistent for older adults that allows reducing the feeling of loneliness, carrying out tests with end-users (older adults), thus obtaining information on their needs, and how they interact with this technology. To achieve this, a prototype of a simple, low-cost voice assistant is proposed and implemented.

In the next section, our theoretical framework is presented, Sect. 3 presents the problem and objectives, in Sect. 4 the project solution is presented, Sect. 5 discusses the results and in Sect. 6 we present the conclusions, all supported by current bibliography.

2 Theoretical Framework

In Chile, the law N° 19.828 created the Servicio Nacional del Adulto Mayor (SENAMA), and defined as an older adult any person who has reached the age of 60, regardless of gender [14].

These older adults, mostly self-reliant, have a greater sense of loneliness [4, 5], mainly due to the lack of company, which is a result of how they perceive, experience, and evaluate their social isolation and lack of communication with others, either because they feel misunderstood and rejected or because they lack the company to carry out an activity they like [6, 12].

Although technology will not replace the affection or company that a human being provides, it can help mitigate this feeling [15]. Under this premise, different technologies of Support of In-Home Care for Older Adults have appeared [15].

One of them is the "voice assistant", technology based on artificial intelligence, which through a voice interface allows users to interact with the internet or with other devices [15], others allow seek advice from health professionals, such as in telemedicine systems [8].

In simple terms, a voice assistant allows a natural and close interaction to how human beings communicate since with it users can make inquiries and interact with different platforms depending on the availability of services that this system has.

The most popular are Alexa, Google Assistant, Cortana, and Siri, however, these are not segmented to older adults. Even though Alexa added a tool called "Alexa We Care" aimed at older adults, which invites users to interact daily through questions, reminders, and advice related to their physical and mental well-being, as well as through conversation, from the information that the user provides [16].

Several studies show that these voice assistants reduce the feeling of loneliness and increase social interaction [17–19]. Although they present limitations in terms of their representativeness, the literature shows that these devices can be easy to use by older adults, allowing them to interact and make inquiries.

On the other hand, Curtis et al. [20] conducted a literature review examining the design features of virtual health assistants, and the effects generated by these interactions. Among the findings, the need to generate a human-looking avatar is observed, this must be empathic and present information about itself, which will generate greater confidence in its use. Finally, they realize that linguistic aspects influence user engagement.

On the same, Humphry and Chesher [21] point out that the voices contain a positive or negative significance, and, therefore, the user creates associations of these with their experiences, so it is recommended to pay attention to the voice used.

Jovanovic et al. [22], in their work on the implementation of technologies in older adults, his work points out to consider the user and the environment in which it is developed since it will present characteristics that will influence the design of the assistant and their specific needs.

That means, a person-centered design must be adopted [23]. Other authors emphasize that what is important is how easy the app is to use since this will encourage its use and increase confidence in it [24].

Regarding privacy, Abou et al. [15], point out that older adults would be willing to tolerate lower levels of privacy in exchange for achieving greater autonomy at home, however, it is unclear whether they are aware of what this means [24].

It also describes that the relationship with this technology generates affective ties, a situation that is still under discussion [15].

Regarding its implementation, Kadylak and Cotten [25] shows a high willingness to use these technologies, especially in those older adults who have a health problem or limitations to their autonomy.

The former is consistent with the benefits found in the use of virtual help systems, where an increase in safety and autonomy has been observed [26]. Also increased self-confidence to move around and learn new tasks, especially to find out about one's illnesses has been shown [27, 28].

Finally, Garcia-Moreno et al. [29] shows that this technology saves costs for continuous monitoring, such as temperature, heart rate, among others.

3 Problem Description

Loneliness, as we have pointed out, has multiple consequences in older adults, including loss of autonomy, security, and decreased physical activity, among others [9]. In the following subsection we identify the cause of the problem, to later show the proposed solution.

3.1 Causes of Loneliness

The main causes of the feeling of loneliness in older adults are:

Social Isolation: Produced by various situations, such as living alone, being abandoned, having some type of illness, or inactivity. The data in Chile indicate that 459.686 older adults live alone, which is equivalent to 13,4% of older adults. In addition, 227,991 older adults share a room with an older adult, of which 18.3% indicated that they did not have any relatives with whom to talk [4, 30]. Although living alone does not necessarily mean loneliness, authors like Steed et al. [31], point out that people who spend a lot of time alone are vulnerable to loneliness. Similarly, Hughes et al. [32] indicate that older people who live alone feel more alone than people of the same age who live with someone.

Environmental Barriers: They correspond to barriers that restrict the social contact of older adults and could lead them to experience loneliness, these barriers could be financial or the fear of leaving home [10, 30]. Especially if we consider that only 21.2% of older adults have enough income to live comfortably [4, 33].

Lack of Communication: It is affected by two variables, the first related to the difficulty older adults face in manipulating technological products that allow them to communicate, and the second related to the fact that they do not have someone close to whom they can talk. Growth from Knowledge [3], points out that 46% of older adults in Chile recognize that they do not get along with technology and 47% of older adults lose interest in any technological product that is too complicated to use.

3.2 Proposed Solution and Objectives

From the science of design, considering that applications must respond to real problems [34, 35], a traditional development methodology is followed, in which older adults are the target users. The defined objective was "to develop a communication and support system for older adults that includes a voice assistant in Spanish, in which the basic commands necessary for these users are integrated".

For this objective, the key indicators of success were identified, the Spanish language, the correct answer delivered by the voice system, the cost of the assistant, and that it contains 20 basic commands. Table 1 identifies four objectives and assigned metrics.

Table 1. Objectives and metrics. Source: Own elaboration.

Objective	Metric	Success criteria
1. Language	Spanish = 1 Other = 0	Language = 1
2. Right Answers (RA)	RA = (A/Q) * 100 RA = Percentage of correct answers over the total number of attempts A = Number of correct answers Q = Number of queries	RA ≥ 75%
3. App cost	Unitary Cost (UC)	UC ≤ 200 USD
4. 20 Basic existing commands (EC)	Number of existing commands Comandos (EC)	EC > 20

Regarding objective 2, the percentage of correct answers was obtained from the evaluations carried out on the voice assistants Alexa, Echo Show, Cortana, Google Assistant, and Siri, which have shown an average of 75% of correct answers [36]. It should be noted that the tests were performed by people of all ages and not exclusively by older adults.

Regarding objective 3, we intend to make it accessible to people with lower incomes (Environmental barriers), a final development cost will be estimated considering 5,000 units, this cost must be less than 50% of a minimum monthly income in Chile.

Objectives 1 and 4, are obtained from the general objective of the app, which is aimed at a specific user segment Older adults Spanish-speaking.

4   Project Solutions

The requirements were cataloged into three categories: functional, non-functional, and business requirements [34, 35]. The programming language was Python to reduce costs, using free libraries and, the system was a desktop application, without major memory and processor requirements, but internet connection, speakers, and microphone were necesary.

In Fig. 1, we show a diagram of the operation process of the voice assistant prototype. This process begins when the user decides to use a command, which is entered by voice, the application makes a voice recognition using the "speechrecognition v3.8.1" library, which recognizes the content of the message said by the user and converts it into a string of text, then comes the command detection, in which the text string is compared with the previously established commands, allowing the function associated with that command to be executed.

One of the advantages of this library is that it has built-in functions "that are used to identify the background noises – like whispering, or people talking in the background, or loud footsteps, or construction noises, etc. – and cancel those ambient noises in order to focus on the foreground data which is basically the user-recorded speech" [37]. Which guarantees a high accuracy of understanding between the user and the assistant [38] along side a Hidden Markov Model (HMM) that reduces time calculations? [39].

Fig. 1. Operation of the prototype voice assistant. Source: Own elaboration.

To achieve certain functions that require running apps or services on the computer, such as playing YouTube content, sending WhatsApp messages, or opening websites, specific libraries will be used, such as "pywhatkit" and "PyAutoGUI" [40–45].

Figure 2 presents the deployment diagram, which shows the requirement for a sound device. The interface use Tkinder (see Sect. 4.3). The database presented in the diagram is used in the conversation function, which is presented in Sect. 4.4 and consists of a set of questions and answers.

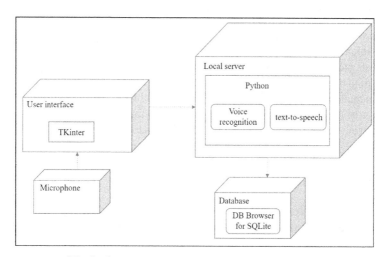

Fig. 2. Deployment diagram Source: Own elaboration.

4.1 Functions

From the design of the use cases, 20 functionalities that the user can select were determined. Table 2, lists the functions, additionally, the Python library used and the command to be used are presented.

Table 2. Voice assistant functions, Python library used, and voice command to execute (translated command). Source: Own elaboration.

Function	Library (s)	Translated voice command
Play music	Pywhatkit	Play + (Song)
Search wikipedia	Wikipedia	Search + (Name)
Activate alarm	Datetime, pygame	Set alarm at + (time)
Write notes	N/A	Write
Hear notes	N/A	Open note
Open website	webbrowser	Open + (Webpage from a predefined set)
Check time	strftime	What time is it?
Check date	strftime	What date is it?
Tell jokes	chistesESP	Tell me a joke
Timer	Pyautogui, webbrowser, time	Timer in + (minutes)
Calculator	AppID de wolfram alpha	Calculate + (mathematical operation)
Find addresses	webbrowser	Where is + (address)?
Weather	API de OpenWeatherMap	Weather in + (city)
Dictionary	PyDictionary, translator	Meaning of + (word)
Conversation	chatterbot, sqlite3 con consulta a Base de datos (ver sección 4.4)	Let's talk
Search google	Pywhatkit	Information about + (topic)
Send whatsapp message (to registered contacts)	Newsapi	Send message + (message)
News	Newsapi	News
Close browser		Close browser
Close voice assistant		Bye

4.2 Materials

The software used consisted of:

- Operating system: Windows 10
- Programming language: Python v3.9
- Source code editor: Visual Studio Code V1.6
- DB Browser for SQLite 3.12.2

The Hardware used consisted of:

- Processor: Pentium i5 de 1,8 GHz
- RAM: 8 GB
- HDD: 256 GB SSD
- Microphone: Generic Via USB
- Speakers: Generic
- Internet connection

4.3 App Interface

As mentioned, the interface was developed using the TKinter library and works like a PC application in which the user can interact with it by pressing the "Escuchar" button. We would like to remind the reader that the interface and commands are in Spanish since the target group of users are Spanish-speaking older adults.

The goal of the interface was to keep it as simple as possible, which is why consisted of just one window from which commands were executed.

In Fig. 4 we present the interface, in which two additional icons will be appreciated. The first of them allows the user to review the list of available commands and the second allows to add a WhatsApp contact to later be able to use the send message command (Fig. 3).

Fig. 3. App interface. Source: Own elaboration.

4.4   Conversation Function

The "conversation" function is designed as a Chatbot, through pre-established questions and answers [40, 46–48]. A database was created which cointans questions and answer that the user can made. This database is used for trainning the chatbot.

Figure 5 shows an example of the content stored in the database, in which we show some of the possible questions and responses. It should be noted that this list is customizable and is part of the future work to be developed.

	Questions	Responses
	Filter	Filter
1	hola	hola, qué tal?
2	quién eres	soy tu asistente de voz
3	gracias	no hay de que, fui programada para ...
4	hola asistente	hola, cómo estás?
5	dime algo	sabías que fui programada de ...
6	bien y tú	bien, aquí lista para lo que necesites
7	cuéntame algo	La jirafa duerme tan sólo 7 minutos p...
8	háblame de ti	soy un prototipo de asistente de voz ...
9	bien	me alegra oír eso, que haz hecho hoy?

Fig. 4. Example of the content stored in the database for the conversation function in Spanish. Source: Own elaboration.

Regarding the functionality of the Chatbot, sentences were created in the code so that it does not memorize all the records of the database, to modify the information if necessary. Once the ChatBot has been trained, the microphone is activated to start a conversation with the user.

5   Results and Discussion

We followed a Software Quality process, documenting risks and stages of the development process [49–51]. The voice assistant tests were carried out in two stages, in both of them, the tests were designed considering the abilities of those who will test them, as recommended by Gerrard [52].

In the first one a development environment and later with a group of objective users, who volunteered to carry out the test. In the following sections, we present the results of each stage.

5.1   Development Tests

The first set of tests are Alpha Tests [53], which consisted of 40 queries to each of the commands. These consultations were carried out by a middle-aged woman, in an environment with moderate noise. Table 3 shows the results of the tests carried out.

Table 3. Test set results. Source: Own elaboration.

Function	Right answer ratio	Percentage
Play music	40/40	100%
Search wikipedia	40/40	100%
Activate alarm	37/40	92.5%
Write notes	35/40	87.5%
Hear notes	36/40	90%
Open website	35/40	87.5%
Check time	37/40	92.5%
Check date	36/40	90%
Tell jokes	40/40	100%
Timer	31/40	77.5%
Calculator	35/40	87.5%
Find addresses	40/40	100%
Weather	40/40	100%
Dictionary	34/40	85%
Conversation	31/40	77.5%
Search google	40/40	100%
Send whatsapp message	32/40	80%
News	37/40	92.5%
Close browser	40/40	100%
Close voice assistant	39/40	97.5%

Regarding the results obtained, it is observed that in all the commands the obtained right answer ratio percentage is greater than 75%, so objective 2, presented in Table 1, would be fulfilled.

As for the lowest percentages, these were given in the "Timer" and "Conversation" functions, which, are the ones that require more user interaction, an additional consideration to take into account for future work is that the voice assistant systems prefer short and concise commands in order not to reduce the number of hits.

5.2   Users Test

The Beta tests [53], were carried out with 6 people, all over 65 years of age, 3 men and 3 women. All noted that they had not previously interacted with a voice assistant.

The objective of this test is to approach a "real world with real customers" scenario, for feedback on each element of the software, evaluating bugs, crashes and complete features, obtaining "a good idea of what your customers think about the product and what would they likely experience when they purchase it" [53].

The test set consisted of 3 queries for each of the functionalities by each user. The result of the tests is presented in Table 4, users are described by a number.

Table 4. User test results. source: own elaboration.

Functionl User	1	2	3	4	5	6	Function success percentage
Play music	3/3	3/3	3/3	2/3	3/3	2/3	88.89%
Search wikipedia	3/3	3/3	2/3	2/3	3/3	3/3	88.89%
Activate alarm	2/3	3/3	3/3	3/3	2/3	2/3	83.33%
Write notes	2/3	2/3	3/3	3/3	2/3	2/3	77.78%
Hear notes	3/3	3/3	2/3	3/3	3/3	3/3	94.44%
Open website	2/3	2/3	3/3	2/3	3/3	2/3	77.78%
Check time	3/3	3/3	3/3	3/3	3/3	2/3	94.44%
Check date	3/3	3/3	3/3	3/3	3/3	2/3	94.44%
Tell jokes	3/3	3/3	2/3	2/3	3/3	3/3	88.89%
Timer	2/3	3/3	2/3	2/3	3/3	2/3	77.78%
Calculator	3/3	3/3	2/3	3/3	3/3	3/3	94.44%
Find addresses	3/3	3/3	3/3	2/3	2/3	3/3	88.89%
Weather	3/3	3/3	3/3	3/3	3/3	2/3	94.44%
Dictionary	2/3	2/3	3/3	3/3	2/3	2/3	88.89%
Conversation	2/3	2/3	3/3	3/3	2/3	1/3	72.22%
Search google	3/3	2/3	3/3	3/3	3/3	3/3	94.44%
Send whatsapp message	2/3	3/3	3/3	3/3	1/3	2/3	77.78%
News	3/3	3/3	2/3	3/3	3/3	2/3	94.44%
Close browser	3/3	3/3	3/3	2/3	2/3	3/3	88.89%
Close voice assistant	3/3	3/3	3/3	3/3	3/3	2/3	94.44%
User success percentage	88.33%	91.67%	90.00%	88.33%	86.67%	76.67%	86.94%

The average number of correct answers was 86.9%, again the conversation function is within the fewest values, which is due to the number of interactions that increase the probability of error. Unlike the development tests, none of the functions had a 100% success, which accounts for a variation in the tone, volume, and pronunciation of users depending on the age group.

Subject 6 corresponds to the oldest person, so the low individual metrics may have multiple causes which should be studied in future work.

Regarding the "open website" function, we observed that the errors were caused by having to pronounce words in another language, so we recommend using only words in the user's language to minimize mistakes.

It was observed that users had trouble remembering all the commands, a situation that should be integrated into a new use case to evaluate possible solutions.

We also observed that when the app initiated and says "hi", the users responded "hi" or "good morning", and when they ask something, they usually say words like "please" or "thanks", commands that the assistant does not recognize.

Once the interaction with the voice assistant was over, users were asked two questions, the first was about their experience in general terms, to which they pointed out that at first, they felt fear and discomfort, by having to interact with something that they did not know how it worked, but as they repeated the commands and got a response from the assistant they felt more comfortable and enjoyed the activity, Additionaly, the users pointed out that the assistant could be a good company in their daily activities.

The second question related to what they think of the experience of interacting by voice, in which they indicated that it facilitates their access to different functions that they could not perform on their own.

The results with the group of users are consistent with results observed in the literature, especially concerning the increase in confidence as the application is used. [15, 23, 27], increased confidence and security to perform other activities [26, 27], and decreased loneliness [19].

5.3 General Results of the Objectives

In Table 5 we present the results of the metrics associated with the proposed objectives. It should be noted that, regarding the cost, an 18-month cash flow estimate was made, with the sale of 5,000 units, which resulted in an estimated sale price of 150 USD, with an Internal Rate of Return (IRR) of 10%.

Table 5. Objectives and metrics. Source: Own elaboration.

Objective	Metric	Success criteria	Conclusion
1. Language	Spanish	Language $= 1$	Achieved
2. Right Answers (RA)	86.94%	RC $\geq 75\%$	Achieved
3. App cost	150 USD	CU ≤ 200 USD	Achieved
4. 20 Basic existing commands (EC)	1	(CE/20) ≥ 1.0	Achieved

6 Conclusions

This research, whose objective has been to design and test with users a voice accompanying system for older adults, using low-cost technology and open-source software, has additionally generated contributions to the literature regarding the impact and considerations that should be taken with this group of users.

Within our conclusions we can point out that it is an appropriate indicator to consider 75% as a correct answer metric, although in the optimum, the error rate should be closer to zero, our tests show that the probability that the voice system fails, given the tones, volumes and even languages involved, is high. It is for this reason that our recommendation is to use simple commands that do not complicate the user, as well as that the words used are in the same language at all times, to reduce the minimize errors. Our tests also show the need to prefer short and concise commands, but also familiar to the user, with everyday words that facilitate memorizing them, or the intuitive type so as not to depend on memory.

Our tests suggest that it is relevant to consider the user and their environment, in special, the moral and behavioral norms in which they operate, so it is important to investigate how to consider these situations and their implications in the development of support systems.

Regarding the implementation of technology, our tests conclude that users, once they gained confidence in its use, had no problems manipulating the application, which would indicate that this age group does not have a negative predisposition to technology, on the contrary, they would be willing to use it and interact with it.

User tests revealed the benefits of these assistants, including increased security and confidence, carrying out new activities, and accompaniment for those who live alone.

For future work, we recommend exploring the interaction processes for Chatbot training, as well as identifying functions that were not included but were suggested, such as a panic button in an emergency, and even associating it with home automation.

It is necessary to continue investigating the processes of technology adoption by older adults and how it improves their quality of life, in particular, it is suggested to carry out a test with the voice assistant for a longer time to conclude if effectively reduces their feeling of loneliness. In addition, a qualitative evaluation of the users should be included to obtain more feedback on the use and possible improvements of the assistant.

Finally, we must point out that due to Covid-19 contingency a low number of tests were carried out. This is why we are working on an extended version of the assistant, in which a greater number of tests will be considered alongside time response and qualitative evaluations by the users.

Acknowledgements. This research was funded by University of Bio-Bio grant number 2060222 IF/R and 2160277 GI/EF. And the Research Department (VRI) of Universidad Andres Bello grant number DI-12-20/REG.

References

1. World Health Organization: 10 Datos sobre le envejecimiento y la salud. https://www.who.int/features/factfiles/ageing/es/. Accessed 20 Jan 2022

2. Ministerio de Salud de Chile: Subsecretario Burrows en ONU: El año 2025 más del 20% de la población chilena será mayor de 60 años. https://www.minsal.cl/subsecretario-bur rows-en-onu-el-ano-2025-mas-del-20-de-la-poblacion-chilena-sera-mayor-de-60-anos/#:~: text=Al. Accessed 18 Jan 2022
3. Cuneo, C.: El Tercer Acto de la Vida. Una Radiografía a la Adultez. Departamento de Comunicaciones, GfK (2018)
4. Centro UC Estudios de Vejez y Envejecimiento: Chile y sus mayores: 10 años de la Encuesta Calidad de Vida en la Vejez: V Encuesta Calidad de Vida en la Vejez (2019)
5. Bravo, D.: Las Personas Mayores en Chile: Resultados Preliminares de la Aplicación del Protocolo Armonizado de Evaluación Cognitiva. Centro UC de Encuestas y Estudios Longitudinales, Santiago (2020)
6. Pinazo, S., Bellegarde, M.: La soledad de las personas mayores. Conceptualización, Valoración e Intervención. Estudios de la Fundación Pilares Para la Autonomía Personal (2018)
7. Valarezo Carrión, J.L., Silva Maldonado, J.C., Medina Muñoz, R.P.: Influencia de la soledad en el estado cognitivo y emocional en las personas de la tercera edad residentes en una institución geriátrica. Rev. Espac. 41, 2 (2020)
8. Castillo Sepúlveda, J., Reyes, M.I.: Repertorios interpretativos de la teleasistencia domiciliaria (TAD) como práctica de cuidado. Rev. Latinoam. Psicol. Soc. Ignacio Martín-Baró. 2, 1–31 (2013)
9. Iglesias de Ussel, J., Lopez Doblas, J., Díaz conde, M.P., Alemán Bracho, C., Requena, A., Castor, P.: La soledad en las personas mayores. Influencias Personales, Familiares y Sociales. Análisis Cualitativo. Instituto de Migraciones y Servicios Sociales, Madrid (2001)
10. Observatorio del Envejecimiento: Personas Mayores en Contexto de Pandemia y Aislamiento Social. Pontificia Universidad Catolica de Chile (2020)
11. Rodríguez Martín, M.: La soledad en el anciano. Gerokomos 20 (2009). https://doi.org/10. 4321/S1134-928X2009000400003
12. Rubio Herrera, R., Cerquera Córdoba, A.M., Muñoz Mejía, R., Pinzón Benavides, E.A.: Concepciones populares sobre soledad de los adultos mayores de España y Bucaramanga, Colombia. Diversitas. 7, 307 (2011). https://doi.org/10.15332/s1794-9998.2011.0002.08
13. Rojas-Navarro, S., Energici, M.-A., Schöngut-Grollmus, N., Alarcón-Arcos, S.: Imposibilidades del cuidado: reconstrucciones del cuidar en la pandemia de la covid-19 a partir de la experiencia de mujeres en Chile. Antípoda. Rev. Antropol. y Arqueol. 101–123 (2021). https://doi.org/10.7440/antipoda45.2021.05
14. SENAMA: Servicio Nacional del Adulto Mayor. http://www.senama.gob.cl/servicio-nac ional-del-adulto-mayor. Accessed 25 Jan 2022
15. Abou Allaban, A., Wang, M., Padır, T.: A systematic review of robotics research in support of in-home care for older adults. Information 11, 75 (2020). https://doi.org/10.3390/info11 020075
16. Rundoom I + D: El futuro de los asistentes virtuales en salud: Alexa we care, la skill para personas mayors. https://www.runroom.com/cases/asistentes-virtuales-salud-personas-mayores. Accessed 26 Jan 2022
17. Greenwood Campbell: Voice for loneliness. https://www.greenwoodcampbell.com/what/voi ceforloneliness/. Accessed 25 Jan 2022
18. Mizak, A., Park, M., Park, D., Olson, K.: Amazon "Alexa" pilot analysis report. Front Porch Center for Innovationand Wellbeing (2017)
19. Elza, R., Barton, C., Fehskens, C., Silsby, J.: Reducing social isolation in affordable senior housing using voice assistant technology. LeadingAge Center for Aging Services Technologies (2019)
20. Curtis, R.G., et al.: Improving user experience of virtual health assistants: scoping review. J. Med. Internet Res. 23, e31737 (2021). https://doi.org/10.2196/31737

21. Humphry, J., Chesher, C.: Preparing for smart voice assistants: cultural histories and media innovations. New Media Soc. **23**, 1971–1988 (2021). https://doi.org/10.1177/146144482092 3679
22. Jovanović, M., De Angeli, A., McNeill, A., Coventry, L.: User requirements for inclusive technology for older adults. Int. J. Hum.-Comput. Interact. **37**, 1947–1965 (2021). https://doi.org/10.1080/10447318.2021.1921365
23. Bedaf, S., Marti, P., Amirabdollahian, F., de Witte, L.: A multi-perspective evaluation of a service robot for seniors: the voice of different stakeholders. Disabil. Rehabil. Assist. Technol. **13**, 592–599 (2018). https://doi.org/10.1080/17483107.2017.1358300
24. Acikgoz, F., Vega, R.P.: The role of privacy cynicism in consumer habits with voice assistants: a technology acceptance model perspective. Int. J. Hum.–Comput. Interact. 1–15 (2021). https://doi.org/10.1080/10447318.2021.1987677
25. Kadylak, T., Cotten, S.R.: United States older adults' willingness to use emerging technologies. Inf. Commun. Soc. **23**, 736–750 (2020). https://doi.org/10.1080/1369118X.2020.171 3848
26. Kivimäki, T., Stolt, M., Charalambous, A., Suhonen, R.: Safety of older people at home: An integrative literature review. Int. J. Older People Nurs. **15** (2020). https://doi.org/10.1111/opn. 12285
27. Göransson, C., et al.: Testing an app for reporting health concerns-Experiences from older people and home care nurses. Int. J. Older People Nurs. **13**, e12181 (2018). https://doi.org/10.1111/opn.12181
28. Pradhan, A., Lazar, A., Findlater, L.: Use of intelligent voice assistants by older adults with low technology use. ACM Trans. Comput. Interact. **27**, 1–27 (2020). https://doi.org/10.1145/3373759
29. Garcia-Moreno, F.M., Bermudez-Edo, M., Rodríguez-García, E., Pérez-Mármol, J.M., Garrido, J.L., Rodríguez-Fórtiz, M.J.: A machine learning approach for semi-automatic assessment of IADL dependence in older adults with wearable sensors. Int. J. Med. Inform. **157**, 104625 (2022). https://doi.org/10.1016/j.ijmedinf.2021.104625
30. Observatorio del Envejecimiento: Salud Mental y Principales Preocupaciones de las Personas Mayores en Contexto de Pandemia. Pontificia Universidad Catolica de Chile (2020)
31. Steed, L., Boldy, D., Grenade, L., Iredell, H.: The demographics of loneliness among older people in Perth, Western Australia. Australas. J. Ageing. **26**, 81–86 (2007). https://doi.org/10.1111/j.1741-6612.2007.00221.x
32. Hughes, M.E., Waite, L.J., Hawkley, L.C., Cacioppo, J.T.: A short scale for measuring loneliness in large surveys. Res. Aging. **26**, 655–672 (2004). https://doi.org/10.1177/016402750 4268574
33. Centro UC Estudios de Vejez y Envejecimiento: Chile y sus mayores 10 años de la Encuesta Calidad de Vida en la Vejez: IV Encuesta Calidad de Vida en la Vejez (2017)
34. Jansen, A., Malavolta, I., Muccini, H., Ozkaya, I., Zimmermann, O. (eds.): ECSA 2020. LNCS, vol. 12292. Springer, Cham (2020). https://doi.org/10.1007/978-3-030-58923-3
35. Khalid, L.: Software Architecture for Business. Springer International Publishing, Cham (2020). https://doi.org/10.1007/978-3-030-13632-1
36. Enge, E.: Calificando la inteligencia de los asistentes personales digitales en 2019. https://www.perficient.com/insights/research-hub/digital-personal-assistants-study
37. Datta, D., David, P.E., Mittal, D., Jain, A.: Neural machine translation using recurrent neural network. Int. J. Eng. Adv. Technol. 9, 1395–1400 (2020). https://doi.org/10.35940/ijeat. D7637.049420
38. Sinha, Y., Siegert, I.: Improving the Accuracy for Voice-Assistant conversations in German by combining different online ASR-API outputs. In: Human Perspectives on Spoken Human-Machine Interaction, pp. 11–16 (2021). https://doi.org/10.6094/UNIFR/223823

39. Amos, D.: The Ultimate Guide To Speech Recognition With Python (2021)
40. Hamed AlSaedi, A.K., AlAsadi, A.H.H.: A new hand gestures recognition system. Indones. J. Electr. Eng. Comput. Sci. **18**, 49 (2020). https://doi.org/10.11591/ijeecs.v18.i1.pp49-55
41. Sridhar, S., Sanagavarapu, S., Chitrakala, S.: Cross-platform remote desktop sharing with IP tunneling. In: 2020 11th International Conference on Computing, Communication and Networking Technologies (ICCCNT), pp. 1–7. IEEE (2020). https://doi.org/10.1109/ICCCNT 49239.2020.9225437
42. Nagpal, A., Gabrani, G.: Python for data analytics, scientific and technical applications. In: 2019 Amity International Conference on Artificial Intelligence (AICAI), pp. 140–145. IEEE (2019). https://doi.org/10.1109/AICAI.2019.8701341
43. Stancin, I., Jovic, A.: An overview and comparison of free Python libraries for data mining and big data analysis. In: 2019 42nd International Convention on Information and Communication Technology, Electronics and Microelectronics (MIPRO), pp. 977–982. IEEE (2019). https://doi.org/10.23919/MIPRO.2019.8757088
44. Hug, N.: Surprise: A Python library for recommender systems. J. Open Source Softw. **5**, 2174 (2020). https://doi.org/10.21105/joss.02174
45. Bahit, E.: Introduccion al lenguaje python. http://escuela.eugeniabahit.com (2018)
46. Nhu, T.V., Sawada, H.: Development of vietnamese voice chatbot with emotion expression. In: 2018 International Symposium on Micro-NanoMechatronics and Human Science (MHS), pp. 1–7. IEEE (2018). https://doi.org/10.1109/MHS.2018.8886954
47. Bilgin, T.T., Yavuz, E.: Conceptual design of python ide with embedded turkish spoken chatbot that analyzes and corrects the syntax errors. Eur. J. Sci. Technol. (2021). https://doi.org/10.31590/ejosat.1035421
48. Chawla, A., Varshney, A., Umar, M.S., Javed, H.: ProBot: an online aid to procurement. In: 2018 International Conference on System Modeling and Advancement in Research Trends (SMART), pp. 268–273. IEEE (2018). https://doi.org/10.1109/SYSMART.2018.8746954
49. Galin, D.: Software Quality: Concepts and Practice. IEEE/Wiley (2018)
50. O'Regan, G.: Introduction to Software Quality. Springer International Publishing, Cham (2014). https://doi.org/10.1007/978-3-319-06106-1
51. Goericke, S., (ed.): The Future of Software Quality Assurance. Springer International Publishing, Cham (2020). https://doi.org/10.1007/978-3-030-29509-7
52. Gerrard, P.: The tester skills program: teaching testers to think for themselves. In: Goericke, S. (ed.) The Future of Software Quality Assurance, pp. 39–60. Springer International Publishing, Cham (2020). https://doi.org/10.1007/978-3-030-29509-7_4
53. Mitev, M.: Measure twice, cut once: acceptance testing. In: The Future of Software Quality Assurance, pp. 93–104. Springer International Publishing, Cham (2020). https://doi.org/10.1007/978-3-030-29509-7_7

Design of a Wearable Assistive System for Visually Impaired People

Yigay He-Astudillo[1], Marcelo Reyes-Rogget[1(✉)], Felipe A. López[2],
Ignacio N. López-Martínez[3], Rodrigo Linfati[4], Daniel Morillo[5], and Gustavo Gatica[1]

[1] Engineering Faculty, Universidad Andres Bello, Antonio Varas 880, Providencia, Santiago de Chile, 7500971 Santiago, Chile
{marcelo.reyes,ggatica}@unab.cl

[2] Instituto de Humanidades, Universidad Academia Humanismo Cristiano, Av. Condell 282, Providencia, Santiago de Chile, Chile
felipe.lopez@uacademia.cl

[3] Instituto de Física, Pontificia Universidad Catolica de Chile, Santiago, Chile
inlopez1@uc.cl

[4] Universidad del Bío-Bio, Concepción, Chile
rlinfati@ubiobio.cl

[5] Pontificia Universidad Javeriana de Cali, Cali, Colombia
daniel.morillo@javerianacali.edu.co

Abstract. At least 2.2 billion people are visually impaired, with the main problem being a lack of autonomy and safety when moving around the city. To solve those needs, a wearable assistive system for vision impairment people, with low cost and open-source applications, integrating machine learning and deep learning was developed. We used a mixed methodology, including semi-structured interviews with visually impaired people and specialists in visually impaired needs, including them both in the design process. This allowed us to have an understatement of the specific needs and to generate improvements in the design. The results are auspicious for the feasibility of this type of development, the main considerations and lessons learned are noted, leaving some opportunities for future research.

Keywords: Visual impairment · Machine learning · Face recognition · Obstacle detection · Ultrasonic sensor · Identifying objects

1 Introduction

"Vision is the most dominant of the five senses and plays a crucial role in every facet of our lives" [1]. According to figures from World Health Organization, globally, at least 2.2 billion people have a near or distance vision impairment and 36 million are blind, and those numbers are increasing [1, 2]. Studies have shown that impaired vision may be the initial manifestation of COVID-19 [3] and others that this increase is one more of the consequences of the pandemic on society and health [4, 5].

When an eye condition affects the visual system and alters one or more of its vision functions we define it as vision impairment [1]. The main causes of vision impairment

K. Saeed and J. Dvorský (Eds.): CISIM 2022, LNCS 13293, pp. 123–135, 2022.
https://doi.org/10.1007/978-3-031-10539-5_9

are uncorrected refractive errors; cataracts; age-related macular degeneration; glaucoma; diabetic retinopathy; corneal opacity; and trachoma [6]. The classification of visual impairment is based on the distance to the object, separating them into Distance vision impairment (mild, moderate, severe and blindness) and Near vision impairment [7].

This condition is unequally distributed according to the income level of the countries [1]. It has serious public policy implications, being associated with poorer living conditions and poorer health [8] and even a greater impact on the COVID-19 [5].

Some of the consequences associated with visual impairment are three times more likely to be involved in a collision with a vehicle and twice as likely to trip and fall while walking. [6]. These problems are increased by the emotional situation and dependency suffered by the visually impaired, as they are not even sure who they are talking to, and by the lack of autonomy when carrying out tasks that are routine for the rest of the people, all of which generates greater personal dissatisfaction [9]. Another of the main difficulties is travelling abroad, as cities are poorly prepared for the needs of this type of person [8, 10]. For this reason, specially designed aids must be used, the most common of which are canes, guide dogs, and mobility training, as well as the use of IoT and sensors [11].

Measurements of visual acuity and visual field allow various types and levels of impairment to be established, as indicated in the following list [7]:

- Mild: visual acuity less than 6/12
- Moderate: visual acuity less than 6/18
- Severe: visual acuity less than 6/60
- Blindness visual acuity less than 3/60 or inability to perceive light.

This research focuses on people with severe visual impairment or blindness. Using a mixed research method, through semi-structured interviews and the development of a prototype, we propose wearable hardware connected to an algorithm that contains artificial intelligence functions (deep learning and machine learning) which allow the recognition of faces, objects, text, and the use of an ultrasonic sensor.

Our objective was to evaluate the technical feasibility of developing and integrating different tools to generate a system that helps visually impaired people make decisions at a low-cost.

This paper is an early-stage development of the system, our goal is to generate discussion about the solution and contribute with our preliminary results.

The following section presents the theoretical framework. Section 3 describes the problem feature. Section 4 describes the methodology. Section 5 describes the development process of each component. Section 6 discusses the process and findings. Section 7 reports the conclusions.

2 Related Work

Vision has different activities and occupations (see details clearly; allowing differentiation of objects of a similar size and shape; etc.) [1]. However, we will deal with factors that measure efficiency:

- Visual acuity: the sharpness or detail with which objects are perceived (clarity).
- Visual field: space covered by vision when looking straight ahead (peripheral vision).

For people with severe visual impairment, blindness, or whose visual field is so small that they cannot see, technology is an option, which is the set of techniques, knowledge, and resources to provide visually impaired people with the appropriate means for the correct use of technology [12]. These consider character magnification, screen readers, and Braille converters, among others.

Riazi's research [13] reports some situations that annoy and frustrate visually impaired people and that are their main drawbacks:

- Need to ask others and ask for help in routine activities.
- Route identification, having to pay attention to the route and memorize details, including escalators, potholes, and holes in the ground.
- The potential risk of accidents, with bicycles or motorbikes, especially when riding on pavements; scaffolding, and other obstacles both on the ground and overhead (e.g., branches).

Research agrees that lack of autonomy, sense of place, and insecurity when traveling are the main limitations faced by visually impaired or blind people in cities [13–15]. The following are observed to help the visually impaired person: infrared sensors [16], ultrasonic sensors [17], stereo cameras [16, 18], RGB-D sensors [19, 20], and radar sensors [20]. In which the use of stereoscopic cameras or cameras with RGB-D sensors gives a good result for alerting about stairs or the distance of an obstacle, but usually a notebook is used to process the images, which means additional weight to be carried. The literature also state that using networks such as 3G is very slow for information to arrive in real-time, but nowadays networks have improved and there is 4G with speeds reaching 100 Mbps [21, 22], and soon 5G. So, cloud processing could be an option. On the other hand, the use of technologies with high processing and small calculation time as in the project of Jafri [16] using a Tablet, called Tango project, created by Google, that involves an interesting use of stereoscopic cameras and a video card inside the device. This has the disadvantage that it has to be held in a certain way to capture the environment correctly, another concern is the long-term support of this tool, considering that Google may not continue its development. Another alternative is ARcore, a mobile application developed by Google that provides an understanding of the environment, which could allow finding unevenness in the ground, however, it would not meet the criteria of an adaptative architecture [23].

Other research focuses only on object recognition such as in [24] they even consider voice commands, but that has the disadvantage of forcing the person to speak loudly in public which can be embarrassing for the person. Or the apps do not meet the requirements of visually impaired people [25, 26]. Table 1 summarizes solutions found in other published works.

Table 1. Solutions found in other published works. The problems are listed in the first column and appear with a ticket if they are solved in the respective publication. Source: Own elaboration

Problem	[19]	[27]	[17]	[24]	Our solution
Distance sensor	✓	X	✓	X	✓
Face recognition	X	✓	X	X	✓
Step recognition	X	X	✓	X	✓
Object recognition	X	X	X	✓	✓
Light	X	X	✓	✓	✓
Emotion recognition	X	✓	X	X	X
Voice commands	X	X	X	✓	X

3 Methodology

The methodology used is based on the science of design, using metrics that validate the previously defined objectives [23, 35]. Thus, this work consists of three main steps: identification of needs, development of the artefact, and evaluation.

For the first step, weekly meetings were held with the specialist in visually impaired people to determine the different requirements. This resulted in the identification of 22 functional requirements, non-functional, business considerations, and project requirements.

To determine the characteristics of the application, we used as references the requirements set out in the Fundación Auna [36], Schrott [37], and Lopez Delgado et al. [38], these recommendations include the use of large screens, appropriate keyboards, ergonomics, depending on the type of disability being addressed, i.e. characterize the application and develop it through the selected degree of interaction [26].

The requirements were associated with each of the proposed objectives, the system is intended to be a wearable sensor device at head level, which has 2 modes, i) focus mode for obstacle detection, calculating distances, and warning through vibrations or audio in case of danger; ii) recognition mode, which processes the image and indicates to the user the object in front of him/her through audio. A third option is to turn it off when no information is desired.

For quality assurance, the followed standard are reported in IEEE 8282–1998 Software Configuration Management Plans [39]; 730–1998 Standard for Software Quality Assurance Plans; 1233–1998 Guide for Developing System Requirements Specifications; 829–1998 Software Test Documentation, and 12207 -2017 Software life cycle processes.

4 Problem Feature

Having defined our target group (people with severe visual impairment or blindness) and their major problems (lack of autonomy and insecurity), we focus on determining the root cause of these problems. Using the fishbone "Ishikawa" methodology [28, 29], by conducting semi-structured interviews [30] with a blind person and a professional specialist in the field.

With this information, we determined three main causes, as shown in Fig. 1. This analysis allows us to estimate the level of effort and time required for its execution. Each root cause defines an objective alongside the requirements identified. These causes are:

- C1: Difficulty in distance perception: visually impaired people mainly use touch and while walking the cane fulfills this function. However, there are risks due to obstacles above ground or overhead.
- C2: Difficulty in recognizing objects: memory plays an important role in recognizing objects, therefore the necessity to find features to distinguish between objects with similar characteristics.
- C3: Difficulty in recognizing people: the visually impaired person must rely on their memory to remember voices, leading to confusion and misidentification.

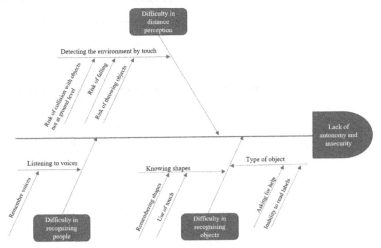

Fig. 1. Ishikawa diagram for root-cause analysis. Source: Own elaboration.

Our objective was to develop and integrate different tools to create a system that helps visually impaired people make decisions.

In Table 2, we show the specific objectives, expected result, and how it will be measured (Metric), and the last column presents the reported accuracy from published literature (APL) for each metric. In Table 3, we associate each of the objectives with the causes (C).

5 Development Process

The schematic of the solution is shown in Fig. 2, and the description about each component is presented in following sub-sections. Figure 3 depict the location of the equipment in the user.

Table 2. Specifics objectives. Source: Own elaboration

Objectives	Expected result	Metric	APL
O1: Recognize the person in front of him/her	Identifying the person through a camera	% Face recognition efficiency (FRE)	FRE ≥ 96% [24, 31]
O2: Inform of the objects in front of him/her	Identifying objects through a camera	% Object recognition efficiency (ORE) % Efficiency in tag reading (ETR)	ORE ≥ 58% [32] ETR ≥ 92% [33]
O3: Information about obstacles that are not at ground level	Identify and alert the visually impaired person to a possible obstacle	% Accuracy of obstacle alerts (AOA)	AOA ≥ 97,95% [34]
O4: Inform about the existence of a staircase in front	Identifying and alerting about stairs ahead	% Staircase Alert Accuracy (SAA)	SAA ≥ 98,6% [18]

Table 3. Associate each of the objectives (O) with the causes (C). Source: Own elaboration

	C1	C2	C3
O1			X
O2		X	
O3	X	X	
O4	X		

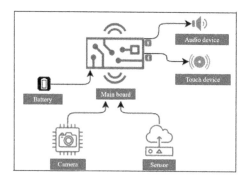

Fig. 2. Schematic solution. Source: Own elaboration.

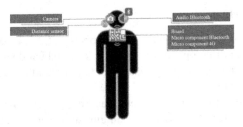

Fig. 3. Location of equipment. Source: Own elaboration.

The following sections present the selection process of the software, hardware and the tests carried out.

5.1 Software Selection

Open-source software and python language are used. In particular the Computer Vision and Digital image processing libraries for python. Three methods were selected based on Deep Learning (Fast R-CNN 2015 y Yolo V3 2018), both use Common objects in context (COCO) a dataset for object detection and segmentation [40]. In the case of Fast R-CNN, it has two two-stage and one-stage approaches (e.g., SSD), both are tested [40].

The pre-trained function for Fast R-CNN, Luminoth, was used to optimize the development process. In both methods, COCO was used as a test set, complemented by a set of images of common objects [40].

We observed that Fast R-CNN in its single-process mode (SSD) delivered immediate results but with a higher error rate. In the case of Fast R-CNN with two parts and YOLO, it took between 1 and 2 s for processing, with a lower error rate. Table 4 shows a comparison of the results after hardware adjustments. This result led us to select YOLO as the visual recognition method.

Table 4. Comparison of results. Source: Own elaboration

	Yolo	Sdd
Average time	1,19 s	2,21 s
Objects	Success rate	Success rate
Mug	4/5	4/5
Mouse	2/5	2/5
People	4/5	4/5
Table	3/5	3/5
Keyboard	4/5	3/5

Text recognition is done by machine learning, using automatic reasoning, natural language processing, and computer vision (similar to the one used in object recognition), using Tesseract.

5.2 Hardware Selection

The hardware environment corresponds to a Raspberry PI 3+. To take advantage of its resources, the Raspbian Lite operating system is used, which does not have a desktop interface, this Debian-based operating system contains default libraries and Python. Part of the code is removed to optimize it.

A Steelseries audio input card was used as audio input. (USB soundcard V2 Model NO.: SC-00003). For obstacle recognition, an ultrasonic sensor is used, with 5V input (VDC), decreasing its response (echo) to 3.3V to not damage the board.

Additionally, buttons are included, which will allow activating the distance measurement, among other actions, for example, On-Off, change function. The sensor and camera are attached to thick glasses. The final prototype is shown in Fig. 4.

Fig. 4. Final prototype. Source: Own elaboration.

5.3 Tests Carried

In addition to the system and hardware tests carried out to verify the functionality of the prototype, we worked alongside a specialist in visual impairment and cane use. User tests were designed by this specialist.

The tests consisted of:

- Moving towards an object above ground level.
- Recognition of people around.
- Reading an emergency sign.
- Recognition of objects.
- Use of buttons, to switch between modes.

Some of the user feedbacks were:

- The system provides extra security by receiving information that the cane does not provide.

- It is a technology that allows more actions to be performed.
- Not having to contract other applications or additional internet plans is especially useful.
- It is necessary to improve aesthetics, and performance and to standardise the outputs so that the visually impaired person can memorise them.
- Notwithstanding the above, the system provides security, autonomy, and independence.

Concerning the metrics of compliance with the objectives set (see Sect. 3), the results are shown in Table 5.

Table 5. Metrics objectives. Source: Own elaboration

Objectives	Metric	APL	Accuracy
O1: Recognise the person in front of him/her	% Face recognition efficiency (FRE)	FRE $\geq$ 96%	FRE = 90%
O2: Inform of the objects in front of him/her	% Object recognition efficiency (ORE) % Efficiency in tag reading (ETR)	ORE $\geq$ 58% ETR $\geq$ 92%	ORE = 60% ETR = 46%
O3: Information about obstacles that are not at ground level	% Accuracy of obstacle alerts (AOA)	AOA $\geq$ 97,95%	AOA = 90%
O4: Inform about the existence of a staircase in front	% Staircase Alert Accuracy (SAA)	SAA $\geq$ 98,6%	SAA = Not tested

6 Preliminary Results and Discussion

There is a broad spectrum of open-source libraries and functionalities, however, we focused on a few that are recommended in the scientific literature, thus, for example, our results regarding the comparison between YOLO and Fast R-CNN are in agreement with those presented by Zhang et al. [40].

In the same way, we took into consideration Sharma et al. [41], regarding the use of machine learning algorithm for facial recognition, which allowed us to reduce the size of the images to optimise processing time in the device.

In data privacy, we agree with Zhao et al. [42], regarding the complications that the facial recognition process brings, however, our prototype does not have interactions with other networks, allowing users to maintain their privacy.

For the objective O1, although the FRE was measured at 90%, the objective is considered to have been met, understanding that the algorithm was trained with only one image for each person, also achieving 90% recognition of the subjects, without considering that facial expressions can complicate recognition [41], and therefore increasing the number of images will increase the accuracy.

O2 is determined as partially achieved, because ORE was achieved, however, further optimisation of the algorithm is required. It should be noted that the ultrasonic sensor allows the user to be alerted to the object, even if it does not allow for full recognition, increasing the level of range and security, as demonstrated by Cardillo et al. [43].

O3 is determined as achieved, as every object with an angle less than 40° was detected, however, when searching for this angle limitation in the literature, no information was found. It should be noted that as in Cardillo et al. [43], the radar system only takes into consideration the existence of the object, not its recognition as to what it is, which motivates us to declare the objective approved.

O4 was not tested because the acquired technology, adjusted to the budget, did not consider this variable when the ladder was descending, so using a conservative criterion it was preferred to leave it as untested.

7 Conclusions

The process described above shows the importance of considering the user in the early stages of software engineering and the importance of understanding the user's needs. In this way, technologies will be an enabler of their development and not an imposition.

Our research demonstrates the feasibility of developing a wearable assistive system for vision impaired people, using open-source tools and low-cost technology such as Arduino systems, integrating machine learning and deep learning technologies in a "pocket-sized" device. The cost of hardware did not exceed 400 dollars.

From this work some lessons were learned, lack of official relays for certain AMD cards meant that applications had to work on unofficial versions and therefore we had to install additional software and utilities, increasing the disk space used.

Notwithstanding the above, the test results were adequate for the time spent and the imaging set proved to be appropriate for the mobility environment.

In addition to that, the mixed strategy of tests on visually impaired users and with experts on this ailment was considered a success, and we consider that is fundamental to consider them in future developments, because placing the user at the center of the technology allows for modifications on the system or knowledge that would otherwise be impossible to obtain. In this respect, we can point out, for example, the need to place sensitive identifiers on buttons so that the user can distinguish them. Therefore, ergonomic knowledge should be considered in future developments.

Future research should address the scalability of the facial recognition system, in particular by increasing the base set of images to improve this process and keep the base updated to the user's needs.

This opens up a field of research associated with the use of Cloud IaaS technologies, as well as integration with 4G and 5G networks, to distribute the processing load, with the hypothesis that this will increase performance.

The limitations of this work are related to the limited test set and therefore, we require further testing in uncontrolled environments that allows for more realistic scenarios.

Although this prototype is working disconnected from the internet, the feasibility of its integration must be evaluated to increase the number of images to be recognized, without the necessity to increase disk space.

Finally, we must point out that our preliminary results cannot be generalized, given the limited number of tests carried out. It is for this reason that our working group is developing a prototype, for which different testing and validation methods have been developed, both quantitative (performance) and qualitative (user impression).

Acknowledgements. This research was funded by University of Bio-Bio grant number 2060222 IF/R and 2160277 GI/EF. And the Research Department (VRI) of Universidad Andres Bello grant number DI-12-20/REG.

References

1. World Health Organization: World Report on Vision (2019)
2. Bourne, R., et al.: Trends in prevalence of blindness and distance and near vision impairment over 30 years: an analysis for the global burden of disease study. Lancet Glob. Heal. **9**, e130–e143 (2021). https://doi.org/10.1016/S2214-109X(20)30425-3
3. Finsterer, J., Scorza, F.A., Scorza, C.A., Fiorini, A.C.: SARS-CoV-2 impairs vision. J. Neuro-Ophthalmology. **41**, 166–169 (2021). https://doi.org/10.1097/WNO.0000000000001273
4. Toro, M.D., et al.: COVID-19 outbreak and increased risk of amblyopia and epidemic myopia: Insights from EUROCOVCAT group. Eur. J. Ophthalmol. **32**, 17–22 (2022). https://doi.org/10.1177/11206721211053175
5. Shalaby, W.S., et al.: The impact of COVID-19 on individuals across the spectrum of visual impairment. Am. J. Ophthalmol. **227**, 53–65 (2021). https://doi.org/10.1016/j.ajo.2021.03.016
6. World Health Organization: Blindness and vision impairment, https://www.who.int/news-room/fact-sheets/detail/blindness-and-visual-impairment. Accessed 05 Jan 2022
7. World Health Organization: International Classification of Diseases 11th Revision. https://icd.who.int/en
8. Hernández Flores, M.: Ciegos conquistando la ciudad de México: vulnerabilidad y accesibilidad en un entorno discapacitante. Nueva Antropol. **25** (2012)
9. Galarce Muñoz, M.I., Pérez-Salas, C.P., Sirlopú, D.: Análisis Comparativo de la participación escolar y bienestar subjetivo en estudiantes con y sin discapacidad en chile. Psykhe (Santiago). **29**, 1–16 (2020). https://doi.org/10.7764/psykhe.29.2.1444
10. Aguilar Díaz, M.Á.: Centralidad de los sentidos. Encartes. **3**, 29–55 (2020). https://doi.org/10.29340/en.v3n5.136
11. Sandoval-Pillajo, L., Pusdá, M., Garrido, F., Herrera, E.: Sistema embebido para movilidad de personas con discapacidad visual. Rev. Ibérica Sist. e Tecnol. Informação. **19**, 328–340 (2019)
12. Ministerio de Educación Española: Educación Inclusiva: Tiflotecnología. http://www.ite.educacion.es/formacion/materiales/129/cd/unidad_10/m10_tiflotecnologia.htm. Accessed 28 Dec 2021
13. Riazi, A., Riazi, F., Yoosfi, R., Bahmeei, F.: Outdoor difficulties experienced by a group of visually impaired Iranian people. J. Curr. Ophthalmol. **28**, 85–90 (2016). https://doi.org/10.1016/j.joco.2016.04.002

14. Dunai, L., Lengua, I., Tortajada, I., Brusola, F.: Obstacle detectors for visually impaired people. In: International Conference on Optimization of Electrical and Electronic Equipment (OPTIM), pp. 809–816 (2014)
15. Alvarado, J.D., Mosquera, V.H.: Sistema de detección de obstáculos para invidentes. Visión Electrónica, Algo Más que un Estado Sólido. **10**, 7 (2016)
16. Jafri, R., Campos, R.L., Ali, S.A., Arabnia, H.R.: Visual and infrared sensor data-based obstacle detection for the visually impaired using the google project tango tablet development kit and the unity engine. IEEE Access. **6**, 443–454 (2018). https://doi.org/10.1109/ACCESS. 2017.2766579
17. Gbenga, D.E., Shani, A.I., Adekunle, A.L.: Smart walking stick for visually impaired people using ultrasonic sensors and arduino. Int. J. Eng. Technol. **9**, 3435–3447 (2017). https://doi. org/10.21817/ijet/2017/v9i5/170905302
18. Filipe, V., Fernandes, F., Fernandes, H., Sousa, A., Paredes, H., Barroso, J.: Blind navigation support system based on microsoft kinect. Procedia Comput. Sci. **14**, 94–101 (2012). https:// doi.org/10.1016/j.procs.2012.10.011
19. Yang, K., Wang, K., Lin, S., Bai, J., Bergasa, L.M., Arroyo, R.: Long-range traversability awareness and low-lying obstacle negotiation with realsense for the visually impaired. In: Proceedings of the 2018 International Conference on Information Science and System, pp. 137–141. ACM, New York, NY, USA (2018). https://doi.org/10.1145/3209914.3209943
20. Long, N., Wang, K., Cheng, R., Yang, K., Hu, W., Bai, J.: Assisting the visually impaired: multitarget warning through millimeter wave radar and RGB-depth sensors. J. Electron. Imaging. **28**, 1 (2019). https://doi.org/10.1117/1.JEI.28.1.013028
21. Agiwal, M., Kwon, H., Park, S., Jin, H.: A survey on 4G–5G dual connectivity: road to 5G implementation. IEEE Access. **9**, 16193–16210 (2021). https://doi.org/10.1109/ACCESS. 2021.3052462
22. Zafarullah Noohani, M., Ullah Magsi, K.: Review of 5G technology: architecture, security and wide applications. Int. Res. J. Eng. Technol. **7**, 3440–3471 (2020). https://doi.org/10. 5281/zenodo.3842353
23. Araya, S., et al.: Design of a system to support certification management with an adaptive architecture. In: 2021 16th Iberian Conference on Information Systems and Technologies (CISTI), pp. 1–6 (2021). https://doi.org/10.23919/CISTI52073.2021.9476390
24. Nagarajan, A., Sindhuja, K., Balamurugan, C.R.: Smart glass with voice recognition and visual processing facility for visually imparied people. SEEE Digib. Eng. Technol. **1** (2018)
25. Vasquez Salazar, R.D., Cardona Mesa, A.A.: Dispositivos de asistencia para la movilidad en personas con discapacidad visual: una revisión bibliográfica. Rev. Politécnica. **15**, 107–116 (2019). https://doi.org/10.33571/rpolitec.v15n28a10
26. Esparza-Maldonado, A., Margain-Fuentes, L., Álvarez-Rodríguez, F., Benítez-Guerrero, E.: Desarrollo y evaluación de un sistema Interactivo para personas con discapacidad visual. TecnoLógicas. **21**, 149–157 (2018)
27. Márquez-Olivera, M., Juárez-Gracia, A.-G., Hernández-Herrera, V., Argüelles-Cruz, A.-J., López-Yáñez, I.: System for face recognition under different facial expressions using a new associative hybrid model amαβ-knn for people with visual impairment or prosopagnosia. Sensors. **19**, 578 (2019). https://doi.org/10.3390/s19030578
28. Escaida Villalobos, I., Jara Valdés, P., Letzkus Palavecino, M.: Mejora de procesos productivos mediante lean manufacturing. Trilogía. **28**, 26–55 (2016)
29. Khalid, L.: Software Architecture for Business. Springer International Publishing, Cham (2020). https://doi.org/10.1007/978-3-030-13632-1
30. Corbetta, P.: Metodología y Técnicas de Investigación Social. McGraw-Hill, Madrid (2007)
31. Solanki, K., Pittalia, P.: Review of face recognition techniques. Int. J. Comput. Appl. **133**, 20–25 (2016)

32. Ren, S., He, K., Girshick, R., Sun, J.: Faster R-CNN: towards real-time object detection with region proposal networks. IEEE Trans. Pattern Anal. Mach. Intell. **39**, 1137–1149 (2017). https://doi.org/10.1109/TPAMI.2016.2577031
33. Fan, K., Baek, S.J.: A robust proposal generation method for text lines in natural scene images. Neurocomputing **304**, 47–63 (2018). https://doi.org/10.1016/j.neucom.2018.03.041
34. Ahmad, N.S., Boon, N.L., Goh, P.: Multi-sensor obstacle detection system via model-based state-feedback control in smart cane design for the visually challenged. IEEE Access. **6**, 64182–64192 (2018). https://doi.org/10.1109/ACCESS.2018.2878423
35. Hevner, A., Chatterjee, S.: Design Research in Information Systems. Springer US, Boston, MA (2010). https://doi.org/10.1007/978-1-4419-5653-8
36. Fundacion Auna: Las Personas con Discapacidad Frente a las Tecnologías de la Información y las Comunicaciones en España. Fundación Auna-Ministerio de Trabajo de Asuntos Sociales, Madrid (2003)
37. Schrott, H.: Diseñar para los discapacitados. Rev. la OMPI. **5**, 32 (2009)
38. López Delgado, A., Olmedo, E., Tadeu, P., Fernández Batanero, J.M.: Propuesta de las condiciones de las Aplicaciones móviles, para la construcción de un Entorno de Accesibilidad Personal para usuarios con discapacidad visual en las Smart Cities. Aula Abierta. **48**, 193 (2019). https://doi.org/10.17811/rifie.48.2.2019.193-202
39. IEEE: Standard Glossary of Software Engineering Terminology (Std 610.12–1990). IEEE (1990)
40. Zhang, S., Wen, L., Bian, X., Lei, Z., Li, S.Z.: Single-shot refinement neural network for object detection. In: 2018 IEEE/CVF Conference on Computer Vision and Pattern Recognition, pp. 4203–4212. IEEE (2018). https://doi.org/10.1109/CVPR.2018.00442
41. Sharma, S., Bhatt, M., Sharma, P.: Face Recognition system using machine learning algorithm. In: 2020 5th International Conference on Communication and Electronics Systems (ICCES), pp. 1162–1168. IEEE (2020). https://doi.org/10.1109/ICCES48766.2020.9137850
42. Zhao, Y., Wu, S., Reynolds, L., Azenkot, S.: A Face recognition application for people with visual impairments. In: Proceedings of the 2018 CHI Conference on Human Factors in Computing Systems, pp. 1–14. ACM, New York, NY, USA (2018). https://doi.org/10.1145/3173574.3173789
43. Cardillo, E., et al.: An electromagnetic sensor prototype to assist visually impaired and blind people in autonomous walking. IEEE Sens. J. **18**, 2568–2576 (2018). https://doi.org/10.1109/JSEN.2018.2795046

Drivers of Eco-innovation in Industrial Clusters - A Case Study in the Colombian Metalworking Sector

Nohora Mercado-Caruso[1,2]($\boxtimes$), Marival Segarra-Oña[2], Ángel Peiró-Signes[2]($\boxtimes$), Ivan Portnoy[1], and Evaristo Navarro[3]($\boxtimes$)

[1] Productivity and Innovation Department, Universidad de la Costa, Barranquilla, Colombia
nmercado1@cuc.edu.co
[2] Department of Business Administration and Management, Universidad Politécnica de Valencia, Valencia, Spain
anpeisig@omp.upv.es
[3] Economic Sciences Department, Universidad de la Costa, Barranquilla, Colombia
enavarro3@cuc.edu.co

Abstract. Eco-innovation is the development of products and processes that contribute to searching for solutions to differentiate and position companies or businesses in the market sustainably. The cluster is considered a cooperative strategy for businesses to achieve competitive efficiency. Nowadays, companies have the intrinsic responsibility of reducing their environmental impact significantly, creating novel, enhanced products and services.

This work aims to identify the drivers or determinant factors fostering the eco-innovation within industrial clusters for a Case Study in Colombia, South America. The study was applied to 40 companies in the Colombian metalworking sector. The Fuzzy-set Qualitative Comparative Analysis (fsQCA) methodology was implemented, allowing the identification of underlying causal relationships ruling the levels of eco-innovation in industrial clusters.

Results show that the capacity, the regulatory policies, and the competitive pressure are the main drivers for the clusters to reach high innovation levels, achieving the desired economic and environmental outcomes. Furthermore, even with low-demand conditions and unclear policies, companies in the cluster can successfully generate profits and stay competitive depending strongly on the three identified factors. Future research will focus on extrapolating the study to industrial clusters in different countries, regions, and business sectors.

Keywords: Sustainable innovation · Eco-innovation · Cluster · Competitivity · Metalworking sector

1 Introduction

According to Huppes (2009), eco-innovation or environmental innovation is the (positive) transformation of activities that have economic, environmental, and social impacts.

K. Saeed and J. Dvorský (Eds.): CISIM 2022, LNCS 13293, pp. 136–145, 2022.
https://doi.org/10.1007/978-3-031-10539-5_10

That definition highlights the reduction of the environmental impact through the implementation of policies and organizational strategies aiming to enhance operational efficiency, which is necessary to gain access to new markets and improve the enterprise reputation with customers, suppliers, and employees [2].

René Kemp (2007) defines eco-innovation as *"the production, assimilation, or exploitation of a good, service, productive process, organizational structure, or business management method that is novel for the enterprise or the user, and that leads (throughout its lifecycle) to reducing environmental risk, pollution, and negative impacts arising from the use of resources."*

Moreover, the Organization for Economic Development and Cooperation [4] asserts that eco-innovation not only renders environmental benefits, but it also adds value within the organizations as it contributes to increasing productivity and competitiveness, reducing costs, and granting access to new markets (Bessant et al., 2012; González-Benito et al., 2016; Löfsten, 2014; Segarra-Oña et al., 2011; Solleiro & Castañon, 2005; Wang et al., 2008). Nevertheless, companies going through big challenges must face a globalized world and be competitive via strategies that foster their growth, establishing core policies aligned with international markets' demands, such as environmental quality requirements, certifications, training, clean technologies implementation, and innovation processes that increase the companies' response capacity.

1.1 Study Conceptualization

The metalworking sector comprises the tasks of production, manufacturing, and assembling of goods used by other sectors in their activities and, to a lesser extent, by the final user. It could be stated that metalworking depends on third parties' activities. It is a derived-demand sector, which must have the technological capacity and infrastructure to respond to its customers' needs [11]. According to the Colombian metalworking and shipyard chamber (Fedemetal), which is attached with the Colombian association of entrepreneurs (ANDI), the metalworking sector is one of the most productive sectors, as it has strengthened its export chain, expanding to new countries while increasing sales in countries such as Ecuador and the US. As of 2018, more aggressive strategies, such as innovating within the value chain and implementing new demand models, were implemented, setting out the path to the aerospace industry and strengthening the automotive industry [12].

The Colombian metalworking cluster was conceived and is coordinated by the Colombian Association of Micro, Small, and Medium Enterprises (ACOPI). Among the Colombian metalworking cluster's goals are: *"to promote cooperation, innovation, and entrepreneurial capacity to strengthen the business, as well as generate strategies to foster the competitiveness of metalworking products and services in the local, national, and international market."*

These goals aim to stimulate the sector's competitiveness through cooperation, entrepreneurial capacity, visibility, and the generation of strategies to boost the cluster's supply chain via sustainability-enabling technologies that also improve the cluster's good image. This study is in line with the cluster's goals, making it relevant in the Colombian metalworking sector. Nevertheless, this sector still experiences considerable technological gaps that make it difficult to fully implement eco-innovation. Thus, it is essential to establish strategic alliances with other organisms, universities, regional R&D centers, and implement strategies to enhance innovation capabilities and infrastructure, and gain governmental entities' support to conduct R&D.

2   Methodology

Qualitative comparative analysis (QCA) is among the most used methodologies within social sciences, particularly in the administrative area [13]. QCA is based on analyzing the necessary and sufficient conditions to model causal complexity. QCA is a fuzzy sets-based comparative research method that has evolved to perform high-throughput quantitative analysis on datasets with dichotomic variables and different settings. Moreover, QCA uses equifinality principles, setting different configurations regarding causal interactions to achieve a goal. Using this technique renders the necessary and sufficient conditions to achieve an outcome, making the relationships between the conditions explicit.

Rihoux & Ragin (2008) introduced the QCA as an efficient way to carry out hypothesis testing based on set-theoretic relations. This study proposes a model to measure and analyze the factors involved in eco-innovation and their influence on the performance (eco-innovation-wise) of the companies belonging to the Colombian metalworking cluster. The model is validated with real data from the cluster. Figure 1 illustrates the conceptual model with all the factors ruling the eco-innovation levels in industrial clusters— in contrast, most studies on industrial eco-innovation feature linear analysis such as linear regression or structural equations [15–18].

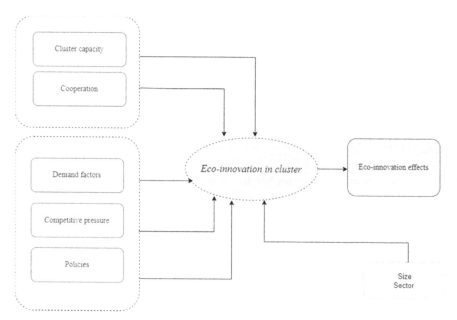

Fig. 1. Eco-innovation model for industrial clusters (Adapted from Mercado-Caruso et al., 2020)

The Fuzzy-set Qualitative Comparative Analysis (fsQCA) methodology tackles some limitations featured by regression-based methods, such as asymmetry and variables interdependence [19], being ideal to complement regression analysis, as variables exhibit interactions or "cooperation" to achieve an outcome. This model is based on five factors that boost eco-innovation-related activities: i) demand, ii) cluster capacity, iii) cooperation level, iv) competitive pressure, and v) environmental policies and regulations. In addition, the model includes three output factors: i) economic effects, ii) eco-innovative effects, and iii) access to new markets. The analysis is applied to 40 metalworking companies from Barranquilla, Colombia, belonging to the previously mentioned cluster. Data was gathered via in-person visits to the companies, all of which are classified as Small and medium-sized enterprises (SMEs). The software fs/QCA 3.0 was used to analyze the factors' contribution to the cluster's eco-innovation performance and their interactions.

The gathered data contains a rich set of measures on the demand, competitiveness, cooperation, policies, and cluster capacity, which allows studying these factors' influence on the cluster's sustainable innovation, economic benefits, and access to new markets. Data is constrained to metalworking companies from the Colombian Caribbean region, which guarantees comparability between operations. Furthermore, as data comes from companies offering services, this poses a natural variability and uncertainty in the competitive environment.

The instrument to assess the eco-innovation drivers is a structured survey based on the Likert scale with a 1–7 range, containing 29 questions appraising the input and output factors according to their importance (1 is for less important and 7 is for most important). Other authors have validated this measurement instrument [20–22]. A sensitivity test was conducted using Cronbach's alpha coefficient, obtaining values above 80%, as seen in Table 1, which validates the use of the instrument in this study.

Table 1. Results from survey to measure sensitivity

Variable	Mean	Items	Deviation	Cronbach's alpha coef.
Capacity	3,62778	1–9	1,362118	0,847
Demand	4,49000	10–14	1,762836	0,847
Cooperation	3,40000	15	2,296039	0,895
Competitive pressure	4,04375	16–18	1,926627	0,844
Policies	3,77500	19–26	1,923872	0,852
OUTEFFECTS	4,76563	27–29	1,521530	0,862

For the FsQCA analysis, inputs must be "calibrated" or re-scaled from 1–7 to 0–1. As suggested by [23], this study calibrates inputs with polytomous variables. The fuzzy membership scores range from 0–1. Three anchor points define a full membership set with a score, a full non-membership, and a crossover point [24].

The scores obtained from the 40 companies are averaged and used as a calibration baseline. This study defines the cutoff values shown in Table 2, which are based on percentiles, as suggested by [13, 25].

Table 2. Calibration of polytomous variables

Calibration variable	Full membership (percentile 90)	Crossover (percentile 50%)	Full non-membership (percentile 90)
Conditions and outcomes	0,95	0,5	0,05

The membership is computed using the following equation [26, 27]:

$$membership = \exp(\log(probability))/(1 + \exp(\log(probability))) \tag{1}$$

Results are fed to the software Fs/QCA 3.0, and it yields a truth table displaying all the evaluated conditions. Only those conditions complying with a consistency of at least 0.8 and a frequency of at least two (2) observations are considered. Hence, conditions with a consistency equal to or greater than 0.8 were coded as 1 and otherwise as 0. The software removes inconsistent configurations and cases that are not comparable with other case studies, as well as redundant conditions. Rows of the truth table are compared against those sufficient configurations.

The software renders three Boolean minimization results: i) the complex solution, ii) the parsimonious solution, and iii) the intermediate solution. The latter is considered the best solution to unravel the relationship between conditions and outcomes, according to [28]. For this solution, only some of the no-case configurations yield valuable results. Therefore, this study only considers intermediate solutions.

On the other hand, the model will have the following structure (Eq. (2)):

$$Y = f(Capacity, Demand, Competitiveness, Policies, Cooperation) \tag{2}$$

Using the QCA, it is possible to pinpoint those configurations that are (if any) necessary conditions to attain the desired eco-innovation levels within the cluster, as well as the combinations of causal antecedents that can explain the eco-innovation levels in the cluster.

3   Results and Discussion

As stated in the literature, a condition is necessary if it is present in all causal configurations that explain a given outcome [29]. A single condition might be necessary, but rarely will it be sufficient to explain a given outcome. Table 3 summarizes the analysis of necessary conditions. The tilde (~) represents the absence or negation of a condition, i.e., a variable preceded by ~ within a model indicates the effects of its absence on the modeled outcome.

From Table 3, we observe that all conditions exhibit a consistency smaller than 0.9. This implies that none of them is (strictly) necessary. However, some conditions exhibit a consistency close to (yet smaller than) 0.9, making them *quasi-necessary* conditions, such as *Policies* and *Capacity*. This reaffirms the importance of companies investing in eco-innovative technologies to reduce costs and comply with environmental regulations, thus rendering positive economic effects and granting the companies access to other markets.

As for the sufficient conditions, we analyze the combination of causal conditions relative to environmental effects (OUTEFFECTS) which can contribute to reaching the sufficient conditions for cluster eco-innovation.

Table 3. Analysis of necessary conditions

Outcome	OUTEFFECTS	
Analyzed conditions	Consistency	Coverage
Capacity	0.730224	0.831338
Demand	0.793324	0.823055
Competitive pressure	0.488797	0.564116
Policies	0.746228	0.793003
Cooperation	0.716964	0.766373
~Capacity	**0.821291**	0.716210
~Demand	0.794264	0.761099
~Competitive pressure	0.544402	0.468884
~Policies	0.765030	0.714212
~Cooperation	0.736349	0.683214

Along with sufficiency, equifinality is considered as several combinations of conditions may lead to a common outcome, and the causal configurations explain such outcome [30].

Table 4 presents the intermediate solution. The model shows the sufficient conditions to achieve eco-innovative effects in the cluster, as it exhibits a consistency of 0.86, indicating that the assessed configurations are highly consistent subsets for the outcome. The configuration-wise consistency values are also above 0.85, indicating that such configurations are essential for reaching the outcome. The Solution Coverage indicates the extent to which the configuration explains the eco-innovative effects on the cluster. In this case, roughly 70% of the conditions explain such effects. As for the Raw Coverage, the third configuration stands out with a greater value than that of the others. Sufficiency analysis reveals that there is not a single path to appraising eco-innovation, but there are rather four alternative paths leading to the desired outcome.

The first solution, CAPACITY*COOPERATION* ~ COMPETITIVE PRESSURE, highlights the importance of enterprises' cooperation and capacity to reach eco-innovation. Even with low competitive pressure, positive effects on eco-innovation are

Table 4. Sufficient conditions, OUTEFFECTS

MODEL: OUTEFFECTS = f(CAPACITY, DEMAND, COMPETITIVE PRESSURE, POLICIES, COOPERATION)

Configurations	Raw coverage	Unique coverage	Consistency
CAPACITY*COOPERATION* ~ COMPETITIVE PRESSURE	0.232739	0.035665	0.902482
DEMAND*COOPERATION*COMPETITIVE PRESSURE	0.331962	0.031092	0.847141
DEMAND*COMPETITIVE PRESSURE*POLICIES	**0.576132**	**0.259259**	**0.903874**
CAPACITY* ~ DEMAND* ~ COOPERATION*POLICIES	0.189758	0.027434	0.810547
SOLUTION COVERAGE: 0.708733			
SOLUTION CONSISTENCY: 0.860156			

not penalized. It is worth pinpointing the major role of the companies' capacity, arising from personnel training, creation of R&I centers, and innovation experience and know-how. Acquiring such capacities and getting access to innovation-intended resources is essential for both SMES and large enterprises to thrive and evolve into a more sustainable production paradigm; the commitment and capacities of governments to promote technological innovation is crucial to create internal capacities in the companies of the cluster, and thus be able to stay competitive and access new markets.

The fourth solution, CAPACITY* ~ DEMAND* ~ COOPERATION*POLICIES, reveals a configuration that contains Capacity, Policies, and the absence of Demand and Cooperation; It is the result that exhibits the lowest coverage to achieve environmental effects with a consistency of 81%. The absence of cooperation and demand do not seem to penalize the path towards environmental innovation; although the literature highlights as barriers to innovation the absence of commercial partners, networks of collaborators, as well as little cooperation with research centers and universities and uncertain market demand, companies with high organizational capacity and with the development of policies that provide incentives and regulate activities are relevant to achieve environmental effects.

The third solution of the model (see Table 4), DEMAND*COMPETITIVE PRESSURE*POLICIES, is the best solution elucidated by the model. This solution exhibits the greatest Raw Coverage (0.58) and Consistency (0.9); combining demand, competitive pressure, and regulatory policies is key for achieving eco-innovation in clusters.

These results are aligned with some literature studies that pinpoint the advantages of alliances and cooperation between companies belonging to the same sector (or subsector), jointly creating projects that advance innovation and competitiveness [31]. According to [32] and Porter's hypothesis, the legal and political environment is fundamental for enterprises to advance their processes to eco-innovative activities, proving the need for demand and regulatory policies and actions.

In conclusion, as outlined by [33], environmental policies make enterprises "be the first to act" by offering eco-innovative products and services and creating new markets. Hence, the right environmental policies can promote eco-innovation and compensate for non-compliance costs. In addition, environmental regulations introduce cleaner technologies and processes, improving process efficiency and promoting growth and profitability.

Finally, we must highlight that, although the model was implemented for a particular economic sector in Colombia, its implementation can be easily extrapolated to other sectors and regions. The case study was for validation purposes, but the model's input variables are common to any kind of clusters within a wide spectrum of economic sectors in different regions.

4   Conclusions

The FsQCA method provides an alternative approach to analyzing data compared to traditional methods such as the analysis of variance (ANOVA). The causal relationships among variables are analyzed using fuzzy sets theory instead of feeding on traditional correlational analysis. Thus, FsQCA can unravel underlying interactions even in situations where there is asymmetry and equifinality (Fiss, 2011; I. O. Pappas & Woodside, 2021; Rihoux & Ragin, 2008).

For a metalworking sector cluster located on the north coast of Colombia, the FsQCA method was implemented, giving special attention to the intermediate solution, as it best captures the relationship between conditions and outcomes. Such a solution retrieved the consistency values for the outcome variable OUTEFFECTS. The model found that the Capacity and (environmental) Policies are quasi-necessary conditions to promote eco-innovation within a cluster. The model found four alternative paths leading to the desired outcome regarding sufficient conditions. In addition, one particular solution found by the model (see Table 4), Demand*Competitive Pressure*Policies, exhibits the greatest Raw Coverage (0.58) and Consistency (0.9); this implies that combining demand, competitive pressure, and regulatory policies is key for achieving eco-innovation in clusters. Moreover, the conducted analysis demonstrates the importance of combining the presence or absence of relevant predictors. Therefore, this information helps discover asymmetric conditions that cannot manifest in multiple regression.

Results revealed different paths to achieving eco-innovation in the cluster's enterprises and implementing a proactive (rather than reactive) strategy. The companies must not look at the compliance of environmental regulations as additional costs but as a need. Additionally, companies must realize the mid-term and long-term opportunities, benefits, and competitive advantages arising from advancing eco-innovation.

The metalworking sector stands out in the Colombian Caribbean region due to its high capacity to advance innovation. These results can help governmental entities, competitiveness centers, universities, and the cluster's companies to strengthen their eco-innovation capacities, enhance productivity, and get important investment funding. Therefore, it is proposed that the cluster carry out open innovation practices to establish activities where different actors are involved, including society, to generate learning processes to transfer knowledge in the company.

This work contributes to the literature by proposing a model to measure eco-innovation in industrial clusters based on environmental results. Therefore, this study contributes to the field of innovation, strategy, and competitiveness in the companies of a cluster.

References

1. Huppes, G.: Eco-efficiency: from focused technical tools to reflective sustainability analysis. Ecol. Econ. **68**(6), 1572–1574 (2009)
2. Calia, R.C., Guerrini, F.M., Moura, G.L.: Innovation networks: from technological development to business model reconfiguration. Technovation **27**(8), 426–432 (2007)
3. Kemp, R.: Final report MEI project about measuring eco-innovation. UM Merit, Maastricht **32**(3), 121–124 (2007)
4. OEDC: Propuesta Norma Práctica Para Encuestas de Investigación y Desarrollo Experimental de la OECD. Frascati, Italia (2003)
5. Segarra Oña, M.V., Peiró Signes, A., Albors Garrigós, J., Miret Pastor, P.: Impact of innovative practices in environmentally focused firms: moderating factors. Int. J. Environ. Res. **5**(2), 425–434 (2011)
6. Wang, C., Lu, I.-Y., Chen, C.-B.: Evaluating firm technological innovation capability under uncertainty. Technovation **28**(6), 349–363 (2008)
7. Löfsten, H.: Product innovation processes and the trade-off between product innovation performance and business performance. Eur. J. Innov. Manag. **17**(1), 61–84 (2014)
8. González-Benito, Ó., Muñoz-Gallego, P.A., García-Zamora, E.: Role of collaboration in innovation success: differences for large and small businesses. J. Bus. Econ. Manag. **17**(4), 645–662 (2016)
9. Bessant, J., Alexander, A., Tsekouras, G., Rush, H., Lamming, R.: Developing innovation capability through learning networks. J. Econ. Geogr. **12**(5), 1087–1112 (2012)
10. Solleiro, J.L., Castañon, R.: Competitiveness and innovation systems: the challenges for Mexico's insertion in the global context. Technovation **25**(9), 1059–1070 (2005)
11. Antuña, G.: Un paso al frente: el sector metalmecánico asturiano ante la reconversión industrial, 1978–2000. Investig. Hist. Econ. (2021). https://doi.org/10.33231/j.ihe.2021.02.002
12. Fedemetal: Sector metalmecánico, el de mayor proyección en Colombia: fedemetal. Internacional Metalmecanica (2018)
13. Fiss, P.C.: Building better causal theories: a fuzzy set approach to typologies in organization research. Acad. Manag. J. **54**(2), 393–420 (2011)
14. Rihoux, B., Ragin, C.C.: Configurational Comparative Methods Qualitative Comparative Analysis (QCA) and Related Techniques. SAGE Publications (2008)
15. Cao, H., Chen, Z.: The driving effect of internal and external environment on green innovation strategy–the moderating role of top management's environmental awareness. NANKAI Bus. Rev. Int. **10**(3), 342–361 (2019)
16. Arranz, N., Arroyabe, C.F., Arroyabe, J.C.F.: The effect of regional factors in the development of eco-innovations in the firm. Bus. Strategy Environ. 1406–1415 (2019)
17. Kesidou, E., Demirel, P.: On the drivers of eco-innovations: Empirical evidence from the UK. Res. Policy **41**(5), 862–870 (2012). https://doi.org/10.1016/j.respol.2012.01.005
18. da Rabelo, O.S., de Azevedo Melo, A.S.S., da Silva Rabêlo, O., de Azevedo Melo, A.S. S.: Drivers of multidimensional eco-innovation: empirical evidence from the Brazilian industry. Environ. Technol. **40**(19), 2556–2566 (2019)

19. Emmenegger, P., Schraff, D., Walter, A.: QCA, the truth table analysis and large-N survey data: the benefits of calibration and the importance of robustness tests (2014)
20. Hojnik, J., Ruzzier, M.: The driving forces of process eco-innovation and its impact on performance: insights from Slovenia. J. Clean. Prod. **133**, 812–825 (2016)
21. Kemp, R., Pearson, P.: Final report MEI project about measuring eco-innovation. UM Merit, Maastricht **32**(3), 121–124 (2007)
22. Sanni, M.: Drivers of eco-innovation in the manufacturing sector of Nigeria. Technol. Forecast. Soc. Change **131**, 303–314 (2018). https://doi.org/10.1016/j.techfore.2017.11.007
23. Pappas, I.O., Woodside, A.G.: Fuzzy-set Qualitative Comparative Analysis (fsQCA): guidelines for research practice in information systems and marketing. Int. J. Inf. Manage. **58**, 102310 (2021). https://doi.org/10.1016/j.ijinfomgt.2021.102310
24. Legewie, N.: An introduction to applied data analysis with qualitative comparative analysis (QCA). Forum Qual. Soc. **14**(3), 1–30 (2013)
25. Dul, J.: Identifying single necessary conditions with NCA and fsQCA. J. Bus. Res. **69**(4), 1516–1523 (2016)
26. Woodside, A.: Moving beyond multiple regression analysis to algorithms: calling for a paradigm shift from symmetric to asymmetric thinking in data analysis and crafting theory. J. Bus. Res. **66**, 463–472 (2013)
27. Beynon, M.J., Jones, P., Pickernell, D.: Country-based comparison analysis using fsQCA investigating entrepreneurial attitudes and activity. J. Bus. Res. **69**(4), 1271–1276 (2016)
28. Peiró-Signes, Á., Trull, Ó., Segarra-Oña, M., García-Díaz, J.C.: Attitudes towards statistics in secondary education: findings from fsQCA. Mathematics **8**(5), 1–17 (2020)
29. Pappas, I., Woodside, A.: Fuzzy-set qualitative comparative analysis (fsQCA): guidelines for research practice in information systems and marketing. Int. J. Inf. Manage. **58**, 102310 (2021)
30. Urueña, A., Hidalgo, A.: Successful loyalty in e-complaints: FsQCA and structural equation modeling analyses. J. Bus. Res. **69**(4), 1384–1389 (2016)
31. Murcia, C., Guzmán, A.: La innovación tecnológica: mecanismo de competitividad para la creación de un clúster en el sector metalmecánico de los municipios de Cali y Yumbo. Gestión Desarro. **9**(1), 27–35 (2015)
32. Jaffe, A., Palmer, K.: Environmental regulation and innovation: a panel data study. Nat. Bur. Econ. Res. (1996)
33. Porter, M.E., Van Der Linde, C.: Green and competitive: ending the stalemate green and competitive. Harv. Bus. Rev. **73**(5), 120–134 (1995)

International Purchase Transactions: An Analysis of the Decision Cycles in Colombian Companies' Operations

Danielle Nunes Pozzo[1](✉) 🄳, Rafael Antonio Muñoz Aguilar[2] 🄳,
Julián Alberto Acosta Libreros[2] 🄳, Diana Marcela García Tamayo[1] 🄳,
Jenny Romero Borre[1] 🄳, and Uiliam Hahn Biegelmeyer[3] 🄳

[1] Universidad de La Costa, 080002 Barranquilla, ATL, Colombia
`dnunez8@cuc.edu.co`
[2] Universidad Antonio Nariño, 760043 Cali, Colombia
[3] Universidade de Caxias Do Sul, Caxias Do Sul, RS 99200-000, Brazil

Abstract. Although the understanding of decision-making as a key aspect of high-performance supply chain operations is not new, context variables that interfere with the decision process are still a relevant aspect to expand. Specially in Latin America, where mature supply chains are a goal but not the norm, the majority of the companies are SMEs that do not hold a formal decision-making process to support logistics and operations decisions. Therefore, the present study aims to analyze the decision cycles applied in operations for international purchase transactions. Data collection was conducted with a total of 86 companies currently operating in Buenaventura Port, Colombia. Results show the visibility of each of the critical processes that articulate the decision-making process within the import process, thus, identifying all logistic process associated in three cycles: (i) purchase process, (ii) international physical distribution process and (iii) customs clearance process. Lack of operations planning and high focus on the same incoterms without proper context assessment are the most critical issues found on the sample companies. Based on the data obtained, a model is proposed to estimate the costs and risks and support formal decision-making processes while taking context variables into consideration.

Keywords: Decision cycles · International purchase transactions · Operations management · Supply chain management

1 Introduction

International competitiveness is a constant concern that motivates a permanent search for solutions to improve organizational and operational performance. Logistics and operations costs are still a challenge, especially when it comes to SMEs and emerging markets [11, 22]. In a general analysis, there is still a visible improvisation in the import and export operations, caused by the predominance of informality and use of empiric-based practices that result in loss of both financial and capital resources [1, 20].

© The Author(s), under exclusive license to Springer Nature Switzerland AG 2022
K. Saeed and J. Dvorský (Eds.): CISIM 2022, LNCS 13293, pp. 146–159, 2022.
https://doi.org/10.1007/978-3-031-10539-5_11

In the case of the Colombian economy, the absence of planning strategies that allow the articulation between the different components of the International Physical Distribution (IPD) and the cycles of international purchase, causes inefficient management made by the actors who intervene within the operational dynamics between the sellers and the buyers; this is reflected in the Doing Business Report [26], in which it is shown that the big problem of Colombia compared to other countries, are the logistical costs of IPD, because on average their import costs are around of USD $ 595. If these costs are compared with those of a country like Chile, a leader in the region and which reports USD $ 275 respectively, the country's lack of competitiveness in logistics is evident.

Among the main barriers that impact logistics, argued by Colombian businessmen in the National Logistics Survey [6], 53.4% correspond to the country's infrastructure (high transport costs, insufficient road, port and airport infrastructure), 34.8% are business management type (lack of logistics information systems, untrained human talent, shortage of services offered), and 11% are customs related barriers (ignorance of regulations).

Regarding their level of logistics development, the same source notes that the 27% of companies plan little or nothing their import and export operations, given that their approach is to meet customer's requirement without control of their logistics costs; 43% use some type of control and monitoring, and only 30% see logistics as a strategic axis in the company. In this context, the lack of a strategic logistic planning approach to cost and measure variables and their lead time as well as the marked tendency to outsource the coordination of logistic services of foreign trade: 54.8% according to the National Survey Logistics [6] are the main factors that have triggered the generation of cost overruns throughout the entire IPD chain.

In Colombia there are few SMEs that have formal foreign trade departments as indicated by a study by the Colombian Association of Micro, Small and Medium Enterprises [2], which indicates that only 27% of microenterprises and 35% of small companies have specialized teams and formal internationalization processes within their companies. This scenario, associated with the numbers of ENL [6], reveal that the lack of specialized profiles, lack of training and the distribution of functions is one of the reasons why there isn't a specific knowledge of the phases that make part of an international physical distribution operation, which makes it difficult to plan correctly the import logistic process.

Also, according to the information provided by the National Association of Foreign Trade of Colombia (ANALDEX) entrepreneurs struggle to prepare a quotation because they ignore the INCOTERMS, making SMEs take great risks, not only in terms of costs, but also in tax and legal matters [4]. Currently, Colombia is on the bottom of the ranking of Latin America countries in terms of Logistics performance [25], a position that can be at least partially explained by the aforementioned data. The problem outlined above requires a broader knowledge of the situation of port logistics related to importing processes, which is why the need arises to carry out an exploratory and descriptive study.

Therefore, the present study intends to characterize the decision cycles in international purchasing processes in Colombian companies based on the Buenaventura Port customers database, which consists of a sample entirely formed by SMEs. As a final goal, this study proposes a model considering context-specific variables for international purchase transactions.

2 Theoretical Background

Decision-making modelling to support the understanding of phenomena, as well as support management is a recurring topic, since complexity is increasing along the speed of market and its variables' behaviors [5, 13]. Considering that operations involve a significant amount of factors, it is not a surprise that current literature proposes models adapted to specific operations and environments [19].

Yazdani et al. [24] stated a proposal for a new model for logistics centers decision under the perspective that previous literature lacked this approach. Additionally, previous work on the topic did not bring substantial concrete validation and did not present the integration of the same variables as addressed by Yazdani [24]. Lack of solid literature is also the main foundation to establish preliminary case studies in specific contexts, which was the case for Aksoy and Durmusoglu [3] and Maden and Alptekin [16]. A similar scenario is faced by this study, since a specific approach towards international purchase selection integrating these variables is not observed in previous publications.

The lack of historical data on specific cases as well as single or short sample phenomena also affects the use of classical AHP models, motivating the publication of new model proposals, such as Tuljak-Suban and Bajecand [23] and the one intended on this study.

Also, not only tangible variables are relevant, but also human cognitive processes, that can be implicit or explicit but certainly impact decisions and performances [14]. This aspect motivates another trend of current literature in decision models at the same time that it provides an opportunity for non-exclusive mathematical proposals to support decisions. This is even more appropriate when it comes to scenarios with a predominance of SMEs, which tend to present limited resources and require more qualitative, simplified solutions [10, 21].

Regarding decision processes in international purchase transactions, it is possible to establish, based on literature, three pillars that consolidate into specific cycles: (i) purchasing process, (ii) international physical distribution process and (iii) customs clearance process (Fig. 1) [8, 9].

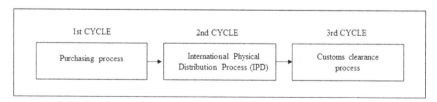

Fig. 1. Logistics decision cycles

Therefore, the decision in international purchase transactions would be a sequence of this factors, however specific variables are still an important part of the operationalization of this process.

As already established, the discussion is not new. However, the topic is still representing a challenge when it comes to context-specific models that could support practitioners and reduce decision risks [17, 18]. In Latin America more specifically, literature is still restricted and represents a suitable gap for research, since context-specific variables interact with main factors in such a way that can change its outcomes and behavior [11, 22].

3 Methodology

This is a cross-sectional study, that can be characterized as mixed method since data was processed both statistically and qualitatively. Data collection was conducted in Colombia, considering regular importers and exporters from Buenaventura Port Society (SPBUN), which resulted in a database of 144 companies, all SMEs. In order to achieve higher answering rates, a face-to-face data collection was conducted, using port service providers as intermediaries. A total of 86 valid cases were considered for this analysis. Considering the type of company and cultural preferences to centralize decisions in the strategic level of the organization, the owner was interviewed in all cases. The access to SMEs in Colombia is a challenge since companies tend to manifest resistance towards sharing information and public data about them is almost non-existent. Therefore, the number of responses obtained can be considered quite relevant to the academia, since previous studies do not provide this sort of information under this perspective in the Colombian context. Although, it is also relevant to emphasize that this represents approximately 3,26% of the total of the current exporters in Colombia [7]. Therefore, this sample can be considered as a local case study as well as a preliminary or exploratory phase for a future national study.

Literature review supported the development of a framework of decision cycles dimensions resulting on a total of 22 variables, as shown on Table 1.

Table 1. Dimensions and variables of logistics decisions cycles considered for this study

Decision cycle	Variable
1st	Formality in selecting international suppliers
	Critical factors for choosing an international supplier
	Import cost pre-feasibility
	International purchase payment method
2nd	Volume of annual purchase
	Selection of the international commercial term (INCOTERM)
	Frequency of use of each INCOTERM
	Mode of transportation
	International freight contracting
	Critical variables in international freight contracting
	Original quotation versus final cost of operation

(*continued*)

Table 1. (*continued*)

Decision cycle	Variable
	Local costs related to ocean container use
	Exchange rate mitigation
	Insurance
	Involvement of customs clearence agent
	Critical factors in selecting a customs clearence agent
	Processing of import registry
3rd	Modality of payment of import duties and taxes
	Lead time of customs clearance while at port
	Delays in the clearance processes
	Previous inspections of merchandise
	Highest percentage of costs within the customs clearance process

These variables were the foundation to develop a semi-structured interview containing 29 questions. The decision to use a qualitative instrument was based on the intention to deepen the discussions that support the proposal of the decision model (the main product of the study), as well as the lack of an already validated scale that could lead to the proper measure of these variables. Due to this context, it is expected that this study leads to a future proposal of scales to suffice the measure of these variables in the dynamics shown in the final model.

In this step, data was processed using coding and frequency analysis, resulting in a statistical output that allowed researchers to integrate responses and better understand sample behavior. At the same time, the results were used as a guide to map a secondary data collection: following the interview analysis, additional document research was conducted, both to validate and deepen the understanding of phenomena. Document research was based on companies' internal files and government documents and systems outputs, also provided by companies via access to reports from the suitable system platforms.

4   Results and Discussions

Results will be presented according to its respective decision cycle in the following subsections.

4.1   First Cycle: Decisions Related to the Purchasing Process

The decision to initiate an international purchasing process through imports is an indicator of the level of formality given to foreign trade operations. 25% of interviewees stated that they had carried out a strategic planning exercise, either based on a projected study of demand (12.5%) or that they have a budget for international purchases formally defined in a strategic plan (12.5%). 33.3% carries out a periodic review of inventory levels and when they reach critical levels defined in the policies, the decision is made to start the international purchase.

Regarding process for selecting international suppliers: 68% states that they do have a defined formal process. In terms of critical factors for choosing an international supplier: Price is still the most relevant factor when choosing an international supplier. So are the delivery times, the diversity in the forms of payment and the total import lead time, that is, the time elapsed between the date of placing the order to the date the order is in the importer's warehouse. Each of these reasons exceeded 60% relevance.

When asked if they carried out a cost pre-feasibility process to make the purchase decision, 92% said that they did. For them, the most relevant analysis variables involve cost analysis to define the sale price and analysis of previous customs requirements, which exceed 60% of relevance.

Additionally, almost 46% of the sample states that they make their payments by bank transfer (Swift), denoting trust in international suppliers. 50% does by using international money orders through the international banking system, (29.2% does by making the money order after they are shipped, and 20.8% before the goods are shipped). Only 4.2% does by using a letter of credit, which is the safest method, but also the one that carries the most financial costs.

4.2 Second Cycle: Decisions Related to the International Physical Distribution Process (IPD)

The majority of companies (83.2%) carries out more than five (5) imports in the year, which represents a constant process of making international purchases (one arrives and the other begins). Of these, 42% were between 5–20 imports. 12.5% stated that they made less than four annual imports.

Regarding the selection of the international commercial term (INCOTERM, only 8.3% stated that the supplier determines it, which indicates that the remaining 91.7% gives the importer the power to have inference in the decision-making process. Of this percentage, 41.7% is defined after a negotiation period, while 29.2% is carried out after a cost analysis; The management of the company defines the remaining 20.8%.

EXW and FOB incoterms with 83% have been used at least once by the interviewed importers. Regarding to the use of CFR and CIF INCOTERMS, little more than 60% reveal that they have been used. The terms FAS, DAT (now DPU) and DAP were rarely used.

Since the entire sample has made at least one maritime import, the study looked to validate what other means of transportation are used. Results shown that 75% at least used air transport and only 29% terrestrial transport. It is important to note that multimodal operations (which in Colombia are customs transit operations to a free zone) have been used only by 38% of the sample.

International forwarders (96%) and customs clearance agents (92%) are foreign trade operators that were used at least once to hire international freight. Shipping companies and airlines are hired via intermediaries by 75% and 71% of the sample, respectively. Among the variables that were considered very important at the time of hiring the international freight, it was found that they were, in their order, the price (96%), service level (88%), granting of credit (79%), speed in delivering the quotation offer (75%) and level of experience in the market (71%).

Once an international freight hiring process has finished, the idea is to make a comparison between the cost declared in the quotation by the foreign trade operator against the real cost generated during the operation, thus avoiding hidden costs not mentioned. 75% stated that they always check it, and 20.8% does it frequently. Only 4.2% do not realize this procedure.

In the use of containers for import, local conditions (like detention and demurrage costs) represent cost overruns that, if not known in advance, can generate a high percentage of the import cost, the most critical being: the release or issuing the transport document or bill of lading -BL- (without the original transport document customs clearance cannot be done) and detention. For this study sample, it was noted that all the conditions related to costs are known to the importer, since they have been verified at least once (above 80%).

Regarding to the inquiry of whether they make any kind of forecast to mitigate the effects of the exchange rate, 54.2% plans and estimates an exchange rate at the time of arrival of the goods, 20.8% does not make any forecast, 16.8% purchases forwards on currencies (forwards are banking products that allow the importer to secure the value of the exchange rate at a predetermined time), 12.5% negotiates a Currency adjustment factor –CAF- (surcharge for adjustment of currency) with foreign trade operators (which is similar to the forward used between the importer and the operator).

The final topic of the second cycle was insurance: 87.5% of the companies used insurance for their imported goods. Of this total, the type of insurance used is: i) a global policy of its own (71.4%) and ii) a purchase of a specific policy for shipment (28.6%). When asked about what the contracted insurance policy covers, 40.9% indicates that covers 100% of the value of the goods and transportation costs from leaving the seller's warehouse until it reaches the purchaser's warehouse, while another 40.9% in addition to this negotiates a loss of profit in case of damages, breakdowns, or losses. Only 9.1% is unaware of the conditions of the insurance policy.

4.3   Third Cycle: Decisions Related to the Process of Customs Clearance

Moment in which the customs clearance agent is involved in an import: 96% inform their custom clearance agent before the goods reaches the national customs territory. Of this percentage, 63% does it before the goods departs from country of origin, while 33% does it once they have already left.

Another important aspect of the third cycle is the level of importance of value proposal by customs agents. When it comes to choose a customs agent, the major aspects considered were the agility in the process of customs clearance in port (92% considers it very important), and the previous experience of the customs agent with the type of merchandise which is object of importation (83%) considers it very important. The first relates to a process of customs clearance done with planning (where the importer takes more importance), while the second has to do with managing the agent own customs requirements of the product (where customs agent takes more importance).

This discussion is followed by the analysis of the process of import registry at the Ventanilla Unica de Comercio Exterior – VUCE. The VUCE is the foreign trade platform for importers and exporters where they process entry permits, import registries and import licenses for all government dependencies related to foreign trade. According to the data obtained, 66% of importers must request some type of approval either through an import registry or a prior license to clear their goods. This means that additional planning process and lead time before arrival must be made in order to comply with customs regulations.

Before requesting selectivity to the customs clearance system, the importer pays the import taxes and duties (formerly customs duties) whose method used influences the total clearance time, being the fastest direct payment of taxes via electronic payment (PSE in Spanish). The research showed that traditional (face-to-face) methods prevail, where 58.3% delegates the customs agent to pay taxes and its amount is included in the customs advance requested at the beginning of the customs clearance operation, while 25% does it through a letter of taxes presented to the bank. Only 16.7% uses the online payment method, also the fastest one.

Regarding the lead time that the process of customs clearance takes once the goods arrive at Buenaventura until they are removed from port, 58.3% does it in 4–6 days, while 20.8% does it in 7–10 days. Only 16.7% does it within the three free days of warehousing granted by the port, which implies that 83% pays additional costs for warehousing of goods.

Among the activities that cause delays in the clearance process are those related to inspections at the port, which presented a certain frequency, namely: i) Inspection by the Tax authorities and National Customs (DIAN) after the application for selectivity to the customs clearance system (71%), ii) carrying out previous inspections or recognitions of merchandise requested by the importer (63%), iii) mandatory inclusion of the DIAN at the time of unloading of straight out from the vessel (54%). Another aspect that also occurred with some frequency has been the delay in which the transport document is transmitted to the customs system (71%), which depends on the management of the shipping line and the customs system.

The previous inspections or recognitions of merchandise are processes that generate an additional cost to the importer since they increase both the total time of customs clearance, as well as the port expenses, since it is necessary to manage mobilizations and container openings in inspection yards. 42% of the companies carries out inspections and 50% does not. Of those which do, 33.3% say they do so to avoid DIAN sanctions, 16.7% because it requires extracting information from the merchandise to complete the minimum descriptions necessary for the import customs declaration, while 16.7% does so by recommendation of the customs agent. Goods inspections by the customs authority DIAN are randomly requested by the customs system at the time of requesting selectivity, which is when the import customs declaration is presented once the customs duties and taxes are paid. 70.8% indicated that several times they were asked to do it (and pay for it), of which 12.5% stated that almost always that they have to do it for every import made.

At this point, it is important to emphasize the variables that present the highest percentage of costs within the customs clearance process. The costs generated during a port clearance operation are: i) port expenses (which includes container movements, energy, warehousing, use of facilities and others that involve the use of port terminal) which is variable and is directly proportional to the time the goods last inside the terminal, ii) import registration processing and/or import license if the sub-item requires it, iii) customs commission and customs agent fees, iv) the payment of import duties and taxes, v) merchandise inspections (either through a prior inspection requested by the importer, or DIAN inspections that may be (1) forced inclusions at the time of unloading the goods from the vessel, (2) mandatory customs clearance inspection at the time of selectivity in the customs system, and (3) Tax and Customs Police (POLFA) at the time of removal of the goods from the terminal. The research said that importers consider port expenses as the major determinants of cost (45.8%), followed by the payment of taxes and import duties (41.7%). 12.5% consider mandatory DIAN inspections to be the biggest determining variable.

The result obtained indicates that companies constantly carry out import processes, 83% of the sample carries out more than five (5) annual imports. The formal planning of the international purchasing process continues to be a low percentage as only 25% of interviewees stated that it was because of a previous planning study. 70% of companies declared having a formal process established for the selection of international suppliers, which is consistent with the form of payment used, since 46% use Swift-type bank transfers denoting full trust in suppliers.

Financial expenses resulting from bank procedures are costs inherent to the import process subject to being paid for from the planning process, even more so when 54.2% of importers stated that they will use the modality of use of bank intermediation subject to conditions, such as they are money orders and credit cards. The same with the use of Swift-type payments, banks generate commissions based on the value of the transaction. The purchase of foreign currency forwards used as a method of mitigating the exchange rate also generates related bank charges and their use was evidenced in the investigation.

A sum of 92% of companies carried out a preliminary analysis before starting the international purchase process where the price of the goods and customs requirements are the main variables of analysis. The most relevant reasons when choosing a supplier are the price offered, the total import lead time and that the supplier has flexibility in the delivery of the order as required by the level of service.

Importers have the power to decide on selecting INCOTERM negotiation term, since 92% interviewees expressed it in some way. However, a relatively low percentage of 29% performs a cost analysis of various INCOTERMS. The most frequent term is FOB and together with the term EXW they have been used at least once, which indicates that the importer is the one who selects and pays the international freight, and therefore has the possibility of optimizing it.

The contracting of international freight is delivered to the freight forwarder and/or customs agent in a percentage higher than 90%, the most considered variables are the price, the service level, the credit granted, the speed of delivery. of the quotation and the agent's endorsement. A sum of 83.5% of respondents used a method of mitigating the exchange rate by the Representative Market Rate (TRM). Among the most used methods are the future estimation based on a projection method, the negotiation of an exchange rate surcharge or Currency Adjustment Factor (CAF) with foreign trade operators, and the purchase of forwards on currencies in banks. More than 90% declared to insure their merchandise, being the use of a contracted global policy the most used method. There is a consensus among interviewees regarding involving the customs agent in the process before the arrival of the goods, however, 33% does it after the goods are shipped, increasing the risk of cost overruns by not having all the customs requirements necessary at the time of customs clearance, even leading to situations of legal desertion or destruction of goods when they cannot be re-shipped within the period given by customs to clear customs. Important to note that 66% of respondents transacted any prior import registration or import license at the VUCE.

Eighty-three percent (83%) of the companies indicated that customs clearance processes exceed three (3) days free of storage in port, which represents a latent need to reduce import times, even more so when port expenses are considered as the greatest determinant of cost with the payment of import duties and taxes (concept that depends on the HS code (tariff number) of the goods and not on the agile management in port). DIAN customs inspections, which are also representative of costs in both money and time, depend on the randomness of the customs system, but are influenced by both the HS code and the risk degree of certain importer within the customs system.

Focusing on the previous goods inspections, almost 50% continues to carry them out, indicating that more work must be done on planning customs requirements by the supplier. Previous inspections are a 100% controllable and mitigable factor for the importer.

4.4 A Proposed Model for Context-Specific Decisions

Regarding context-specific elements, variables were grouped into 2 factors: restrictions and mechanisms and agents. As shown on Table 2, restriction and mechanisms consist of norms, laws, agreements and guidelines (from local, bilateral and international sources) that will interfere with the development of alternatives for the decision process.

Table 2. Restrictions and mechanisms that affect import operations decisions

Variable code	Description
R1	Colombian classification code guidelines
R2	Law 0925/2013
R3	Law 390/2016
R4	Complementary product-specific customs norms and procedures
R5	IATA's DGR Manual
R6	IMO IMDG Manual
R7	NTC Norm No. 1692
R8	NFPA Norm No. 704
R9	Free trade agreements established by Colombia with other countries

(continued)

Table 2. (*continued*)

Variable code	Description
R10	Transportation capacity according to local market regulations
R11	Law 2147/2016
R12	Corporate policies
R13	Currency exchange policy

In a similar sense, the agents involved in these operations will establish parameters and preferences that will interfere in the shape of alternatives and final decisions. For the studied environment, the agents were coded as represented on Table 3.

Table 3. Agents that interact in import operations decisions

Variable code	Description
M1	Importer
M2	Service provider specialists for cargo classification and norm mapping
M3	Operations manager (main service provider)
M4	Provider
M5	International cargo agent
M6	Customs agency
M7	Customs warehouse
M8	Free zone
M9	Multimodal Transport Operator – MTO
M10	Bank

Based on data, a model was proposed, integrating decision steps -that expand the 3 cycles model- and context-specific variables, as presented in Fig. 2.

As presented on Fig. 2, the decision-making process starts by mapping and assessing context requirements that involve legal issues as well as needs and specificities under strategic and operative perspectives of customs. After that, the characteristics of cargo will be the focus, followed by the analysis of different packages proposed by logistics providers. This integrated data leads to the definition of transportation settings, followed by specificities in terms of determining the customs point of entrance (which can represent a significant variation in minor customs operations procedures). By concluding this step, it is feasible to establish the best provider, incoterm and the operation's lead time, which leads to a vision of the preliminary costs. Summing financial and administrative costs, the flow is complete.

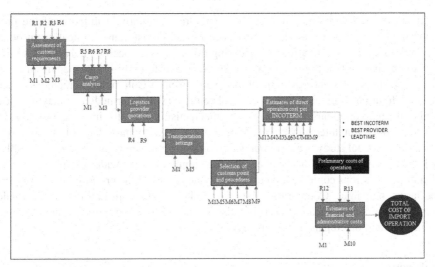

Fig. 2. Proposed model for a context-specific decision-making process in international purchase transactions

This proposed model shows a more hierarchical and detailed process than the original cycles, which can support the development of managerial tools to support this organizational routine.

5 Conclusions

The present study characterized the decision cycles of international purchase transactions based on data from Buenaventura Port importers and exporters. First cycle decisions emphasize the predominance of prices and flexibility as key factors, also highlighting the lack of long-term projections.

In the second cycle, the classical EXW and FOB INCOTERMS are found as predominant, with ocean freight as a preference. Although cargo details were not deeply discussed, it is pertinent to clarify that this is a rather frequent response for medium to large cargos as it is the most efficient in the studied context [2], however specific cargos might present a different optimal scenario. These results differ deeply from those found in Poland by Hajdukiewicz and Pera [12], and in Ukraine, by Khalipova et al. [15]. Unfortunately, data from other Latin American countries was not available in previous research, impeding a proper comparison within the same region.

In the third cycle, the lack of proper planning is present in more than one third of responses, which can lead to a massive increase of unexpected costs and risks in the operation [13]. This reinforces preliminary data informed by ANALDEX [4].

Finally, the proposed model shows that the same context variable can affect different steps of the decision cycle, now designed as a more detailed 8-step process. Restrictions and mechanisms were grouped since the same source can have dual function during the process.

It is expected that data could support a future quantitative validation of the proposed model, as well as provide a reference for comparison and replication in other contexts with similar scenarios. Considering this is a case-specific analysis, it is relevant to emphasize that these variables may behave differently in other environments. Moreover, the agents and restrictions may vary, even in Colombian companies, since other configurations in the supply chain and contracts with intermediaries may increase or alter the map of agents, restrictions, and mechanisms. It is also important to observe that data collection antecedes covid-19, which can be a potential factor to change this dynamic. A sequel study is recommended in order to compare results so these variables and its impacts can be further analyzed in this sample. Also, a wider sample or a study in multiple locations could be able to compare the results of the proposed flow in SMEs and large companies. Comparative data from other locations in Latin America would require a significant research effort but also would provide more understanding about similarities and discrepancies in this region.

References

1. Abubakari, A., Ofori, K. S., Boateng, H., N'Da, K., Hinson, R. E.: The effect of foreign market knowledge on SME export performance: a study of non-traditional SMEs in Ghana. Glob. Knowl., Mem. Commun. (2021). https://doi.org/10.1108/GKMC-03-2021-0054
2. ACOPI: Estudios económicos. https://www.acopi.org.co/estudios-economicos/. Last Accessed 1 March 2022
3. Aksoy, S., Durmusoglu, Y.: Improving competitiveness level of Turkish intermodal ports in the frame of green port concept: a case study. Marit. Policy Manag. **47**(2), 203–220 (2020). https://doi.org/10.1080/03088839.2019.1688876
4. ANALDEX: Exponotas. https://www.analdex.org/category/exponotas/. Last Accessed 1 March 2022
5. Christiansen, B.: Handbook of research on global supply chain management. Handbook of research on global supply chain management. IGI Global, Hershey, PA, USA (2016). doi:https://doi.org/10.4018/978-1-4666-9639-6
6. Departamento Nacional de Planeación: Encueesta Nacional de Planeación. https://onl.dnp. gov.co/es/Publicaciones/Documents/Encuesta%20Nacional%20Log%C3%ADstica%202 015%20%E2%80%93%20Libro%20de%20resultados.pdf (2021). Last Accessed 2 March 2022
7. DIAN: Estadísticas de comercio exterior. https://www.dian.gov.co/dian/cifras/Paginas/Estadi sticasComEx.aspx. Last Accessed 2 March 2022
8. Farahani, R., Rezapour, S., Kardar, L.: Logistics Operations and Management. Elsevier, Amsterdam (2011). https://doi.org/10.1016/C2010-0-67008-8
9. Friedrich, H., Tavasszy, L., Davydenko, I.: Distribution structures. In: Modelling Freight Transport, pp. 65–87. Elsevier (2014). https://doi.org/10.1016/B978-0-12-410400-6.00004-5
10. Garg, C.P., Kashav, V.: Modeling the supply chain finance (SCF) barriers of Indian SMEs using BWM framework. J. Bus. Ind. Mark. **37**(1), 128–145 (2021). https://doi.org/10.1108/ JBIM-05-2020-0248
11. Gutierrez-Franco, E., Mejia-Argueta, C., Rabelo, L.: Data-driven methodology to support long-lasting logistics and decision making for urban last-mile operations. Sustainability (Switzerland) **13**(11), 6230 (2021). https://doi.org/10.3390/su13116230
12. Hajdukiewicz, A., Pera, B.: Factors affecting the choice of Incoterms: the case of companies operating in Poland. Int. Entrepreneurship Rev. **7**(4), 35–50 (2021)

13. Hult, T., Closs, D., Frayer, D.: Global Supply Chain Management: Leveraging Processes, Measurements, and Tools for Strategic Corporate Advantage. Default Book Series. McGraw-Hill, New York (2013)
14. Jung, S., Hong, S., Lee, K.: A data-driven air traffic sequencing model based on pairwise preference learning. IEEE Trans. Intell. Transp. Syst. **20**(3), 803–816 (2019). https://doi.org/10.1109/TITS.2018.2829863
15. Khalipova, N., Bosov, A., Progonyuk, I.: Development of a model for the integrated management of the international delivery chains formation. Eastern-European J. Enterp. Technol. **93**, 59–72 (2018). https://doi.org/10.15587/1729-4061.2018.132683
16. Maden, A., Alptekin, E.: Evaluation of factors affecting the decision to adopt blockchain technology: a logistics company case study using fuzzy DEMATEL. J. Intell. Fuzzy Syst. **39**(5), 6279–6291 (2020). https://doi.org/10.3233/JIFS-189096
17. Mathirajan, M., Reddy, S., Rani, M.V.: An experimental study of newly proposed initial basic feasible solution methods for a transportation problem. Opsearch **59**, 102–145 (2021). https://doi.org/10.1007/s12597-021-00533-5
18. Pereira, D.F., Oliveira, J.F., Carravilla, M.A.: Merging make-to-stock/make-to-order decisions into sales and operations planning: a multi-objective approach. Omega **107**, 102561 (2022). https://doi.org/10.1016/j.omega.2021.102561
19. Qaiser, F.H., Ahmed, K., Sykora, M., Choudhary, A., Simpson, M.: Decision support systems for sustainable logistics: a review & bibliometric analysis. Ind. Manag. Data Syst. **117**(7), 1376–1388 (2017). https://doi.org/10.1108/IMDS-09-2016-0410
20. Salazar-Araujo, E.J., Pozzo, D., Cazallo-Antunez, A.M.: Innovation capacity vs. internationalization capacity: the case of Colombian manufacturing SMEs of the Atlantic region. In: 15th Iberian Conference on Information Systems and Technologies (CISTI), pp. 1–6. Iberian Association for Information Systems and Technologies, Portugal (2020). https://doi.org/10.23919/CISTI49556.2020.9141016
21. Schiffer, M., Wiendahl, H.-H., Saretz, B.: Self-assessment of industry 4.0 technologies in intralogistics for SME's. In: Ameri, F., Stecke, K.E., von Cieminski, G., Kiritsis, D. (eds.) APMS 2019. IAICT, vol. 567, pp. 339–346. Springer, Cham (2019). https://doi.org/10.1007/978-3-030-29996-5_39
22. Snoeck, A., Winkenbach, M.: The value of physical distribution flexibility in serving dense and uncertain urban markets. Transport. Res. Part A: Policy Pract. **136**, 151–177 (2020). https://doi.org/10.1016/j.tra.2020.02.011
23. Tuljak-Suban, D., Bajec, P.: Integration of AHP and GTMA to make a reliable decision in complex decision-making problems: application of the logistics provider selection problem as a case study. Symmetry **12**(766), 1–19 (2020). https://doi.org/10.3390/SYM12050766
24. Yazdani, M., Chatterjee, P., Pamucar, D., Chakraborty, S.: Development of an integrated decision making model for location selection of logistics centers in the spanish autonomous communities. Expert Syst. Appl. **148**, 1–45 (2020). https://doi.org/10.1016/j.eswa.2020.113208
25. World Bank: Logistics performance index. https://datos.bancomundial.org/indicator/LP.LPI.OVRL.XQ. Last Accessed 2 March 2022
26. World Bank: Doing Business Report 2020. https://documents1.worldbank.org/curated/en/688761571934946384/pdf/Doing-Business-2020-Comparing-Business-Regulation-in-190-Economies.pdf. Last Accessed 1 March 2022

Knowledge Management: Effects on Innovation in Micro, Small, and Medium-Sized Export Enterprises

Gabriel Velandia Pacheco[1] (ID), Adalberto Escobar Castillo[1](✉)(ID),
Evaristo Navarro Manotas[1] (ID), Cristina Logreira Vargas[2],
Wendell Archibold Barrios[3] (ID), Carlos Recuay Salazar[4] (ID), Diana García Tamayo[1],
and Rubén Hernández Burgos[1]

[1] Universidad de la Costa CUC, Barranquilla 08003, Colombia
aescobar2@cuc.edu.co
[2] Fundación Universitaria Ceipa Business School, Barranquilla 08003, Colombia
[3] Universidad del Atlántico, Barranquilla 08003, Colombia
[4] Universidad Continental, Huancayo 12000, Perú

Abstract. Despite their informality, studies have shown the impact of knowledge management activities on innovative performance in SMEs. Consequently, the objective of the study is to establish whether knowledge management processes affect the innovation capability in micro, small, and medium-sized export enterprises in Departamento del Atlántico. This is achieved through a positivist, non-experimental, cross-sectional, and explanatory research, which applies a Likert-type survey to 71 managers. The results show the direct effect of the acquisition, exploitation, and transfer of knowledge, as well as the negative relationship of internalization and the non-significance of the measurement. This makes it possible to show that, although SMEs carry out knowledge management activities, they do not formally apply it, which can be explained from their nature and ways of responding to the demands of the environment.

Keywords: Knowledge acquisition · Knowledge internalization · Knowledge exploitation · Knowledge transfer · Knowledge measurement

1 Introduction

The literature allows us to identify the effect of innovative performance on competitiveness, mediated by the adaptation capability [1–5]. Likewise, knowledge management, understood as the acquisition, internalization, exploitation, transfer, and measurement of knowledge, is one of the main variables that explains innovation [5–8].

On the other hand, Matlay [9], Alegre et al. [6] and Castillo et al. [10], affirm that the survival of Micro, Small and Medium Enterprises (SMEs) requires a flexible structure, which facilitates the fluidity of knowledge within it (Adaptation capability) facilitating its innovative performance, thanks to the search of solutions to the demands of the environment. However, authors such as Durst and Runar [11], Velandia et al. [12]

K. Saeed and J. Dvorský (Eds.): CISIM 2022, LNCS 13293, pp. 160–171, 2022.
https://doi.org/10.1007/978-3-031-10539-5_12

Granados et al. [13] highlight that, due to resource limitations, they normally do not develop a formal knowledge management structure, therefore, their learning strategies are generally short term.

Despite this informality, authors such as Grimsdottir and Edvardsson [14], Soto-Acosta et al. [5], Hassan and Raziq [15] showed that, in SMEs, there is a positive relationship between knowledge management processes and innovation. However, most of the studies found in the literature refer to companies located in European markets, generating research gaps due to the lack of studies that refer to companies in Latin America. Consequently, the objective of this work is to establish whether knowledge management processes affect the innovation capability in micro, small, and medium-sized export enterprises in Departamento del Atlántico; through a positivist research, non-experimental design, transversal and explanatory scope.

These approaches suggest that the study is necessary because the results help explain the relationship between knowledge management processes and innovation in SMEs in Latin American context. Pointing out the aspects that managers must consider for improving their innovative performance. In addition, it becomes relevant, due to these organizations represent 99% of formal Latin American companies and create 61% of jobs in the region [16]. Initially, the literature that supports the initial approaches related to the capability for innovation and knowledge management is presented. Subsequently, the methodology is presented to continue with the results and conclusions.

2 Literature Review

This section presents the theoretical fundament used to model the relationship be-tween knowledge management and innovation capability. On literature it is observed that acquisition, internalization, exploitation, and transfer are the basic learning processes in organizations. In addition, it could be understood as the main process to manage knowledge and generate intellectual capital when it is formalized across measurement and supported by information and communication technologies (ICT).

2.1 Innovation Capability

The rapid technological changes and high competition establish that the capability for innovation is a key success factor which forces organizations to implement strategic surveillance processes [5]. It is defined as organizational skill used for developing products and services, production methods, market identification, supply sources and organizational structure; new or substantially improved. An effective capability for innovation allows the organization to materialize economic benefits [17].

2.2 Knowledge Management

Knowledge management is a systematic and formal process, which directs the innate capacities of organizational learning towards the generation of value, from the efficient use of technology and intellectual capital, mediated by the acquisition, internalization, exploitation, transfer, and measurement of knowledge with potential value. Generating

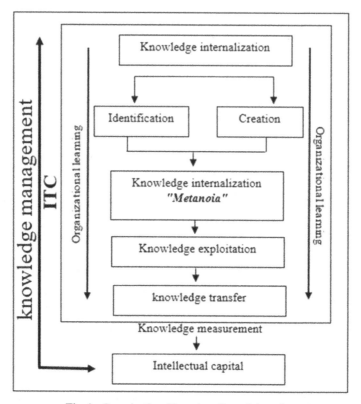

Fig. 1. Organizational learning. Own elaboration

distinctive capabilities that are difficult to imitate (innovation), thanks to the peculiarities of the learning processes and the accessibility of resources [18–26] (see Fig. 1).

Knowledge Acquisition. Knowledge acquisition is carried out internally or externally. The first materializes when the organization intends to absorb knowledge through the efficient use of human capital, creating capabilities that generate competitive advantages, and the second, implementing strategic surveillance, which allow identifying new knowledge with potential value for the organization [23, 27, 28].

Through the studies developed by Durst and Runar [11], Harris [7], Soto-Acosta [5] and Hussain et al. [8], it has been established that in turbulent environments where processes that optimize innovative performance are required, business success is related to the ability to acquire knowledge. Therefore, it can be established that:

H_1: knowledge acquisition has a positive effect on the innovation capability of SMEs.

Knowledge Internalization. It is constituted in the appropriation of acquired knowledge, which arrives tacitly and is transform in explicit by the learning administration [19]. Although the support of ICT is important at this stage, effective internalization requires much more than the simple distribution of information throughout the organization, since it requires the development of the ability to use the new knowledge in the problem solving, and sometimes this activity, requires unlearning consolidated processes (metanoia) [29]. Consequently, knowledge internalization materializes in the execution of new products, services, methods, or strategies, which contribute to efficient innovative performance [30]. Based on this, it can be deduced that:

H_2: knowledge internalization has a positive effect on the innovation capability of SMEs.

Knowledge Exploitation. It constitutes the ability to use knowledge as a critical element that conditions innovative performance [27]. The effectiveness of the knowledge exploitation materializes when the organization develops the capability to apply it economically [31]; through routines that tend to redefine, improve, or create competencies [32]. Based on these approaches, it can be stated that:

H_3: knowledge exploitation has a positive effect on the innovation capability of SMEs.

Knowledge Transfer. It is an intrinsic quality of knowledge that can be used to transfer it to different parts of the organization or in an interorganizational way, with the aim of taking advantage of its economically. This is achieved through the support of ICT, from the collective use of databases and memories. In this way, concepts are structured, synthesized, and systematized, generating communication processes through which innovative performance is increased [33]. In this order of ideas, it is coherent to say that:

H_4: knowledge transfer has a positive effect on the innovation capability of SMEs.

Knowledge Measurement. For Gómez [34] measurement refers to the evaluation process of the value that is generated from applying knowledge economically. Along the same lines, Larios [35] highlights that this process becomes a mediating variable in the recognition of intangibles with critical value for the company and that potentially enables the development of competitive advantages; making privileged information available to management that facilitates the decision-making process, which has repercussions on innovative performance. These fundamentals allow to state that:

H_5: knowledge measurement has a positive effect on the innovation capability of SMEs.

Figure 2 presents the model made up of the hypotheses proposed in the theoretical framework.

3 Methods and Material

The study was applied to seventy-one (71) micro, small, and medium-sized export enterprises from Departamento del Atlántico, which were selected through simple random probabilistic sampling, supported by the database of the Cámara de Comercio de Barranquilla, conformed for a population of 87 companies. The parameters to define the sample were: margin of error 5%, confidence interval 95% and estimated percentage of 50%.

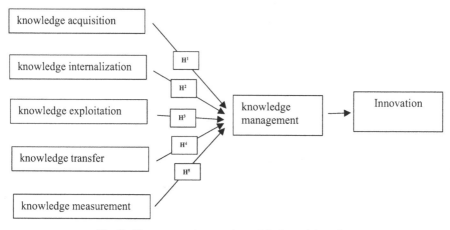

Fig. 2. The proposed research model. Own elaboration

Considering previous studies on knowledge management and innovation showed on Table 1, where there is evidence of use of the Likert scale for its measurement, a survey with this type of scale was used. Designed with five response options and an index of Cronbach's alpha of 0.944. Which suggests a non-experimental, cross-sectional research. The statistical support program was the Statistical Package for the Social Sciences (SPSS) version 24.

Table 1. Scales used in the measurement of the variables

Variable	Scale	Values	Research background
Innovation	Ordinal	5: Totally agree 4: Agree 3: Neither agree nor disagree 2: In disagreement 1: Strongly disagree	Lekhanya [36]; Oskouei [37]; Ngibe and Lekhanya [38]; Sonmez et al. [39]; Soewarno et al. [40]
Knowledge management			Hussain et al. [15]; Al Ahbabi et al. [41]; Maryani et al. [42]; Tamana [43]; Chawla [44]

Source: own elaboration

The survey was built supported by the coherence matrix and the theoretical framework, obtaining a total of 143 statements, which were validated by the judgment of five (5) experts. Subsequently, through the Cronbach's Alpha reliability test, it was reduced to 82 statements, that constitute empirical indicators that tend to measure the processes of knowledge management and the capability for innovation in the empirical reality of the organizations involved in the study. The final instrument was delivered to the 71 managers of the SMEs studied, through email and in person, achieving a response rate of 100%.

The data collected was analyzed through statistical tools such as measures of central tendency, dispersion, and correlation coefficients (Pearson). On the other hand, the hypotheses were contrasted through a multiple linear regression model, from which it was sought to estimate the pattern that adequately explains innovation in micro, small, and medium-sized export enterprises, through the acquisition, internalization, exploitation, transfer, and measurement as elements of knowledge management. To estimate the *betas* (β) and the error (ε) of the model, the method of ordinary least squares (OLS) was used Eq. (1).

$$INNV_t = \beta_0 + \beta_1 ACQ_t + \beta_2 INT_t + \beta_3 EXP_t + \beta_4 TRA_t + \beta_5 MEA_t + \varepsilon \qquad (1)$$

where:

INNV: Innovation.
ACQ: knowledge acquisition.
INT: knowledge internalization.
EXP: knowledge exploitation.
TRA: knowledge transfer.
MEA: knowledge measurement.

In the model validation process, it was verified, through the Kolmogorov - Smirnov normality test, that the distribution of errors is normal. In addition, it is observed that the assumption of linearity and the lack of self-correlation between the explanatory variables are met. Besides, the latter do not have collinearity. Finally, it was confirmed that the model meets the criteria of homoscedasticity.

4 Finding

The correlation coefficient 0.864 indicates that there is a statistically strong linear correlation between the explanatory and the dependent variables. In addition, the R^2 determines the model explains the innovation in 74.6%, through the dimensions of knowledge management considered in this study. On the other hand, the typical frequency error was 0.4783. Finally, the value of the Durbin Watson statistic is 2.055, complying with the independence parameters (Table 2). Also, since the P-value is less than 0.05, there is a statistically significant relationship between the means of the variables (Table 3).

Table 2. Model summary

R		R square	R squared square	Standard error of the estimate	Durbin-watson
0.864		0.746	0.726	0.4783	2.055

Source: own elaboration based on the data processed with the Statistical Package for the Social Sciences (SPSS)

Table 3. ANOVA variance analysis test

Model	Sum of squares	gl	Quadratic mean	F	Sig.
Regression	43.610	5	8.722	38.130	0.000^b
Residue	14.868	65	0.229		
Total	58.479	70			

Source: own elaboration based on the data processed with the Statistical Package for the Social Sciences (SPSS)

To test the hypotheses, the p-values were taken as a reference. In Table 4 it is observed that, the incidence of knowledge acquisition in innovation capability is positive and significant at 1% (β: 0.794, p-values: 0.000), thus confirming H_1. Similarly, a positive influence of knowledge exploitation is noticed, becoming evidence that supports H_3 (β: 0. 608, p-values: 0.000). On the other hand, the relationship between knowledge transfer and innovation is direct and presents a level of significance of 5% (β: 0.163, p-values: 0.040), which supports H_4 (Table 4).

Alternatively, the results do not present empirical evidence that supports H_2, because there is a negative incidence of knowledge internalization on innovation, significant at 1% (β: -0.833, p-values: 0.000). Finally, the causal relationship between the knowledge measurement variable and innovation does not have statistical significance, therefore, H_5 does not present empirical support in the context of the study (β: -0.140, p-values: 0.073) (Table 4).

Table 4. Hypothesis testing

Hypothesis	Model	Std. beta	Std. error	Sig.	Decision
	(Constant)	1.741	0.228	0.000**	
H_1	Knowledge acquisition	0.794	0.089	0.000**	Supported
H_2	Knowledge internalization	-0.833	0.130	0.000**	Not supported
H_3	Knowledge exploitation	0.608	0.119	0.000**	Supported
H_4	Knowledge transfer	0.163	0.078	0.040^*	Supported
H_5	Knowledge measurement	-0.140	0.077	0.073	Not supported

Note: * $p < 0.05$ ** $p < 0.01$.
Source: own elaboration based on data

5 Discussion

The study contributes to the literature related to knowledge management and innovation in the context of SMEs, highlighting that the acquisition, exploitation and transfer of knowledge direct the innate capabilities of organizational learning towards innovative performance, which has repercussions on the development of competitive advantages; confirming that, from these processes, organizational knowledge is aligned with corporate objectives, affecting its strategic positioning, according to the approaches of Cohen and Levinthal [27], Lane and Lubatkin [31], Zahra and George [32], Durst and Runar [11], Lopera and Ledi [33], Harris et al. [7], Soto-Acosta et al. [5] and Hussain et al. [8].

On the other hand, it was established that knowledge internalization has a negative effect on innovation. In addition, the measurement does not present statistical significance, which may be associated with resource limitations in SMEs, which makes it difficult to implement technological tools for storage, coding, and evaluation. This is consistent with what was expressed by Durst and Runar [11], Velandia et al. [12] and Granados et al. [13]. These results do not imply that these organizations do not take advantage of knowledge; in fact, Matlay [9], Alegre et al. [6] and Castillo et al. [10], affirm that their survival requires that internal fluidity be facilitated; however, due to their informality, they solve the demands of the environment, without implementing systematic and planned knowledge management processes, giving little importance to internalization and measurement processes, since they do not find immediate useful results in them.

In this order of ideas, it is valid to make a separation of the dimensions of knowledge management: those that provide immediate results, easy and economical implementation and those of long-term results, difficult and expensive implementation. Thus, the acquisition, exploitation and transfer of knowledge represent, for SMEs, an economic and effective opportunity to cope with the demands of the environment, contrary to the processes of measurement and internalization, which due to their complexity, high costs and lack of results immediate, they are usually despised.

The efficient measurement of knowledge requires the integration of all the processes inherent to its management, however, SMEs to respond to the demands of the environment with scarce resources, assign greater importance to processes of relatively easy applicability, which contribute to solve circumstantial problems (acquisition, exploitation, and transfer). For this reason, it is possible that the decomposition of intellectual capital is not useful, but expensive and not very significant for decision making. Scenario that is consistent with the results obtained. That is, if a process is not formally and completely implemented, how is it measured?

Finally, knowledge internalization is a process that, in addition to demanding technological resources, requires changes in the core competencies of the organization, which aims to affect the organizational culture, which usually requires investment of time and money that will yield long-term results, little related to the efforts. This is contradictory to the nature of these organizations. Under this perception, it is consistent that in the model it has a negative effect on innovation.

6 Conclusions

The objective of the study was to establish whether knowledge management processes have a positive effect on the capability for innovation in export SMEs. The results allow to conclude that the variables acquisition, exploitation, and transfer have a direct and significant effect, while the internalization has a negative impact, and the measurement has no statistical significance in the model. The latter may be related to the nature of the organizations that participated in the study, which give value to strategies that present short-term and low-cost solutions.

It was evidenced that in the analyzed SMEs there is no formal knowledge management process, however, they have activities related to organizational learning. Normally in literature these concepts tend to be confused; however, managing knowledge requires a formal, planned, and systematized process. On the other hand, learning is an activity that occurs naturally, which can be unplanned and informal and, likewise, present results that affect innovation.

In this sense, export SMEs mainly take advantage of those aspects of learning that are easy to apply and low cost, to respond circumstantially to the demands of the environment. Thus, for this type of companies it is sufficient to acquire, use (exploit) and transfer, normally informally the knowledge that is useful to meet their needs without incurring greater efforts that does not mean for their managers an immediate tangible result, which makes sense within the analyzed model.

The limited use that SMEs give to the dimensions of knowledge management, constitutes a competitive strategy that tends to maximize resources and opportunities, in a type of organization that is characterized by the relative scarcity. The implementation of formal internalization and measurement processes, from the cost-benefit logic, can be negative for the administration. Therefore, from the point of view of SME managers, knowledge management processes can be divided into those of short-term results of economic application (acquisition, exploitation, and transfer), relatively effective to cover short-term needs and the expensive that give long term results (internalization and measurement).

7   Implications

The findings highlight that, to strengthen innovative performance in the context of SMEs, activities related to the acquisition, exploitation and transfer of knowledge become more relevant for managers; nevertheless, it is suggested to extrapolate this research to other contexts, implementing experimental and longitudinal designs that include a larger population and allow the behavior of the explanatory variables to be analyzed over a given period. In addition, it is recommended to include variables such as size and sector, as well as qualitative studies that complement their understanding, when considering the subjectivities included by managers that affect the processes of organizational learning, knowledge management and innovation.

References

1. Aguiar, T., Moreno, S., Picazo, P.: How could traditional travel agencies improve their competitiveness and survive? a qualitative study in Spain. Tourism Manag. Perspect. **20**, 98–108 (2016). https://doi.org/10.1016/j.tmp.2016.07.011
2. Husain, Z., Dayan, M., Di Benedetto, A.: The impact of networking on competitiveness via organizational learning, employee innovativeness, and innovation process: a mediation model. J. Eng. Technol. Manag. **40**, 15–28 (2016). https://doi.org/10.1016/j.jengtecman.2016.03.001

3. Carlan, V., Sys, C., Vanelslander, T.: How port community systems can contribute to port competitiveness: developing a cost–benefit framework. Res. Transport. Bus. Manag. **19**, 51–64 (2016). https://doi.org/10.1016/j.rtbm.2016.03.009

4. Tong Ha, S., Chiun Lo, M.: An empirical examination of knowledge management and organizational performance among Malaysian manufacturing SMEs. Int. J. Bus. Innov. Res. **17**(1), 23–37 (2018). https://doi.org/10.1504/IJBIR.2018.094196

5. Soto-Acosta, P., Popa, S., Martínez-Conesa, I.: Information technology, knowledge management and environmental dynamism as drivers of innovation ambidexterity: a study in SMEs. J. Knowl. Manag. **22**(4), 824–849 (2018). https://doi.org/10.1108/JKM-10-2017-0448

6. Alegre, J., Sengupta, K., Lapiedra, R.: Knowledge management and innovation performance in a high-tech SMEs industry. Int. Small Bus. J. **31**(4), 454–470 (2011). https://doi.org/10.1177/0266242611417472

7. Harris, R., McCausland, I., Reid, R.: Knowledge management as a source of innovation and competitive advantage for SMEs in peripheral regions. Entrepreneurship Innov. **14**(1), 49–61 (2013). https://doi.org/10.5367/ijei.2013.0105

8. Hussain, I., Qurashi, A., Mujtaba, G., Waseem, M.A., Iqbal, Z.: Knowledge management: a roadmap for innovation in SMEs' sector of Azad Jammu & Kashmir. J. Glob. Entrep. Res. **9**(1), 1–18 (2019). https://doi.org/10.1186/s40497-018-0120-8

9. Matlay, H.: Organizational learning in small organizations an empirical overview. Educ. Train. **42**(4/5), 202–211 (2000). https://doi.org/10.1108/00400910010373642

10. Castillo, A., Velandia, G., Hernández, P., Archibold, W.: Gestión del conocimiento e innovación en las PYME exportadoras del sector industrial en Colombia. Espacios **38**(34), 24–37 (2017)

11. Durst, S., Runar, I.: Knowledge management in SMEs: a literature review. J. Knowl. Manag. **16**(6), 879–903 (2012). https://doi.org/10.1108/13673271211276173

12. Velandia, G., Hernández, L., Portillo, R., Alvear, L., Crissien, T.: Rasgos de la administración de la microempresa en Barranquilla Colombia. Espacios **37**(9), 7–22 (2016)

13. Granados, M., Mohamed, S., Hlupic, V.: Knowledge management activities in social enterprises: lessons for small and non-profit firms. J. Knowl. Manag. **21**(2), 376–396 (2017). https://doi.org/10.1108/JKM-01-2016-0026

14. Grimsdottir, E., Edvardsson, I.: Knowledge management, knowledge creation, and open innovation in Icelandic SMEs. SAGE Open **8**(1), 1–13 (2018). https://doi.org/10.1177/2158244018 88073

15. Hassan, N., Raziq, A.: Effects of knowledge management practices on innovation in SMEs. Manag. Sci. Lett. **9**, 997–1008 (2019). https://doi.org/10.5267/j.msl.2019.4.005

16. Dini, M., Stumpo, G.: Mipymes en América Latina: un frágil desempeño y nuevos desafíos para las políticas de fomento, Documentos de Proyectos (LC/TS.2018/7). Comisión Económica para América Latina y el Caribe (CEPAL), Chile (2018)

17. Teece, D.: Business models, business strategy and innovation. Long Range Plan. **43**(2–3), 172–194 (2010). https://doi.org/10.1016/j.lrp.2009.07.003

18. Barney, J.: Firm resources and sustained competitive advantage. J. Manag. **17**(1), 99–120 (1991)

19. Nonaka, I., Takeuchi, H.: The Knowledge Creation Company. Oxford University Press, Nex York, USA (1995)

20. Sveiby, K.: The New Organizational Wealth. Berrett-Koehler Publishers Inc, San Francisco, USA (1997)

21. Teece, D., Pisano, G., Shuen, A.: Dynamic capabilities and strategic management. Strateg. Manag. J. **18**(7), 509–533 (1997)

22. Davenport, T., Prusak, L.: Working Knowledge: How Organizations Manage What They Know. Harvard Business Press, Boston, USA (1998)

23. Probst, G., Raub, S., Romhardt, K.: Administre el conocimiento: los pilares del éxito. Pearson Educación, México (2001)
24. Garzón, M.: Aproximaciones a la gestión del conocimiento en empresas colombianas. Universidad & Empresa **5**(10), 232–256 (2006)
25. Iddy, J., Alon, I.: Knowledge management in franchising: a research agenda. J. Knowl. Manag. **23**(4), 763–785 (2019). https://doi.org/10.1108/JKM-07-2018-0441
26. López-Zapata, E., López-Moros, G.P., Agudelo-Muñoz, S.M.: Relación entre estrategias competitivas y tipos de aprendizaje organizativo en empresas colombianas. Información tecnológica **30**(5), 191–202 (2019). https://doi.org/10.4067/S0718-07642019000500191
27. Cohen, W.M., Levinthal, D.A.: Absorptive capacity: a new perspective on learning and innovation. Adm. Sci. Q. **35**(1), 128–152 (1990). https://doi.org/10.2307/2393553
28. Garzón, M.: Modelo de capacidades dinámicas. Revista Dimensión Empresarial **13**(1), 111–131 (2015). https://doi.org/10.15665/rde.v13i1.341
29. Senge, P.: La quinta disciplina: el arte y la práctica de la organización abierta al aprendizaje. Granica S.A., Buenos Aires, Argentina (1990)
30. Martínez-Costa, M., Jiménez-Jiménez, D., Dine-Rabeh, H.: The effect of organizational learning on interorganizational collaborations in innovation: an empirical study in SMEs. Knowl. Manag. Res. Pract. **17**(2), 137–150 (2019). https://doi.org/10.1080/14778238.2018.1538601
31. Lane, P., Lubatkin, M.: Relative absorptive capacity and interorganizational learning. Strastegic Manag. J. **19**(5), 461–477 (1998)
32. Zahra, S., George, G.: Absorptive capacity: a review, reconceptualization and extension. Acad. Manag. Rev. **2**(27), 185–203 (2002). https://doi.org/10.2307/4134351
33. Lopera, M.: Ledis, N: Caracterización de un modelo de gestión del conocimiento aplicable a las funciones universitarias de investigación y extensión: Caso Universidad CES. Universidad del Rosario, Bogotá, Colombia, Tesis de Maestría (2013)
34. Gómez, M.: Desarrollo de un modelo de evaluación de la gestión del conocimiento en empresas de manufactura. Universidad Politécnica de Madrid, Escuela técnica superior de ingenieros industriales, Tesis doctoral (2009)
35. Larios, J.: El capital intelectual: Un modelo de medición en las empresas del nuevo milenio. Criterio Libre **7**(11), 101–121 (2009)
36. Lekhanya, L.: The support structures for strengthening social innovation in South Africa. Inte. J. Entrepreneurship **23**(4) (2019)
37. Oskouei, Z.: Linking social and economic responsibilities and financial performance: the assisting role of innovation for an oil engineering and development company. Int. J. Financ. Econ. **24**(3), 1345–1354 (2019). https://doi.org/10.1002/ijfe.1722
38. Ngibe, M., Lekhanya, L.: Critical factors influencing innovative leadership in attaining business innovation: a case of manufacturing smes in kwazulu-natal. International Journal of Entrepreneurship **23**(2) (2019)
39. Sonmez Cakir, F., Adiguzel, Z.: Evaluation of open leadership and innovation orientation on employees and culture of the organization. Bus.: Theor. Pract. **20**, 432–445 (2019). https://doi.org/10.3846/btp.2019.40
40. Soewarno, N., Tjahjadi, B., Fithrianti, F.: Green innovation strategy and green innovation: The roles of green organizational identity and environmental organizational legitimacy. Manag. Decis. **57**(11), 3061–3078 (2019). https://doi.org/10.1108/MD-05-2018-0563
41. Al Ahbabi, S., Singh, S., Balasubramanian, S., Gaur, S.: Employee perception of impact of knowledge management processes on public sector performance. J. Knowl. Manag. **23**(2), 351–373 (2019). https://doi.org/10.1108/JKM-08-2017-0348
42. Maryani, B., Mahesworo, B., Samsinga, A., Hendarti, H: (2019). User Interface Evaluation on Government Knowledge Management Portal Using Webqual 4.0. In: International Conference on Information Management and Technology (ICIMTech), pp. 244–249. Jakarta/Bali, Indonesia. https://doi.org/10.1109/ICIMTech.2019.8843780

43. Tamanna, S.: Impact of knowledge management and organizational learning on performance in healthcare sector. Int. J. Emerg. Technol. **10**(4), 416–421 (2019)
44. Chawla, A.: Knowledge management enablers practices among Indian higher educational institutions. Int. J. Knowl. Manag. Stud. **10**(4), 415–425 (2019). https://doi.org/10.1504/IJKMS.2019.103356

Evaluation of Educational Quality Under a Six Sigma Approach to Engineering Degrees in Colombia

Rohemi Zuluaga-Ortiz[1](✉) (ID), Enrique Delahoz-Dominguez[2] (ID),
Arantxa Periñan-Luna[2] (ID), Jey Escorcia[4] (ID), Francisco Moreira-Villegas[3] (ID),
and Ana Arteta[4] (ID)

[1] Engineering Faculty, Universidad del Sinú, Cartagena, Colombia
rohemi.zuluaga@unisinu.edu.co
[2] Engineering Faculty, Universidad Tecnológica de Bolívar, Cartagena, Colombia
[3] Faculty of Natural Sciences and Mathematics, Escuela Superior Politécnica del Litoral,
Guayaquil, Ecuador
[4] Faculty of Business Sciences, Universidad de La Costa, Barranquilla, Colombia

Abstract. In this research, a methodology is developed to measure the quality of the Colombian educational system by analyzing universities and their academic programs. For the above, a Six Sigma approach is used as a tool for educational management in order to classify, evaluate and analyze the educational system having two approaches: universities and academic programs. Consequently, this article is divided into 5 sections: In the first section, a review of research carried out on quality and HEIs is carried out. The second section presents the research methodology, describes the study population and variables. The third section shows the results derived from the application of the Six Sigma methodology. The fourth section presents the discussion and recommendations. Finally, the fifth section presents the conclusions. Now, within the most significant findings, it is found that the sigma level of the Colombian educational system is found at $Z = 2.17$ and $Y = 75\%$ and is considered, according to what is established in the methodology of this work, as an acceptable level.

Keywords: Six Sigma · Higher education · Learning analytics · Continuous improvement · Quality

1 Introduction

The increase in competitive pressure in the goods and services industries constantly forces the search for new ways to improve their performance, be competitive, and thus, sustain in the long term [1–4]. This unleashes several requirements and challenges for all organizations, for example, to have in their work team a skilled staff that manages to help the company grow. Consequently, Higher Education Institutions (HEIs) are not exempt from these requirements, since they are the ones that provide professionals with the competencies and skills required by companies [2, 5, 6].

© The Author(s), under exclusive license to Springer Nature Switzerland AG 2022
K. Saeed and J. Dvorský (Eds.): CISIM 2022, LNCS 13293, pp. 172–188, 2022.
https://doi.org/10.1007/978-3-031-10539-5_13

According to the above, the objective of HEIs should be framed in the training of competent professionals who are capable of adapting to the volatility of the environment; in this way, these professionals will help industry and society in their development [7, 8]. Amador and Martínez [9] affirm that the supplier-client relationship between HEIs and organizations is of vital importance, due to the creation of a collaborative work culture called "win-win". Consequently, one of the main concerns of HEIs is to comply with the minimum standards associated with factors such as infrastructure, projection, relevance, and resources, which respond to institutional accreditations, which are granted by independent agencies [10]. But first, HEIs must prepare themselves to be evaluated, for this, they must have tools that are useful for educational management and to be able to meet the objectives set.

Therefore, in this research, a Six Sigma approach is used as a tool for educational management to classify, evaluate and analyze the educational system with two approaches: universities and academic programs. It should be noted that this research takes into account only the academic results of the national standardized assessments in Colombia (SABER PRO). Accordingly, this article is divided into 5 sections: In the first section, the review of research conducted around quality and HEIs are carried out. The second section presents the research methodology and describes the population and variables of the study. In the third section, the results derived from the application of the Six Sigma methodology are shown. In the fourth section, the discussion and recommendations are presented. Finally, the fifth section presents the conclusions.

2 Literature Review

2.1 Assessing Quality in the Service Industry

Throughout these last years, new concepts and approaches to service quality have been added to the literature, in addition to the vast existence of comments on the interpretation, contributions, and variants of quality in services, and how important it is nowadays in competitive scenarios. On the other hand, services for [11] are a means to deliver value and benefits to customers at a specific time and place producing the desired change in favor of the service. Services must have a tactical approach and function in managing the nature of the service, as well as having a clear scope of service quality, customer expectations, and quality particularities. However, when evaluating service quality, customer perception is the ideal and most commonly used perspective. The Service Quality (SERVQUAL) model proposed more than two decades ago is still in force and is still an important reference for the evaluation of quality in various services [12].

Service quality in organizations is the measure of the degree to which the service provided meets customer expectations [13]. The success of business activity will depend on the perceived quality of service delivery. Therefore, the ability of a company or organization to estimate the quality of service is a prerequisite for achieving a high level of quality in that service provision [14, 15].

2.2 Application of Six Sigma in the Service Industry

Six Sigma applies the Define, Measure, Analyze, Improve, and Control (DMAIC) methodology, which is a perfect fit for effective process improvement. Likewise, to permeate quality in products must be done from the design phase, a preventive app-roach to design for Six Sigma (DFSS) De-sign for Six Sigma [16] is needed. The main objective of Six Sigma is to increase the sigma level by reducing defects per million opportunities (DPMO) [17]. This quality tool aims to achieve as close to perfection as possible, is used in many organizations, and is based on evidence, analytics of inputs, and procedures [18]. Likewise, throughout the implementation of Six Sigma, statistical tools are used for the characterization and study of the processes (hence the name of the tool), since sigma is the standard deviation that gives a clue of how the variability is in the process and the main objective is to reduce it so that the process is in the limits established by the customer requirements [19].

Now, implementing Six Sigma allows the elimination of all activities that do not add value to the process. Six Sigma makes significant contributions in the main areas of the organizations that influence the long and medium-term performance periods, such as process design, process approach and improvement, broad participation in problem-solving, knowledge sharing, goal setting, supplier selection, and data-driven decision making [20].

Six Sigma is a powerful methodology that ultimately helps to reduce costs due to defect prevention and improvement of products and processes, leading to increased profitability, where customer satisfaction and competitiveness are at the center of focus for any quality improvement practice and performance measurement. Likewise, the relationship between Six Sigma and service in some research is named as Six Sigma Transactional Service because it provides organizations with a disciplined approach to improve service efficiency and effectiveness [21–23].

2.3 Application of Six Sigma in Higher Education

When talking about quality and the terms of Six Sigma in education, it is established that the IES is completely different from what usually the quality of services and the Six Sigma tool face. In that same order of ideas, the experience to be evaluated is divided into two areas: the evaluation of the quality in the teaching and learning process, and the evaluation of the quality taking into account the student's experience. The latter involves the development of specific instruments and mechanisms for service quality assessment for the environment of higher education institutions. Education is an impor-tant organization to give a change to the economy through knowledge. The market of higher education institutions has led to their students being highly regarded as cus-tomers/consumers. Additionally, in the education sector where even though there is no product involved, the service provided will impact the competitive demarcation between institutions in terms of their superiority. The evaluation of service quality in HEIs can provide an important contribution and inputs which will be of excellent help for the administrative side to make decisions to further improve the quality of their education [13].

Although most of the concepts of the Six Sigma tool are built for manufacturing industries, they are related to the educational service. The scope given to Six Sigma in education is commonly used in very specific cases of improvement or in conjunction with the Baldrige Criteria for Performance Excellence to facilitate application to educational structures [24].

However, there are divided opinions regarding the implementation of six sigma in the field of education, for example, waste and rework in the educational environment differs in terms of tangibility to how it is in manufacturing industries, wherein the latter has a physically noticeable impact [25].

3 Methodology

The present research is evaluative and consists of five stages (see Fig. 1). The first stage is contextualization; here we seek to establish the units of the study and determine the dimensions of quality. The second stage seeks to apply the evaluation metrics to universities and academic programs. The third stage seeks to analyze the universities and academic programs in terms of the results of the metrics. And finally, the fourth stage consists of performing an analysis of the compliant and non-compliant units of the study.

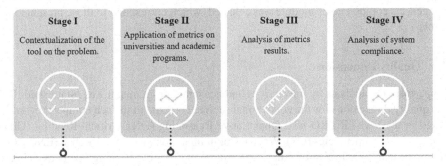

Fig. 1. Research methodology

3.1 Population

The database used contains 12,411 observations, each one representing one student. These observations come from 135 universities and 8 academic programs (Industrial, Civil, Mechanical, Chemical, Chemical, Electronic, Electrical, Aeronautical, and Control Engineering). In this research the database is summarized combining universities and academic programs, leaving a total of 265 observations to analyze (academic programs taking into account the university). It should be noted that the analysis of the research has two approaches, the first is an analysis by universities (135 observations) and the second is by academic programs (265 observations).

3.2 Academic Competencies

The SABER PRO tests are designed by the Colombian Institute for the Evaluation of Education (ICFES) and seek to measure the quality of public and private universities, whether they are accredited or not. The tests are applied to students who complete their

Table 1. Information on the study variables.

Variable	Name	Mean
QR	Quantitative reasoning	77,42
CR	Critical reading	62,20
CS	Citizenship skills	59,19
ENG	English	67,50
WC	Written communication	53,70

Source. Information taken from Dataset of academic performance evolution for engineering students [26].

professional training and consist of two parts: the first evaluates the generic competencies of all professionals, the second evaluates the specific competencies of the academic program to which a student belongs; consequently, for the development of this research, the generic competencies module was selected, which correspond to those presented in Table 1.

3.3 Quality Dimensions

To perform the analysis by universities and academic programs, it was established that the quality dimensions for the educational service correspond to each competency evaluated in the SABER PRO test: Quantitative Reasoning (QR), Critical Reading (CR), Citizenship Competencies (CS), Written Communication (WC) and English (ENG). On the other hand, Table 2 shows the conforming and non-conforming levels associated with the academic competencies. It should be noted that the information contained in the orientation guide for the SABER PRO tests offered by ICFES (2020) was used to establish the levels of conformity and non-conformity. These levels correspond to the achievement reached by the student in each competency, with the lowest level being those students with the lowest scores in the evaluation results, while the highest level corresponds to the students with the highest scores in the evaluation results. On the other hand, an additional interpretation of the levels corresponds to the measurement of the development of academic competencies for problem-solving.

Table 2. Information on the configuration of skill levels.

Competencies	Number of levels	Non-conforming levels	Conforming levels
QR	3	I, II	III
ENG	5	I, II, III	IV, V
CR	3	I, II	III
CS	5	I, II, III	IV, V
WC	8	I, II, III, IV, V	VI, VII, VII

Now, taking into account Table 2, the proportion of compliant and non-compliant observations of the universities in the study is presented at the global level as shown in Table 3.

Table 3. Proportion of compliant and non-compliant results in the universities of the study example at the global level.

Universities	Proportion of compliant	
	Compliant	Non-compliant
Universidad de Los Andes	88,79%	11,21%
Universidad de La Sabana	78,31%	21,69%
Universidad Nacional Sede Medellín	82,67%	17,33%
Universidad del Norte	82,96%	17,04%
Corporación Universitaria Comfacauca	41,20%	58,80%
Universidad Autónoma de Manizales	55,87%	44,13%
Fundación Universitaria Los Libertadores	41,72%	58,28%
Universidad de La Guajira	34,80%	65,20%

4 Results

In this chapter it is important to align the concepts of the Six Sigma methodology to the objective of this research, that is why it is necessary to relate each metric of the model with the study group and educational context, as shown in Table 5.

Table 4. Description of performance in relation to Sigma Level and Yield for the dimensions to be evaluated.

Performance	Sigma level	Yield
Deficient	$Z < 2$	$Y < 69,1\%$
Acceptable	$2 \leq Z \leq 3$	$69,1\% \leq Y \leq 93,3\%$
Good	$3 \leq Z \leq 4$	$93,3\% \leq Y \leq 99,4\%$
Excellent	$Z > 4$	$Y \geq 99,4\%$

Source. Adapted from Evaluation of service quality through Six Sigma in a university document service center [27].

On the other hand, the relationship between the Six Sigma metrics and the educational context in Table 5 is done as follows [28, 29]: The parameter U is the study population, for this research it is the universities. Parameter O corresponds to the opportunities for error found in the competencies evaluated in the SABER PRO test and means the number of times that an observation (student) can fail (see Table 4). Parameter n, on the other hand, is the non-compliant observations. The parameter Y is the performance of the university that varies between 0 and 1, taking into account the reference values established in Table 5. Finally, Defects Per Million Opportunities (DPMO) is the number of observed defects extrapolated to every million opportunities for defects.

Table 5. Quantitative relation of the different concepts of the Six Sigma in the variables of the study.

Metrics	Study definition
U	Total number of universities evaluated (Tests evaluated)
O	Chance of error
n	Total unsatisfactory results (for each competency)
Y	Yield of evaluated universities
DPMO	Defects per million opportunities metric

4.1 Six Sigma Results Analysis

Now, in the same sense, for the representation and application of the Six Sigma metrics in this study, 8 universities were taken as examples, under the criteria that 4 are the universities with the best performances in the SABER PRO tests and the other 4 are universities with average performances in these tests.

Table 6 shows that the Quality Dimension evaluated with the best performance on average is the English proficiency where the highest Yield is 99.79% obtained by the Universidad de Los Andes. On the other hand, the Quality Dimension with the lowest average performance is Critical Reading, where the lowest Yield is 60.20%, which corresponds to the Universidad de La Guajira.

Table 6. Six Sigma Metrics for the Universities taken as an example for this study.

University	Metrics	Quality dimensions evaluated				
		QR	CR	CS	ENG	WC
Universidad de Los Andes	DPMO	31828,47	368018,87	192639,4	14860,3	316693,19
	YIELD	99,46%	93,86%	95,9%	99,79%	94,71%

(continued)

Table 7 shows the proportion of conformity of the results of the academic programs of the universities in the study. The quality dimension with the highest proportion of conformity is English in all academic programs, and the program with the highest proportion

Table 6. (*continued*)

University	Metrics	Quality dimensions evaluated				
		QR	CR	CS	ENG	WC
Universidad de La Sabana	Z	4,43	3,06	3,46	4,48	3,11
	DPMO	223328,7	223328,7	172313,7	23046,3	77197,8
	YIELD	88,82%	88,82%	91,38%	98,84%	96,13%
Universidad de Nacional Sede Medellin	Z	2,73	2,73	2,85	3,81	3,27
	DPMO	15625	477087,73	339160,51	93370,42	486857,47
	YIELD	99,68%	90,44%	93,21%	97,90%	90,25%
Universidad del Norte	Z	4,73	2,85	3	3,54	2,80
	DPMO	195631,11	379779,95	333763,64	44227,22	321505,44
	YIELD	96,08%	90,02%	93,31%	99,11%	93,56%
Corporación Universitaria Comfacauca	Z	3,26	2,79	2,40	4,87	3,08
	DPMO	235294,12	1663348	196078,43	176470,59	164705,88
	YIELD	76,47%	66,73%	80,39%	82,35%	83,52%
Universidad Autónoma de Manizales	Z	2,22	1,93	2,35	2,42	2,47
	DPMO	138235,2	814705,88	629411,76	145098,03	377647,05
	YIELD	95,3%	72,8%	79,01%	95,16%	87,00%
Fundación Universitaria Los Libertadores	Z	3,66	2,10	2,31	3,63	2,65
	DPMO	868007,1	663348	1094315	670994,8	741295,2
	YIELD	78,29%	66,73%	78,11	86,58%	78,11
Universidad de La Guajira	Z	2,29	1,93	2,27	2,62	2,27
	DPMO	893752	1518120	751164,6	751054,6	407095
	YIELD	70,20%	60,28%	81,22%	74,96%	78,82%
	Z	2,03	1,80	2,40	2,18	2,78

Table 7. Proportion of compliance with results by academic program.

Academic program	Percentage of compliance of academic competencies assessed				
	QR	CR	CS	ENG	WC
Industrial engineering	84,73%	67,72%	73,76%	87,91%	69,47%
Civil engineering	90,58%	76,47%	78,52%	86,17%	62,94%
Mechanical engineering	89,76%	73,22%	72,04%	88,58%	62,2%
Chemical engineering	92,55%	79,78%	82,26%	97,87%	71,98%
Electronic engineering	90,54%	81,08%	78,37%	95,94%	55,4%
Electrical engineering	91,66%	81,66%	83,33%	96,66%	76,66%
Control engineering	72,09%	44,18%	44,18%	69,76%	32,55%
Aeronautical engineering	100%	63,63%	72,72%	90,9%	45,45%

of conforming results for this dimension is Chemical Engineering. On the other hand, the quality dimension with the lowest proportion of compliant results in the academic programs is Written Communication, being Chemical Engineering the program with the highest proportion of compliant results for this dimension and Control Engineering the one with the lowest proportion for this dimension (Table 8).

In terms of Six Sigma, the dimension evaluated with the highest performance is the English competency, on average for all academic programs, being Chemical Engineering and Electrical Engineering the programs with the highest performance in this dimension and competency, with Yield = 99.17% and Yield = 99.27% respectively. On the other hand, the Quality Dimension evaluated with the lowest performance on average for all academic programs is Critical Reading. However, the program with the highest performance in this dimension is Electrical Engineering with a Yield = 92.75% and the program with the lowest performance for this dimension is Aeronautical Engineering with a Yield = 72.09%.

4.2 Conformity Analysis

This section analyzes the system according to the level of conformity. Consequently, Fig. 2 shows each competency associated with its percentage of compliant units per level.

Figure 3 shows the percentage of compliant units taking into account the accreditation of the HEI.

On the other hand, Table 9 shows the average results of the competencies by the accredited and non-accredited universities. Note that the competencies with the highest average correspond to ENG and QR for both accredited and non-accredited universities; on the other hand, the competencies with the lowest average are WC and CS for accredited universities and CR and CS for non-accredited universities.

Similarly, as Table 9 is developed, an analysis is performed for the average of compliant and non-compliant units (see Table 10). As can be seen, the competencies with

Table 8. Six Sigma metrics for the academic programs of the Universities used in the study at a global level.

Academic program	Metrics	Quality dimensions assessed				
		QR	CR	CS	ENG	WC
Industrial engineering	DPMO	1122120,01	1869111,87	3384732,63	789371,82	721147,4
	YIELD	85,95%	76,38%	85,81%	90,01%	90,98%
	Z	2,93	1,78	2,31	3,13	2,88
Civil engineering	DPMO	264873,18	483218,27	265633,21	229794,36	290451,56
	YIELD	93,37%	84,94%	93,27%	94,25%	92,73%
	Z	3,69	2,66	3,03	3,40	2,96
Mechanical engineering	DPMO	659191,17	1310864,36	956860,22	540641,80	672267,10
	YIELD	89,01%	78,15%	94,12%	99,17%	94,08%
	Z	3,47	2,82	3,06	3,96	3,06
Chemical engineering	DPMO	100951,81	291231,46	176226,80	24722,03	77383,50
	YIELD	96,63%	90,28%	94,12%	99,17%	96,08%
	Z	3,47	2,82	3,06	3,96	3,06
Electronic engineering	DPMO	260683,75	697115,38	437179,36	111111,11	486495,71
	YIELD	93,48%	82,57%	87,81%	97,22%	87,83%
	Z	3,88	2,56	2,75	4,43	2,78
Electrical engineering	DPMO	54347,82	144409,93	72463,76	14492,75	100621,11
	YIELD	97,28%	92,75%	96,37%	99,27%	94,96%
	Z	4,05	3,01	3,97	4,34	3,14
Control engineering	DPMO	0	181818,18	90909,09	30303,03	109090,90
	YIELD	100%	81,81%	90,90%	96,96%	89,09%
	Z	5	2,40	2,83	3,37	2,73
Aeronautical engineering	DPMO	139534,88	279069,76	186046,51	100775,19	134883,7
	YIELD	86,04%	72,09%	81,39%	89,92%	86,51%
	Z	2,58	2,08	2,39	2,77	2,60

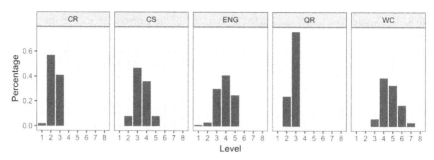

Fig. 2. Distribution of the study population.

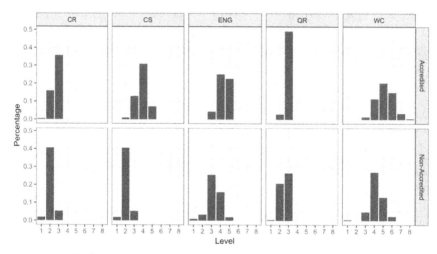

Fig. 3. Proportion of accreditation of the universities in the study.

Table 9. Average of competencies by accreditation.

Competencies	Accredited	Non-accredited
QR	81,83	65,26
CR	67,02	48,98
ENG	72,40	53,16
WC	61,42	49,39
CS	63,54	47,58

the highest averages are CR and CR for both the group of compliant and non-compliant units. On the other hand, the competencies with the lowest averages are WC and CS for the conforming group and ENG and CS for the non-conforming group.

Table 10. Average of competencies per compliance.

Competencies	Compliant	Non-compliant
QR	79,43	57,41
CR	74,65	49,55
ENG	72,68	48,46
WC	69,83	49,25
CS	69,66	46,15

Now, with the support of Fig. 3, Table 11 is constructed, showing the averages of the competencies according to the conformity and accreditation of the unit. It is observed that the highest averages of the competencies for the accredited and compliant universities correspond to CR and CR; the lowest averages correspond to the competencies WC and CS. For the non-accredited and compliant universities, the highest averages are for CR and CR; in contrast, the competencies with the lowest averages are WC and CS. On the other hand, for the accredited and non-compliant universities, the highest averages are for the competencies QR and CR, in contrast, the competencies with the lowest averages are ENG and CS. Finally, the competencies with the highest averages of the non-accredited and non-compliant universities are ENG and QR, in contrast, the competencies with the lowest averages are WC and CS.

Finally, an analysis is presented in the Pareto diagram (see Fig. 4), in the diagram it can be observed that 76.81% of the non-compliant results are concentrated in the first

Table 11. Average of competencies by compliance and accreditation.

Competencies	State	Accredited	Non-accredited
QR	Compliant	83,95	74,90
	Non-compliant	61,11	57,09
CR	Compliant	75,08	72,03
	Non-compliant	56,84	47,84
ENG	Compliant	74,87	68,73
	Non-compliant	53,61	48,06
WC	Compliant	70,54	68,23
	Non-compliant	54,86	47,43
CS	Compliant	70,54	67,27
	Non-compliant	51,72	44,96

three competencies which are Written Communication (WC), Critical Reading (CR), and Citizenship Competencies (CS). Therefore, this indicates that the performance of the study population can be improved if they focus on these three competencies, and consequently the quality level of the HEIs will increase.

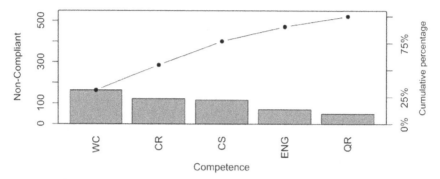

Fig. 4. Cause analysis using the Pareto diagram.

5 Discussion

As is well known, the success of the application of the Six Sigma methodology depends mainly on the identification and selection of the factors that influence the quality of the system being evaluated [30]. In this regard, our research takes as a premise that professional performance and success depends on the development of students' core competencies [31, 32], therefore, the analysis resources for this research are students' professional core competencies: Quantitative Reasoning, Critical Reading, English, Written Communication, and Citizenship Competencies.

Reviewing the applications of Six Sigma in the literature to evaluate educational quality we found that: Paramasivam and Muthusamy [33] develop research that aims to identify the critical factors that are necessary in the working world, and because of this, engineers must have them in their curriculum, through the DMAIC approach of Six Sigma, they manage to identify that the critical factors are: Washington Accord, Outcome Based Education (OBE), Problem Based Learning (PBL), Theory for Inventive Problem Solving (TRIZ), Project-Based Learning, Case-Based Learning (CBL), internships and Continuous Quality Improvement (CQI). Mehrabi [30] in his work identifies that the success of Six Sigma implementation in the educational sector depends on the selection of factors, therefore, the author proposes to consider in the implementation of Six Sigma factors such as management participation, organizational commitment, project management, skills management, cultural change, and continuous training. In contrast to the works presented, Adina-Petruta and Roxana [34] in their work present how the Six Sigma methodology integrated with the ISO 9000 quality model helps the development, continuous improvement, and success of HEIs. On the other hand, Ameen Abdulla et al. [35] in their research seek to ensure quality according to the criteria proposed by the

National Board of Accreditation India (NBA), to achieve their objective the authors used various Six Sigma techniques under the DMAIC methodology, within their results they identified that the versatility of the program curriculum, laboratories, workshops and credibility among universities are important factors for quality assurance, in addition, they add that with the Six Sigma tool it is possible to mitigate the defects found. Finally, we can highlight the research of MacIel-Monteon et al. [36], these authors propose the design and validation of an instrument to evaluate the implementation of the critical success factors during the execution of the Six Sigma methodology for the improvement of HEIs. Of eleven factors studied in their work, the authors determined as truly critical the participation, managerial commitment, linkage of Six Sigma with the institutional strategy, linkage of Six Sigma with suppliers, communication, and selection of team members.

From the works presented above, it can be pointed out that specific factors are selected that are mostly applied to a particular area of knowledge; on the other hand, in MacIel-Monteon's research, a significant contribution is generated by proposing a methodology to validate the implementation of Six Sigma according to the selected factors. Considering the above, it can be highlighted that the present research makes use of the basic competencies as inputs of the Six Sigma methodology to generate a greater opportunity for improvement on the system. In addition, our methodology can be applied to any area of knowledge because these basic competencies are transversal for all professionals.

6   Conclusions

The significant contribution of this research is the evaluation of the educational quality of universities in Colombia and their respective programs with the Six Sigma tool. The tool is usually applied to the manufacturing sector and gradually has been implemented in other sectors such as education. In this research, the evaluation process of the educational quality is highlighted using as inputs of our system the results obtained in the standardized tests SABER PRO in the Colombian universities of the engineering programs.

In the same way, the results of this research show the pertinence that exists to combine and structure concepts of educational quality with the metrics of Six Sigma, allowing to design a standard of the performance of the universities for the improvement of the quality of the educational system employing the contextualization of Six Sigma. This is important because it allows improving the education sector in Colombia, allowing to continue forming and building the professionals of the country that will contribute from their different knowledge for the development of the society.

Following this same order of ideas, the following conclusions can be drawn: first, the quality of the education sector presents an acceptable performance, taking into account its sigma level and Yield (2.17 and 75%). Surely, the methodology applied for this study allowed a quantitative analysis, through the use of the dimensions of quality proposed for this study (academic competencies) and the relationship with the metrics of the Six Sigma tool, which made it possible to perform a holistic evaluation and analysis of the educational service. However, this research is left as a basis for future works related to the evaluation of the educational quality in universities and its contribution to the quality of the Colombian educational sector.

References

1. Cardiel-Ortega, J.J., Baeza-Serrato, R., Lizarraga-Morales, R.A.: Development of a system dynamics model based on Six Sigma methodology. Ingeniería e Investigación **37**, 80–90 (2017). https://doi.org/10.15446/ing.investig.v37n1.62270
2. Costa, L.B.M., Filho, M.G., Fredendall, L.D., Ganga, G.M.D.: The effect of Lean Six Sigma practices on food industry performance: implications of the Sector's experience and typical characteristics. Food Control **112**, 107110 (2020). https://doi.org/10.1016/j.foodcont.2020.107110
3. Costa, L.B.M., Filho, M.G., Fredendall, L.D., Ganga, G.M.D.: Lean six sigma in the food industry: Construct development and measurement validation. Int. J. Prod. Econ. **231**, 107843 (2021). https://doi.org/10.1016/j.ijpe.2020.107843
4. Gastelum-Acosta, C., Limon-Romero, J., Maciel-Monteon, M., Baez-Lopez, Y.: Seis Sigma en Instituciones de Educación Superior en México. Información tecnológica **29**(5), 91–100 (2018). https://doi.org/10.4067/S0718-07642018000500091
5. De La Hoz, E., Zuluaga, R., Mendoza, A.: Assessing and classification of academic efficiency in engineering teaching programs. ERIES J. **14**, 41–52 (2021). https://doi.org/10.7160/eriesj.2021.140104
6. Guzman, J.H.E., Zuluaga-Ortiz, R.A., Barrios-Miranda, D.A., Delahoz-Dominguez, E.J.: Information and communication technologies (ICT) in the processes of distribution and use of knowledge in higher education institutions (HEIs). Procedia Comput. Sci. **198**, 644–649 (2022). https://doi.org/10.1016/j.procs.2021.12.300
7. Bourner, T., Rospigliosi, A., Heath, L.: The fully functioning university. In: Bourner, T., Rospigliosi, A., Heath, L. (eds.) The Fully Functioning University, pp. 7–39. Emerald Publishing Limited (2020). https://doi.org/10.1108/978-1-83982-498-220201003
8. Moreno-Brid, J.C., Ruiz-Nápoles, P.: La educación superior y el desarrollo económico en América Latina. Revista iberoamericana de educación superior. **1**, 171–188 (2010)
9. Amador Muñoz, L.V., Martínez Rodríguez, F.M.: Educación y desarrollo socio-económico. Contextos educativos **83**, 83–97 (2010) https://doi.org/10.18172/con.628
10. Delahoz-Dominguez, E.J., Fontalvo, T., Zuluaga, R.: Evaluation of academic productivity of citizen competencies in the teaching of engineering by using the Malmquist index. Formación Universitaria **13**, 27–34 (2020). https://doi.org/10.4067/S0718-50062020000500027
11. Stanescu, C.L.V.: Modelos de evaluación de la calidad del servicio: Caracterización y análisis. **21**, 57–76 (2015)
12. Chui, T.B., Ahmad, M.S.B., Bassim, F.B.A., Zaimi, N.B.A.: Evaluation of service quality of private higher education using service improvement matrix. Procedia – Soc. Behav. Sci. **224**, 132–140 (2016). https://doi.org/10.1016/j.sbspro.2016.05.417
13. Yousapronpaiboon, K.: SERVQUAL: measuring higher education service quality in Thailand. Procedia. Soc. Behav. Sci. **116**, 1088–1095 (2014). https://doi.org/10.1016/j.sbspro.2014.01.350
14. Hien, N.M.: A study on evaluation of e-government service quality. World Acad. Sci., Eng. Technol. Int. J. Humanit. Soc. Sci. **8**(1), 16–19 (2014)
15. Lee, H., Kim, C.: Benchmarking of service quality with data envelopment analysis. Expert Syst. Appl. **41**, 3761–3768 (2014). https://doi.org/10.1016/j.eswa.2013.12.008
16. Suresh, K.M., Asokan, P., Vinodh, S.: Application of design for Six Sigma methodology to an automotive component. Int. J. Six Sigma Competitive Advantage **10**(1), 1 (2016). https://doi.org/10.1504/IJSSCA.2016.080446

17. Suman, G., Prajapati, D.R.: Statistical analysis of the researches carried out on Lean and Six Sigma applications in healthcare industry. Int. J. Qual. Eng. Technol. **7**, 1–38 (2018). https://doi.org/10.1504/IJQET.2018.094667

18. Ishak, A., Siregar, K., Asfriyati, H.N.: Quality control with Six Sigma DMAIC and grey failure mode effect anaysis (FMEA): a review. IOP Conf. Series: Mater. Sci. Eng. **505**(1), 012057 (2019). https://doi.org/10.1088/1757-899X/505/1/012057

19. Zambrano, N., Alá, A.: Implementación de la metodología seis sigma para el mejoramiento continuo del proceso de venta de servicios tecnológicos y comunicacionales en Ecuadortelecom S.A. (2014)

20. Zare Mehrjerdi, Y.: Six-Sigma: methodology, tools and its future. Assem. Autom. **31**, 79–88 (2011). https://doi.org/10.1108/01445151111104209

21. Hsieh, Y.-J., Huang, L.-Y., Wang, C.-T.: A framework for the selection of Six Sigma projects in services: case studies of banking and health care services in Taiwan. Serv. Bus. **6**, 243–264 (2012). https://doi.org/10.1007/s11628-012-0134-1

22. Shokri, A.: Six Sigma in supply chain. In: Ramanathan, U., Ramanathan, R. (eds.) Supply Chain Strategies, Issues and Models, pp. 63–98. Springer, London, London (2014)

23. Surange, V.G.: Implementation of Six Sigma to reduce cost of quality: a case study of automobile sector. J. Fail. Anal. Prev. **15**(2), 282–294 (2015). https://doi.org/10.1007/s11668-015-9927-6

24. LeMahieu, P.G., Nordstrum, L.E., Cudney, E.A.: Six Sigma in education. Qual. Assur. Educ. **25**, 91–108 (2017). https://doi.org/10.1108/QAE-12-2016-0082

25. Svensson, C., Antony, J., Ba-Essa, M., Bakhsh, M., Albliwi, S.: A Lean Six Sigma program in higher education. Int. J. Qual. Reliab. Manag. **32**, 951–969 (2015). https://doi.org/10.1108/IJQRM-09-2014-0141

26. Delahoz-Dominguez, E., Zuluaga, R., Fontalvo-Herrera, T.: Dataset of academic performance evolution for engineering students. Data Brief **30**, 105537 (2020). https://doi.org/10.1016/j.dib.2020.105537

27. Delahoz-Dominguez, E.J., Fontalvo, T.J., Fontalvo, O.M.: Evaluación de la calidad del servicio por medio de seis sigma en un centro de atención documental en una universidad. Form. Univ. **13**, 93–102 (2020). https://doi.org/10.4067/S0718-50062020000200093

28. Darmawan, A., Bahri, S., Putra, A.T.B.: Six Sigma Implementation in quality evaluation of raw material: a case study. IOP Conf. Series: Mater. Sci. Eng. **875**(1), 012065 (2020). https://doi.org/10.1088/1757-899X/875/1/012065

29. Tenera, A., Pinto, L.C.: A Lean Six Sigma (LSS) project management improvement model. Procedia. Soc. Behav. Sci. **119**, 912–920 (2014). https://doi.org/10.1016/j.sbspro.2014.03.102

30. Mehrabi, J.: Application of Six-Sigma in educational quality management. Procedia. Soc. Behav. Sci. **47**, 1358–1362 (2012). https://doi.org/10.1016/j.sbspro.2012.06.826

31. Jury, M., Smeding, A., Stephens, N.M., Nelson, J.E., Aelenei, C., Darnon, C.: The experience of low-SES students in higher education: psychological barriers to success and interventions to reduce social-class inequality: low-SES students in higher education. J. Soc. Issues **73**, 23–41 (2017). https://doi.org/10.1111/josi.12202

32. Nagy, M., Molontay, R.: Predicting dropout in higher education based on secondary school performance. In: 2018 IEEE 22nd International Conference on Intelligent Engineering Systems (INES). pp. 000389–000394. IEEE, Las Palmas de Gran Canaria (2018)

33. Paramasivam, S., Muthusamy, K.: Study of critical success factors in engineering education curriculum development using Six-Sigma methodology. Procedia. Soc. Behav. Sci. **56**, 652–661 (2012). https://doi.org/10.1016/j.sbspro.2012.09.700

34. Adina-Petruţa, P., Roxana, S.: Integrating six sigma with quality management systems for the development and continuous improvement of higher education institutions. Procedia. Soc. Behav. Sci. **143**, 643–648 (2014). https://doi.org/10.1016/j.sbspro.2014.07.456

35. Ameen Abdulla, M.S., Mohammed Navas, O.P., Amal, M.S., Nizam, B., Kavilal, E.G.: Quality assurance in education based on six sigma tool. In: Proceedings of the International Conference on Industrial Engineering and Operations Management, pp. 2347–2360 (2020)
36. MacIel-Monteon, M., Limon-Romero, J., Gastelum-Acosta, C., Tlapa, D., Baez-Lopez, Y., Solano-Lamphar, H.A.: Measuring critical success factors for six sigma in higher education institutions: development and validation of a surveying instrument. IEEE Access. **8**, 1813–1823 (2020). https://doi.org/10.1109/ACCESS.2019.2962521

Machine Learning and Artificial Neural Networks

A Recommender System for Digital Newspaper Readers Based on Random Forest

Enrique Delahoz-Dominguez[1] (ID), Rohemi Zuluaga-Ortiz[2(✉)] (ID),
Adel Mendoza-Mendoza[3] (ID), Jey Escorcia[4] (ID), Francisco Moreira-Villegas[5] (ID),
and Pedro Oliveros-Eusse[6] (ID)

[1] Engineering Faculty, Universidad Tecnológica de Bolívar, Cartagena, Colombia
edelahoz@utb.edu.co
[2] Engineering Faculty, Universidad del Sinú, Cartagena, Colombia
rohemi.zuluaga@unisinu.edu.co
[3] Engineering Faculty, Universidad del Atlántico, Barranquilla, Colombia
[4] Faculty of Business Sciences, Universidad de la Costa, Barranquilla, Colombia
[5] Faculty of Natural Sciences and Mathematics, Escuela Superior Politécnica del Litoral,
Guayaquil, Ecuador
[6] Faculty of Social Sciences and Humanities, Universidad de la Costa, Barranquilla, Colombia

Abstract. In this research, the potential of machine learning methods based on decision trees (DT) and Random Forest (RF) models developed in the context of classifying readers of a digital newspaper. For this purpose, the number of visits of users to each section of the newspaper in a 3-month interval has been taken into account. The models of DT and RF developed in this paper classify the profiles of readers who access the journal with an accuracy of 98.07% and AUC value of 99.27%, thus demonstrating that it serves as a valid tool for making strategic and operational decisions when creating, manage and present content in the user – website interaction.

Keywords: Random Forest · Classification · Newspapers · Supervised learning · Recommender systems

1 Introduction

Machine learning (ML) is an evolving branch of computational algorithms that are designed to emulate human intelligence by learning from the surrounding environment [1, 2]. Also, it's a branch of artificial intelligence (AI) that creates data-based models to identify hidden patterns and non-contextual information about a phenomenon without establishing the intrinsic relationships that characterize the problem [3]. Thus, machine learning algorithms can gradually improve their performance by counting a more significant amount of data and uncovering hidden patterns in complicated, heterogeneous, and high-dimensional data sets [4], these types of algorithms automatically alter or adapt their architecture through repetition, so they become better at achieving the desired task [1]. Machine Learning is gradually evolving, is, and will be a potential game-changer in the history of computing, logical algorithm patterns, and the design of complex data structures [5]. Consequently, the ML has become the key technology for developing many real applications in different fields: from predicting complex diseases [6], the bankruptcy forecast for companies [7], the internet search engines [8] educational data mining [9–11], speech recognition and computer vision [12].

In the field of client management in virtual environments, there are machine learning algorithms, such as Logistic Regression (LR), Gradient Boosting Machines, Support Vector Machines (SVMs), Decision Trees (DTs), and Random Forests (RFs), which can relate variables of non-linear and heterogeneous inputs to a pattern and response, even when relationships between model variables cannot be determined due to their complexity, high variability or lack of business sense [13–15].

Nowadays, sizeable Internet-based companies use Machine learning models, which have the capabilities and resources to develop data collection and modeling. However, it isn't common to find ML models in the context of small businesses. Our research is designed in a regional digital newspaper, categorized as Small and medium-sized enterprises (SME'S), and characterized by a small volume of readers and a low proportion of subscribers. The above features could compromise the algorithm learning process and make unsuitable recommendations for a machine learning model. Among several classification algorithms. As it is cited in the work of Akinsola [16] Decision Trees (DT) are trees that classify instances by sorting them based on feature values. Each node in a decision tree represents a value that the node can assume. Also, instances are classified starting at the root node and sorted based on their feature values. Decision tree learning, that are used in Data Mining and Machine Learning, uses a decision tree as a predictive model which maps observations about an item to conclusions about the item's target value. Moreover, the DT has characteristics that are particularly suited to classifying website users. The DT can be understood intuitively, even without statistical or mathematical training, and can visualize the results, thus reinforcing its understanding. On the other hand, DTs can deal with missing NA values and combine categorical and numeric data in the same model while developing a selection of main characteristics parallel to the modeling.

The transformations in the way people keep themselves informed, associated with the revolution of social networks and the excessive supply of information, force the digital media to understand the behavior of its readers to be competitive [17].

It's not a secret that the newspaper industry has been in a steady decline triggered by a loss in readership and ad revenue which have been migrating to other media, most notably digital [18]. Additionally, according to [19] Digital Innovation has been the engine to drive change in the industry of news and media. Even though the transition from print to digital started more than two decades ago, the changes to news and media companies during this pandemic time have been dramatic. However, to take advantage of this evolution, news and media firms are leveraging the strength of their digital platforms to generate previously unattainable insights into reader behavior. Companies are enhancing both reader engagement and online revenue success by employing this information with greater sophistication. Knowing this, it's important for this type of companies to keep improving their services and intern processes, in order to keep them in force. The Pandemic has accelerated the Digital Transformation for everything and everyone, and only the ones that take this threat as an opportunity will succeed in the present and in the near future. So, to keep with the dynamics of the business in the digital world require digital newspapers to understand their readers' behavior. So, through the present research, the following research questions are answered. How to identify the key variables in the consumption flow of the digital newspaper reader? How to define a machine learning model to classify digital newspaper readers? How to graphically represent the profiles of readers of digital newspapers to have a comprehensive perspective? In correspondence with the previously proposed, a method of classifying readers of digital newspapers is presented, identifying the significant newspaper sections and the representative classification of the readers according to the use of the website.

2 Materials and Methods

2.1 Data

The database comprises six hundred eighty-nine readers who have interacted with the newspaper from January to March 2019. We assessed the number of visits made by each user to each newspaper section (see Table 1) to identify the intensity of use of the website. Thus, the average activity in each section allows defining standardized behavior vectors, independent of the number of visits to the newspaper. For reproducibility purposes, only the information corresponding to users who visited the newspaper six times in the last three months has been used. The Observations corresponding to 70% (482) of the total data used in the study correspond to the model's training phase, and the remaining 30% (207) of readers will be evaluation elements. The new datasets developed in the cross-validation process will train the Decision tree and Random Forest, models.

Table 1. Summary of the predictor variables.

Section	Min	Max	Mean	SD
Main page	0	55.5	16.7	12.1
Politics	0	44.4	24.6	11.1
Economy	0	20	4.2	5.4
Sports	0	25	5.62	6.5
Culture	0	25	6.13	6.8
Interview	0	33.3	13.1	6.5
Opinion	0	44.4	17.4	9.5
International	0	44.4	19.2	8.9
Video	0	100	65	31.6

2.2 Target Variables

The output variables of the classification process represent the reader's profile: Visual, Informed, and Net-NEE, as described in [20].

Readers with a visual profile show a high utilization rate of videos and little relation with reading contents. This profile resembles those known in the literature as digital natives, those who prefer the graphics to the texts; they use external shortcuts to access the Web and frequently share information with their friends on social networks [21].

Consequently, readers in the Informed profile highlight the widespread use of the newspaper sections and show global interest in what happens in their environment; this group represents 50.5% of the total sample of users used for this study. This profile is like that of digital immigrants, who prefer sequential processes. It is as if they learn a new language, culture, and communication approach in social terms.

The NetNee profile responds to the behavior of little interest in the newspaper's contents. It hardly interacts with the other sections; its entrance to the Web is through external platforms, such as social networks or forums, which shows that, at the first moment, he engages with the information. Still, when he enters the Web, he leaves immediately. According to Hernández et al. [22], this profile could be similar to the sniffer visitor, a silent participant, with a passive activity; being there, reading, watching the messages in the forums, stalking, but in no way contributes nor comment on the generated discussion.

2.3 Decision Trees

Decision trees (DT) are machine learning models that resemble the shape of a tree, where the leaves represent the output categories, and the branches represent the partitions of the predictive variables that determine the results of classification or regression. Also, Decision tree classifiers usually employ post-pruning techniques that evaluate the performance of decision trees, as they are pruned by using a validation set [16].

The decision tree implemented is based on the architecture of the "CART" algorithm developed using the rpart package [23] of the software RSTUDIO. The data set was divided repeatedly through the cross-validation technique during the training process, creating ten new data sets, thus generating a trial and error process to characterize the parameters. The Gini Diversity Index (GDI) was considered as an optimization criterion for the models for evaluating the models. The GDI measures the level of impurity of each node; therefore, a node will be pure when all the observations belong to the same category.

The design process of the decision tree has been developed in the following way: The minimum number required for the creation of a participation node is equal to ten and at least one observation for a response node. The tree creation procedure was repeated five hundred times, and each time a different subset of data was tested. Beforehand, it was expected to observe a high variability between the performance of these 500 DT.

Pruning

Pruning methods aim to simplify decisions trees that overfitted data [24] which consists in examining the nodes that have a more negligible effect in the general classification. In other words, pruning means changing the model by deleting the child nodes of a branch node. The pruned node is regarded as a leaf node. Leaf nodes cannot be pruned [25]. In this research, the pruning process was applied to penalize the decision tree's complexity, ensuring significant partitions were involved in the model.

2.4 Random Forest

Random Forest is a well-known and powerful supervised classification method. Due to its high accuracy and robustness, and some ability to offer insights by the ranking of its features, RF has effectively been applied to various Machine Learning applications. RF consists of a set of decision trees, each of which is generated by the bagging algorithm with no pruning, forming a "Forest" of classifiers voting for a particular class [26]. Random Forest models are methods articulated between machine learning algorithms; it entails the repeated and growing building of many decision trees using an aggregation method called bootstrapping [27]. In Breiman's approach, each tree in the collection is formed by first selecting at random, at each node, a small group of input coordinates to split on, and secondly, by calculating the best split based on these features in the training set [28]. Thus, generating several decision trees with varied variable compositions such that each tree provides an independent outcome, followed by a democratic approach in which the category with the most votes is chosen as the final output. The ability to generate different responses for each decision tree and then combine them into general forecast results in robust models that are less susceptible to extreme values than a basic decision tree, boosting the model's prediction and classification capabilities.

Also, to train an RF, it's needed two parameters, the number of tress (ntree) in the forest and the number of randomly selected features/variables used to evaluate at each tree node (mtry), must be supplied, as well as a training database with ground-truth class labels [26].

The RF model incorporates a variable selection strategy, which enables it to handle data sets with many variables if preceding processes are used to minimize dimensions. Additionally, the model allows for determining the importance of each variable for correctly classifying observations using a permutation test.

The Random Forest model used consists of 500 trees created under the following guidelines. We considered three as the minimum number of observations that give rise to a response node. The number of variables used to create the trees varied from 4 to 8.

2.5 Performance Metrics

The classification process's success is set by the difference between the anticipated and actual values. The True Positive (VP), True Negative (VN), False Positive (FP), and False Negative (FN) metrics all describe this relationship [2]. The model's evaluation will calculate the Correct classification rate (C), Kappa (K) [29], and the area under the receiver operating characteristic curve (ROC) [30]. The region beneath the curve AUC (area under the ROC curve) shows the rate of TP and FP at various thresholds of discrimination. An AUC value equal to one indicates a model with perfect classification. Meanwhile, an AUC equivalent to 0.5 represents an utterly rando model.

3   Results

3.1   Exploratory Data Analysis

A visual representation of the data was created using Principal Component Analysis (PCA). Initially, we arranged data according to the frequency of viewing and use of newspaper sections. The first two principal components (PCs) account for 80.4% of the data. Figure 1 depicts the reader's activity in two dimensions. As a result, the plot's points represent readers, and the shapes respond to each profile.

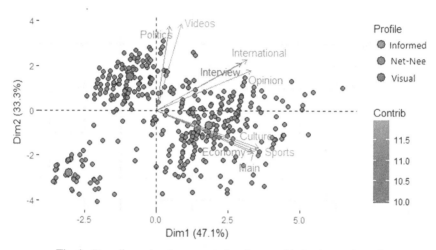

Fig. 1. Two-dimensional representation for users' behavior on the web.

The greater the contribution value, the more significantly the variable contributes to the principal components. As a result, the variable that has the tiniest information is Interview. The informed group (circles) is distributed throughout the horizontal axis, in the growing direction of the Main, Sports, Culture, Economic, International, Opinion, and Interview sections. This location maximizes the relations of these users with the newspaper, representing high visiting frequency and interaction. On the other hand, the Visual readers (triangles) allocated on the top of the vertical axis interact with the videos and Politics sections but in the lower position of the growing vectors. On the opposite, the NetNee users (squares), are located in the third quadrant of the plane; this allocation reduces the bulk of sections since they are growing in the opposite direction of their growth, indicating a lack of interest in interacting with the newspaper.

3.2   Decision Tree Results

The decision tree shown in Fig. 2 was developed after creating 500 trees, trained in different subsets of data, exchanging the roles of training and evaluation among them. The decision tree correctly predicted the type of reader with 93.1% for training and

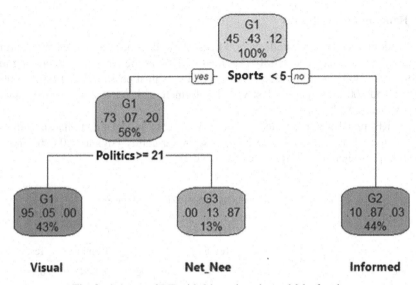

Fig. 2. Schema of DT with 3 branch nodes and 3 leaf nodes.

88.1% for the test. So, the decision tree DT can identify reader types G1, G2, and G3 with 81%, 100%, and 90.4% sensitivity, respectively.

In Fig. 3, we can see the ROC results with an AUC-TRAIN = 0.97 and AUC-TEST = 0.95 for the decision tree predictions. From the nine sections of the diary used for the classification process, the decision tree identifies the "sports" and "politics" sections as the critical discrimination variables. None of the remaining seven sections has been used by the decision tree model to predict the reader's profile.

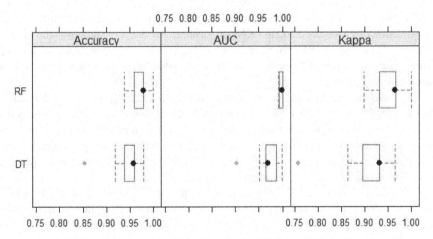

Fig. 3. Boxplot illustrating the results for the three metrics selected

3.3 Random Forest Results

The Random Forest model, built on 500 trees, showed an accuracy of 98.55% during the training phase and successfully classified 97.10% of the test cases, improving the performance of the decision tree. The specificity evaluation shows values of 100%, 94.68%, and 100% for the profiles, Visual, Informed, and NetNee, respectively, and a global value of AUC-test = 99.27%.

The RF model was replicated ten times to test the model's compliance with the decision tree. The results indicate a decrease in variability (sigma = 0.006) and an overall improvement in performance (see Table 2).

Table 2. Performance metrics of DT and RF models.

Metric	DT		RF	
	Training	Test	Training	Test
Accuracy (%)	0.9376	0.8696	0.9751	0.9807
Kappa	0.8963	0.7899	0.9588	0.9685
The area under the ROC curve (AUC)	0.9724	0.9519	0.9967	0.9927

4 Discussion

The AUC performance metric of 99.27%, achieved by the model for the test phase, demonstrates the relevance of the machine learning model presented in this research to be replicated and reproduced in other web user classification environments. The results obtained are similar to those found by Adeniyi et al. [31] in their study on the classification of web users using the KNN algorithm; the object of study was the Simple Syndication system (RSS), achieving 70% accuracy in the recommendations' quality, which means the level of fit of the news recommended to the user according to their immediate requirements.

The Random Forest model yielded a robust result, significantly improving the performance of the DT-based model. The structure of the model makes it possible to identify the Visual, Informed, and NetNee reader profiles with very high precision. The robustness of the model allows its implementation as a system for recommending content to users of a digital newspaper, generating a continuous learning process for updating profiles according to readers' interaction with the website.

It is essential to express the particularities to the development of this study, which makes it interesting for small digital businesses, which do not have the resources or the infrastructure necessary to access advanced recommendation systems.

As far as the researchers' knowledge is concerned, the scientific community is presented with a novel model for classifying readers in a digital newspaper, using profiles associated with the frequency and use of newspaper sections as classification variables. The predictions reached by the DT and RF models are generated from the real behavior of readers, resulting in a robust model for making strategic and operational decisions in the administration of a digital newspaper. Therefore, using this model by other means of digital communication and comparing results will generate a scalable model.

5   Conclusion

The interaction between users and the newspaper's website has been modeled effectively, using the nine sections of the newspaper as predictor variables, using the frequency of visit, and use of the sections to make up the dataset of 489 users. The policy and sports sections have the most significant discrimination capacity to determine user profiles: Visual, Informed and NetNee.

The model identifies users using the sports section less than 5% and the policy section greater than 21% as a reader of the "Visual" profile with a 95% probability. Those readers with 5% or more use of the sports section will classify for the "Informed" profile with an 87% probability. Users who consume the politics section greater than 21% and sports less than 5% will be in the NetNee profile.

The Random Forest model consistently presented better results than the Decision Tree for the three-performance metrics. The model based on 500 trees yielded a 98.07%, 96.85%, and 0.9927 for accuracy, Kappa and AUC, respectively, evidencing a robust, replicable, and reproducible model.

This research could help this newspaper to fully take advantage of this new insights to improve the User Interface and Experience, so they can build a strong engagement with their readers and keep new readers into the newspaper by offering a tailor-made service for each group of readers that the newspaper has. This kind of study allow the newspaper to take decisions based on data, meaning that all the decisions taken would be fully substantiated and efficient. Taking decisions based on the results of this research would allow resources saving for the newspaper at the time to make or implement any strategies for gaining or retaining their clients well known as readers. This kind of approach is a combination of innovation, technology, statistical methods and Data Science. A solution up to the mark in this digital transformation era.

References

1. El Naqa, I., Murphy, M.J.: What is machine learning? In: El Naqa, I., Li, R., Murphy, M.J. (eds.) Machine Learning in Radiation Oncology, pp. 3–11. Springer, Cham (2015). https://doi.org/10.1007/978-3-319-18305-3_1
2. De La Hoz, E., Zuluaga, R., Mendoza, A.: Assessing and classification of academic efficiency in engineering teaching programs. J. Effi. Responsib. Educ. Sci. **14**, 41–52 (2021)
3. Escorcia Guzman, J.H., Zuluaga-Ortiz, R.A., Barrios-Miranda, D.A., Delahoz-Dominguez, E.J.: Information and Communication Technologies (ICT) in the processes of distribution and use of knowledge in Higher Education Institutions (HEIs). Procedia Comput. Sci. **198**, 644–649 (2022)
4. Suthaharan, S.: Big data classification: problems and challenges in network intrusion prediction with machine learning. ACM SIGMETRICS Perform. Eval. Rev. **41**, 70–73 (2014)
5. Nayak, A., Dutta, K.: Impacts of machine learning and artificial intelligence on mankind. In: 2017 International Conference on Intelligent Computing and Control (I2C2) pp. 1–3. IEEE, Coimbatore (2017)

6. Obermeyer, Z., Emanuel, E.J.: Predicting the future — big data, machine learning, and clinical medicine. N. Engl. J. Med. **375**, 1216–1219 (2016)
7. Yu, Q., Miche, Y., Séverin, E., Lendasse, A.: Bankruptcy prediction using extreme learning machine and financial expertise. Neurocomputing **128**, 296–302 (2014)
8. Mahdavinejad, M.S., Rezvan, M., Barekatain, M., Adibi, P., Barnaghi, P., Sheth, A.P.: Machine learning for internet of things data analysis: a survey. Digit. Commun. Netw. **4**, 161–175 (2018)
9. De-La-Hoz, E.J., De-La-Hoz, E.J., Fontalvo, T.J., De-La-Hoz, E.J., De-La-Hoz, E.J., Fontalvo, T.J.: Methodology of machine learning for the classification and prediction of users in virtual education environments. Inf. Tecnológica. **30**, 247–254 (2019)
10. Delahoz-Dominguez, E.J., Fontalvo, T., Zuluaga, R.: Evaluation of academic productivity of citizen competencies in the teaching of engineering by using the Malmquist index. Form. Univ. **13**, 27–34 (2020)
11. Delahoz-Dominguez, E., Zuluaga, R., Fontalvo-Herrera, T.: Dataset of academic performance evolution for engineering students. Data Brief **30**, 105537 (2020)
12. Kourou, K., Exarchos, T.P., Exarchos, K.P., Karamouzis, M.V., Fotiadis, D.I.: Machine learning applications in cancer prognosis and prediction. Comput. Struct. Biotechnol. J. **13**, 8–17 (2015)
13. Erevelles, S., Fukawa, N., Swayne, L.: Big Data consumer analytics and the transformation of marketing. J. Bus. Res. **69**, 897–904 (2016)
14. Stalidis, G., Karapistolis, D., Vafeiadis, A.: Marketing decision support using artificial intelligence and knowledge modeling: application to tourist destination management. Procedia Soc. Behav. Sci. **175**, 106–113 (2015)
15. Sundsøy, P., Bjelland, J., Iqbal, A.M., Pentland, A.", de Montjoye, Y.-A.: Big data-driven marketing: how machine learning outperforms marketers' gut-feeling. In: Kennedy, W.G., Agarwal, N., Yang, S.J. (eds.) SBP 2014. LNCS, vol. 8393, pp. 367–374. Springer, Cham (2014). https://doi.org/10.1007/978-3-319-05579-4_45
16. Osisanwo, F.Y., Akinsola, J.E.T., Awodele, O., Hinmikaiye, J.O., Olakanmi, O., Akinjobi, J.: Supervised machine learning algorithms: classification and comparison. Int. J. Comput. Trends Technol. **48**(3), 128–138 (2017)
17. Allcott, H., Gentzkow, M.: Social media and fake news in the 2016 election. J. Econ. Perspect. **31**, 211–236 (2017)
18. Adgate, B.: Newspapers Have Been Struggling and then Came the Pandemic. https://www.forbes.com/sites/bradadgate/2021/08/20/newspapers-have-been-struggling-and-then-came-the-pandemic/
19. Deloitte: Digital Transformation Through Data for News and Media Companies. http://www2.deloitte.com/us/en/pages/consulting/articles/digital-transformation-through-data-for-news.html
20. De La Hoz Domínguez, E., Mendoza Mendoza, A., Ojeda De La Hoz, H.: Classification of readers profiles of a digital journal. Rev. UDCA Actual. Amp Divulg. Científica. **20**, 469–478 (2017)
21. Ahn, J., Jung, Y.: The common sense of dependence on smartphone: a comparison between digital natives and digital immigrants. New Media Soc. **18**, 1236–1256 (2016)
22. Hernández, D.H., Ramírez-Martinell, A., Cassany, D.: Categorizando a los usuarios de sistemas digitales. Pixel-Bit Rev. Medios Educ. (2014). https://doi.org/10.12795/pixelbit.2014.i44.08
23. Therneau, T., Atkinson, B., Ripley, B.: rpart: Recursive partitioning and regression trees (Version R package version 4.1-10). URL HttpsCRAN R-Proj. Orgpackage Rpart (2015)
24. Esposito, F., Malerba, D., Semeraro, G., Kay, J.: A comparative analysis of methods for pruning decision trees. IEEE Trans. Pattern Anal. Mach. Intell. **19**, 476–493 (1997)

25. IBM: Pruning Decision Tress. https://prod.ibmdocs-production-dal-6099123ce774e59 2a519d7c33db8265e-0000.us-south.containers.appdomain.cloud/docs/en/db2/10.5?topic= view-pruning-decision-trees
26. Petkovic, D., Altman, R., Wong, M., Vigil, A.: Improving the explainability of Random Forest classifier – user centered approach. In: Biocomputing, pp. 204–215. WORLD SCIENTIFIC, Kohala Coast, Hawaii, USA (2018)
27. Breiman, L.: Random forests. Mach. Learn. **45**, 5–32 (2001)
28. Biau, G.: Analysis of a random forests model. J. Mach. Learn. Res. **13**, 1063–1095 (2012)
29. Araújo, F.H.D., Santana, A.M., de Pedro, A., Neto, S.: Using machine learning to support healthcare professionals in making preauthorisation decisions. Int. J. Med. Inf. **94**, 1–7 (2016)
30. Faraggi, D., Reiser, B.: Estimation of the area under the ROC curve. Stat. Med. **21**, 3093–3106 (2002)
31. Adeniyi, D.A., Wei, Z., Yongquan, Y.: Automated web usage data mining and recommendation system using K-Nearest Neighbor (KNN) classification method. Appl. Comput. Inform. **12**, 90–108 (2016)

Analysis of Pre-trained Convolutional Neural Network Models in Diabetic Retinopathy Detection Through Retinal Fundus Images

José Escorcia-Gutierrez[1](✉) ⓘ, Jose Cuello[1] ⓘ, Carlos Barraza[1],
Margarita Gamarra[2] ⓘ, Pere Romero-Aroca[3] ⓘ, Eduardo Caicedo[4] ⓘ, Aida Valls[5] ⓘ,
and Domenec Puig[5] ⓘ

[1] Electronic and Telecommunications Engineering Program, Universidad Autónoma del Caribe,
Barranquilla 080001, Colombia
jose.escorcia23@gmail.com
[2] Department of Computational Science and Electronic, Corporación Universitaria de la Costa,
CUC, Barranquilla 080001, Colombia
[3] Ophthalmology Service, Universitari Hospital Sant Joan, Institut de Investigacio Sanitaria
Pere Virgili [IISPV], 43204 Reus, Spain
[4] School of Electrical and Electronic Engineering, Universidad del Valle, Cali 760032, Colombia
[5] Departament d'Enginyeria Informàtica i Matemàtiques, Escola Tècnica Superior
d'Enginyeria, Universitat Rovira i Virgili, 43007 Tarragona, Spain

Abstract. Diabetic Retinopathy (DR) is a disease on the rise; as this is a complication of diabetes, it becomes an imminent fate in people who have not been treated correctly for the disease, resulting in possible loss of vision if not is detected in time. This disease affects the retina, and the diagnosis is made based on fundus images of patients, through which various lesions and anomalies can be visualized. Visual inspection is a challenging task, and the diagnosis is expert dependent. This article proposes a convolutional neural network (CNN) model to detect DR, a common illness in diabetic patients. This work allows estimating the capacity of a pre-trained CNN (VGG16) using the transfer learning technique to detect symptoms and injuries caused by DR. For learning and feature extraction we used a set of retinal images obtained from the APTOS 2019 Blindness Detection competition in Kaggle. This network is trained and learns to identify between healthy retina and RD with high performance, overcoming other works. The best experimentation we obtained reached an accuracy value of 96.86% for DR detection tasks.

Keywords: Diabetic retinopathy · Retinal imaging · Image recognition · Convolutional neural network · Transfer learning

1 Introduction

Diabetes is a severe chronic disease that occurs when the pancreas does not produce enough insulin (a hormone that regulates the level of sugar, or glucose, in the blood),

K. Saeed and J. Dvorský (Eds.): CISIM 2022, LNCS 13293, pp. 202–213, 2022.
https://doi.org/10.1007/978-3-031-10539-5_15

or the body cannot effectively use the insulin it produces [1, 2]. People with diabetes may have an eye disease called diabetic retinopathy (DR). This disease occurs because high blood sugar levels cause damage to the blood vessels in the retina. These blood vessels can swell and leak fluid. They can also close and prevent blood from flowing. New abnormal blood vessels are sometimes generated in the retina (see Fig. 1) [3]. All these changes and damages can cause individuals to lose their vision if not diagnosed in time [4].

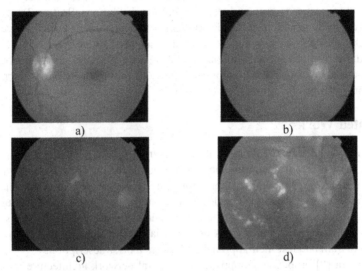

a)   b)   c)   d)

Fig. 1. Retinal fundus images from APTOS dataset. a) and b) healthy images; c) and d) images with DR.

Given the impact of this disease, greater agility, efficiency, and accuracy of diagnoses are necessary for the timely detection of diabetic retinopathy. According to World Health Organization data, diabetes in the world population went from being present in 108 million people, in 1980, to the alarming number of 422 million people in 2014 [5]. Therefore, with early detection of DR, there is a greater chance that the patient will not lose part of their vision or all of it in the worst case, thanks to the timely treatment provided.

Currently, health professionals mainly use traditional methods to detect DR. They perform manual detection of DR using eye fundus images, from where experts identify lesions associated with abnormalities in the blood vessels caused by diabetes. This method is useful but requires many resources, including special cameras. The specific infrastructure needed to manage DR is always limited in places where diabetes is high. As the rate of people with diabetes continues to grow, the expertise and equipment needed to alleviate blindness caused by DR will be even more scarce [6].

Including computer-assisted detection using artificial intelligence through the application of Deep Learning techniques would help in the DR diagnosis. These techniques have shown outstanding performance in other areas of detection of anomalies and diseases of the human body, such as detecting cancer or tumors [7, 8]. In addition to this, it is worth mentioning that the cost of time and money for detection tasks would be greatly reduced, alleviating the effects of variability as well of results due to differences between experts.

The main contribution of this work is to present a DR detection system based on deep transfer learning through different pre-entrained convolutional neural network in APTOS database. More than thirteen CNN models are tested to determine high performance in DR detection. Hence, this article is organized as follows. Section 2 reviews the related works of other authors who have researched and developed their networks using the same set of images to train and test their proposed solutions. Section 3 exposes our proposed solution methodology for the problem of DR detection in retinal images. Evaluation metrics to compare our proposal with other approaches are described in Sect. 3.4. Afterward, the results achieved with our model are discussed in Sect. 4. Finally, Sect. 5 describes our conclusions about automated DR detection through Deep Learning and the recommendations for future lines of research.

2 Related Work

The creation, development, and innovation of alternatives for detecting DR has greatly increased since it is a growing problem and the human resource available for this task is not enough to cover the entire population waiting for an evaluation on time. Many studies available in the literature include artificial intelligence applications, through Deep Learning (DL) oriented to this task. This section shows the recent developments in Deep Learning that used the set of images of the Asia-Pacific Teleophthalmology Society (APTOS) to train and test their approaches, besides a brief description.

Authors in [9] propose a composite deep neural network architecture with gated-attention mechanism for automated diagnosis of diabetic retinopathy. The model focused on the sections of the images that present lesions, with less attention on the areas without any alteration or lesion. Each input descriptor presents a different emphasis according to the corresponding section. Then the "Gated attention" technique is applied. To make this possible, they use attention blocks with layers with properties to distinguish specific features of the given input. The proposed model recorded an accuracy of 82.54%, and a Kappa score of 79 for diabetic retinopathy severity level prediction.

The research developed in [10] presents a binary classification for the detection of DR using Deep Learning models through texture features. They used the local binary patterns (LBP) method for feature extraction. LBP was applied to each image in the preprocessing stage. Finally, the networks tested for the binary classification of retinopathy diabetes are DenseNet [11] and ResNet [12]. The results show that ResNet, DenseNet and DetNet can obtain 0,9635%, 0,8405% and 0,9399% of accuracy, respectively.

The authors in [13] investigated deep transfer learning models for medical DR detection and made a comparison of the most common pre-trained Deep Learning models due to the few layers they present in their structure, among these, VGG16 [14], VGG19 [15], and ResNet. The data augmentation technique was applied for the input retinal images to convert the most robust networks and thus avoid the overfitting problem. The AlexNet model achieved the highest testing accuracy at 97.9%.

The work in [16] exposes a method for the solution of the problem of DR detection that consists of 4 fundamental stages: image preprocessing, data augmentation, transfer learning using the modified Inception-ResNetV2 network [17] ("hybrid network"), and finally the prediction of the image which determines if it has signs of DR. The results show an accuracy of 72.33% and 82.18% on Messidor-1 and APTOS dataset, respectively. Bear in mind that our methodological proposal is considered as a preliminary stage for future work on the multiclass classification of the different types of RD based on their pathologies. Despite being a preliminary proposal, our results exceed those recorded in the literature, as shown in the results section of this work.

3 Methodology

3.1 Work Environment

All the processes were carried out in the Google Collaboratory environment [18], which provides an execution environment with Google's GPU, considerably reducing the resources needed for tasks with high processing capacity. This platform randomly assigns us one of the available processors, NVIDIA's K80, T4, P4, and P100, with up to 12.72 GB of RAM. Although it allows to carry out tasks more efficiently, it has limits in some respects, such as processing capacity, storage, and the duration of active sessions, to guarantee the most significant possible availability to the public. Google's virtual machine limits its users to 12 h of availability of its hardware resources for processing. In our case, our sacrifices were the epoch numbers, image resolution, and the non-possibility of pre-processing methods that require GPU.

3.2 Dataset Description and Processing

The set of images used in this work was obtained from Kaggle, corresponding to the APTOS 2019 Blindness Detection competition [19], which contains a folder with 3,662 fundus images to be used for the network training process and another folder with 1,928 images for testing. However, as it is a competition in Kaggle that consists of making predictions about the test group, these last images are not labeled, so there is no way to make comparisons using them.

The original images have diverse dimensions, resulting in an obstacle to the network's learning. Then, it is necessary to submit them to preprocessing to guarantee optimal training in the network. For this task, we rely on the techniques studied by [20], which provides a way to cut out the dark areas of the images as much as possible, and then readjust their size to the desired size (for this project, we chose to work with sizes of 224 × 224 pixels); In addition, we used masks and added Gaussian noise to obtain processed images with more prominent blood vessels and lesions. Figure 2 shows the changes that these images present.

The APTOS dataset competition has a.csv file where the images are labeled in 5 classes, having levels 0, 1, 2, 3, and 4, corresponding to the classes: i) No RD; ii) Medium; iii) Moderate; iv) Severe; and v) Proliferative RD, respectively (see Fig. 3). The dataset is imbalanced in terms of the number of samples belonging to each class, being distributed as shown in Fig. 4a. This aspect must be taken into account when dividing the set of images into groups for network training, validation, and evaluation.

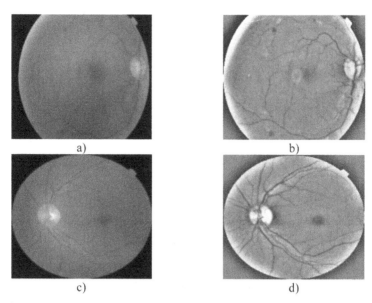

Fig. 2. The pre-processing methodology applied to APTOS dataset: a) and c) original RGF images, b) and d) output images after Gaussian filter.

These three subsets take a part of the whole dataset, distributed as shown in Fig. 4b, and each subset must retain the same proportions of examples of each class as given

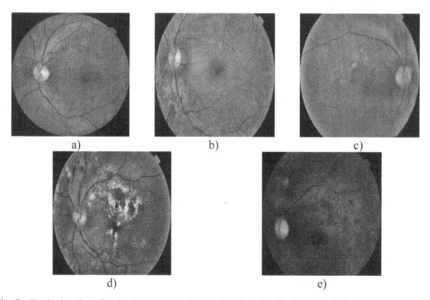

Fig. 3. Typical retinal fundus images: (a) Normal retina, (b) Retina in middle phase NPDR, (c) Moderate phase NPRP, (d) Severe phase NPRP, (e) Proliferative diabetic retinopathy (PDR).

in Fig. 4a. The training group is divided because the APTOS dataset only has ground truth records on this group of images, allowing us to validate the system against different images that are not part of its knowledge base (i.e., the training dataset is composed of 3662 and the testing dataset with 1928 images).

3.3 Proposed Approach

For constructing the Convolutional Neural Network (CNN), we used some techniques described by [21], such as Transfer Learning, Feature Extraction, and Fine-Tuning, which facilitate the development of new networks based on previously created models and thus reduce the computational resources required to train the CNN.

Transfer Learning. It is a technique that uses a model that is open to the public and has been previously trained and evaluated with a large set of data. To do this, we turn to Keras [22], an open-source neural network library that has a series of applicable models for Deep Learning practices.

In our work, we used the ResNet50, Xception, VGG16, DenseNet121, and EfficientNetB0 models, which have their weights in each layer, predefined based on a set of images used by Keras, known as "Imagenet".

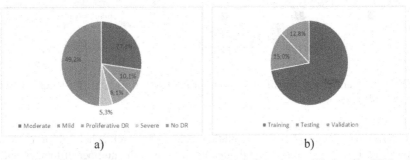

a)   b)

Fig. 4. APTOS dataset distribution percentage per DR. a) Percentage of images by DR level, b) Percentage of images for training, validation, and testing.

Feature Extraction. It consists of applying the patterns that the pre-trained network uses to recognize the features of an image based on generic concepts, such as shapes, contours, colors, and others. To this end, a technique recognized as "layer freezing" is implemented, which specifies that the weights in the layers of the pre-trained network are maintained, preserving the knowledge they have acquired to interpretate the information in the images.

Additionally, it is necessary to eliminate a set of layers belonging to the last blocks of layers of the network, known as the final classifier. These layers are used to identify the different classes with which the network was originally trained. Then, it is necessary to omit them and define a new classifier specific to the task in question. For our purpose, recognition of RD, we used a simple classifier [23], with three layers: 2-dimensional Global Average Pooling, a Dropout layer that allows us to indicate the desired total percentage of interconnections between the neurons of the network in order to reduce overfitting effects, and a Dense layer with sigmoid activation, which works thanks to the multiple label implementation properly.

Fine-Tuning. It consists of enabling some of the layers that precede the final classifier to trained. Their weights are updated to values that allow distinguishing more abstract characteristics typical of the retina images during the process.

Thus, Fig. 5a represents a diagram that helps interpret the modifications in the five network models evaluated in this work, taking as a starting point the five pre-trained networks: ResNet50, Xception, VGG16, DenseNet121, and EfficientNetB0. Figure 5b uses the EfficientNetB0 network to exemplify the five models' structure to be trained.

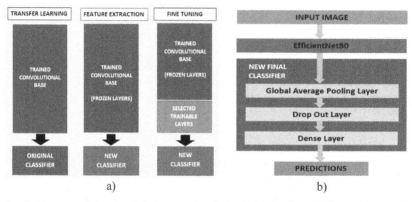

Fig. 5. a) Diagram of the simplified structure of the CNN, b) Scheme for training based on EfficientNetB0

Finally, we used the Data Augmentation technique, which is helpful for a few samples. With this. it is possible to synthetically "increase" the number of images that the model uses during training. It consists on, taking the same image several times but with alterations that help the network analyze it from different perspectives. In this case, we applied zoom, rotations, and flipping the image vertically and horizontally, with the aim that the network does not take images in only one direction and that it can classify appropriately with any new images. Based on 3,368 available training images, the knowledge base increased by 20%, and the learning process of 50 epochs.

Figure 6 summarizes the methodology for the construction of the networks. The results achieved and their evaluation will be discussed in the following sections.

3.4 Performance Indicators

To establish a comparison of our experiments and to know which of these presented the best results, it is necessary to obtain a series of metrics, to have the correct criteria for evaluating the results obtained.

The metrics considered in this study are accuracy, sensitivity, specificity [24], precision, F1 score [25], kappa coefficient [26], and area under the curve. These are related in Eqs. (1–6).

$$Accuracy (Acc) = \frac{TP + TN}{TP + TN + FP + FN} \tag{1}$$

$$Precision = \frac{TP}{TP + FP} \tag{2}$$

$$Sensitivity (Se) = \frac{TP}{TP + FN} \tag{3}$$

$$Specificity (Sp) = \frac{TN}{TN + FP} \tag{4}$$

$$F1 - Score = 2 * \frac{Precision * Se}{Precision + Se} \tag{5}$$

$$Kappa\,coef = \frac{(Obs\,Acc - Exp\,Acc)}{(1 - Exp\,Acc)} \tag{6}$$

where TP is true positives, TN is true negatives, FP is false positives, and FN is false negatives.

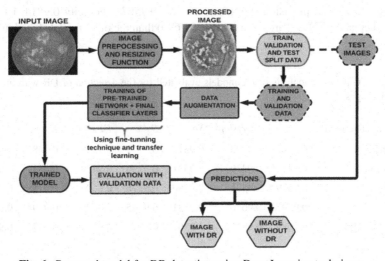

Fig. 6. Proposed model for DR detection using Deep Learning techniques.

4 Results and Discussion

4.1 Comparative Between Evaluated Models

The results obtained using the APTOS 2019 Blindness Detection image set were categorized according to the most complex networks in terms of the number of parameters. Table 1 shows the number of parameters that make up each model from largest to smallest.

Table 1. Number of parameters of the pre-trained networks.

Pre-trained network	Parameters		Overall parameters
	Trained	Untrained	
ResNet50	14,976,000	8,611,712	23,587,712
Xception	16,472,240	4,389,240	20,861,480
VGG16	7,079,424	7,635,264	14,714,688
DenseNet121	5,524,224	1,513,280	7,037,504
EfficientNetB0	1,129,392	2,920,179	4,049,571

These models had a personalized classifier in the last layers, the same for all networks (detailed in the Proposed Approach section). We can see in Table 2 that the number of parameters that make up a network does not indicate that high results will be achieved with such a network. In this case, the EfficientNetB0 model has the least number of trainable parameters and it is the best in in detecting DR in retinal images, which can be seen in all the evaluated indicators, achieving better results than ResNet50, Xception, VGG16, and DenseNet121 networks. Therefore, EfficientNetB0 is the model selected in our method due to its performance at level of all measure metrics are superior (i.e., in accuracy 0.9689, precision 0.9815, sensitivity 0.9567 specificity 0.9814, F1 score 0.9689, kappa 0.9377 and area under curve 0.9690) than the other models listed in Table 2.

Table 2. Comparative analysis of the models evaluated for the detection of DR with the set of APTOS images.

Pre-trained network	Acc	Precision	Sn	Sp	F1 score	Kappa	AUC
ResNet50	0.9542	0.9773	0.9314	0.9777	0.9538	0.9085	0.9546
Xception	0.9414	0.9329	0.9531	0.9294	0.9429	0.8827	0.9412
VGG16	0.9579	0.9774	0.9386	0.9778	0.9576	0.9158	0.9582
DenseNet121	0.9597	0.9670	0.9531	0.9665	0.9600	0.9194	0.9598
EfficientNetB0	0.9689	0.9815	0.9567	0.9814	0.9689	0.9377	0.9690

To better appreciate the results obtained and how they were obtained, Fig. 7 shows the confusion matrix with the set of test images. The values of 0 and 1 on the axes of this matrix correspond to the "No DR" and "DR" classes, respectively.

These results are indicative of the high efficiency achieved with the tested networks. Using the selected configuration of the final classifier and the hyperparameters configured in a custom way, we obtained a light network in terms of the number of trainable parameters and easy to understand for users. At the same time, the network achieved suitable performance to take as a baseline for future studies.

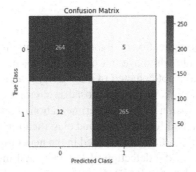

Fig. 7. Confusion matrix for detection using the EfficientNetB0 network.

4.2 Comparative with Related Works

Additionally, concerning with literature exposed in Sect. 2, we made a comparison between the results achieved by the EfficienteNetB0 network proposed by us, with some of these state-of-the-art works to establish how close we are to their metrics and have a notion of the efficiency of our tests and configurations on each network. The summary of this comparison can be seen in Table 3.

Table 3. Comparative between our model and the state-of-the-art.

Model	Acc	Precision	Sn	Sp	F1 score	Kappa	AUC
EfficientNetB0 (Our best accuracy)	0.9689	0.9815	0.9567	0.9814	0.9689	0.9377	0.9690
[9]	0.9782	–	–	–	–	–	–
[10] (ResNet)	0.9635	–	–	–	–	–	–
[10] (Densenet 121)	0.8405	–	–	–	–	–	–
[13] (VGG 19)	0.9740	0.9464	0.9576	–	0.9520	–	–
[13] (VGG 16)	0.9780	0.9519	0.9602	–	0.9560	–	–
[27]	0.9437	–	–	–	–	–	–

Table 3 shows that the work that has overcome our model is [9] (only accuracy), since [13] surpasses us in terms of accuracy but not in the other metrics. These results indicate that in this study, we achieved a suitable fitting of a pre-trained network with a simple final classifier configuration and established hyperparameters, achieving the same level of performance, robustness, and efficiency as other state-of-the-art works.

Regarding accuracy metrics, our results is comparable with the state-of-the-art, but it was not possible to obtain a statistic comparison as the values reported in the other works did not include information about standard deviation to define a significant difference. The validation process was performed with new data, not included in the training stage, and we obtained a F1 score and precision higher than the results exposed in [13].

5 Conclusion

Diabetic retinopathy is a complication of diabetes and is a disease that is increasing every day. It mainly affects people who have not treated the disease correctly, resulting in a possible loss of vision if it is not detected in time. Early diagnosis of DR is essential to prevent such damage. Therefore, we have proposed an alternative solution to this problem from the field of computer vision with the experimentation of different pre-trained neural networks specifically designed for detection and classification tasks.

We introduced a final classifier personalized in the network according to the task we expect the network to reach (the detection of DR in retinal images). We trained these networks with the public dataset of APTOS 2019 Blindness Detection obtaining very challenging and competitive results in comparison with the results obtained by other state-of-the-art works available to date that used the same dataset as ours. We emphasize that the proposed methodology allows a reasonably fast image classification system without too many complications, such as the implemented transfer learning models (i.e., ResNet50, Xception, VGG16, DenseNet121, and EfficientNetB0).

Between the different experimentations with pretrained networks that we performed, the best experimentation that we obtained, reached an accuracy value of 96.86% for RD detection tasks, which indicates that it is a suitable network for this purpose, as to reach higher values, it is necessary to have resources and more specialized knowledge configure a CNN. Even so, this research work is considered a suitable baseline for future research in the field of automated DR detection using Deep Learning techniques.

References

1. Romero-Aroca, P., et al.: Cost of diabetic retinopathy and macular oedema in a population, an eight year follow up. BMC Ophthalmol. **16**, 1–7 (2016). https://doi.org/10.1186/S12886-016-0318-X
2. Pelullo, C.P., Rossiello, R., Nappi, R., Napolitano, F., Di Giuseppe, G.: Diabetes prevention: knowledge and perception of risk among italian population. Biomed. Res. Int. **2019** (2019). https://doi.org/10.1155/2019/2753131
3. Thapa, R., et al.: Prevalence and risk factors of diabetic retinopathy among an elderly population with diabetes in Nepal: the Bhaktapur Retina Study. Clin. Ophthalmol. **12**, 561 (2018). https://doi.org/10.2147/OPTH.S157560
4. Sneha, N., Gangil, T.: Analysis of diabetes mellitus for early prediction using optimal features selection. J. Big Data **6**(1), 1–19 (2019). https://doi.org/10.1186/s40537-019-0175-6
5. Diabetes. https://www.who.int/news-room/fact-sheets/detail/diabetes. Accessed 21 Feb 2022
6. Wang, Y., Wang, G.A., Fan, W., Li, J.: A deep learning based pipeline for image grading of diabetic retinopathy. In: Chen, H., Fang, Q., Zeng, D., Wu, J. (eds.) ICSH 2018. LNCS (LNAI and LNB), vol. 10983, pp. 240–248. Springer, Cham (2018). https://doi.org/10.1007/978-3-030-03649-2_24
7. Muthumayil, K., Manikandan, S., Srinivasan, S., Escorcia-Gutierrez, J., Gamarra, M., Mansour, R.F.: Diagnosis of leukemia disease based on enhanced virtual neural network. Comput. Mater. Contin. **69**, 2031–2044 (2021). https://doi.org/10.32604/CMC.2021.017116
8. Orlando, J.I., Prokofyeva, E., Del Fresno, M., Blaschko, M.B.: An ensemble deep learning based approach for red lesion detection in fundus images. Comput. Methods Program. Biomed. **153**, 115–127 (2017)

9. Bodapati, J.D., Shaik, N.S., Naralasetti, V.: Composite deep neural network with gated-attention mechanism for diabetic retinopathy severity classification. J. Ambient. Intell. Humaniz. Comput. **12**(10), 9825–9839 (2021). https://doi.org/10.1007/s12652-020-02727-z
10. Adriman, R., Muchtar, K., Maulina, N.: Performance evaluation of binary classification of diabetic retinopathy through deep learning techniques using texture feature. Proc. Comput. Sci. **179**, 88–94 (2021). https://doi.org/10.1016/j.procs.2020.12.012
11. Huang, G., Liu, Z., Van Der Maaten, L., Weinberger, K.Q.: Densely connected convolutional networks. In: Proceedings - 30th IEEE Conference on Computer Vision and Pattern Recognition, CVPR 2017, pp. 2261–2269. Institute of Electrical and Electronics Engineers Inc. (2017). https://doi.org/10.1109/CVPR.2017.243
12. He, K., Zhang, X., Ren, S., Sun, J.: Deep residual learning for image recognition. In: Proceedings of the IEEE Computer Society Conference on Computer Vision and Pattern Recognition, pp. 770–778. IEEE Computer Society (2016). https://doi.org/10.1109/CVPR.2016.90
13. Khalifa, N.E.M., Loey, M., Taha, M.H.N., Mohamed, H.N.E.T.: Deep transfer learning models for medical diabetic retinopathy detection. Acta Inform. Medica. **27**, 327–332 (2019). https://doi.org/10.5455/aim.2019.27.327-332
14. VGG16 - Convolutional Network for Classification and Detection
15. VGG-19 convolutional neural network - MATLAB vgg19
16. Gangwar, A.K., Ravi, V.: Diabetic retinopathy detection using transfer learning and deep learning. Presented at the (2021). https://doi.org/10.1007/978-981-15-5788-0_64
17. Google AI Blog: Improving Inception and Image Classification in TensorFlow
18. Google colab is a free cloud notebook environment. https://bcrf.biochem.wisc.edu/2021/02/05/google-colab-is-a-free-cloud-notebook-environment/#:~:text=Google. Colab is a free cloud-based service that allows, and install new python libraries. &text=Colab is heavily used for, a platform to learn Python
19. APTOS 2019 Blindness Detection | Kaggle
20. APTOS: Eye Preprocessing in Diabetic Retinopathy | Kaggle
21. Torres, J.: Deep learning, introducción práctica con Keras (SEGUNDA PARTE) - Jordi TORRES.AI
22. Keras: The Python deep learning API. https://keras.io/
23. Montereal, Q.: APTOS 2019: DenseNet Keras Starter | Kaggle
24. Kassani, S.H., Kassani, P.H., Khazaeinezhad, R., Wesolowski, M.J., Schneider, K.A., Deters, R.: Diabetic retinopathy classification using a modified xception architecture. In: 2019 IEEE 19th International Symposium on Signal Processing and Information, ISSPIT 2019, pp. 1–6 (2019). https://doi.org/10.1109/ISSPIT47144.2019.9001846
25. Cuello Navarro, J., Barraza Peña, C., Escorcia-Gutiérrez, J.: Una revisión de los métodos de deep learning aplicados a la detección automatizada de la retinopatía diabética. Rev. SEXTANTE **23**, 14–33 (2020)
26. Bodapati, J.D., Shaik, N.S., Naralasetti, V.: Deep convolution feature aggregation: an application to diabetic retinopathy severity level prediction. Signal Image Video Process. **15**(5), 923–930 (2021). https://doi.org/10.1007/s11760-020-01816-y
27. Dekhil, O., Naglah, A., Shaban, M., Ghazal, M., Taher, F., Elbaz, A.: Deep learning based method for computer aided diagnosis of diabetic retinopathy. In: IST 2019 - IEEE International Conference on Imaging Systems and Techniques Proceedings, pp. 19–22 (2019). https://doi.org/10.1109/IST48021.2019.9010333

User Interface-Based in Machine Learning as Tool in the Analysis of Control Loops Performance and Robustness

John Gómez Múnera[2]📖, Javier Jiménez-Cabas[1]📖, and Luis Díaz-Charris[1(✉)]📖

[1] Universidad de la Costa - CUC, Calle 58 # 55 - 66, Barranquilla, Colombia
{jjimenez41,ldiaz28}@cuc.edu.co
[2] Corporacion Estudiantes Universitarios y Profesionales de Marinilla - CORUM, Calle 30 San José # 25 - 118, Marinilla, Antioquia, Colombia
gomezmunera@corum.org.co

Abstract. The monitoring of control loops in industrial processes is of great importance, considering that the correct operation of the productive procedures is related to the control loops that make up the system. Mostly, industrial processes are composed of a large amount of control loops that interact with each other, that means both are coupled, therefore, if one of the loops does not work properly it can negatively affect the system performance, leading the other loops into setpoints that were not designed for them. It has been found that many responsible causes for poor system performance can be identified by stochastic or deterministic performance indices. These performance indices, from a theoretical perspective, allow making relevant decisions, such as design parameters adjustment of the controllers or actuators maintenance. The most known are the stochastic performance index, it requires only normal operation and knowledge of the process. However, the performance analysis in a lot of cases is not conclusive and can present scale problems. On the contrary, deterministic performance index are easier to interpret, favoring the analysis and deduction of the operator. Nevertheless, it is necessary to perform invasive tests to get them, which makes it impractical.Therefore, this work obtains a deterministic index through a inferential model built with machine learning-based neural networks that use as input the stochastic index acquired throughout recollecting the normal operational data in closed loop and in the knowledge process. furthermore, count with a graphic interface that allows the operator interactively to get performance and robustness values represented in the deterministic indices. The strategy is put on test in a real study case of sensing levels for the industrial control process FESTO® MPS-PA Compact Workstation.

Keywords: Control loop performance · Performance indices · Machine learning · Neural networks · User interface

K. Saeed and J. Dvorský (Eds.): CISIM 2022, LNCS 13293, pp. 214–230, 2022.
https://doi.org/10.1007/978-3-031-10539-5_16

1   Introduction

The objective of a control system is to achieve that the outputs behave in a prescribed way by manipulating the inputs of the system, this is reflected in maximizing profits by transforming raw materials into products, minimizing production costs. The design, setting and strategies control are implemented during the first phase of control problems solutions, many industries use PID controllers, even though other studies based in optimal control for linear problems [9,10,18,28], trajectory linearization for nonlinear problems [19] and others using Kalman filter when stochastic process is involved [34]. Then after the appropriate setting, the result in this phase must be a control system working correctly. However, after some time in operation, changes in the material/product characteristics, modifications in the operational strategy and adjustments in plant status can turn the system control performance into degradation. Problems can appear even in well-designed control loops for several reasons, ranging from the need to tune in or design the control strategy to degradation of the elements acting in the control loop [5]. For this reason, in the second phase appears the supervision of the control loops, the early detection in the deterioration of their performance and the monitoring of the outputs of the process to verify that it is not too different from the desired reference [8]. Control systems are increasingly recognized as capital assets that must be routinely and automatically maintained, monitored and reviewed. These tasks are taken up today in the Control System Performance Monitoring (CPM), which has received considerable recognition from the academic and industrial communities in recent decades. This work aimed to use stochastic indices, which are non-invasive but not easy to interpret, to determine deterministic indices that are more understandable but are invasive to the systems. The reason for using deterministic indices is that this shows an idea of the robustness and performance of a system. This means that the precision for analysis over a system using deterministic indices is more precisely, quickly, and adjusted for a particular process. Therefore, a graphic interface helps technicians and engineers analyze the robustness and performance of a system without formal instruction over CPM techniques.

2   Control Performance Monitoring

The term CPM used by Harris [20] and implemented through the Minimum Variance Index (MVI) to obtain the best control design has led to a boom in the monitoring of control loops and their relationship with the functioning of systems; all this, given the need for reliable and efficient control systems in industrial environments. Consequently, many of the investigations have opted for the study, development, and monitoring of control loops in feedback systems. Thus, tools or frameworks such as those suggested by Moudgalya have been obtained [31], which automatically and systematically evaluate the MVI, enabling to detect and diagnosis causes of poor system performance and provide measures to improve control performance monitoring [26]. The CPM then provides the necessary information to determine if the target or performance index is being achieved and if the response times of the controlled variables of the control system are adequate.

There are three significant methodologies used in the monitoring and evaluating processes given the classification of Jelali methods [27]: stochastic, deterministic, and advanced techniques.

2.1   Stochastic Stationary Processes

Stationary processes are implemented with time series models; an essential feature in the development of these models is the assumption of some form of statistical equilibrium. A series of stationary time may be described in a useful and practical way through its mean, variance, and autocorrelation function (ACF) or equivalently as its mean, its variance and its spectral density function [6].

Mean and Variance of a Stationary Process. Stationary assumption implies that the probability distribution $p(Z_t)$ is the same for all times t and may be written as $p(z)$. Therefore, the stochastic process has a constant mean

$$\mu = E[z_t] = \int_{-\infty}^{\infty} zp(z)dz, \tag{1}$$

which defines the level at which it fluctuates, and a constant variance as Eq. 2

$$\sigma_z^2 = E\left[(z_t - \mu)^2\right] = \int_{-\infty}^{\infty} (z - \mu)^2 p(z)dz, \tag{2}$$

which measures spreading.

The mean μ of a stochastic process may be determined by the mean of samples

$$\bar{z} = \frac{1}{N} \sum_{t=1}^{N} z_t, \tag{3}$$

with N as the total number of samples and the variance σ_z^2 of the stochastic process could be estimated by the sample variance

$$\hat{\sigma}_z^2 = \frac{1}{N} \sum_{t=1}^{N} (z_t - \bar{z})^2, \tag{4}$$

of time series obtained through closed-loop process measurement.

Autocovariance and Autocorrelation Coefficients. Autocovariance in delay k is defined in Eq. 5 as

$$\gamma_k = \text{cov}\,(z_t, z_{t+k}) = E\left[(z_t - \mu)\,(z_{t+k} - \mu)\right],\tag{5}$$

similarly autocorrelation may be defined as the cross correlation of the signal with itself

$$\rho_k = \frac{E\left[(z_t - \mu)\,(z_{t+k} - \mu)\right]}{\sqrt{E\left[(z_t - \mu)^2\right]E\left[(z_{t+k} - \mu)^2\right]}}$$
$$= \frac{E\left[(z_t - \mu)\,(z_{t+k} - \mu)\right]}{\sigma_z^2},\tag{6}$$

for stationary processes, the variance $\sigma_z^2 = \gamma_0$ is the same at the instant $t + k$ as at the time t. Therefore, the autocorrelation function at delay k, defined in Eq. 7, is the correlation between z_t y z_{t+k} as

$$\rho_k = \frac{\gamma_k}{\gamma_0},\tag{7}$$

which implies that $\rho_0 = 1$.

The ACF is used to determine how the data in the time series are related, allowing to discover the nature of the disturbances that act in the process and how they affect the system by comparing the measurement patterns of the current process, with those presented in the former one during "normal" operation. The ACF indicates when it is necessary to perform AR, MA, ARMA, ARMAX models, as shown in Table 3.2 of the box book [6].

A fundamental test to evaluate the performance of control loops is to check the autocorrelation of the output samples: the autocorrelation should disappear beyond the delay time τ if the control is of minimum variance.

2.2 Performance Indices

Performance indices should be sensitive to weaknesses in the tuning and aging of the model, regardless of disturbances or set-point spectrum, which may vary widely in a process. Also, they must be calculated from data obtained under normal operating conditions (closed-loop); some indices used must be non-invasive; for others, it is necessary to apply invasive tests to the process.

Performance indices must be realistic, and it must be possible to calculate them under physical constraints. They should provide evidence of the reasons for poor performance in control systems and measure performance improvements due to changes in the controller.

Stochastic Performance Indices. In the evaluation of the performance of control systems in relation to the minimum variance, it is necessary to find the minimum variance control (**MVC**), it is concerned with the design of controllers that minimize the error variance in the process output, this controller is not concerned about the control effort required to achieve the objective, therefore the signal sent by the controller may not be limited, that is why the minimum variance controller is used as a benchmark, to be compared with the performance of other controllers, and the minimum variance controller is used as a benchmark, to be compared with the performance of other controllers [31].

The minimum variance control is the best possible feedback control for linear systems because it minimizes the output variance. For this, several indices have been defined; among them, the most known and used is the Harris index [11], given in Eq. 8, which compares the variance of a system output, σ_y^2 , with the minimum variance σ_{MV}^2 obtained using a time series model estimated with the operating data.

$$\eta_{Harris} = \frac{\sigma_{MV}^2}{\sigma_y^2}, \tag{8}$$

The index varies in the interval $[0, 1]$, where values close to 1 indicate good control regarding the minimum variance and those close to 0 indicate the worst performance, including unstable control.

Even though the Harris index has been extended to **MIMO** systems (multiple inputs and multiple outputs) [21, 25, 30], the emergence of the interaction or equivalence matrix plays an important role. It may not be determined by knowledge of time delays alone but from data in closed-loop [24]. A practical solution to the MIMO architecture and for the Control Performance Assessment (**CPA**) is to do the first procedure through time series analysis for control loops with a Single Input and Single Output (**SISO**), to estimate the output variable of the process independently for each y_i output [14]. These models are commonly AR/ARMA types. From these models, the response to a process impulse is calculated as shown by Jelali in [27], where the first τ terms of the response are not a function of the process model or the controller; these depend exclusively on the characteristics of the disturbance acting on the process. The variance for this portion is calculated as follows

$$\sigma_{MV}^2 = \sum_{i=0}^{\tau-1} e_i^2 \sigma_\epsilon^2, \tag{9}$$

where e_i are the coefficients of impulse response and σ_ϵ is the variance of the noise. Equivalently, the total variance may be calculated as

$$\sigma_y^2 = \sum_{i=\tau}^{\infty} e_i^2 \sigma_\epsilon^2 \tag{10}$$

Knowing the value of both variances, might be calculated the Harris index. The same results may be obtained by regression using the least-squares method [22, 33].

Farenzena proposes in [15] to decompose the output signal of the process into three parts according to the Eq. 11

$$y = w + g + f,\tag{11}$$

where w is the random component of the signal, g is the part that can be accessed by the feedback control, and f is the influence of the delay.

According to the Eq. 11, the total variance of the signal can be defined as:

$$TSV = \sigma^2(w) + \sigma^2(g) + \sigma^2(f).\tag{12}$$

From the Eq. 12 3 stochastic indices are defined, the first of them is

$$\text{Nosi} = \frac{\sigma^2(w)}{TSV},\tag{13}$$

that quantify the influence of noise on the control loop, the second is

$$\text{Deli} = \frac{\sigma^2(g)}{TSV},\tag{14}$$

that quantify the effect of transport delay in the control loop, and the third

$$\text{Tuni} = \frac{\sigma^2(f)}{TSV},\tag{15}$$

that quantify the impact of the performance of feedback control.

Other stochastic indices defined in [16], are determined from the autocorrelation function. The first index is **AcorSl**, which takes the form

$$\text{AcorSl} = \frac{\rho_\tau - CI}{\theta_{cross} - \tau},\tag{16}$$

which is the ratio of the autocorrelation value in the process delay time (ρ_τ) minus the Confidence Interval (CI) and the difference between the process delay value (τ) as well as the delay or lag value before the curve reaches the confidence interval θ_{cross}. The second index is **AcorAr**,

$$\text{AcorAr} = \int \begin{cases} |\rho_k| - CI, \; si \; |\rho_k| > CI \\ 0, \qquad\qquad si \; |\rho_k| < CI \end{cases} dLag,\tag{17}$$

which represents the area under the curve outside the confidence interval of the ACF.

The main reason for the failure of stochastic performance indices is the absence of a common and absolute target for quantifying performance. Conclusive indices are available in the literature, however, determining them in a real plant is impractical, because invasive tests are necessary.

Deterministic Indices. Deterministic indices are based on: closed and open-loop rise time relation R_{tr}, closed and open-loop settling time relation S_{tr}, gain margin GM, phase margin PM, maximum sensitivity MS, etc. It is mentioned in [13] that the MVC-based driver performance rating was challenging to interpret and could not assess the effect of deterministic changes on a closed-loop system. That is why some alternative indices are presented that required the exact models of the process and the controller.

In [2] it is mentioned that the deterministic indices provides a better estimate of loop performance than stochastic methods. Nonetheless, real-time quantification of deterministic indices is costly since it requires intrusive testing.

Performance: For stable systems, loop performance can be managed using classic parameters that describe dynamic systems. In this case, it is of particular interest to calculate the rise time (R_t) and (S_t), which is the time required by the response to rising and settling time from 5% to 95% of its final value.

Robustness: In the same way, there are parameters that can also be used to determine the robustness of the loop, that is, to measure how much the loop differs from the marginal stability, for this we analyze indices obtained from the bode diagram in which the phase margin and the gain margin are determined. Another way to determine robustness is through the maximum sensitivity, which is based on the graph of the Nyquist diagram, for which the minimum distance r from the curve to the critical point -1 is calculated, thus, the maximum sensitivity is based on the inverse of r. Robustness allows handling uncertainty, which means that a system correctly functions although uncertain parameters or disturbances are found. i.e., indicating how much the loop differs from marginal stability. In this way, the advantage of inferring the deterministic indices from the stochastic indices is obtaining a measure of the robustness of the system and a quick performance evaluation, all without having to make plant stoppages as required by the pure calculation of deterministic indices.

3 Machine Learning

In machine learning, it is essential to choose a suitable model, for which it is necessary to follow the steps of postulation, identification, estimation, diagnosis, and verification. Subsequently, the model can be used in a production environment.

3.1 Supervised Learning

A supervised learning builds a model that makes predictions based on evidence in the presence of uncertainty. An algorithm takes a known set of input data and known responses for these data (outputs). As a result, it trains a model to generate reasonable predictions in response to new data. Machine learning techniques are used in classification and regression problems, respectively, to predict discrete and continuous responses; in both cases, neural networks may be used [4].

Neural Networks. The use of artificial neural networks (**ANNs**) has been widely implemented in areas that allow prediction or classification purposes to a great extent to their inherent capacity for nonlinear modeling without any presumption about statistical distribution. The model that bests fits is adaptively generated according to the data and must reproduce numerical values that resemble the importance of some physical system.

Inferential Model with Neural Networks. The inferential model is a nonlinear model that estimates deterministic indices from stochastic ones to evaluate the performance and robustness of the system.

Neural networks with three layers are used for the construction. The first is the input layer, the second is the hidden layer, and the third is the output layer [23]. The output of the model is based on linear combinations of the inputs of a nonlinear fixed-base function; where the coefficients in the linear combination are adaptive parameters, the output takes the form of Eq. 18

$$y_t = \alpha_0 + \sum_{j=1}^{q} \alpha_j g \left(\beta_{0j} + \sum_{i=1}^{p} \beta_{ij} y_{t-i} \right) + \varepsilon_t, \forall t \tag{18}$$

with $y_{(t-i)}(i = 1, 2, \ldots, p)$ as p inputs and y_t is the output. Integer values p, q are the number of inputs and hidden nodes or neurons respectively. The $\alpha_j(j = 0, 1, 2, \ldots, q)$ and $\beta_{ij}(i = 0, 1, 2, \ldots, p; j = 0, 1, 2, \ldots, q)$ are the weights of connections and ε_t is a random change. Constants α_0, β_{0j} are usually known as the term bias [36]. The term g corresponds to the activation function, which determines the behavior of the node.

Least-squares methods are used to estimate the weights of neuron connections, which are based on the minimization of the error function, for which a cost function of the form is used:

$$J(\Theta) = MSE = \sum_{i=1}^{m} e_i^2 = \sum_{i=1}^{m} (y_i - \hat{y}_i)^2, \tag{19}$$

with Θ as a vector of all parameters to be found or connection weights.

Optimization techniques to minimize the error function or the cost functional 19 are referred to as learning rules, the best known in the literature are the backpropagation algorithms or the generalized delta rule [3].

4 Results

4.1 A Case Study

For the case study, we worked with a physical system, based on industrial control process FESTO® MPS-PA Compact Workstation of the automation laboratory of the Universidad de la Costa, that provide Exploration facilities from an academic point of view, allowing us testing the strategies of the inferential model

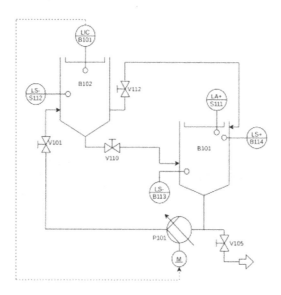

Fig. 1. Simplified PI&D level system diagram.

to obtain the performance and robustness measures of the control technique. A comparison between the plant and the model that infers the deterministic indices was carried out for this work. The model was trained over the process data. To probe the model's effectiveness, this was compared to the process directly. The plant was subjected to set-point changes while the process was executed, and the model was monitored to verify the correct output.

The Fig. 1 represents the PI&D diagram [1], in which the components related to the level control process are indicated, the pump P101 the one that supplies the fluid from a storage tank B101 to a tank B102 through a piping system. The fluid level inside the tank B102 is monitored with an analog ultrasonic BL1 sensor set in the measuring point LIC B102 and transduced to volume [L]. The current signal [4 - 20 mA] from the sensor is sent to a measuring transformer that converts it into a voltage signal [0 a 10 V], that can be used in the pump as the final control element. The value must be kept at a certain level even when there are disturbances or changes in the set point [7].

Open Loop Process Data and Extraction with Fluid-Lab Software. The "Fluid-Lab PA" software is used to obtain the data, it allows to study the open-loop dynamics. It is necessary to disturb the system to obtain a reaction curve to a change in setpoint in the FESTO MPS-PA workstation, with a change in dynamic volume of 0.5 L, that is, raise the level from 2.1 L to 2.6 L, as shown in Fig. 2.

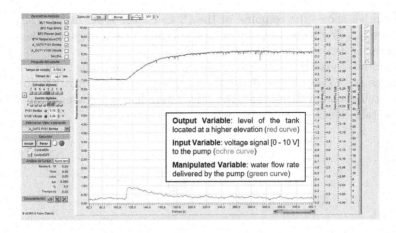

Fig. 2. Process reaction curve.

Model Identification. From the dynamic response of the system, we look for a first order model and dead time of the form of Eq. 20

$$G = \frac{Ke^{-\theta s}}{\tau s + 1}, \tag{20}$$

with τ as time or rate constant of process response, θ as dead time or delay and K as gain model of the plant.

To find the model and the parameters that characterize the model, the Smith's two-point method [29], is performed, based on the reaction curve, with which the values of $K = 4.7\frac{L}{V}$, $\theta = 1.27s$ y $\tau = 36.36s$.

Design of PI and PID Controllers for Verification of the FESTO®️ MPS-PA Workstation. The values for parameters adjustment depends on the closed loop responses wanted. The dynamics characteristics of the process and the elements involved, PI and PID type controllers are proposed [12,32]. In order to penalize the error of the oscillations around time for long periods of time from the beginning of the response, the ITAE criterion and the integral adjustment formulas of minimum error for disturbance-type inputs are used, proposed in Smith-Corripio [35]. The values found are shown in Table 1

Table 1. Controller parameters

Controller type	K_c	τ_i	τ_d
PI	4.2	6.3	-
PID	3.8	6.6	0.5

Figure 3a, shows the response of the PI controller type, in the graphic the right axis represents the set-point values, controlled variable, manipulated variable in dimensionless form $[0-1]$.

Figure 3b, shows the same procedure for an PID controller, but in this one was necessary to adjust the derivative constant value, when it presented sustained oscillations in the output, the values were lowered gradually until found an acceptable behavior at the output.

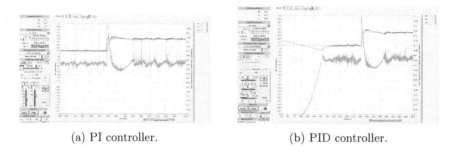

(a) PI controller.   (b) PID controller.

Fig. 3. System response

Table 2 shows the values obtained during the level process while using the two types of controllers proposed, these measures will help to compare with those obtained through the machine learning model.

Table 2. Values obtained from the plant for performance analysis

Process	$t_{Rise}[s]$	$t_{Settling}[s]$
Open loop	101	121
Close loop PI	4.4	9.2
Close loop PID	6.5	39

4.2   The Model with Machine Learning

For the machine learning model were used neural networks such as those described in Sect. 3.1 through MATLAB and based on strategies for the pursuit of control systems performance [17], working with a dataset in which the plant parameters and disturbance were varied according to the values described in Table 3, changing regarding to the preliminary tests in the inclusion of the identified gain in the plant. The data generated was a total of 80000, from the combinations made to the variations, to obtain the values of the stochastic indices raised that allow obtaining the corresponding deterministic index.

Table 4 shows the variables used in each machine learning model input to determine the differents deterministic index.

Table 3. Variation of process parameters to design the machine learning model

Parameter	Value
τ	[5:5:200]
θ	[1:5:100]
τ_d	[10:20:100]
K	[1:5:100]

Table 4. Variables selected to build the neural network model for each deterministic index

Output (deterministic index)	Variables
R_{tr}	$[\tau\ \theta\ Deli\ AcorSL]$
S_{tr}	$[\tau\ \theta\ Deli\ AcorSL]$
PM	$[\tau\ \theta\ MVI\ AcorAr]$
GM	$[\tau\ \theta\ MVI\ Deli\ AcorAr]$
MS	$[\tau\ Deli\ Tuni\ AcorSl\ AcorAr]$

A pre-processing of the data was done, which included carrying out a cleaning and reducing those that had generated unstable systems, in addition to those that were different from the decimal number 5, for this reason many data had variations in high decimal numbers, which can represent a repeated data for the models, leading to an overestimation. Thus, a dataset of 3961 is obtained for the R_{tr} and S_{tr} models, 4000 for the MS model, 4001 for the deterministic GM index model, and 4000 for the model representing the PM index.

The data used is divided into three subsets in such a way that 70% is used for training (used to update the weights and the bias of the inputs and neurons), 15% is used for validation (the error in the validation set is monitored while the network is training) and 15% for testing the machine learning model. The network architecture, the training algorithm and the activation functions are defined with three layers. The first layer corresponds to the inputs. In the second layer, a hidden layer is set up, with 20 neurons, and in the last one the output is defined. A model for each deterministic index and for each type of controller is built in such a way as to obtain a reduction in the cost function 19. Figure 4a and Fig. 4b show the performance that is obtained with the increase in epochs for the PI type controller. Therefore, the Mean Squared Error (MSE) metric is used in the training model to minimize function cost.

4.3   User Interface for Deterministic Indices Prediction

Figure 5 shows a graphical interface elaborated in the MATLAB app designer for the prediction of deterministic indices implementing data from normal operation of the plant and the characteristics identified with the first order model and dead time as tools. For this case, those corresponding to the plant were loaded when it was operating with the PI controller type. In the section called "Datos de la

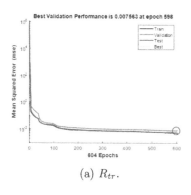

(a) R_{tr}.

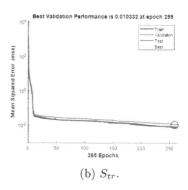

(b) S_{tr}.

Fig. 4. Performance for the index model

planta" of the interface the operator can enter the data that characterizes the plant, which correspond to the process time constant defined as τ, the process dead time defined as θ, and the reference value or set-point for which the plant is operating. The sampling time value is fixed and cannot be modified by the operator or user. The interface has a button to import the data, it is necessary for the operator to load the data and enter the characteristics of the plant, in case the data is not loaded, an error modal appears on the screen.

When the data is loaded, it is displayed on the axis named Controlled Variable. After viewing the data and defining the characteristics, it is possible to first perform the calculation of the stochastic indexes using the button identified as "Calcular índices estocásticos". They are displayed in the panel below the button. For the Estimate with Neural Networks panel, after selecting the type of controller with which the system is operating, there is a button to Calculate the proposed deterministic indices, using for this the model loaded in the code environment of the app designer.

Figures 5 and 6 show the predictions for the two types of controllers that were tested in the plant.

Table 5 shows the differences between the values obtained for the PI and PID type controllers, directly measuring the behavior in the level process, and that obtained with the estimation of the models built with machine learning. At this point, only the R_{tr} index and the S_{tr} are analyzed, thus being able to determine the values of the real process with a step change and determining the relationships by observing the reaction curve of Figs. 3a and 3b.

Table 5. Valuations of actual and estimated measures

Controller type	Deterministic index	Process measurement	Estimation	Relative error
PI	R_{tr}	22.955	24.98	8.85%
	S_{tr}	13.1522	15.74	19.66%
PID	R_{tr}	15.5	13.38	13.5%
	S_{tr}	3.1	3.053	1.5%

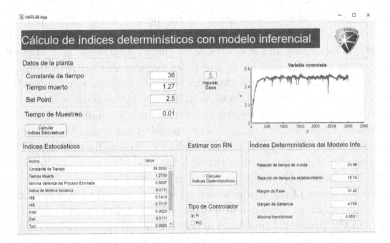

Fig. 5. Interactive interface for the prediction of deterministic indices, with a PI controller.

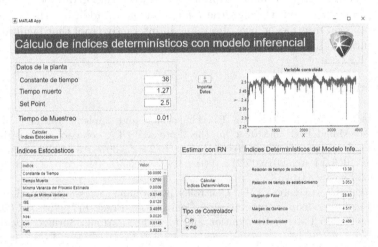

Fig. 6. Interactive interface for the prediction of deterministic indices, with a PID controller.

The deterministic indices obtained with the model based on machine learning techniques and the deterministic indices calculated directly with the plant's operating point variation present a low margin of error, as shown in table 5, Which indicates that the model is capable of calculating these indices with reasonable accuracy.

5   Conclusions

The performance analysis of control loops has been conditioned to the calculation of stochastic indices, such as the minimum variance index, which in many cases does not show conclusive information on the behavior and performance of the loop. For this reason, deterministic indices gain strength, because they directly relate the performance and robustness of the control loop and also offer an easier interpretation for operators and plant engineers, thus providing decision criteria on the corrective actions that can be taken necessary in the control loop for optimal operation. The problem with deterministic indices lies in the fact that to obtain them it is necessary to change the set point or invasive tests on the system, therefore, in the approach, models were created through machine learning techniques based on neural networks that allows finding or predict these indices, also allowing visualization through the graphical user interface, giving a possibility to evaluate them in industrial environments.

The construction of the model was worked with neural networks that needed as input some stochastic indices and other variables corresponding to the characteristics of the process. The neural network is made up of a single hidden layer with 20 neurons that formed the entire layer, a model was obtained that minimizes the functional cost. The model was validated in an industrial level control process, obtaining acceptable measurements between the prediction and the real model, comparing them through the relative error. In addition, the realization of the graphical interface allows obtaining an interactive tool that facilitates the implementation and decision-making by the operator.

References

1. Ahmad, S., Ali, S., Tabasha, R.: The design and implementation of a fuzzy gain-scheduled PID controller for the Festo MPS PA compact workstation liquid level control. Eng. Sci. Technol. Int. J. **23**(2), 307–315 (2020). https://doi.org/10.1016/j.jestch.2019.05.014. https://www.sciencedirect.com/science/article/pii/S221509861831615X
2. Bezergianni, S., Georgakis, C.: Controller performance assessment based on minimum and open-loop output variance. Control Eng. Pract. **8**(7), 791–797 (2000)
3. Bishop, C.M.: Pattern Recognition and Machine Learning. Springer, Heidelberg (2006)
4. Bonaccorso, G.: Machine Learning Algorithms. Packt Publishing Ltd (2017)
5. Borrero-Salazar, A.A., Cardenas-Cabrera, J.M., Barros-Gutierrez, D.A., Jimenezénez-Cabas, J.A.: A comparison study of MPC strategies based on minimum variance control index performance (2019)
6. Box, G.E., Jenkins, G.M., Reinsel, G.C., Ljung, G.M.: Time Series Analysis: Forecasting and Control. Wiley, Hoboken (2015)
7. Bustos Pulluquitin, S.P.: Modelación matemática para un control robusto de la planta Festo MPS-PA Compact Workstation mediante la normativa IEC-61499. Ph.D. thesis, Universidad Técnica de Ambato, Ambato, Ecuador (2021). https://repositorio.uta.edu.ec/handle/123456789/32221
8. Cardenas-Cabrera, J., et al.: Model predictive control strategies performance evaluation over a pipeline transportation system. J. Control Sci. Eng. **2019** (2019)
9. Costanza, V., Rivadeneira, P.S., Gómez Múnera, J.A.: An efficient cost reduction procedure for bounded-control LQR problems. Comput. Appl. Math. **37**(2), 1175–1196 (2018)

10. Costanza, V., Rivadeneira, P.S., Gómez Múnera, J.A.: Numerical treatment of the bounded-control LQR problem by updating the final phase value. IEEE Latin Am. Trans. **14**(6), 2687–2692 (2016)
11. Desborough, L., Harris, T.: Performance assessment measures for univariate feedforward/feedback control. Can. J. Chem. Eng. **71**(4), 605–616 (1993)
12. Dorf, R.C., Bishop, R.H.: Modern Control Systems. Pearson (2011)
13. Eriksson, P.: Some aspects of control loop performance monitoring. In: IEEE Conference of Control Applications, Glasgow, UK, 1994 (1994)
14. Ettaleb, L.: Control loop performance assessment and oscillation detection. Ph.D. thesis, University of British Columbia (1999)
15. Farenzena, M., Trierweiler, J.: Quantifying the impact of control loop performance, time delay and white-noise over the final product variability. In: Cancun, Mexico: International Symposium on Dynamics and Control of Process Systems (2007)
16. Farenzena, M.: Novel methodologies for assessment and diagnostics in control loop management. Ph.D. thesis, Universidade Federal Do Rio Grande Do Sul (2008)
17. Gómez-Múnera, J.A., Díaz-Charris, L., Ruiz-Ariza, J., Cárdenas-Cabrera, J., Romero, E., Jiménez-Cabas, J.: Stochastic performance indices to infer deterministic indices through machine learning in the performance analysis of control loops. Adv. Mech. **9**(3), 616–626 (2021)
18. Gómez Múnera, J.A., Giraldo Quintero, A.: Parallel computing for rolling mill process with a numerical treatment of the LQR problem. Comput. Electron. Sci. Theor. Appli. **1**(1), 11–30 (2020)
19. Gómez Múnera, J.A., Rivadeneira Paz, P.S., Costanza, V.: A cost reduction procedure for control-restricted nonlinear systems. Int. Rev. Autom. Control (IREACO), **10** (2017)
20. Harris, T.J.: Assessment of control loop performance. Can. J. Chem. Eng. **67**(5), 856–861 (1989)
21. Harris, T.J., Boudreau, F., MacGregor, J.F.: Performance assessment of multivariable feedback controllers. Automatica **32**(11), 1505–1518 (1996)
22. Harris, T.J., Seppala, C., Desborough, L.: A review of performance monitoring and assessment techniques for univariate and multivariate control systems. J. Process Control **9**(1), 1–17 (1999)
23. Haykin, S.: Neural Networks and Learning Machines, 3/E. Pearson Education India, Noida (2010)
24. Huang, B., Shah, S.L.: Performance Assessment of Control Loops: Theory and Applications. Springer, Heidelberg (1999). https://doi.org/10.1007/978-1-4471-0415-5
25. Huang, B., Shah, S.L., Kwok, E.: Good, bad or optimal? performance assessment of multivariable processes. Automatica **33**(6), 1175–1183 (1997)
26. Jelali, M.: An overview of control performance assessment technology and industrial applications. Control Eng. Pract. **14**(5), 441–466 (2006)
27. Jelali, M.: Control Performance Management in Industrial Automation: Assessment, Diagnosis and Improvement of Control Loop Performance. Springer, Heidelberg (2012). https://doi.org/10.1007/978-1-4471-4546-2
28. Jiménez-Cabas, J., et al.: Robust control of an evaporator through algebraic Riccati equations and D-K iteration. In: Misra, S., et al. (eds.) ICCSA 2019. LNCS, vol. 11620, pp. 731–742. Springer, Cham (2019). https://doi.org/10.1007/978-3-030-24296-1_58
29. López Guillén, M.E.: Identificación de Sistemas. Aplicación al modelado de un motor de continua

30. McNabb, C.A., Qin, S.J.: Projection based MIMO control performance monitoring: II–measured disturbances and setpoint changes. J. Process Control **15**(1), 89–102 (2005)
31. Moudgalya, K.M.: Digital Control. Wiley, Hoboken (2007)
32. Ogata, K.: Modern Control Engineering. Prentice hall (2010)
33. Qin, S.J.: Control performance monitoring-a review and assessment. Comput. Chem. Eng. **23**(2), 173–186 (1998)
34. Rivadeneira, P.S., Gómez Múnera, J.A., Costanza, V.: Dynamic allocation of industrial utilities as an optimal stochastic tracking problem. Chem. Eng. Sci. **160**, 121–130 (2017)
35. Smith, C.A., Corripio, A.B.: Principles and Practices of Automatic Process Control. Wiley, Hoboken (2005)
36. Zhang, G.P.: A neural network ensemble method with jittered training data for time series forecasting. Inf. Sci. **177**(23), 5329–5346 (2007)

Predictive Model of Cardiovascular Diseases Implementing Artificial Neural Networks

Carlos Henriquez[1], Johan Mardin[2]([✉]), Dixon Salcedo[2], María Pulgar-Emiliani[3], Inirida Avendaño[4], Luis Angulo[2], and Joan Pinedo[2]

[1] Faculty of Engineering, Universidad del Magdalena, Santa Marta, Colombia
chenriquezm@unimagdalena.edu.co
[2] Computer Science and Electronics Department, Universidad de La Costa, Barranquilla, Colombia
jmardini@cuc.edu.co
[3] Clínica Centro, Barranquilla, Colombia
[4] Humanities Department, Universidad de La Costa, Barranquilla, Colombia

Abstract. Currently, there is a growing need from health entities for the integration of the use of technology. Cardiovascular disease (CEI) identification systems allow a large extent to predict diseases associated with the heart, thus allowing early identification of cardiovascular diseases (CVD) to improve the quality of life of patients.

In this research, a comparative analysis of the results obtained after implementing a series of feature selection techniques (Info. Gain, Gain ratio), and classification techniques based on artificial neural networks (SOM and GHSOM) was carried out, using the same data set "Heart Cleveland Kaggle Disease Data Set" hosted in the Machine Learning UCI repository and under the same test environment. Thus, to establish which of the techniques mentioned achieve a higher percentage of accuracy and precision when identifying patients who suffer from the disease under study. For the performance of the tests, cross-validation was used to select a percentage of the data set to perform them and another for training.

Through the implementation of load balancing, normalization, and attribute selection techniques, it was possible to reduce the number of characteristics used in the classification process of the predictive model of cardiovascular diseases, which generated a reduction in computational requirements. Based on the above, 81.45% of successes were obtained with the hybridization of the Gain ratio feature selection technique and the GHSOM training techniques with the use of 7 features.

Keywords: SOM neural networks · GHSOM neural networks · Feature selection · Cardiovascular disease

1 Introduction

According to a report from the National Health Organization (ONS), cardiovascular diseases (CVD), along with cancer, diabetes, and chronic lung diseases, are identified

K. Saeed and J. Dvorský (Eds.): CISIM 2022, LNCS 13293, pp. 231–242, 2022.
https://doi.org/10.1007/978-3-031-10539-5_17

as non-communicable diseases (NCDs), which have shown a rapid increase, classifying them as the main causes of death in the world [1].

Worldwide, 42% of deaths from cardiovascular diseases are related to ischemic heart disease, and 34% to cerebrovascular diseases. It is estimated that in 2015, 17.7 million people died from this cause, which represents 31% of all deaths registered in the world. Of these deaths, 7.4 million were due to coronary heart disease. More than three-quarters of cardiovascular diseases deaths occur in low- and middle-income countries. Of the 17 million deaths in people under 70 years of age attributable to noncommunicable diseases, 82% are in low- and middle-income countries and 37% are due to CVD [2].

Acute Myocardial Infarction (AMI) is a frequent disease of uncertain evolution whose mortality during the acute phase is estimated between 20 and 50% despite the progress achieved, which justifies the dedication of efforts and resources to improve your prognosis and refine your therapy [3]. There are drugs and procedures of proven effectiveness in it, which are intended to improve the survival and quality of life of patients affected by this disease, but their effectiveness decreases when they are not applied early.

In addition, patients with preexisting cardiovascular disease and risk factors are more likely to experience adverse outcomes associated with the novel coronavirus disease-2019 (COVID-19). Likewise, these patients can develop various cardiovascular complications related to COVID-19 that increase their associated morbidity and mortality, making them more vulnerable [4].

It is a fact that the COVID-19 pandemic is currently dominating the attention of the health system. We are focusing our resources and efforts on combating COVID-19. In addition, various organizations are working hard for a vaccine. However, as the virus spreads, many patients will need medical attention for traditional or COVID-19-related cardiovascular problems [5]. Therefore, there is a need for a well-distributed approach to treat traditional cardiovascular and other problems associated with COVID-19 during this period. Many non-urgent but required cardiovascular tests and procedures are significantly delayed, which can have an adverse long-term impact.

In this way, the models become preventive tools that avoid leaving only the therapeutic approach to clinical judgment, allowing the objective evaluation of the patient in his clinical context, including both the burden and the severity of the disease, thus allowing a better identification in In terms of safety and cost-benefit characteristics, the optimal treatment is the one that allows the best extent to reduce the probability of the occurrence of cardiovascular events with fewer adverse effects. In addition to the above, the models improve communication between doctor and patient since they allow clarifying expectations, changes in lifestyle, and general recommendations. It's worth mentioning that the creation of these tools enabled the definition of current traditional cardiovascular risk factors, as well as the identification and evaluation of both new markers and potential therapeutic targets [6].

On the other hand, in the research field, machine learning algorithms have been widely implemented in the prognosis and prediction of cardiovascular diseases. The interest that has been aroused lately is due to the advance of algorithmic programming, the increase in the processing capacity of modern computers, and the increase in the capacity to store large volumes of data [7].

The use of these machine learning techniques for disease prediction is generating positive results considering that they automate the cognitive work of humans quickly and with great precision. The development in the field of machine learning with the aim of applying algorithmic techniques to the study of health-related problems has made great progress, mainly in Europe, where the great utility of these tools in the development of predictive models for health has been demonstrated. This development is possible thanks to the articulation between health professionals (doctors, psychologists, biotechnologists, etc.), computer scientists specializing in big data and e-health consultants.

This scientific article has been structured as follows: Sect. 2 describes the related research. Section 3 presents the pre-processing of the data used for the development of the model. In Sect. 4 the used feature selection techniques are presented, in Sect. 5 the training and classification techniques are denoted. Section 6 presents the methodology implemented for the construction of the model, in Sect. 7 the simulation scenarios are presented with their respective results and finally in Sect. 8 the conclusions are presented.

2 Related Research

When consulting related research, we noticed that some documents analyze very specific approaches from the point of view of technology (LM and hybridization techniques [8, 9], comparative studies of cardiovascular risk techniques [10, 11], cardiovascular monitoring systems [12]). Other reviews, although not exhaustive, are limited in evaluating classification techniques in terms of accuracy for predicting cardiovascular disease from data sets [13, 14], and [15].

However, there is no evidence proposing the hybridization of feature selection techniques (Info. gain and Gain ratio) with machine learning techniques based on artificial neural networks (SOM and GHSOM). A detailed description of the studies mentioned above.

In [16], they implement computer-assisted techniques providing fast and accurate tools to identify the electrocardiogram (ECG) signals of a patient. They summarize and compare diagnostic techniques using data preprocessing, feature engineering, classification, and application.

In addition, in [17], an end-to-end model is made by integrating the extraction and classification of features into learning algorithms, which not only greatly simplifies the data analysis process but also shows an accuracy evaluated at a good level.

In the same way, in [17], extraction of multivariate clinical characteristics of patients with acute coronary syndrome (ACS) registered in a database registry was implemented, and they used several machine learning algorithms to develop several models that had an appreciable performance in predicting cardiac arrest in patients with acute coronary syndrome (ACS).

3 Data Pre-processing

The simulation process used to validate the detection rates of a classifier involves the execution of a series of phases: pre-processing, selection, training, classification, and evaluation of the performance of the classifier.

The preprocessing phase involves the use of a data set from which the data to be analyzed comes. The Heart Cleveland Kaggle Disease Data Set has been used in this type of research, as it is widely endorsed by the scientific community that evaluates correlated studies.

The improvements that the HEART CLEVELAND KAGGLE KDD has with respect to other datasets are the fact that it does not include redundant records in the data collection in the field of data training; the number of records selected from each difficulty level group is inversely proportional to the percentage of records in the original KDD dataset; and the number of records in the data collections for training and testing is reasonable.

To tune the HEART CLEVELAND KAGGLE KDD ensemble, preprocessing, load balancing, and normalization techniques were applied. Load balancing is intended to balance the number of normal predictions with the number of abnormal predictions to avoid overtraining.

Therefore, a load balancing technique called Synthetic Minority Oversampling TEchnique-SMOTE, defined in [17], was implemented. According to [18], this technique is responsible for adding random information to the data set training process, generating new data instances. In the present investigation, SMOTE adds new instances of the "diagnosis" class, at a percentage of 4.27 of the current ones, from the HEART CLEVELAND KAGGLE KDD training data set, calculating each new instance from the mean of the five nearest neighbors and with a seed initialized to one.

4   Feature Selection Techniques

According to [19], feature selection refers to a concept used in data mining with the aim of reducing the size of the input data to facilitate the processing and analysis of said information. Feature selection not only considers the decrease in coordination, that is, maintaining a partial or predefined limit on the number of attributes considered when creating a model, but also allows the attributes to be discarded appropriately based on their usefulness for carrying out a good analysis process.

In addition to this classification, feature selection methods can also be divided into three models according to [20]:

According to [21], the filter-based feature selection technique (filter) is used to find the best subset of features from the original set. Filtering methods seem to be good at selecting a large subset of data because they do not depend on the algorithm of classification and its computational cost is lower for large data sets. The wrapper-based feature selection techniques defined in [22, 23] use the performance prediction of the learning algorithm for feature selection. It improves the results of the corresponding predictors and achieves better recognition rates, in some cases outperforming filter-based techniques; however, they are dependent on the classification algorithm, and the method has a higher computational cost for large datasets of wrappers.

Finally, the embedded methods (embedded), also defined in [24], are based on the evaluation of the performance of the metric calculated directly from the data without direct reference to the results of the data analysis systems. In them, there is a marriage of feature selection techniques with the learning process for a given learning algorithm. Embedded methods are less prone to overfitting and depend on the sort algorithm.

The ability to use feature selection is paramount for effective analysis because the data contains information that is not needed for model generation. The Info. Gain and Gain Ratio techniques have been selected due to that in the preliminary exploration of the state of the art, it was observed that when they were implemented in topics related to the detection of cardiovascular diseases, their results were promising. However, they were implemented in hybridization. In this paper, we apply SOM and GHSOM neural networks to analyze the performance metrics that the proposed model yields.

Next, the Info. Gain and Gain Ratio feature selection techniques are presented in detail, since they support the model proposed in this research.

4.1 Info. Gain

It is a filter-based feature selection technique defined in [24]. It is also known as information gain and is used to identify the level of relevance or ranking of the characteristics of a data collection. Equation No. 1 defines this level of relevance. The attribute with the highest information gain is chosen as the split attribute for node N. This attribute minimizes the information needed to classify the pairs in the resulting partition and reflects the least randomness or impurity in these partitions.

$$IG\,(D, X\_3) = entropy(D) - \sum\nolimits_{\_v} (|D\_v|entropy(D\_v))/(|D|) \qquad (1)$$

Implementing the selection technique on the data set, the order of characteristics is as follows: Induced depression, electrocardiogram result, maximum heart rate reached, resting blood pressure, type of chest pain, sugar level, age, cholesterol, maximum curve slope of exercise, number of major vessels, angina induction exercise, sex, thal.

4.2 Gain Ratio

According to [25], gain ratio belongs to the category of filtering feature selection techniques and is a measurement method to weight the features in the data set with high dimensionality. When there are many different values, the information gain ratio is used to account for these features. This method is widely used because, through its application, very good results are obtained, which are later used in the classification phase. Its greatest peculiarity is that the modification of the information gain reduces the bias. The gain ratio considers the number and size of branches to choose from in an attribute.

Implementing the selection technique to the data set, the order of characteristics is as follows: blood pressure at rest, sugar level, maximum heart rate reached, number of major vessels, cholesterol, angina inducing exercise, induced depression, curved slope maximum exercise, age, electrocardiogram result, thal, sex, type of chest pain.

5 Training Techniques and Classification

In this phase, in the first instance, the classifier is trained based on the selected learning algorithm and using the data set already normalized and reduced to the most relevant characteristics to generate more efficient learning.

Once the model has been trained, the classifier determines the diagnosis of heart disease, performing the subsequent classification of each of the connections in the data set (HEART CLEVELAND KAGGLE KDD). Quality metrics are then calculated to assess the performance of the classification technique.

In this research we will deal with the SOM and GHSOM Artificial Neural Networks. Therefore, it is necessary to define the concept of neural network. According to [26], neural networks are represented by a directed graph with four (4) conditions: (1) the links are called connections and operate as instantaneous unidirectional paths; (2) the nodes are called process elements (EP), which can have any number of connections and have local memory; (3) all connections coming out of the EP must have the same signal; (4) each EP has a transfer function, which, based on the inputs and the local memory, produces an output signal, thus altering the local memory.

5.1   Neural Networks SOM (Self-organizing Map)

It is an efficient neural algorithm (unsupervised) that allows the projection of data from a multidimensional space into a two-dimensional grid called "map", qualitatively preserving the organization (topology) of the original set [29].

In 1982, T. Kohonen [29] presented a network model called self-organizing maps or SOM (Self-organizing Maps), with which he wanted to show that an external stimulus (input) can force the formation of maps, assuming a structure is determined and a functional description. According to [28], the most important characteristic of SOMs is that they learn to classify the data through an unsupervised learning algorithm (a SOM learns to classify the training data without any type of external control).

5.2   Neural Networks GSOM (Growing Hierarchical Self Organizing Maps)

According to [30], GHSOM is a hierarchical and dynamic structure, developed to overcome the weaknesses and problems that SOM presents. The GHSOM structure consists of multiple layers composed of several independent SOMs whose number and size are determined during the training phase. The adaptive growth process is controlled by two parameters that determine the depth of the hierarchy and the breadth of each map. Therefore, these two parameters are the only ones that must be set initially in GHSOM (Fig. 1).

These types of maps are born as an improved version of the SOM architecture, according to [29] there are two purposes for the GHSOM architecture:

1. SOM has a fixed network architecture, that is, the number of units of use, as well as the distribution of the units must be determined before training.
2. Input data that is hierarchical in nature should be represented in a hierarchical structure for clarity of representation. GHSOM uses a multi-layered hierarchical structure, where each layer is made up of several independent SOMs. Only one SOM is used in the first layer of the hierarchy.

For each map unit, a SOM could be added to the next layer in the hierarchy. This principle is repeated with the third level of the map and the other layers of the GHSOM, as shown in Fig. 2.

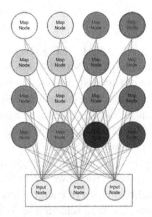

Fig. 1. Network SOM [29]

According to [31], for each map unit, a SOM could be added to the next layer in the hierarchy. This principle is repeated with the third level of the map and the other layers of the GHSOM. To carry out the process of inserting columns or rows in a GHSOM, the following steps must be followed:

1. The weights of each unit are initialized with random values.
2. The standard SOM algorithm is applied.
3. The unit with the largest deviation between the weight vector and the input vectors is chosen to represent the unit error.
4. A row or column is inserted between the error unit and the most different neighbor unit in terms of input space.
5. Steps 1 to 3 are repeated until the Mean Quantization Error (MQE) reaches a certain threshold, a fraction of the average quantization error of Unit i, at the procedure layer of the hierarchy.

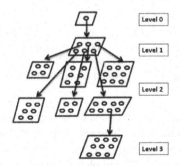

Fig. 2. Structure of a GHSOM network [29]

6 Methodology

The data set (HEART CLEVELAND KAGGLE KDD) was taken at 100% in its pure state and the preprocessing techniques SMOTE (Synthetic Minority Oversampling Technique) and normalization were applied, applying normalization to zero mean.

Once the refined data is obtained, a series of feature selection techniques are applied (Info. gain, Gain Ratio) to identify the attributes that have the greatest impact on the performance of the classifier. Two (2) techniques were applied for classification based on artificial neural networks, SOM and GHSOM.

The testing process was carried out through the implementation of cross-validation using 10 folds and the results obtained from it were represented in the respective confusion matrices, allowing the quality metrics of each of the experimental scenarios to be calculated. From this, the techniques (both selection and classification) that yielded the best results were identified. Figure 3 describes this process.

7 Simulation Scenarios and Results

For the development of this research, I imply the use of two (2) sets of experimental tests. The SOM classifier was used for the first set of tests, varying the previously mentioned feature selection techniques. Once the corresponding feature selection technique was applied, the order of the most relevant attributes could be identified, and from this a series of variables were simulated. series of experimentation scenarios, varying the number of attributes for each of the implemented selection techniques, see Table 1.

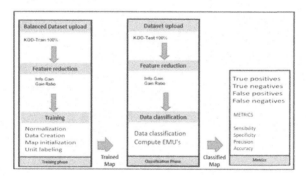

Fig. 3. Training and classification process

For the second set of tests, the GHSOM classifier was used, also varying the previously mentioned feature selection techniques. After identifying the order of relevance of the attributes, the corresponding experimentation scenarios were carried out, varying the number of attributes for each of the implemented selection techniques (see Table 1).

The different experiments were carried out on a DELL LATITUDE 3470 computer with an Intel Core i7 6500U processor at 2.5 Ghz, 8 GB of DDR3 Ram at 2400 MHz and an NVIDIA GeForce 920 M video card with 2 GB of DDR3 capacity. Each experiment

Table 1. Results with implementation of cross validation fold 10 for SOM and GHSOM classifiers

Training technique	T. feature selections	Cant.	Hit percentage (%)	Sensitivity (%)	Specificity (%)	Precision (%)
SOM	Info. Gain	7	71,21 ± 0,033	73,84 ± 0,009	79,56 ± 0,027	77,32 ± 0,051
		8	73,9 ± 0,030	74,50 ± 0,016	74,66 ± 0,024	75,82 ± 0,038
		9	74,35 ± 0,028	74,39 ± 0,012	75,59 ± 0,016	81,10 ± 0,027
		10	**75,03 ± 0,019**	**75,05 ± 0,049**	**78,65 ± 0,014**	**83,56 ± 0,037**
		11	74,19 ± 0,045	73,92 ± 0,043	77,24 ± 0,036	76,46 ± 0,009
		12	73,99 ± 0,023	73,29 ± 0,010	76,62 ± 0,018	77,01 ± 0,036
		13	72,37 ± 0,027	74,49 ± 0,008	77,42 ± 0,022	76,86 ± 0,037
	Gain ratio	5	73,16 ± 0,021	76,84 ± 0,007	75,4 ± 0,017	78,8 ± 0,098
		6	75,15 ± 0,028	75,76 ± 0,009	81,37 ± 0,047	78,79 ± 0,076
		7	78,12 ± 0,022	76,8 ± 0,010	75,36 ± 0,018	78,76 ± 0,029
		8	**78,35 ± 0,009**	**76,89 ± 0,003**	**79,35 ± 0,008**	**77,23 ± 0,013**
		9	77,68 ± 0,002	75,11 ± 0,005	76,83 ± 0,003	81,2 ± 0,022
		10	73,23 ± 0,003	74,47 ± 0,091	73,44 ± 0,005	75,35 ± 0,028
		11	74,56 ± 0,002	74,59 ± 0,052	73,3 ± 0,083	79,35 ± 0,019
GHSOM	Info. Gain	**7**	**81,45 ± 0,016**	**82,12 ± 0,005**	**77,91 ± 0,049**	**80,46 ± 0,011**
		8	80,12 ± 0,078	78,68 ± 0,018	74,12 ± 0,015	76,45 ± 0,014
		9	74,98 ± 0,004	75,96 ± 0,006	75,01 ± 0,031	81,99 ± 0,016
		10	74,89 ± 0,005	79,12 ± 0,005	81,69 ± 0,005	74,90 ± 0,010
		11	78,19 ± 0,003	75,84 ± 0,006	74,63 ± 0,003	75,21 ± 0,007
		12	74,60 ± 0,031	80,59 ± 0,008	74,60 ± 0,006	74,60 ± 0,025
		13	78,86 ± 0,010	75,21 ± 0,007	76,68 ± 0,006	83,92 ± 0,019
	Gain ratio	5	74,75 ± 0,005	74,80 ± 0,014	74,71 ± 0,007	74,75 ± 0,011
		6	74,41 ± 0,005	75,13 ± 0,022	75,65 ± 0,008	75,41 ± 0,014
		7	78,16 ± 0,004	76,12 ± 0,009	76,19 ± 0,004	76,16 ± 0,016
		8	**82,24 ± 0,046**	**78,14 ± 0,019**	**83,32 ± 0,035**	**81,24 ± 0,010**
		9	75,76 ± 0,014	79,13 ± 0,008	76,30 ± 0,003	75,76 ± 0,007
		10	76,04 ± 0,003	75,41 ± 0,027	76,58 ± 0,081	76,04 ± 0,035
		11	75,77 ± 0,005	75,06 ± 0,009	76,38 ± 0,010	75,77 ± 0,019

was carried out 10 times, thanks to which the values of the metrics that allowed evaluating the quality of the processes were obtained. See Tables 1 and 2 that contain each quality metric by technique of selection of characteristics and by method of classification, with their respective standard deviation.

In the classification process of both sets of tests, the 10-fold cross-validation technique was used, applying to the HEART CLEVELAND KAGGLE KDD training data set, and generating simulations that allow evaluating the diagnosis of heart disease.

At the end of each experimentation scenario, the evaluation of the proposed functional models was carried out, calculating the sensitivity, specificity, precision, and accuracy evaluation metrics. Figure 3 describes the process.

8 Conclusions

Considering that the most appropriate metric to evaluate the performance of a classifier is the success rate, since it is the ratio of true positives to true negatives. For the set of tests carried out with the SOM classifier, the best results have been obtained by using the Gain ratio feature selection technique with 8 attributes, reaching a percentage of correct answers of 78.35 ± 0.009, as shown in Table 2.

For the set of tests carried out with the GHSOM classifier, the best results have been obtained by using the Gain ratio feature selection technique with 7 attributes, reaching a percentage of correct answers of 81.45 ± 0.016, as shown in the Table 2.

The most significant simulation scenarios are provided in Table 2, where it can be verified that, using the GHSOM classifier and the GAIN RATIO feature selection technique, better values are obtained in the metrics that allow evaluating the quality of the proposed method.

Table 2. Best result

Training technique	T. feature selections	Cant.	Hit percentage (%)	Sensitivity (%)	Specificity (%)	Precision (%)
SOM	Info. gain	10	75,03 ± 0,019	75,05 ± 0,049	78,65 ± 0,014	83,56 ± 0,037
	Gain ratio	8	78,35 ± 0,009	76,89 ± 0,003	79,35 ± 0,008	77,23 ± 0,013
GHSOM	Info. gain	8	78,35 ± 0,009	76,89 ± 0,003	79,35 ± 0,008	77,23 ± 0,013
	Gain ratio	7	81,45 ± 0,016	82,12 ± 0,005	77,91 ± 0,049	80,46 ± 0,011

With GAIN RATIO, the 7 characteristics that best contribute to the classification process have been identified, in order of priority, from highest to lowest. These are: number of major vessels, resting blood pressure, sugar level, maximum heart rate, number of major vessels, cholesterol, angina-inducing exercise.

The quality metrics obtained with this distribution were: a success rate of 81.45%; sensitivity of 82.12%; specificity of 77.91%; and precision of 80.46%. The fact of using only the 7 most relevant characteristics of the 13 possible attributes of the data set (Heart Cleveland Kaggle Disease Data set) contributes to generating a lighter cardiovascular disease identification system, which will require fewer hardware resources for the process of classification.

References

1. World Health Organization. https://www.who.int/es/news-room/fact-sheets/detail/cardiovas cular-diseases-(cvds). Accessed 15 Jan 2022
2. Pan American Health Organization. https://www.paho.org/es/temas/hipertension. Accessed 16 Jan 2022
3. PLOS One Staff. Correction: comparison of risk models for mortality and cardiovascular events between machine learning and conventional logistic regression analysis. PloS One, **14**(10), e0223931 (2019)
4. Mukherjee, T., Robbins, T., Keung, S.N.L.C., Sankar, S., Randeva, H., Arvanitis, T.N.: A systematic review considering risk factors for mortality of patients discharged from hospital with a diagnosis of diabetes. J. Diabetes Complications **34**, 107705 (2020)
5. Yao, L., et al.: Enhanced automated diagnosis of coronary artery disease using features extracted from QT interval time series and ST–T waveform. IEEE Access **8**, 129510–129524 (2020)
6. Strodthoff, N., Strodthoff, C.: Detecting and interpreting myocardial infarction using fully convolutional neural networks. Physiological **40**(1), 015001 (2019)
7. Kitchenham, B., Brereton, O.P., Budgen, D., Turner, M., Bailey, J., Linkman, S.: Systematic literature reviews in software engineering—a systematic literature review. Inf. Softw. Technol. **51**(1), 7–15 (2009). https://doi.org/10.1016/j.infsof.2008.09.009
8. Manterola, C., Astudillo, P., Arias, E., Claros, N.: Systematic reviews of the literature: what should be known about them. Cir. Esp. **91**(3), 149–155 (2013). https://doi.org/10.1016/j.cir esp.2011.07.009
9. García-Pérez, L., et al.: Systematic review of health-related utilities in Spain: the case of mental health. Gac. Sanit. **28**(1), 77–83 (2013). https://doi.org/10.1016/j.gaceta.2013.04.006
10. Merlano-Porras, C.A., Gorbanev, L.: Health system in Colombia: a systematic review of literature. Rev. Gerencia Políticas Salud **12**(24), 74–86 (2013)
11. Sanchez, A., Neira, D., Cabello, J.J.: Frameworks applied in quality management—a systematic review. Rev. Espacios **37**(9), 17 (2016)
12. Grams, M.E., et al.: Validation of CKD and related conditions in existing data sets: a systematic review. Amer. J. Kidney Dis. **57**(1), 44–54 (2011). https://doi.org/10.1053/j.ajkd.2010.05.013
13. Crimi, G., et al.: Percutaneous coronary intervention techniques for bifurcation disease: network meta-analysis reveals superiority of double-kissing crush. Can. J. Cardiol. **36**(6), 906–914 (2020)
14. Kandasamy, S., Anand, S.S.: Cardiovascular disease among women from vulnerable populations: a review. Can. J. Cardiol. **34**(4), 450–457 (2018)
15. Retnakaran, R.: Novel biomarkers for predicting cardiovascular disease in patients with diabetes. Can. J. Cardiol. **34**(5), 624–631 (2018)
16. Kramer, A.I., Trinder, M., Brunham, L.R.: Estimating the prevalence of familial hypercholes-terolemia in acute coronary syndrome: a systematic review and meta-analysis. Can. J. Cardiol. **35**(10), 1322–1331 (2019)
17. Ordovas, K.G., Baldassarre, L.A., Bucciarelli-Ducci, C., et al.: Cardiovascular magnetic resonance in women with cardiovascular disease: position statement from the Society for Cardiovascular Magnetic Resonance (SCMR). J. Cardiovasc Magn. Reson **23**, 52 (2021). https://doi.org/10.1186/s12968-021-00746-z
18. Chawla, N.V., Bowyer, K.W., Hall, L.O., Kegelmeyer, W.P.: SMOTE: synthetic minority over-sampling technique. J. Artif. Intell. Res. **16**, 321–357 (2002)
19. Liu, A., Ghosh, J., Martin, C.: Generative oversampling for mining imbalanced datasets. In: de International Conference on Data Mining-DMIN (2007)

20. Sánchez-maroño, V.B.N.: A review of feature selection methods on synthetic data, pp. 483–519 (2013). https://doi.org/10.1007/s10115-012-0487-8

21. Spolaˆ, N., Monard, M.C.: Label construction for multi-label feature selection (2014). https://doi.org/10.1109/BRACIS.2014.52

22. Kaur, R., Kumar, G., Kumar, K.: A comparative study of feature selection techniques for intrusion detection. In: de 2nd International Conference on Computing for Sustainable Global Development (2015)

23. Singh, R., Kumar, H., Singla, R.K.: Analysis of Feature Selection Techniques for Network Traffic Dataset. In Machine Intelligence and Research Advancement (ICMIRA), 2013 International Conference on, (pp. 42–46). IEEE (2013)

24. Bolón-Canedo, V., Sánchez-Maroño, N., Alonso-Betanzos, A.: A review of feature selection methods on synthetic data. Knowl. Inf. Syst. **34**(3), 483–519 (2013). https://doi.org/10.1007/s10115-012-0487-8

25. Kumar Kundu, M., Mohapatra, D.P., Konar, A., Chakraborty, A. (eds.): Advanced Computing, Networking and Informatics- Volume 1. SIST, vol. 27. Springer, Cham (2014). https://doi.org/10.1007/978-3-319-07353-8

26. Ibrahim, H.E., Badr, S.M., Shaheen, M.A.: Adaptive layered approach using machine learning techniques with gain ratio for intrusion detection systems. arXiv preprint arXiv:1210.7650 (2012)

27. Chen, A.M., Lu, H.M., Hecht-Nielsen, R.: Sobre la geometría de las superficies de error de red neuronal de avance. Cálculo neuronal **5**(6), 910–927 (1993)

28. Kohonen, T.: Associative memory: a system-theoretical approach, vol. 17. Springer, Heidelberg (2012). https://doi.org/10.1007/978-3-642-96384-1

29. Kohonen, T.: Essentials of the self-organizing map. Neural Netw. **37**, 52–65 (2013)

30. Kohonen, T.: Analysis of a simple self-organizing process. Biol. Cybern. **44**(2), 135–140 (1982)

31. Dittenbach, M., Merkl, D., Rauber, A.: Organizing and exploring high-dimensional data with the growing hierarchical self-organizing map. In: FSKD, pp. 626–630 (2002)

Bird Identification
from the Thamnophilidae Family
at the Andean Region of Colombia

Sara Virginia Martinez Ortega and Milton Sarria-Paja[(✉)][iD]

Universidad Santiago de Cali, Cali, Colombia
{sara.martinez01,milton.sarria00}@usc.edu.co

Abstract. Colombia, with more than 1900 known bird species, is amongst the countries with the highest diversity of this biological group worldwide. It is important to promote environmental conservation to help protect wildlife and biodiversity. In order to promote environmental conservation we need to characterize the areas of interest, by identifying the wildlife species populating such areas. Bioacoustics plays an important role in this area, as it uses non-invasive methods, thus reducing the impact while collecting data. In the case of characterizing bird population, bioacoustics helps to analyze their vocalizations and characterize the species by using their calls and songs. In this research, we center attention on the western mountain range of Colombia, in order to identify and classify the 30 species of the Thamnophilidae family inhabiting this area. We use audio recordings from Xenocanto (www.xeno-canto.org), by filtering the metadata it was possible to select 3689 recordings labeled as birdsongs from the Thamnophilidae family and collected in the area of interest. We compare different classification approaches, ranging from classical machine learning techniques such as logistic regression and support vector machine classifiers to modern techniques based on deep learning. For the task at hand, we use pre-trained models to evaluate the usability of models trained on other domains. According to the results, good performance was achieved when using transfer learning for feature extraction and use classical machine learning schemes for classification. Nevertheless, best performance was achieved using a support vector machine classifier and a feature representation based on the mel-frequency cepstral coefficients as feature vectors. Other deep learning approaches have poor performance or were unable to converge given the low amount of data.

Keywords: Bird identification · Thamnophilidae family · Transfer learning · Deep embedding · MFCC

1 Introduction

Acoustics is essential for many living beings, as it plays an important role for communications [14]. Acoustics allows spatial navigation, prey localization,

K. Saeed and J. Dvorský (Eds.): CISIM 2022, LNCS 13293, pp. 243–257, 2022.
https://doi.org/10.1007/978-3-031-10539-5_18

defend the territory, raise attention for predators, find couple, among other important social functions [19]. The analysis of acoustic signals advances knowledge and gives insights from many species. It helps to study behavior, quantify and monitor populations, as well it helps in taxonomic identification [14].

Monitoring the State and trend of animal diversity and population levels is paramount to evaluate the health of ecosystems [12]. For many reasons, one of the most studied groups of wildlife are birds. Birds are a good indicator of ecosystem health, as they help with insect and rodent control, seed dispersal and plant pollination [22]. The use of acoustic techniques for bird monitoring is growing due to different reasons. For example, there is no physical contact with species [29], and it does not induce alterations in the behavior of individuals [37]. Furthermore, it allows to estimate population density as well as monitoring endangered species and the impact of human activity [14].

There are bird families that hinder their observation because they have rapid movements and prefer areas with a great density of vegetation. An example is the Thamnophilidae family, also known as antbirds, even though its feeding is not currently based on ants their biological function is pest control [11]. Birds of the Thamnophilidae family are weakly distinguished by the plumage, however, they show vocal differences [11]. This family is composed of 62 genera, and for the present work it is of special interest the 19 genera composed of 30 species that inhabit the western mountain range in the Andean region of Colombia [16].

Colombia has a great diversity of birds, approximately 1900 species, and therefore it is important to promote its protection and conservation. However, to the best of our knowledge, the number of studies aiming at a better understanding and analysis of bird populations in Colombia is limited. There are different factors hampering this type of studies, such as absence of data or difficulty to access existing databases, low-quality recordings, lack of funding to collect new information and advance research in this field, security risks for researchers to access protected areas, among others [31]. Recently, technologies and digital tools have made a huge impact on different fields, including biology [1,17,34]. These technologies facilitate and streamline different tasks that have typically been carried out manually [18,29].

When done manually, the analysis of bird songs takes considerable time in order to process and extract the biological information of importance [28,29]. Even though there are different computer tools for the acoustic analysis of certain species. Most bird vocalization studies are based on visual spectrogram inspection [6,12,28]. Furthermore, one of the top challenges present at the time of obtaining the sounds of monitoring in nature, is that they tend to be polyphonic because it contains a vocalization of different species or the recording contains a mix of different sound sources (wind, water sources, population sounds, between others) [2].

This research work aims to explore the use of modern signal processing and pattern recognition techniques to automate the analysis and recognition of bird calls from the Andean region of South West Colombian. The remainder of this paper is organized as follows. Section 2 describes different research works using signal processing and machine learning techniques in the area of bioacoustics. Section 3 presents the specific details of this research such as the dataset, the preprocessing techniques and the classification schemes. Section 4 presents the results of our experiments, and finally Sect. 5 presents the conclusions and final remarks.

2   Related Work

There are different research works addressing this problem in detail. Solutions based on classical approaches, including support vector machines (SVM), K-nearest neighbors (KNN), Gaussian mixture models (GMM), among others. Recent works present important advances using modern techniques such as deep learning. Some of these research works are discussed in this section

The work presented in [28] reviews different paradigms and algorithms existing up to the year 2016. The authors highlight the need to design automatic systems to speed up the required tasks for the detection and classification of birds from acoustic recordings. They also present some technical considerations to be taken into account. As an example, we can mention ambient noise variability. Normally, constant noise levels are assumed in the automatic segmentation process. This assumption can have important effects on final results, as we can include acoustic events that do not correspond to the species of interest.

Next, the work presented in [7] compares the performance of different classical methods. In this work, the authors select a sub-set from the Xenocanto database, this subset contains 14027 audio records belonging to 501 species. The authors perform experiments comparing different classification systems by increasing the number of classes and using the mel-frequency cepstral coefficients as feature vectors. According to the results, the performance of classification systems degrades as the number of classes increases. For example, by including only 5 species, all systems achieve accuracy greater than 40%. But when including 100 species, the accuracy drops to values below 20%.

Another important research work is the one presented in [37]. In this work, the authors use dissimilarity measures combined with a support vector machine-based classifier. The authors select different subsets of the database presented in the *LifeClef 2015 Bird Task*, which in turn contains songs from 999 species taken from the Xenocanto database. Spectrogram images were used to extract textural features such as Local Binary Pattern (LBP), Robust Local Binary Pattern (RLBP), and Local Phase Quantization (LPQ). To use a dissimilarity framework, the authors convert the multiclass task to a binary classification problem. Different scenarios were evaluated, and authors report an identification rate of 71% considering 915 species, which they consider the hardest scenario. As reported by [7], in this work authors also conclude that classification rate drops as the number of classes increases.

On the other hand, it is important to mention recent research works using modern signal processing and classification techniques based on deep learning. Here, we present some relevant recent research where the main focus is the use of deep learning techniques.

The most recent work is [12], where authors combine recordings from two well-known data-sets, i.e., the Macaulay Library and Xenocanto, totaling 984 species. Authors use a residual neural network to classify spectrogram images. Frequency values are grouped into 64 bands distributed according to the Mel frequency scale in the range of 150 to 15 kHz. The model is trained to classify around 1000 classes, including not only bird songs but also other acoustic events. As a result, authors report a classification rate of 77%.

Convolutional neural networks (CNN) architectures have been used to classify not only birdsongs but also other wildlife such as mammals. That is the case of the work presented in [18], where authors classify sounds from 14 species including birds and mammals using spectrogram images from sound segments of 12 s. The manuscript reports accuracy and ROC curves per species. Best results for some species surpass 90% accuracy, however that is not the case for all species as in some cases it barely surpass 50%, thus showing how difficult can be this task even with modern techniques.

Another work of interest is [36] where authors use a CNN to analyze and classify birdsongs of the species Phylloscopus cantator and Spelaeornis caudatus from Nepal. In this work, authors use 100 audio samples from the target species and more than 300 acoustic events from other sound sources. Similarly to previous works using DNN, authors use spectrogram images from audio segments of 2–4 s. It is important to mention that this work uses a pre-trained DNN (ResNet50 [8]) and apply fine tuning and data augmentation in order to adapt the model to the task at hand. Authors report specificity, sensitivity, and accuracy superior to 90%. This work is important for us, as it uses transfer learning to compensate for the lack of sufficient data for training a DNN as is the case we explore in this paper.

Above mentioned research works show the potential of signal processing, acoustic analyses, and machine learning techniques applied to biology. However, we also noticed that previous works use manually annotated data-sets [18]. Audio recordings have a high signal-to-noise-ratio (SNR) [12], which allows using fairly simple methods such as energy detection, which analyze the strength of the signal to isolate the events. In the literature we did not find works addressing the problem of detecting acoustic events with low SNR or polyphonic audio recordings.

3   Experimental Setup

In this work we explore the use of pre-trained models for classifying birdsongs from the Thamnophilidae family. The Thamnophilidae family inhabits the western mountain range of the Colombian Andes, and to the best of our knowledge, there are no related works exploring this problem in this geographical area and for this specific bird family. Our experimental design has different stages

First, we need to define the data-set for our experiments. Next, given the audio recordings, it is necessary to define the pre-processing pipeline in order to isolate the relevant acoustic events. Finally, we define the machine learning techniques in order to achieve the automatic classification from the acoustic signal.

3.1 Data-Set

In this work, we used as a primary data source the collection stored in Xeno-canto (www.xeno-canto.org). Xeno-canto is a community-curated collection of recordings from around the world. This collection features more than 680,000 recordings of over 10,000 bird species totaling over 11000 h of audio data. We selected a subset of 3689 audio recordings, For this purpose, we use a Python script to automate the process, however, manual supervision was necessary in order to ensure that the audio recordings audio recordings were from the 30 species of interest.

During this process we noticed that the audio files have different quality, as they have been recorded by different users with different methods, not everyone has the ideal microphone or recorder for this of task. In addition to this, the recordings were taken at different times of the year, in different places, some of them close to populated areas. These factors affect the task at hand, as we can face different artifacts, i.e., audio events belonging to other sound sources different to the species of interest, and different noise levels, this represents a challenge [32].

To explore the information available, and perform a preliminary analysis, we compute the average long term spectral envelope. This allows to select the frequency range of interest, and re-sample all audio recordings to an uniform sampling rate of 16 kHz. Results are depicted in Fig. 1, as we can see, there is an energy concentration between the frequency range 2 kHz–8 kHz. This result is inline with previously reported analyzes, for most birds, the vocalizations contain information 250 Hz to 8.3 kHz [9]. For the Thamnophilidae family it has been reported that vocalizations contain relevant information below 8 kHz [10,11].

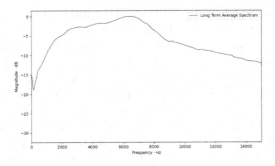

Fig. 1. Long term average spectral envelope for a random sample of audio recordings

Next, we establish a strategy to isolate the audio events of interest, i.e., those acoustic events belonging to individuals of the Thamnophilidae family. The audio recordings downloaded from the Xeno-canto data-set contain different sound sources as well as background noise. First, we use the algorithm presented in [21] to reduce the noise levels. Figure 2 depicts an example of applying this technique to an audio recording. We can see at the top left of the figure a waveform and at the bottom left its respective spectrogram. It shows different acoustic events as well high noise levels in between the acoustic events. At the top right we can see the filtered waveform, and at the bottom right its respective spectrogram. As we can see, this technique can be useful for the task at hand to reduce the background noise.

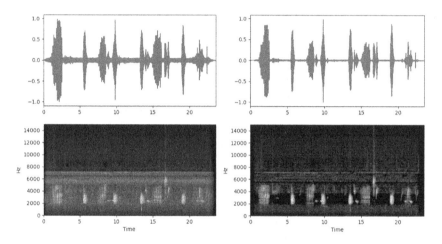

Fig. 2. Waveform and spectrogram examples showing the effects of the de-noising algorithm

After reducing the noise levels, it is necessary to isolate the acoustic events of interest. In the literature we can find different approaches, however, most of them are based on energy levels. In [36,37] the authors propose and algorithm that combines the spectral centroid and the energy level (signal strength) to identify the acoustic events of interest. After a pilot experiment, we found that this technique can present some drawbacks. First, this technique requires a complete removal of the background noise. This is not always possible, as many noise reduction techniques require an initial audio segment to estimate the noise contaminating the whole audio segment [33], and this small segment is not always available. Second, the technique assumes that all audio events have stable values for the energy and spectral centroid. That is not the case, specially if we are unable to completely remove the background noise. To illustrate this problem we present two examples in the Fig. 3.

For this experiment we set the same configuration as suggested by [36,37], i.e., non-overlaping windows with 50 ms duration. The Fig. 3 depicts two waveform examples after applying the noise reduction algorithm. From top to bottom we can see the waveform, the normalized energy and the spectral centroid. First, we observe that the energy level is very small for some some acoustic events, so it is difficult to determine a criteria to discriminate between silence and acoustic events. Another important observation is that the spectral centroid is not consistent. As can be seen, for the waveform at the left, the spectral centroid takes values around 6 kHz in the segments where there is an acoustic event of interest. While the non acoustic events take values around 4 kHz. However, for the waveform at the right, the spectral centroid takes values between 2 kHz and 4 kHz. And the non acoustic events take values close to 5 kHz.

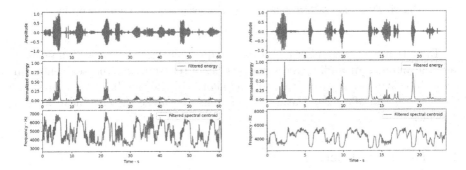

Fig. 3. Waveform, energy envelope and spectral centroid for two waveforms

This is not a problem commonly addressed in previous works. Considering the noise levels and the multiple sound sources that can be present in an audio recording. In a previous work, we proposed to use an approach to automatically isolate only those acoustic events belonging to the Thamnophilidae family taking the following considerations.

There are two types of bird vocalizations, i.e., calls and songs. For the case of bird songs, it refers to a complex structure with several acoustic events, with small pauses in between. Bird songs play important roles such as attracting a mate or defend the territory. Bird calls on the other hand, usually are monosyllabic acoustic events, have shorter duration than songs and usually means danger or establish location. [5,13]. Previous works such as the presented in [37], do not take into account this difference. For a given audio recording, authors suppress all segments with low energy and concatenate all acoustic events in one single utterance. Another approach is to segment the audio recording in short segments of fixed duration [12]. These works do not considerate other sound sources or short duration acoustic events.

In this work we use a previously proposed algorithm to isolate acoustic events of interest and discard those events that do not correspond to bird songs or bird calls [15]. The algorithm uses sound source separation based on Robust Principal Component Analysis (RPCA) [4], combined with the Hilbert envelope to isolated those acoustic events that can be considered either as bird songs or bird calls. After having these events isolated, there is a chance many are noise or artifacts coming from the environment. In this case a binary classifier is trained to discriminate between bird songs or bird calls and non-bird acoustic [15]. Figure 4 depicts the building blocks of the algorithm proposed in [15].

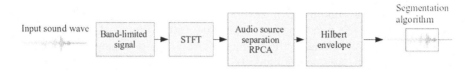

Fig. 4. Detection of bird-related acoustic events in the audio recording

Table 1 shows the number of audio recordings downloaded from Xeno-canto, and the number of audio events per species after applying the segmentation algorithm. We can see that there is unbalance in the number of samples per species, this can affect the learning algorithms and make the classification task difficult.

3.2   Feature Extraction

In this work we use the classical Mel-frequency cepstral coefficients (MFCC) as feature vectors. The MFCCs are the most widely used features specially for speech enabled systems. Here, the recordings were pre-emphasized using a first order finite impulse response filter with constant $a = 0.97$, in order to reduce the dynamic range of the frequency representation. In our experiments, 27 triangular band-pass filters spaced according to the mel scale were used in the computation of 13 MFCC features including the 0-th order cepstral coefficient (log-energy). We did not include the derivatives. As a result, the feature representation for a single audio recording can be expressed as a $P \times T$ matrix, where $P = 13$ (the number of MFCC) and T the number of frames for such audio recording.

Given the MFCC feature representation, it is necessary to use a feature mapping strategy in order to use the MFCC in a classical classification. For this purpose, it is required to map the matrices of $P \times T$ to a fixed dimension vector, considering that the number of frames is variable. A suitable technique that has been used to describe images [30], and later successfully extended to audio applications [23,35], is to use the covariance matrix. The idea is to compute the covariance matrix from a short-time feature representation such as MFCCs. Next, we collapse it into a vector by taking the upper (or lower) triangular of the covariance matrix, including the diagonal. It is important to note that this vector may be subject to dimension reduction by applying Principal Component Analysis (PCA) [23].

Most recent works use images from spectrograms as pre-processing technique to feed modern deep-learning models. Training a deep model also requires a considerable number of training examples. In many cases, the lack of training data

Table 1. Number of audio recordings and number of audio events after segmentation per species of the Thamnophilidae family

Species	Number of audio recordings	Number of audio events
Cercomacra nigricans	98	117
Cercomacroides parkeri	79	455
Cercomacra tyrannina	303	991
Cymbilaimus lineatus	186	516
Drymophila striaticeps	131	725
Dysithamnus occidentalis	49	57
Dysithamus mentalis	391	561
Dysithamnus puncticeps	63	75
Epinecrophyla fulviventris	91	365
Gymnocichla nudiceps	173	160
Gymnopithys bicolor	83	321
Hafferia inmaculata	57	178
Hafferia zeledoni	118	465
Hepsilochmus axillaris	48	162
Hylopylax naerioides	87	422
Microhopias quixensis	202	1237
Myrmotherula axillaris	257	759
Myrmotherula ignota	61	193
Myrmotherula pacifica	54	271
Myrmotherula schisticolor	58	227
Phaenostictus mcleannani	57	309
Poliocrania exsul	242	502
Sipia berlepschi	43	229
Sipia nigricauda	57	297
Taraba major	354	136
Terenura callinota	24	158
Thamnistes anabatinus	52	203
Thamnophilus atrinucha	191	403
Thamnophilus multistratus	88	200
Thamnophilus unicolor	126	206
TOTAL	**3685**	**11800**

is compensated by artificially creating new training samples, this is also known as data augmentation [24]. Also, another requirement we usually have is to use fixed dimension data. This is difficult to maintain specially for audio, as audio recordings usually have variable length. Some authors use fixed-length audio segments by truncating the signal or by zero padding, also by warping the frequency or time axis of a given spectrogram image to fit a standard dimensionality. In this work we use the mel-spectrogram, with 27 bands and window length of 25 ms, with 10 ms hop time.

Having the covariance matrix, we can use this representation as an image to feed any system based on deep neural networks. By doing this, we do not have the restriction to have always same duration audio recordings or alter the time and frequency axis of the spectrogram images to fit a given dimension. We propose to evaluate this approach, by using the covariance as and array-like image in gray scale.

3.3   Classification Stage

Figure 5 depicts the building blocks of a general-purpose classification system. This system can be used for the task at hand, i.e., given an isolated audio event, we want to identify the bird species producing that sound. As we can see, there is an input acoustic event to the system, and the purpose of the feature extraction stage is to get relevant and discriminative information from the acoustic signal. These features can be manipulated in a post-processing stage. This post-processing allows fitting the feature representation to the requirements of any given classification scheme. Next, we have the inference o classification stage, where a decision is made.

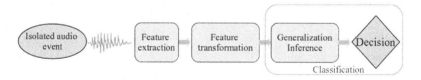

Fig. 5. Building blocks for a general purpose pattern recognition system that can be applied to the task at hand

For the classification stage, we propose to evaluate different schemes, from classical machine learning techniques to modern deep-learning models. First, two classification systems were implemented using logistic regression [3,20] and support vector machines [3,26]. A detailed description of these techniques are out of the scope of this paper. These schemes serve us as baseline to compare against deep-larning based classification schemes. In this work, we use pre-trained deep-learning models for two main reasons. First, the lack of sufficient training data to completely train a DNN. Second, because we want to explore the potential of different pre-trained models in this particular task. By doing this, we explore feasible solutions aiming at monitoring and preserving not only bird species, but also other endemic species, without the need of massive amounts of data to train a classification system.

There are two approaches we explore with pre-trained models. First, use the DNN as a feature extractor, this can be done by feeding to the DNN an image-like array containing a feature representation of the acoustic signal. Then, the DNN role is to encode such representation into a embedding which results from a feed-forward pass through the layers of the DNN. This embedding can be used as a highly discriminative feature vector to be used in a standard classification system. Second, we can use fine tuning to adjust the output parameters of a pre-trained DNN in order to perform the classification task.

We evaluate three different architectures in different scenarios. First, two well known pre-trained models such as RESNET50 [8] and VGG19 [25]. These two architectures use as input an image-like array, which is compatible with two previously mentioned feature representation for an acoustic signal, i.e., spectrogram images or covariance matrix computed from short-time features such as MFCC. We also explore a third architecture more related to audio applications. Recent state-of-the-art speaker verification systems use deep-learning models to compute fixed-length embeddings from variable length acoustic signals without altering important information such as time or frequency. A robust DNN embedding was proposed in [27], these embeddings also known as *x-vectors*, are the current state-of-the-art representation for applications such as speaker verification.

We propose to use *x-vectors* as a feature vector in a standard classification system. Even though there are evident differences between human speech and bird songs, we want to explore the use of a pre-trained model devoted to an acoustic application (such as speaker verification) in the task of bird identification. To the best of our knowledge, this has not been explored before.

Summarizing, we are interested in the Thamnophilidae family of the western Andean region of Colombia. In our experiments we will compare the following settings in order to determine the best approach to solve this problem:

- Feature extraction: Covariance matrix from short-term features (MFCC). For classical machine learning approaches, this representation is subject of dimensionality reduction using PCA, retaining 98% of cumulative variance. For deep-learning models we maintain the full covariance matrix re-scaling its values to the range 0–1.
- Deep embeddings: Embeddings can be computed from image-like arrays or directly from the spectrogram image or from the covariance matrix computed from the MFCC.
- Classical machine learning approaches: Logistic regression and Support vector machine based classifiers.
- Fine tuned pre-trained models: VGG19 and RESNET50.

4 Results

Table 2 reports the classification results for all classification schemes. We report accuracy ± the standard deviation. As we can see, average classification results

Table 2. Accuracy results for all approaches

Approach	Accuracy (%)	
	Features from MFCC	Features from spectrogram images
Classical approach		
Logistic regression	45.52 ± 0.68	42.02 ± 1.47
SVM	58.47 ± 0.69	44.15 ± 0.89
Embeddings		
Logistic regression + VGG19	21.47 ± 0.47	50.44 ± 0.84
Logistic regression + RESNET50	27.93 ± 0.50	53.17 ± 0.93
Logistic regression + x-vectors	50.52 ± 0.64	
SVM + VGG19	36.58 ± 0.69	48.49 ± 1.09
SVM + RESNET50	48.03 ± 0.64	54.19 ± 1.22
SVM + x-vectors	55.46 ± 0.88	
Fine tuning pre-trained models		
VGG19	36.79 ± 3.30	21.50 ± 3.30
RESNET50	18.36 ± 2.87	15.50 ± 3.30

vary across the approaches we are evaluating with significant differences. Considering the number of species we aim to classify and the limited amount of data, results are inline with the literature.

By examining in detail the results, we can observe that the classical approaches, i.e., logistic regression +MFCC and SVM + MFCC, exhibit a good performance when comparing with approaches using deep embeddings or fine-tuned pre-trained models. In fact, best result are achieved by using SVM + MFCC, next we have SVM + x-vectors. These results show that classical classification schemes are useful for difficult classification tasks in absence of sufficient training examples.

Another important observation is that deep-embeddings are a feasible feature representation to combine with classical classification schemes. However, the best seems to be x-vectors, as we can see this feature representation achieves acceptable performance when combined either with logistic regression or SVM. This may be due to the fact that x-vectors are embeddings designed to extract information from audio recordings. Hence, there is a direct relationship between the task at hand and the domain for which the x-vector extractor was trained.

When comparing the feature representation, we can see that using images from spectrograms have better performance than the use of the covariance matrix to feed the DNN. This is particularly true when using DNN to extract embeddings and combine this feature representation with SVM or logistic regression classifiers. However, when using fine tuning to adjust a pre-trained DNN, we observe that the covariance matrix perform better than the use of spectrogram images. Notwithstanding, performance for fine-tuned DNNs was below the average the approaches using classical approaches for classification.

We can see that fine-tuning is not a good alternative for the task at hand. We can hypothesize that the number of training samples is not enough to train the parameters comprising the output layer of these architectures. More experiments are necessary to get insights and better understand this behavior in these architectures.

5   Conclusions

Herein, we have addressed the problem of bird identification from audio recordings using digital signal processing and machine learning techniques. We propose to evaluate different classification schemes in order to find a simple and effective architecture to solve this problem. We propose to use classical machine learning techniques combined with modern deep-learning models. More specifically, we propose to use pre-trained models as feature extractors, then use these embeddings to feed a logistic regression or SVM classifiers.

According to the results, a simple scheme, consisting of a SVM based classifier combined with a fixed length feature vector derived from the MFCC, achieves the best results for the task at hand. These results show that the covariance matrix representation to summarize the information encoded in MFCC is a powerful feature representation. This approach has shown to be effective in other applications and given the results and the simplicity of the approach we consider it is necessary to continue exploring in this direction.

On the other hand, pre-trained models have shown to be a powerful tool for similar tasks. However, in this case, it lacks effectiveness as results do not outperform the classical scheme. Only the x-vector embedding shows to be a highly discriminative feature representation. Regardless of these results, the problem addressed in this work is yet an unexplored problem, as there are few references in the literature applying DNN to solve bioacoustic problems. Results reported in the literature differ in many different ways. There are reports for a considerable number of classes and high accuracy, but also we encounter some research where the number of classes is lower and the results are around 50%. This confirms our conclusion that more research is needed in the field of bioacoustics applications using deep learning models.

Acknowledgements. We would like to acknowledge the Universidad Santiago de Cali for funding this research.

References

1. Agrawal, R., Archak, S., Tyagi, R.: An overview of biodiversity informatics with special reference to plant genetic resources. Comput. Electron. Agric. **84**, 92–99 (2012)
2. Arriaga, J.G., Cody, M.L., Vallejo, E.E., Taylor, C.E.: Bird-db: a database for annotated bird song sequences. Eco. Inform. **27**, 21–25 (2015)

3. Bishop, C.M., Nasrabadi, N.M.: Pattern Recognition and Machine Learning, vol. 4. Springer, Cham (2006)
4. Candés, E.J., Li, X., Ma, Y., Wright, J.: Robust principal component analysis? J. ACM (JACM) **58**(3), 1–37 (2011)
5. Catchpole, C.K.: The biology and evolution of bird songs. Perspect. Biol. Med. **30**(1), 47–64 (1986)
6. Furnas, B.J.: Rapid and varied responses of songbirds to climate change in California coniferous forests. Biol. Cons. **241**, 108347 (2020)
7. Guo, X., Liu, Q.Z.: A comparison study to identify birds species based on bird song signals. In: ITM Web of Conferences, vol. 12, p. 02002. EDP Sciences (2017)
8. He, K., Zhang, X., Ren, S., Sun, J.: Deep residual learning for image recognition. In: Proceedings of the IEEE Conference on Computer Vision and Pattern Recognition, pp. 770–778 (2016)
9. Hu, Y., Cardoso, G.C.: Are bird species that vocalize at higher frequencies preadapted to inhabit noisy urban areas? Behav. Ecol. **20**(6), 1268–1273 (2009)
10. IsLER, M., Isler, P.R., Whitney, B.M.: Use of vocalizations to establish species limits in antbirds (passeriformes: Thamnophilidae). Auk **115**(3), 577–590 (1998)
11. Isler, M.L., Maldonado-Coelho, M.: Calls distinguish species of antbirds (Aves: Passeriformes: Thamnophilidae) in the genus Pyriglena. Zootaxa **4291**(2), 275–294 (2017)
12. Kahl, S., Wood, C.M., Eibl, M., Klinck, H.: Birdnet: a deep learning solution for avian diversity monitoring. Eco. Inform. **61**, 101236 (2021)
13. Marler, P.: Bird calls: their potential for behavioral neurobiology. Ann. N. Y. Acad. Sci. **1016**(1), 31–44 (2004)
14. Martínez-Medina, D., et al.: Estado, desarrollo y tendencias de los estudios en acústica de la fauna en colombia. Biota Colomb. **22**(1), 2021 (2021)
15. Martínez-Ortega, S.V., Sarria-Paja, M.: Automatic segmentation and classification of the thamnophilidae's family of the western andean region of colombia. In: 2021 XXIII Symposium on Image, Signal Processing and Artificial Vision (STSIVA), pp. 1–6. IEEE (2021)
16. McMullan, M., Donegan, T.M., Quevedo, A.: Field Guide to the Birds of Colombia. Fundación ProAves (2010)
17. Nazir, S., Kaleem, M.: Advances in image acquisition and processing technologies transforming animal ecological studies. Ecol. Inf. **61**, 101212 (2021)
18. Ruff, Z.J., Lesmeister, D.B., Appel, C.L., Sullivan, C.M.: Workflow and convolutional neural network for automated identification of animal sounds. Ecol. Ind. **124**, 107419 (2021)
19. Rundus, A.S., Hart, L.A.: Overview: animal acoustic communication and the role of the physical environment. J. Comp. Psychol. **116**(2), 120 (2002)
20. Rymarczyk, T., Kozłowski, E., Kłosowski, G., Niderla, K.: Logistic regression for machine learning in process tomography. Sensors **19**(15), 3400 (2019)
21. Sainburg, T., Thielk, M., Gentner, T.Q.: Finding, visualizing, and quantifying latent structure across diverse animal vocal repertoires. PLoS Comput. Biol. **16**(10), e1008228 (2020)
22. Sekercioglu, C.H.: Increasing awareness of avian ecological function. Trends Ecol. Evol. **21**(8), 464–471 (2006)
23. Senoussaoui, M., Saria-Paja, M.O., Cardinal, P., Falk, T.H., Michaud, F.: 1. state-of-the-art speaker recognition methods applied to speakers with dysarthria. In: Voice Technologies for Speech Reconstruction and Enhancement, pp. 7–34. De Gruyter (2020)

24. Shorten, C., Khoshgoftaar, T.M.: A survey on image data augmentation for deep learning. J. Big Data **6**(1), 1–48 (2019). https://doi.org/10.1186/s40537-019-0197-0

25. Simonyan, K., Zisserman, A.: Very deep convolutional networks for large-scale image recognition (2014). arXiv preprint arXiv:1409.1556

26. Smola, A.J., Schölkopf, B.: Learning with Kernels, vol. 4. Citeseer, Princeton (1998)

27. Snyder, D., Garcia-Romero, D., Sell, G., Povey, D., Khudanpur, S.: X-vectors: Robust dnn embeddings for speaker recognition. In: 2018 IEEE International Conference on Acoustics, Speech and Signal Processing (ICASSP), pp. 5329–5333. IEEE (2018)

28. Stowell, D., Wood, M., Stylianou, Y., Glotin, H.: Bird detection in audio: a survey and a challenge. In: 2016 IEEE 26th International Workshop on Machine Learning for Signal Processing (MLSP), pp. 1–6. IEEE (2016)

29. Szymański, P., Olszowiak, K., Wheeldon, A., Budka, M., Osiejuk, T.S.: Passive acoustic monitoring gives new insight into year-round duetting behaviour of a tropical songbird. Ecol. Ind. **122**, 107271 (2021)

30. Tuzel, O., Porikli, F., Meer, P.: Region covariance: a fast descriptor for detection and classification. In: Leonardis, A., Bischof, H., Pinz, A. (eds.) ECCV 2006. LNCS, vol. 3952, pp. 589–600. Springer, Heidelberg (2006). https://doi.org/10.1007/11744047_45

31. Vélez, D., et al.: Distribution of birds in colombia. Biodivers. Data J. **9**, e59202 (2021)

32. Vellinga, W.P., Planqué, R.: The xeno-canto collection and its relation to sound recognition and classification. In: CLEF (Working Notes) (2015)

33. Xie, J., Colonna, J.G., Zhang, J.: Bioacoustic signal denoising: a review. Artif. Intell. Rev. **54**(5), 3575–3597 (2020). https://doi.org/10.1007/s10462-020-09932-4

34. Xie, J., Hu, K., Guo, Y., Zhu, Q., Yu, J.: On loss functions and cnns for improved bioacoustic signal classification. Ecol. Inf. **64**, 101331 (2021)

35. Ye, C., Liu, J., Chen, C., Song, M., Bu, J.: Speech emotion classification on a riemannian manifold. In: Huang, Y.M.R. (ed.) PCM 2008. LNCS, vol. 5353, pp. 61–69. Springer, Heidelberg (2008). https://doi.org/10.1007/978-3-540-89796-5_7

36. Zhong, M., et al.: Acoustic detection of regionally rare bird species through deep convolutional neural networks. Ecol. Inf. **64**, 101333 (2021)

37. Zottesso, R.H., Costa, Y.M., Bertolini, D., Oliveira, L.E.: Bird species identification using spectrogram and dissimilarity approach. Eco. Inform. **48**, 187–197 (2018)

Blood Pressure Estimation from Photoplethysmography Signals by Applying Deep Learning Techniques

Roy Rodriguez-Marquez[1,2] and Silvia Moreno[1(✉)]

[1] Universidad Simon Bolivar, 080001 Barranquilla, Colombia
smoreno12@unisimonbolivar.edu.co
[2] Universidad San Martin, 080001 Barranquilla, Colombia

Abstract. Blood Pressure is one of the physiological parameters that are significant to assess a person's health status, so it is of importance to control this parameter and monitor blood pressure in intensive care units. There is an interest to develop non-invasive methods that allow the continuous monitoring of this vital sign. In this work, Convolutional Neural Networks (CNNs) are used to estimate Blood Pressure from photoplethysmography signals (PPG) from the University of Queensland's dataset. The PPG signal values of 5590 samples recorded in this dataset were used to plot images of the PPG signal over predetermined intervals of time, and then these images were used as input for a CNN. Our method predicts Systolic Blood Pressure (SBP) and Diastolic Blood Pressure (DBP) by applying Regression techniques from Artificial Intelligence as the last layer of the CNN. Our best model achieves an R2 coefficient of 0.79 for SBP and 0.93 for DBP. This demonstrates that our solution has the potential to predict these physiological parameters in a non-invasive, continuous way.

Keywords: Photoplethysmography · Deep Learning · Blood pressure

1 Introduction

Blood pressure is one of the physiological parameters that are most significant to determine a person's health status, along with heart rate, body temperature, and respiratory rate. It is of great importance to control these parameters and especially to monitor blood pressure in intensive care units. Frequently, in these units there are patients with great hemodynamic instability that may cause organ or even multiple organ failure.

The two usual ways to measure blood pressure in intensive care units are: invasive, through artery cannulation, and non-invasive, through a sphygmomanometer, which in most cases is connected for patient monitoring. In clinical practice, there are health risks associated with cannulation and reliability problems with the sphygmomanometer, since this approach is not continuous. For these reasons, research is being performed to find other methods to measure blood pressure, however, these are still in study and their effectiveness is not confirmed.

In this study a method is proposed for blood pressure estimation from the photo-plethysmography signal (PPG), so we can measure Systolic Blood Pressure (SBP) and Diastolic Blood Pressure (DBP). For this purpose, a systemic approach is taken to inter-act with the problem and to determine the fundamental elements involved in the subject matter. The proposed method applies Deep Learning, specifically Convolutional Neu-ronal Networks (CNNs) combined with Regression techniques to predict the values for SBP and DBP, taking as input the PPG signal.

2 Previous Work

Photoplethysmography is a non-invasive optical technique that allows to measure vari-ations in volume and perfusion of blood through the skin by measuring changes in light absorption. The PPG signal contains components that are synchronous to the cardiac and respiratory rhythms [1]. Photoplethysmography produces an optical signal related to arterial volumetric pulsations of blood, and its analysis can be used as an alternative to estimate Blood Pressure in a simple, continuous and non-invasive way. Therefore, PPG can be used for the detection and early evaluation of non-invasive cardiovascular and peripheral micro-circulation pathologies [2].

However, despite the improvements achieved by many authors that have attempted to measure Blood Pressure without a cuff, there is still a need to find reliable methods that can be used in clinical practice. Some of these authors have applied signal features such as Pulse Transit Time (PTT), which is the time that takes the pulse to travel from the heart to the finger, Vascular Transit Time (VTT) that is calculated from the difference in time from the PPG measured in the finger and the Electrocardiogram (ECG) measured in the chest. Other authors have used multiple magnetic sensors to measure the Pulse Wave Velocity (PWV) achieving acceptable measures, but using at least two sensors, which makes it inappropriate to some applications since it implies carrying two sensors at the same time during, for example, exercise or sleep [3]. So developing a method that uses only the PPG signal with enough precision would be very useful.

Other previous studies have attempted to optimize the selection of feature points of the PPG signal to better predict Blood Pressure, and have designed a function to evaluate its quality. The results of this study showed that the fusion method (Kalman filter) is capable of obtaining a raw sub-product more precisely than traditional methods, using fixed unique PPG feature points [4].

Another previous work in Blood Pressure estimation applies the Support Vector Machine algorithm (SVM). In this study, it was found that there are two PPG signals according to their waveform: evident dicrotic pulse and non-evident, and the signal of the non-evident dicrotic pulse was selected as the subject of study since it was more universal. Signal features were extracted and then reduced from 21 to 9 to improve precision and reduce the algorithm's complexity [5].

In another study, a new method was researched for the continuous estimation of two main features of the Systolic and Diastolic Blood Pressure waveforms. For this purpose, the peaks of the PPG signal were used to model Systolic Blood Pressure (SBP) and the troughs of the signal to model Diastolic Blood Pressure (DBP). Then an Autoregressive Moving Average (ARMA) model was used to predict the values [6].

In the work of Khalid et. al., the performance of three machine learning algorithms was compared (Regression Trees, Multiple Linear Regression, and Support Vector Machine). The three more significant pulse features were used (pulse area, pulse rising time, and width 25%). Besides, three types of Blood Pressure were considered: hypotension, hypertension, and normal. The Regression Tree algorithm achieved higher accuracy in the Blood Pressure estimation [3].

Another study by Martinez et. al. presents the similarities, both in time and frequency domains, of Invasive Blood Pressure (IBP) and PPG. It was found that the PPG signal is the one that has more informative features in comparison with the ones of IBP. Three hypotheses were tested, H1, H2, and H3. H1: The amplitudes of the PPG waveforms and their corresponding IBP waveforms are not correlated, showing thus that the PPG amplitudes cannot substitute the IBP amplitudes. H2: If the PPG morphology (lineal time-domain analysis) is correlated with the IBP morphology, then the morphology of the PPG waveform contains valuable information that can be used to evaluate Blood Pressure. H3: If the waveforms of PPG and IBP have mutual and coherent information (non-linear dependency analysis), then the PPG waveform morphology contains useful information to predict Blood Pressure. The rejection of hypothesis 1confirmed and validated the other two hypotheses since there is great similarity between the two signals [2].

None of the previous studies applied Deep Learning techniques, such as Convolutional Neural Networks, which is a contribution of this work.

3 Materials and Methods

To estimate Blood Pressure, a training phase is needed where the proposed Convolutional Neural Network model learns in an intelligent and supervised way the elements and features that relate the input data with the outputs. For this Deep Learning task, we used as input the dataset of vital signs from Queensland University (Australia) that contains a wide range of vital sign monitoring data registered during 32 surgical cases in which patients were subjected to anesthesia at the Royal Adelaide Hospital [7]. Included in this data were values for PPG, SBP, and DBP (among others).

For the effective utilization of this dataset, extraction, cleaning, preparation, transformation, and load algorithms were applied. These algorithms were implemented as instructions (scripts) in the programming language Python. Figure 1 describes the overall process.

As a result of the previous process, a depurated training dataset with 5500 records (structured data with PPG, SBP, and DBP information) was obtained for this study.

3.1 Preprocessing Stage

Since raw data was not usable in its original form, a preliminary process of cleaning, mapping, and transformation was necessary. A python script was coded to perform this task. In this first algorithm, the original dataset was taken with the records of the 32 patients. For each case, there was a different number of readings that varied according to the length of the patient monitoring. The program registered a CSV (comma separated

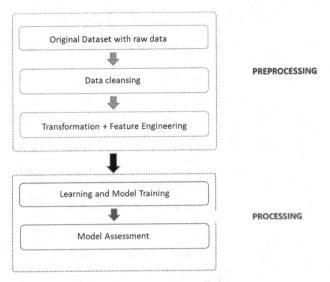

Fig. 1. Overview of the applied process

values) file for every 10 min of continuous reading. The algorithm parsed through the readings of every case, performed a cleaning process of empty values, applied range selection filters of blood pressure values, and generated the depurated files for each case and patient. The summary data of this process can be observed in Table 1.

After this first pre-processing of the original dataset, a set of record segments from the PPG signal was obtained for a time-lapse of 10 s for a range of 689 pairs of SBP-DBP values for each of the cases in the dataset. With this data registered in CSV files, a second algorithm was applied to generate plot images of each segment of the PPG readings during 10 s. This is, for each CSV file, a new JPG file is created with the image of the PPG signal that matches a Blood Pressure value (both Systolic and Diastolic values), similar to the ones presented in Fig. 2. This stage of the pre-processing is also known as Feature Engineering and has the goal to enrich the data to adapt them to the type of Deep Learning technique to be utilized, and so improving the performance of the predictive model proposed as a solution to this problem.

Next, an exhaustive visual inspection (one by one) of all the generated images was performed to detect patterns or atypical waveforms of the PPG signal. The images with unusual waveforms were removed from the dataset that was used for the training stage of the Convolutional Neural Network (CNN) proposed in this study. Finally, 5590 images were used for the training phase and 500 images were used for the test phase.

3.2 Processing Stage

For this stage, we started with a training dataset of 5590 images, which is sufficiently robust to perform the model generation with a two-dimensional Convolutional Neural Network. This CNN was designed to automatically learn the intrinsic features present in the generated PPG images and perform the required prediction. The network predicts

Table 1. Summary data of preprocessing step.

Cases	Total samples	Filtered	Normal BP	High BP	Low BP	Lost
1	729600	690513	86314		604199	39087
2	101376	69149			69149	32227
3	1498522	1280733	188690		1092043	217789
4	876578	801804	445318	87069	269417	74774
5	600000	419556		419556		180444
6	632116	487194	96531	65278	325385	144922
7	322816	322816	31041		291775	0
8	349389	323192	102938		220254	26197
9	654832	602608	26139		576469	52224
10	258487	241080	17812	33637	189631	17407
11	540660	503712	349427	34202	120083	36948
12	1771628	1653431	151541	100515	1401375	118197
13	594536	565089	136034	16779	412276	29447
14	533215	475493	177573	285353	12567	57722
15	158958	134924	62216		72708	24034
16	1148642	976827			976827	171815
17	122266	107537	14666	16259	76612	14729
18	69427	61760		17715	44045	7667
19	139674	123804	32604		91200	15870
20	675123	605711	196470	18380	390861	69412
21	458547	346848	64787		282061	111699
22	977954	891051	64308	776642	50101	86903
23	167733	160379	37434		122945	7354
24	372308	354575		57005	297570	17733
25	633856	521600	226083	94403	201114	112256
26	997822	858241	457631	31950	368660	139581
27	1538143	1000663	126148	37683	836832	537480
28	446111	413942	187561	34007	192374	32169
29	730761	675702	309465	34096	332141	55059
30	368272	316437	64278	46192	205967	51835
31	1264544	1237224	919194	55429	262601	27320
32	496022	451351	353047	65228	33076	44671

Typical Waveform PPG

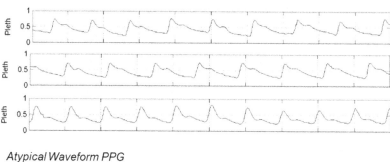

Atypical Waveform PPG

Fig. 2. Examples of typical and atypical PPG signal images

the 2 values related to blood pressure: diastolic (DBP) and systolic (SBP), both in millimeters of mercury (mmHg), according to the units of the input labels, from the image representation of the PPG signal obtained numerically as a continuous, non-invasive reading of a patient during a time interval.

In the Deep Learning field, several techniques and architectures have been proposed with specific applications. One of the most popular is Convolutional Neural Networks. CNNs were inspired by a mammal's visual cortex research and how they perceive the world by using a layered neuron architecture in their brains [8]. In this study, the visual cortex model is imagined as groups of neurons specifically designed to recognize different patterns, features, and distinctive shapes. Each group of neurons is triggered when an object is perceived and they communicate with each other to develop a holistic understanding of the object. In more simple terms, when an object is seen, the system has different groups of neurons that are activated by different traits of the object and they communicate with each other to create a global image [8].

Intuitively, convolutional neural networks take images as input and attempt to find different small features (local connections), independently of their position (space invariant), by applying a series of mathematical operations (stratification, clustering) to understand the whole image and its context. These mathematical operations model an image as a matrix of numbers where each number represents the intensity of the pixels. In our case, the object to perceive and analyze is the image corresponding to the waveform of the PPG signal, and then we proceed to associate it with a pair of SBP and DBP values through linear regression.

3.3 Proposed Convolutional Neural Network

For this Regression Problem, the proposed Convolutional Neural Network takes as input a 64×64 pixels image. The first filter with 3×3 dimensions has a stride of one over our images along the X and Y axis, applying a convolution operation from which we obtain a resulting matrix or feature map with a depth of 16 and 16×16 dimensions. Then we apply max pooling with 2×2 filters, followed by a non-linear activation function (ReLU) which offers better performance over other activation functions.

To this 16×16 matrix a new filter of 3×3 is applied with the convolution operation two more times with depths of 32 and 64, obtaining a reduced matrix by a process of max pooling of 8×8 pixels. From these operations the filters can find different features such as borders, shapes, blurs, sharpness, among others, that will be obtained during learning in the training stage.

To each of these convolutions, a Batch Normalization layer is applied, as can be seen in Fig. 3. This layer helps to coordinate the updates of the weights through many layers, and reduces the number of parameters to which max pooling is applied. The max pooling layer takes the maximum value selecting the most important features in the input matrix by dividing it into segments of the same size.

After this process, a flattening of the matrix is performed, that is, the matrix is turned into a vector and we apply a Fully Connected Layer (FC). Finally, to the output parameters, two neurons will be applied that perform multiple linear Regression, and the outputs of Diastolic and Systolic pressure will be obtained from the model. Figure 3 summarizes the proposed architecture.

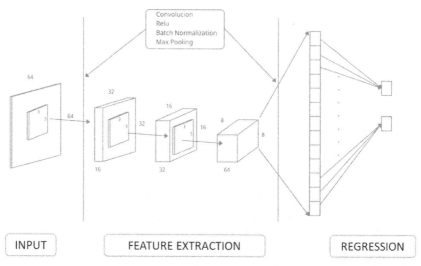

Fig. 3. Proposed CNN architecture

4   Results

Using Convolutional Neural Networks with an architecture inspired by VGGNet [9], three models are implemented that vary in the number of Convolutional Layers, Filters (Kernels) to apply, and Initial Learning Rate as a hyperparameter of the training stage of the model. The Convolutional Neural Network was implemented in the programming language Python using the library Keras with TensorFlow backend.

4.1   2D-CNN Model 1

This Convolutional Neural Network inspired by the VVGNet [9] architecture has 3 convolutional layers, with filters of 16, 32, and 64 kernels respectively. This 2D-CNN model is trained with 3 different initial learning rates of 0.1, 0.001, and 0.001. Figure 4 presents the specific architecture of this network and the results obtained during the training stage.

The Mean Absolute Error (MAE) of this first model presents a significantly high value with the first learning rate. This metric shows an important difference between the real value (target) and the predicted value, but this indicator gets lower when the learning rate decreases (LR). The R2 value or coefficient of determination shows, with high negative values, that the model does not fit the data with the first learning rate, and like the MAE indicator, it improves by lowering the learning rate.

4.2   2D-CNN Model 2

This Convolutional Neural Network has 4 Convolutional Layers, with filters of 16, 32, 64, and 128 kernels respectively. This 2D-CNN model is trained with 3 different learning

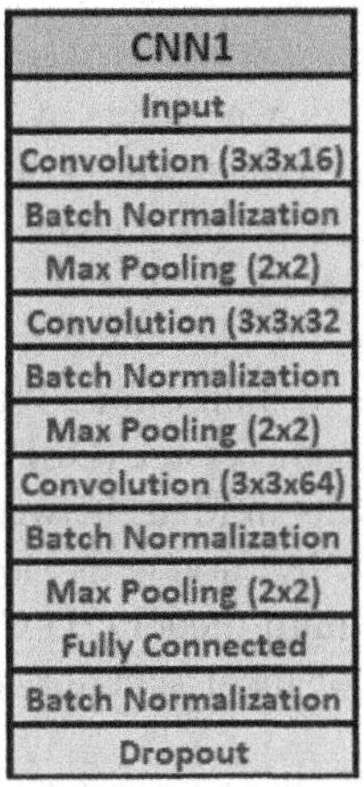

CNN1
Input
Convolution (3x3x16)
Batch Normalization
Max Pooling (2x2)
Convolution (3x3x32
Batch Normalization
Max Pooling (2x2)
Convolution (3x3x64)
Batch Normalization
Max Pooling (2x2)
Fully Connected
Batch Normalization
Dropout

LR:1e-1	CNN1	SBP	DBP
	MAE	19,1	115,3
	R2	-563	-244

LR:1e-2	CNN1	SBP	DBP
	MAE	9,3	14,25
	R2	0,3	0,49

LR:1e-3	CNN1	SBP	DBP
	MAE	10,66	14,55
	R2	0,05	0,37

Fig. 4. 2D-CNN model 1 architecture and results with the training dataset

rates as well: 0.1, 0.01, and 0.001. Figure 5 presents the specific architecture of the second model and the results obtained during the training stage.

In this second model (2D-CNN2) there is a significant improvement in the values of the different metrics when this model is trained with the 3 proposed Learning Rates (LR). The Mean Absolute Error (MAE) obtained with the 3 learning rate settings show a mean value of 9 between the real values (target) and the predicted values for the Systolic Blood Pressure (SBP), and a mean value of 13 for the Diastolic Blood Pressure (DBP). The coefficient of determination R2 shows values that indicate an improvement of the adjustment of the model between 2D-CNN1 and 2D-CNN2.

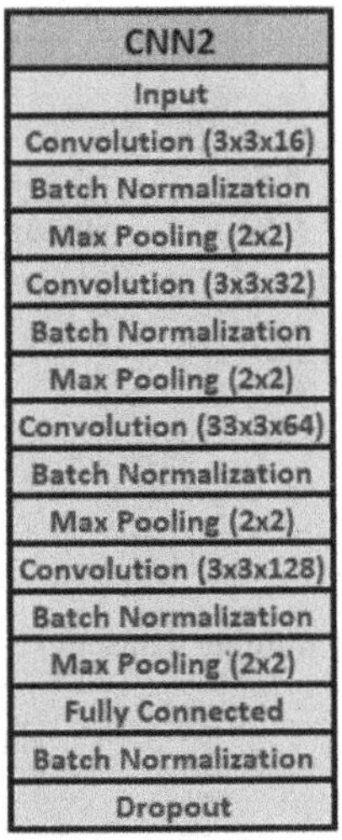

CNN2
Input
Convolution (3x3x16)
Batch Normalization
Max Pooling (2x2)
Convolution (3x3x32)
Batch Normalization
Max Pooling (2x2)
Convolution (33x3x64)
Batch Normalization
Max Pooling (2x2)
Convolution (3x3x128)
Batch Normalization
Max Pooling (2x2)
Fully Connected
Batch Normalization
Dropout

LR:1e-1	CNN2	SBP	DBP
	MAE	8,98	13,9
	R2	0,3	0,54

LR:1e-2	CNN2	SBP	DBP
	MAE	9,27	13,6
	R2	0,19	0,4

LR:1e-3	CNN2	SBP	DBP
	MAE	9,46	12,11
	R2	0,34	0,59

Fig. 5. 2D-CNN model 2 architecture and results with the training dataset

4.3   2D-CNN Model 3

This Convolutional Neural Network has 5 Convolutional Layers, with filters of 16, 32, 64, 128, and 256 kernels respectively. This 2D-CNN model is trained with 3 different learning rates as well: 0.1, 0.01, and 0.001. Figure 6 presents the specific architecture of the third model and the results obtained during the training stage.

For the third model (2D-CNN3) a Mean Absolute Error of 8 was obtained as an absolute difference between real and predicted values for the Systolic Blood Pressure (SBP) and a difference of 12 was obtained for the Diastolic Blood Pressure (DBP). This was the best result of the three models. The difference in results in MAE between the three models indicates that it is possible to improve this metric by varying the network architecture. About the coefficient of determination R2, the third model (2D-CNN3) shows an improvement with all positive values, almost all of them superior to 0.3, indicating a better adjustment of the model.

Comparing all the models, the one with the best results in the training stage was model 2D-CNN3 with a learning rate of 0.001. This model had a MAE of 8.31 to predict Systolic Blood Pressure and of 12.63 for Diastolic Blood Pressure, and coefficients of determination R2 of 0.34 and 0.56 respectively. However, to assess the real prediction capability of the model we have to assess their performance with unseen data, so an evaluation stage was performed with the test dataset after training.

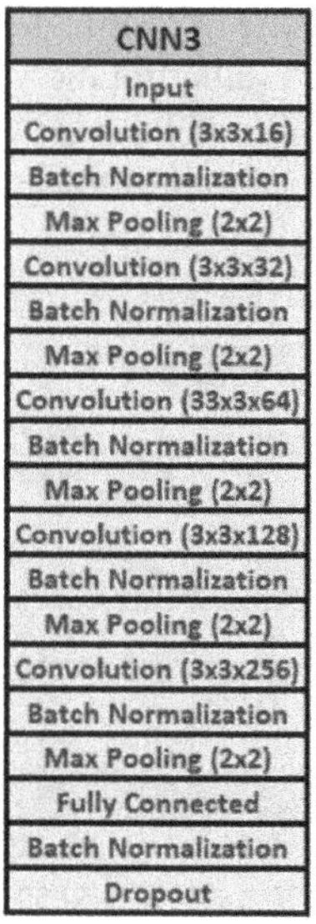

CNN3
Input
Convolution (3x3x16)
Batch Normalization
Max Pooling (2x2)
Convolution (3x3x32)
Batch Normalization
Max Pooling (2x2)
Convolution (33x3x64)
Batch Normalization
Max Pooling (2x2)
Convolution (3x3x128)
Batch Normalization
Max Pooling (2x2)
Convolution (3x3x256)
Batch Normalization
Max Pooling (2x2)
Fully Connected
Batch Normalization
Dropout

LR:1e-1

CNN3	SBP	DBP
MAE	9,79	12,38
R2	0,34	0,59

LR:1e-2

CNN3	SBP	DBP
MAE	8,82	12,41
R2	0,36	0,54

LR:1e-3

CNN3	SBP	DBP
MAE	8,31	12,63
R2	0,34	0,56

Fig. 6. 2D-CNN model 3 architecture and results with the training dataset

4.4   Evaluation Stage

For the three trained models, 2D-CNN1, 2D-CNN2, and 2D-CNN3, an evaluation stage is performed with a test dataset of 500 samples, not used in the previous training cycle, to validate the model's behavior with unseen data. Figure 7 presents the results obtained after applying model 2D-CNN3 with LR 1e-3 with the test dataset of 500 unseen during training samples. This was our best model, and a MAE of 17.62 and 11.51 was obtained for Systolic and Diastolic Blood Pressure estimation. A good performance was also indicated by the coefficient of correlation R2 with values close to 1. An R2 coefficient of 0.79 and one of 0.93 were obtained for SBP AND DBP respectively, as can be seen in Fig. 7.

MAE_SBP	17,6
MAE_DBP	11,61
R2_SBP	0,79
R2_DBP	0,93

Fig. 7. 2D-CNN model 3 results with test dataset

5 Conclusions

A method to estimate Blood Pressure through PPG signal processing and Deep Learning has been proposed. The evaluation of the different models applied to predict Systolic and Diastolic Blood Pressure allows us to determine that using a two-dimensional Convolutional Neural Network is a valid method to solve these types of problems.

During the implementation of the algorithm to define the different models, it was established that there exists a functional relationship between the graphical representation of the PPG signal (the image with the waveform) and the values of Systolic Blood Pressure (SBP) and Diastolic Blood Pressure (DBP). The three models of 2D-CNNs show an R2 coefficient with positive values between 0 and 1 with the training dataset, which indicates that there is at least a minimum adjustment of the models. The performance in the test dataset shows a significant improvement with R2 values close to one, which indicates that the model is generalizing well and there are minimum errors between the real values and the predicted ones.

This research indicates that it is possible to measure blood pressure in a continuous and non-invasive way in conditions favorable to the patient and useful for diagnostic interpretation.

References

1. Moreno, S., Quintero, A., Ochoa, C., Bonfante, M., Villareal, R., Pestana, J.: Remote monitoring system of vital signs for triage and detection of anomalous patient states in the emergency room. In: 2016 21st Symposium Signal Processing Images Artificial Vision STSIVA 2016, pp. 1–5 (2016)
2. Martínez, G., Howard, N., Abbott, D., Lim, K., Ward, R., Elgendi, M.: Can photoplethysmography replace arterial blood pressure in the assessment of blood pressure? J. Clin. Med. 7(10), 316 (2018)

3. Khalid, S.G., Zhang, J., Chen, F., Zheng, D.: Blood pressure estimation using photoplethys-mography only: comparison between different machine learning approaches. J. Healthc. Eng. **2018**, 1548647 (2018) .

4. Xu, L., Gao, K.: Continuous cuffless arterial blood pressure measurement based on PPG quality assessment. Int. J. Comput. Biol. Drug Des. **8**(2), 150–158 (2015)

5. Zhang, Y., Feng, Z.: A SVM method for continuous blood pressure estimation from a PPG signal. In: Proceedings of the 9th International Conference on Machine Learning and Computing, pp. 128–132 (2017)

6. Zadi, A.S., Alex, R., Zhang, R., Watenpaugh, D.E., Behbehani, K.: Arterial blood pressure feature estimation using photoplethysmography. Comput. Biol. Med. **102**, 104–111 (2018)

7. Liu, D., Görges, M., Jenkins, S.A.: University of Queensland vital signs dataset: development of an accessible repository of anesthesia patient monitoring data for research. Anesth. Analg. **114**(3), 584–589 (2012)

8. Hubel, D.H., Wiesel, T.N.: Receptive fields, binocular interaction and functional architecture in the cat's visual cortex. J. Physiol. **160**(1), 106–154 (1962)

9. Simonyan, K., Zisserman, A.: Very deep convolutional networks for large-scale image recognition. In: 3rd International Conference on Learning Representations, ICLR 2015-Conference Track Proceedings (2015)

Food Classification from Images Using a Neural Network Based Approach with NVIDIA Volta and Pascal GPUs

Ewa Tusień, Aleksandra Wilke, Joanna Woźna, and Pawel Czarnul[✉][iD]

Faculty of Electronics, Telecommunications and Informatics,
Gdańsk University of Technology, Narutowicza 11/12, 80-233 Gdańsk, Poland
`pczarnul@eti.pg.edu.pl`

Abstract. In the paper we investigate the problem of food classification from images, for the Food-101 dataset extended with 31 additional food classes from Polish cuisine. We adopted transfer learning and firstly measured training times for models such as MobileNet, MobileNetV2, ResNet50, ResNet50V2, ResNet101, ResNet101V2, InceptionV3, InceptionResNetV2, Xception, NasNetMobile and DenseNet, for systems with NVIDIA Tesla V100 (Volta) and NVIDIA GTX 1060 (Pascal) GPUs. We presented inference times corresponding to training the various considered network models, both using a desktop NVIDIA GTX 1060 GPU and an Intel i7-7000 CPU. Subsequently, we investigated the InceptionV3 model in more detail, best in the preliminary tests, regarding the impact of both learning rates (including both various fixed and variable rates) as well as batch sizes on the accuracy of classification, along with training times for various batch sizes. This allowed to identify better learning rate configurations as well as classification performance versus training time.

Keywords: Deep neural networks · Food classification · GPUs · Inference · Neural network training

1 Introduction

Topics related to food have become very important, especially in the context of globalization, when we have opportunities to visit many places that considerably differ in terms of cuisine. Food recognition, which is the subject of this paper along with modern deep learning based algorithms, is of interest to many people as it helps to identify what we eat. Development of an effective classifier as well as assessment of inference performance is important in the context of wide adoption of mobile devices. Mobile devices are widely used, therefore these constitute the best medium for reaching future users for such applications.

In this article, we discuss the problem of image recognition using a convolutional neural network approach. Convolutional neural networks are a type of deep neural networks which are mostly applied to the problem of image classification, as shown in [10]. The contribution of this paper is as follows:

K. Saeed and J. Dvorský (Eds.): CISIM 2022, LNCS 13293, pp. 269–283, 2022.
https://doi.org/10.1007/978-3-031-10539-5_20

1. Initial assessment of performance of 11 various network models: MobileNet, MobileNetV2, ResNet50, ResNet50V2, ResNet101, ResNet101V2, Inception V3, InceptionResNetV2, Xception, NasNetMobile and DenseNet for food classification using transfer learning, specifically regarding models' ability to obtain top-1 and top-5 accuracies, in the context of learning time, for two distinct and representative hardware setups: server/workstation NVIDIA Tesla V100 and desktop NVIDIA GTX 1060. Comparison of times gives an indication of what performance we can expect in a datacenter/cloud versus home environment, the latter could be engaged in volunteer systems.
2. Investigation of the performance of all the models for the Food-101 vs a data set of the Food-101 extended with 31 additional Polish food classes, downloaded from the Internet. The latter can be thought of the type of images taken by users with their smartphones on daily basis.
3. Comparison of inference times using all the models for the NVIDIA GTX 1060 GPU and Intel(R) Core(TM) i7-7700 CPU, of interest to end users of food classification applications.
4. Detailed investigation of the impact of various learning rates including variable learning rates as well as batch sizes on both final performance of the best identified model among the tested ones – InceptionV3, including assessment of training times for various settings.

2   Related Work and Motivations

In this section, progress on algorithms as well as benchmarking of food detection and classification is summarized, especially in the context of accuracy obtained for particular algorithms as well as, what is important, numbers of food categories.

Authors of paper [6] proposed a very practical approach to food image recognition (aimed at recording eating habits) using mobile phones. Specifically, a Multiple Kernel Learning (MKL) method was used for integration of image features such as color, texture as well as SIFT. They obtained the accuracy of 61.34% for 50 types of food.

In paper [7] authors focused on exploration of hyper parameters for accuracy of food recognition using a Convolutional Neural Network (CNN), specifically number of layers, kernels, sizes of kernels and normalization. For a data set with 10 most frequent food items from a 170 000 set of images acquired from FoodLog. Images were scaled to 64×64. Best accuracy obtained was 73.7% while food detection 93.8%.

Authors of [1] used a Random Forest to cluster superpixels of a training set. For classification, superpixels of an input image are scored using component models and a multi-class SVM with spatial pooling is used to predict the final class. The Food-101 data set (101 food categories with 1000 images each) with 750 images of each class are used for training and the remaining 250 for testing. The authors achieved an average accuracy of 50.76% which is better than MLDS and IFV by 8.13% and 11.88% but worse than CNN (56.40%).

In work [9] authors combined features obtained from a pre-trained Deep Convolutional Neural network on a LSVRC 1000-class dataset with Fisher Vectors with HoG and Color patches. For the UEC-FOOD100 100-class food dataset they achieved the top-1 accuracy of 72.26% and the top-5 accuracy of 92.00%. The same authors, in paper [24] extended their previous work and used a finetuned DCNN pre-trained with 2000 categories in the ImageNet (with 1000 food categories). They achieved the top-1 accuracy of 78.77% for the UEC-FOOD100 set and 67.57% for the UEC-FOOD256 dataset. They also mentioned the 0.03 s time for food image classification using a GPU (NVIDIA Titan Black).

Authors of [25] used a five-layer CNN for recognition using a 100-class food dataset with about 15000 for accuracy of 80.8% and a fruit dataset with approximately 40000 images (30 kinds) for accuracy of 60.9%. A part of research included by [23], apart from food/non-food classification, was recognizing the type of a food in an image. A dataset called Food-11 with 11 classes and 16643 images was used to train and test a model. A modified CNN GoogLeNet was used: 11 classes learning rate of 0.001 and policy polynomial. The authors obtained the maximum accuracy of 83.5%, the maximum values of F-measure and kappa coefficients of 0.911 and 0.816 respectively. In paper [13] the author used a dataset with 5822 images of ten categories. A bag-of-features (BoF) model together with a support vector machine (SVM) returned accuracy of 56% while a plain fivelayer CNN gave accuracy of 74%. Furthermore, data augmentation techniques through geometric transformations allowed to increase the training data size and accuracy to over 90%.

In paper authors [12] presented a CNN based solution for food image recognition. The solution uses two Inception modules (with additional convolutional layers) connected via an additional max pooling layer. The network has 22 layers with parameters. 70% dropout is used in the approach. For the UEC-256 set with 256 categories with a total of 28375 images, the proposed approach allowed to obtain top-1 accuracy of 54.7%, top-5 accuracy of 81.5%. For UEC-100, corresponding results were 76.3% and 94.6% while for Food-101 77.4% and 93.7%. Adding bounding boxes improved top-1 accuracy for UEC-256 to 63.8%.

Authors of [5] used a tuned Inception V3 network architecture for food recognition using the ETH Food-101, UEC FOOD 100 and UEC FOOD 256 data sets, for which they obtained the top-1 accuracies of 88.28%, 81.45% and 76.17% while top-5 accuracies of 96.88%, 97.27% and 92.58%.

In paper [2] authors used UNIMIB2016 food data set collected in a real canteen environment and performed segmentation into 73 food classes. Finally, they used 1010 tray images and 65 classes with partitioning into 70% for training and 30% testing sets. CNN4096 features with the combination of posterior probability strategy (from global and local) returned the best performance of 78.9% (SVM).

In paper [19] authors proposed a new network model Ensemble Net that includes histogram and equalization layer followed by parallel assessment using fine tuned AlexNet, fine tuned GoogLeNet and fine tuned ResNet. Experimental results were performed on two data sets: ETH Food-101 with 1000 images per class with 101 classes as well as an Indian food database which includes images divided into 50 food classes, each with 100 images. For the former, Ensemble Net reached 72.12% top-1 accuracy and 91.61% top-5 accuracy while for the latter it reached 73.5% top-1 and 94.4% top-5 accuracy, outperforming AlexNet, GoogLeNet and ResNet.

This work is similar to [4] where authors combined a new Turkish cuisine dataset with Food-101 and deep learning was applied for the combined set of 113 classes. Tests were performed for learning rates of 0.1, 0.3 and 0.7 with batch size equal to 100. In that comparison the best accuracy of 62.7% was obtained for the learning rate of 0.3 which was further improved in longer training to 68.2%. Validation cross entropy of around 1.3 was reported while for training around 0.7.

Authors of [15] performed comparison of performance of various models for food and drink recognition. Specifically, they compared four architectures including AlexNet, GoogLeNet, ResNet and NutriNet. Three solvers were tested: SGD, NAG and AdaGrad. For 512×512 images, best test accuracies were obtained by the 512×512 version of ResNet with NAG that achieved the accuracy of 87.96% as compared to the best NutriNet with AdaGrad of 86.72% which turned out to be 1.93% better than its AlexNet version. On the other hand the authors argue that NutriNet si significantly faster (approx. 5x) to train than ResNet. The dataset was divided into training, validation and testing sets proportionally to 70%, 10% and 20%, for a total of 225953 images of 520 food and drink items.

The research shown by authors of [17] confirms that food recognition using neural networks for a small number of categories can result in really high accuracy values. Specifically, for food images taken from personal life archives from life loggers, for a total of 14760 images of just eight different foods, the authors obtained 91.67% for AlexNet and 95.97% for GoogLeNet for test sets.

Authors of paper [20] proposed a Deep Convolutional Neural Network food recognition model, K-foodNet for recognition of Korean food and conducted experimental comparison vs AlexNet, GoogLeNet, VGG-19 and ResNet-18. For a data set with 23 food categories, which was divided into training and test images with 69000 and 23000 images in each set respectively, the proposed model achieved best results obtaining the test accuracy of 91.3% albeit with a noisy loss function. The authors argue that Korean food is reasonably complex to recognize, especially to other national food items. The authors struggled with the problem of too many similar, augmented images.

In paper [18] authors used the Food-41 dataset (4100 images and 41 classes) and partitioned it into parts 60% – training, 20% – validation and 20% – testing after resizing into 640×480 pixel images. They used Keras, GTX 1070 and a proposed CBNet that uses output from auxiliary classifiers (such as ResNet50, VGG19, DenseNet121) and performs fusion for final prediction. Generally, CBNet solutions returns better accuracies than best single models, both for tuning the last layer: CBNet-VD with 89.47% vs VGG19-AVG with 88.82% and the overall network: CBNet-RD with 95.28% vs DenseNet121 with 93.78%.

3 Problem Formulation and Approach

The main purpose of this research is to investigate a neural network based app-roach to food classification. We considered 11 models of artificial neural networks: MobileNet, MobileNetV2, ResNet50, ResNet50V2, ResNet101, ResNet101 V2, InceptionV3, InceptionResNetV2, Xception, NasNetMobile and DenseNet. Dur-ing analysis the following parameters are taken into consideration: prediction accuracy, the time of training a neural network and the time of models' infer-ence. All of the measurements are taken on each of the following hardware: two GPUs: NVIDIA Tesla V100 and NVIDIA GTX 1060; and Intel(R) Core(TM) i7-7700 CPU. The implementations of models are obtained from Keras Appli-cations. The library contains popular deep learning models which are available with pre-trained weights. Each model selected for this research is prepared as follows: import a model from Keras Applications with weights trained on Ima-geNet, attach classification layers: *GlobalAveragePooling2D, Dense* with argu-ments: *units* - number of classes and *activation* - an element-wise activation function activation (with value *softmax*).

The main assumption adopted for the design of this investigation is the app-roach to the problem of food recognition based on pictures of dishes. The problem has non-trivial solutions because of the similarity of classes in a dataset. There is a strong conviction that the complexity of this classification problem will con-vey much more valuable results of tests in comparison with many elementary problems, e.g. a binary classification task.

In machine learning, classification is an example of the common problem of pattern recognition. The popularity of classification problem and significant resources of pre-trained models on various data have a tremendous impact on the decision of applying transfer learning in the presented solution. Transfer learning speeds up training, improves the performance of neural networks and circumvents the need for lots of new data. It is for these reasons that pre-trained models are commonly used for obtaining better results.

4 Training and Validation Data

The Food-101 dataset – the first public collection of dishes with such a large number of photos - has been chosen as the base dataset for network training. It is owned by the Federal Institute Technology in Zurich (ETHZ). It contains 101 ordered food categories with 1000 images each. Dimensions of a single image from this dataset are not uniform - photos reach range between 512×317 pixels and 512×512 pixels, while the size of the photo is approximately 45 KB. We further created an extended data set containing 31 Polish dishes using script downloading photos based on Google search results and manual selection of suitable photos to use.

The images in the dataset had been pre-processed. A change to the RGB from [0, 255] to range [0, 1] value range was used on the extended dataset. Another important aspect of pre-processing is swapping RGB order values to BRG order.

Table 1 presents the characteristics of the pre-processing used to transform data into various models in the Keras library. Data augmentation was also used on the extended dataset through cropping, padding and horizontal flipping.

Table 1. Pre-processing dedicated to models from Keras library

Model name	Photo size (pixels, pixels)	Order RGB value	Range RGB value	Other transformations
VGG16, VGG19	(224, 224)	BGR	No scaling	Pixel values scaled to an average equal zero
ResNet 50, 101	(224, 224)	BGR	No scaling	Pixel values scaled to an average equal zero
ResNetV2 50, 101	(224, 224)	RGB	$[-1, 1]$	—
InceptionV3	(299, 299)	RGB	$[-1, 1]$	—
Xception	(299, 299)	RGB	$[-1, 1]$	—
InceptionRes NetV2	(299, 299)	RGB	$[-1, 1]$	—
MobileNet	(224, 224)	RGB	$[-1, 1]$	—
MobileNetV2	(224, 224)	RGB	$[-1, 1]$	—
DenseNet 121	(224, 224)	RGB	$[0, 1]$	Normalization
NASNetMobile	(224, 224)	RGB	$[-1, 1]$	—

The dataset has been divided into the three parts: training data (70%), test data (15%) and evaluation data (15%).

5   Experimental Results

5.1   Preliminary Results for Various Models

During training, all models were tested for top-1 and top-5 accuracy and cross-entropy loss function recommended in classification problems. Cross entropy has been favorably compared to quadratic loss for classification by [3], using the CIFAR 100 dataset. For the optimizer, it was decided to use the Stochastic Gradient Descent (SGD) method. It is a very popular and common algorithm used in various machine learning algorithms. Its popularity is due to the introduction of randomization in the algorithm, which significantly contributed to reducing the number of computational operations. The study used the SGD method with two parameters: learning rate of 0.01 and momentum parameter of 0.9. To prevent over-training of the network, the early stopping method was used. If the loss function on the validation dataset does not receive smaller values for 5 learning periods, then the training process stops. Furthermore, to get the best result that the model can achieve, the evaluation accuracy was checked every epoch, and if the result was better than in the previous model, the model was saved. Thanks to this, at the end of each training process we obtained the best model. After each training an evaluation process started. The evaluation dataset consisted of unique photos of dishes, which were used neither in the training nor in the validation process.

Firstly, all models were trained on the Food-101 dataset, all of which exceeded 80% top-1 accuracy as indicated in Table 2. The InceptionV3 model obtained top-1 accuracy 87.63%, which renders it as the best of all tested models.

Table 2. Test top-1 and top-5 accuracies for dataset Food-101

Model name	Epochs	top-1	top-5
InceptionV3	20	0.876	0.969
DenseNet	17	0.859	0.973
MobileNet	18	0.844	0.965
Xception	10	0.832	0.965
ResNetV50	15	0.830	0.966
ResNet101V2	18	0.828	0.963
ResNet101	19	0.826	0.963
ResNet50V2	13	0.822	0.954
InceptionResNetV2	10	0.819	0.961
NASNetMobile	18	0.818	0.957
MobileNetV2	27	0.813	0.958

Table 3. Test top-1 and top-5 accuracies for extended dataset

Model name	Epochs	top-1	top-5
InceptionV3	19	0.833	0.954
MobileNetV2	16	0.797	0.942
MobileNet	16	0.793	0.941
ResNet101	20	0.793	0.940
NASNetMobile	17	0.782	0.933
ResNetV50	17	0.775	0.927
ResNet101V2	19	0.764	0.924
Xception	9	0.751	0.922
ResNet50V2	11	0.748	0.921
InceptionResNetV2	8	0.732	0.921
DenseNet	10	0.694	0.886

Then all models were trained on an extended set of Food-101 with 31 additional dish classes. Results are presented in Table 3. As in the previous study, the InceptionV3 model obtained the best accuracy equal to 83%, whereas other models' results have not dropped below 70%. It is noteworthy that for all architectures, the accuracy of top-1 and top-5 has decreased compared to only Food-101.

Figure 1 presents the top-1 accuracy of the Food-101 dataset compared to the trainable number of parameters. The latter is usually used to approximate learning time because it tells us how many parameters need to be calculated and corrected during the learning process.

Table 4 presents the average training time per epoch for each model. The test was carried out on Nvidia's graphic cards GTX 1060 with 6 GB memory and Tesla V100 with 16 GB memory. Due to the difference in memory size, the batch size for each model for the GTX card is 12 and for Tesla is 32. Besides, the determining factor may be the input size of the model because, for InceptionV3, Xception and InceptionResNetV2 the size is 299×299 pixels, while for the rest of models is 244×244 pixels. These models were designed in this size, thus the difference was accepted in this experiment.

Whereas the number of different factors, the results can only be used to estimate the duration of learning on these machines. This result shows that if on Tesla V100 full training of InceptionV3 takes 20 epochs what overall is 3.5 h that on GTX 1060 it could take more than 9 h.

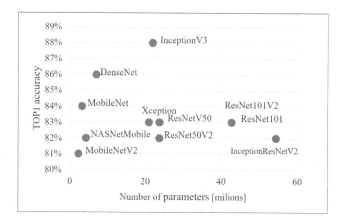

Fig. 1. top-1 accuracy compared to the number of parameters

Table 4. Training time on GTX 1060 and Tesla V100 graphic card

Model name	Average training time per one epoch [s]	
	Tesla V100	GTX 1060
MobileNet	330.06	1095.86
ResNet50V2	351.26	1160.27
MobileNetV2	379.84	806.40
ResNet50	402.86	1367.44
DenseNet	465.09	1376.77
InceptionV3	586.05	1642.05
ResNet101V2	601.94	2024.22
ResNet101	649.88	2242.47
NasNetMoblie	839.12	1379.56
InceptionResNetV2	1236.61	2317.98
Xception	1502.04	3691.54

5.2 Inference Times Using CPU vs GPU

Following the preliminary tests for various models, we carried out experiments for inference time tests on the CPU and GPU. A desktop class Intel(R) Core(TM) i7-7700 CPU and NVIDIA GTX 1060 with memory 6 GB were used which can be regarded as representative of desktop systems that could be used by typical end users. Two virtual Python environments were created, in which Tensorflow on a CPU was installed on one, and Tensorflow on a GPU on the other. The test was carried out in such a way that one image and one network model were loaded into memory, after which the inference process was started. Time was measured only during the prediction process, 10 times for each model. Results are

Table 5. Inference times using CPU vs GPU

Model name	Average time per picture [s]		Comparison GPU to CPU
	GPU Nvidia GTX 1060	CPU Intel Core i7-7700	
InceptionV3	0.223	0.198	11.24%
NASNetMobile	0.921	0.882	4.17%
DenseNet	0.954	0.936	1.83%
ResNet50V2	0.435	0.436	−0.28%
ResNet50	0.398	0.404	−1.54%
MobileNetV2	0.189	0.192	−1.57%
MobileNet	0.135	0.137	−1.71%
Xception	0.168	0.171	−1.73%
InceptionResNetV2	0.544	0.561	−3.06%
ResNet101V2	0.648	0.681	−5.07%
ResNet101	0.572	0.608	−6.23%

presented in Table 5 and are very similar between CPU and GPU, not exceeding 11.3% (0.12 s) – the largest for InceptionV3. Differences between GPU vs CPU times typically stem from additional CPU-GPU copy and specific GPU kernel configuration like grid size, memory usage etc. and could be further investigated for more details.

5.3 Training and Results for Various Parameters for InceptionV3 Model

Following the preliminary results, we have decided to analyze the InceptionV3 model in more detail, using NVIDIA Tesla V100. Specifically, we present detailed results for various training parameters such as various batch sizes as well as learning rates, including variable learning rates showing how these affect the final performance of the model.

Firstly, we have performed learning for various constant values of the learning rate observing final top-1 accuracy, after 25 epochs, for learning rates 0.2, 0.01 and 0.001 respectively. As a reference at this point, for the learning rate of 0.001 the following precision and recall values were obtained:

- batch size 16: precision 0.972 and recall 0.947 for training and 0.852 and 0.811 for validation,
- batch size 32: precision 0.980 and recall 0.960 for training and 0.857 and 0.805 for validation,
- batch size 64: precision 0.979 and recall 0.954 for training and 0.860 and 0.801 for validation.

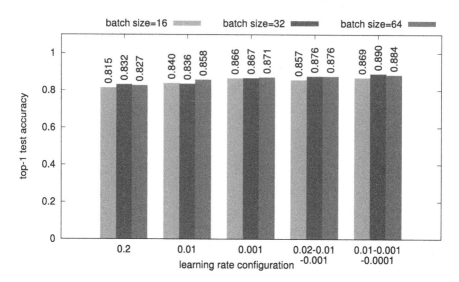

Fig. 2. top-1 test accuracy for InceptionV3 – various learning rate configurations

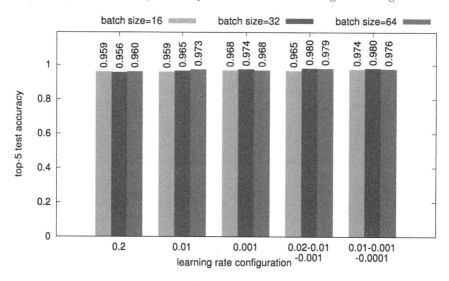

Fig. 3. top-5 test accuracy for InceptionV3 – various learning rate configurations

Subsequently, we have varied learning rate values along the process:

– 0.02 (epochs 1–7), 0.01 (epochs 8–17), 0.001 (epochs 18–25),
– 0.01 (epochs 1–10), 0.001 (epochs 11–20), 0.0001 (epochs 21-25).

All the results for top-1 and top-5 test accuracies and various batch sizes are shown in Fig. 2 and Fig. 3 respectively. We can draw the following conclusions based on the presented results:

1. In terms of accuracy in the transfer learning used in this work, we can see that for the constant learning rate 0.01 allows to achieve slightly higher accuracy than 0.02 and the learning rate of 0.001 marginally higher than for 0.01. On the other hand, even better results have been possible with decreasing the learning rate i.e. 0.02-0.01-0.001 gives even better accuracy and marginally best out of the tested sets was obtained by 0.01-0.001-0.0001 for top-1 and very similar ones for the last two configurations for top-5 accuracy, which is very high.

2. In terms of batch size, for the best tested learning rate configuration (0.01-0.001-0.0001), best performance of the model was obtained for batch size 32 with the top-1 accuracy of 0.89, followed by 0.884 for batch size 64 after 25 epochs. top-1 accuracy for training and test as well as corresponding losses for batch size 32 are shown in Fig. 4. Corresponding top-1 and top-5 accuracies obtained in various epochs are shown in Fig. 5.

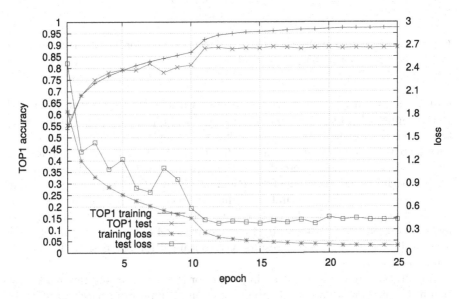

Fig. 4. top-1 accuracy and loss (training and test) vs epoch for InceptionV3 – learning rate = 0.01-0.001-0.0001, batch size = 32

Batch size is limited due to GPU memory size. We have tested configurations fitting into the given GPU memory size. Our results and observing increasing accuracies up to the tested batch size of 32 are similar to those presented in [14] where, for MNIST and CIFAR-10 and batch sizes 16, 32, 50, 64, 100 and 128 increasing accuracies are observed up to the batch size of 100 and a drop for 128. Furthermore, authors of paper [21] tested various learning rates for batch sizes of 32 and 64 for training a LeNet network for detecting exudate in eye fundus images, achieving visibly better results for batch size 64 and learning

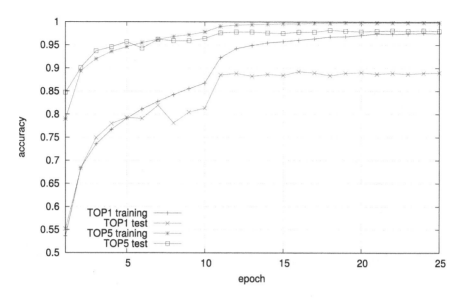

Fig. 5. top-1 and top-5 accuracy (training and test) vs epoch for InceptionV3 – learning rate = 0.01-0.001-0.0001, batch size = 32

rate 0.01. Within this paper we tested even variable learning rates, compared to that approach. Results seen in the charts in this paper are also in line with top-1 accuracy versus batch size for a fixed learning rate of 0.01 shown in [16] with increasing values from 32 through 64, 128 and 256 and visible drop for 512 and 1024 – not observed here due to the fact that such large values were not possible to be tested. Authors of [8] concluded that for CNNs, for larger learning rates larger batch sizes perform better and they recommend small batch sizes for smaller learning rates. In the case of our experiments with fixed learning rate, for 0.01 best accuracy was obtained for batch size 64 out of 16, 32 and 64 while for learning rate 0.001 better results were obtained for batch sizes 32 and 16, compared to 64.

Finally, we present model training times for the best learning rate configuration in Fig. 6, showing a considerable reduction of times from batch size 8 to 16 and smaller for 32 and 64. In general, training performance for selected neural networks depends on both batch sizes as well as architectural advancements such as the I/O subsystem, as reported by [22]. Accuracy/training time is best for batch size 64.

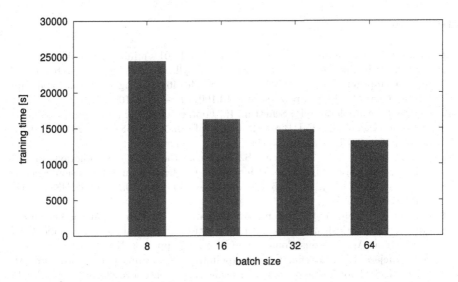

Fig. 6. Training times for best tested learning rate = 0.01-0.001-0.0001

6   Conclusions and Future Work

In the paper, we presented a neural network based approach for classification of food categories from images, both for Food-101 as well as Food-101 extended with 31 additional Polish dishes. Training and comparison was initially performed for several models including MobileNet, MobileNetV2, ResNet50, ResNet50V2, ResNet101, ResNet101V2, InceptionV3, InceptionResNetV2, Xception, NasNetMobile and DenseNet, using both NVIDIA Tesla V100 and GTX 1060 GPUs. Then we analyzed in detail the model giving best results – InceptionV3 and performed detailed assessment of model performance and training times for various learning rate configurations (both constant and variable) and various batch sizes finding the best (out of the tested ones) variable learning rate configuration 0.01–0.001–0.0001 and batch size 32. Finally, we presented comparison of inference times for Intel i7-7700 CPU and NVIDIA GTX 1060 GPU that are typical of desktop systems used by end users nowadays.

Future work will cover the following areas: incorporation of energy measurements into assessment of performance-energy trade-offs such as presented in [11] as well as extending focus on deployment and inference time measurements for mobile devices.

Acknowledgment. In this work, we used facilities located at the Faculty of Electronics, Telecommunications and Informatics – especially the DGX Station with NVIDIA V100 cards as well as GTX 1060 cards located at the lab of the Department of Computer Architecture of the aforementioned faculty.

References

1. Bossard, L., Guillaumin, M., Van Gool, L.: Food-101 - mining discriminative components with random forests. In: Fleet, D., Pajdla, T., Schiele, B., Tuytelaars, T. (eds.) Computer Vision - ECCV 2014, pp. 446–461. Springer International Publishing, Cham (2014). https://doi.org/10.1007/978-3-319-10599-4_2
2. Ciocca, G., Napoletano, P., Schettini, R.: Food recognition: a new dataset, experiments and results. IEEE J. Biomed. Health Inform. **21**(3), 588–598 (2017). https://doi.org/10.1109/JBHI.2016.2636441
3. Demirkaya, A., Chen, J., Oymak, S.: Exploring the role of loss functions in multiclass classification. In: 2020 54th Annual Conference on Information Sciences and Systems (CISS), pp. 1–5 (2020). https://doi.org/10.1109/CISS48834.2020.1570627167
4. Gungor, C., Baltaci, F., Erdem, A., Erdem, E.: Turkish cuisine: a benchmark dataset with turkish meals for food recognition. In: Signal Processing and Communications Applications Conference (SIU) 2017, pp. 1–4. IEEE (2017)
5. Hassannejad, H., Matrella, G., Ciampolini, P., De Munari, I., Mordonini, M., Cagnoni, S.: Food image recognition using very deep convolutional networks. In: Proceedings of the 2nd International Workshop on Multimedia Assisted Dietary Management. pp. 41–49. MADiMa 2016, Association for Computing Machinery, New York, NY, USA (2016). https://doi.org/10.1145/2986035.2986042
6. Joutou, T., Yanai, K.: A food image recognition system with multiple kernel learning. In: ICIP, pp. 285–288. IEEE (2009). http://dblp.uni-trier.de/db/conf/icip/icip2009.html#JoutouY09
7. Kagaya, H., Aizawa, K., Ogawa, M.: Food detection and recognition using convolutional neural network. In: Proceedings of the 22nd ACM International Conference on Multimedia, pp. 1085–1088. MM 2014, Association for Computing Machinery, New York, NY, USA (2014). https://doi.org/10.1145/2647868.2654970
8. Kandel, I., Castelli, M.: The effect of batch size on the generalizability of the convolutional neural networks on a histopathology dataset. ICT Express, **6**(4), 312–315 (2020). https://doi.org/10.1016/j.icte.2020.04.010. https://www.sciencedirect.com/science/article/pii/S2405959519303455
9. Kawano, Y., Yanai, K.: Food image recognition with deep convolutional features. In: Proceedings of the 2014 ACM International Joint Conference on Pervasive and Ubiquitous Computing: Adjunct Publication, pp. 589–593. UbiComp 2014 Adjunct, Association for Computing Machinery, New York, NY, USA (2014). https://doi.org/10.1145/2638728.2641339
10. Krizhevsky, A., Sutskever, I., Hinton, G.E.: Imagenet classification with deep convolutional neural networks. Commun. ACM **60**(6), 84–90 (2017). https://doi.org/10.1145/3065386
11. Krzywaniak, A., Czarnul, P., Proficz, J.: Extended investigation of performance-energy trade-offs under power capping in HPC environments. In: 2019 International Conference on High Performance Computing Simulation (HPCS), pp. 440–447 (2019). https://doi.org/10.1109/HPCS48598.2019.9188149
12. Liu, C., Cao, Yu., Luo, Y., Chen, G., Vokkarane, V., Ma, Y.: DeepFood: deep learning-based food image recognition for computer-aided dietary assessment. In: Chang, C.K., Chiari, L., Cao, Yu., Jin, H., Mokhtari, M., Aloulou, H. (eds.) ICOST 2016. LNCS, vol. 9677, pp. 37–48. Springer, Cham (2016). https://doi.org/10.1007/978-3-319-39601-9_4

13. Lu, Y.: Food image recognition by using convolutional neural networks (cnns) (2016)
14. Radiuk, P.M.: Impact of training set batch size on the performance of convolutional neural networks for diverse datasets. Inf. Technol. Manag. Sci. **20**(1), 20–24 (2017). https://ideas.repec.org/a/vrs/itmasc/v20y2017i1p20-24n3.html
15. Mezgec, S., Koroušić Seljak, B.: Nutrinet: a deep learning food and drink image recognition system for dietary assessment. Nutrients, **9**(7) (2017). https://doi.org/10.3390/nu9070657.https://www.mdpi.com/2072-6643/9/7/657
16. Mishkin, D., Sergievskiy, N., Matas, J.: Systematic evaluation of CNN advances on the imagenet. CoRR abs/1606.02228 (2016). http://arxiv.org/abs/1606.02228
17. Nguyen, B.T., Dang-Nguyen, D., Tien, D.X., Phat, T.V., Gurrin, C.: A deep learning based food recognition system for lifelog images. In: De Marsico, M., di Baja, G.S., Fred, A.L.N. (eds.) Proceedings of the 7th International Conference on Pattern Recognition Applications and Methods, ICPRAM 2018, Funchal, Madeira - Portugal, 16–18 January 2018, pp. 657–664. SciTePress (2018). https://doi.org/10.5220/0006749006570664
18. Pan, L., Li, C., Pouyanfar, S., Chen, R., Zhou, Y.: A novel combinational convolutional neural network for automatic food-ingredient classification. Comput. Mater. Continua, **62**(2), 731–746 (2020). https://doi.org/10.32604/cmc.2020.06508. http://www.techscience.com/cmc/v62n2/38273
19. Pandey, P., Deepthi, A., Mandal, B., Puhan, N.B.: Foodnet: recognizing foods using ensemble of deep networks (2017). CoRR abs/1709.09429. http://arxiv.org/abs/1709.09429
20. Park, S.J., Palvanov, A., Lee, C.H., Jeong, N., Cho, Y.I., Lee, H.J.: The development of food image detection and recognition model of Korean food for mobile dietary management. Nurs. Res. Pract. **13**(6), 521–528 (2019). https://doi.org/10.4162/nrp.2019.13.6.521
21. Perdomo, O., Arevalo, J., González, F.A.: Convolutional network to detect exudates in eye fundus images of diabetic subjects. In: Romero, E., Lepore, N., Brieva, J., Brieva, J. (eds.) 12th International Symposium on Medical Information Processing and Analysis, vol. 10160, pp. 235–240. Int. Soc. Opt. Photonics, SPIE (2017). https://doi.org/10.1117/12.2256939
22. Rościszewski, P., Iwański, M., Czarnul, P.: The impact of the ac922 architecture on performance of deep neural network training. In: 2019 International Conference on High Performance Computing Simulation (HPCS), pp. 666–673 (2019). https://doi.org/10.1109/HPCS48598.2019.9188164
23. Singla, A., Yuan, L., Ebrahimi, T.: Food/non-food image classification and food categorization using pre-trained googlenet model. In: Proceedings of the 2nd International Workshop on Multimedia Assisted Dietary Management, pp. 3–11. MADiMa 2016, Association for Computing Machinery, New York, NY, USA (2016). https://doi.org/10.1145/2986035.2986039
24. Yanai, K., Kawano, Y.: Food image recognition using deep convolutional network with pre-training and fine-tuning. In: 2015 IEEE International Conference on Multimedia Expo Workshops (ICMEW), pp. 1–6 (2015). https://doi.org/10.1109/ICMEW.2015.7169816
25. Zhang, W., Zhao, D., Gong, W., Li, Z., Lu, Q., Yang, S.: Food image recognition with convolutional neural networks. In: 2015 IEEE 12th Intl Conf on Ubiquitous Intelligence and Computing and 2015 IEEE 12th Intl Conf on Autonomic and Trusted Computing and 2015 IEEE 15th Intl Conf on Scalable Computing and Communications and Its Associated Workshops (UIC-ATC-ScalCom), pp. 690–693 (2015)

Application of Continuous Embedding of Viral Genome Sequences and Machine Learning in the Prediction of SARS-CoV-2 Variants

Piotr Tynecki[1]($\boxtimes$) and Marcin Lubocki[2]

[1] Faculty of Computer Science, Bialystok University of Technology, Białystok, Poland
p.tynecki@doktoranci.pb.edu.pl
[2] Laboratory of Virus Molecular Biology, Intercollegiate Faculty of Biotechnology, University of Gdańsk, Medical University of Gdańsk, Gdańsk, Poland

Abstract. Since the beginning of the novel coronavirus pandemic, Severe Acute Respiratory Syndrome Coronavirus 2 (SARS-CoV-2) has spread to 224 countries with over 430 million confirmed cases and more than 5,97 million deaths worldwide. One of the crucial reasons why the spread of the virus was difficult to stop was the viral evolution over time. The emergence of new virus variants is hindering the development of effective drugs and vaccines. Moreover, they contribute e.g. to virus transmissibility or viral immune evasion. This fact has led to increased importance of understanding genomic data related to SARS-CoV-2. In this study, we are proposing *sarscov2vec*, a new application of continuous vector space representation on novel species of coronaviruses genomes. With its core methodology of genome feature extraction step and being supervised by a Machine Learning model, this tool is designed to distinguish the most common five different SARS-CoV-2 variants: Alpha, Beta, Delta, Gamma and Omicron. In this research we used 367,004 unique genome sequence records from the official virus repositories, where 25,000 sequences were randomly selected and used to train the Natural Language Processing (NLP) algorithm. The next 36,365 samples were processed by a Machine Learning pipeline. Our research results show that the final hiper-tuned classification model achieved 99% of accuracy on the test set. Furthermore, this study demonstrated that the continuous vector space representation of SARS-CoV-2 genomes can be decomposed into 2D vector space and visualized as a method of explaining Machine Learning model decisions.

Keywords: SARS-CoV-2 · COVID-19 · Continuous embedding

1 Introduction

The COVID-19 pandemic, caused by Severe Acute Respiratory Syndrome Coronavirus 2 (SARS-CoV-2), is one of the biggest changes the world has experienced in the 21st century. According to the worldometer data on 26 February 2022, the virus which emerged in December 2019 from Wuhan, infected over 430 million people within two years, resulting in the death of almost six million people [1].

© The Author(s), under exclusive license to Springer Nature Switzerland AG 2022
K. Saeed and J. Dvorský (Eds.): CISIM 2022, LNCS 13293, pp. 284–298, 2022.
https://doi.org/10.1007/978-3-031-10539-5_21

The respiratory system is mainly affected by the virus and manifestation of an infection varies from an asymptomatic infection to a severe respiratory failure. However, with time new evidence emerged suggesting that the virus infection should rather be considered as systemic, as other organs are also reported to be affected [2]. Moreover, many survivors struggle with the problem of the post-COVID-19 syndrome, which can include e.g. pulmonary, cardiovascular or neurological impairments [3, 4]. It is still difficult to estimate the long-term health effects of a past infection. The US Centers for Disease Control and Prevention (CDC) mentions older people and people with a list of certain medical conditions as being at higher risk for severe illness. The list consists of e.g. cancer, chronic kidney disease, cystic fibrosis, neurological conditions, diabetes (type 1 or type 2), heart conditions, immunocompromised states, mental health conditions, overweight, obesity or pregnancy among others [5]. Unfortunately, we still do not have an effective antiviral drug, and the vaccines available on the market are losing their effectiveness against emerging new lineages of the virus [6, 7].

The International Committee on Taxonomy of Viruses (ICTV) classified the novel virus emerged from Wuhan in order *Nidovirales*, family *Coronaviridae*, genus *Betacoronavirus* as Severe Acute Respiratory Syndrome Coronavirus 2 (SARS-CoV-2) (ICTV, Virus Metadata Repository number 18, October 19 2021; MSL36). The genome of SARS-CoV-2 consists of positive sense, non-segmented, single-stranded RNA with 5' cap structure and 3' poly-A tail, and contains 12 open reading frames encoding 27 proteins. The genome length usually varies between 29.0 kb to 29.9 kb [8].

It is generally observed that RNA viruses tend to have a higher mutation rate than DNA viruses [9]. Mutations arise as a result of errors in the replication of the genetic material of the virus and can lead to changes in amino acid sequences of proteins. If a mutation proves beneficial, providing the virus with traits that will favor its spread, it begins to persist in the population. Consequently, newly emerging variants of SARS-CoV-2 are constantly observed and implicate clinical outcomes [10–12]. These variants can be associated with increased transmissibility, disease severity or viral escape from the host immune system. The SARS-CoV-2 variants describe certain mutation patterns within the Spike protein sequence. As the coronavirus Spike protein is responsible for binding the host cell receptor and the fusion between the viral and host cell membranes, it is the main factor determining the host range [13]. Simultaneously, the viral Spike protein is the main target for neutralizing-antibody and T-cell responses. As a consequence, the Spike protein is the main interest for vaccine development [14, 15]. It brings the need of monitoring the emergence of novel variants, which can evade vaccine or past infection derived immunity, as it was already observed [16]. The SARS-CoV-2 variants of the highest significance are called the variants of concern (VOCs). To date, we have faced five different VOCs: Alpha, Beta, Gamma, Delta and Omicron, and others are expected to emerge [17].

The impact of the COVID-19 pandemic on all spheres of human life has been so significant that attempts to develop effective therapeutics were quickly started, and interdisciplinary measures were taken to fight the spreading virus. These days we are witnessing how IT tools enabling the storage and analysis of Big Data turned out to be particularly significant in the fight against the pandemic [18, 19].

In this paper, we focus on the SARS-CoV-2 variants' prediction based on genome sequence data. We propose an unsupervised NLP model trained on virus genomes for biological feature extraction and Machine Learning classification algorithm, as an alignment-free pipeline for distinguishing five different variants: Alpha, Beta, Gamma, Delta and Omicron. We achieved 99% of confidence level measured on an independent test set. Furthermore, our method was able to differentiate BA.2 - a sub-variant of Omicron not used in language model training - proving to have a potential in novel sub-variants detection.

2   Materials and Methods

2.1   Dataset Preparation and Preprocessing

In this study we used SARS-CoV-2 genomes sequences and meta-data from three independent open data sources:

- **National Center for Biotechnology Information (NCBI Virus):** community portal for viral sequence data from RefSeq, GenBank and other NCBI repositories;
- **GISAID Initiative (GISAID):** rapid sharing of data from all influenza viruses and the coronavirus causing COVID-19, including genetic sequence and related clinical and epidemiological data associated with human viruses;
- **COVID-19 Data Portal (CDP):** the European COVID-19 data platform facilitating data sharing and analysis in order to accelerate coronavirus research.

These data sources (combined together) shared more than 15M samples classified by 11 variants of SARS-CoV-2 virus, including Variant Of Concern (VOC), Variant Of Interest (VOI) and Variant Under Monitoring (VUM). After merging the data, we analyzed the corpus and discovered that the origin format of it was insufficiently representative, because the data included duplicate observations, viruses with incomplete genomes (fragments, contigs), DNA with low coverage %, as well as SARS-CoV-2 samples with limited information about the lineage, collection date, country or accession number (meta-data).

Our motivation for this research was to select enough representative subset of viruses from the global sources to present the possibilities of NLP methods in SARS-CoV-2 variants classification and discovery. We focused mostly on the VOC variants - Alpha, Beta, Gamma, Delta and Omicron - which are related to extensive transmission. That is why a customized data processing pipeline was required to develop and handle several steps such as downloading, filtering and rating the samples in order to build the corpus for this research.

Building Research Corpus. All the samples in our research were downloaded as nucleotide sequences in FASTA format and CSV files using source's Application Programming Interface (API) or web portals. On 26 February 2022, after the data crawling procedure, it allowed us to collect 372,721 unique SARS-CoV-2 virus genomes and associated meta-data in total. This number is represented by five virus variants and one sub-variant, as shown in detail in Table 1.

Table 1. SARS-CoV-2 variants distribution in raw corpus.

Pango lineage	WHO label	Number of samples
B.1.1.7	Alpha	159,014
B.1.351	Beta	21,495
P.1	Gamma	12,814
B.1.617.2	Delta	46,481
BA.1	Omicron	131,552
BA.2	Omicron (sub-variant)	1,365
Total	–	372,721

To reproduce the creation of the data collection in the study, each of the search engines in source's repositories has to be setup using proper filters:

- NCBI Virus subset finally represented by 212,602 samples, was available after adopting:

  - "Nucleotide Completeness" filter as "complete";
  - "Pango lineage" filter as "B.1.1.7", "B.1.351", "P.1", "B.1.617.2", "BA.1" or "BA.2".

- GISAID subset finally represented by 18,643 samples, was available after adopting:

  - "complete" filter as "checked";
  - "high coverage" filter as "checked";
  - "low coverage exclude" filter as "checked";
  - "collection date complete" filter as "checked";

- "Variants" filter as "VOC Alpha GRY (B.1.1.7 + Q.*)", "VOC Beta GH/501Y.V2 (B.1.351 + B.1.351.2 + B.1.351.3)", "VOC Gamma GR/501Y.V3 (P.1 + P.1.*)". "VOC Delta GK (B.1.617.2 + AY.*)" or "VOC Omicron GRA (B.1.1.529 + BA.*)".

• CDP subset finally represented by 141,476 samples, was available after adopting:

  - "Data types" filter as "Sequences";
  - "lineage" filter as "B.1.1.7", "B.1.351", "P.1", "B.1.617.2", "BA.1" or "BA.2";
  - "Coverage %" filter in 90–100 range.

Next, we executed two steps on the collected SARS-CoV-2 samples: removal samples with incomplete genome or empty meta-data and removal sequence duplicates.

Sequences with smaller length seem to be incomplete, even if they have a "complete" phrase in description. Hence all observations of the sequences with genome's length (bp) shorter than 29,000 bp were excluded. Likewise, samples with nullable lineage, country, collection date or accession number values (i.e. "N/A", "NaN" or empty) were also removed.

It was crucial for us to work with the virus samples possible to be recognized by the ID in global databases and in scientific papers, as well as locatable on a geographic map. Information about the location of samples is correlated with a specific population, which was another significant aspect to us in terms of keeping democratized complex statistical and computational models' development. To make sure that the corpus had unique samples, the SHA-256 algorithm from Python 3.8.10 standard library (module "hash") was applied directly on normalized genomic sequences. For genome normalization we used a custom method, which transformed each raw genome sequence (containing "A", "C", "T" and "G" chars) to uppercase and removed white spaces and other blank characters. After that, SHA checksum was calculated for each SARS-CoV-2 genome and assigned to a sample. All the viruses with duplicated hash values were removed from the corpus. The final dataset, after normalization and cleaning procedures, was represented by 367,004 unique and complete samples.

Exploratory Data Analysis. The final dataset was represented by the samples contributed from 120 countries, where 91,55% of data were shared by the USA and the United Kingdom scientists. The top-10 countries' sample distributions are listed in Table 2. The collection date, when the sample was contributed to data sources, covers 2020, 2021 and 2022 years, where 2021 makes up 87,32% of data. The distributions of samples per year are listed in Table 3.

Table 2. SARS-CoV-2 virus samples distribution in 10 most numerous subsets of countries in the final dataset.

Country	Number of samples	% of samples in corpus
USA	194,864	54,17
UK	137,017	37,38
Germany	8,402	2,29
Switzerland	3,900	1,06
Slovakia	3,371	0,92
Philippines	2,121	0,58
France	1,928	0,53
Sweden	1,868	0,51
Reunion	1,625	0,44
Finland	1,000	0,27

Table 3. SARS-CoV-2 virus samples distribution between 2020–2022 in final dataset.

Year	Number of samples	% of samples in corpus
2022	37,461	10,22
2021	320,026	87,32
2020	9,017	2,46

The genomic sequences of SARS-CoV-2 viruses exhibit a diverse length in the corpus from 29,001 to 30,255 base pairs (bp). These values indicate the diversity of biological data in the final set, which is advisable for building unsupervised NLP models with minimized bias.

Dataset for NLP Model Training. To train the NLP model we used 25,000 SARS-CoV-2 virus samples from the final dataset. They were selected from 367,004 samples using a custom method based on semi-auto stratified random sampling. The number 42 was set as a seed for a random number generator. In order to keep a high diversity level of data the NLP dataset included 5,000 samples. They were taken from each subset of variants (B.1.1.7, B.1.351, P.1, B.1.617.2 and BA.1) including all of the sources and countries where they came from and all years of contribution.

This policy of data selection is common in the NLP domain and solving text classification problems. Crucially for this research we decided to adapt it to a biological problem, assuming that not only it should allow modern models to learn common and repetitive patterns of nucleotide sequences, but also to be sensitive to mutations and deletions related to a region or a population. Furthermore, the data balance in SARS-CoV-2 variants was kept to mitigate unintended bias to the most representative subsets ("Alpha" and "Omicron"), during the unsupervised NLP model training.

Train and Test Sets in Machine Learning. To train the Machine Learning (ML) model for SARS-CoV-2 variants prediction we used 36,365 virus samples from the final dataset. But this time, observations were selected from 367,004 dataset, after excluding 25,000 viruses used for training NLP models. To be precise, the ML dataset did not include samples used for the NLP model, which helped avoid data leakage in this research. Data leakage is a serious and widespread problem in data mining and ML, which needs to be handled carefully in order to obtain a robust and generalized predictive model [20].

This time also, a custom method based on semi-auto stratified random sampling was used to prepare a set of 36,365 viruses for classification purpose. The number 42 was set as a seed for a random number generator. The ML dataset included 7,000 samples from each subset of variants (B.1.1.7, B.1.351, P.1, B.1.617.2 and BA.1) and extra 1,365 samples from Omicron sub-variant (BA.2). All the samples covered most of the sources and countries where they came from and years of contribution, so that a high diversity level of data was kept.

The ML dataset represented by 36,365 viruses were shuffled and splitted to train and test the sets in 80:20 ratio. This means we used 29,092 (80%) of the observations for training and 10-fold cross-validation and the rest 7,273 (20%) for testing the prediction model. The distribution of variants in train/test sets are listed in Table 4.

Table 4. SARS-CoV-2 variants distribution in train and test sets used for training a Machine Learning model.

Pango lineage	WHO label	Train set	Test set
B.1.1.7	Alpha	5,600	1,400
B.1.351	Beta	5,600	1,400
P.1	Gamma	5,600	1,400
B.1.617.2	Delta	5,600	1,400
BA.1	Omicron	5,600	1,400
BA.2	Omicron (sub-variant)	1,092	273

2.2 Ngrams-Based SARS-CoV-2 Genome Vectorization

Natural language processing refers to the branch of artificial intelligence concerned with giving computers the ability to understand text (documents, sentences and words) in much the same way human beings can do. This combines statistical, machine and deep learning models with computational linguistics. Thanks to AI research it is possible for computers to process human language in the form of text to "understand" its full meaning.

Genome Text Corpus. While in standard language processing applications, sentences contain words and each of them have some meaning (depending on the context), in nucleotide sequences, the concept of words does not exist, which makes a significant difference for application of NLP methods. To transform SARS-CoV-2 genome sequence to numerical vector space we treated each individual virus nucleotide sequence as a long sentence. Next, we implemented and executed a tokenizer - a custom word extractor dedicated for this problem - to deliver a bag of words, in which case a nucleotide sequence was represented by small fragments of the genome called "k-mers".

At the input of the tokenizer there was a normalization step which transformed each genome sequence containing chars from the set {"A", "C", "T", "G"} to uppercase format with removed white spaces and other blank characters. Next, the sequence was scanned from the left to right, to extract fixed-length overlapping words. Finally, all extracted words with length of 7 nucleotides (k-mers with $k = 7$) were joined by a space separator to simulate standard sentence format. k value was selected empirically. Figure 1 presents the tokenizer workflow on a short sequence fragment. This procedure was executed on each SARS-CoV-2 sample in this experiment.

Input:
attaaaggttt (...)

Normalization:
ATTAAAGGTTT (...)

Output:
ATTAAAG TTAAAGG TAAAGGT AAAGGTT AAGGTTT (...)

Fig. 1. k-mer based tokenizer usage example with k = 7.

Finally, all the transformed virus sequences were combined into one text file (each sample as a new line) named "NLP corpus". This NLP corpus file was used in the next step to train the NLP model with an unsupervised approach.

Continuous Embedding of Viral Genomes. SARS-CoV-2 genome sequences were treated as documents with sentences, and 7-mers tokens - as words to learn unsupervised embedding. To extract feature space from the prepared corpus we decided to use fastText v0.9.2. The fastText is an open-source library implemented in C++ - from Facebook's AI Research lab - for representation and classification of text. There are other powerful methods in NLP for text vectorization like One-Hot encoding, Word2Vec or Glove. Nonetheless, fastText is the only one of them that supports n-grams, which was proven to introduce better performance in word representations.

In fastText, each word (k-mer) is represented as a bag of character n-grams in addition to the word itself, for example, for the word"ATTAAAG", with $n = 3$, the fastText representations for the character 3-g (codons) is {"<AT", "ATT", "TTA", "TAA", "AAA", "AAG", "AG>"}. < and > are added as boundary symbols to distinguish the n-gram of a word from a word itself, for example, if the word "ATT" is part of the vocabulary, it is represented as <ATT>. This helps preserve the meaning of shorter tokens that may show up as n-grams of other words. Inherently, this also allowed us to capture the meaning of suffixes or prefixes. In the case of this work, it translates into a better sensitivity in the detection of mutations.

Parameters setup used for fastText unsupervised model training:

{input=<corpus_text_file>, model="skipgram",
dim=200, epoch=10, lr=0.05, thread=32, loss="ns",
minCount=5, ws=5, t=1e-3, neg=10, verbose=1}

The NLP model was trained for 10 epochs with a skip-gram approach and with a negative sampling technique. The skip-gram model was able to learn words based on how they occur in the sentence, specifically the words they hang out with (context). In turn, negative sampling modified the optimization objective by each training sample to update only a small percentage of the model's weights.

The fastText library was also used as a technique for delivering multidimensional vectors for each SARS-CoV-2 genome sequence. After loading the trained fastText model (.bin file), its instance shared the method, which divided each word (token) vector in sentence by its norm and then averaged them as sequence vectors. At the end, each virus genome was represented by a vector of 200 floating numbers.

2.3 Supervised Machine Learning

As an algorithm for multi-class classification we used a Support Vector Machine (SVM) with a radial kernel. This is an effective approach when the data are not linearly separable. The SVM classifier implementation was delivered by NVIDIA RAPIDS v22.02 scientific ecosystem for data science. The hyper-parameters of the SVM classifier were tuned by the Optuna framework, which scanned the entire space of available parameter combinations (i.e. *C*, *gamma* and *delta*). SVM training with Optuna was executed with 50 trials and 10-fold cross-validations driven by a stratified shuffle split using a train set (29,092 virus samples represented by 200 dimensional numerical vectors each). The Optuna framework implements a Bayesian optimization algorithm called Tree-structured Parzen Estimator (TPE). The TPE uses a history record of trials to determine which hyperparameter values to try next, estimating an even more fitet params setup for the model. Consequently, it brings more accurate results measured by F1-weighted metric score.

To evaluate the performance of the final SVM model we used a separate test set, which covered 7,273 SARS-CoV-2 samples. None of them were used in NLP, ML training or even cross-validation. Furthermore, the test set introduced a new Omicron sub-variant class BA.2, which was not presented for the fastText model during the NLP training. In the quality control step we calculated accuracy (TP + TN)/(TP + TN + FN + FP), precision (TP/TP + FP), recall (TP/TP + FN) and F1-score (harmonic mean of precision and recall) metrics for the test set. Moreover, we generated a confusion matrix - to summarize prediction results on a classification problem, and ROC UAC - to illustrate the diagnostic ability of a classifier.

3 Results and Discussion

The NLP model based on continuous embedding of nucleotide sequence, driven by fastText, k-mers and n-grams "words" extraction strategy, was trained using a corpus file covered by 25,000 unique SARS-CoV-2 samples. The corpus text file took up 5.1 GB disk space. It was represented by 16,384 unique words (7-mers), which together defined the corpus vocabulary. 10 epochs training processes for the NLP model used 32 CPU threads and took 15 h to complete in total. After the training, a model was serialized as a *.bin* file for further purposes (virus genome vectorization). The final embedding model file size was 1.6 GB.

The training of a supervised Machine Learning model for SARS-CoV-2 variants prediction, including hyper-parameter tuning with 10-fold cross-validation, as well as evaluation on an independent test set, took 11h in total. To create a SVM model 36,365 virus samples were used, while each of them was represented by a 200 dimensional numeric vector and a label (variant name). The best parameters setup used for the final SVM model instance computed by Optuna framework are as follows:

{'C': 96.16125714544324, 'break_ties': False, 'cache_size': 200, 'class_weight':
'balanced', 'coef0': 0.0, 'decision_function_shape': 'ovr', 'degree': 8, 'gamma':
99.86390194515234, 'kernel': 'rbf', 'max_iter': -1, 'probability': True, 'random_state':
42, 'shrinking': True, 'tol': 0.001, 'verbose': False}

3.1 Evaluation on Test Set

The final SVM model was calibrated to fit multiple copies of the model, using 10-fold cross-validation, and graduate the probabilities predicted by these models using the test set. The nonparametric "isotonic" method was used as a type of probability calibration. The final SVM model achieved **99,79% accuracy** on an independent test set (7,273 virus samples). The detailed classification report, including precision, recall and F1-score metrics for each SARS-CoV-2 variants class, are described in Table 5. All the metrics were calculated using *classification_report* method from scikit-learn v1.0.2 scientific Python package.

The final SVM model was less precise in predictions, which we were able to confirm by deeper evaluation using a confusion matrix, Receiver Operator Characteristic (ROC) and Learning curve presented in Fig. 2, 3 and 4.

3.2 2D Projection of 61,365 SARS-CoV-2 Samples

Data visualization is a powerful method of graphical representation of information. It is an important step in the NLP model evaluation process, offering practical benefits. Projecting multidimensional data in 2D or 3D space can deliver deeper insight about the samples, potential clusters and embedding model sensitivity in their distinguishing.

To confirm the results from Machine Learning models, we decided to reduce 200 dimension vectors to 100 dimension space of each SARS-CoV-2 virus using the Principal

Table 5. SVM classification report for 7,273 SARS-CoV-2 virus samples from test set.

Pango lineage	WHO label	Precision	Recall	F1-score	Samples
B.1.1.7	Alpha	1,00	1,00	1,00	1,400
B.1.351	Beta	1,00	1,00	1,00	1,400
B.1.617.2	Delta	1,00	1,00	1,00	1,400
BA.1	Omicron	1,00	1,00	1,00	1,400
BA.2	Omicron (sub-variant)	1,00	1,00	1,00	273
P.1	Gamma	1,00	1,00	1,00	1,400
Macro avg		1,00	1,00	1,00	7,273
Weighted avg		1,00	1,00	1,00	7,273

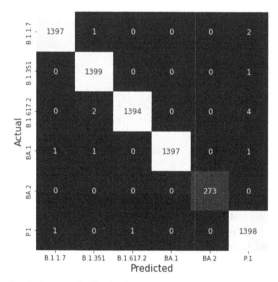

Fig. 2. Confusion matrix for the best SVM model evaluated in this paper.

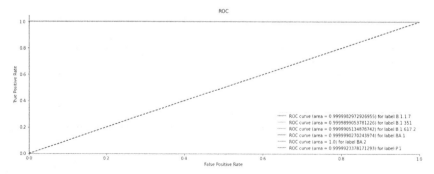

Fig. 3. ROC curves for the multiclass SVM classifier evaluated in this paper.

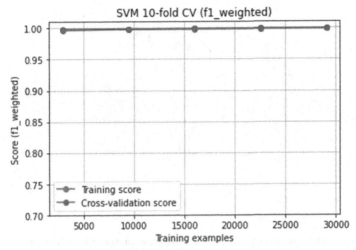

Fig. 4. Learning curve for 10-fold cross-validation of a multiclass SVM classifier evaluated in this paper.

Component Analysis (PCA) algorithm. This method reduces the dimensionality of large datasets and increases the data interpretability. Information loss was minimized in this case and confirmed by our calculation of explained variance ratio of 97,39%. Next, we trained the Uniform Manifold Approximation and Projection for Dimension Reduction (UMAP) model using vectors from PCA output and *euclidean* metric, to prepare 2-dimensional vectors for each virus sample, possible to display as a point in 2D interactive plot. The achieved result proves that SARS-CoV-2 feature space extracted from the genome sequences by the NLP model from this paper creates separated clusters per variant and sub-variant. The 2D projection screen is presented in Fig. 5.

3.3 Limitations and Future Research

In this work we present initial research results of our team for prediction of SARS-CoV-2 variants. We are aware that our tool *sarscov2vec,* which combines custom NLP embedding and Machine Learning classifier, has some limitations.

For the training NLP model we used samples limited to 25,000, which probably does not include all the possible virus mutations shared by global repositories. We also did not include Variant Of Interest and Variant Under Monitoring in this research, which could introduce a deeper historical context of viruses evolution for the NLP model. Moreover, we did not compare how proposed in this paper fastText n-grams approach for genome vectorization fares against the baseline techniques in NLP like One-Hot, TF-IDF encoding or Word2Vec. We did not check how the embedding model would react to smaller or bigger k-mers than 7. All of these aspects will be covered by further research work, which is ongoing.

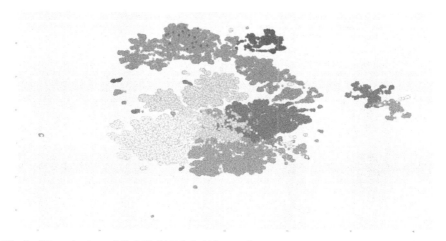

Fig. 5. 2D projection of 61,365 SARS-CoV-2 samples combined with NLP and ML datasets, performed by PCA and UMAP. Legend of virus variants: light green "BA.1", dark green "BA.2", red "B.1.617.2", pink "B.1.1.7", blue "P.1", yellow "B.1.351". (Color figure online)

4 Conclusions

In this paper, we demonstrated the tool *sarscov2vec* for distinguishing SARS-CoV-2 variants using their genome sequences. It combines custom NLP embedding driven by fastText and Support Vector Machine - a supervised Machine Learning algorithm - Our method is alignment free and uses numeric vectors of 7-mers and 3-g as a fixed sized feature space. We handled the class imbalance problem by semi-auto stratified random sampling of sequences per variant class. Our training and testing corpus included virus samples from 120 countries, deposited from 2020 to 2022, which helped us to keep high diversity of biological data that caused minimized bias.

The presented results show that our tool achieved a 99% confidence level in the prediction of variants of the highest significance (Alpha, Beta, Gamma, Delta and Omicron). An additional benefit important to highlight is the *sarscov2vec* tool's possibility of Omicron sub-variant (BA.2) detection with the same accuracy as the main Variant Of Concern. It proves that the NLP model demonstrates the ability to generalize and at the same time to confirm and discover new variants, which was not reported by other similar papers focused on AI-aided identification of SARS-CoV-2 variants [21, 22].

All the computations have been performed on Ubuntu 20.04 operating system, Python v3.8.10 and NVIDIA RAPIDS v22.02 scientific environment. The PC was equipped with high performance hardware for Machine Learning: AMD Ryzen Threadripper 1950x, 128 GB RAM, GPU NVIDIA RTX A6000 and 1TB SSD M.2. The GPU-enable environment and hardware parameters both significantly boosted this research work.

Acknowledgment. This work was supported by the Białystok University of Technology through the Polish Ministry of Science and Higher Education under Grant WI/WI-IIT/5/2020 and WZ/WI-IIT/3/2020. We gratefully acknowledge both the originating and submitting laboratories for the sequence data in NCBI Virus, GISAID and CDP on which the SARS-CoV-2 variants data are partially based.

Authors' Contributions. PT designed and developed the NLP and Machine Learning pipeline, as well as the *sarscov2vec* tool code base. ML was responsible for the biological context of the research, established data repositories, collected the datasets and compiled the high quality criteria for them. Both of us gathered materials about the current state of knowledge in SARS-CoV-2 variants prediction.

Data Availability. Open-source code of *sarscov2vec* tool and datasets from our research work are available here: https://github.com/ptynecki/sarscov2vec.

Conflict of Interest. The authors declare that they have no conflicts of interest.

References

1. Worldometers.info. https://www.worldometers.info/coronavirus/. Accessed 26 Feb 2022
2. Synowiec, A., Szczepański, A., Barreto-Duran, E., Lie, L.K., Pyrc, K.: Severe acute respiratory syndrome Coronavirus 2 (SARS-CoV-2): a systemic infection. Clin. Microbiol. Rev. **34** (2021)
3. Kunal, S., et al.: Emerging spectrum of post-COVID-19 syndrome. Postgrad. Med. J. (2021)
4. Desai, A.D., Lavelle, M., Boursiquot, B.C., Wan, E.Y.: Long-term complications of COVID-19. Am. J. Physiol. Physiol. **322**, C1–C11 (2022)
5. National Center for Immunization and Respiratory Diseases. https://www.cdc.gov/coronavirus/2019-ncov/need-extra-precautions/people-with-medical-conditions.html. Accessed 26 Feb 2022
6. Malik, J.A., et al.: The SARS-CoV-2 mutations versus vaccine effectiveness: new opportunities to new challenges. J. Infect. Public Health **15**, 228–240 (2022)
7. Li, M., Lou, F., Fan, H.: SARS-CoV-2 variant Omicron: currently the most complete "escapee" from neutralization by antibodies and vaccines. Signal Transduct. Target. Ther. **7**, 28 (2022)
8. Rahimi, A., Mirzazadeh, A., Tavakolpour, S.: Genetics and genomics of SARS-CoV-2: A review of the literature with the special focus on genetic diversity and SARS-CoV-2 genome detection. Genomics **113**, 1221–1232 (2021)
9. Sanjuán, R., Nebot, M.R., Chirico, N., Mansky, L.M., Belshaw, R.: Viral mutation rates. J. Virol. **84**, 9733–9748 (2010)
10. Tao, K., et al.: The biological and clinical significance of emerging SARS-CoV-2 variants. Nat. Rev. Genet. **22**, 757–773 (2021)
11. Harvey, W.T., et al.: SARS-CoV-2 variants, spike mutations and immune escape. Nat. Rev. Microbiol. **19**, 409–424 (2021)
12. Boehm, E., et al.: Novel SARS-CoV-2 variants: the pandemics within the pandemic. Clin. Microbiol. Infect. **27**, 1109–1117 (2021)
13. Lu, G., Wang, Q., Gao, G.F.: Bat-to-human: spike features determining 'host jump' of coronaviruses SARS-CoV, MERS-CoV, and beyond. Trends Microbiol. **23**, 468–478 (2015)
14. Du, L., et al.: The spike protein of SARS-CoV - a target for vaccine and therapeutic development. Nat. Rev. Microbiol. **7**, 226–236 (2009)
15. Duan, L., et al.: The SARS-CoV-2 spike glycoprotein biosynthesis, structure, function, and antigenicity: implications for the design of spike-based vaccine immunogens. Front. Immunol. **11**, 576622 (2020)

16. Bian, L., et al.: Effects of SARS-CoV-2 variants on vaccine efficacy and response strategies. Expert Rev. Vaccines **20**, 365–373 (2021)
17. WHO Tracking SARS-CoV-2 variants. https://www.who.int/en/activities/tracking-SARS-CoV-2-variants/. Accessed 26 Feb 2022
18. Abubaker Bagabir, S., Ibrahim, N.K., Abubaker Bagabir, H., Hashem Ateeq, R.: Covid-19 and artificial intelligence: genome sequencing, drug development and vaccine discovery. J. Infect. Public Health **15**, 289–296 (2022)
19. Zhang, Q., Gao, J., Wu, J.T., Cao, Z., Dajun Zeng, D.: Data science approaches to confronting the COVID-19 pandemic: a narrative review. Philos. Trans. R. Soc. A Math. Phys. Eng. Sci. **380**, 20210127 (2022)
20. Elangovan, A., He, J., Verspoor, K.: Memorization vs. generalization: quantifying data leakage in NLP performance evaluation (2021)
21. Nagpal, S., et al.: Genomic surveillance of COVID-19 variants with language models and machine learning. Front. Genet. **13** (2022)
22. Basu, S., et al.: Classifying COVID-19 variants based on genetic sequences using deep learning models. bioRxiv preprint (2021). https://doi.org/10.1101/2021.06.29.450335

Modelling and Optimization

Hybrid Model of Tourism Recommendation Software Development

Isabel Arregocés[1]($\boxtimes$) ⓘ, Jaime Daza[2] ⓘ, Jan Charris[2] ⓘ, Asly Cantillo[2] ⓘ,
Juan Amaya[2] ⓘ, and Margarita Gamarra[2] ⓘ

[1] Universidad de la Guajira, Riohacha, Guajira, Colombia
icarregoces@uniguajira.edu.co
[2] Universidad de la Costa, CUC, Barranquilla, Atlántico, Colombia
{Jdaza17,jcharris32,Acantil137,Jamaya9,mgamarra3}@cuc.edu.co

Abstract. Technological progress implies a revolution for many economic sectors. Among them, the tourism industry is one of the activities that depend on the online interaction of users as a promotion and marketing strategy. Recommender systems have gained great importance as an engine to promote visits to tourist sites according to certain user preferences. This study proposes a hybrid development model that addresses software that provides information about tourist sites, cultural and historical interest of any city. The hybrid methodology is based on the classic waterfall model and the agile Scrum and Kanban methodologies, which allows incorporating the linear sequential scheme, but with the advantages of agile methodologies. The hybrid methodology was applied to the analysis and planning phase of the tourist recommendation software case study. Different functionalities were proposed aimed at providing information on the most important aspects for tourists. The proposed model maintains the cascading sequential structure, taking organizational and methodological aspects of the Scrum and Kanban proposal. Additionally, the software application proposal will allow the user to have an experience where they obtain multiple options, from budgeting trips to planning them, in the same application.

Keywords: Mobile applications · Software engineering · Tourism · Recommendation systems · Web sites

1 Introduction

Tourism can be closely related to relaxation and enjoyment activities such as, for example, getting to know new places, going to the beach, enjoying the landscape and gastronomy, and even promoting knowledge of new cultures. The term tourism encompasses a broader field of action that involves the socioeconomic development of developing countries. This is due to its transformative power, the generation of business opportunities, and the possibility of boosting entrepreneurship in each region. However, the contribution of tourism to economic development depends on the quality of the services, spaces, resources, and profits it offers [1, 2].

Currently, the quality of tourism services is being enhanced by technology, since it is constantly evolving, changing the way we interact with the world. So, the contribution of technologies to the tourism industry is significant, that the study conducted by Google Travel reflects that, in 2015, "74% of leisure travelers plan their trips online, while only 13% do so through travel agencies" [3].

For this reason, more tourism applications have been developed, allowing the tourist to be more informed about his destination and to take a proactive role in the organization of the trip. This has created that the tourist requires more data to have diverse destination options and finally make a decision [4]. Generally, during the vacation period, tourists prefer to do recreational activities out far from the cities of origin. However, those who cannot go out, take their vacations locally, in places that are enabled for such activities [5]. Through tourism applications, each person can to choose the travel option according to their preferences, make ratings of the establishments and services offered in the places they visit, and even know the post-trip experience of other travelers [6, 7].

The frequent use of smartphones allows for an enriched experience before, during, and after the trip. Therefore, digital applications contribute to the tourism sector boosting the economy of the regions while satisfying the needs of travelers. Existing applications facilitate access to points of interest in an interactive way through algorithms that facilitate the implementation of prototypes based on Artificial Intelligence and Big Data techniques. Likewise, digital storytelling, 3D images, mixed reality, sensors, and recommendation systems, among others, are increasingly used to attract visitors. Despite the technological advances in the tourism context, there are opportunities for improvement in the development of applications related to the data used in the system, the design, and the type of recommendation for the end-user. Thus, the use of an appropriate methodology in the process of software development is essential to obtain high-quality software in the tourism context.

Considering the exposed before, this article proposes a hybrid model for the development of tourism recommendation software, to achieve a final product with the desired quality, under criteria of competitiveness and usability.

2 Related Work

Several studies on tourism in different areas have been published, however, for the development of this study, we focused on Software Engineering and related disciplines. A tourism information system similar to our proposal is detailed in [8]. The authors observed that many applications in the sector require detailed information of the region in which they operate, although they can incorporate the latest advances in Data Mining and Machine Learning. Therefore, they proposed an information system based on an Application Programming Interface (API) to obtain information on different points of interest, events, and itineraries, and to facilitate the interaction between users and the different tourism stakeholders. This is a suitable option given that this system pursues to solve the scarcity of information on many points of interest for cultural tourism.

Part of this scarcity of information is because, in regions where tourism is underestimated, there is not enough statistical data, as shown in [9]. In the case of the department of Casanare, Colombia, although investments can positively affect tourism, there is no projection to enhance the tourism potential of the different points of interest. Furthermore, although it is recognized that tourism has had an impact on the department's economy, there is no information to prove it.

Tourist destinations that, physically or virtually, have reconstructed the tangible and intangible elements of their culture have expanded their demand, generating local dynamics associated with the socioeconomic level. New forms of visitor-centered interaction enrich the experience [10–12] regardless of the type of tourism activity selected. Optimized content and the functionalities of the platforms or applications created are considered decisive elements when selecting the destination.

Regarding the use of APIs for the tourism sector, the CitySDK project [13] is a precedent. This project was initially available for the cities of Amsterdam (Netherlands), Helsinki (Finland), Lameia (Greece), Lisbon (Portugal), and Rome (Italy), and was also used by some companies in the sector. Despite the effort, the main challenge lies in the fact that each city usually publishes its information in different formats, which forces developers to deal with each of them.

In that sense, alternatives have been proposed in this research regarding the way to obtain the information, presenting a system where users' opinions are recorded when planning a trip [14]. This system proposes to create a space where users can register the different places and their sincere impressions about them, an element that can help in the planning of a trip. The developed system seeks to encourage these actions in all types of sites, considering that many existing solutions in the market only focus on one type of site (hotels, restaurants, nightspots, historical sites, etc.).

The work presented in [15] analyzes other studies with a methodology in the development of computer applications for tourism supported by augmented reality technology. The result of the research was a mixed methodology prototype for the development of computer applications in augmented reality applied in tourism.

Other works have explored and reviewed the impact of to introduce agile methodologies in a traditional environment [16–18]. These works concludes that the implementation of a hybrid Agile methodology might benefit large organizations.

As part of the creation process of the tourist recommendation software and to reach quality criteria on the final product, it is necessary to define a software development methodology that allows addressing all the requirements, taking advantage of the resources within the process, and reaching the objectives in the desired time.

There are numerous methodologies for software development, and the tourism industry adopt some of them in the creation of information systems [19]. Nevertheless, to the best of our knowledge, a methodology specifically for the case of tourism recommender systems, adjusted to this context and to the user needs has not been specified. This paper proposes a hybrid methodology that allows to carry out an adequate software development process, considering functional and non-functional requirements in the time defined for this purpose, both in the context of tourist recommendation systems and for other types of applications with high requirements for usability and agility in development.

3 Proposed Approach

In the software development process for tourist recommendation, it is necessary an adequate analysis of the user requirements, according to the needs of the tourist and the region; to have a correct organization of the work team; to identify, organize, and assign the tasks to be developed; to achieve a complete risk analysis and to define the support tools for project management and software development [20]. A literature review has shown that the inclusion of different methodologies of software development, could help the software team to reach the objectives, fulfilling quality standards [21, 22]. In several cases [23, 24], software methodologies are combined with new standards, which have increased team productivity and customer satisfaction, through improving the software development process.

To reach these requirements, the proposed hybrid model combines the waterfall methodology, as a base methodology, and two agile methodologies, Scrum and Kanban. The waterfall methodology allows to perform the corresponding operations in a more delayed way, but with greater efficiency at the time of obtaining the results, since it makes hypotheses in each phase and checks them for less risk of loss because it verifies the results that they are yielding [25].

On the other hand, the Scrum methodology proposes iterations for the development of the most important functionalities of the application, while it is more flexible in terms of change control than the waterfall methodology. In this case study, the application's usage environment is highly changeable (as it is highly dependent on user input), Scrum gives greater user participation within the development process [26]. In addition, the typical control of the waterfall methodology would be transformed into the controls of the review of each iteration, in which improvements in the process and functionalities are proposed. These aspects of the Scrum methodology would be applied specifically to the coding phase since the planning process should define the aspects to be considered in each platform (web or mobile) [27].

Finally, the Kanban methodology would be applied mainly in the analysis and design processes, although it can also be applied to the iterations proposed by Scrum. Given the nature of the waterfall methodology, each phase is defined and must be completed to advance to the next [25], and when using the pure waterfall methodology, there is no possibility of backward jumps. Kanban allows controlling the tasks to be developed in each of these phases, using a board where the workflow is visualized. In this way, bottlenecks are reduced, while establishing a limit called Work in Progress Limit, which limits the number of tasks that can be in each stage of the development process [26].

A schematic of the proposed hybrid methodology for the tourism recommender system is shown in Fig. 1. In this hybrid methodology, the main aspects of the Scrum methodology are taken in terms of the structure of the iterations and the organization of the work team. For the execution of tasks during the development of the project, the proposed Kanban methodology is used through the activities board and assigned responsible persons. From the waterfall methodology, the rigorousness of the processes and the detailed definition of the requirements at the beginning of the project are taken.

Compared with Waterfall and agile methodologies, the hybrid model could offer less flexibility, it shows a weak structure and planning of the project could be incomplete. In addition, communication, collaboration, and personal involvement are needed to ensure the success of an agile process. This can be negative in case of having an uncollaborative team. On the other hand, agile methodologies are very dependent on the members of the work team themselves, so that if any of the team members fails, the project would be delayed [28]. Then, from the agile model, communication between team members in the distributed environment and the skill and expertise requirements, are still limitation in the hybrid model. Other drawback of the hybrid model is the implementation, as it includes part of both approaches, is hard identify the elements that are contained in the hybrid model [29].

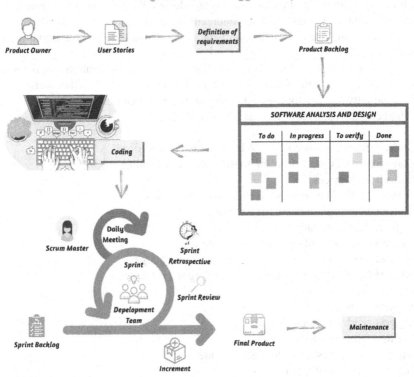

Fig. 1. Hybrid methodology (own elaboration)

By the other hand, the hybrid model offers several advantages which have a positive effect on the project. For example, project planning, from Waterfall approach, and scheduling charts along with task level of documentation using user story and Kanban card, provides accurate estimation which is essential for product owner in identifying risk with the project.

Other advantage of the hybrid model is that in terms of user satisfaction, the agile methodology fosters the communication and interaction with the customer so that they can see how the product satisfices their needs and reach an effective solution.

The hybrid model maintains the agility of the scrum approach as the plan for the project can change through the software development cycle. Each change may affect the cost and time of the development [30]. For those changes that increase the cost and/or time a new project plan is presented immediately to maintain the project in acceptable limits.

4   Case Study: RioTour

The proposed model is adopted in the development process of the web application RioTour, currently in the stage of analysis and design. RioTour intends to give cultural touristic recommendations (routes, monuments, and cultural attractions) adapted to the visitor's needs through a tourist recommendation system, based on the initial profiling of each visitor.

The waterfall methodology proposes a rigorous analysis of requirements in the planning stage. We adopted this feature for our model. For the case study of the tourism recommendation software, RioTour, the following are the proposed functionalities, considering the characteristics and requirements for the project:

- Consult travel costs according to location and destination
- Compare travel costs according to transportation (land or air)
- Consult hotel prices
- Consult medical centers and medical insurance costs
- Consult entry requirements for a region
- Suggest travel itinerary and places of interest
- Suggest hotels according to places of interest
- Suggest restaurants according to food tastes and budget
- Suggest cultural places of interest according to preferences
- Suggest nearby events
- Suggest car rental prices
- Suggest nearby gas stations
- Weather forecast information
- Suggest the shortest route to places of interest
- Gallery of places of interest
- Know the opinion of other users about the places of interest.

These functionalities are proposed based on the experience of customers with the different existing applications in the market and the common needs of many tourists [31].

Due to the characteristics of the project, a team with the following roles is proposed, based on the Scrum methodology:

- Project Manager (Product Owner)
- Scrum Master (for the development process)
- Graphic Designer
- User Interface Designer (UI)
- Interaction Designer (IxD)
- User Experience Designer (UX)
- Development team:

  - Software Analyst and Architect
  - Database Administrator
  - Mobile Developer
  - Frontend Web Developer
  - Backend Web Developer
  - Quality Engineer
  - Tester and Quality Assurance (QA).

The team, given the positions, will have a controlled decentralized structure [25]. This allows at the same time, to coordinate the team internally, and to give a prudent margin to its members to solve the different concerns. Secondary managers can also be appointed for different tasks: Design and architecture tasks (User Interface (UI), User Experience (UX) and interaction designers are involved, as well as the software architect), development (involving developers and the database administrator), testing and quality assurance.

4.1 Metrics of the Software Project

The objective of the project is to design a web application for tourist travel information. Table 1 shows the metrics for monitoring the project, for each activity, and the tools for verifying compliance with these metrics.

Table 2 shows the different metrics according to their category, to track the project and how they can be obtained. Quality metrics for software products should be easy to measure in practice and should be able to be validated theoretically and empirically [32].

These metrics allow to have a deep vision of the effectiveness of the processes already existing in the project, this is key for the improvement of the software quality and the performance of the organization. For this reason, it is important to be clear about the project objectives and to understand the information shown by the metrics.

On the other hand, the metrics measure the responses and functionalities, verifying that they comply with the requirements. Finally, the quality metrics are necessary because we want to provide an adequate service to the users that access the tourism page and that they are satisfied, in addition to work on different aspects of the software with the lowest possible cost.

Table 1. Indicators for project monitoring

Activities	Indicators	Verification tools
• Facilitate access to information on tourist trips offered • Determine the requirements for the design of applications (The website is focused on travel) • Use this methodology (waterfall) to design travel web applications • Determine the commercial and touristic information of the software • Show different offers, services, and prices offered by the Tourism and Business website	• It has efficiency concerning the behavior of time and resources of the project • Apply a flexible development process that adapts to customer needs. Obtain user feedback quickly • Display in a visual and understandable way for the user the travel catalog • A drop-down tab will be displayed to show the different offers and services offered	• Annual reports of weather behavior and others • Table with all user records • At the end of the first test phase, see if it was effective • Customer experience survey

Table 2. Software metrics [25].

Elements	Software Metric
Process	• All errors and defects from different projects are categorized by origin • The cost of correcting each error or defect is recorded • The number of errors and defects in each category are counted and sorted in decreasing order • The overall cost of errors and defects in each category is computed • The resulting data are analyzed to detect the categories that produce the highest cost
Function	• The process is modified to try to eliminate the costliest defects or errors • These metrics are obtained by considering the productivity measures and normalizing them by a measure of the functionality delivered by the application
Quality	• The functionality is derived from other direct measures • The capability of error detection and correction • Attempt to measure the usability attribute • Increase in productivity when the system is used in a moderately efficient manner

4.2 Risks Identification and Management

The first risks that the project will face are those associated with planning, specifically those associated with the estimation process, due to its uncertainty. The most important estimation risks are those of cost and effort and those of human resources. In the first risk group, some costs will likely exceed the estimated value, while in the second group, it is possible to have insufficient staff, untrained or inexperienced staff, or unwilling staff.

Other risks category that the project may face is a technical risk. These risks are associated with potential problems in the design, implementation, interface, verification, and maintenance stages. In addition, regulatory ambiguity, technical uncertainty, obsolete technology, and new technology are also risk factors to consider.

The probability and impact of each risk were evaluated. The scale for Probability and Impact are: Very high, High, Moderate, Low and Very low. It represents a qualitative assessment of the probability and consequences of the risk. Considering the occurrence of events in previous projects [33].

For each risk, numerical values of probability and impact have been assigned. The probability and impact matrix will be used to prioritize the identified threats. Through this analysis, we quantify whether the risk is classified as high, medium, or low. The assigned values are set based in previous experience and expert criteria. The equivalent values in the Probability were given, the very high valuation is 0.9 and it goes down two by two. A similar assignation was done for Impact values. The final matrix is shown in Table 3.

Table 3. Probability and impact matrix of the risks in the software.

Probability and impact matrix		Impact				
		Very high 0.05	High 0.1	Moderate 0.2	Low 0.4	Very low 0.9
Probability	Very high 0.9	0.045	0.09	0.18	0.36	0.72
	High 0.7	0.035	0.07	0.14	0.28	0.56
	Moderate 0.5	0.025	0.03	0.1	0.2	0.4
	Low 0.3	0.015	0.03	0.06	0.12	0.24
	Very low 0.1	0.005	0.01	0.02	0.04	0.08
Low Risk----Moderate Risk----High Risk						

Considering the context where the project will be developed, Table 4 establishes the different risks of the project and their relationship between probability and impact:

Finally, the different risks are related in the matrix shown in Table 5, where the probabilities and impact of the different project risks are assessed as tools for developing the risk analysis. Probability and Impact values are multiplied to obtain the risk assessment.

The risk management is an important aspect considered in project management standards and frameworks as PMBOK, PRINCE2 and ISO 1006. These standards propose exhaustive documentation to identify and minimize risk. This is helpful in complex software development projects, but the in an agile proposal the documentation is limited.

Table 4. Risks of the project and their relationship between probability and impact.

Project risks	Probability/Impact
Lack of information due to regions where tourism is underestimated	Low
Possible failures in the software during its development	Moderate
Low end-user acceptance and high market competition	Moderate
Each city usually publishes its information in different formats, so the project could be delayed	Moderate
Requirement changes that redo the design. Customers do not share the change that has been made	Very low
The time required to develop the software, the defect repair rate, and the size of the software, are underestimated	Low
The used database cannot handle as many transactions per second as expected	Moderate

Table 5. Risk assessment by the product of probability and impact.

No.	Risk	Probability (P)	Impact (I)	P x I
1	Lack of information in regions where tourism is not fostered	0.3	0.8	0.24
2	Possible failures in the development software	0.5	0.8	0.4
3	Competitors and apathy of users	0.5	0.8	0.4
4	Delay due to different formats of the information in each City	0.5	0.5	0.25
5	Changes in the requirements	0.1	0.3	0.1
6	The time to develop the software is underestimated	0.3	0.4	0.14
7	Fails in database	0.5	0.8	0.4

In our hybrid methodology, despite include some aspect of waterfall method, we define the risk management based in an agile context [34].

In our hybrid model, all risks are identified and placed in the risk backlog, using the probability and impact matrix. Then, the risks are prioritized based on factors determining priority, as the context, the teamwork, the user need, and others. When the risks are prioritized (see Table 3), the risks with higher priority enter the Scrum iteration cycle to be considered for risk management. In this iteration, the strategy to overcome the risk is planned. Afterward, the strategy is applied and finally, the risk elimination is observed and controlled.

4.3 Control Version

It is proposed to use Git to perform version control, since it works appropriately in a wide variety of software development environments, i.e., it runs on different operating systems, and it is integrated into most code editors and integrated development environments (IDEs). A large number of software projects rely on Git for version control, including commercial and open-source projects [35]. Git is a version control software designed by Linus Torvalds for version maintenance of applications when they have many sources code files, so that code realization is much more reliable and compatible among the development team.

According to a survey of 69,808 professional developers conducted by the Stack-overflow platform [36], it was found that 88.4% of professionals prefer to use Git for version control of software projects. Since the percentage of professionals who voted for Git is too high, it can be deduced that it has become the dominant option for version control for developers today. For this reason, the development team decided to use Git for version control of the tourism information system RioTour. In addition, the platform offers great benefits such as the possibility of teamwork, collaboration in different projects, greater autonomy when working, it is free software, and multiplatform.

Likewise, it is proposed to store the application code in GitHub, firstly, because it is the largest software repository service in the world and, secondly, because its storage is in the cloud and thus avoids having the code in local storage, with the corresponding risk of losing all the project files in case of problems in the physical media. Normally, the central repository of the project is created on GitHub, and through Git, each team member can have a copy of these on their workstations. It also allows you to create private or public projects.

4.4 Rio Tour Application

As a result of the implementation of our hybrid model, the requirement analysis was completed and a prototype of the web application RioTour was designed. This development intends to create a profile of the tourist using personal and contextual information as shown in Fig. 2a. One of the outputs in the software is the suggested route to the destination selected by the user, as shown in Fig. 2b.

The use of the hybrid methodology in the development and implementation of Rio-Tour led to the creation of a robust system and allowed to clearly detect the possible risks in cost and time given the amount of person-hours in the development of the software and the complexity of the algorithms used. Several collaborators and experts worked in the development, then the control version tool opened the possibility of having stable starting points of the software to make variations when a new layer was added and thus return if necessary to the point of origin, in case of failures or development errors.

The implementation of metrics was useful to detect and discard unused modules and options in the system and reduce the waste of time developing modules of little use. The Scrum and Kanban methodologies were used to overcome the limitations due to

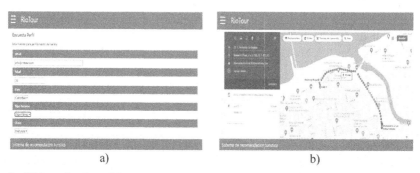

Fig. 2. Web application of the touristic recommendation software, RioTour. a) Input of the user profile. b) Suggestion of the route to the selected destination.

the lack of information or partial data found. The structure proposed in the application, is adjustable to other recommendation systems given its capacity of hybridization and data analysis to generate a response according to the needs of each user of the system.

Finally, RioTour is a tangible tool of the theories of algorithms and recommender systems and software development methodologies. This application can be considered as a contribution to the creative economy of tourism in the regions, since it is a tool that can be used in places where the income depends largely on tourism. This application can also generate valuable information for capital investment in tourist destinations.

5   Conclusions

The proposed hybrid software development methodology includes significant elements of the traditional waterfall methodology and two agile methodologies, that is, Scrum and Kanban. Incorporating different elements of each methodology allows having an adequate adjustment to the tourism recommendation system. On the one hand, the process defined in the waterfall model is quite complete and allows to specify an appropriate software design. On the other hand, the Scrum methodology provides a guide to performing the iterations in permanent contact with the client, in an environment where the software must be created in the client-developer team and the Kanban proposal includes an appropriate distribution of activities in the process.

The case study of the Tourism Information Software Rio Tour provides the user with a new experience, with multiple options, from making a travel budget to buying tickets for hotel reservations, offers travel plans among other services, all so that the user has confidence and security when making use of it.

Furthermore, this hybrid methodology could be extended to other recommendation system, different to tourism context, as our proposal focus on identifying the changing needs of the users, involve the client into the software development and manage the task in an efficient manner, containing aspect of waterfall, Scrum and Kanban methodologies. This makes the hybrid method more flexible and suitable for other context with similar features.

The definition of the functionalities of the Tourist Information Software was carried out considering the needs of the users and the characteristics and requirements for the project in a complete way with expert professionals. The relevant risks were identified where a high category is assigned if the risk were to occur during and after the development of the project.

It is proposed to use Git to perform version control since it works very well in a wide variety of software development environments, that is, it works in different operating systems, and it is integrated into most code editors and development environments.

As future work, it is proposed to apply the proposed methodology completely in the design, coding, and testing phases of the tourism recommendation software, which will facilitate the organization of the work team and the inclusion of quality criteria in the development methodology.

References

1. Brida, J.G., Brindis, M.A.R., Mejía-Alzate, M.L.: La contribución del turismo al crecimiento económico de la ciudad de Medellín – Colombia. Rev. Econ. Rosario. **24**, 1–23 (2021). https://doi.org/10.12804/REVISTAS.UROSARIO.EDU.CO/ECONOMIA/A.8926
2. Chanquey, Y., Lagos, N., Llanco, C., Chanquey, Y., Lagos, N., Llanco, C.: Analysis of economic growth as a function of tourism in Chile, period 2000–2018. Rev. Interam. Ambient. Tur. **17**, 34–46 (2021). https://doi.org/10.4067/S0718-235X2021000100034
3. "Internet está transformando los servicios de turismo en el mundo y Colombia no es la excepción": David Luna. https://mintic.gov.co/portal/inicio/Sala-de-prensa/Noticias/12631: Internet-esta-transformando-los-servicios-de-turismo-en-el-mundo-y-Colombia-no-es-la-excepcion-David-Luna. Accessed 04 Mar 2022
4. Pantano, E., Priporas, C.V., Stylos, N.: 'You will like it!' using open data to predict tourists' response to a tourist attraction. Tour. Manag. **60**, 430–438 (2017). https://doi.org/10.1016/J.TOURMAN.2016.12.020
5. Streimikiene, D., Svagzdiene, B., Jasinskas, E., Simanavicius, A.: Sustainable tourism development and competitiveness: The systematic literature review. Sustain. Dev. **29**, 259–271 (2021). https://doi.org/10.1002/SD.2133
6. Vellingiri, J., Suraj, A., Gopal, J.: A Novel smart meal planner website with online store and dietician consultancy-for this modern era-from the human-computer interaction practitioners' perspective. Int. J. Adv. Trends Comput. Sci. Eng. **9**, 2947–2954 (2020). https://doi.org/10.30534/ijatcse/2020/70932020
7. Ip, C., Lee, H., Law, R.: Profiling the users of travel websites for planning and online experience sharing. **36**, 418–426 (2010). http://dx.doi.org/10.1177/1096348010388663, https://doi.org/10.1177/1096348010388663
8. Lopes, P., et al.: Open tourist information system: a platform for touristic information management and outreach. Inf. Technol. Tour. **21**(4), 577–593 (2019). https://doi.org/10.1007/s40558-019-00159-w
9. Barrios, O.S., González, L.A.Á.: Determinación de indicadores pertinentes para utilizar en un sistema de gestión de información turística para el departamento de Casanare. Tur. Soc. **20**, 191–209 (2017). https://doi.org/10.18601/01207555.N20.10
10. Shin, J., Kim, J., Woo, W.: Narrative design for rediscovering Daereungwon: a location-based augmented reality game. In: 2017 IEEE International Conference on Consumer Electronics, ICCE 2017 pp. 384–387 (2017). https://doi.org/10.1109/ICCE.2017.7889364
11. Liestol, G.: Sequence & access, storytelling & archive in mobile augmented reality. In: Proceedings of 2017 23rd International Conference on Virtual System & Multimedia, VSMM 2017, vol. 2018-January, pp. 1–7 (2018). https://doi.org/10.1109/VSMM.2017.8346305

12. Gutierrez, J.M., Molinero, M.A., Soto-Martín, O., Medina, C.R.: Augmented reality technology spreads information about historical Graffiti in temple of debod. Proc. Comput. Sci. **75**, 390–397 (2015). https://doi.org/10.1016/J.PROCS.2015.12.262
13. Pereira, R.L., Sousa, P.C., Barata, R., Oliveira, A., Monsieur, G.: CitySDK tourism API - building value around open data. J. Internet Serv. Appl. **6**, 1–13 (2015). https://doi.org/10.1186/S13174-015-0039-Z/FIGURES/4
14. Mirza, A.A.: Collaborative tourist information sharing system. Int. J. Adv. Trends Comput. Sci. Eng. **9**, 5565–5569 (2020). https://doi.org/10.30534/IJATCSE/2020/203942020
15. Rios, M.D.G., Villegas, J.J.T., Martinez, M.A.Q., Vazquez, M.Y.L.: Methodology for the development of computer applications with augmented reality in the tourism sector. In: Ahram, T., Taiar, R. (eds.) IHIET 2021. LNNS, vol. 319, pp. 797–804. Springer, Cham (2022). https://doi.org/10.1007/978-3-030-85540-6_101
16. Mahadevan, L., Kettinger, W.J., Meservy, T.O., Mahadevan, L., Kettinger, W.J.: Running on hybrid: control changes when introducing an agile methodology in a traditional "waterfall" system development environment. Commun. Assoc. Inf. Syst. **36**, 5 (2015). https://doi.org/10.17705/1CAIS.03605
17. Shimoda, A., Yaguchi, K.: A method of setting the order of user story development of an agile-waterfall hybrid method by focusing on common objects. In: Proceedings - 2017 6th IIAI International Congress on Advanced Applied Informatics, IIAI-AAI 2017, pp. 301–306 (2017). https://doi.org/10.1109/IIAI-AAI.2017.149
18. Schuh, G., Rebentisch, E., Riesener, M., DIels, F., Dölle, C., Eich, S.: Agile-waterfall hybrid product development in the manufacturing industry - introducing guidelines for implementation of parallel use of the two models. In: IEEE International Conference on Industrial Engineering and Engineering Management, vol. 2017-December, pp. 725–729 (2018). https://doi.org/10.1109/IEEM.2017.8289986
19. Brankica, P., Zlatko, L.: Contemporary information system development methodologies in tourism organizations. In: Cvijanović, D., Grigorievna, A., Ruţić, P., Gnjatović, D., Stanišić, T. (eds.) Tourism International Scientific Conference Vrnjačka Banja – TISC, pp. 467–481. University of Kragujevac - Faculty of Hotel Management and Tourism (2016)
20. Gamarra, M., Zurek, E., Nieto, W., Jimeno, M., Sierra, D.: Spiral-based model for software architecture in bio-image analysis: a case study in RSV cell infection. In: Saeed, K., Dvorský, J. (eds.) CISIM 2020. LNCS, vol. 12133, pp. 25–38. Springer, Cham (2020). https://doi.org/10.1007/978-3-030-47679-3_3
21. Kuhrmann, M., et al.: Hybrid software development approaches in practice: a european perspective. IEEE Softw. **36**, 20–31 (2019). https://doi.org/10.1109/MS.2018.110161245
22. Kuhrmann, M., et al.: Hybrid software and system development in practice: waterfall, scrum, and beyond. In: ACM International Conference on Proceeding Series, Part F128767, pp. 30–39 (2017). https://doi.org/10.1145/3084100.3084104
23. Esteki, M., Gandomani, T.J., Farsani, H.K.: A risk management framework for distributed scrum using PRINCE2 methodology. Bull. Electr. Eng. Inform. **9**, 1299–1310 (2020). https://doi.org/10.11591/EEI.V9I3.1905
24. Gandomani, T.J., Sarpiri, M.N.: A case study of using the hybrid model of scrum and six sigma in software development. Artic. Int. J. Electr. Comput. Eng. **11**, 5342–5350 (2021). https://doi.org/10.11591/ijece.v11i6.pp5342-5350
25. Pressman, R.S., Bruce, R.M.: Software Engineering A Practitioner's Approach. McGraw-Hill Education, New York (2015). 1, 53
26. Sommerville, I.: Software Engineering: Pearson New International Edition, p. 816 (2015)
27. Dalal, S., Solanki, K., Sudhir, Diksha: Exploring the essentials and principles of software development. Int. J. Adv. Trends Comput. Sci. Eng. **8**, 3504–3510 (2019). https://doi.org/10.30534/IJATCSE/2019/129862019

28. Ramingwong, S., Ramingwong, L., Cosh, K., Eiamkanitchat, N.: A comparative study on scrum simulations. In: Unger, H., Sodsee, S., Meesad, P. (eds.) IC2IT 2018. AISC, vol. 769, pp. 317–326. Springer, Cham (2019). https://doi.org/10.1007/978-3-319-93692-5_31

29. Bhavsar, K., Gopalan, S., Shah, V.: Scrumbanfall: an agile integration of scrum and kanban with waterfall in software engineering. Int. J. Innov. Technol. Explor. Eng. **9**, 2075–2084 (2020). https://doi.org/10.35940/IJITEE.D1437.029420

30. Hassanein, E.E., Hassanien, S.A.: Cost efficient scrum process methodology to improve agile software development. J. Comput. Sci. **18** (2020)

31. Yachin, J.M.: The 'customer journey': learning from customers in tourism experience encounters. Tour. Manag. Perspect. **28**, 201–210 (2018). https://doi.org/10.1016/J.TMP.2018.09.002

32. Castaño, J.: Métricas en la evaluación de la calidad del software: una revisión conceptual. Comput. Electron. Sci. Theory Appl. **2**, 21–26 (2021). https://doi.org/10.17981/CESTA.02.02.2021.03

33. Kassem, M.A., Khoiry, M.A., Hamzah, N.: Using probability impact matrix (PIM) in analyzing risk factors affecting the success of oil and gas construction projects in Yemen. Int. J. Energy Sect. Manag. **14**, 527–546 (2020). https://doi.org/10.1108/IJESM-03-2019-0011

34. Gandomani, T.J., Afshari, M.: A novel risk management model in the Scrum and extreme programming hybrid methodology. Artic. Int. J. Electr. Comput. Eng. **12**, 2911–2921 (2022). https://doi.org/10.11591/ijece.v12i3.pp2911-2921

35. ¿Qué es el software de control de versiones GIT? - Base de Conocimientos – ICTEA. https://www.ictea.com/cs/index.php?rp=%2Fknowledgebase%2F3484%2FiQue-es-el-software-de-control-de-versiones-GIT.html. Accessed 04 Mar 2022

36. Stack Overflow Developer Survey 2018. https://insights.stackoverflow.com/survey/2018/#work-version-control. Accessed 25 Apr 2022

Integrated Models-Driven Framework to Generate Various Online and Print Tests

Daniela Borissova[1]($\boxtimes$) (ID), Nikolay Buhtiyarov[1] (ID), Radoslav Yoshinov[2] (ID), Magdalena Garvanova[3] (ID), and Ivan Garvanov[3] (ID)

[1] Institute of Information and Communication Technologies at the Bulgarian Academy of Sciences, 1113 Sofia, Bulgaria
{daniela.borissova,nikolay.buhtiyarov}@iict.bas.bg
[2] Laboratory of Telematics at the Bulgarian Academy of Sciences, Sofia, Bulgaria
yoshinov@cc.bas.bg
[3] University of Library Studies and Information Technologies, 1784 Sofia, Bulgaria
{m.garvanova,i.garvanov}@unibit.bg

Abstract. The ongoing digital transformation influence all fields from education to economics. That is why many efforts are taken to develop different business models to reflect the new reality. The e-tests are the core of contemporary e-learning and are suitable to conduct proper checks about the level of competency for different occupations. In this regard the current article describes an integrated framework based on different optimization models to select a set of questions to compose e-tests or print tests. The basic workflow algorithm of this framework is described. The framework' distinguish feature is the possibility to generate different levels of tests' complexity thanks to the specifics of formulated single criterion mixed-integer and multi-criteria models. The applicability of the integrated models-driven framework is demonstrated by using a test bank with predefined questions with different difficulties. The obtained results prove the possibility to generate tests with different degrees of complexity accordingly to the formulated models.

Keywords: Integrated framework · Model-driven design · Mixed-integer linear programming · Multi-criteria optimization · Tests generation

1 Introduction

ICTs together with advances in operations research, allow the development of new tools to support various aspects of smart decision-making in line with the digitalization process [1]. New business challenges require the incorporation of state-of-the-art technology into business intelligence tools to improve product quality and user satisfaction. Therefore, the current trends in e-learning are focused not only on the provision of content for e-learning, but as an integral part of the training are the tools for verification and assessment level of knowledge [2, 3]. Process of assessment could be executed in different way including proper tests, writing code, or construct of algorithms. It is worth to mention that some e-learning courses in the area of mathematics and programming require special

K. Saeed and J. Dvorský (Eds.): CISIM 2022, LNCS 13293, pp. 316–329, 2022.
https://doi.org/10.1007/978-3-031-10539-5_23

kind of tools for algorithms visualization [4] or automated design algorithms [5]. Another suitable tool useful for testing in programming is the existing of proper environment where some software code can be tested [6]. The computer science should be mention too as an area with highly dynamic of learning content. To cope with such challenges, a learning model with a couple of learning blocks containing axiomatic lessons for a particular subject together with set of problems that students need to solve is proposed [7].

Modern Learning Management Systems (LMS) enable the creation and management of learning content, including various forms of exams and tests [8]. Tests can be designed and developed with automatic classification options. Although setting up a question bank is a time-consuming activity, the test elements can be reused and students' exams are automatically assessed. In addition, immediate assessment of online exams allows students to receive quick feedback on their achievements. The authors show that students who use the tests during training have better results than other students [9]. Different types of questions could be used like questions of multiple-choices type, true-false selection, short-answer, essay all of them provided by test banks. It should be noted that true-false questions have a 50% chance of guessing the correct answer, so multiple choice questions are often preferred. The use of multiple-choice questions provides an opportunity to learn new information from the test: for example, the learner may not know the answer to the question, but may be able to justify the answer, based on the knowledge gained [10]. Another promising direction in questions construction is the usage of some kind of gamification [11, 12]. An analysis of algorithms used to generate test questions in e-testing systems can be found in [13].

Given the fact that ICTs are so widespread, e-learning is probably the most appropriate area for the introduction of new technologies. The use of different mathematical methods makes it possible to formulate different tests using quizzes or open-ended questions to check the level of knowledge. The e-testing could be used not only at the universities or at the schools, but it is also a suitable tool to establish the level of competency for different occupations [14]. Along with the availability of e-learning materials and e-tests, a special role is given to the e-facilitator. It contributes to facilitating access to various electronic services, maintains virtual libraries and forms communities involving all stakeholders [15].

The design of any system could be represented via proper business model that contribute for better understanding the essence of processes [16, 17]. Special attention needs to be paid to mobile applications that are widely spread recently. In this regard, a systematic review of model driven development techniques and methodologies to support mobile app development and their usage is given in [18]. The development of stand-alone application is costly and time-consuming due to the diversity and complexity of the requirements. To cope with such problems, a promising technique known as software-as-a-service could be used. Similar approach is used in proposed framework composed of context-as-a-service reference model, a context service meta-model, a graphical modeling tool, a code generation tool, and a context service management tool [19]. Model-driven development was also utilized to facilitate simulation modeling via high-level modeling languages providing reusable building blocks [20]. The authors show that model-driven development is a promising direction to ease the development and increase productivity in agent-based simulation development. Evaluations of model-oriented programming are challenging as there is a need to provide sophisticated development environments for realistic evaluation and experienced users are to be involved [21]. Due to the advantages of model-driven development, the Umple technology for model-oriented programming is established. Umple is modeling tool for open source and education targeted to agile developers and software engineering education [22, 23]. In the e-learning domain, content recommender systems suggest appropriate learning resources based on learners' preferences and learning goals. A literature review on the recent studies on personalized and adaptive learning systems is presented in [24].

Given the importance of e-learning, it is important to provide an integrated and flexible e-testing tool. To guarantee such flexibility a promising approach is the usage of different mathematical models. In this regard, the current article proposes an integrated model-driven framework for generating and evaluating online tests with different levels of complexity is proposed. The proposed approach could be used in the regime of self-testing or as an official examination. The core idea of the described framework is based on several optimization models used to generate the questions to compose the tests of different levels of complexity realised by corresponding scenarious.

The rest of the article is structured as follows: Sect. 2 provide description of integrated model-driven framework including the formulation of the used optimization models for test generation, Sect. 3 contains the input data and relust from the conducted numerical application, and Sect. 4 contains the conclusion and some future directions for developments.

2 Integrated Models-Driven Framework for Tests Generation

The purpose of the proposed approach is to provide a flexibility in the selection of questions for the purposes of generating tests with varying degrees of complexity in e-learning. In order to realize the generation of tests with different degrees of complexity, it is necessary to formulate in advance a large number of questions with different degrees of difficulty, from which to make the appropriate choice, consistent with the set levels of complexity of the tests.

2.1 Models-Driven Framework for Generating Different e-Tests

The proposed integrated framework is based on different scenarios, each of them realized by a specific mathematical model. Each of these models could be tuned in a such way to generate test with different level of complexity. The basic workflow algorithm of proposed framework for generating various tests with different level of complexity is illustrated in Fig. 1.

This approach can be applied when: 1) the total number of questions and 2) their corresponding difficulty level score, available through databases in different subject areas, are known. In the presence of already prepared databases with questions, the user can choose the appropriate subject area for which it will be tested to establish and assess the level of acquired knowledge.

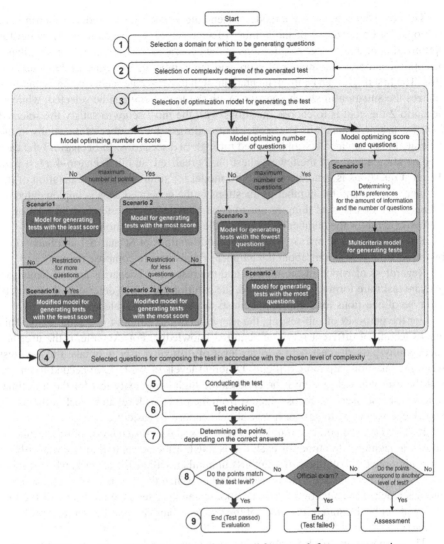

Fig. 1. Basic workflow algorithm of proposed framework for tests generation

The next step is to select the level of complexity of the generated test. Tests with different levels of complexity can be generated to match different grades. Several levels of complexity of the generated tests have been proposed in accordance with the rating scale, namely an average test (3), a good test (4), a very good grade test (5) and an excellent test (6). It should be noted that there are no obstacles to defining more levels of complexity of the generated tests, if necessary. The choice of the level of complexity of the test is not related to the condition that the user has successfully passed the lower test level, i.e. there is no limit to the sequence of when choosing a test, according to its complexity.

The next step is to choose a model to generate a test. 3 main models are proposed: 1) model for optimization of the number of score in the generated tests, 2) model for optimization of the number of questions in the generated tests, 3) model for simultaneous optimization of the number of score and the number of questions in the generated tests. The first model can be implemented through two separate scenarios. In Scenario-1 realizes the situation in which questions with the least score can be selected, while in Scenario-2 the goal is to choose questions with the most score to satisfy the selected level for testing/evaluation. The model that optimizes the number of questions in the generated tests can also be implemented through two scenarios. In Scenario-3 the case of generating a test with the fewest questions is realized, and in Scenario-4 a test with the most questions is generated. The third model for simultaneous optimization of the number of score and the number of questions in the generated tests is implemented by Scenario-5. The essential thing in it is to determine the user' preferences in relation to the two criteria for the number of score and the number of questions.

Scenario-1a and Scenario-2a represent modifications of Scenario-1 and Scenario-2 by introducing restrictions about the number of questions to compose the tests.

Regardless of which of the models and the respective scenarios are implemented, relevant tasks are formulated and solved, the solutions of which determine the quantity and type of questions for compiling the tests, according to the selected level.

For the purposes of self-testing, the user can choose different test complexity. This allows testing of different levels of acquired knowledge. For example, if the user has successfully passed a test with a lower level of difficulty, user may take the next test when the questions are more difficult. Different levels of the test are needed to ensure that the user will not give up if he chooses the high complexity test for the first time. In this case, the user can choose the test from the previous level and check if the user's knowledge is enough to pass or he/she should choose an easier test.

It should also be borne in mind that regardless of the chosen mode of self-testing or official assessment, the time for each test is fixed. This means that the time to solve a test with more difficult questions, but less in number, will be the same as when solving a test with easier questions, but more in number. When the user is in official test mode and has reached the situation where he chooses another test, the total time of the two tests will not be the sum of the times of the two tests but will have the set time provided for the test.

The proposed approach to generating tests is applicable in cases of using multiple choice, short answer, or true-false questions.

2.2 Mathematical Models for Generating Tests with Different Levels of Complexity

The needed input data for the realization of the different levels of complexity of tests are shown in Table 1.

The set of questions is denoted by $Q = \{q_1, q_2, ..., q_M\}$ and is composed of M number of questions with different difficulty levels. Each question is assigned a corresponding level of difficulty, and which occupies values in the interval $1 \leq d_i \leq N$, where the lowest level of difficulty of the questions is denoted by 1, and the value corresponding

Table 1. Questions, complexity of questions, levels of complexity of tests.

Total number of questions	Degree of questions' difficulty	Binary integer variables	Level of complexity of the test (L^k)		
			L^1 excellent	L^2 very good	L^3 good
q_1	d_1	x_1	$L^1_{min} < L^1$	$L^2_{min} < L^2$	$L^3_{min} < L^3$
q_2	d_2	x_2	$L^1 < L^1_{max}$	$L^2 < L^2_{max}$	$L^3 < L^3_{max}$
...	...	...			
q_i	d_i	x_i			
...	...	...			
q_M	d_M	x_M			

to the highest level of difficulty is expressed by N. It should be noted that there is no relationship between the total number of questions (Q) and the levels of difficulty.

The difficulty index (p) of the questions can be determined using the proposed formula [25]:

$$p = (U_p + L_p)/2n \tag{1}$$

where U_p and L_p are the number of learners who answered the question correctly in the upper and lower group, and n is the value of the total number of learners in the groups.

Three levels of difficulty are often used in the implementation of such tests, and the corresponding allowable intervals for these difficulties are as follows: easy ($1.00 - 0.65$), medium ($0.65 - 0.35$) and difficult ($0.35 - 0.0$) [26].

An essential feature in determining the questions that make up the respective test is that the sum of the score for the difficulty of the questions must be greater than the required value, corresponding to an excellent grade, i.e. $L^k < \sum d_M$. Each question is assigned control binary variables x_i, through which the choice of questions is realized, according to the required level of complexity of the test. In the general case, as many levels of complexity can be used, but to demonstrate the applicability of described approach, 3 types of levels of complexity are defined, namely: level for excellent assessment, level for very good, and level for good. For each level it is necessary to determine the permissible range of score obtained from the tests performed by setting the respective lower (L_{min}) and upper limits (L_{max}) for the total number of score. There are no restrictions on the levels of tests that can be generated, but for each level it is necessary to determine the relevant limits.

The proposed mathematical model, that realize Scenario-1 which optimizing the amount of information and determining the number of questions for tests with different levels of complexity is as follows:

$$max\left(L^k = \sum_{i=1}^{M} x_i d_i\right) \tag{2}$$

Subject to

$$\sum_i^M d_i = D \tag{3}$$

$$L_{max}^k < D \tag{4}$$

$$L^k \geq L_{min}^k \tag{5}$$

$$L^k \leq L_{max}^k \tag{6}$$

$$x_i \in \{0, 1\} \tag{7}$$

where L^k is the level of complexity of the selected test, x_i is the binary integer variables that can take a value of 0 or 1, d_i is the level of difficulty of the questions, and D is the total number of score for all questions, of which the test will be generated.

The use of binary integer variables x_i guarantees the single choice of questions in the generation of the specific test. The objective function (2) seeks to maximize the total score number of questions for the test taking into account the predetermined degree of difficulty for each of the questions. The total amount of possible score for the respective difficulties of all questions (D) is represented by the constraint (3). It should be noted that this total sum of the difficulty score of all questions (D) is not the upper limit (L_{max}^k) for the highest complexity of tests (test for excellent grade). Therefore, this upper limit L_{max}^k for the test with the selected level of difficulty must always be less than the total number of points for all questions.

Constraints (4) and (5) determine the lower and upper limit for the number of score that form the chosen level of complexity of the test for which the learner is tested. The constraint (7) was used to determine the questions for the specific test using the binary integer variables x_i.

The formulated model (2)–(7) can be modified by changing the direction of the objective function (2) and instead of looking for a maximum of the number of score for the generated test, we can look for its minimum (Scenario-2).

In order to implement Scenario-1a and Scenario-2a, it is necessary to add additional restrictions on the number of selected questions that make up the specific test. An upper limit on the number of questions in the generated tests can be added to the first formulated model (2)–(7). In this case (Scenario-1a), the model will use the objective function (2) subject to constraints (3)–(7) and an additional constraint:

$$\sum_{i=1}^{M} x_i \leq K_{max} \tag{8}$$

To realize Scenario-2a where objective function (2) is minimizing, the additional restriction is about the lower limit for the number of questions for the generated tests as follows:

$$\sum_{i=1}^{M} x_i \geq K_{min} \tag{9}$$

Constraints (8) and (9) provide flexibility by providing options for choosing a small number of questions, but with great difficulty and vice versa – choosing more questions and not so difficult.

To implement the Scenario-3, another mathematical model is used, which minimizes the number of questions that make up the respective test and has the following form:

$$min\left(K^k = \sum_{i=1}^{M} x_i \right) \tag{10}$$

Subject to

$$\sum_{i}^{M} x_i d_i \leq L^k \tag{11}$$

$$L^k \leq L^k_{max} \tag{12}$$

$$L^k \geq L^k_{min} \tag{13}$$

$$x_i \in \{0, 1\} \tag{14}$$

$$L^k_{max} < D \tag{15}$$

$$\sum_{i}^{M} d_i = D \tag{16}$$

It is also possible to introduce an additional restriction on this model regarding the minimum number of generated questions ($K > K^*$).

To implement Scenario-4, where as many test questions as possible are identified, the target function is changed to maximize (10) under the same constraints. In this realization, it is possible also to add additional restriction could be introduced regarding the admissible maximum number of questions that will constitute the generated test ($K < K^*$).

Scenario-5 requires using multicriteria optimization as two parameters need to be optimized simultaneously. The corresponding model that realizes this scenario is as follows:

$$\begin{cases} max\left(L^k = \sum_{i=1}^{M} x_i d_i \right) \\ min\left(K^k = \sum_{i=1}^{M} x_i \right) \end{cases} \tag{17}$$

Subject to

$$L^k \leq L^k_{max} \tag{18}$$

$$L^k \geq L^k_{min} \tag{19}$$

$$L^k_{max} < D \tag{20}$$

$$\sum_{i}^{M} d_i = D \tag{21}$$

$$x_i \in \{0, 1\} \tag{22}$$

The essence of this formulation is that the objective function simultaneously seeks to maximize the score (L^k) and minimize the number of questions (K^k) of the questions that will make up the test. The two criteria formulated are contradictory, as the first criterion for score will seek to rely on as many questions as possible, and the second will seek to minimize the total number of questions for the test. The limitations of this model are similar to the previous models and are related to the satisfaction of the required number of score for the respective level of complexity of the test.

In multicriteria optimization problems, several criteria are optimized simultaneously and in the general case, there is no single alternative to optimize all criteria. Unlike single-criteria optimization, the solution of a multi-criteria problem can be considered as a concept rather than a definition. In this type of optimization, there is usually no optimal solution and it is necessary to determine a set of ones that satisfy the user's preferences toward the optimality expressed as Pareto-optimality [27].

Among the variety of methods able to cope with such problems, the weighted sum approach is the easiest to understand. For simplicity, it is assumed that the used two criteria are of equal importance. The usage of the weighted sum approach requires transforming multiple objective functions (17) into single aggregated objective function as follows:

$$max\left(w_1 \left(\frac{L^{max} - L}{L^{max} - L^{min}} \right)_k + w_2 \left(\frac{K - K^{min}}{K^{max} - K^{min}} \right)_k \right) \tag{23}$$

An additional restriction is also added:

$$w_1 + w_2 = 1 \tag{24}$$

where w_1 and w_2 are weighted coefficients that express the importance of the criteria.

3 Numerical Application

All described models that express specific scenarios for generating different tests are numerically tested. The applicability of the proposed integrated model-driven framework is demonstrated by using a set-up test bank with 40 questions from computer science area. The corresponding difficulties of the questions are shown in Table 2.

A specific feature of the proposed approach to generating different tests is the fact that each time the questions from the specific domains are updated, it is necessary to check the total amount of points that form the difficulty of the individual questions. This is necessary to ensure that the set upper and lower limits of the respective test can be realized by the questions used and their difficulties. This is due to the core of the combinatorial nature of all models included in the proposed integrated models-driven framework.

Distinguish feature of all models is the requirement for setting up upper and lower limits for the different tests, according to their degree of difficulty. For the formation of the different tests it is necessary to achieve a certain number of score. Considering

Table 2. Set of question and their difficulty.

#	Question' difficulty	#	Question' difficulty	#	Question' difficulty	#	Question' difficulty
1	5	11	6	21	6	31	8
2	7	12	7	22	3	32	4
3	10	13	8	23	5	33	8
4	9	14	3	24	4	34	10
5	7	15	10	25	7	35	6
6	6	16	5	26	5	36	5
7	3	17	7	27	10	37	10
8	5	18	10	28	6	38	6
9	8	19	9	29	8	39	7
10	9	20	8	30	3	40	7

the given input data about the questions and their difficulties (see Table 2) the used admissible limits about three levels of complexity for generated e-tests are shown in Table 3.

Table 3. Upper and lower limits for the different tests.

Test for excellent		Test for very good		Test for good	
L_{max}^{E}	L_{min}^{E}	L_{max}^{VG}	L_{min}^{VG}	L_{max}^{G}	L_{min}^{G}
200	190	189	176	175	160

The number of selected questions for the different levels of complexity of generated e-tests using all the proposed single-criteria and multi-criteria optimization models is shown in Fig. 2.

From the obtained results it can be established that the number of questions constituting the generated tests when using the multi-criteria model differs from the number of questions determined by the single-criteria models. This proves that the use of multi-criteria optimization can be used as well to generate tests as single-criteria optimization, as it allows finding other combinations of questions that satisfy the corresponding level of complexity of the tests. For example, in a test for good, the number of questions when using the multi-criteria model is set at 28, in contrast to the results in single-criteria models – respectively 26, 24, 19, 24, 18 and 30 questions. In the tests for very good and good, the result is similar (see Fig. 2).

A similar comparison of the score for the generated tests using the formulated single-criterion and multi-criteria optimization models is shown in Fig. 3.

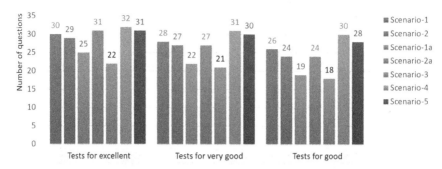

Fig. 2. Selected number of questions for the generated tests by using different models

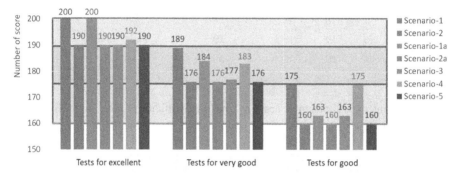

Fig. 3. Permissible point limits for the different levels of complexity of the tests and the results obtained using the proposed models

When using the model implementing Scenario-1, the results show that the generated tests at all three levels of complexity tend to reach the upper limit for the respective level. This is an expected result, as the objective function seeks to satisfy the maximum level of complexity. In the model implementing Scenario-2, the result for the value of the objective function is not unambiguous. For the model implementing Scenario-1a and the model implementing Scenario-2a they use additional limits for the number of questions included in the generated tests.

When using the model implementing Scenario-3, the aim is to determine the smallest possible number of questions satisfying the required number of points for the respective level, which is evident from the results of Fig. 2. In this model, the main idea is to choose issues that are more difficult. The model implementing Scenario-4 seeks to identify as many questions as possible that will have less difficulty, but will still be able to satisfy the required number of points for the respective level. In the model that implement Scenario-5, the objective function seeks to satisfy simultaneously both criteria expressed with equal importance. That means a compromise between number of questions and number of score is needed that should conform the required test complexity level.

For two of the formulated models (implementing Scenario-1a and Scenario-2a), using limitations for the number of questions, it may not be possible to find a solution if the set lower/upper limits for the questions cannot be satisfied. If such a situation arises, the relevant restriction needs to be changed. The use of other models allows only by changing the direction (min/max) and the expression for the objective function (number of score/number of questions) to generate the relevant tests.

From the obtained results in Fig. 3, it is easy to establish that the number of score for the generated tests when using the multicriteria model does not differ from the others. This is a confirmation that multicriteria optimization can be used just as well to generate tests, as the score of the defined combinations of questions satisfy the set levels of test complexity (Fig. 3).

A distinctive feature of the proposed approach is the ability to choose different mathematical models, leading to the determination of different combinations of questions that make up the generating tests. It should be noted that in self-test mode, when another test level or a new test of the same level is selected, it is possible to use appropriate flags for the already selected questions, so that the next generated test consists of questions other than the previous test. This would guarantee the uniqueness of the tests and crawl the entire range of content if the number of questions for the specific area is large enough.

All formulated models are of the type of mixed-integer linear programming. Determining whether a question will be part of the test or not is realized through the use of binary integer variables that uniquely define the question. From the conducted numerical testing, it can be established that tests with the same level of complexity can be realized by using a different number of questions. This is due to the fact that the questions in the database have different degrees of difficulty and it is possible to implement different combinations of questions that meet the set limits for the number of score for different levels of complexity of the tests.

The advantage of the proposed approach, respectively of the formulated mathematical models is the flexibility to generate tests of varying degrees of complexity using binary integer variables. Given the huge amount of diversity of electronic content in the disciplines in both schools and universities, the proposed approach can be applied to different curricula, where it is necessary to generate appropriate tests to verify the acquired knowledge.

4   Conclusions

E-testing is the most used tool not only in universities and schools but also as a tool for establishing the level of competence of employees from different areas. Taking into account the importance of e-tests, the main contribution of the current article is focused on a combination of different mathematical models integrated within a framework to generate a variety of e-tests. Several combinatorial models are formulated that compose the core for the realization of various scenarios to generate tests with different degrees of complexity. The advantage of these models is the possibility to modify the lower and upper limits for different levels of tests complexity.

The applicability of the proposed model-driven framework is illustrated by using a test bank with a predefined number of questions with corresponding difficulties. The used questions are from the area of computer science. The obtained results demonstrate the planned functionality of the framework in the generation of different e-tests.

There are no obstacles to including other models for generating e-tests as each of the used models is coded in a separate module. The usage of such an approach contributes to better digitalization in learning.

Acknowledgements. This work is supported by the Bulgarian National Science Fund by the project "*Mathematical models, methods and algorithms for solving hard optimization problems to achieve high security in communications and better economic sustainability*", KP-06-N52/7/19-11-2021.

References

1. Saeed, K.: Limits to growth concepts in classical economics. In: Cavana, R.Y., Dangerfield, B.C., Pavlov, O.V., Radzicki, M.J., Wheat, I.D. (eds.) Feedback Economics. CST, pp. 217–246. Springer, Cham (2021). https://doi.org/10.1007/978-3-030-67190-7_9
2. Petrova, P., Kostadinova, I., Alsulami, M.H.: Embedded intelligence in a system for automatic test generation for smoothly digital transformation in higher education. In: Sgurev, V., Jotsov, V., Kacprzyk, J. (eds.) Advances in Intelligent Systems Research and Innovation. SSDC, vol. 379, pp. 441–461. Springer, Cham (2022). https://doi.org/10.1007/978-3-030-78124-8_20
3. Kostadinova, I., Rasheva-Yordanova, K., Ivanov, I., Petrova, P.: Automated system for generating and validation a learning tests. In: ICERI2017 Proceedings, pp. 414–424 (2017). http://dx.doi.org/10.21125/iceri.2017.0160
4. Borissova, D., Mustakerov, I.: E-learning tool for visualization of shortest paths algorithms. Trends J. Sci. Res. **2**(3), 84–89 (2015)
5. Meng, W., Qu, R.: Automated design of search algorithms: learning on algorithmic components. Expert Syst. Appl. **185**, 115493 (2021). https://doi.org/10.1016/j.eswa.2021.115493
6. Mustakerov, I., Borissova, D.: A framework for development of e-learning system for computer programming: application in the C programming language. J. e-Learn. Knowl. Soc. **13**(2), 89–101 (2017). https://doi.org/10.20368/1971-8829/142
7. Yoshinov, R., Iliev, O.: How to learn computer science, using computer science. Int. J. Comput. **2**, 223–228 (2017)
8. Aldiab, A., Chowdhury, H., Kootsookos, A., Alam, F., Allhibi, H.: Utilization of learning management systems (LMSs) in higher education system: A case review for Saudi Arabia. Energy Proc. **160**, 731–737 (2019)
9. Hennig, S., Staatz, C., Bond, J.A., Leung, D., Singleton, J.: Quizzing for success: evaluation of the impact of feedback quizzes on the experiences and academic performance of undergraduate students in two clinical pharmacokinetics courses. Curr. Pharm. Teach. Learn. **11**, 742–749 (2019). https://doi.org/10.1016/j.cptl.2019.03.014
10. Marsh, E.J., Cantor, A.D.: Learning from the test: dos and don'ts for using multiple-choice tests. In: McDaniel, M., Frey, R., Fitzpatrick, S., Roediger, H.L. (eds.) Integrating Cognitive Science with Innovative Teaching in STEM Disciplines (2014). http://dx.doi.org/10.7936/K7Z60KZK
11. Tuparov, G., Keremedchiev, D., Tuparova, D., Stoyanova, M.: Gamification and educational computer games in open source learning management systems as a part of assessment. In: 17th International Conference Information Technology Based Higher Education and Training (ITHET), pp. 1–5 (2018). https://doi.org/10.1109/ITHET.2018.8424768
12. Borissova, D., Keremedchiev, D., Tuparov, G.: Multi-criteria model for questions selection in generating e-education tests involving gamification. TEM J. – Technol. Educ. Manag. Inform. **9**(2), 779–785 (2020). https://doi.org/10.18421/TEM92-47

13. Kostadinova, I., Rasheva-Yordanova, K., Garvanova, M.: Analysis of algorithms for generating test questions in e-testing systems. In: 11th International Conference on Education and New Learning Technologies, EDULEARN 2019, pp. 1714–1719 (2019). http://dx.doi.org/10.21125/edulearn.2019.0498

14. Borissova, D.: A group decision making model considering experts competency: an application in personnel selections. Compt. Rendus l'Acad. Bulgare Sci. **71**(11), 1520–1527 (2018)

15. Yoshinov, R., Chehlarova, T., Kotseva, M.: The e-facilitator as a key player for interactive dissemination of STEAM resources for e-learning via webinar. In: Auer, M.E., Tsiatsos, T. (eds.) IMCL 2019. AISC, vol. 1192, pp. 675–686. Springer, Cham (2021). https://doi.org/10.1007/978-3-030-49932-7_63

16. Andreev, R., Borissova, D., Shikalanov, A., Yorgova, T.: Model-driven design of eMedia: virtual technology transfer office. In: Lugmayr, A., Stojmenova, E., Stanoevska, K., Wellington, R. (eds.) Information Systems and Management in Media and Entertainment Industries. ISCEMT, pp. 279–298. Springer, Cham (2016). https://doi.org/10.1007/978-3-319-49407-4_14

17. Khider, H., Hammoudi, S., Meziane, A.: Business process model recommendation as a transformation process in MDE: conceptualization and first experiments. In: 8th International Conference on Model-Driven Engineering and Software Development – MODELSWARD, pp. 65–75 (2020). http://dx.doi.org/10.5220/0009155600650075

18. Shamsujjoha, M., Grundy, J., Li, L., Khalajzadeh, H., Lu, Q.: Developing mobile applications via model driven development: a systematic literature review. Inf. Softw. Technol. **140**, 106693 (2021). https://doi.org/10.1016/j.infsof.2021.106693

19. Moradi, H., Zamani, B., Zamanifar, K.: CaaSSET: a framework for model-driven development of context as a service. Futur. Gener. Comput. Syst. **105**, 61–95 (2020). https://doi.org/10.1016/j.future.2019.11.028

20. Santos, F., Nunes, I., Bazzan, A.L.C.: Quantitatively assessing the benefits of model-driven development in agent-based modeling and simulation. Simul. Model. Pract. Theory **104**, 102126 (2020). https://doi.org/10.1016/j.simpat.2020.102126

21. Badreddin, O., Lethbridge, T.C.: Combining experiments and grounded theory to evaluate a research prototype: lessons from the umple model-oriented programming technology. In: First International Workshop on User Evaluation for Software Engineering Researchers (USER), pp. 1–4 (2012). https://doi.org/10.1109/USER.2012.6226575

22. Lethbridge, T.C., et al.: Umple: model-driven development for open source and education. Sci. Comput. Program. **208**, 102665 (2021). https://doi.org/10.1016/j.scico.2021.102665

23. Orabi, M., Orabi, A., Lethbridge, T.: Umple as a template language (Umple-TL). In: Proceedings of 7th International Conference on Model-Driven Engineering and Software Development – MODELSWARD, pp. 98–106 (2019). http://dx.doi.org/10.5220/0007382000980106

24. Joy, J., Pillai, R.V.G.: Review and classification of content recommenders in E-learning environment. J. King Saud Uni. – Comput. Inf. Sci. (2021). https://doi.org/10.1016/j.jksuci.2021.06.009

25. Bachman, L.F.: Statistical Analyses for Language Assessment. Cambridge University Press, Cambridge (2004)

26. Tasci, T., Parlak, Z., Kibar, A., Tasbasi, N., Cebeci, H.I.: A novel agent-supported academic online examination system. Educ. Technol. Soc. **17**(1), 154–168 (2014)

27. Marler, R.T., Arora, J.S.: Survey of multi-objective optimization methods for engineering. Struct. Multidiscip. Optim. **26**, 369–395 (2004)

Application of Graph Document Model for Classification of Agricultural Scientific Papers in Polish

Waldemar Karwowski[✉] ⓘ and Piotr Wrzeciono ⓘ

Institute of Information Technology, Warsaw University of Life Sciences, Nowoursynowska 166, 02-787 Warsaw, Poland
{waldemar_karwowski,piotr_wrzeciono}@sggw.edu.pl

Abstract. In the paper, the problem of classification of texts in the Polish language based on graph document model is discussed. A set of agricultural scientific texts in the Polish language are normalized and converted into directed graphs with words as vertices. Paths in the graph are assigned weights depending on how often words appear next to each other. The phrases with the highest weight are selected to represent the particular text in every graph. Only phrases with nouns, a verb, or an adjective were selected to use semantics connected with the relationship between different parts of speech. Methods for determining the similarity of phrases and documents were discussed and appropriate formulas were defined. For the representation of a document as a set of phrases, similarity between texts are calculated. The documents have been used to create an undirected graph whose edge weights equal the similarity values. On this basis, the documents are classified with the Chinese Whispers clustering algorithm. A series of experiments were performed for different versions of document similarity and different versions of the algorithm. In the final part it was concluded that increasing the length of phrases does not improve the results, but taking into account the grammatical category of words has a positive effect. Moreover, for clustering, the number of selected edges is more important than changes in the formulas for calculating weights.

Keywords: Knowledge management · Graph databases · Classification and clustering · Text analysis

1 Introduction

Currently, the Internet provides us with a huge number of websites and gives access to multiple documents in electronic form. Despite applications like Google search, a reader cannot select and review all interesting content. For example, reviewing all the opinions related to the specific issue is sometimes impossible on social media pages. We often need a brief description of the document; many documents, for example, scientific publications, have titles, summaries, and keywords (tags), but they do not always reflect the searched content. Natural language processing (NLP) algorithms are a helpful tool for extracting keywords or text summarization in such situations. A typical example is

© The Author(s), under exclusive license to Springer Nature Switzerland AG 2022
K. Saeed and J. Dvorský (Eds.): CISIM 2022, LNCS 13293, pp. 330–344, 2022.
https://doi.org/10.1007/978-3-031-10539-5_24

the analysis of a group of texts; to discover dependencies between them; we define the distance between two texts for comparing their similarity. Algorithms for such tasks are based on different text data representations. Common document representation is based on vectors. In this model, each term in a document becomes a dimension. Since the number of dimensions in such a representation is huge, many methods have been developed to reduce the number of dimensions by selecting the most important features. Many machine learning algorithms uses such a reduction. They are nowadays common tools used for text analysis, but they require a lot of documents to train the model.The graph model is one of the other possibilities. Graph models for text allow performing NLP tasks for even single text, where other methods may not be used [1].

A graph is a data structure representing a set of related objects. The objects that make up a graph are called vertices, and the links between them are known as edges [2, 3]. The graph model is connected with networks in the real world. Web pages create a huge network connected by hyperlinks, and it can be described as a graph. The most famous example of using a graph model is the PageRank algorithm used by Google Search to rank web pages in their search engine results [4]. However, this algorithm does not analyze the page content but only hyperlinks. The best known graph-based ranking model for text documents is TextRank [5]. It exploits the structure of the text itself for extraction of keywords or sentences, which appear "important" to the text, similar to how PageRank selects important Web pages.

Our goal is to analyze and classify agricultural scientific papers written in the Polish language. First we want to extract the most "important" phrases from the text document. This task goes somewhat beyond the closely related tasks of keywords extraction or text summarization. In this paper, our approach is based on text graph representation presented in [6, 7]. Then for texts represented by the extracted most "important" phrases, we calculate distances between texts, and build an undirected graph, the vertices of which are texts and edge weights are distances. On this basis, we classify documents with a clustering algorithm. Our method is an extension of the method presented in [8]. The method for documents in the Polish language was based on a so-called artificial sentence, which was built from the most frequent noun, the most frequent verb, and the second most frequent noun. This method was utilized for text classification in the form of a non-directed graph with analyzed papers as vertices and distances between them as weighted edges [9]. In this paper, our method is similar, but we replace one short sentence with a set of phrases.

In the next sections of this paper, the graph model for analyzed text and processing method are presented, then experimental results are described. In the final section the conclusions are formulated.

2   Graph Document Model and Sentence Distance

The basis of our application is a graph document model. Some basic rules of graph-based ranking applications to natural language texts are formulated in [5]. The application should consist of the following main steps:

1. Identify text units that best define the task at hand, and add them as vertices in the graph.

2. Identify relations that connect such text units and use these relations to draw edges between vertices in the graph. Edges can be directed or undirected, weighted or unweighted.
3. Iterate the graph-based ranking algorithm until convergence.
4. Sort vertices based on their final score. Use the values attached to each vertex for ranking/selection decisions.

These rules are quite general; text units can be whole text, sentence, word, or any other part of the text. For example in [5], for keyword extraction task, lexical units (words) extracted from text were used as vertices, and co-occurrence relation was used for edges. Experiments were performed with various syntactic filters, and the best performance was achieved with the filter that selects nouns and adjectives only. The second example was sentence extraction for automatic summarization. This time text units were entire sentences, and as a connection between two sentences, a "similarity" relation between them was taken, where "similarity" was measured as a function of their content overlap. Such a relation between two sentences can be seen as a process of "recommendation": a sentence that addresses certain concepts in a text gives the reader a "recommendation" to refer to other sentences in the text that address the same concepts [5, 10]. New alternatives to the similarity function for the TextRank algorithm for automated summarization of texts are discussed in [11]. The authors generalized the algorithm from [5] and proposed different similarity functions. Some of these variants achieved a significant improvement using the same dataset [5]. Other modifications of TextRank are presented in [12, 13]. Methods presented in [14] used adjacency of terms as edges. On this base, six algorithms were described and discussed: standard, simple, n-distance, n-simple distance, absolute frequency, and relative frequency. More extensive discussion about a graph-based model for extracting information-rich sentences from the original texts is performed in [15].

Distance between documents, sentences, or words is as significant as the graph document model and is needed to determine their similarity in the classification process. Generally, the similarity of the texts should be proportional to the standard part of the texts concerning the size of texts. However, this concept must be formalized. Sentence similarity can be measured at different levels of granularity: word-level, phrase-level, analogously for whole documents with additional sentence level. Word distance can be defined as string distance. The most well-known measure of this type is Hamming distance, i.e., the number of positions the corresponding symbols are different [16]. Another known measure is Levenshtein distance [17], roughly speaking the minimum number of single-character insertions, deletions, or substitutions required to change one word to the other. However, in many cases, it is not enough; similarity at the semantic level is also essential. In [18] exhaustive introduction to the tasks of computing word and sense similarity was presented. We are interested in whether the subject matter of sentences is similar. It is clear that the similarity of sentences or whole texts is most often based on the similarity of the words. Lin [19] has discussed the basic intuitions and assumptions about similarity from the information theory point of view, and he formulated the Similarity Theorem in the general form:

$$sim(A; B) = \frac{log\, P(common(A; B))}{log\, P(description(A; B))}$$

The similarity between A and B is measured by the ratio between the amount of information needed to state the commonality of A and B and the information needed to fully describe A and B. The theorem, in general, shows how the similarity between the texts can be defined. The simple similarity measure consistent with the mentioned formula is based on the Jaccard index. We take into account only the occurrence of a term in the texts and ignore how often it occurs. The similarity is expressed in the form:

$$sim(A; B) = \frac{|A \cap B|}{|A \cup B|}$$

In other words, in the Jaccard index, documents are represented as vectors where each dimension corresponds to a separate term and 0 means that term is not present, and 1 otherwise. In the Vector Space Model [17, 20], documents are represented as vectors $(a_1, ..., a_n)$ and $(b_1, ..., b_n)$ of features, typically terms that occur in both documents. The value of each feature is called the feature weight and is usually the term's frequency in the document. The other common and popular weight is the Term Frequency–Inverse Document Frequency (TF-IDF) weighting scheme (the frequency of the terms appearing in the document TF and the importance of those terms through the entire set of documents IDF). As the similarity between documents, cosine similarity between representing vectors is standardly used in the vector representation:

$$sim(A; B) = \frac{\sum_{i=1}^{n} (a_i * b_i)}{\sqrt{\sum_{i=1}^{n} (a_i)^2 * \sum_{i=1}^{n} (b_i)^2}}$$

We have to note that the Euclidean distance is not helpful in this situation.

The Jaccard index and cosine measure are useful, but information from the syntax and semantics of the sentence is lost. Sentences similarity can be based on syntactic and semantic information of the sentences. A frequently used way of maintaining relationships between words is the n-gram model, in which groups of adjacent words are taken as units instead of individual words. The semantic similarity of words can be measured using ontology e.g. WordNet. In [21] authors proposed an algorithm that takes advantage of grammatical rules and corpus-based ontology. In [22] is presented approach connected with the fact that certain parts of speech and certain relationships between different parts of speech are semantically more important than others, weights of different POS and weights of POS relation have been proposed. The method allows comparing texts, but the semantic similarity must be based on a large text corpus.

3   Graph Model for Text and Processing Method

We model text data as a directed graph where each word is a vertex, and an edge between two vertices indicates that the words appear next to each other in the sentence. Words are the smallest language units having semantic value. They form phrases and sentences and have a grammatical category. This graph model makes it possible to achieve our goal of extracting phrases. We have only one type of vertices: word, and one type of relation: next. Every vertex has a name; it is exactly word and property - the number of times word appears in the document. Every relation connects two words w1 and w2, and has a property – weight; a number of times, the word w2 appears exactly after the word w1 in some sentence for all sentences in the document. We can illustrate our model on the following text in Polish; *"Ala ma kota. Jan ma psa. Ala ma rower. Ala lubi psa. Jan ma bardzo dobre oceny."* ("Ala has cat. Jan has dog. Ala has bicycle. Ala likes dog. Jan has very good scores."). Our graph model is presented in Fig. 1.

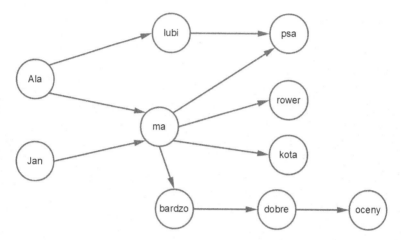

Fig. 1. Graph model for sample document in Polish.

The words in the sample document were not changed into base form, but here the goal is only an illustration of the model. All edges (with start and end vertices) can be presented in the text form:

```
[{"Ala", "number":3}, {"weight":2}, {"ma", "number":4}]
[{"Jan", "number":2}, {"weight":2}, {"ma", "number":4}]
[{"ma", "number":4}, {"weight":1}, {"kota", "number":1}]
[{"ma", "number":4}, {"weight":1}, {"psa", "number":2}]
[{"lubi", "number":1}, {"weight":1}, {"psa", "number":2}]
[{"ma", "number":4}, {"weight":1}, {"rower", "number":1}]
[{"Ala", "number":3}, {"weight":1}, {"lubi", "number":2}]
[{"ma", "number":4}, {"weight":1}, {"bardzo", "number":1}]
[{"bardzo", "number":1}, {"weight":1}, {"dobre", "number":1}]
[{"dobre", "number":1}, {"weight":1}, {"oceny", "number":1}]
```

This model is very similar to the model presented in [6, 7]. The basic idea implemented by this model is that we analyze paths in such a graph. We can see that paths in our sample directed graph represent phrases. For example, we have three-word phrases: *"Jan"* → *"ma"* → *"psa"* or *"Jan"* → *"ma"* → *"kota"*. We have to note that phrases obtained from the model may not appear in the original text i.e., *"Jan"* → *"ma"* → *"kota"* ("Jan" → "has" → "cat").

Paths can consist of many edges. To evaluate the importance of the phrase, we take the average weight of its edges:

$$w(p) = \sum_{i=1}^{n} \frac{w_i}{n} \tag{1}$$

In this formula w(p) denotes the total score for path p, which consists of n edges, w_i is the weight of edge i. Where w(p) denotes the total score for path p, which consists of n edges, wi is the weight of edge i. Formula (1) is very similar to presented in [7]. On this basis, main phrases, i.e., with the highest weights, are extracted, and the document is represented only by the most important phrases. This method is unsupervised and can be applied to individual texts.

It is easy to see that the method for more advanced sentences may not be so simple. Sentences contain many frequent words without special meaning. For example, in English, there are auxiliary words like prepositions, pronouns, interjections, and conjunctions. In the processing of natural language data, such words are called stopwords and are generally removed before the analysis. The situation is similar in the Polish language. Moreover in Polish the verbs, the nouns, and the adjectives all have inflection. The number of possible forms is enormous. For example, the verbs have about one hundred inflection forms, including the past and passive participle, with their grammar rules. This means that the text before we build the graph must be preprocessed. Preprocessing contains four steps. The first is text cleaning, which includes the elimination of punctuation marks and the changing of all capital letters into lower case. The second is stop-word removal which decreases the total number of different words in the text. As a result, the relations between semantically important words become more emphasized. Next, during the third step, we have to overcome the issues associated with inflection. Because we cannot use algorithms specific for the English language, for this task, the custom algorithm is applied described in [8]. It is based on the dictionary of Polish [23]; that freely available dictionary consists of words with inflection forms. After this step, all words are reduced to their base form. The last step is part of speech tagging; it is also performed with the algorithm described in [8]. As a result of the preprocessing, we obtained a set of sentences with words in the base form marked by part of speech for particular text. For preprocessed text, we can prepare a graph model as a set of edges in the text form:

```
[{"lubić",    "number":1,    "VERB"},    {"weight":1},    {"pies",
"number":2, "NOUN"}]
```

For such document representation, distances between texts are calculated. The process was the following. For every document, we selected the n-words phrases, i.e., paths connected from n-1 edges, with the highest weight. However, only phrases with a fixed number of nouns, verbs and adjectives were included. Thanks to this fact, our method uses not only the word statistics but also the syntactic and semantic features of the text. During experiments, we extended the weight given in formula (1) by adding weights of vertices, i.e., frequency of words. Formula modified from formula (1) has the form:

$$w(p) = \sum_{i=1}^{n} \frac{w_i}{n} + \alpha \sum_{i=0}^{n} \frac{v_i}{n} \tag{2}$$

In formula (2), w_i is the weight of edge i and v_i is the weight of vertex i, n is the number of vertices, and α is from $<0; 1>$. Of course for α equals zero it is identical to the formula (1).

For documents represented by sets of phrases, we defined similarity between two documents. Two similarity functions based on the similarity of phrases were tested. The document similarity functions should be normalized so that they have values from the interval $<0; 1>$.

First, for two n-word phrases $p = (p_1, p_2,..., p_n)$ and $q = (q_1, q_2,..., q_n)$ we define similarity between them

$$simH(p, q) = \frac{1}{n * n} \sum_{i=1}^{n} \sum_{j=1}^{n} \delta(p_i, q_j)$$

where $\delta(p_i, q_j) = 1$ if and only if $p_i = q_j$ and $\delta(p_i, q_j) = 0$ for $p_i \neq q_j$. This similarity measure is connected with modified Hamming distance

$$distH(p, q) = 1 - simH(p, q)$$

In our approach each text is represented by a fixed number of k highest-weighted phrases. On this base we define similarity between two texts in the following way

$$SimH(t, s) = \frac{1}{k * k} \sum_{i=1}^{k} \sum_{j=1}^{k} simH(t_i, s_j) \tag{3}$$

where text t is represented by k phrases $(t_1, t_2, ..., t_k)$, and text s is represented by k phrases $(s_1, s_2, ..., s_k)$.

Next, we defined modified similarity between two n-word phrases using weights of phrases

$$sim(p, q) = \frac{1}{n * n} \sum_{i=1}^{n} \sum_{j=1}^{n} \delta(p_i, q_j) * w_p * w_q$$

where w_p and w_q are weights of phrase p and q relatively. Modified similarity between two texts with weights is given by formula

$$Sim(t, s) = \frac{1}{\sum_{i=1}^{k} \sum_{j=1}^{k} w_{t_i} * w_{s_j}} \sum_{i=1}^{k} \sum_{j=1}^{k} sim(t_i, s_j) \tag{4}$$

After then, we count distances between every pair of documents. A graph in which documents are vertices, and distances are the weights of edges was created. On this basis, the documents can be classified with a clustering algorithm. We decided to use the Chinese Whispers algorithm [24]. Chinese Whispers is an efficient graph clustering algorithm to identify communities of vertices. We utilized the implementation of this algorithm from DLib library. This implementation has two versions of input data; the first version simply uses only edges without weights (i.e., we only set if an edge exists or not), the second version uses edges with weights.

4 Experimental Results

To test the presented method small set of agriculture scientific papers in Polish was chosen. The selected publications in Polish were taken from Agricultural Engineering Journal (Inżynieria Rolnicza - IR). The first group, related to the cultivation and processing of maize, consisted of seven papers (A-G). The second group was taken from the same journal, and there are twelve papers (H-S) generally connected with potatoes. These publications were analysed and used in [8] and [9] as test set.

A. "Assessment of the operation quality of the corn cobs and seeds processing line" [25]
B. "Methodological aspects of measuring hardness of maize caryopsis" [26]
C. "Evaluation of results of irrigation applied to grain maze" [27]
D. "Extra corn grain shredding and particle breaking up as a method used to improve quality of cut green forage" [28]
E. "Comparative assessment of sugar corn grain acquisition for food purposes using cut off and threshing methods" [29]
F. "Information system for acquiring data on geometry of agricultural products exemplified by a corn kernel" [30]
G. "A decision support system in maize silage production" [31]
H. "Application of Computer Image Processing to Determine the Physical Properties to Potato Tubers" [32]
I. "New Technology of the Potatoes Production – the bed tillage" [33]
J. "The impact of microwave irradiation on growth dynamics of potato tuber germs" [34]
K. "Evaluation of physical properties of potato bulbs" [35]
L. "The impact of potato plantation irrigation on selected physical attributes of tubers which are significant in crop separation and sorting process" [36]
M. "Evaluation of yield, chemical composition and quality of tubers of medium early, medium late and late starch potato cultivars" [37]
N. "The impact of selected agrotechnical factors on the quantitative characteristics of potato tuber crop" [38]
O. "Using the canvassing of the image to assessing losses in the nursery of the potato" [39]
P. "Relations between tuber density growth and selected potato properties during storage" [40]
Q. "Assessment technique and statistic modelling of the degree of potato damage caused by Colorado beetle" [41]
R. "Design parameters of a roller-type potato cleaning separator" [42]
S. "Potato as a cultivated plant - fragments of history" [43].

We selected a set of phrases with the highest scores from every text. After a series of experiments, we limited the size of phrases to three-word phrases. We have observed that cycles are formed on the basis of the edges with the highest weights. In the case of phrases longer than three words, phrases with circulation dominate, and do not contribute more information about the text. Moreover, we filtered phrases only with at least two nouns, and verb or adjective. This choice was made to ensure similarity with artificial sentence analyzed in [8]. For example, int text A, three-word best score phrase with formula (2) for $\alpha = 0$ (i.e., formula (1)) is: *ocena* (NOUN) *jakość* (NOUN) *praca* (NOUN), with score 7. For $\alpha = 1$, it is: *ziarno* (NOUN) *kukurydza* (NOUN) *ziarno* (NOUN) with score 61,5. Analogously for text D we have for $\alpha = 0$ *wskaźnik* (NOUN) *rozdrobnić* (VERB) *ziarno* (NOUN) with score 17,5, and for $\alpha = 1$ *rozdrobnić* (VERB) *ziarno* (NOUN) *kukurydza* (NOUN) with score 47. For text R we have for $\alpha = 0$ *nacisk* (NOUN) *spiralny* (ADJECTIVE) *występ* (NOUN) with score 3.5, and for $\alpha = 1$ *bulwa* (NOUN) *ziemniak* (NOUN) *walec* (NOUN) with score 203. There is clearly a predominance of nouns. Even in phrases of three words, there are phrases with noun circulation, the same noun occurs twice. As a result of this step, we received sets of three-word phrases with the highest weights for each document.

Another problem arose when testing clustering. We have prepared graphs based on specific document representation formulas for a different number of hight weighted phrases. Because similarities are normalized, all edge weights are not more than one. Similarity equals 0 means that there is no edge between documents. In such a situation we noticed that the algorithm implementation version with weighted edges does not cluster any documents. It is because the differences between weights are not very large. It caused us to use algorithm version without edge weights. We filter edge weights on a few levels to follow the clustering process. For example, for level 0.5, all edges with weights less than 0.5 were removed, but edges with weights equal to or greater than 0.5 were treated equally.

Table 1 shows the clusters for similarity defined in formula (3) and modified similarity defined in formula (4) for Dlib implementation of the Chinese Whispers algorithm version with unweighted edges, suitably for multiple filter levels. It means that we filter only edges with a weight greater equal level. As document representation, the 15 highest-weighted phrases were chosen according to formula (2) with $\alpha = 0$. Of course, for level 1 all vertices are isolated except situations when document representations are identical. For our sample papers there are 19 clusters. For level 0, all documents would be connected into one cluster, except when the similarity is zero with any other document. It is easy to observe that clusters are almost identical. Sequentially for descending levels, several clusters are combined into the bigger one.

To compare the clustering process, we set the value $\alpha = 0.2$ in the formula (2) and performed a set of analogous tests for selected the best 15 phrases. Table 2 is analogous to Table 1, and shows the clusters for similarity according to formula (3) and formula (4) for the version of Dlib implementation of the Chinese Whispers algorithm with unweighted edges, suitably for multiple filter levels.

This time results are identical for both similarity formulas. As for Table 1 at each subsequent level, several clusters are combined into one. We have to note that results for formula (2) with $\alpha = 0.2$ are more interesting. Strengthening the phrase weights by adding vertex weights accelerated the clustering process. Papers about maze and potato have been separated. Since word weights have been added, and therefore primarily noun weights, the more frequent occurrence of the noun has a more significant impact on the similarity of the texts.

Table 1. Cluster comparison for the formula (2) and (3) for unweighted edges with a = 0.0.

Level	Number of clusters	Similarity based on Hamming formula (3) - phrases for $\alpha = 0$	Similarity with edge weights formula (4) - phrases for $\alpha = 0$
0.9	18	{A} {B} {C} {D} {E} {F} {G} {H} {I} {J} {K} {L} {M} {N} {O, Q} {P} {R} {S}	{A} {B} {C} {D} {E} {F} {G} {H} {I} {J} {K} {L} {M} {N} {O, Q} {P} {R} {S}
0.6	16	{A} {B} {C, E} {D} {F} {G} {H} {I} {J} {K, L} {M} {N} {O, Q} {P} {R} {S}	{A} {B} {C, E} {D} {F} {G} {H} {I} {J} {K, L} {M} {N} {O, Q} {P} {R} {S}
0.3	11	{A} {B} {C, D, E} {F} {G} {H, K, L, N, O, Q, S} {I} {J} {M} {P} {R}	{A} {B} {C, D, E} {F} {G} {H, K, L, N, O, Q, S} {I} {J} {M} {P} {R}
0.2	7/8	{A} {B} {C, D, E, G} {F} {H, I, J, K, L, N, O, Q, R, S} {M} {P}	{A} {B} {C, D, E} {F} {G} {H, I, J, K, L, M, N, O, Q, S} {P} {R}
0.1	4	{A} {B} {C, D, E, G} {F, H, I, J, K, L, M, N, O, P, Q, R, S}	{A} {B} {C, D, E, G} {F, H, I, J, K, L, M, N, O, P, Q, R, S}

Table 2. Cluster comparison for the formula (2) and (3) for unweighted edges with a = 0.2.

Level	Number of clusters	Similarity based on Hamming formula (3) - phrases for $\alpha = 0.2$	Similarity with edge weights formula (4) - phrases for $\alpha = 0.2$
0.9	18	{A} {B} {C} {D} {E} {F} {G} {H} {I} {J} {K} {L} {M} {N} {O, Q} {P} {R} {S}	{A} {B} {C} {D} {E} {F} {G} {H} {I} {J} {K} {L} {M} {N} {O, Q} {P} {R} {S}
0.6	10	{A, C, D, E} {B} {F} {G} {H, K, L, M, R} {I} {J} {N} {O, Q, S} {P}	{A, C, D, E} {B} {F} {G} {H, K, L, M, R} {I} {J} {N} {O, Q, S} {P}
0.3	7	{A, C, D, E, G} {B} {F} {H, K, L, M, N, R} {I, O, Q, S} {J} {P}	{A, C, D, E, G} {B} {F} {H, K, L, M, N, R} {I, O, Q, S} {J} {P}
0.2	4	{A, C, D, E, G} {B} {F} {H, I, J, K, L, M, N, O, P, Q, R, S}	{A, C, D, E, G} {B} {F} {H, I, J, K, L, M, N, O, P, Q, R, S}
0.1	4	{A, C, D, E, G} {B} {F} {H, I, J, K, L, M, N, O, P, Q, R, S}	{A, C, D, E, G} {B} {F} {H, I, J, K, L, M, N, O, P, Q, R, S}

Because the Chinese Whispers algorithm for weighted edges does not cluster any documents if similarity is normalized, we tested similarity without normalization.

$$SimH^*(t, s) = \sum_{i=1}^{k} \sum_{j=1}^{k} simH(t_i, s_j) \qquad (5)$$

$$Sim^*(t, s) = \sum\nolimits_{i=1}^{k} \sum\nolimits_{j=1}^{k} sim(t_i, s_j) \qquad (6)$$

Since the values were not normalized, their range has been selected to illustrate trends in clustering. For our set of sample papers, the maximum value of formula (5) between two different documents is 466, for formula (6) it is 103257.67. Of course, in this situation, the results for two similarity formulas are non-comparable. In this situation, we decided to compare each algorithm version for a fixed similarity formula. We set the value $\alpha = 0.2$ in the formula (2) in both cases. Table 3 shows the result clusters according to the formula (6) for multiple levels. Because the values of the edge weights in this case are very large we set filter levels in a big range. In graph we removed all edges with weights less than level. In Chinese Whispers clustering algorithm for unweighted graph all other edges were treated equally, in the second version edges were with weights.

Table 3. Results for weighted and unweighted edges without normalization for the formula (6).

Level	Number of clusters	Similarity with formula (6) -algorithm without edge weights	Similarity with formula (6) - algorithm with edge weights
60000	13/15	{A} {B} {C, E} {D} {F} {G} {H} {I, Q, S} {J} {K, L, M, N} {O} {P} {R}	{A, C, E} {B} {D} {F} {G} {H, K, L} {I} {J} {M} {N} {O} {P} {Q} {R} {S}
50000	10/14	{A, C, D, E} {B} {F} {G} {H, K, L, M, N} {I, Q, S} {J} {O} {P} {R}	{A, C, E} {B} {D} {F} {G} {H, K, L, M} {I} {J} {N} {O} {P} {Q} {R} {S}
40000	9/11	{A, C, D, E} {B} {F} {G} {H, K, L, M, N} {I, O, Q, S} {J} {P} {R}	{A, C, D, E} {B} {F} {G} {H, K, L, M, N} {I} {J} {O, Q} {P} {R} {S}
30000	9/10	{A, C, D, E} {B} {F} {G} {H, K, L, M, N} {I, O, Q, S} {J} {P} {R}	{A, C, D, E} {B} {F} {G} {H, K, L, M, N} {I} {J} {O, Q, S} {P} {R}
20000	8/10	{A, C, D, E} {B} {F} {G} {H, K, L, M, N, P} {I, O, Q, S} {J} {R}	{A, C, D, E} {B} {F} {G} {H, K, L, M, N} {I} {J} {O, Q, S} {P} {R}
10000	4/8	{A, C, D, E, G} {B} {F} {H, I, J, K, L, M, N, O, P, Q, R, S}	{A, C, D, E} {B} {F} {G} {H, J, K, L, M, N, R} {I} {O, Q, S} {P}
0	1/7	{A, B, C, D, E, F, G, H, I, J, K, L, M, N, O, P, Q, R, S}	{A, C, D, E, G} {B} {F} {H, J, K, L, M, N, R} {I} {O, Q, S} {P}

Clustering for modified similarity with the Chinese Whispers algorithm with edge weights has limit of 7 clusters. The reason is that the values of similarity vary greatly. However, the second algorithm may determine a smaller number of clusters. As before at each subsequent level, several clusters are combined into one. Generally, taking into account, the analysis of the texts, papers about maze and potato have been separated except when we take into account all edges.

Analogously Table 4 shows the clusters for the formula (5) for two versions of Dlib implementation of the Chinese Whispers algorithm. This time, the range of levels has also been adjusted to the achieved similarity values.

Table 4. Results for weighted and unweighted edges without normalization for the formula (5).

Level	Number of clusters	Similarity with formula (5) - algorithm without edge weights	Similarity with formula (5) - algorithm with edge weights
400	18/18	{A} {B} {C} {D} {E} {F} {G} {H} {I} {J} {K} {L} {M} {N} {O} {P} {Q, S} {R}	{A} {B} {C} {D} {E} {F} {G} {H} {I} {J} {K} {L} {M} {N} {O} {P} {Q, S} {R}}
300	14/17	{A, C, E} {B} {D} {F} {G} {H} {I} {J} {K, L} {M} {N} {O, Q, S} {P} {R}	{A} {B} {C} {D} {E} {F} {G} {H} {I} {J} {K} {L} {M} {N} {O, Q, S} {P} {R}
200	8/17	{A, C, D, E} {B} {F} {G} {H, I, K, L, M, N, R, S} {J} {O, Q} {P}	{A} {B} {C} {D} {E} {F} {G} {H} {I} {J} {K} {L} {M} {N} {O, Q, S} {P} {R}
100	7/10	{A, C, D, E, G} {B} {F} {H, K, L, M, N, R} {I, O, Q, S} {J} {P}	{A} {B} {C} {D} {E} {F} {G} {H, I, K, L, M, N, O, Q, R, S} {J} {P}
0	1/8	{A, B, C, D, E, F, G, H, I, J, K, L, M, N, O, P, Q, R, S}	{A} {B} {C} {D} {E} {F} {G} {H, I, J, K, L, M, N, O, P, Q, R, S}

We can conclude that clustering for similarity according to the formula (5) with Chinese Whispers algorithm with edge weights has limit of 8 clusters. The other remarks are analogous to Table 3.

5   Conclusion and Future Work

Graph document model in which the words are vertices, and an edge between two vertices indicates that the words appear next to each other in the sentence proved to be useful for phrase generation. A collection of phrases (paths from this graph) is an interesting representation of the text document. Preliminary experiments have shown that increasing the length of phrases does not improve the results in the clustering process, and phrases composed of three words proved to be the most useful. Two types of similarity between the documents were defined. The first definition, formula (3), does not take into account the weights of words, the second, formula (4), takes into account these weights. Every similarity formula was tested with the Chinese Whispers clustering algorithm as a verification method. Tests have shown that the selection of phrases with the highest weights is important. For clustering, the number of selected edges with highest weights is important. Formula versions have a much smaller impact on the results. Moreover, we concluded that taking into account the grammatical category of words and choosing phrases only with nouns, verbs and adjectives impacted the results primarily when the weights of words in the phrase were taken into account. During the experiments, we also found some interesting features of the clustering algorithm from Dlib library. We concluded that the algorithm for weighted graphs does not work well because all the values for normalized similarity were small. It was necessary to use a version for graphs without weights (i.e. all equals 1). The edges with the smallest weights were successively removed for subsequent levels. Moreover, it turned out that the algorithm does not work well when the distances between documents are not normalized. In many cases only one cluster was obtained. Removing edges with lower weights improves the results, but removing too many edges causes documents not to be combined into clusters. Graph document model allows selection of the most important phrases from the text and specifies semantic similarity between documents even for a small number of documents.

Our goal is to analyze documents connected with agriculture in the Polish language on the semantic level. However, including only parts of speech adds little semantics, which is insufficient for our research. In further research, we want to modify the weights of phrases using the ontology of concepts in the field of agriculture. Moreover, we plan to perform a test for more diverse documents collection.

References

1. Nastase, V., Mihalcea, R., Radev, D.: A survey of graphs in natural language processing. Nat. Lang. Eng. **21**, 665–698 (2015)
2. Robinson, I., Webber, J., Eifrem, E.: Graph Databases. 2nd edn. O'Reilly Media, Inc. (2015)
3. Hodler, A.E., Needham, M.: Graph Algorithms. O'Reilly Media, Inc. (2019)
4. Brin, S., Page, L.: The anatomy of a large-scale hypertextual Web search engine. Comput. Netw. ISDN Syst. **30**, 1–7 (1998)
5. Mihalcea, R., Tarau, P.: TextRank: bringing order into texts. In: Proceedings of the 2004 Conference on Empirical Methods in Natural Language Processing, Barcelona, Spain, pp. 404–411 (2004)
6. Lyon W.: Natural Language Processing With Neo4j - Mining Paradigmatic Word Associations. https://www.lyonwj.com/2015/06/16/nlp-with-neo4j/
7. Lyon W.: Webinar Natural Language Processing With Graphs & Neo4j. https://info.neo4j.com/natural-language-processing-with-graphs.html
8. Wrzeciono, P., Karwowski, W.: Automatic indexing and creating semantic networks for agricultural science papers in the Polish language. In: 2013 IEEE 37th Annual Computer Software and Applications Conference Workshops: COMPSACW 2013, Kyoto, Japan, 22–26 July 2013, Kyoto, pp. 356–360 (2013)
9. Wrzeciono, P., Karwowski, W.: Pattern recognition method for classification of agricultural scientific papers in Polish. In: Chmielewski, L.J., Kozera, R., Orłowski, A., Wojciechowski, K., Bruckstein, A.M., Petkov, N. (eds.) ICCVG 2018. LNCS, vol. 11114, pp. 499–511. Springer, Cham (2018). https://doi.org/10.1007/978-3-030-00692-1_43
10. Mihalcea, R.: Graph-based ranking algorithms for sentence extraction, applied to text summarization. In: Proceedings of the 42nd Annual Meeting of the Association for Computational Lingusitics (ACL 2004) (companion volume), Barcelona, Spain (2004)

11. Barrios, F., López, F., Argerich, L., Wachenchauzer, R.: Variations of the similarity function of TextRank for automated summarization. In: Proceedings of Argentine Symposium on Artificial Intelligence, ASAI (2016)
12. Boudin, F.: A comparison of centrality measures for graph-based keyphrase extraction. In: Proceedings of the Sixth International Joint Conference on Natural Language Processing, pp. 834–838 (2013)
13. Zheng, H., Lapata, M.: Sentence centrality revisited for unsupervised summarization. ArXiv, abs/1906.03508 (2019)
14. Schenker, A.: Graph-theoretic techniques for web content mining. Ph.D. thesis, University of South Florida (2003)
15. Yang, K.C., Al-Sabahi, K., Xiang, Y., Zhang, Z.: An integrated graph model for document summarization. Information 9, 232 (2018)
16. Hamming, R.W.: Error detecting and error correcting codes. Bell Syst. Tech. J. 29(2), 147–160 (1950)
17. Jurafski, D., Martin, J.H.: Speech and Language Processing, 2nd edn. Prentice Hall, Hoboken (2008)
18. Navigli, R., Martelli, F.: An overview of word and sense similarity. Nat. Lang. Eng. 25(6), 693–714 (2019)
19. Lin, D.: An information-theoretic definition of similarity. In: ICML 1998 Proceedings of the Fifteenth International Conference on Machine Learning, pp. 296–304. Morgan Kaufmann (1998)
20. Manning, C.D., Raghavan, P., Schütze, H.: Introduction to Information Retrieval. Cambridge University Press, Cambridge (2008)
21. Lee, M., Chang, J.W., Hsieh, T.: A grammar-based semantic similarity algorithm for natural language sentences. Sci. World J. 2014 (2014). https://doi.org/10.1155/2014/437162
22. Batanović, V., Bojic, D.: Using part-of-speech tags as deep-syntax indicators in determining short-text semantic similarity. Comput. Sci. Inf. Syst. 12, 1–31 (2015)
23. The Polish language dictionary (Słownik Języka Polskiego) Homepage, sjp.pl. Accessed 10 Feb 2022
24. Biemann, Ch.: Chinese whispers - an efficient graph clustering algorithm and its applications to natural language processing problems. In: Proceedings of TextGraphs: the First Workshop on Graph Based Methods for Natural Language Processing, pp. 73–80 (2006)
25. Bieniek, J., Zawada, J., Molendowski, F., Komarnicki, P., Kwietniak, K.: Ocena jakości pracy linii technologicznej do obróbki kolb i ziarna kukurydzy. Inżynieria Rolnicza 4(147), 17–26 (2013)
26. Czachor, G., Bohdziewicz, J.: Metodologiczne aspekty pomiaru twardości ziarniaka kukurydzy. Inżynieria Rolnicza 4(147), 53–62 (2013)
27. Dudek, S., Żarski, J.: Ocena efektów zastosowania nawadniania w uprawie kukurydzy na ziarno. Inżynieria Rolnicza 3(63), 159–164 (2005)
28. Lisowski, A., Kostyra, K.: Dodatkowe rozdrabnianie ziaren i rozrywanie cząstek kukurydzy sposobem na poprawienie jakości pociętej zielonki. Inżynieria Rolnicza 9(107), 189–195 (2008)
29. Szymanek, M.: Ocena porównawcza pozyskiwania ziarna kukurydzy cukrowej na cele spożywcze metoda odcinania i omłotu. Inżynieria Rolnicza 8(117), 215–222 (2009)
30. Weres, J.: Informatyczny system pozyskiwania danych o geometrii produktów rolniczych na przykładzie ziarniaka kukurydzy. Inżynieria Rolnicza 7(125), 229–236 (2010)
31. Zaliwski, A., Hołaj, J.: System wspomagania decyzji w produkcji kiszonki z kukurydzy. Inżynieria Rolnicza 2(90), 327–332 (2007)
32. Kiełbasa, P., Budyń, P.: Zastosowanie techniki wideo-komputerowej przy wyznaczaniu cech fizycznych bulw. Inżynieria Rolnicza 8(68), 143–152 (2005)

33. Jabłoński, K.: Nowe technologie produkcji ziemniaka – uprawa zagonowa. Inżynieria Rolnicza 1(61), 75–83 (2005)
34. Jakubowski, T.: Wpływ napromieniowania mikrofalowego na dynamikę wzrostu kiełków bulwy ziemniaka. Inżynieria Rolnicza 5(103), 7–13 (2008)
35. Kiełbasa, P.: Ocena wybranych cech fizycznych bulw ziemniaków. Inżynieria Rolnicza 6(66), 305–313 (2005)
36. Klamka, K.: Rad M: Wpływ nawadniania plantacji ziemniaka na wybrane cechy fizyczne bulw istotne w procesie separacji i sortowania plonu. Inżynieria Rolnicza 11(109), 127–134 (2008)
37. Kołodziejczyk, M., et al.: Ocena plonowania, składu chemicznego i jakości bulw wybranych odmian ziemniaka skrobiowego. Inżynieria Rolnicza 3(146), 123–130 (2013)
38. Krzysztofik, B., Marks, N., Baran, D.: Wpływ wybranych czynników agrotechnicznych na ilościowe cechy plonu bulw ziemniaka. Inżynieria Rolnicza 5(114), 123–129 (2009)
39. Rut, J., Szwedziak, K.: Zastosowanie akwizycji obrazu do szacowania strat w uprawie ziemniaka. Inżynieria Rolnicza 7(105), 179–184 (2008)
40. Sobol, Z., Baran, D.: Relacje pomiędzy przyrostem gęstości bulw a wybranymi właściwościami ziemniaka w okresie przechowywania. Inżynieria Rolnicza 9(97), 203–210 (2007)
41. Szwedziak, K., Rut, J.: Technika oceny i modelowanie statystyczne stopnia uszkodzeń ziemniaka przez stonkę ziemniaczaną. Inżynieria Rolnicza 6(104), 203–210 (2008)
42. Tanaś, W.: Parametry konstrukcyjne rolkowego separatora czyszczącego do ziemniaków. Inżynieria Rolnicza 10(108), 261–267 (2008)
43. Zalewski, P.: Ziemniak jako roślina uprawna - fragmenty historii. Inżynieria Rolnicza 5(114), 311–318 (2009)

Mobile Phone as a 6DoF Motion Controller

Maciej Kopczynski[(✉)]

Faculty of Computer Science, Bialystok University of Technology,
Wiejska 45A, 15-351 Białystok, Poland
`m.kopczynski@pb.edu.pl`

Abstract. This paper presents results and describes a solution allowing for using an Android-based mobile phone as a precise six degrees of freedom motion controller in **V**irtual **R**eality (**VR**) applications that are running on PC computer. This approach is focused on creating versatile system devoted to different types applications, that are additionally accessible by wireless communication (no cables connecting PC and mobile device), therefore giving freedom of movements and allowing to use mobile device as a high-precision motion controller. The obtained results show possibility of achieving good compromise between low latency of tracked movements and high prediction rate, giving small delay in movements tracking.

Keywords: Virtual Reality · Motion control · Small delay · Prediction · Mobile device

1 Introduction

One of the main challenges of the VR industry is price of required devices, e.g. headset or controllers. Most high-quality applications like games are made for PC because of their computing power and ways of interaction in virtual space with available peripherals. Because of the limited computing power and lack of basic keyboard or mouse interaction known from games, virtual reality mobile solutions are not used by most high-quality developers. Currently PCs are most popular medium to create solutions for professional VR helmets like HTC Vive or Oculus Rift. Both of these solutions cost hundreds of euro. For most home users, these solutions are still not available due to the high price. The idea of developing technology described in this paper is to drastically reduce the price of entry into the VR for PC entertainment. It will be possible to extend potential market and overcome previously mentioned challenges by developing a solution that enables the use of a mobile device cooperating with PC in the effective way, focusing mainly on low latency and high image quality. Additionally, the **I**nertial **M**easurement **U**nits (**IMU**) sensors in most mobile devices are not designed to provide high precision of motion tracking, what is crucial for virtual reality to achieve satisfactory levels of immersion.

K. Saeed and J. Dvorský (Eds.): CISIM 2022, LNCS 13293, pp. 345–359, 2022.
https://doi.org/10.1007/978-3-031-10539-5_25

The next problem in the mobile VR helmet and controller simulation is the excessive delay of the image in relation to the head and body movements (including hands) which results in motion sickness and prevents the comfortable gameplay. In order to overcome this effect, the strong focus have to be put on optimization both the VR image transmission algorithms from the computer to the phone, as well as motion tracking in the controllers to reduce image delay. Motion sickness can be seen for most people, when delay is bigger than 50 ms [5].

At the moment there are not many ready-to-use solutions for transforming Android mobile device to high-precision motion controller using wireless network as transmission medium and focusing on low CPU usage, high prediction rate and low latency of movement tracking. Of course, there are many controller devices available on the market, but those are either expensive units or parts of VR helmet sets. Implementation details related to motion tracking, filtering and prediction algorithms are held as producing company secrets. In the literature one can find mainly descriptions of concepts or partial solutions for transformation of mobile device into high-precision and low latency motion controllers.

Approach to remote motion controller with visual feedback on mobile devices was presented in [3]. Description of motion-based remote control device for interaction with 3D multimedia content can be found in [9]. Analysis of degrees of freedom using mobile phone for VR is described in [1]. 9DoF customly designed motion controller based on **Micro-Electro-Mechanical Systems (MEMS)** chips is described in [6]. General concepts and descriptions of coders and decoders for fast video encoding is in [10,14] and [15]. Latency analysis for H.264 coding standard is described in [13] and [12]. Optimizations for fast wireless image transfer using H.264 codec to Android mobile devices can be found in [8]. IP networks usage as a basis for sending encoded image can be found in [16] and [17].

The paper is organized as follows. In Sect. 2 some information about the basic definitions are presented. The Sect. 3 focuses on description of implemented solution and optimizations made in test application, while Sect. 4 is devoted to presentation of the experimental results.

2   Basic Definitions

For the purpose of measuring obtained results related to precision of motion tracking and movements prediction, some definitions have to be introduced. Selected formulas are presented below.

2.1   6 Degrees of Freedom

Six degrees of freedom in motion description (6DoF) refers to the axes of movement of a rigid body in three-dimensional space. The body is able to change position as forward/backward (surge), up/down (heave), left/right (sway) translation in three perpendicular axes, combined with changes in orientation through rotation in three perpendicular axes, often called yaw (normal axis), pitch (transverse axis), and roll (longitudinal axis). Name of the movements are shown on Fig. 1.

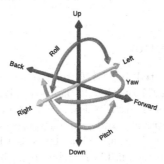

Fig. 1. Naming convention for movement types based on 6DoF [4].

Basic IMU chip in mobile phone allows to track three degrees of freedom (3DoF) in rotational motion only: pitch, yaw, and roll. Solution described in this paper allows to translate 3DoF produced by mobile phone IMU into 6DoF using inverted body model described later in this paper.

2.2   Kalman Filtering

Kalman filter is an algorithm proposed by R.E. Kalman. It is based on recursive determination of the minimal-variance estimate for state vector of a linear model, mostly discrete dynamic system, based on the measurements of the system's input and output. It is assumed that both the measurement and the processing inside the system are affected by an error with the Gaussian distribution. Kalman filtering has many technological applications, e.g. guidance, navigation, and control of vehicles, particularly aircraft, spacecraft and ships that are positioned dynamically. Furthermore, Kalman filtering is a concept much applied in time series analysis used for topics such as signal processing based on sensor readings and can be used for trajectory optimization. Because of space limitations in this paper, more details about Kalman filtering can be found in original article of R.E. Kalman [7] or general review like [2].

2.3   Quality Assesment

An important aspect of 3DoF to 6DoF conversion is smallest possible difference between perfect theoretical movement and the one that was created by using the algorithm. Additional aspect is the time delay required for data processing. Too big delay can cause nausea and motion sickness when using controllers in VR environment. Error in movement measurement is summarized by using standard deviation on set of collected samples:

$$\sigma = \sqrt{\frac{1}{N} \sum_{i=1}^{N} (x_i - \mu)^2} \tag{1}$$

where N is number of collected samples, x_i is i-th sample, while μ is the average of the samples.

3   Solution Description

Test application was created in .NET technology using C# language and Microsoft Visual Studio 2017 on the PC side. Mobile device running Android operating system part was created in Java using Android Studio 3 IDE. Technologies that were used for data and graphics processing based extensively on low-level APIs for IMU raw data, as well as Direct3D 11 for visual part. For the precise and repeatable motion simulation, based on 3 different types of movements, which are described in details in Sect. 4, simple 1-axis robotic arm was used. Range of constant speed rotational movement was limited to range 0–90°. Each tested mobile device was attached to the end of the arm.

Figure 2 presents general architecture of solution.

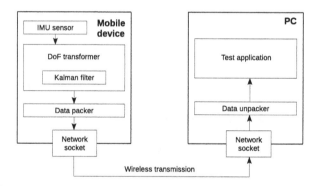

Fig. 2. Solution architecture in general.

System consists of two parts - test application running on PC and sensor data collecting and processing application on mobile device. Main functional parts of mobile client are:

– *IMU sensor* – main sensor of the mobile device,
– *DoF transformer* – transforms 3DoF data into 6DoF according to described algorithms,
– *Kalman filter* – Kalman filter for sensor data,
– *Data packer* – responsible for preparing collected and processed sensor data int MTU-sized frames.

Main functional parts of PC server are *Data unpacker* responsible for unpacking data from network stream and prepare it for processing and visualisation by *Test application*.

3.1   3DoF to 6DoF Transformation

The input is for the algorithm is head and hand data. The hand is dependent on the body position, which is unknown. For this reason, before estimation of hand to head relation, it is necessary to determine the approximate body direction. This process is divided into two stages - body position estimation and wrist position estimation.

Body Direction Estimation. The direction of the body is estimated basing on assumption, that wrist and head rotation is independent of the body itself, but with angular restrictions. Head defines the direction of moving body, which is derived from spherical linear interpolation between the currently supposed body direction and the direction of the head. Additionally, intensity of the hand movements determine the body rotation speed. This approach prevents a false-estimated body rotation in a situation, where the player only looks to the side without directing his hand there, e.g. quickly looking back in response to an event in the played game. Pseudocode of algorithm for body direction estimation is presented below.

INPUT: Head position M_H, transformation matrix M_C
OUTPUT: Body rotation Q_B
1:   $Q_H \leftarrow Extract_XY_Rotation(M_H)$
2:   $Q_B \leftarrow Q_H$
3: **for** each frame n in stream **do**
4:     $Q_\Delta \leftarrow Angle(M_{C_{n-1}}, M_{C_N})$
5:     **if** $Q_\Delta < THRESHOLD_\Delta$ **then**
6:       $StaticBodyFrames \leftarrow StaticBodyFrames + 1$
7:     **else**
8:       $StaticBodyFrames \leftarrow 0$
9:     **end if**
10:    **if** $StaticBodyFrames > THRESHOLD_F$ **then**
11:      $L \leftarrow 0$
12:    **else**
13:      $L \qquad\qquad\qquad\qquad\qquad\qquad\qquad\qquad\qquad\qquad \leftarrow$
         $Clamp(Q_\Delta, 0, MAX\_BODY\_MOVEMENT\_PER\_FRAME\_DEG)$
14:    **end if**
15:    $Q_B \leftarrow Slerp(Q_B, Q_H, L)$
16: **end for**

Input to the algorithm is a transformation matrix M_H representing the head position and a transformation matrix M_C describing controller rotation in 3DoF. Output is the estimated body rotation quaternion Q_B, that should follow the head and hand, assuming human speed of movements. At the beginning, in line 1, head rotation Q_H in X and Y axes is calculated. The same value is assigned to body rotation Q_B. Loop in lines 3–16 is iterates over each sensor sample from data stream. Line 4 is responsible for calculating Q_Δ angle difference between subsequent data frames. Number of frames, when the the controller was relatively stationary is checked in condition defined in lines 5–9 by comparing current value of angle difference Q_Δ to the constant threshold $THRESHOLD_\Delta$, which defines minimum angle the controller must travel each frame to recognize its movement. In the event of a standstill, the number of consecutive frames $StaticBodyFrames$ is reset. Next condition, defined in lines 10–14, is for checking maximum angular velocity of body rotation. If the number of consecutive frames exceeds $THRESHOLD_F$, then interpolation coefficient L is set to 0, what results in "cutting off the body" the controller. Otherwise, the interpolation coefficient L is calculated in line 12 and limited by the *Clamp* function assigning value in the range between $<0, MAX\_BODY\_MOVEMENT\_PER\_FRAME\_DEG>$. Line 14 calculates Q_B value as a result being spherical linear interpolation supported by the *Slerp* estimation function using current body direction Q_B and the current head direction Q_H with the interpolation factor L.

3DoF to 6DoF. After estimating the body position, it is possible to proceed to estimating the full position of the controller itself. For this purpose, a series of constants should be adopted in terms of body structure, e.g. the height from the elbow to the rotational center of the head, the horizontal distance from the center of the head to the elbow, or the length of the forearm with the wrist. Some constants are assigned to the controller (the structure of the controller body), and others are assigned to a specific player (anatomical differences between players).

Assuming hand in the welcome position (e.g. for a handshake) it can be seen, that the wrist has relatively small rotation in the X and Z axes (pitch and roll). In the Z axis (roll), the rotation is connected with the radius and ulna bones. X axis (pitch) has similarly small rotation range. When making a gesture of aiming (e.g. with a weapon in the game) it is easy to notice that when making changes in these axes, the entire forearm has to be moved. Only the Y axis (yaw) has a nearly 180° rotation field without changing the position of the forearm.

With these limitations in mind, it was assumed that each wrist movement is a direct result of the forearm movement. Thus, the position of the elbow will be a direct result of wrist rotation.

The pseudocode describing the above process is described below.

INPUT: controller quaternion Q_C, body quaternion Q_B, vector V_A
OUTPUT: Controller position matrix M_C
1: $Q_L \leftarrow Normalize(Inverse(Q_B) \cdot Q_C)$
2: $V_E, Q_E \leftarrow CalculateElbow(V_A, Q_L, Q_B)$
3: $V_W \leftarrow V_E + (Q_E \cdot WRIST\_OFFSET)$
4: $V_C \leftarrow Q_L \cdot CONTROLLER\_CENTER\_OFFSET$
5: $M_{CRot} \leftarrow RotationMatrix(Q_C)$
6: $M_{WPos} \leftarrow TranslationMatrix(V_W)$
7: $M_{CPos} \leftarrow TranslationMatrix(V_C)$
8: $M_C \leftarrow M_{CRot} \cdot M_{WPos} \cdot M_{CPos}$

Input to the algorithm is absolute controller rotation quaternion Q_C, estimated body rotation quaternion Q_B and vector $V_A = [-1, 1, 1]$ for the left controller and $[1, 1, 1]$ for the right controller. Output is the M_C matrix that represents controller position in three-dimensional space, including it's direction.

In line 1 quaternion Q_L representing local rotation of the controller with respect to the body, is computed. Then, in line 2, the elbow displacement vector V_E relative to the head along with the elbow quaternion Q_E is estimated on the basis of hand side multiplier V_A, controller rotation Q_L relative to the body, and estimated body rotation Q_B. Line 3 is responsible for calculating V_W vector, which describes head to wrist offset. This calculation is weighted by the anatomical user constant $WRIST\_OFFSET$. The goal of line 4 is to calculate the V_W vector offset from the wrist to the center of the controller rotation, which is constant for the controller and is based on its physical grip location. Given all the shift vectors and the quaternions of rotation, three transformation matrices are created on lines 5–7. M_{CRot} represents the absolute rotation of the controller, M_{Wpos} represents the offset to the wrist relative to the head, and M_{CPos} represents the offset to the center of the controller body relative to the wrist. In line 8, matrices are folded into a final transformation matrix M_C, which describes approximate 6DoF controller.

Kalman Filtering. Kalman filtering was used to make the tracking of the hand position smoother and with less perceptible delays, what included controller position data and its velocity. Results returned by filter allows to determine the predicted position for drawing the next frame. Next important advantage is the possibility of using existing measurements in the event of a delay in reading new data from stream and determining a new position at fixed time intervals.

Pseudocode for Kalman filter prediction used for sensor data stream is is described below.

INPUT: matrix M_C, frame time F_T
OUTPUT: vector V_{PF}
1: $KalmanStateSize \leftarrow 6$
2: $KalmanMeasurementSize \leftarrow 3$
3: $F_p \leftarrow GetCurrentTime()$
4: $M_p \leftarrow M_C$
5: **while** *working* **do**
6:   $Wait\ until\ M_C = M_p\ and\ F_P + F_T < GetCurrentTime()$
7:   $F_{Dt} \leftarrow GetCurrentTime() - F_p$
8:   $KalmanDeltaTime \leftarrow F_{Dt}$
9:   $V_{PT} \leftarrow KalmanPredict()$
10:   **if** $M_C \neq M_p$ **then**
11:     $V_M \leftarrow ExtractPosition(M_C)$
12:     $KalmanMeasurement \leftarrow V_M$
13:     $V_{PT} \leftarrow KalmanCorrect()$
14:     $M_P \leftarrow M_C$
15:   **end if**
16:   $V_{PF} \leftarrow V_{PT} + F_t \cdot KalmanGetState()$
17:   $F_P \leftarrow GetCurrentTime()$
18: **end while**

According to the previously presented approach, input for the algorithm is M_C matrix that represents controller position in three-dimensional space (including it's direction) and single frame time F_T. Output of the algorithm is vector V_{PF} representing filtered and predicted value of controller position. Kalman filtering in this approach is based on 6-element state size and 3-element data size. In the initial phase of the algorithm, the Kalman filter is configured to a 6-element state size (line 1) and a 3-element measurement data size (line 2). The status data is the position and velocity (3 components for each), while only measured parameter is the position. As part of the initialization (line 3) the start time (F_P) is saved, which is used to store the time of the last update. In line 4, the M_P variable saves initial controller position. Loop in lines 5–18 repeats the sequence of steps until it is interrupted. In the beginning, algorithm waits for the state of the controller position matrix to be changed or for the duration of a single frame to expire, what is shown in line 6. Then, the time elapsed since the previous update (F_{Dt}) is determined. In line 9, the temporary forecast position (V_{PT}) is derived. If the update is done as a result of a change of the controller state matrix, a new controller position vector is extracted from this matrix (line 11). This vector is then stored in the first three elements of the measurement vector. As the filter now has new data, the previously calculated temporary position can be corrected based on this data (line 13). Then, the final predicted controller position (V_{PF}) is determined. Temporary position is updated by the product of the time of a single frame and the speed in context of individual axes. Values are taken from the filter state vector (line 15). When the loop ends, predicted controller position (V_{PF}) contains final value, which is output of the algorithm.

4   Experimental Results

Presented results were obtained using a PC equipped with an 8 GB RAM, 4-core Intel Core i5-6600k processor and Nvidia GeForce GTX 970 graphics card running Windows 10 operating system. Mobile devices used in tests were Google Pixel XL, Nexus 5X and Xperia Z1 Compact with the same version of Android operating system. Google Pixel XL is considered as mobile device with best quality IMU sensors, Nexus 5X with medium quality and Xperia Z1 Compact has lowest grade sensors. Wireless network connection between PC and phone was established using TP-Link WDR3600 router configured to provide WiFi 802.11ac 5 GHz network.

Each of the controller movement measurements were 2 basic types:

- type 1 - swing of right hand over the left shoulder,
- type 2 - right hand rotation left to a ground parallel plane,

Each of the described movements were assuming 3DoF to 6DoF transformation using different mobile devices. Additionally, Kalman filtering was added in process of movement prediction. All collected samples were send using wireless network to specially written data processing application running on the PC. Purpose of the application was collecting IMU sensor data stream (raw and

processed on the mobile device), as well as visualization of received data using
3 planes (XYZ). During rotational phase of the movement, each sample was
acquired every 3° in the angle range of 0 to 90°, so 31 samples were collected for
every single test phase. All data samples were first collected on mobile device to
avoid any delays in transmission.

Because of paper size limitations, tables with data contain every third sample,
but images are built on basis of full collected data.

Time needed by the mobile device to finish calculations on all implemented
algorithms for each data sample was lower than 0.5 ms for each case.

Initial test set was performed for type 1 of the movement - swing of right
hand over the left shoulder. First mobile device tested was Xperia Z1 Compact.
Table 1 presents results acquired by test application.

Each presented table shown rotation in degrees for 3 axes - pitch, yaw and
roll in column *Rotation*. *Reference* is the column describing ideal single point
description using XYZ coordinates after transformation from 3DoF to 6DoF,
the same as for following columns. *Raw data* column shows non-filtered data,
while *Kalman* column represents points after Kalman filtering. It should be
additionally noted, that reference data was collected every time after arm or
mobile device reconfiguration took place.

Table 1. Results acquired for type 1 movement for Xperia Z1 Compact

Sample	Rotation			Reference			Raw data			Kalman		
	Pitch	Yaw	Roll	X	Y	Z	X	Y	Z	X	Y	Z
1	0.013	0.008	0.002	0.262	−0.399	−0.438	0.282	−0.392	−0.430	0.282	−0.392	−0.430
4	6.351	6.398	0.364	0.208	−0.358	−0.447	0.211	−0.350	−0.439	0.211	−0.341	−0.443
7	12.629	12.948	1.441	0.158	−0.317	−0.448	0.172	−0.294	−0.445	0.160	−0.285	−0.447
10	18.732	19.822	3.302	0.110	−0.281	−0.439	0.125	−0.269	−0.424	0.117	−0.246	−0.438
13	24.555	27.200	6.030	0.062	−0.248	−0.423	0.062	−0.248	−0.405	0.069	−0.231	−0.419
16	29.998	35.271	9.740	0.023	−0.216	−0.403	0.041	−0.207	−0.401	0.033	−0.202	−0.401
19	34.893	44.232	14.569	−0.013	−0.189	−0.371	−0.005	−0.176	−0.349	−0.005	−0.170	−0.369
22	39.051	54.229	20.596	−0.042	−0.167	−0.338	−0.021	−0.161	−0.333	−0.033	−0.149	−0.336
25	42.261	65.336	27.846	−0.068	−0.148	−0.296	−0.065	−0.129	−0.282	−0.061	−0.134	−0.291
28	44.292	77.373	36.120	−0.083	−0.136	−0.252	−0.071	−0.126	−0.245	−0.083	−0.116	−0.251
31	44.998	90.011	45.010	−0.092	−0.131	−0.203	−0.088	−0.128	−0.192	−0.094	−0.113	−0.201

Standard deviation for type 1 movement for Xperia Z1 Compact based on
all originally collected samples (31) and compared on basis of errors to reference
data is equal to:

- raw sensor data - $\sigma_{X_R} = 0.00632, \sigma_{Y_R} = 0.00677, \sigma_{Z_R} = 0.00671$,
- filtered sensor data - $\sigma_{X_F} = 0.00489, \sigma_{Y_F} = 0.00706, \sigma_{Z_F} = 0.00234$.

Table 2 presents results acquired by test application for Nexus 5X mobile
device.

Standard deviation for type 1 movement for Nexus 5X based on all originally
collected samples (31) and compared on basis of errors to reference data is equal
to:

Table 2. Results acquired for type 1 movement for Nexus 5X

Sample	Rotation			Reference			Raw data			Kalman		
	Pitch	Yaw	Roll	X	Y	Z	X	Y	Z	X	Y	Z
1	0.001	0.009	0.006	0.262	−0.399	−0.439	0.264	−0.399	−0.438	0.264	−0.399	−0.438
4	6.352	6.391	0.368	0.209	−0.356	−0.446	0.212	−0.352	−0.442	0.212	−0.354	−0.445
7	12.630	12.944	1.446	0.156	−0.320	−0.447	0.157	−0.320	−0.446	0.157	−0.315	−0.453
10	18.734	19.828	3.315	0.110	−0.280	−0.439	0.113	−0.276	−0.436	0.105	−0.276	−0.449
13	24.556	27.194	6.032	0.063	−0.247	−0.424	0.065	−0.244	−0.422	0.060	−0.240	−0.433
16	30.004	35.281	9.754	0.021	−0.216	−0.400	0.021	−0.214	−0.396	0.018	−0.210	−0.408
19	34.898	44.231	14.561	−0.012	−0.188	−0.373	−0.008	−0.185	−0.372	−0.018	−0.182	−0.378
22	39.046	54.225	20.588	−0.044	−0.165	−0.337	−0.042	−0.162	−0.333	−0.049	−0.157	−0.343
25	42.253	65.322	27.835	−0.066	−0.147	−0.297	−0.063	−0.144	−0.295	−0.071	−0.138	−0.303
28	44.295	77.383	36.123	−0.085	−0.138	−0.253	−0.084	−0.137	−0.253	−0.089	−0.128	−0.257
31	44.986	90.007	45.009	−0.092	−0.130	−0.203	−0.090	−0.129	−0.196	−0.099	−0.121	−0.205

- raw sensor data - $\sigma_{X_R} = 0.00323, \sigma_{Y_R} = 0.00357, \sigma_{Z_R} = 0.00422$,
- filtered sensor data - $\sigma_{X_F} = 0.00234, \sigma_{Y_F} = 0.00224, \sigma_{Z_F} = 0.00153$.

Table 3 presents results acquired by test application for Google Pixel XL mobile device.

Table 3. Results acquired for type 1 movement for Google Pixel XL

Sample	Rotation			Reference			Raw data			Kalman		
	Pitch	Yaw	Roll	X	Y	Z	X	Y	Z	X	Y	Z
1	0.013	0.001	0.004	0.262	−0.396	−0.437	0.261	−0.398	−0.438	0.261	−0.398	−0.438
4	6.355	6.396	0.361	0.208	−0.356	−0.447	0.207	−0.357	−0.447	0.208	−0.357	−0.448
7	12.627	12.949	1.447	0.158	−0.319	−0.448	0.157	−0.319	−0.448	0.157	−0.318	−0.455
10	18.733	19.826	3.306	0.109	−0.282	−0.440	0.108	−0.282	−0.440	0.107	−0.280	−0.452
13	24.553	27.205	6.041	0.064	−0.246	−0.423	0.063	−0.247	−0.424	0.060	−0.245	−0.436
16	30.006	35.274	9.752	0.022	−0.215	−0.400	0.021	−0.216	−0.401	0.017	−0.212	−0.412
19	34.897	44.232	14.561	−0.012	−0.190	−0.371	−0.013	−0.190	−0.372	−0.019	−0.185	−0.382
22	39.059	54.237	20.596	−0.043	−0.165	−0.336	−0.044	−0.166	−0.338	−0.051	−0.161	−0.346
25	42.252	65.332	27.842	−0.067	−0.148	−0.296	−0.068	−0.149	−0.297	−0.076	−0.144	−0.305
28	44.294	77.381	36.126	−0.083	−0.135	−0.251	−0.084	−0.136	−0.252	−0.093	−0.131	−0.259
31	44.998	90.015	45.012	−0.092	−0.128	−0.204	−0.093	−0.130	−0.204	−0.102	−0.123	−0.209

Standard deviation for type 1 movement for Google Pixel XL based on all originally collected samples (31) and compared on basis of errors to reference data is equal to:

- raw sensor data - $\sigma_{X_R} = 0.00043, \sigma_{Y_R} = 0.00053, \sigma_{Z_R} = 0.00042$,
- filtered sensor data - $\sigma_{X_F} = 0.00034, \sigma_{Y_F} = 0.00025, \sigma_{Z_F} = 0.00037$.

Second test set was performed for type 2 of the movement - right hand rotation left to a ground parallel plane. First mobile device tested was Xperia Z1 Compact. Table 4 presents results acquired by test application.

Table 4. Results acquired for type 2 movement for Xperia Z1 Compact

Sample	Rotation			Reference			Raw data			Kalman		
	Pitch	Yaw	Roll	X	Y	Z	X	Y	Z	X	Y	Z
1	0.014	0.013	0.006	0.263	−0.397	−0.438	0.284	−0.382	−0.424	0.284	−0.382	−0.424
4	0.008	9.005	0.000	0.204	−0.398	−0.433	0.221	−0.391	−0.415	0.210	−0.380	−0.426
7	0.003	18.009	0.009	0.146	−0.396	−0.423	0.149	−0.375	−0.421	0.139	−0.372	−0.421
10	0.008	27.002	0.016	0.093	−0.399	−0.403	0.100	−0.395	−0.397	0.081	−0.372	−0.409
13	0.007	36.009	0.010	0.044	−0.399	−0.373	0.061	−0.398	−0.351	0.041	−0.382	−0.376
16	0.006	45.001	0.015	−0.000	−0.399	−0.340	0.010	−0.395	−0.321	0.002	−0.385	−0.334
19	0.003	54.000	0.012	−0.039	−0.397	−0.304	−0.023	−0.380	−0.298	−0.037	−0.384	−0.298
22	0.005	63.005	0.016	−0.071	−0.398	−0.260	−0.050	−0.390	−0.255	−0.060	−0.390	−0.253
25	0.006	72.009	0.009	−0.098	−0.399	−0.212	−0.092	−0.391	−0.200	−0.093	−0.387	−0.208
28	359.993	81.000	0.012	−0.115	−0.398	−0.162	−0.102	−0.384	−0.141	−0.114	−0.390	−0.152
31	0.003	90.007	0.0131	−0.124	−0.397	−0.113	−0.106	−0.382	−0.108	−0.124	−0.386	−0.106

Standard deviation for type 2 movement for Xperia Z1 Compact based on all originally collected samples (31) and compared on basis of errors to reference data is equal to:

- raw sensor data - $\sigma_{X_R} = 0.00617, \sigma_{Y_R} = 0.00667, \sigma_{Z_R} = 0.00641$,
- filtered sensor data - $\sigma_{X_F} = 0.00723, \sigma_{Y_F} = 0.00629, \sigma_{Z_F} = 0.00529$.

Table 5 presents results acquired by test application for Google Nexus 5X mobile device.

Table 5. Results acquired for type 2 movement for Nexus 5X

Sample	Rotation			Reference			Raw data			Kalman		
	Pitch	Yaw	Roll	X	Y	Z	X	Y	Z	X	Y	Z
1	0.013	0.005	0.011	0.263	−0.399	−0.437	0.267	−0.399	−0.433	0.267	−0.399	−0.433
4	0.005	9.005	0.007	0.204	−0.398	−0.434	0.206	−0.396	−0.432	0.201	−0.395	−0.436
7	0.008	18.005	0.008	0.145	−0.396	−0.422	0.146	−0.391	−0.420	0.135	−0.395	−0.436
10	0.008	27.002	0.016	0.093	−0.397	−0.402	0.096	−0.393	−0.399	0.081	−0.394	−0.421
13	0.007	36.003	0.011	0.044	−0.397	−0.373	0.046	−0.393	−0.369	0.035	−0.394	−0.389
16	0.010	45.007	0.007	−0.002	−0.397	−0.340	−0.002	−0.393	−0.335	−0.007	−0.393	−0.349
19	−0.003	54.004	0.011	−0.041	−0.397	−0.301	−0.040	−0.393	−0.297	−0.044	−0.393	−0.308
22	−0.001	62.997	0.011	−0.070	−0.397	−0.260	−0.066	−0.394	−0.260	−0.077	−0.393	−0.263
25	0.003	72.008	0.018	−0.098	−0.399	−0.213	−0.097	−0.397	−0.212	−0.103	−0.397	−0.215
28	0.001	80.995	0.019	−0.113	−0.399	−0.162	−0.109	−0.398	−0.159	−0.121	−0.397	−0.164
31	0.003	89.994	0.009	−0.126	−0.396	−0.113	−0.126	−0.392	−0.112	−0.132	−0.393	−0.114

Standard deviation for type 2 movement for Nexus 5X based on all originally collected samples (31) and compared on basis of errors to reference data is equal to:

- raw sensor data - $\sigma_{X_R} = 0.00324, \sigma_{Y_R} = 0.00343, \sigma_{Z_R} = 0.00418$,
- filtered sensor data - $\sigma_{X_F} = 0.00423, \sigma_{Y_F} = 0.00297, \sigma_{Z_F} = 0.00321$.

Table 6 presents results acquired by test application for Google Pixel XL mobile device.

Table 6. Results acquired for type 2 movement for Google Pixel XL

Sample	Rotation			Reference			Raw data			Kalman		
	Pitch	Yaw	Roll	X	Y	Z	X	Y	Z	X	Y	Z
1	0.000	0.010	0.006	0.262	−0.397	−0.436	0.261	−0.398	−0.438	0.261	−0.398	−0.438
4	0.005	9.012	0.006	0.204	−0.399	−0.433	0.203	−0.399	−0.434	0.202	−0.399	−0.436
7	0.002	18.003	0.009	0.148	−0.399	−0.422	0.146	−0.399	−0.423	0.143	−0.400	−0.431
10	0.002	27.008	0.008	0.094	−0.398	−0.401	0.093	−0.399	−0.402	0.088	−0.400	−0.416
13	0.001	36.000	0.014	0.043	−0.399	−0.376	0.043	−0.399	−0.376	0.037	−0.399	−0.389
16	0.004	45.004	0.008	−0.001	−0.398	−0.342	−0.002	−0.399	−0.343	−0.007	−0.399	−0.353
19	0.001	54.000	0.011	−0.039	−0.399	−0.301	−0.040	−0.399	−0.303	−0.047	−0.399	−0.311
22	0.002	63.001	0.016	−0.072	−0.399	−0.258	−0.073	−0.399	−0.259	−0.080	−0.399	−0.266
25	0.003	72.009	0.003	−0.097	−0.396	−0.211	−0.098	−0.398	−0.212	−0.106	−0.398	−0.218
28	0.005	80.992	0.004	−0.115	−0.397	−0.163	−0.116	−0.398	−0.164	−0.125	−0.398	−0.168
31	−0.001	89.998	0.012	−0.126	−0.398	−0.112	−0.126	−0.399	−0.113	−0.136	−0.399	−0.116

Standard deviation for type 2 movement for Google Pixel XL based on all originally collected samples (31) and compared on basis of errors to reference data is equal to:

- raw sensor data - $\sigma_{X_R} = 0.00045, \sigma_{Y_R} = 0.00049, \sigma_{Z_R} = 0.00048$,
- filtered sensor data - $\sigma_{X_F} = 0.00029, \sigma_{Y_F} = 0.00009, \sigma_{Z_F} = 0.00041$.

Figure 3, Fig. 4 and Fig. 5 shows visualization of acquired data points for two types of movements for Xperia Z1 Compact, Nexus 5X and Google Pixel XL mobile devices respectively. Green line is data points for type 1 movement, while blue line is for type 2 movement. Part a) on each image presents reference set of data points, part b) is for raw and non-filtered data, while part c) is for data after Kalman filtering process.

According to obtained results, both results in tables and standard deviation, it can be clearly seen, that 3DoF to 6DoF algorithm works properly, but quality of the IMU sensor used by the mobile device has big impact on the output stability of 6DoF conversion. Google Pixel XL equipped with very precise sensor needs almost no converted data filtering comparing to Xperia Z1 Compact mobile device. Nexus 5X gives average results and can be placed between Google Pixel XL and Xperia Z1 Compact. Use of Kalman filtering allows removing noise, but adds small delay to the output stream in terms of real position of controller.

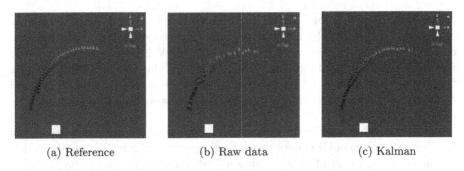

(a) Reference   (b) Raw data   (c) Kalman

Fig. 3. Sensor data points visualization for two types of movement for Xperia Z1 Compact

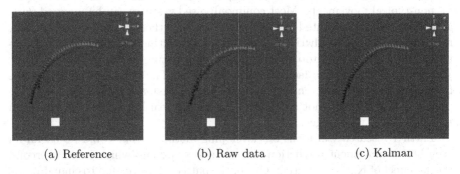

(a) Reference   (b) Raw data   (c) Kalman

Fig. 4. Sensor data points visualization for two types of movement for Nexus 5X

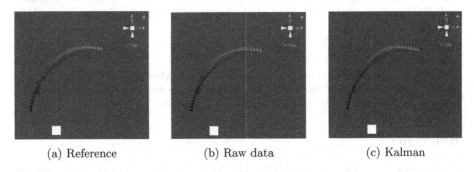

(a) Reference   (b) Raw data   (c) Kalman

Fig. 5. Sensor data points visualization for two types of movement for Google Pixel XL

5   Conclusions

Performed research shows, that creating efficient and versatile methods of using 3DoF mobile devices as 6DoF controllers is possible, when specified limitations are assumed and by using properly designed 3DoF to 6DoF transformation algorithm. Additionally, using Kalman filtering approach allows to improve quality of predicted movements by removing mobile device sensor noise. Computational cost has very small effect on player immersion in VR world and allows using mobile device as a fully functional 6DoF controller. Only one limitation coming from Kalman filtering used for processing sensor data is a small delay related to nature of Kalman filter algorithm. This can be especially problematic in very dynamic FPP games.

The main advantage is the cost of this solution. It does not require strong hardware (in terms of CPU data processing), so even older mobile phone models can be used as an controller. An additional advantage is the simplicity of installation and use of such system. User needs to install an application on the phone, as opposed to having to set up cameras or other devices needed for an external tracking system. The disadvantage, of course, is the accuracy of mapping for non-typical movements. Most commonly used gestures can be mapped fairly accurately, as it is presented in this paper. However, there are some sophisticated movements, such as handwriting, painting, or simulating the use of advanced virtual tools, that may be too challenging to map naturally from 3DoF to 6DoF. Another drawback is the lack of tactile feedback. The touch screen allows you to display buttons and even respond with haptic feedback of the phone's vibration motor, but this is not comparable to feeling real buttons, scroll wheels or joysticks under your finger.

Further research will focus on developing methods, that could be useful for even better movement prediction and noise filtering and which could overcome the lag-effect of Kalman filtering. One of the paths will be related to changing and optimizing body model limitations that are used in 3DoF to 6DoF conversion. Another path of research will be related to testing more mobile devices to check, how IMU sensor quality impacts final results and allow to change algorithms parameters.

Acknowledgments. The work was supported by the grant WZ/WI-IIT/2/2020 from Bialystok University of Technology. Research results are based on the project "Development of new, innovative tools and interaction mechanisms in VRidge technology" financed by National Center of Research and Development.

References

1. Benzina, A., Toennis, M., Klinker, G., Ashry, M.: Phone-based motion control in VR: analysis of degrees of freedom, Proceeding of CHI EA 2011: CHI 2011 Extended Abstracts on Human Factors in Computing Systems, pp. 1519–1524. ACM (2011)
2. Campestrini, Ch., Heil, T., Kosch, S., Jossen, A.: A comparative study and review of different Kalman filters by applying an enhanced validation method. J. Energy Storage **8**, 142–159 (2016)
3. Sravan, M.S., Moolam, S., Sreepathi, S., Kokil, P.: Implementation of remote motion controller with visual feedback. In: 2017 8th International Conference on Computing, Communication and Networking Technologies (ICCCNT), pp. 1–7. IEEE (2017)

4. Wikimedia Commons homepage. https://commons.wikimedia.org/wiki/File: 6DOF.svg. Accessed 05 May 2022
5. Hell, S., Argyriou, V.: Machine learning architectures to predict motion sickness using a virtual reality rollercoaster simulation tool. In: 2018 IEEE International Conference on Artificial Intelligence and Virtual Reality (AIVR), Taichung, Taiwan, pp. 153–156 (2018)
6. Jayaraj, L., Wood, J., Gibson, M.: Engineering a mobile VR experience with MEMS 9DOF motion controller. In: 2018 IEEE Games, Entertainment, Media Conference (GEM), pp. 1–9 (2018)
7. Kalman, R.E.: A new approach to linear filtering and prediction problems. Trans. ASME-J. Basic Eng. **82**, 35–45 (1960)
8. Kopczynski, M.: Optimizations for fast wireless image transfer using H.264 codec to android mobile devices for virtual reality applications. In: Zamojski, W., Mazurkiewicz, J., Sugier, J., Walkowiak, T., Kacprzyk, J. (eds.) DepCoS-RELCOMEX 2021. AISC, vol. 1389, pp. 203–212. Springer, Cham (2021). https://doi.org/10.1007/978-3-030-76773-0_20
9. Santos, R.A., Rasteiro, M.A., Castro, H.F., Bento, L.B., Barata, M., Assunção, P.A.: Motion-based remote control device for enhanced interaction with 3D multimedia content. In: Proceedings of Conference on Telecommunications - ConfTele, Aveiro, Portugal, pp. 1–4 (2015)
10. Ribas-Cobera, J., Chou, P.A., Regunathan, S.L.: A generalized hypothetical reference decoder for H.264/AVC. IEEE Trans. Circ. Syst. Video Technol. **13**(7), 674–687 (2003)
11. VRidge application homepage. https://riftcat.com/vridge. Accessed 05 May 2022
12. Schreier, R., Rothermel, A.: Motion adaptive intra refresh for the H.264 video coding standard. IEEE Trans. Consum. Electron. **52**(1), 249–253 (2006)
13. Schreier, R.M., Rothermel A.: A latency analysis on H.264 video transmission systems. In: 2008 Digest of Technical Papers - International Conference on Consumer Electronics, pp. 1–2. IEEE, Las Vegas (2008)
14. Sullivan, G.J., Wiegand, T.: Video compression - from concepts to the H.264/AVC standard. Proc. IEEE **93**(1), 18–31 (2005)
15. Sullivan, G.J., Ohm, J., Han, W., Wiegand, T.: Overview of the high efficiency video coding (HEVC) standard. IEEE Trans. Circ. Syst. Video Technol. **22**(12), 1649–1668 (2012)
16. Wenger, S.: H.264/AVC over IP. IEEE Trans. Circ. Syst. Video Technol. **13**(7), 645–656 (2003)
17. Zheng, H., Boyce, J.: An improved UDP protocol for video transmission over internet-to-wireless networks. IEEE Trans. Multimed. **3**, 356–365 (2001)

An Efficient Data Distribution Strategy for Distributed Graph Processing System

Aradhita Mukherjee[1][✉] [iD], Rituparna Chaki[2], and Nabendu Chaki[1] [iD]

[1] Department of Computer Science and Engineering, University of Calcutta JD - II,
Sector III, Salt Lake City, Kolkata 700106, India
aradhita.mukherjee.2016@gmail.com, nabendu@ieee.org
[2] A. K. Choudhury School of Information Technology, University of Calcutta JD - II,
Sector III, Salt Lake City, Kolkata 700106, India
rchaki@ieee.org

Abstract. Big data applications like social networks, biological networks, etc. are often realized on graphs. Graph processing, if done on a single node, increases time complexity. Partitioning of graphs has been proved to be useful towards handle this well-known issue. There are several partitioning algorithms that are used to partition a graph. Each partition is assigned to a node within a cluster. However, the storage capacity of a node is limited. Therefore, an effective data distribution mechanism is required. This work aims to propose a novel strategy that would define an efficient distribution of graphs into nodes using genetic algorithms. The proposed data distribution strategy, when applied on two benchmark data set, shows improved data availability without increasing the number of replicas. It has also observed that the execution time will almost became half after applying the proposed method.

Keywords: Distributed graph processing · Data placement · Genetic algorithm

1 Introduction

The growth of Big Data applications demands huge amount computed nodes for data processing. Distributed graph processing [8] system is composed by a series of compute node having different processing speed, load and altogether connected through a high bandwidth network. In distributed graph processing system a graph has been partitioned and placed randomly at different compute nodes. Placement of partition has a great impact on the performance of real-time applications. Most researchers focus on task scheduling to improve the success rate of real-time application, with very little consideration for availability of data. On the other hand, availability should get more attention to increase the performance of the overall system. Many fault-tolerant systems define the availability of each compute node as a ratio of execution time to total turnaround time within a given period. The replication of compute node is considered as one

K. Saeed and J. Dvorský (Eds.): CISIM 2022, LNCS 13293, pp. 360–373, 2022.
https://doi.org/10.1007/978-3-031-10539-5_26

of the approaches to increase the availability of the overall system. This helps to enhance data availability. Replication of data leads to high maintenance costs and storage costs. To decrease replica number sometimes replication of data is based on the popularity of data which lead to data unavailability due to its highly skewed distribution. Availability is also defined as the probability of nodes are available within a given period of time. This is hampered by data hammering, which happens due to machine failures including correlated machine (multiple nodes fails concurrently) and non-correlated machine failures (Individual nodes).

In this work, we have considered availability as a scenario where a request for data is more than what is available. We proposed an availability approached partition placement algorithm to cope with the above-defined problems. In order to partition, a graph agglomerative hierarchical clustering has been used here. Silhouette score has been used here to find optimal number partition numbers. Here, we have divided a graph into several sub-graphs and placed each sub-graph into individual computing nodes based on a fitness function. Each partition has its own set of tasks. Each task has its own instruction set. Genetic algorithm has been used here to minimize total execution time by assigning partition into a proper processor. The goal of the partition placement scheduling algorithms is to increase parallelization and decrease execution time.

The rest of the paper is organized as follows: In Sect. 2, a brief description of related work in this domain is presented. Section 3 describes the proposed system. Simulation results of our experiments are presented in Sect. 4. Finally, in Sect. 5, the concluding remarks have been recorded.

2   Related Work

Graphs are used in many fields of application like social networks, biological networks and path-finding in road networks. Extremely large graphs for such applications cannot fit in a single node [15]. Graph partition are the only solution. A large majority of the existing graph partitioning algorithms follows the divide-and-conquer [3] approach. Subsequently, each partition is assigned to a different computing node of the cluster. Graph partitioning is an NP-complete problem. Until now, there is no efficient algorithm that can find an optimal solution in polynomial time [2]. However, the choice of a partitioning algorithm depends on the system. Vertex-centric Systems follows vertex cut partition. Efficiency of vertex-cut partitioning algorithms is based on minimum number of replicas [10]. Many researchers have used genetic algorithm for partitioning a graph which is suitable only for static graphs. Genetic algorithms have been designed by researchers to allocate replica. It has been observed that by using this mechanism the latency and bandwidth in social networks is reduced [17]. Hybrid genetic algorithm is another variant, which considers current replica distribution as input and makes it suitable for dynamic environments. Problem of scheduling job and data replication greatly affects the performance of wide-area distributed systems that have been addressed in [14]. The focus of some of existing works is to reduce data scheduling between cloud data-centers and also to lower the transaction costs. They have used data placement strategies based on genetic algorithm for optimal data placement. However, such works have not been designed for the placement of the social network data in the cloud. Another work [4] addressed the problem of placing the components of SaaS in cloud environment. However, the authors did't consider data replication issue. In paper [16], the authors have proposed a new graph-partitioning algorithm to divide a social connected user network into different partitions based on connectivity of users. This graph-partitioning algorithm has been devised to optimize data placement and replication in cloud data-centers. However, the authors did not consider the optimization of the partitions. The focus of this work is to optimally place data in computation nodes to reduce data scheduling between the data centers. They have used data placement matrix to reduce the computation time. However, the frequency of transactions, data access history and access heat, which increased the cost of data management, have not been considered. In [6], the authors aim to reduce the cooperation cost among data slices, to eventually lower the distributed transaction cost produced by data placement. This strategy has been developed mainly for global load balance in data center. Here, the authors have designed a mechanism towards achieving high availability in the presence of partitions. They have concluded that the data accessing pattern greatly affect availability of data in a network partition.

Challenges Identified: The study of some of the most noted works in field prompts us to infer that mostly all the existing data placement algorithms addresses the issue of placement of data so that the scheduling time is reduced. Ease of availability of data and its correlation with execution time is hardly explored towards designing a better partitioning algorithm with minimum number of partitions. In fact, some of the partitioning algorithm replicates to increase availability. However, these often suffer from huge space complexity as the two issues are not addressed in an integrated approach.

Problem Statement: In this work, we consider the problem of data placement to reduce computation time as well as to increase availability of data besides enhanced scheduling of tasks.

Objective of the Proposed Work: The two major objectives of the work have been presented below to summarize the novelty of the proposed work.

Contribution 1: Devise a methodology to find minimum number of partitions and placed them properly as opposed to the other algorithms where the partition placement is decided randomly.

Contribution 2: Derived a correlation between availability and execution time for improved scheduling.

Algorithm 1: Parttion Creation

Input   : Input: Graph $G(v,e)$
Output: Set of partition P
$P_i \leftarrow$ Calculate distances using $BFS(G(v,e))$
$k \leftarrow$ Find optimal number of clusters using $Silhouette\_score()$
$linkage \leftarrow$ 'average'
$Agglomerative\_Hierarchical\_Clustering(P_i, k, linkage)$

---

3   Methodology

In this work, we have proposed a partition placement mechanism for Distributed graph processing system. Initially, we have partitioned the graph into multiple partitions and used genetic algorithm for proper placement of partition. A set of processors is represented as a chromosome. The availability of each processor has been calculated and based on which we have sorted the processor position within a chromosome. At first, each partition has been assigned to the processor randomly. Then basic operations of the genetic algorithm like selection, crossover, and mutation are followed. After certain number of generations, we have obtained a near-optimal best solution.

The proposed work has been divided into two phases:

1. Phase I or Partitioning: Divided the graph into several partitions.
2. Phase II or Partition allocation: Allocating each partition into a processor.

Phase I: Partitioning. In this phase, we have divided the graph into several partitions. A Graph partitioning problem is an NP-hard problem. Here at first, we have created an adjacency matrix; value of the adjacency matrix has been calculated through Breadth-First Search (BFS). This adjacency matrix has been fed as input to an agglomerative hierarchical clustering algorithm to get the appropriate partition [5, 7, 12]. The optimal number of clusters has been decided using the Silhouette score [11, 18]. Algorithm 1 explains the working of the Phase 1.

Phase II or Partition Allocation. In this phase, we have proposed a mechanism to maximize the availability of the computed nodes for job execution. The proposed Availability model is built based on the trust model followed in literature [1, 15]. Availability is defined as the possibility that the nodes are available for a given time period [19]. Availability depends on MTTF (Average time to failure means expected time required for two consecutive failures), and MTTR is (Average time to recovery or mean time to restore means expected time required for consecutive repairs from failure) of a compute node. Availability of a node n at a time t has been defined in Eq. 1 $A_i(t)$, of the i the node for time t.

$$A_i(t) = MTTF_i/(MTTF_i + MTTR_i) \qquad (1)$$

The proposed systems follow M/M/s Model [15], and therefore, each compute node has its own load and service rate. T_i is the average number of tasks arriving per unit of time, Ser_i is the average number of Tasks completing the service per unit time and L_i is considered as a system load (total number of instruction already assigned to a compute node). So, the first part of Eq. 2 states the waiting time for each node. Consequently, to find the total execution time of each node i for executing p number of tasks allocated to a particular partition (pr) is defined as in Eq. 2.

$$\sum_{j=1}^{p}(L_i/(Ser_i - T_i) + (1/Ser_i) * INT_j)) \qquad (2)$$

INT_j is the number of instructions present in the j task. Here, we have selected the number of compute nodes based on partition number and consider that each partition node must be allocated to a single compute node.

N_1	N_2	N_3	N_4	N_5
P_4	P_1	P_2	P_3	P_0
T_1-T_{20}	T_1-T_{50}	T_1-T_{14}	T_1-T_{30}	T_1-T_{15}

Fig. 1. Phase II: initial population

In this phase, we have used a genetic algorithm for proper placement of partition into a compute node so that the execution time reduces and availability of the overall system increases. We have considered each chromosome containing a compute node, partitions, and allocated tasks for each partition as depicted in Fig. 1. Initially, we have determined the availability of each node by using Eq. 1. The first part of the chromosome contains compute node whose position in a chromosome is sorted in descending order based on the availability of the compute node and has been fixed for all generations. Here, each iteration is called a generation. At first, all partitions are allocated to the computed node randomly. Later, the other three operations: Selection, crossover, and mutation were performed to get the best solution. In the selection phase, parents are selected. The selection of parents depends on execution time computed through Eq. 2. In the crossover, the parents are crossover to produce a new child and then in mutation, the offspring has been altered based on the mutation rule. The above steps have been drafted in Algorithms 2 and 3.

Selection: For selection operation, the genetic algorithm [20] uses plenty of selection functions like Rank Selection, Elitism, and Roulette-wheel. Among all Roulette-wheel method has been chosen mostly as a selection operator [1]. In this

---

Algorithm 2: GA-PS (Efficient genetic algorithm for partition scheduling)

Input: A set of partition
Crossover Probability
Mutation Probability
Size of Gen_Number
Size of Population
Number of Processors
Load of each processors
Service rate for each processor
Number of task allocated for each partition
Task size for each partition
Output: Proper placement of partition and accordingly execution time is
        evaluated
1. call Initial Population.
2. repeat
3. Selection
4. Crossover
5. Mutation
6. until Gen_Number

Algorithm 3: Initial Population

Input: A set of partition, MTTR, MTTF
Output: Initial population
1. **for** *each processor* **do**
  | Calculate *availability* $= MTTF/(MTTF + MTTR)$
    end
2. Sort processor in descending order based on availability
3. Generate an initial population by random partition allocated to each processor

---

method, at each iteration, a point has been chosen on the wheel circumference and the wheel is rotated. The region which comes in front of the fixed point has been chosen as the first parent. The same procedure has been followed for the second parent selection. Individual solution thus has a greater part on the wheel and thus has a greater chance of selection. In this proposed algorithm, Roulette-wheel method has been chosen for selection. Here, we have placed each solution on the wheel. Individual chromosome calculates their fitness by using Eq. 2. Based on fitness value, some solution has been selected as the best solution. The mechanism has been explained in Algorithm 4.

Crossover: In the 3rd phase Crossover operation has been performed to produce new chromosomes. We have created two children chromosomes from two parent chromosomes. Here, we have used single point cross-over. Some parts of the first parent and some parts of the second parent are directly transmitted

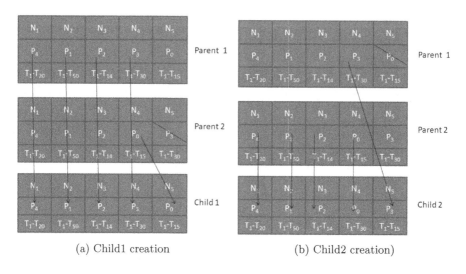

(a) Child1 creation   (b) Child2 creation)

Fig. 2. Crossover

Algorithm 4: Selection

Input: Current population
Output: New Selected Population
1. The fitness value of each individual in the population is calculated by using Eq. 2
2. Select best chromosomes based on execution time and add them to the Selected Population
3. Calculate the sum of fitness.
4. From the first population, continue add partial sum with finesses
5. The individual for whom Partial fitness are small have been chosen as individual.

---

to the child1. The constraint associated with such transmission is no repeated occurrence of partitions in a given chromosome. We followed the same procedure to create a child2 and maintaining the same constraint. The only difference is that the transmission mechanism is reversed. The phrase is thoroughly explained in Algorithm 5 and Fig. 2.

Mutation: The 4th phrase of the genetic algorithm is Mutation. It has been used to maintain genetic diversity from one generation of a population of chromosomes to the next. Based on probability, it alters the genes. The sample size has been increased to avoid local optimums. Here, a gene or partition is randomly selected in each chromosome and is altered with another partition. Details are explained in Algorithm 6 and Fig. 3.

Algorithm 5: Crossover

Input: Two parents from the current population
Output: Two new children
1. Randomly crossover point i has been selected.
2. Cut both parent's chromosomes from the i th position
3. First, part genes from father's chromosome have been stored in son's chromosome
4. The part from the mother's chromosome that does not appear in the father's chromosome has been copied to the right part of the son's chromosome.
5. The first part of the mother's chromosome has been stored into daughter's chromosome
6. The part from the fathers' chromosome that does not appear in the mother's chromosome has been copied to the right part of the daughter's chromosome.
7. Replace any two randomly selected chromosomes with these two new children

Algorithm 6: Mutation

Input: A randomly chosen chromosome
Output: A new chromosome
1. Choose randomly a partition/gene p_i
2. Generate a new child by interchanging the partition p_i with another partition p_j of same chromosomes

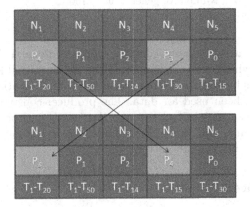

Fig. 3. Mutation

4   Experimental Observations

The proposed failure recovery method has been evaluated on two benchmark data-sets. Data-set 1 and data-set 2 have been derived from two email data-sets from two departments of a European research institution [13]. Each data-set has a set of nodes and edges, where connecting edges between two nodes A and B describe that user connectivity. An edge has been created between A and B when A has sent an email to user B [9]. The number of nodes and edges of each data-set has been explained in Table 1.

Table 1. Dataset description

Dataset#	#Nodes	#Edges
Dataset 1	309	3031
Dataset 2	142	1375

Table 2. Parameter description

Parameter#	#Values
MTTR	10–240S
MTTF	900–2400S
Probability of crossover	0.6
Probability of mutation	0.1
Number of generation	100

The communication between compute nodes is done through the peer-to-peer mechanism, which has been simulated through a virtual local area network (VLAN). UDP has been used for connection less communication between nodes. Transfer TCP has been used for data. The producer-consumer model of communication has been maintained through the Gossip protocol. A node pushes data into the channel and the receiver pulls data from the channel. Message generation follows the pub-sub pattern.

4.1 Performance Evaluation

The proposed data placement strategy has been evaluated on two benchmark data-sets. Initially, for each data-set, partitioning is performed through an agglomerative hierarchical clustering algorithm. We have varied the value from 2 to 10 to find the optimal number of partition pr and partition number have been fixed by using seen Silhouette score as shown in Fig. 4. Here, the performance of the proposed data placement technique is evaluated by changing its parameters. In each experiment, we have changed one particular parameter keeping the other parameters unchanged. Data used in the experiments are randomly generated and the parameter list is given in Table 2. Here, we consider that each partition has been assigned in a single compute node. We have calculated availability by using MTTF and MTTR. We have set computed node position in chromosomes based on descending order of their availability.

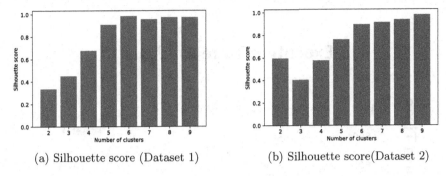

(a) Silhouette score (Dataset 1)   (b) Silhouette score(Dataset 2)

Fig. 4. Optimal number of clusters for the three datasets

In our experiment, we have considered three parameters like task size, number of task assigned to a partition and load of a computed node which greatly influences execution time. We have varied one of the parameter at a time and compare its performance with randomly placed partition technique.

Experiment with Varying Load of Compute Node. In Fig. 6, We here perform our experiment on Data-set1 having 309 nodes. It has been shown that if we place the partition randomly when load of each computed node is 50 to 100 the execution time is 998 s but after applying proposed algorithm at Data-set1 execution time is converge below 610 s. After changing the load from 10–50, Data-set1 execution time is converge below 400 s after 100 generations, without proposed mechanism the value is around 600 s. To validate our experiment, the same mechanism is tested on Data-set2 which have 142 nodes, it has been observed that after varying the load within the range of 10–50, Data-set2 execution time is below 150 s which above 300 s if they are placed randomly. Subsequently by changing the load 50 to 100 the execution time reaches 200 s.

Experiment with Varying Task Size: In next phase of our experiment, we vary the size of the task assigned to each partition from 80–100 and 100–150 assigned for each partition to show the effect on execution time. Initially by assigning task with Size of 80–100 without Genetic algorithm, the execution time will become 998 s for Data-set1 and for Data-set2 1350 s. We have defined that task execution time minimization indirectly implies that partition have been placed in proper compute node. By using genetic algorithm, the task size is below 100 KB data-set1 converges within 610 s and for Data-set2 it is less than 210 s. By increasing the size to 150 KB after 100 generations, Data-set1 converges within 1010 s and Data-set2 converges and takes less than 740 s. This has been shown in Fig. 5.

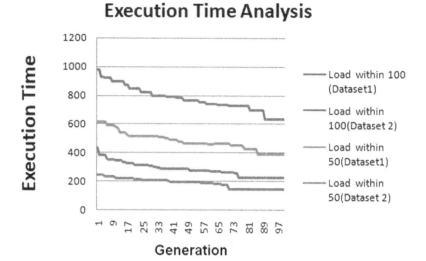

Fig. 5. Execution time analysis by varying load of each compute node

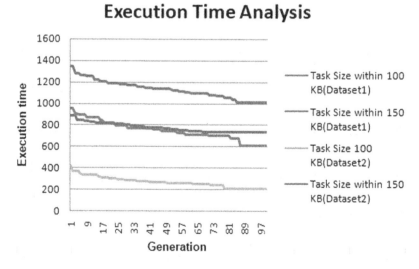

Fig. 6. Execution time analysis by varying task size of each task assigned to a particular partition

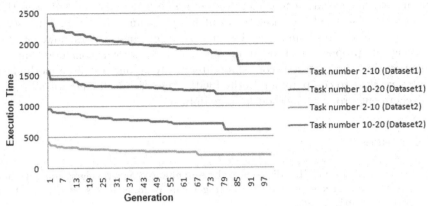

Fig. 7. Execution time analysis by varying number of task allocated for each partition

Experiment with Varying Number of Tasks: In this experiment, we have changed only numbers of tasks assigned to each partition whereas the other parameters are remain constant, which has been shown in Fig. 7. It has been observed that when number of tasks is less than 20, Data-set1 converges at 100 generation and execution time became 650 s, for Data-set2 the time is 250 s. Whereas if we placed them normally without using proposed algorithm, then the execution time has been reaches 1000 s for Data-set1 and 400 s for Data-set2. In another variant, when the number of tasks is varied from 20–60, the execution time for Data-set1 converges in less than 1700 s and for Data-set2 within 1200 s whereas without proposed algorithm the execution time reaches 2300 s for Data-set1 and 1600 s for Data-set2.

5   Conclusion

Now a days, in many big data applications uses graph representation. Such graph is divided into several partitions and placed at compute node. Proper placement of such partitions in the compute nodes indirectly decreases execution time of any request. This also indicates that proper placement increases availability of data. Availability is an important factor that has been being highly neglected. Here, we have emphasized how to increase availability of data by placed them properly. We have used meta-heuristic technique genetic algorithm for placement. At first, we have partitioned the graph by using agglomerative hierarchical clustering where the optimal number of partitions has been decided through Silhouette Score. After the partition, availability of each compute node has been compute through MTTF and MTTR. Based on availability, we have fixed the position of compute node in a chromosome. The initial population creates schedules randomly. The crossover and mutation has been performed to optimize execution time in genetic algorithm selection. The proposed method has been evaluated through two benchmark data-sets. It has been evident that after changing several parameters, the execution time converges to a minimal value that indicates that proper data placement increases the availability. As an example for Data-set1if we placed the partition randomly then the execution time is 900 s, however after applying our proposed method it became 600 s. So we can conclude that the execution time has almost become half after applying our proposed method. In future, we want to compare our method with other standard methods and want to execute our proposed method in large data-sets.

References

1. Akbari, M., Rashidi, H., Alizadeh, S.H.: An enhanced genetic algorithm with new operators for task scheduling in heterogeneous computing systems. Eng. Appl. Artif. Intell. **61**, 35–46 (2017)
2. Alekseev, V.E., Boliac, R., Korobitsyn, D.V., Lozin, V.V.: NP-hard graph problems and boundary classes of graphs. Theoret. Comput. Sci. **389**(1–2), 219–236 (2007)
3. Bentley, J.L.: Multidimensional divide-and-conquer. Commun. ACM **23**(4), 214–229 (1980)
4. Cameron, K., Eschen, E.M., Hoàng, C.T., Sritharan, R.: The complexity of the list partition problem for graphs. SIAM J. Discret. Math. **21**(4), 900–929 (2008)
5. Day, W.H., Edelsbrunner, H.: Efficient algorithms for agglomerative hierarchical clustering methods. J. Classif. **1**(1), 7–24 (1984)
6. Golab, L., Hadjieleftheriou, M., Karloff, H., Saha, B.: Distributed data placement to minimize communication costs via graph partitioning. In: Proceedings of the 26th International Conference on Scientific and Statistical Database Management, pp. 1–12 (2014)
7. Gowda, K.C., Krishna, G.: Agglomerative clustering using the concept of mutual nearest neighbourhood. Pattern Recogn. **10**(2), 105–112 (1978)
8. Kalavri, V., Vlassov, V., Haridi, S.: High-level programming abstractions for distributed graph processing. IEEE Trans. Knowl. Data Eng. **30**(2), 305–324 (2017)
9. Leskovec, J., Mcauley, J.: Learning to discover social circles in ego networks. Adv. Neural Inf. Process. Syst. **25** (2012)
10. Lu, W., Shen, Y., Wang, T., Zhang, M., Jagadish, H.V., Du, X.: Fast failure recovery in vertex-centric distributed graph processing systems. IEEE Trans. Knowl. Data Eng. **31**(4), 733–746 (2018)
11. Margo, D., Seltzer, M.: A scalable distributed graph partitioner. Proc. VLDB Endow. **8**(12), 1478–1489 (2015)
12. Murtagh, F., Contreras, P.: Algorithms for hierarchical clustering: an overview, II. Wiley Interdisc. Rev.: Data Min. Knowl. Discov. **7**(6), e1219 (2017)
13. Paranjape, A., Benson, A.R., Leskovec, J.: Motifs in temporal networks. In: Proceedings of the tenth ACM International Conference on Web Search and Data Mining, pp. 601–610 (2017)
14. Phan, T., Ranganathan, K., Sion, R.: Evolving toward the perfect schedule: co-scheduling job assignments and data replication in wide-area systems using a genetic algorithm. In: Feitelson, D., Frachtenberg, E., Rudolph, L., Schwiegelshohn, U. (eds.) JSSPP 2005. LNCS, vol. 3834, pp. 173–193. Springer, Heidelberg (2005). https://doi.org/10.1007/11605300_9

15. Prakash, S., Vidyarthi, D.P.: Maximizing availability for task scheduling in computational grid using genetic algorithm. Concurr. Comput.: Pract. Exp. **27**(1), 193–210 (2015)
16. Rahimian, F., Payberah, A.H., Girdzijauskas, S., Jelasity, M., Haridi, S.: A distributed algorithm for large-scale graph partitioning. ACM Trans. Auton. Adapt. Syst. (TAAS) **10**(2), 1–24 (2015)
17. Sajjad, H.P., Rahimian, F., Vlassov, V.: Smart partitioning of geo-distributed resources to improve cloud network performance. In: 2015 IEEE 4th International Conference on Cloud Networking (CloudNet), pp. 112–118. IEEE (2015)
18. Shahapure, K.R., Nicholas, C.: Cluster quality analysis using silhouette score. In: 2020 IEEE 7th International Conference on Data Science and Advanced Analytics (DSAA), pp. 747–748. IEEE (2020)
19. Sun, J., Dong, X., Zhang, X., Wang, Y.: An availability approached task scheduling algorithm in heterogeneous fault-tolerant system. In: 2014 9th IEEE International Conference on Networking, Architecture, and Storage, pp. 275–280. IEEE (2014)
20. Whitley, D.: A genetic algorithm tutorial. Stat. Comput. **4**(2), 65–85 (1994)

Embedded Processor Design in FPGA by ASMD-FSMD and FSM-Single Techniques

Valery Salauyou[✉] [iD]

Bialystok University of Technology, Wiejska 45A, 15-351 Bialystok, Poland
v.salauyou@pb.edu.pl

Abstract. The ASMD-FSMD technique for designing digital devices consists in building an algorithmic state machine with data-path (ASMD) describing the behavior of the device, and creating a project code in Verilog language in the form of a finite state machine with data-path (FSMD). The ASMD-FSMD technique significantly reduces the design time and increases the speed of digital devices when the device can be presented as an operating unit (data-path) and a control unit in the form of a finite state machine (FSM). The paper considers the use of ASMD-FSMD technique for designing embedded processors on the example of PIC-processors on FPGA. The ASMD-FSMD technique is compared to the traditional approach and the *FSM-single* technique, which uses the control unit of the single-cycle processor to build the multi-cycle processors. For each technique, the design features of the one-, two-, three-, and four-cycle PIC-processors are described. It has been shown that although the FSM-single and ASMD-FSMD techniques are slightly inferior to the traditional approach in terms of implementation cost, they allow significantly (5–8 times) to reduce design time. In addition, the ASMD-FSMD technique allows you to increase the performance of processors, in some cases by 40%. Recommendations are given on the use of the considered techniques of design of embedded processors on field programmable gate array (FPGA).

Keywords: Algorithm state machine with data-path (ASMD) · Finite state machines with data-path (FSMD) · Embedded processor · Field programmable gate array (FPGA) · Design technique · Verilog language · Finite state machine (FSM)

1 Introduction

To execute programs and algorithms, modern field-programmable gate arrays (FPGAs) often include processors called embedded processors. The need to design a processor in the FPGA may arise when

- the processor implements the application-specific instruction set;
- the processor is required to execute one particular program, in which case the FPGA resources used can be significantly reduced;
- the original processor with its instruction set is implemented.

K. Saeed and J. Dvorský (Eds.): CISIM 2022, LNCS 13293, pp. 374–389, 2022.
https://doi.org/10.1007/978-3-031-10539-5_27

In addition, prototypes of new processors are often implemented on FPGA for their subsequent research.

Usually, when developing a new processor, a single-cycle processor project is first built. The prototype single-cycle processor tests the main ideas (concepts) that form the basis of the processor being developed, examines the effectiveness of the processor architecture, clarifies the processor instruction set, etc. Then, on the basis of a single-cycle processor, multi-cycle processors are built, which are the basis for creating pipeline processors.

Developing a new processor requires a lot of time and effort from the developer. The question arises: is it possible to reduce the development time of a new processor? This paper is intended to answer this question.

For this purpose, three embedded processor design techniques are considered in the paper: the traditional approach, the FSM-single (FSM – finite state machine) technique and the ASMD-FSMD technique. The original PIC-processor was chosen as the design object. For each technique, the design features of the single-, two-, three-, and four-cycle PIC-processors (PIC – peripheral interface controller) are described.

The main contributions of this paper are

- the concept of PIC-processor based on the instruction set architecture of PIC16F84A microcontroller is proposed;
- the structural scheme of the single-cycle PIC-processor is proposed;
- the design algorithms for single-cycle and multi-cycle PIC-processor in the case of traditional approach are developed;
- the FSM-single design technique for multi-cycle processors based on a single-cycle processor is proposed;
- the generalized ASMDs for single- and multi-cycle PIC-processor is developed;
- PIC-processor designs have been developed using the traditional approach as well as the ASMD-FSMD and FSM-single techniques;
- developed PIC processor designs were investigated in their implementation on FPGAs;
- the recommendations are given on the practical use of the traditional approach, the ASMD-FSMD technique and the FSM-single technique in designing embedded processors on FPGA.

The novelty of the proposed paper is for the first time the problem of reducing the development time of embedded processors is considered; for this purpose two techniques are proposed: the ASMD-FSMD technique and the FSM-single technique; for the first time it is shown by means of experimental research (as well as explained theoretically) that ASMD-FSMD and FSM-single techniques can reduce the development time of embedded processors by 5–8 times.

The main goal of the proposed paper is to reduce the development time of embedded processors, possibly at the expense of a small increase in implementation cost.

The article is organized as follows. Section 2 presents the most popular techniques for designing embedded processors. Section 3 discusses the PIC-processor. Section 4 describes the traditional approach to processor design and Sect. 5 describes the FSM-single technique. Section 6 deals with the ASMD-FSMD methodology. Section 7 presents the results of experimental studies.

2 Related Works and Hypothesis

The design of embedded processors plays an important role in the development of embedded systems on the FPGA. A huge number of papers are devoted to this topic. Only some of them are considered here.

In [1], the LISA language is proposed to describe application-specific instruction set processor (ASIP) this allows you to automatically create the software and hardware parts of the embedded system on the FPGA. The FPGA prototyping of a RISC processor core for embedded applications is discussed in [2]. The control device is presented as communicating finite state machines (FSMs), each FSM controlling a separate stage of the pipeline.

Several design techniques of application-specific processors (ASPs) are known. In [3], the ASP is created by extending the instruction set of the base processor. The design of a speed- and power-optimized ASP, using the digital signal processing (DSP) problem as an example, is described in [4].

Many works are also devoted to multiprocessor systems. In [5], a pipeline multiprocessor system design technique is proposed for data transfer applications. An overview of methodologies and algorithms for designing multiprocessor system-on-chip (MPSoC) is given in [6].

Techniques for designing embedded processors are described in many works. In [7], the design technique for FPGA modular processor with very long instruction word (VLIW) is proposed. In [8], the architecture and the design methodology for FPGA for real-time embedded systems are described. A technique for designing a fault-tolerant processor that uses the reconfiguration property of modern FPGAs is discussed in [9].

In a number of papers, it is proposed to use hardware accelerators on FPGA to improve the performance of embedded systems. The technique LegUp for high-level synthesis of the embedded system on the FPGA, which consists of an integrated processor and hardware accelerators, is presented in [10]. The technique of designing a service-oriented system on a chip, which combines embedded processors and hardware accelerators, is discussed in [11].

Recently, much attention has been paid to designing processors on FPGA with the open instruction set RISC-V [12]. In [13], the RISC-V processor for vector systems on the FPGA is described. The techniques for designing the RISC-V processors based on high-level synthesis using the C language and an universal verification methodology (UVM) are offered in [14] and [15].

The reconfigurable architecture of the embedded processor on the FPGA to reduce power consumption is discussed in [16]. The same problem is solved by reconfiguring at the thread and memory level in [17].

In [18], the high-performance convolution neural networks (CNN) processor on FPGA for solving computer vision problems is offered. The technique of the choice of microarchitecture of processors for the Internet of things (IoT) is presented in [19].

None of the papers reviewed investigates the problem of reducing the development time of embedded processors.

Hypothesis: ASMD-FSMD and FSM-single technologies can significantly reduce the development time of embedded processors.

3 PIC- Processor

The instruction-set architecture of the popular microcontroller PIC16F84A [20] is taken as the basis of the implemented PIC-processor. In this architecture (Fig. 1) one of the operands always is in an accumulator W, and the other operand arrives from a register file (RF). The location of the result is determined by the value of the bit d, which is in the instruction code. When $d = 0$, the result is placed in the accumulator W, and at $d = 1$, the result is written back to the register file.

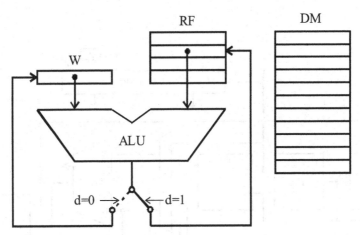

Fig. 1. The architecture of the PIC-processor instruction set.

The PIC-processor [21], unlike the microcontroller PIC16F84A, uses traditional data memory (DM) of the type RAM. To interact the processor with data memory, two additional instructions are entered into the PIC-processor instruction set: lw – load the value to the accumulator W from the data memory and sw – store the value of the accumulator W into the data memory. To be able to branch programs, two new commands were added to the PIC-processor instruction set: $gotoz$ - go to the address if the result of the previous operation is zero, and $gotonz$ - go to the address if the result of the previous operation is not zero. The PIC-processor instruction set is shown in [21].

4 Traditional Approach to Embedded Processor Design

The technique for designing processors on the FPGA is described in [22], which is repeated in [23]. This technique will be called the *traditional approach*, with which we will compare the proposed techniques.

4.1 Designing of the Single-Cycle Processor

The main feature of the single-cycle processor is that all instructions are executed during one clock cycle. The design of a single-cycle processor begins with the definition of processor memory elements. Such elements are the program counter (PC), the instruction memory (IM), the register file (RF), the data memory (DM), and the accumulator W.

The single-cycle PIC-processor is shown in Fig. 2, where *ffc* is flip-flop, *we* is write enable. The data-path components are connected by buses and multiplexers. The controller, based on the instruction word, the zero flag z and the zero flag of the previous operation pz, generates selection signals for multiplexers, as well as control signals for the memory elements and the circuit PC-logic. The detailed description of the design process for the single-cycle PIC-processor using the traditional approach and the Verilog-code of the design are presented in [21].

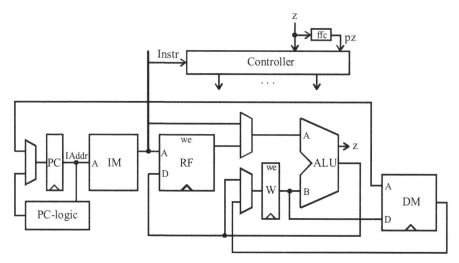

Fig. 2. The diagram of the single-cycle PIC-processor.

The design of a single-cycle processor consists in the development of the circuit for determining the address of the next instruction (PC-logic), the operating device (data-path), the arithmetic logic unit (ALU) and the control device (controller). All these devices are developed in parallel. In this case, separate groups of PIC-processor instructions are sequentially considered and the necessary components are added to the structure of each device to implement this group of instructions. The technique of designing a single-cycle processor can be presented in the form of the following algorithm.

Algorithm 1. Designing the single-cycle PIC-processor using the traditional approach.

1. Define of processor memory elements.
2. Create the circuit PC-logic to determine the address of the next instruction.
3. Define the data-path components to implement the certain groups of instructions.
4. Create the ALU.
5. Create the controller as the combinational circuit.

4.2 Designing of the Multi-cycle Processor

In a multi-cycle processor, the execution of each instruction is divided into stages. Typical stages for executing multi-cycle instructions are Fetch, Decode, Execute, and Memory.

The data-path components of the single-cycle and multi-cycle processors largely coincide. The main differences between a single-clock and a multi-clock processor are in their control devices. The multi-cycle processor control device in case of the traditional approach is presented as the Moore finite state machine (FSM).

Designing of the multi-cycle processor consists in sequential determination of the FSM states (Fig. 3): for fetching the instruction (state S0), for decoding the instruction (state S1), as well as for implementing the certain groups of the instructions (states S2–S15). The transition paths from state S1 are determined by the hallmarks (codes) of the instruction or the group of instructions. In each state, control signals are determined that must be set to 1 to implement the corresponding instruction (the group of instructions).

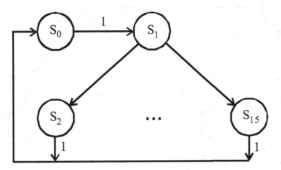

Fig. 3. The FSM graph of the multi-cycle PIC-processor

The technique of designing a multi-cycle processor can be presented in the form of the following algorithm.

Algorithm 2. Designing the multi-cycle PIC-processor using the traditional approach.

1. Define of processor memory elements.
2. Create the circuit PC-logic to determine the address of the next instruction.
3. Define the data-path components to implement the certain groups of instructions; add registers to the operating device necessary to build a multi-clock processor.
4. Create the ALU.
5. Create the controller as the Moore FSM.

In the multi-cycle processor, the circuit PC-logic and the ALU completely coincide with similar components of the single-cycle processor. The differences are the addition to the data-path of the registers necessary to build a multi-cycle processor.

Each instruction in Fig. 3 corresponds to a path through three states of the FSM. Therefore, the multi-cycle PIC-processor built according to the above technique is a three-cycle processor, since each instruction in the multi-cycle PIC-processor is executed in three clock cycles. The detailed description of the design process for the multi-cycle PIC-processor using the traditional approach and the Verilog-code of the design are presented in [21].

In the PIC-processor, decoding the instruction is performed by a simple wired connection and does not require a separate clock cycle. Therefore, in the traditional approach, the two-cycle PIC-processor is built by simply combining the states S0 and S1 in Fig. 3.

To build a four-cycle PIC-processor, register A is entered in the structure of the data-path at the input A of the ALU, as well as register O at the output ALU. Recording of data in the registers A and O is controlled by signals awe and owe, respectively. Note that the sw and lw instructions are executed at the Execute stage as normal instructions (Fig. 4).

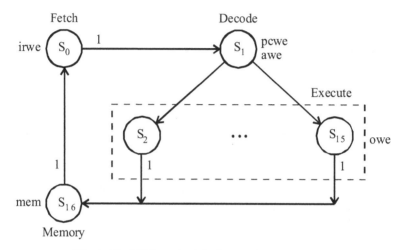

Fig. 4. The FSM graph of the four-cycle PIC-processor

In the Fetch stage (Fig. 4), the instruction is read from the instruction memory IM by the signal *irwe*. In the Decode stage, the operand is written to the register A by signal *awe* and the address of the next instruction is written to the register PC by signal *pcwe*. In the Execute stage, the instruction is executed, and the result is written to the register O by the signal *owe*. In the Memory stage, the result from the register O is placed either in the register file RF or in the accumulator W by the signal *mem*.

5   The FSM-Single Design Methodology for Multi-cycle Processors

Developers spend considerable time designing the control device, since many components of the data-path are standard functional blocks, and the control device for each project needs to be designed again every time. The question arises: is it impossible to use the control device of the single-cycle processor in the multi-cycle processor project? This is possible, and such a technique is called *FSM-single* (combining a FSM and the controller of one-clock processor).

The structure of the four-cycle PIC-processor, which was created using the FSM-single technique, is shown in Fig. 5a. In this structure, the controller is completely the same as the controller of the single-cycle PIC-processor, and the data-path is the same as the data-path of the four-cycle PIC-processor from Subsect. 4.2. In the structure of the PIC-processor in Fig. 5, the FSM is added, which generates signals F, D, E and M, corresponding to the stages of the four-cycle processor.

a)   b)

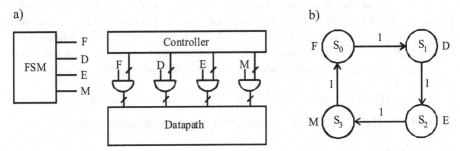

Fig. 5. The four-cycle PIC-processor built according to the FSM-single technique: a – the structure, b – the FSM graph

In Fig. 5a, the control signals of the Data-path are generated by combining (by means of gates AND) the signals F, D, E, and M of the FSM and the signals which are generated by the Controller. The FSM is a simple cyclic Moore FSM (Fig. 5b). The states S0, S1, S2 and S3 of the FSM correspond to the stages of the multi-cycle PIC-processor, the transitions between states are unconditional. In states S0, S1, S2 and S3, the signals F, D, E and M are generated, respectively. The FSM in Fig. 5b is very simple, so the FSM-single technique allows you to significantly reduce the design time of multi-cycle processors, since there is no need to develop a control device.

The two-cycle PIC-processor according to the FSM-single technique is built by combining in the FSM the states S0 and S1, as well as the states S2 and S3 together and using the data-path of the two-cycle PIC-processor from Subsect. 4.2. The Verilog-codes of the two-cycle and four-cycle PIC-processors built using the FSM-single methodology are given in [21].

The three-cycle PIC-processor according to the FSM-single technique is built by combining the states S0 and S1 or S2 and S3 together.

6   ASMD-FSMD Design Technique for Embedded Processors

The development of digital devices by means of the ASMD-FSMD technique consists in creation a flowchart of an algorithmic state machine with data-path (ASMD) and in the description of the Verilog-code in the form of the finite state machine with data-path (FSMD) [24].

The ASMD flowchart consists of ASMD blocks. Each ASMD block describes the behavior of the FSMD in one state during one clock cycle. The ASMD block includes one state box (rectangle) and can have several decision boxes (rhombs) and conditional output boxes (ovals). The ASMD block has only one input, which is the input to the state box, and can have one or more outputs. The inputs and outputs of the boxes are connected by arcs. Feedbacks are prohibited inside the ASMD block. The algorithm loops and waiting states in the ASMD flowchart are implemented by external feedbacks.

For a Moore-type machine, the operations performed in this FSMD state are written inside the state box (rectangle). For the Mealy-type machine, operations performed on this FSMD transition are written inside the conditional output boxes (ovals). Logical expressions are written inside the decision boxes (rhombs). The outputs of the decision box are denoted by values 0 and 1, which correspond to transitions in the case of a false or true value of the logical expression. As the operations which are written down in rectangles and ovals and also as the logical expressions which are written down in rhombuses any operations and logical expressions admissible in the Verilog language can be used.

The ASMD-FSMD technique is presented as the following algorithm.

Algorithm 3. The ASMD-FSMD technique for designing of digital devices.

1. The FSMD states are determined.
2. The ASMD block is constructed for each FSMD state.

   a. In the ASMD decision boxes, the logical expressions are written, the values of which are checked in this state.
   b. For the Moore FSMD, the operations are written in the state box that are performed on the content of the registers in this state.
   c. For the Mealy FSMD, the operations are written in the conditional output box that are performed on the content of the registers on these transitions.

3. The ASMD blocks are connected to each other in accordance with the algorithm of the device operation. Each output of the ASMD block can be connected to only one input of this or other ASMD block.
4. If necessary, the ASMD is modified for increase the performance or the area of the designed device. For example, the algorithm loops are analyzed and the ASMD is changed in such a way as to minimize the number of states in the loop.
5. The Verilog-code of the FSMD is built directly by ASMD. In Verilog code, the variables correspond to the device registers. The logical expressions in the **if** statements correspond to the logical expressions checked in the ASMD conditional boxes. The actions performed in ASMD blocks are described as procedural blocks **begin...end**. For the Moore FSMD, the operations, which are performed in the corresponding ASMD block, are described in state box, and the next states are determined in according to the ASMD transitions. For the Mealy FSMD, all the actions, which are performed in the corresponding ASMD block, are described in the style of the algorithmic description.
6. The FSMD is implemented using the appropriate design tool.
7. End.

Figure 6 shows a general view of the ASMD flowchart for implementing single-cycle PIC-processor instructions. The flowchart in Fig. 6 consists of one ASMD block for the

Mealy FSMD. In Fig. 6, the instruction hallmarks ($i\_1, \ldots, i\_k$) are checked in rhombs, and the actions ($ex\_1, \ldots, ex\_k$) required to implement the particular instruction (in the form of assignment statements assigning expression values to certain variables) are written in ovals. The ASMD flowchart in Fig. 6 can be described as a chain of **if-else-if** statements or with a single **case** statement in Verilog language.

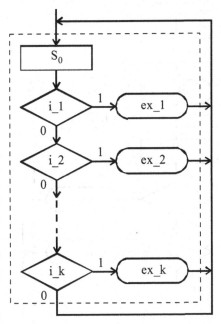

Fig. 6. The ASMD flowchart for implementing single-cycle PIC-processor instructions

In the Verilog-code of the single-cycle PIC-processor created by the ASMD-FSMD technique, the memory elements (the program counter PC, the register file RF, the accumulator W, triggers of the flags c and z, and the stack) are described as separate modules. The main module instantiates memory elements and generates instruction hallmark based on the instruction word. The circuit PC-logic and the implementation of the instruction are described as separate processes (blocks **always**).

The ASMD flowchart of the four-cycle PIC-processor consists of four ASMD blocks, which correspond to the stages of the four-cycle processor (Fig. 7).

The ASMD Execute block in Fig. 7 repeats the ASMD block diagram for a single-cycle PIC-processor, except for the instructions read *lw* and write *sw* of data memory that are implemented in the Memory block.

The ASMD-FSMD two-cycle PIC-processor is built by combining blocks Fetch and Decode, and also Execute and Memory in Fig. 7. The three-cycle PIC-processor can be built either by combining blocks Fetch and Decode, or by combining blocks Execute and Memory in Fig. 7.

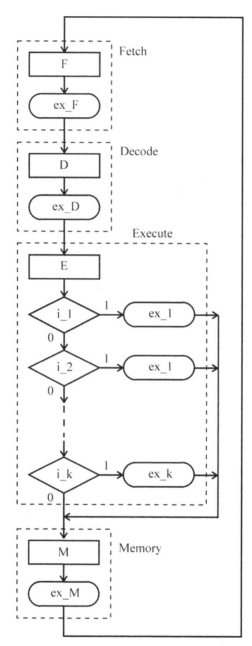

Fig. 7. The ASMD flowchart for four-cycle PIC-processor

7 Experimental Research

The following PIC-processor designs have been developed to test the effectiveness of the embedded processor design techniques reviewed:

- PIC_1_cycle_Tr, PIC_2_cycle_Tr, PIC_3_cycle_Tr, PIC_4_cycle_Tr – single-, two-, three-, and four-cycle PIC-processor designs built using the traditional approach;
- PIC_2_cycle_FSM, PIC_3_cycle_FSM, PIC_4_cycle_FSM – two-, three-, and four-cycle PIC-processor designs built using the FSM-single technique;
- PIC_1_cycle_ASMD,   PIC_2_cycle_ASMD,   PIC_3_cycle_ASMD, PIC_4_cycle_ASMD – single-, two-, three-, and four-cycle PIC-processor designs built using the ASMD-FSMD technique.

Studies of the effectiveness of the techniques considered were carried out when implementing PIC-processors on the family FPGA Cyclone IV E using the system Quartus Prime Standard version 21.1. The PIC-processor designs were investigated with data width N equal to 4, 8, 16, 32, 64 and 128 bits.

The results of the studies are given in Table 1, where L_T, L_F, L_A are the number of FPGA logic elements used (an implementation cost) in the case of the traditional approach, as well as using the techniques FSM-single and ASMD-FSMD, respectively; F_T, F_F, F_A - the maximum synchronization frequency (in megahertz) of the PIC-processor designs in the case of the traditional approach, as well as using the techniques FSM-single and ASMD-FSMD, respectively; L_F/L_T, L_A/L_T, F_F/F_T and F_A/F_T are respective parameter ratios. Table 1 accepts the following design designation: PIC_k_cycle_N, where k is the number of processor cycles, N is the width of the data bus.

Table 2 shows the arithmetic mean values of the respective parameter ratios for the convenience of comparing the various techniques with each other.

Analysis of Table 2 shows that the traditional approach is slightly (by 3–4%) superior to the FSM-single technique in terms of implementation cost. This result is predictable because the FSM is added to the PIC-processor structure. The traditional approach also surpasses the FSM-single technique in speed (by 19–21%). This is due to the fact that the delay of the signals of the processor built using the traditional approach increases by the value of delay of the signals in the FSM (Fig. 5).

Comparing the traditional approach with the ASMD-FSMD technique shows that the traditional approach exceeds the ASMD-FSMD technique in terms of implementation cost (by 9–15%), but is inferior in speed, with the exception of four-cycle processors. In some cases, the superiority of the ASMD-FSMD technique in speed over the traditional approach reaches 40% (the example PIC_2_cycle_128).

However, the main advantage of the FSM-single and ASMD-FSMD techniques over the traditional approach is a significant reduction in the design development time. To evaluate the design time under the traditional approach and using FSM-single and ASMD-FSMD techniques, all projects were created by one developer. The time in minutes spent developing each design is shown in Table 3, where DT_T is the development time (in minutes) in the case of a traditional approach; DT_F - development time in case of using the FSM-single technique; DT_A - development time in case of ASMD-FSMD technique; DT_T/DT_F and DT_T/DT_A - ratio of corresponding parameters; mid is the average value.

Table 1. The research results of the PIC-processor design techniques on FPGA

Processor	LT	L_F	L_A	F_T	F_F	F_A	L_F/L_T	L_A/L_T	F_F/F_T	F_A/F_T
PIC_1_cycle_4	1002	–	1197	70.67	–	71.89	–	1.19	–	1.02
PIC_1_cycle_8	1653	–	1991	66.80	–	69.25	–	1.20	–	1.04
PIC_1_cycle_16	2978	–	3494	67.85	–	66.97	–	1.27	–	0.99
PIC_1_cycle_32	5561	–	6498	53.58	–	57.33	–	1.17	–	1.07
PIC_1_cycle_64	10804	–	12456	52.59	–	51.83	–	1.15	–	0.99
PIC_1_cycle_128	21290	–	24359	39.08	–	39.54	–	1.14	–	1.01
PIC_2_cycle_4	914	1011	1344	84.40	73.85	79.47	1.11	1.47	0.88	0.94
PIC_2_cycle_8	1571	1656	2143	79.79	65.52	73.03	1.05	1.36	0.82	0.92
PIC_2_cycle_16	2909	2940	3497	67.28	68.85	75.34	1.01	1.20	1.02	1.12
PIC_2_cycle_32	5503	5593	6104	60.02	50.21	69.59	1.02	1.11	0.84	1.16
PIC_2_cycle_64	10706	10787	11300	56.11	53.19	68.61	1.01	1.06	0.95	1.22
PIC_2_cycle_128	21202	21262	21834	42.69	40.95	59.96	1.00	1.03	0.96	**1.40**
PIC_3_cycle_4	920	1015	1359	83.17	70.46	76.09	1.10	1.48	0.85	0.91
PIC_3_cycle_8	1571	1656	2160	76.90	65.79	74.43	1.05	1.37	0.86	0.97
PIC_3_cycle_16	2870	2962	3502	74.58	68.03	71.41	1.03	1.22	0.91	0.96
PIC_3_cycle_32	5509	5602	6157	60.33	56.14	69.31	1.02	1.12	0.93	1.15
PIC_3_cycle_64	10718	10801	11304	58.15	52.24	68.29	1.01	1.05	0.90	1.17
PIC_3_cycle_128	21190	21274	21849	43.04	39.78	59.41	1.00	1.03	092	1.38
PIC_4_cycle_4	898	1002	1325	109.15	88.87	70.49	1.12	1.48	0.81	0.65
PIC_4_cycle_8	1577	16832	2198	97.16	91.89	69.52	1.07	1.39	0.95	0.72
PIC_4_cycle_16	2897	2990	3477	97.42	81.56	67.82	1.03	1.20	0.84	0.70
PIC_4_cycle_32	5506	5601	6111	92.20	79.79	67.34	1.02	1.11	0.87	0.73
PIC_4_cycle_64	10739	10831	11260	89.63	60.87	63.71	1.01	1.05	0.68	0.71
PIC_4_cycle_128	21188	21295	21550	50.87	48.61	55.63	1.01	1.02	0.96	1.09

Table 2. Arithmetic averages ratios the implementation cost and the performance of the PIC-processors

Processor	mid (L_F/L_T)	mid (L_A/L_T)	mid (F_F/F_T)	mid (F_A/F_T)
PIC_1_cycle	–	1.19	–	1.02
PIC_2_cycle	1.03	1.20	0.91	1.13
PIC_3_cycle	1.04	1.21	0.90	1.09
PIC_4_cycle	1.04	1.21	0.85	0.77

Table 3. The development time of the PIC-processors (in minutes)

Processor	DTT	DT_F	DT_A	DT_T/DT_F	DT_T/DT_A
PIC_1_cycle	10560	–	1440	–	7.33
PIC_2_cycle	840	103	120	8.16	7.00
PIC_3_cycle	6240	837	960	7.46	6.50
PIC_4_cycle	980	135	150	7.26	6.53
mid				7.66	6.84

Analysis of Table 3 shows that using the FSM-single technique, the development time of the PIC-processors is reduced by 7 to 8 times. This large reduction in the development time is due to the fact that for the design of multi-cycle processors using the FSM-single technique, the controller and the data-path of a single-cycle processor are used, but only the simple FSM is being developed.

Using the ASMD-FSMD technique allows you to reduce the development time of the PIC-processors by 6–7 times. The significant reduction in the development time when using the ASMD-FSMD technique is due to the fact that there is no need to develop and test all components of the data-path, the controller, as well as the top-level module. The design of the processor, built according to the ASMD-FSMD technique, consists of one module in the Verilog language, plus the modules of the memory elements.

Thus, the hypothesis that the ASMD-FSMD technique and the FSM-single technique significantly reduce the development time of embedded processors has been fully confirmed.

The results allow us to make the following practical recommendations:

- if the main optimization criterion is the implementation cost, then the traditional approach is out of competition;
- if the main optimization criterion is the performance, then you should choose between the traditional approach and the ASMD-FSMD technique;
- if the development time is important and there is already a single-cycle processor design built using the traditional approach, then multi-cycle processors can be quickly developed using the FSM-single technique;
- if the main criterion is the development time and there is no a single-cycle processor design, then use the ASMD-FSMD technique.

8 Conclusions

The conducted research has shown that the ASMD-FSMD technique can be effectively used to design embedded processors on FPGA. Comparison of the ASMD-FSMD technique with the traditional approach and FSM-single technique showed that the ASMD-FSMD technique, in addition to reducing the design time, also allows to increase the processor performance, in some cases by 40%.

The ASMD-FSMD technique can be used to design processors not only on the FPGA, but also on an application-specific integrated circuit (ASIC). The ASMD-FSMD technique can also be used in the case of using VHDL or other hardware description languages, not necessarily Verilog.

Acknowledgements. The present study was supported by a grant WZ/WI-IIT/4/2020 from Bialystok University of Technology and founded from the resources for research by Ministry of Science and Higher Education.

References

1. Hoffmann, A., et al.: A novel methodology for the design of application-specific instruction-set processors (ASIPs) using a machine description language. IEEE Trans. Comput. Aided Des. Integr. Circuits Syst. **20**(11), 1338–1354 (2001)
2. Gschwind, M., Salapura, V., Maurer D.: FPGA prototyping of a RISC processor core for embedded applications. IEEE Trans. Very Large Scale Integr. (VLSI) Syst. **9**(2), 241–250 (2001)
3. Sun, F., et al.: A scalable synthesis methodology for application-specific processors. IEEE Trans. Very Large Scale Integr. (VLSI) Syst. **14**(11), 1175–1188 (2006)
4. Sengupta, A., Sedaghat, R., Zeng, Z.: Hardware efficient design of speed optimized power stringent application specific processor. In: International Conference on Microelectronics-ICM, pp. 173–176. IEEE, Marrakech (2009)
5. Shee, S.L., et al.: Design methodology for pipelined heterogeneous multiprocessor system. In.: 44th ACM/IEEE Design Automation Conference, pp. 811–816. IEEE, San Diego (2007)
6. Wolf, W., Jerraya, A.A., Martin, G.: Multiprocessor system-on-chip (MPSoC) technology. IEEE Trans. Comput. Aided Des. Integr. Circuits Syst. **27**(10), 1701–1713 (2008)
7. Saptono, D., et al.: Concept and development of modular VLIW processor based on FPGA. In.: Second International Conference on Computer and Network Technology, pp. 561–565. IEEE, Bangkok (2010)
8. Oliveira, A.S.R., Almeida, L., de Brito Ferrari, A.: The ARPA-MT embedded SMT processor and its RTOS hardware accelerator. IEEE Trans. Ind. Electron. **58**(3), 890–904 (2009)
9. Psarakis, M., Apostolakis, A.: Fault tolerant FPGA processor based on runtime reconfigurable modules. In.: 17th IEEE European Test Symposium (ETS), pp. 1–6. IEEE, Annecy (2012)
10. Fort, B., et al.: Automating the design of processor/accelerator embedded systems with legup high-level synthesis. In.: 12th IEEE International Conference on Embedded and Ubiquitous Computing, pp. 120–129. IEEE, Milano (2014)
11. Wang, C., et al.: Service-oriented architecture on FPGA-based MPSoC. IEEE Trans. Parallel Distrib. Syst. **28**(10), 2993–3006 (2017)
12. Höller, R., et al.: Open-source RISC-V processor IP cores for FPGAs—overview and evaluation. In.: 8th Mediterranean Conference on Embedded Computing (MECO), pp. 1–6. IEEE, Budva (2019)
13. Johns, M., Kazmierski, T.J.: A minimal RISC-V vector processor for embedded systems. In.: Forum for Specification and Design Languages (FDL), pp. 1–4. IEEE, Kiel (2020)
14. Chen, J., et al.: Design and verification of RISC-V CPU based on HLS and UVM. In.: IEEE International Conference on Computer Science, Electronic Information Engineering and Intelligent Control Technology (CEI), pp. 659–664. IEEE, Fuzhou (2021)
15. Yoshiya, E., Nakanishi, T., Isshiki, T.: RTL design framework for embedded processor by using C++ description. In.: Design, Automation & Test in Europe Conference & Exhibition (DATE), pp. 1208–1211. IEEE, Virtual Conference (2021)

16. Tamimi, S., et al.: An efficient SRAM-based reconfigurable architecture for embedded processors. IEEE Trans. Comput. Aided Des. Integr. Circuits Syst. **38**(3), 466–479 (2018)

17. Jain, S., Lin, L., Alioto, M.: Processor energy-performance range extension beyond voltage scaling via drop-in methodologies. IEEE J. Solid-State Circ. **55**(10), 2670–2679 (2020)

18. Wu, D., et al.: A high-performance CNN processor based on FPGA for MobileNets. In.: 29th International Conference on Field Programmable Logic and Applications (FPL), pp. 136–143. IEEE, Barcelona (2019)

19. Kansakar, P., Munir, A.: Selecting microarchitecture configuration of processors for internet of things. IEEE Trans. Emerg. Top. Comput. **8**(4), 973–985 (2018)

20. Wilmshurst, T.: Designing Embedded Systems with PIC Microcontrollers: Principles and Applications. Elsevier, Oxford (2006)

21. Salauyou, V.V.: Functional block design of embedded systems on FPGA. Hotline– Telecom, Moscow, Russia (2020). (in Russian)

22. Harris, S.L., Harris, D.: Digital Design and Computer Architecture, ARM Morgan Kaufmann, San Francisco (2013)

23. Li, Y., et al.: Computer Principles and Design in Verilog HDL. Wiley, Singapore (2015)

24. Solov'ev, V.V.: ASMD-FSMD technique in designing signal processing devices on field programmable gate arrays. J. Commun. Technol. Electron. **66**(12), 1336–1345 (2021)

Evolutionary Optimization of UAVs Deployment for k-Coverage Problem

Krzysztof Trojanowski[iD], Artur Mikitiuk[iD], and Jakub A. Grzeszczak[(✉)][iD]

Cardinal Stefan Wyszyński University in Warsaw,
Wóycickiego 1/3, 01-938 Warsaw, Poland
jakub.grzeszczak@uksw.edu.pl

Abstract. Unmanned aerial vehicles (UAVs) with base stations can deliver communication and support services in emergency conditions. Their positions over, e.g., a disaster or festive area, are of utmost importance for ground users' connectivity quality. We propose a new model of UAVs deployment optimization problem to minimize the number of UAVs used to provide wireless coverage. An evolutionary approach equipped with the problem-specific representation of solution and perturbation operators reduces the number of UAVs by their smart deployment over the area. For simulations, we propose a new set of benchmark problems. Simulation results show the algorithm's efficiency and reveal the most beneficial values of the algorithm's parameters.

Keywords: Unmanned aerial vehicles · Efficient placement ·
Evolutionary algorithm · k-coverage problem

1 Introduction

Ad-hoc wireless communication systems providing coverage to ground users can be found in several real-world scenarios: disaster or festive areas management, military operations, and more. A swarm of UAVs (Unmanned Aerial Vehicles) carrying MBSs (Mobile Base Stations) represents an instance of such a system. The performance of this network depends on the deployment of UAVs over the users. Our research assumes that users are immobile and previously known to the network. Therefore, we do not adapt UAVs' location over time, calculating neither their speed nor trajectory. We consider a situation where a group of unmoving users has, for example, lost connectivity to the terrestrial base station in a zone, and now several MBSs carried by UAVs are used to establish a new network. The connectivity has to be provided using the minimum number of UAVs, and the main problem to be solved is to establish their positions in the zone.

An approach to the problem of UAV optimal deployment depends on the representation of the search domain. In the proposed model, the space has a structure of many potential location sectors. They do not derive from any regular grid, but they are defined by the users, non-uniformly distributed inside the given zone, and the ranges of MBSs. Together, they divide the zone into regions having an area so that multiple UAVs can occupy a single region. In this model, the deployment of the minimal number of UAVs represents a combinatorial problem. Due to its complexity, we apply a heuristic optimization technique, an evolutionary algorithm with the problem-specific representation of solutions and perturbation operators adjusted to the model. A solution evaluation function promotes solutions with fewer UAVs and a greater variety of the UAVs' locations. For experimental verification, we created a set of benchmark problems and conducted experiments to show the algorithm's efficiency and reveal the most beneficial values of the algorithm's parameters.

The paper consists of six sections. Section 2 discusses related work. The wireless communication system, its model, and optimization criteria are described in Sect. 3. Section 4 presents an evolutionary approach to optimize the deployment of UAVs. The experimental part of the research is described in Sect. 5. Section 6 concludes the paper.

2   Related Work

Research efforts have been made regarding the deployment of UAVs for optimal wireless coverage. Providing communication services for ground users is addressed in [6] where authors maximize users' coverage probability. They find optimal locations of UAVs in 3-D space using particle swarm optimization. A particle in a swarm represents coordinates for an entire group of N UAVs, which is a real-valued vector of $3N$ dimensions. In [1] K-means clustering and a stable marriage approach are used to partition users into clusters and find 2-D coordinates of UAVs first. Then, the third coordinate, altitude, is optimized using search space-constrained exhaustive search and particle swarm optimization (PSO). Triples of real numbers are also used to represent uAVs' locations in [4]. Authors find optimal deployment of UAVs iteratively invoking a clustering algorithm K-means and one of the population heuristics: Particle Swarm Optimization, Genetic Algorithm, or Artificial Bees Colony. Another approach can be found in [3]. The authors propose a problem-specific heuristic optimization method working on a discrete representation of UAV location, where nodes of a square grid of $M \times M$ are considered for discrete locations.

3   The Optimization Problem

3.1   The Model of a Wireless Communication System

In the studied version of the UAVs deployment problem, we have to assure connectivity for a set of n immobile ground users located in the given zone. A swarm of m UAVs carrying MBSs serves as a communication system. Every UAV has its MBS, which is fully operational. The system components are homogenous. That is, all UAVs and MBSs have the same functionality and parameters. The model simplifies a real-world system because we assume that a third-party entity provides connectivity to the UAVs. Hence, the distances between them have no meaning for the network functionality. We also assume that some other aspects that ensure the system's proper functioning, like radio resource management, interference management, channel estimation, prediction, or energy efficiency, are out of the subject of optimization.

The work of UAVs can be intentionally disrupted; therefore, flight safety increases with altitude. On the other side, due to the limited power of the MBSs signal, the higher altitude, the smaller radius of the connectivity area. In this research, we assume that altitude is not a subject of optimization, and all UAVs fly at the same altitude, offering the best compromise between flight safety and productivity. All MBSs transmit with the same power; thus, the round areas with satisfying connectivity offered by MBSs have the same size.

The communication system has to ensure a k-coverage for each user, which means that each user requires at least k MBSs available in its connectivity range. Our goal is to minimize the number of UAVs by optimizing their locations in the zone.

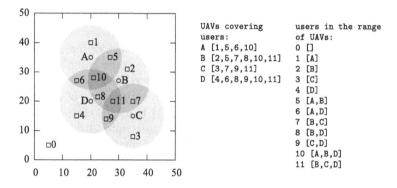

Fig. 1. Example of an operating wireless network with four users: A, B, C and D (circles) and 12 UAVs: $0, 1, 2, \ldots, 11$ (squares)—on the left, and lists of UAVs covering users and users in the range of UAVs—on the right

Figure 1 depicts an example deployment of 12 UAVs over the four users. Gray circles around users have a radius equal to the connectivity radius of MBSs carried by UAVs. Thus, locating MBS wherever in the circle guarantees connectivity to the user in the center of the circle.

The circles divide the zone into sectors. Each sector represents a different set of users, which we can cover by MBS service. The shades of gray of the sectors represent the number of covered users; the darker sector, the more users. In the example, the UAVs are placed one in each sector. For example, UAV no. 10 hovers in the sector where its MBS covers users A, B, and D. MBS of UAV no. 11 covers users B, C, and D. MBS of UAV no. 5—users A and B. And so on. The sector of UAV no. 0 is white, as it has no users in its range. The precise coordinates of a UAV location have no meaning as long as it remains entirely in the respective sector.

3.2 System Hypergraph Representation

The example presented in Fig. 1 can be modeled as a hypergraph where nodes represent users whereas hyperedges—sectors of the zone. There are four nodes and 11 hyperedges in this example. Let us label the hyperedges according to the UAVs' IDs and nodes according to the users. For example, the hyperedge no. 10 connects nodes A, B, and D. The hyperedge no. 11—nodes B, C, and D. The hyperedge no. 5—nodes A and B. And so on. We represent hyperedges like *key-value* pairs in an associative container. The number represents the *key*, and the sequence of covered nodes ordered alphabetically represents the *value*.

In the example, we generated the UAVs' IDs according to the rank based on the growing number of covered users. Thus, UAV no. 0 identifies the sector with no users in the range, and UAVs covering the most significant numbers of users have the highest IDs. In the case of the same number of covered users, the hyperedge IDs are assigned according to the alphabetical order of covered node IDs sequences. This policy of IDs generation was implemented in the optimization method.

3.3 The Optimization Criteria

The optimization aims to find and assign a minimal number of UAVs to the zone sectors to ensure all ground users' connectivity parameters. One can assign zero, one, or more UAVs to each sector. The sector may have assigned no UAVs when UAVs from other sectors deliver connectivity to its ground users. The bandwidth of MBS is large enough to meet all the necessary demands. Therefore, we assume that the number of ground users covered from a sector does not influence service quality. While there is no limit to the number of MBSs allowed in one sector, we try to avoid overcrowding, and this preference is included in the fitness function formula.

The fulfillment of sufficient connectivity conditions depends on the number of UAVs in the user vicinity. Every user needs access to at least k MBSs simultaneously. Therefore, we call this a k-coverage problem. For the example given in Fig. 1, k can be equal at most four because users A and C have four MBSs in their ranges which is the lowest level of coverage among all users. Hence, the proposed deployment of UAVs can also represent a feasible solution for the k-coverage problem where $k = 1, 2, 3, 4$. One can notice that for $k = 4$, the deployment is feasible but not optimal because deployments of fewer UAVs also deliver connectivity for $k = 4$.

4 The Optimization Method

We selected the evolutionary optimization heuristic to optimize the deployment of UAVs in sectors of a zone. An individual represents a solution: a feasible assignment of several UAVs satisfying the k-coverage condition. The population of individuals undergoes an iterative process of improvement, where we repeatedly execute steps of selection, perturbations, and replacement. The following sections describe the problem–specific essential components of an evolutionary algorithm: a solution representation and evaluation and unary and binary perturbation operators. Then, we discuss the main loop of the algorithm.

4.1   Solution Representation, Validation and Repair Procedure

A solution is represented as a variable-length array, and its length equals the number of UAVs used in the network. The values in the array cells represent hyperedge IDs. When we have multiple UAVs in the same hyperedge, its ID will show up in the sequence exactly that many times, in the respective index positions of these UAVs.

A solution is feasible when it satisfies the k-coverage condition. When we have to evaluate an unfeasible solution, it undergoes a repair procedure first. The procedure starts with the identification of the users with insufficient coverage levels. Then, one at a time, we deploy new UAVs in required areas until the condition is met.

Since we want to minimize the number of UAVs, the value of a solution is proportional to the number of UAVs in the network. Additionally, when we have two solutions containing the same numbers of UAVs, we consider the diversity of the UAVs' distribution over sectors. The fewer UAVs occupy the same sectors, the better. Eventually, the fitness function f is evaluated as follows:

$$f(\mathbf{x}) = len(\mathbf{x}) + len(\mathbf{x})/set(\mathbf{x}) \tag{1}$$

where $\mathbf{x}$ represents a solution, $len(\cdot)$ returns the length of the array in the solution, that is, the number of UAVs in the network, and $set(\cdot)$—the number of unique hyperedge IDs in the array cells. When the assignment of UAVs to hyperedges is fully unique, that is, each UAV occupies different sector, the penalty component $len(\mathbf{x})/set(\mathbf{x})$ equals one. Otherwise, it is greater than one and rises as the uniqueness falls.

4.2   Unary and Binary Perturbation Operators

The unary perturbation operator (mutation) of a solution relocates one randomly selected UAV to another sector in the neighborhood. Two sectors are regarded as neighbors when at least one ground user is covered from both sectors. When there is more than one neighboring sector, the transfer destination is selected randomly, and each neighbor has the same chance no matter how many UAVs it contains and how many users remain in its range.

The binary perturbation operator (recombination) starts with converting the variable–length array of a solution into another equivalent structure of a constant number of units. After conversion, the solution representation consists of a series of n UAVs lists containing UAVs for one of n users. As previously, every UAV is identified by its location sector.

For the example in Fig. 1, the deployment of UAVs over the sectors can be converted to a series of four lists: $[1, 5, 6, 10 \| 2, 7, 8, 11 \| 3, 9 \| 4]$, which means that UAVs located in sectors 1, 5, 6, and 10 are bound to the user A, UAVs in sectors 2, 7, 8, and 11—the user B, UAVs in sectors 3 and 9—the user C, and the UAV in sector 4—the user D. Of course, the UAV in sector 10 delivers connectivity for three users: A, B, and D, however, it can be bound to only one of them. Same for UAVs in sectors $5, \ldots, 9, 11$, which also deliver connectivity to multiple users. In the case of these UAVs, we bind them randomly to users selected among the recipients of their connectivity service.

Therefore, more than one sequence of lists may represent the same deployment of UAVs, like the following three for the example in Fig. 1:

$$
\begin{cases}
[1, 5, 6, \mathbf{10} \| 2, 7, 8, 11 \| 3, 9 \| 4], \\
[1, 5, 6 \| 2, 7, 8, \mathbf{10}, 11 \| 3, 9 \| 4], \\
[1, 5, 6 \| 2, 7, 8, 11 \| 3, 9 \| 4, \mathbf{10}].
\end{cases}
$$

The sequences of lists represent the same deployment of UAVs. However, they differ by binding one UAV in sector 10 to users A, B, or D.

We can apply a one–point crossover for the converted solutions described above. We choose a random point between the lists and switch the right parts of lists sequences for each selected pair to create two new hybrid solutions. Finally, the new solutions are converted to the variable–length array representation.

4.3   The Main Loop of Algorithm

The evolutionary algorithm applied in our experiments consists of the following key components: initialization, selection mechanism, perturbation operators, and replacement procedure. The algorithm starts with building the initial population of candidate solutions. Then evaluates the solutions and runs the iterative process of their improvement. In the first step of the main loop, we select and copy solutions with lower fitness values. Next, the selected ones undergo perturbation steps which create new solutions. Finally, new solutions compete with their ancestors in the replacement procedure. This sequence of steps is repeated until the maximum number of fitness function calls is reached. Algorithm 1 presents the pseudocode of the algorithm.

For the selection of candidates for perturbation, we apply tournament selection. We select three random solutions in the current working population and run a tournament among them. A copy of the winner goes to the pool of candidates. The tournament is repeated until the number of candidates equals the population size. Then, we divide the set of candidates into pairs and apply recombination. The recombination procedure produces two new solutions which undergo mutation. Finally, among the two input and two output solutions, the two best ones survive and join the new working population (the replacement step).

Algorithm 1

1: $P \leftarrow$ initial population   ▷ problem class dependent
2: evaluation(P)
3: **repeat**
4:     $P' \leftarrow$ recombination(selection(P))   ▷ representation dependent
5:     $P'' \leftarrow$ mutation(P')   ▷ representation dependent
6:     evaluation(P'')
7:     $P \leftarrow$ replacement(P, P'')
8: **until** termination condition met

5 Experiments

5.1 Benchmark and Plan of Experiments

The test case benchmark, called SCP2 [2], consists of six classes of problems. The users' locations are selected among nodes of a rectangular grid over the square zone of size one unit. There are two densities of grids with grid cell dimensions s_{grid} equal 0.04 by 0.04 or 0.02 by 0.02 units (676 or 2601 nodes in the zone, respectively). To avoid complete regularity in the users' distribution, the number of users is smaller than the number of nodes: 100, 200, or 500 users, and the nodes for users' locations are selected randomly. Additionally, when the node is selected, the final user's location is shifted from the node coordinates toward a random direction by a random distance smaller than 1.5 of s_{grid}. Eventually, we get six classes of users' locations: two grid densities by three sizes of the users' group. For every class, we generated 50 instances having different locations of users.

The round areas around users where MBSs can offer connectivity divide the zone into sectors. The area's radius depends on the MBS signal power, and we arbitrarily set the radius to 0.05 units. The complete list of sectors and users covered by MBSs services when located in each sector defines the structure of hypergraphs obtained for each problem instance. Users are represented as nodes and sectors as hyperedges. Sectors formed from the intersection between round areas around users are represented as hyperedges connecting the nodes corresponding to those users.

Figure 2 presents four graphs with numbers of nodes in connected components of the hypergraphs representing problem instances for the classes of problems with 100 and 200 ground users and two sizes of s_{grid}: 0.04 and 0.02, respectively. Each graph in the figure shows 50 series of connected components sizes for 50 instances of one class of problems. The heights of the bars depict the numbers of nodes in the hypergraph's components.

On average, hypergraphs representing problem instances in the two classes with 100 users have around 18.6 (with a range of 9 to 25 for $s_{\text{grid}} = 0.02$) and 20 (13 to 27 for $s_{\text{grid}} = 0.04$) connected components (Fig. 2a and 2c). For all of these instances, respective hypergraphs consist of multiple components with just a few nodes and several much bigger components, accounting for more than half of the nodes in total. For example, one such hypergraph has four 1-node

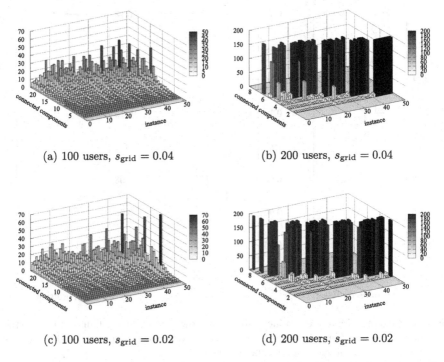

(a) 100 users, $s_{grid} = 0.04$

(b) 200 users, $s_{grid} = 0.04$

(c) 100 users, $s_{grid} = 0.02$

(d) 200 users, $s_{grid} = 0.02$

Fig. 2. Numbers of nodes in connected components of the hypergraphs representing problem instances for classes of problems with 100 ground users—graphs (a) and (c), and with 200 ground users—graphs (b) and (d)

components, five 2-node components, one 3-, 5-, 7- and 12-node component, and a single component with the remaining 59 nodes. Another instance consists of four 1-node, seven 2-node, and five 3-node components. The remaining 67 nodes are divided into singular 4-, 5-, 6-, 7- 14-, 15- and 16-node components.

For hypergraphs representing problem instances in the two classes with 200 users, we got the average of about 3.9 (from 1 to 10 for $s_{grid} = 0.02$) and 3 (from 1 to 6 for $s_{grid} = 0.04$) connected components. In both classes, the average size of the largest component stayed well above 80% of the total number of nodes, but in the case of the $s_{grid} = 0.02$, the smallest of such components consisted of barely 50.5% of them (about 10% smaller than for $s_{grid} = 0.04$). In such cases, the second largest component usually consists of 80% of the remaining nodes.

When we increase the number of users to 500, we always get a hypergraph consisting of one connected component. Such structure is not surprising. When the number of users in the zone grows, so is the density of a hypergraph. Thus, more intersections between areas around users occur.

Figure 3 depicts boxplots (minimum, lower quartile, median, upper quartile and maximum) of Evenness [5] values for the instances sets from classes with 100, 200 and 500 ground users, and for s_{grid} equal 0.02 and 0.04. Precisely, the boxplots show the main component of the Evenness measure, that is, the

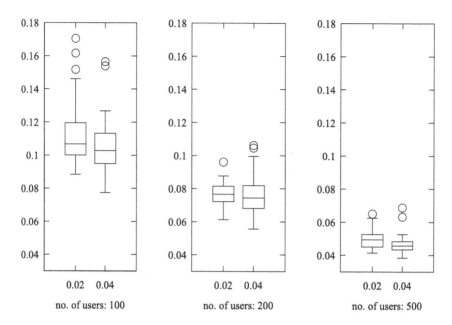

Fig. 3. Boxplots of Evenness values (minimum, lower quartile, median, upper quartile, maximum, and outliers) for the instances sets from classes with 100, 200, and 500 ground users, and for s_{grid} equal 0.02 and 0.04. [5]

Maximum Minimum Distance of the deployment (MMD):

$$\text{MMD} = \max_{\mathbf{x} \in U}(\min_{\mathbf{v} \in V}(d(\mathbf{x}, \mathbf{v}))) \tag{2}$$

where $d(\mathbf{x}, \mathbf{v})$ is an Euclidean distance between $\mathbf{x}$ and $\mathbf{v}$, U is the set of users locations, and V is the set of vertices in the Voronoi polygons for the given U.

One can see from these diagrams that almost all values for $s_{\text{grid}} = 0.04$ are lower than the corresponding values for $s_{\text{grid}} = 0.02$. Smaller grid cell dimensions and the same number of users mean that we have more possibilities to select a user's location. Thus, if user distribution is not uniform, it is likely that the maximum distance between a pair of users will be larger.

Moreover, values for 200 users are smaller than those for 100 users but greater than those for 500 users. The same applies to differences between the median and the lower or the upper quartile. Thus, data sets with more users have higher evenness. Adding more users should decrease the maximum distance between any pair of users on the grid.

The last parameter of the problem is the minimum coverage level k, equal to 1, 2, 5, or 10. Eventually, we get a benchmark consisting of 24 classes of problems: six classes of users' distribution over the zone by four levels of the minimum coverage k.

The algorithm has 2 parameters: population size p_{size} and stopping condition parameter, that is, the maximum number of fitness function calls $max_{\text{nffc}} =$

30000. We repeated the experiment 32 times for every problem instance, excluded the best and worst results, and calculated the mean number of UAVs for the remaining ones.

5.2   The Results

Figure 4 shows the results of our experiments with the benchmark described in Sect. 5.1. In almost every case, the penalty component $len(\mathbf{x})/set(\mathbf{x})$ of the best-found solutions is less than two except from the selected instances of the problems from classes with 100 ground users. For these instances and $k = 5$, the penalty is in the range $[1, 2.5]$, whereas for $k = 10$—in $[1, 3.7]$. Therefore, Fig. 4 shows the mean numbers of UAVs for the best-found solutions rather than the values of $f(\mathbf{x})$ because the number of UAVs interests us the most in this research.

One can see in Fig. 4 that for the larger value of s_{grid}, the mean numbers of UAVs in the best-found solutions are smaller. Only for 200 users and $k = 1$, these numbers are for both values of s_{grid} almost equal.

For the cases with 100 users, our evolutionary algorithm gives the best results for the population size between 500 and 1500 (for $k \leq 2$—between 1000 and 1500, for $k = 5$—750, for $k = 10$—500). With 200 users, the best results are for a population size smaller than 500. Since our termination condition was 30 000 calls to the fitness function, the main loop makes fewer iterations when the population size is greater. It explains why bigger populations produce worse results with 100 and 200 users.

It is also interesting that with 100 users, an optimal population size becomes smaller when k increases. It may be related to the structure of the connected components of the hypergraph corresponding to the network. For small values of k, a larger initial population gives better results due to a greater chance of a good guess. For larger k, we need more UAVs to obtain the required coverage. Then the search capabilities of an evolutionary algorithm play a more important role than a good initial guess. A smaller population means more iterations of the main loop.

However, with 500 users we see the opposite—for $k \leq 2$, the best results are for the population size below 500 but for larger k—for the population 2000. This is probably due to the greater complexity of the problem with so many users. For $k \leq 2$, smaller population size can produce better results due to more main loop iterations. For larger k, the best result is obtained by a good guess. Larger populations increase the chances of such guesses.

6   Conclusions

In this paper, we proposed an evolutionary approach to optimization of UAVs deployment for k-Coverage Problem. The main novelty of our approach lies in a

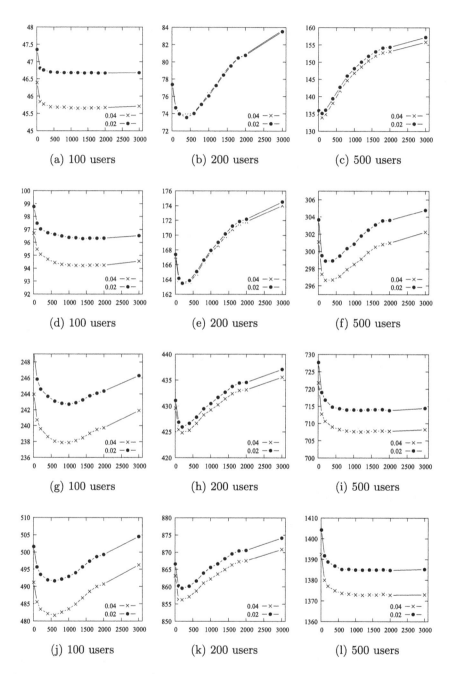

Fig. 4. Mean numbers of UAVs for the best-found solutions for $k = 1$: (a), (b), and (c), $k = 2$: (d), (e), and (f), $k = 5$: (g), (h), and (i), and $k = 10$: (j), (k), and (l); X-axis represents population size

new model of the space where the network formed by UAVs serves the users. The model is based on users' locations and the range of MBSs carried by UAVs. We use a hypergraph representation of the space. The hypergraph nodes represent users, while the hyperedges correspond to possible locations where the UAVs can be deployed. These locations, called sectors, are determined by the MBS range. Hence, the set of users in the range is different for each sector. Each sector transforms to a hyperedge connecting nodes corresponding to the users in the range.

In our evolutionary algorithm, a solution is represented as a variable-length array containing hyperedges which is another novelty. We minimize the number of UAVs and avoid crowding them in the same zones. Thus, the value of a solution (fitness function) is the number of UAVs in the network plus the ratio of this number to the number of unique hyperedge IDs in the array cells. Representation-specific binary and unary perturbation operators (recombination and mutation) in the algorithm are yet another novelty in this paper. We apply a stopping criterion based on limited computational resources for the evolutionary improvement process. Therefore, the evolutionary process ends when we reach the allowed limit of fitness function calls.

In the experimental part of the research, we tested our algorithm efficiency using six classes of test cases. The classes differ in the number of nodes and their deployment, derived from a distribution of nodes in different grids covering the zone. Moreover, we apply different levels of connectivity coverage for the users, which means that each user has to be within the range of k MBSs simultaneously. We performed tests for four values of k—1, 2, 5, and 10.

Results of experiments are correlated with some benchmark problems properties. For example, when the number of users is small regarding the area under consideration and the users are dispersed, the corresponding hypergraph consists of many connected components. In such cases, there is not much room for optimization, and the initial population determines the quality of the solution. On the other hand, when the number of users is large, the corresponding hypergraph is connected. Thus, the task becomes challenging for larger values of k. In this case, a more significant number of UAVs has to be engaged, so the number of alternative UAVs distributions becomes vast. Since we want to avoid clusters of UAVs that make the system more vulnerable, the fitness function penalty component begins to play a more critical role in introducing additional complexity. In the remaining cases, the algorithm performed well—it was possible to determine the best population size given the limit on the number of fitness function calls.

References

1. Hydher, H., Jayakody, D.N.K., Hemachandra, K.T., Samarasinghe, T.: Intelligent UAV deployment for a disaster-resilient wireless network. Sensors **20**(21), 6140 (2020). https://doi.org/10.3390/s20216140
2. Grzeszczak, J., Mikitiuk, A., Trojanowski, K.: Scp2 dataset (2022). https://jaga. blog.uksw.edu.pl/scp2/. Accessed 25 Apr 2022

3. Masroor, R., Naeem, M., Ejaz, W.: Efficient deployment of UAVs for disaster management: a multi-criterion optimization approach. Comput. Commun. **177**, 185–194 (2021). https://doi.org/10.1016/j.comcom.2021.07.006
4. Sawalmeh, A., Othman, N.S., Liu, G., Khreishah, A., Alenezi, A., Alanazi, A.: Power-efficient wireless coverage using minimum number of UAVs. Sensors **22**(1), 223 (2021). https://doi.org/10.3390/s22010223
5. Shen, X.: Evenness evaluation in ad-hoc sensor networks. In: 2010 First International Conference on Networking and Distributed Computing, pp. 53–56. IEEE (2010). https://doi.org/10.1109/icndc.2010.20
6. Yuheng, Z., Liyan, Z., Chunpeng, L.: 3-D deployment optimization of UAVs based on particle swarm algorithm. In: 2019 IEEE 19th International Conference on Communication Technology (ICCT). IEEE (2019). https://doi.org/10.1109/icct46805.2019.8947140

Correction to: Software Product Maintenance: A Case Study

Shariq Aziz Butt, Acosta-Coll Melisa, and Sanjay Misra

Correction to:
Chapter "Software Product Maintenance: A Case Study" in:
K. Saeed and J. Dvorský (Eds.): *Computer Information Systems and Industrial Management*, **LNCS 13293,**
https://doi.org/10.1007/978-3-031-10539-5_6

In an older version of this chapter, the affiliation of Sanjay Misra was presented incorrectly. This has been corrected.

The updated original version of this chapter can be found at
https://doi.org/10.1007/978-3-031-10539-5_6

K. Saeed and J. Dvorský (Eds.): CISIM 2022, LNCS 13293, p. C1, 2022.
https://doi.org/10.1007/978-3-031-10539-5_29

Author Index

Printed in the United States
by Baker & Taylor Publisher Services